I0214153

MANETTE PIONEERING

Published by
MANETTE HISTORY CLUB
Bremerton, Washington

Erv Jensen, editor

Maryjayne Hladky, associate editor

ISBN 978-1-59092-915-5
Copyright 1988, 2023 by Manette History Club
Historic records filed with
Kitsap County Historical Society

TABLE OF CONTENTS

FOREWORD

The inspiration for this book came from Estelle (Mrs. Clyde) Meredith, Manette pioneer, and Gideon Hermanson, past president of the Kitsap County Historical Society. They encouraged the old-timers of Manette to research and publish information about old Port Orchard-Decatur-Manette: information beyond that found in *Kitsap County History* published by the Historical Society in 1977.

The next step was a meeting on February 1, 1983, at the home of Mrs. Meredith on Scott Avenue in Manette. In attendance were Estelle Meredith, Gideon Hermanson, Maryjayne Meredith Hladky, Walter and Mary Fellows, Gladys (Mrs. Lloyd) Solid, Ferris Buchanan, Orville Schultz and Richard Linkletter. The result was formation of the Manette History Club, the ultimate goal being to produce the book.

Interested persons were invited by press, radio and word-of-mouth to come to club meetings and to submit manuscripts and photographs for the book. Meetings were well attended and the mailing list for the club's Newsletter swelled to more than 400. A book committee was formed to steer the project forward. *Manette Pioneering* is the result. The Kitsap County Historical Society agreed to underwrite the project.

A complete review of Manette's bygone days would require many volumes. *Manette Pioneering* aims not to relate all our community's history but rather to provide samples that convey its flavor. The absence of any particular name or event certainly does not mean that the name or event is unimportant.

Some arbitrary committee decisions became necessary, as did exceptions to the decisions. Guidelines generally followed were these:
- "Manette" was considered to extend as far north as Riddell Road.
- "Pioneers" were persons who were here before the Manette bridge opened in 1930.
- A "pioneer business" was one begun before World War II.

Much of the material in the book comes from the memories of the contributors and cannot be verified. Neither the Manette History Club nor the Kitsap County Historical Society can guarantee that the memories are without flaw. But sincere effort has been made to achieve accuracy and has, we believe, been mostly successful.

> The Book Committee:
> Don Atkinson
> Anna Jo Harkins Atkinson
> Ferris Buchanan
> Maryjayne Meredith Hladky
> Ervin Jensen
> Donna Flaugher Jensen
> Estelle Meredith
> Roger Paquette
> Orville Schultz

ACKNOWLEDGEMENTS

We are indebted to the following for help in preparation of the book:

ORGANIZATIONS
    Bremerton School District
    National Archives and Records Administration, Seattle
    King County Auditor's Office
    Kitsap Regional Library
        Laura Boyle, Shirley Bird
    Kitsap County Courthouse personnel
        Ron L. Swedburg, Phil Kirschner, Leslie L. Cline, H.V. (Enzo) Loop
    Kitsap County Historical Society
    Manette Community Church
    Museum of History and Industry, Seattle
    Puget Sound Maritime Historical Society, Inc.
    Kitsap County Retired Teachers Association
    Senior Citizens Recreation Center, Bremerton
    Southern Oregon Historical Society
    U.S. Coast Guard
    University of Washington
        Suzzallo Library
            Government Publications Division
            Pacific Northwest Collection
            Special Collections Division
            Archives and Manuscripts Division
        Forest Resources Library
        Law Library
    Washington State Archives and Record Management Division
    Washington State Historical Society Museum, Tacoma
    Washington State Library, Olympia
    Washington State Parks and Recreation Commission

INDIVIDUALS
    Helen Palmer McCallum for illustrations, Hank Blass for art consultant services, Jan Kerr Arnold for indexing, Susan Schultz Brown for editing assistance and, for many types of assistance, the following:
        Suzanne Anest
        Helga Behr
        Leoda Senn Buckner
        Bremerton Water Superintendent William M. Duffy Jr.
        Garrett Eddy, chairman of board, Port Blakely Tree Farms
        Wells and Alice Ehrhardt
        Dick Hladky
        Rich Hladky
        Iris Senn Hoey
        June Etten Jarstad
        Dick Linkletter
        Valerie Jensen Otheim
        Dianne Robinson
        Norman Rockett, Illahee State Park ranger
        Berenice Bouchard Root
        Fredi Perry
        Joy Jensen Pope
        Randall Schalk, director of office of Public Archaeology Institute for Environmental Studies, U.W.
        Gordon Schroeder, assistant ranger, Illahee State Park
        Jewel Tenge Sollie
        Eleanor Pidduck Ury

IMPROVEMENT JACK

By Bill von Hoene

Thru the green and towering forests,
On the shores of Puget Sound,
Came a band of sturdy yeomen,
Seeking land to call their own.
There were Benders, there were Martins,
There were Petersons and Pitts,
There were Jensens, there were Johnsons,
Jacobsons, and Sheldon Smiths,
Swedes and Irish, Scotch and English,
Sturdy folks as you e'er met,
Settled on this rocky hillside,
Said they'd call the place Manette.

Started building schools and sawmills,
Roads and bridges, slashed a trail,
Seem'd as tho these hardy people
Didn't know a word called fail.
'Bout the time a job was finished,
Folks all tired and money spent,
Up would jump this guy Jack Martin,
Yelping, "More improvements."
Didn't seem to make no difference,
Every place that feller went,
Wouldn't never talk 'bout nothing
But his blamed "improvements."

Said there wa'nt no use a waiting,
Had a town you couldn't beat,
Had the logical location,
For to make a County Seat.
Helped put in a water system,
Charged plenty for it too,
Said he's glad when pro-hi-bition,
Made us drink it 'stead of brew.
Folks got mighty tired of rowing,
Back and Forth to Bremerton,
Jack he figgers out a system,
Do the work with gasoline

'Twasn't long fore Jack, he figgered,
Like to drive to Bremerton,
Talked a guy named Harry Hansen
Put a ferry on the run.
Bought hisself an automobile,
Drove down Californy way,
Got a lot of new ideas,
'Bout improvements round the Bay.
One day got a bright idea,
Said there wa'nt no reason why
We couldn't have a bridge to walk on,
All we had to do was try.

Got some fellers interested,
Started on a big campaign,
Kept a-talkin' bonds and bridges,
Like to drove us all insane,
Pretty soon the bridge was finished,
Folks said, "There's Jack's monument,
Mebby now he'll quit his talkin'
'Bout his danged improvements."
Did that feller shut up, no sir,
Jest set down and started to rub
Out a lot of new ideas ....
'Bout a new Improvement Club.

Talked club day time, talked it night time,
Talked it in his sleep, I guess;
Got Earl Harkins 'lected president,
(Kept hisself clear of that mess)
Come out regular to meetin's,
Telling others what to do,
Even loaned his hall for nothin',
Just to put the matter through.
Talked new street lights, parks, and playgrounds,
Bathing beach and all such truck,
Till the folks began to do things,
Jest to shut the feller up.

That club surely thrived and prospered,
Never saw its like before,
Seems like anything they started,
Was finished 'fore the day was o'er.
Oiled streets and put in sidewalks,
Kept the Mayor on the jump,
Surely crowned theirselves with glory,
When they covered Cora's dump.
Planted flowers upon that hill-side,
Till it bloomed like Sharon's Rose.
Don't know what else might a-happened,
For Jack Martin ups and goes.

Yes, one day he showed up missing,
From the usual haunts of men,
Said his friends, "Jack's work is ended,
With the angels now he sings."
Then there came a distant rumble,
And the earth began to shake,
All the folks rushed from their houses,
For they thought it was a "quake."
Silently they bent and listened,
Heard the old familiar yelp,
"This place surely needs improvements.
Send Earl Harkins down to help."

Chapter 1

EARLY HABITATION

By Fredi Perry

THE FORT

The area of the Manette Bridge has been reputed to have been an Indian fort, and the belief is supported by much evidence, the most recent being information gathered by two professional archaeologists from the University of Washington's Department of Environmental Studies in 1982.

Their study produced no evidence of a permanent settlement. The little historical literature available points to the Erland's Point area as the site of a year-round village in this general area. The Indians were the Saktabsh, a subdivision of the Suquamish belonging to the Nisqually branch of the coastal division of the Salishan linguistic stock, their closest connections being with the Duwamish. This village, used summer and winter, had a longhouse similar to the Old Man House on Agate Passage.

ARTIFACTS

A former resident of the fort area, Bill Schweer, found artifacts consisting of pestles, adzes, bone points, wedges, sandstone abraders and a variety of chipped stone tools. Similar evidence, an adz and a mortar or club head, has been found by Walter LeCompte of 1604 Jacobsen Boulevard near a small creek running through the area. Ann Sleight of Olympic College excavated a burial from the fort locality in 1971.

The University of Washington archaeologists' excavations yielded evidence of at least two distinct occupational episodes at the site, up to 7000 years old. Human skeletal remains were also encountered in this project, but few artifacts were found, strongly suggesting that the site was not a manufacturing site, as the tools seemed only of minor importance during aboriginal occupation, or that most of the evidence had been removed during modern occupation.

When Mrs. L.A. (Ella) Bender arrived in the area in 1888 the fort appeared as a low wall of dirt and rocks overlooking the entrance to the inlet. A site nearer Sheridan has been identified as a location of canoe burials.

The U. of W. report states that food preparation evidence was in abundance, i.e., shells, bones, ovens, and local mollusk shells. Skeletal remains indicated that animals were butchered elsewhere and only selected parts carried to the site for consumption. There was a lack of evidence of residential structures or related domestic artifacts, again suggesting that the location was used only as a temporary seasonal base, most likely, they thought, in late spring.

These Indians of Dyes Inlet were probably totally self-sufficient, given the presence of salmon, their staple food, shellfish, ducks and the many wild berries growing on the hills above the inlet. Berries would have been harvested in conjunction with inland trips to hunt deer or harvest salmon and steelhead.

NORTHERN THREAT

Prior to establishment of William Renton and Daniel Howard's Port Orchard (Enetai Beach) Mill in 1854, the Indians of Dyes Inlet probably used the fort to keep a watchful eye on the narrow channel leading into their bay. Gaining access to Dyes Inlet would be a major coup for enemy Indians from Alaska and Canada, the "Northerns." Ironically, today, at the Naval Regional Medical Center, situated on land once used by the local tribes, a marvelous art collection features examples of the Northerns' art.

Available records do not indicate whether the annual pilgrimages of the Northern tribes to Puget Sound resulted in any confrontations around the village on Dyes Inlet. However, thousands of Indians would camp at Victoria, British Columbia, and in small parties swoop down on the Sound to begin an annual reign of terror. In recorded history, these same Indians would leave their women at the different logging camps and mills on the Sound.

In the summer of 1860, the Northerns came to get their women, who had been left at the Port Orchard Mill site (Enetai Beach). The women didn't want to leave and the white men didn't want to give them up. Angered, the Northerns planned an attack, but the Snohomish and Suquamish had old grievances to avenge and attacked and killed two Northern men and one woman and captured seven of the Northern women. The women who were "saved" were later sent to Victoria.

INDIANS AT THE MILL

At this time there were six Indian families, about 40 persons, living and earning a comfortable livelihood in the vicinity of the Port Orchard Mill.

Daniel Howard's brother-in-law, David Mills, who was enticed to this area by the wages being offered at the Port Orchard Mill, said in a letter to his brother in Scotland in 1861, "There is five Indians employed in the mill for carrying away the slabs and taking the lumber down the wharf. This is the

natives of this country. Their skin is a very dark copper colour and [they] wear very long hair down their back and their heads is flat. The back side and the front side. This is done to them all after they are born. They have articals that they screw on them which is made of wood. All the clothing they wear is a single blanket and they live on clams and fish, musels and venison. There is any quantity of them living up and down here. You could not tell a man from a woman to look at them. Men have no beards. Any of them that have any hair on their face, they pull it all out so that it do not grow. They are very wild in general but round here they are pretty civil."

As the Indians of this particular area had early been assimilated into the working force, the advent of the homesteaders was more of a blessing to them than in other areas, and the two lived then, as now, harmoniously along the shores of Port Orchard and Port Washington Bays. In fact, Captain Renton supposedly advised this particular band to become American citizens and homestead land, which in a number of cases was done.

INDIAN WARS

In the winter of 1855-56, war flared over Puget Sound Indian's discontent with government land policy. Historian Chloe Sutton has noted, however, that Port Orchard was spared even those relatively brief encounters which erupted in some of the other communities on the Sound. She wrote:

"William Renton, of Port Orchard Mill Company, had been on a trip up sound in a large canoe manned by Indians and was returning through Colvos Passage when he was hailed by Indians on the shore who notified him that war was in progress. Renton refused to believe the report and proceeded northward and when nearing the entrance of Port Orchard Bay was hailed from shore by a second band of Indians who delivered the same message. Arriving at the mill, he found the people there in a panic and preparing to desert the mill for the Seattle blockhouse. To this the captain would not agree, saying he would defend his rights and his property to his last breath. Accordingly, squared timbers that had been prepared for shipping were speedily converted into a blockhouse at the east side of Manette Point. An appeal was made to the County Commissioners in Seattle, who provided eleven muskets for defense of the Port Orchard blockhouse. Everything was in readiness but fortunately it was not found necessary to use the blockhouse, excepting as a precautionary measure.

"There was great fear that the Northern Indians might join forces with the Klickitat and allied tribes from east of the mountains. Accordingly a band of soldiers were kept at the Port Orchard blockhouse for awhile to prevent the Saktabsh band, as Chico's people were called, from joining the enemy or from harboring the northern spies who were at work on the sound.... The soldiers stayed... only a week or so, as it was soon very evident that the Port Orchard Indians were devoted to their friends and happy in their work at the mill."

During the crisis, Port Orchard resident Delos Waterman drilled the whites and Indians in defense maneuvers. This instruction took place at a site which is now approximately 1334 Jacobsen Boulevard. The community across the bay from the site is named for Waterman.

CAPT. GEORGE VANCOUVER

May 1792: Capt. George Vancouver's flagship H.M.S. *Discovery* was anchored off the southern end of Bainbridge Island near what the English navigator would later name Restoration Point. Vancouver wrote in his journal:

"On Wednesday the 23rd, we had some lightning, thunder, and rain, from the S.E.; this continued a few hours after which the day was very serene and pleasant. Some of our gentlemen having extended their walk to the cove I had visited the first evening of our arrival, found it to communicate by a very narrow passage with an opening apparently of some extent."

Vancouver's "narrow passage" was what is today Rich Passage, and the "opening" was the water into which the Manette Peninsula extends.

Vancouver's journal continues:

"In consequence of this information, accompanied by Mr. Baker in the yawl, ["Mr. Baker" was Third Lt. Joseph Baker of the *Discovery*] I set out the next morning, Thursday the 24th, to examine it, and found the entrance of the opening situated in the western corner of the cove, formed by two interlocking points, about a quarter of a mile from each other; these formed a channel about half a mile long, free from rocks or shoals, in which there was not less than five fathoms of water. From the west end of this narrow channel the inlet is divided into two branches, one extending to the Southwest about five or six miles, the other to the North about the same distance, constituting a most complete and excellent port, to all appearance perfectly free from danger, with regular soundings from four fathoms near the shore, to nine and ten fathoms in the middle, good holding ground. It occupied us the whole day to row round it....

"The country that surrounds this harbor varies in its elevation; in some places the shores are low level land, in others of moderate height, falling in steep low cliffs on the sandy beach, which in most places binds the shores. It produces some small rivulets of water, is thickly wooded with trees, mostly of the pine tribe, and with some variety of shrubs. This harbor, after the gentleman who discovered it, obtained the name "PORT ORCHARD."

This "gentleman" was Harry Masterman Orchard, clerk on the *Discovery*. And Manette had the first of its three names, Port Orchard.

LT. CHARLES WILKES

In May of 1841 "The U.S. Exploring Expedition" under Lt. Charles Wilkes arrived on the Sound. The ships included the flagship *Vincennes* and the brig *Porpoise,* commanded by Cadwalader Ringgold.

Survey work began May 24. On May 25 the men discovered a northern entrance to Port Orchard—"Agates Passage," named by Wilkes for Lt. Alfred T. Agate, the expedition's artist. Wilkes named the southern entrance "Richs Passage" for W.R. Rich, his botanist. The island separating these passages became Bainbridge, named for Commodore William Bainbridge, U.S. Navy.

On the opposite side of the peninsula—the west side—other boats were sounding the waters Wilkes would name Dyes Inlet, for John W. Dyes, assistant taxidermist on Wilkes' flagship *Vincennes*. (Today part of it is Port Washington Narrows).

Wilkes named the south end of the peninsula Point Herron (commonly called Manette Point) for petty officer Lewis Herron, cooper (barrel maker) on the *Vincennes*.

Wilkes wrote that "Port Orchard is one of the most beautiful of the many fine harbors on these inland waters, and is perfectly protected from the winds.... The sheet of water is very extensive and is surrounded by a large growth of trees, with here and there a small prairie covered by a verdant greensward, and with its honeysuckle and roses just in bloom, resembling a well kept lawn. The soil is superior to that of most places around the Sound and is capable of yielding almost any kind of production. The woods seemed alive with squirrels, while tracks on the shore and through the forest showed that the larger class of animals also were in the habit of frequenting them.... The water was found deep enough for the largest class of vessels, with a bold shore and a good anchorage."

(Port Orchard, as Vancouver named it, included all the tidewater accessible by westward travel through either of its two entrances, Rich Passage or Agate Passage).

Wilkes' diary shows that on May 19 he left the Sound with a small party on an overland trip to the Columbia River. On the 16th of June Wilkes was back on the *Vincennes* and ready to sail. On the 19th of June "anchored off Port Laurence near the entrance to Hood's Canal which I had assigned for a rendezvous with *Porpoise*, which vessel joined us the same day."

RENTON AND HOWARD

William Renton (Born Pictou, Nova Scotia, 1818; Died Port Blakely, 1891) came to the Puget Sound area in September 1852 looking for a load of piles to sell in San Francisco. His enthusiasm for the Puget Sound region was kindled by a realization that it would be far more profitable to establish a mill on the Sound than to share in the profits of loads of unmilled timber sold in San Francisco. He established a mill at Alki Point, Seattle, in the summer of 1853 and employed such Indians and white men as were available.

It took only one winter for him to realize that "New York Alki" with its unprotected point was not ideal for the milling operation. High tides bashed the point that winter and a lack of fresh water made the site even more undesirable. Various new locations were investigated and Enetai Beach was chosen.

On March 26, 1854, Renton drove stakes to claim a mile of waterfront running from north of Enetai Point south nearly to the foot of present day Trenton Avenue and extending inland 1/2 mile: 320 acres. Since the area was then a part of King County, Renton recorded his claim 2 days later at the auditor's office in Seattle. When Slaughter County (later to become Kitsap) was established in 1857, the area became part of it.

The men hired for the moving job included Daniel Sackman, a man who eventually was to play a major role here on the peninsula as well as in the rest of the county.

Renton's partner in the mill was Daniel S. Howard, prominent in the early history of Seattle. It was he who took the first load of piles from Alki to San Francisco in his ship *Leonesa..*

The mill site was well chosen. A small stream supplied water for the mill's boiler and for the mill town. North of the point, off a steeper beach with good holding ground, ships anchored stern to just beyond the face of the company dock and were loaded through stern ports two and three at a time.

In 1855, Captain Ed Howard, brother of mill co-owner Daniel Howard, came to the area with cows, sheep, hogs and chickens. But, he later said in his autobiography, "The skunks killed the chickens and the Indian dogs killed the sheep." He and his family left after a year.

An explosion caused by a boiler with too little water caused considerable damage to the mill in 1857 and cost Mr. Renton the sight in one eye.

It was this same year that a territorial census taker counted 26 residents in this particular area of Slaughter County, including a cooper (barrel maker), two seamen, a cook and 17 lumbermen. Although Indians were employed in this mill, they were not included in this census or any other state census until 1871. Federal census takers didn't count them until 1880 and then counted only those who were taxable. In the 1860 federal census, the non-native population of Port Orchard Bay and Dyes Inlet had grown to 47.

At least two saloons and a hotel were located near the mill for the enjoyment of the millworkers and loggers. Renton was not a prohibitionist but neither did he encourage his workers to spend a lot of time and money at the saloons or waiting for the floating whiskey batteries to drop anchor offshore.

David Mills, brother-in-law of Dan Howard wrote, in a letter to a relative in San Francisco in 1861, "The loggers commence to make a road for themselves from the river side. They draw the logs with oxen into the water and make a large raft of logs 4-500 and bring them to the mill with the tide. This river is called Puget Sound. We keep three vessels sailing all the time between this and Frisco carrying away the lumber. It is the greatest countrys of timber that ever was known."

Renton was granted a deed for the property in 1863, issued in his name and that of his recently deceased partner, Howard. Howard died October 20, 1863, leaving a widow, Elizabeth Howard, age 31, and daughters Caroline, age 3, and Mary, age 1.

In May 1864 Renton and Howard's heirs old the sawmill and all lands surrounding it to N.H. Falk. Renton then moved on to buy a large new mill capable of higher production at Port Blakely on Bainbridge Island. Falk sold his interest in the mill to A.K.P. Glidden and J.M. Colman in September 1867.

A post office was established at Colman and Glidden Mill of Port Orchard, now Enetai, in December 1868, with Nicholas Hale serving as the postmaster.

In August of 1869 Colman and Glidden filed for bankruptcy.

During the ensuing year the pages of Puget Sound newspapers were filled with the drama of life at Port Orchard. A federal judge's wife was thrown overboard while a mill-owned ship was being shanghaied to Victoria as, the *Seattle Intelligencer* reported, "her screams were intolderable." A well-known Puget Sound logger was charged with assault to murder for throwing the ship's captain overboard, and a mysterious explosion rocked the mill.

Trouble had been brewing between the partners, and in the spring of 1870, Glidden, then in San Francisco, issued a statement saying that times were too hard to sell the financially troubled mill.

A valuable watchdog at the mill had been poisoned and one of the watchmen noticed a peculiar odor in the water while making coffee. It was later discovered that the water contained laudanum, an opiate commonly used in murder attempts.

On March 8, 1870, a hired watchman found smoke issuing from under the mill, but before water could reach the structure, it was destroyed. The *Seattle Intelligencer* reported that all that remained was a smoking heap of ruins.

The week following the fire, the Kitsap County sheriff seized what was left of the mill, including machinery, engines and other equipment, for $320 taxes due the county.

By the end of 1871 William Davis had entered the south part of the land under the Homestead Laws. Final proof of his right was submitted and on September 28, 1890, Davis received a patent to these tracts along Enetai Beach. This land was to become McTeigh's Garden Tracts and extend from the Port Orchard mill site to the edge of Decatur.

On August 16, 1884, the Territory of Washington gave a tax deed to Joseph McCarroghee for the north part, including the mill site, which was at the mouth of Micam (Enetai) Creek. On April 10, 1894, Maurice McMicken purchased the land. On April 20, 1906, McMicken sold the land to Thomas Green, and on March 18, 1918, it was purchased by Alvyn L. Croxton, Bremerton's first mayor. Two homes that were built on the land in 1902 are still in use today.

MANETTE HOMESTEADED

In 1865 John Fryberg purchased a 36-acre parcel of land which today is the town of Tracyton. On October 10, 1866, Theodore Williams purchased 38 acres of land behind Point Herron. This was the land that was to become Decatur, and then Manette. Williams built a saloon to cater to the tastes of sailors and Port Orchard mill crews. Daniel Sackman in 1868 filed on a large section of land that would eventually become an additional part of Manette, receiving a patent in May 1869.

In 1883 Joseph Pitt settled north of Manette, later to sell Decatur home sites and business lots.

The 38-acre home of Theodore Williams at Point Herron was purchased by Edwin A. Strout, a Seattle real estate developer, in 1890.

The town that was to become Manette came into existence on April 20, 1891, when Joseph Pitt filed the plat of Decatur.

Chapter 2

TRANSPORTATION

THE WATERWAYS
Mosquito Fleet

The pioneers of the Manette Peninsula necessarily were shoreline dwellers. The land was densely forested, trails and roads were nonexistent and Puget Sound provided the only means of freight and passenger transportation.

In the early part of the 20th century the vessels plying these waters were mostly small steamers, far from the comparatively jumbo-sized ferries which link Bremerton and Seattle today.

The early boats if small were also numerous, as were the ports of call. Wharves stretched into the water at Illahee, Enetai, Waterman, Manette, Sheridan, Tracyton, Fairview, Silverdale and Chico. Some of these have been rebuilt; most have disappeared.

To the assortment of small, busy vessels of the day the term "Mosquito Fleet" has been applied. Some historians refer to "Mosquito Fleet" boats as those owned by one particular company, but the term is also used to describe all the craft collectively.

Just when the Mosquito Fleet era began and ended is likewise indefinite, but the two decades from 1910 to 1930 should at least encompass most of the period.

On the following pages are pictured some of the vessels that served Manette and other nearby ports in the Mosquito Fleet days.

The boat best remembered—or at least most mentioned by various authors later in this book—is the auto ferry *Pioneer*.

Between 1916 and the day the Manette Bridge was opened in 1930, the *Pioneer* was the link between Manette and Bremerton. When taken off the run occasionally for maintenance she was replaced by the passengers-only ferry *Urania*.

The ferry system was owned and operated by Harry Hansen of Tracyton.

Recollections of Jane Ellen Dixon Quinn, a niece of Hansen and current resident of El Cajon, Calif., indicate that the ferry operation was largely a family affair: Alvin Hansen, one of the skippers, was a brother of Harry. Bob Carter, purser, was the husband of Harry's sister Mabel. And Charles E. Dixon, another purser, was the husband of the former Myrtle V. Swisher, sister of Harry's wife Ellen.

Ellen Hansen also sometimes ran the ferry, and in addition was a school teacher, according to Mrs. Quinn.

"She came to Kitsap County in 1906. Her first teaching job was at Tracyton, where she met Harry. Later she taught at Smith School in Bremerton and became principal there," Mrs. Quinn said.

"After the bridge was built, Aunt Ellen and Harry built a lovely brick home at Tracyton on the waterfront. Aunt Ellen invested their money in real estate and they prospered. "She was very good and helpful to all of their many relatives. "Uncle Harry did not go out socially. After the bridge was built and the ferry company went out of business, he had a nice boat built. It was large enough so that 10 or 12 people could sleep on it, had a galley, bathroom, main cabin and wheelhouse. He named her the *Ellen G* of Tracyton. We had nice family times on the *Ellen G*."

Port Washington Narrows (left) and Dyes Inlet, 1920. Photo looks west from Atkinson home in Sheridan Heights. George Morton home is at lower left. To right of Morton home, "Mosquito Fleet" steamer Atlanta *is landing at Sheridan Dock.*

Early Ferries

By Fred Williams

[Fred Williams, now a resident of Warr Acres, Okla., is a grandson of Albert Williams, who came to Manette in 1890. See WILLIAMS, ALBERT, family history.]

Bremerton's main connection with Seattle was the ferry system. I remember some of the older ferries, none of which operate now. A familiar tall-stacked steamer was the *F.G. Reeve*. When our family traveled from Seattle to Bremerton for an evening or a day with Uncle Ed, Uncle Art and Aunt Hattie Holden, Dad would put Mom and my sister Dorothy on the *Chippewa* and he and I would ride the *F.G. Reeve* freight boat. We would come back at night together on the *Chippewa* or the *Commander*. The reason we rode the *Reeve* was that Dad knew the skipper and we rode free. The *Reeve* was bought by the Puget Sound Navigation Company and continued until 1938. The hull now rests in Lake Union.

The *Commander* was a faster steamboat and was strictly for passengers and autos. It was built in 1900 in New Whatcom, Wash., and was brought to Puget Sound by Captain William Mitchell around 1929. It was later bought by Puget Sound Navigation Company in 1936 and soon thereafter was retired.

The original *Chippewa* was a two-stacker. It was a steel passenger ferry and was built by Craig Shipbuilding Company in Chicago. It was brought around Cape Horn in 1907 for Puget Sound Navigation and was rebuilt in 1924 as a regular ferry. It was converted to diesel in 1930.

Another ferry was the steamer *City of Sacramento*. It served on San Francisco Bay until bought by Puget Sound Navigation.

During the war the commander of the navy yard had jurisdiction over all vessels on the Sound, including the ferries. He had told the ferry company to continue as scheduled until notified otherwise by him.

One day they got notified.

There was a draft of sailors who had to proceed with all haste to Seattle to catch a train. The commander commandeered the first ferry to Seattle, which happened to be the *Sacramento*. He told the captain to get there as fast as he could and the navy would stand responsibility for shore damages.

The *Sacramento* was a steamer and could move some faster than a diesel, if pushed. It got pushed. They made the 15-mile trip in 30 minutes. That's moving for a ferry boat. Needless to say, with the bow, spring and stern wakes, there was considerable damage to shore docks and small craft but the navy stood good for it.

Accidents

(Excerpts from the *Bremerton Searchlight*)

December 8, 1919

ONE DEATH AS LANDING FLOAT OVERTURNS

Mrs. Margaret W. Armstrong of Spokane was drowned when the landing float at the Manette Dock capsized last night at 6:40 p.m. as the passengers on the Urania were unloading.

The report was that approximately thirty-five persons were on the float awaiting the arrival of the Urania and they crowded to one side of the 14 x 30 foot float as the passenger boat came alongside. About twenty passengers disembarked and the float tipped under the water as the swift outgoing tide caught and capsized it, thus throwing everyone into the chill waters.

The F.G. Reeve. *Owned by Reeve family of Chico. Carried freight and some passengers in the 1920s. Her many ports of call included Enetai and Manette..*

The City of Manette. *Standing at door is Captain Nathan Williams. Boat was owned by Nathan's brother Theodore, and was used, according to Theodore's son Fred, for freight handling, but a passenger could ride "if he or she didn't mind sitting on freight boxes."*

The Bern (*or Berne, to some historians). One of the boats that carried foot passengers between Manette and Bremerton in the early 1900s. Manette Dock was then at the foot of East 10th Street, a location subsequently occupied by Tracy Lumber Company and its successors, and today is the site of the Narrows Apartments.*

The Swan. Photo taken in 1907. Swan burned at the Manette Dock at the foot of 10th Street in 1917. Flames spread to the dock and destroyed it also.

The Urania. This passengers-only substitute for the Pioneer had a "sawed-off" stern, shortened as a result of fire.

The Pioneer, sentimental favorite of Manette old-timers. She ran between Manette and Bremerton from 1916 until "decommissioned" by Manette Bridge in 1930. Photo shows her leaving Bremerton for Manette, seen in distance.. Pioneer is still afloat today, as a houseboat in Tacoma.

Purser Bob Carter (left) and owner-skipper Harry Hansen on bridge of Pioneer.

Bob Carter (left), friendly purser on the Pioneer, and Alvin Hansen, one of the skippers.

The Hiawatha *at the Second Street landing in Bremerton.*
Photo from Holden album

The steamers skipper immediately whistled for help and many Manette residents responded to help pull the people to safety. J.W.Burt and H.H. Granzier were the first on the scene and a motor steamer from the USS New York also responded with a crew and hospital corpsmen.

Others reported on the boat or on the float at the time were Emery Chase, Margaret Montgomery, Mrs. Fred Diedrich, D.H. Dewey, Velma Dewey, W.L. Rea, Mabel Rea, Jewel Montgomery, Mrs. Hugh Montgomery, Mrs. R.R. Collins, Ernest Collins, Mrs. P. Perry Ross, Kenneth Chase, Burgess Chase, Margaret Young, Modest Harlow, Thomas Cashill, Fred Diedrich, Eugene Chase, Mr. Lyons, and Mr. and Mrs. Ritter and 2-year-old baby.

August 9, 1918

SEDAN PARTY SUBMERGE OFF MANETTE BOAT

Two women and a man were plunged into the bay in a Ford sedan but escaped with no serious hurts when a car belonging to Mrs. M.D. Brewster of Manette shot off the end of the ferry Pioneer as it docked at about 11:20 this morning. H. Dutcher with his wife and Mrs. Agnes Waltenburg of Manette were in the sedan when the accident happened. The car was being brought to Bremerton for slight repairs to the self starter.

The car was at the end of the ferry as it struck the slip slightly sidewise and the failure of the brakes to hold precipitated the car into the bay where it submerged. Dutcher succeeded in getting the car door open and got out and after a little delay the women succeeded in getting free, both partially unconscious.

Thornton Rhodes, a sailor on the Keyport launch, plunged into the water as the women came up and after a hard fight with Miss Waltenburg, who was frightened and struggling, succeeded in bringing her to the float. Rhodes was slight and considerably outweighed by the woman whom he rescued and the feat is a great credit to his bravery and skill as a swimmer. A companion of Rhodes succeeded in bringing Mrs. Dutcher to land by permitting himself to be held by his heels off the float while he reached for the woman.

Mr. and Mrs. Dutcher and Miss Waltenburg were taken to the office of Dr. J.F. Munns, where it was found that they had received no injury save the wetting and shock and a few scratches.

Mrs. Brewster soon arrived to look after the comfort of her friends and superintend the raising of her car which was a comparatively new one.

Final Run of the *Pioneer*

By Orville Schultz

With the building of the Manette Bridge the Bremerton Bridge Company purchased the ferries *Pioneer* and *Urania* from Captain Harry Hansen. The last run of the *Pioneer* was on Saturday, June 21, 1930.

When the last whistle from the *Pioneer* as it left Bremerton on its final round trip was heard, Mrs. E.L. Erickson, 630 Burwell Street, and her son were the only passengers aboard. Charles Heumann, who had been riding the *Pioneer* for 13 years, arrived one minute late for the final going-to-Manette run. Skipper Hansen was not at the wheel; Buddy Meagher took his place. C.E. Dixon was purser.

As the good ship *Pioneer* pushed its way through the water

The Pioneer *made its final trip to the Manette Dock on June 21, 1930.*

Buddy Meagher and C.E. Dixon. Meagher piloted the ferry on its final run and Dixon was purser.

from Manette back to Bremerton, Dixon's daughter Jane Ellen pulled the rope and the old craft tooted its last warning. The boat docked at Bremerton and the passengers were discharged at 3:45 p.m.

Passengers making the last Manette-to-Bremerton trip were: Mr. and Mrs. Michael Harvey; Mrs. R. Larsen and children Marg, Ray and Buddy; Jack Hansen; Mr. and Mrs. A. Sonneland; Mrs. Harry Hansen; Mrs. C.E. Dixon; Jane Dixon, and a *Bremerton Press* representative.

The *Pioneer* was taken to Tacoma for conversion to a houseboat and is still afloat.

Point Herron
Light and Horn

By Roger Paquette

The northern boundaries of Manette have never been too clearly defined and have tended to be flexible over the years. But the southern boundary is a fixed point, Point Herron to be exact. A more obvious and descriptive name is Manette Point because it is the terminus of the whole Manette Peninsula, jutting into Port Orchard Bay. Only the people involved with navigation charts refer to it as Point Herron (named for Lewis Herron, the cooper on the brig *Porpoise* of the Wilkes Expedition in 1841).

The *Bremerton News*, in 1916, tells of a barge being

swamped by the wash of the high-speed ferry, *H.B. Kennedy*, off the "Manette Point." Four big guns and the flat cars on the barge were sent to the bottom. They were being sent to the Naval Gun Factory in Washington, D.C. for relining. The article said this would be an interesting fishing expedition because the guns were worth $10,000 apiece. It was interesting enough for the newsreels to pick up, and the Rex Theater, a month later, advertised movies of the guns being raised off "Manette Point." During World War II the navy eliminated gun-dunking problem by having a railroad spur extended to Bremerton and the shipyard.

In 1904, the *Bremerton News* had reported "Steamer *Advance* went on 'Manette Point' in fog. The Steamer *Manette* grounded trying to help." The need for navigational aid due to the extension of the point into the bay became obvious early on. The records of the 17th Lighthouse District show that a buoy was first placed on the point in 1923. It was a "Red 1st Class Nun." In 1929, the buoy was replaced by a "seven-pile dolphin with a flashing white 2 sec. light." In 1934, a "horn, air, blast 5 sec. silent 5 sec." was added. This was probably too much blast for the people of the area because the follow-

ing year the horn was changed to "blast 5 sec. silent 25 sec." In 1943, a very substantial set of pilings was installed to support the addition of "a white pyramidal house with a red triangle."

Boat builder John Jacobson and his daughter, Edith Ludvigson, lived at 603 Shore Drive and activated the horn when the fog rolled in. Others who lived there and operated the horn over the years were the Hammersburgs, Mr. Jacobson's grandson Harold Halmerson, Bruce Walker and Edith (Mrs. Louis P.) Olsen. Mrs. Olsen was employed as the operator long enough to receive a pension. Louis and Edith had mirrors in their bedroom that enabled them to see the light at night and throw the switch whenever the fog rolled in, without getting out of bed.

John Jacobson and daughter Edith, circa 1926.

The house had been purchased in 1969 by Harry Tangen and his wife Elin, and with relocation of the service cable Elin became the controller. Her job was terminated in 1987 when a new dolphin was installed. The new equipment had its own fog sensing device and a flashing red light in lieu of a white one. Elin was one of the last female lighthouse tenders in the U.S.

ROADS AND VEHICLES
By Orville Schultz

According to research done by Grace Jack Barlow for a Bremerton High School project, the first road in Manette

Combined water-land transportation circa 1898. Scene is at east end of present Manette Bridge. Men and equipment are those of Port Orchard Lumber and Transportation Company (Fellows-Bender mill). Man beside boat at left is unidentified. Next two are believed to be George and Thomas Fellows. Boy at right is unidentified. In background is the original mill building. The mill had been moved across Port Washington Narrows to Smith Cove.   -Photo from Walt Fellows

within today's Bremerton city limits was a wide trail with stumps sawed off at the ground. It started from Bender's mill, ran up Telegraph Avenue (now East 11th Street) to where the Masonic Temple is today, turned and went out what is now Perry Avenue.

The citizens of Seabeck and Port Orchard precincts petitioned for a road to be built from the Seabeck mill to the Port Orchard mill in 1858, but what they got was probably more of a trail than a road.

A new territorial road authorized by the legislature to run

Harry Hansen's bus at bus stop, East 11th Street and Scott Avenue, 1930. House in background is at 1103 Scott Avenue. It is still there.

from Seabeck to the head of Hood Canal at Clifton (Belfair) was finished in 1861. Also, about this time, travelers from Seattle rowed to the Port Orchard mill to walk over a trail to the head of Port Washington Bay (Dyes Inlet) and thence direct (by Anderson Hill Road) to Seabeck to board ships for San Francisco or the Orient. A logger was paid $100 a year to keep the road open.

In 1923 Elton Abernathy started a taxi service from the Manette Dock.

"When the Manette Bridge opened in 1930," according to

Elton Abernathy's taxi on Manette Dock, 1923. Early Puget Sound Steamer in background.

-Photo from Wendell Abernathy

The main drag. In about 1918, East 11th Street looked like this. Meredith's store (now the Gamesters, 2202 East 11th Street) is at the left and J.H. "Jack" Martin's dry goods store is in the background.

Larry Worland, "Harry Hansen started a bus service from Manette to Bremerton. At first the bus ran from the YMCA in Bremerton to East 11th Street and Scott Avenue in Manette. Later the route was extended up Perry Avenue to Sheridan Road. For school children, Harry made a morning and afternoon trip to the old Lincoln School at 11th Street and Ohio Avenue in Bremerton."

MANETTE'S BRIDGES
By Orville Schultz

In the summer of 1925 George Sears, president of the Union Bridge Company of Portland, Oreg., on a visit to Bremerton, investigated the possibility of a bridge from Manette to Bremerton. The idea of a bridge was not new. An article in the *Manette Fog Horn* of April 2, 1921, states:

> The bridge proposition is not dead by any means. It is thought that if the people on this side of the bay would see to it that a first class road was put in between here and Keyport the government would be interested enough to lend its support to the erection of a bridge as it would give a direct route over a first class road from the yard to the Keyport station.

Sears concluded that even with the combined financing of

Manette Bridge under construction, 1929.

An era ending. Ferry Pioneer *and, at lower right, Manette Bridge construction materials and equipment being assembled, 1929.*

the city and the county it was not feasible. He also visited Admiral J.V. Chase, Puget Sound Navy Yard commandant, who assured him that the navy would give any help possible. Admirals Robinson and Ziegemeier in the following years also were cooperative.

Sears died soon after his visit, but Charles G. Huber, Union Bridge Company vice president, took up the work with Ralph Schneelob and W.B. Buell of Portland. One year later the financial studies were nearly completed and in 1926, with the cooperation of Bremerton Mayor Clarence E.B. Oldham, L.A. Bender, E.A. Mills, W.B. Jessup, C.P. Kimball and others, the Bremerton Bridge Company was formed to push the building of the bridge.

The U.S. Congress and President Coolidge approved the project.

Local people sold stock door-to-door county wide, raising

Key participants in Manette Bridge dedication ceremonies, June 21, 1930. Queen for the occasion was Helen Joldersma (back row, third from left). Others in back row are, from left, Genevieve Joyce, Kathryn Alsop, Doris Lamphere, Frances Arney, Constance Oldham and Mary Soyat. Front row: Rear Admiral H.J. Ziegemeier, Puget Sound Navy Yard Commandant; Jane Garrison, 106-year-old granddaughter of Chief Seattle; Bremerton Mayor C.E.B. Oldham, and J.H. "Jack" Martin, Manette businessman.

approximately $200,000. William Abbott of Manette led these teams. On the strength of this success an additional $175,000 was raised by sale of preferred debenture bonds taken over by W.P. Harper and Sons.

The bridge would be of two lanes, 1573 feet long and 80 feet high, with wooden-plank decking and timber-piling approach spans. Tolls would be 25 cents for cars and 5 cents for pedestrians.

Construction began in October 1929 by Union Bridge Company of Portland, low bidder at $525,000.

The bridge opened ahead of schedule June 21, 1930. The event was a gala one: no more driving around through Silverdale via sandy, narrow and sometimes washboard roads, should one miss the last run of the *Pioneer*.

Two views looking Manette-ward from the Manette Bridge center span, taken 56 years apart: the upper one on opening day June 21, 1930 (Bremerton Sun photo), and the lower May 3, 1986 (photo by Lyle Sunderland). Note interim changes in Manette landscape.

TOLL TAKER

George W. Baker was as familiar a figure to the automobile driver and foot pedestrian on the Manette Bridge as Harry Hansen and Bob Carter were to the people who ran to catch the *Pioneer*.

George was a toll taker on the bridge from the moment it opened until the minute it went toll-free. He had a cheery hello for all and if some person (usually a young person who had lost his nickel) came to the toll booth with a long face George immediately knew what was wrong. That person always got to go home, for George always had an extra nickel for a good cause.

He was a loyal member of the East Bremerton Improvement Club and a charter member of American Legion Manette Peninsula Post 68, and in 1938 served as post commander.

George Baker

Bremerton businessman James O. Skirving was the first person to pay a motor vehicle toll to George Baker on June 21, 1930, immediately following the dedication ceremonies, and was the last to pay the car toll across the bridge at 3:59 p.m. on January 28, 1939. A state highway maintenance engineer,

PRICE $1.50   Book N? S 3006
BREMERTON BRIDGE COMPANY
COMMUTATION BOOK
GOOD FOR PEDESTRIAN OR PASSENGER IN VEHICLE CROSSING ONLY

Purchaser.....................

Manette Bridge commuter passbook.

J.C. Bartholet, living in Port Orchard, was the last pedestrian to pay the 5-cent toll to George Baker and walk across the bridge at 3:59 p.m. January 28, 1939.

Some of the other toll takers from Manette were Alonzo Almon, George Pentz, Marion Martin, Charles Klinefelter, Alvin Grove, Frank Hawley and a Mr. Rice.

FREE BRIDGE SOUGHT

Within a few years a campaign to remove the tolls had begun. Lloyd Solid, a staunch member of the East Bremerton Improvement Club (EBIC) and a sparkplug in community affairs, was one of the people advocating going for a free bridge. A committee was formed with J. McDonnell as chairman and members Pliny Allen, C.L. Irwin, Otto Voll and J.H. Martin. Its purpose was to lobby the legislators at Olympia for a free bridge.

The Legislature appropriated $320,000 but a court valued the bridge at $354,000. Tolls were retained until the difference was made up.

On January 28, 1939, tolls were lifted. EBIC sent out the following invitation:

You are cordially invited to join in a

Celebration culminating five years of effort

to make the

Bremerton-Manette Bridge Toll-Free

Exercises at the Manette Bridge-head

on Saturday, January the twenty-eighth, 1939

at four o'clock in the afternoon

R.S.V.P.   EAST BREMERTON IMPROVEMENT CLUB
                                    SPONSORS

NEW BRIDGE?

With the influx of new people into the area before and during World War II the bridge became inadequate for the traffic generated. The EBIC, as spokesmen for the Manette Peninsula, formed a new bridge committee composed of Willard Parker, chairman; Dick Feek, Henry Streutker, E.W. Schweer and Clyde Meredith. They met with Burwell Bantz, state director of highways, to discuss another bridge.

Meanwhile the EBIC, spearheaded by Earl Harkins, had obtained passage by Congress of a law forbidding the re-imposition of tolls on the Manette Bridge.

The *Manette News-Letter* of February 17, 1944, reported that the EBIC favored the construction of a new four-lane bridge.

In 1945 the State Legislature appropriated $750,000 for a Port Washington Narrows bridge. But an additional $1.5 million anticipated from the federal government was not made available, and in 1949 the state funds were used to rebuild the Manette Bridge. Its timber approach pilings and the wooden decking were replaced with steel and concrete. The approach for the pedestrian walk was widened.

The *Kitsap County News* of May 30, 1956, reported that the City of Bremerton and the Washington State Toll Bridge Authority were proceeding with plans to build a new Port Washington Narrows bridge. A $5 to $6 million "package deal" would include the bridge, four-lane approaches, widening of Warren Avenue to Burwell Street, and a four-lane overpass at 11th Street crossing Warren Avenue Playfield. Toll would be 10 cents per car or $1 for 15 commuter crossings.

It was found necessary to have Congress repeal the law which prohibited re-establishing tolls on the Manette Bridge;

a new bridge would not pay for itself if there were a free bridge nearby.

The four-lane Warren Avenue Bridge opened November 25, 1958. Later, its two-way toll was changed to a single entering toll, to facilitate the flow of traffic leaving Bremerton.

The bridges became toll-free October 24, 1972, after 14 years of operation. The expanding growth of the Manette Peninsula produced enough bridge tolls to pay for the bridge construction bonds. Lee Tennison of Manette was the first to drive across the toll-free bridge in a north-south direction. He led the parade in a 1916 Buick.

AIRPLANES
By Larry Worland
Tom Erdman's Lincoln Sport

(including information from an article by Lisetta Lindstrom in the *Kitsap Journal* of July 21, 1976)

Tom Erdman started building a private airplane, the Lincoln Sport, in LaGrande, Wash., in 1929. Later the fuselage and motor were towed to Manette, where he completed the plane in what had been Martin's grocery store on Shore Drive. Tom's uncle, a machinist, designed and built the 40-horsepower, 2100 rpm, three-cylinder radial engine from Harley-Davidson 74 motorcycle parts. It was said to "run like a charm."

The plane was a small bi-plane with one cockpit for the pilot. Brother George and I helped Tom build it.

Tom Erdman's airplane, under construction, about 1930.

After the engine was installed and landing gear was in place, Tom would drive his plane (no wings attached) through the streets of Manette to Bill Sutherland's place (Bill was Tom's brother-in-law) at the north end of Scott Avenue.

Tom would do great going north—uphill—but he had no brakes on his plane, so he would have to pick up the tail end and walk his plane back down.

In 1934 Tom finished the plane. But a 1933 Washington State regulation prevented him from flying a home-built airplane. In 1938 he sold it for $50. It was placed on the roof of a Kitsap County Airport coffee shop with the words HOT

COFFEE on the wing. During World War II the plane was used by the military as a decoy. Later it was lost when a storm destroyed a shed where it was stored. Tom reclaimed the motor components and presented them to the Museum of Flight at Boeing Field in Seattle.

Air Service

An air ferry service between Bremerton and Seattle with Loening amphibians was started in 1929 by Vergne Gorst of Gorst Air Transport Company. On October 31, 1929, one of the planes crashed into the Sound off Trenton Avenue, kill-

An air ferry service between Bremerton and Seattle was started in 1929 with Loening amphibians like the one shown.

ing the two operators, Don Monroe and Al Van Vleet.

"The fact that this plane had crashed off Manette probably saved George Personette's life," Roger Paquette says. "George tipped over in a canoe sometime after the loss of the amphibian. Divers searching for the plane's engine sent a launch from the diving barge and rescued George."

SIGHTSEEING FLIGHTS

Willard Muller recalls: "We boys used to bicycle out past Clare's Marsh on Sunday afternoons to watch a biplane land in a cow pasture and take people for rides for $5 for about 15 minutes. I believe many boys' interest in flying was whetted by seeing that plane and pilot. My brother Ward and John Nelson, both of whom used to bike out there, went into the Army Air Force in World War II, and later I learned to fly a single-engine plane for a hobby. I got away from it soon when we moved to West Germany in 1948 and couldn't fly there."

Sightseeing service in 1930.

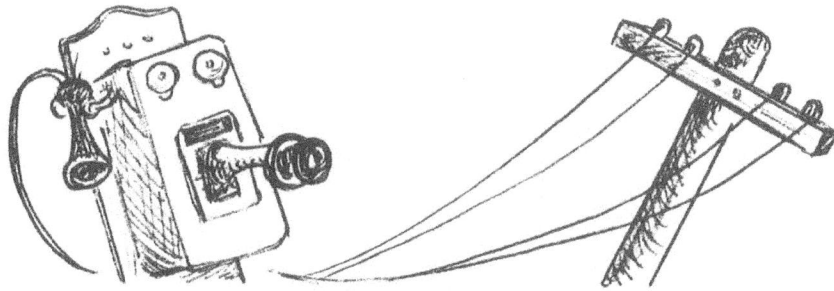

Chapter 3
UTILITIES
By Roger Paquette

WATER, WATER EVERYWHERE

Manette pioneers never had to go too far for their water. In addition to collecting abundant rainfall, which was fairly well distributed through the year, they had access to many streams and springs. Wells and cisterns were dug throughout the area. Windlasses, ropes and buckets were supplanted by pumps where practical. The ultimate was to have an elevated tank or a pressure tank connected to pipes which enabled one to have indoor plumbing.

In 1901, the regular Decatur correspondent to the *Bremerton News* reported "Mr. Smith feels he's on a solid foundation. He has dug a well 40 feet through solid rock and has found plenty of water." In 1903, the same correspondent reported "a cry for well diggers coming from all directions." However, by 1904, he quotes somebody as saying, "if half the money that has been spent digging wells for water in the last two years had been set aside for a water system, Manette would now have a first class system—all we have now is a bunch of holes in the ground."

The Manette Water Works in 1905 had an "excellent supply" of water. In 1906, it was furnishing water for five families. The school opened in September of 1905. In 1906 a new pump had to be put in the schoolhouse.

On November 13, 1906, articles of incorporation were filed for the Manette Water Company, and a relatively large-scale distribution of water began. The first source was actually a shallow well (cistern) "about 30x40 feet and maybe 15 feet deep, covered by planks, located on the west side of Perry just above 11th, the site of the Danel property at a later date," according to Walt Fellows, whose dad, Thomas, was one of the trustees of the company. There was a tank tower at that location to provide wide distribution. By the spring of 1907, the company was reported "laying pipe as fast as possible." The boast was made that "Manette has more water lines than any town near its size."

ELEVATED SOURCE

In 1908 the water company leased a piece of land and right of way above old Manette School on Ironsides Avenue, erected a tower and tank and installed new distribution lines to feed a larger area of Manette. The property was later purchased by the Lloyd Solids. After Manette was annexed to Bremerton and was connected to its water system in 1918,

Water tower (arrow) near Manette School, erected by Manette Water Company in 1908.
-Photo from Edna Hoopes Brookman

private water systems continued to serve a limited clientele. Bright's water system employed a shallow cistern from which water was pumped to a tower. Cherry Bright Baker says her dad was strict about the kids not playing in the cistern, but it was rumored that when the Brights were away some kids did swim in it. Another tank, near 1130 Hayward Avenue, was one Tom Fellows built to supply water for his greenhouse. This tower was a landmark in Manette for many years. The water came from a spring-fed cistern next to Martin's store at about 2109 East 11th Street. (Walt Fellows says he doubts there was ever such a thing as a legal permit to run a line from the cistern up to the tank.) The *Bremerton News* of June 7,

Fellows home and water tower (arrow), early 1900s. They were Manette landmarks for many years. Location was north of East 11th Street and east of Hayward Avenue.

M.R.Brewster's home and 1000-gallon "tank house"
(arrow) about 1911. Site, on Perry Avenue, is occupied
today by Church of Jesus Christ of Latter-Day Saints.
                                    -Photo from Hattie Engstrom.

1911, states that Mr. Brewster on Perry Avenue "has completed a three story tank house with a 1000 gallon capacity and a 2 H.P. gas engine—enough water for his whole ranch." With introduction of electric power in 1912, electric pumps gradually replaced fuel motors. In the 1920s, there were tower tanks and/or compression tanks on Trenton Avenue at the Youngs', Jensens' and Howertons' that fed one or more families.

NO-COST PUMPING

Without doubt the cheapest method of pumping water up to a tank was by hydraulic ram. (An old joke was that steel wool came from hydraulic rams). This device utilizes the energy of a large amount of water to raise a small amount to a great height. The Howerton tank was fed this way. So was the Ammerman tank in Sheridan, where the ram was a homemade wooden device. (It can be remembered as sounding like a gunshot every time it cycled.)

In 1917 the City of Bremerton after some lengthy court hearings purchased the Bremerton Water Company from the private firm of Garrison-Fisher.

On September 10, 1918, in an election by the people of Bremerton and Manette, for annexation of Manette to Bremerton passed easily in both communities. Manette's interest in this affiliation was probably due mostly to the need for adequate water. The growing community had outstripped

Hydraulic ram. Actual
height is about 2 feet.
-Photo from Hattie Engstrom

the ability of the water company to keep the taps running during the dry season, and the other small suppliers also had trouble meeting commitments. The city would supply Manette through the Manette Water Company.

But the annexation did not immediately solve the supply problems, especially during the summer months. The *Bremerton News* of July 12, 1920, said:

MANETTE RESIDENTS AROUSED OVER WATER SUPPLY SHORTAGE:

Committee to appear tonight before city council to demand relief.... Only supply for past weeks has been in buckets from wells.... It is said: Manette residents are aroused and in fighting mood over the water supply to that community across the bay. During the past week 75 percent of the homes on the east side have been without even a trickle from their faucets for several days. According to word from that section of the city today a protesting committee will appear in force before the city council meeting in Bremerton tonight to demand that the city authorities take some action in the matter.

Manette residents say they would not mind the shortage so much if it were not a regular yearly occurrence. They say they are willing to allow for trouble with the water system, but that it is getting to be a case of "too much without any attempt at remedy." During the past week Manette is said to have depended for its water solely on a few wells in the vicinity, supplying their homes through the only method available—that of a water bucket brigade. Water is delivered in Manette from the city water supply, but through a private company which owns the system in that east bay section, and which buys water from the city reservoir and sells it to the Manette homes. Manette people say that on top of the fact that the water supply is always poor in summer, the private company has been charging an additional sum of 50 cents per month over the winter rate of $1.50.

As a result, by June 1921, new wooden water mains, 4-inch and 6-inch, had been installed on the principal streets of Manette. A 6-inch cast iron main was laid across Port Washington Narrows and hooked up to the Manette system. Cost of the project was $53,770.30. This did not spell the end of water troubles in Manette. The Bremerton Water System went through many problems in the twenties, and Manette suffered along with it. The main across the Narrows was subject to swift moving tides. In 1925 a lighthouse tender anchor caused an outage in the supply. Divers had trouble with the main, and temporary service was supplied by a 2-inch pipe. In November of 1927, leaks were discovered again. In February of 1928, more complaints to the city council were made. Divers in 1929 reported the 6-inch main as being "too brittle." "They did their best to fill up the bay with fresh water and finally gave up," says present-day Water Superintendent Bill Duffy.

And they *could* give up, because the Manette Bridge was completed and a 12-inch wooden main was laid on the bridge. This had 36 times the capacity of the 2-incher and furthermore, was unaffected by fast tides and careless anchoring.

The city commissioners had voted in 1925 to buy a lot from Mary Brewster above East 16th Street on Hayward Avenue. Since the purchase was to be used to improve the area by construction of a tank and tower for water supply, she let them have it for half price, $100. The tower was about 50 feet high and probably held about 10,000 gallons when full, though it leaked so much that that figure is probably insignificant. Originally an open tank, it was fitted with a conical roof after a few years.

ANOTHER SUBMARINE LINE

In 1943 the Federal Government brought the submarine water line back into business with a main from the north end of Warren Avenue to the Federal housing project water line in Sheridan Park. In 1945, a new 12-inch steel line across the Manette Bridge replaced the wooden one put on in 1930. In 1948, the city took over the distribution system and all appurtenances and reservoirs from the Sheridan Park Housing Authority and paid the Federal Government $40,000 for the 12-inch submarine main.

On December 2, 1939, the *News Searchlight* reported that T.A. Bright had offered his property to the city for a reservoir site for $1200.

Attention should probably be called to Clifford C. Casad, who was the public works commissioner in 1939. The excellent water system we have today can be credited to his efforts and foresight over many years; this example of buying the Bright property nearly 20 years before it was used is a specific illustration. It was on his recommendation that this was done. It's hard to say how much the property would have cost 10 years later even if it had been available then.

What was finally paid to Bright is not known, but the city took the land and built a reservoir of 2,200,000 gallons. The site is at East 17th Street and Ironsides Avenue. The completed reservoir was accepted by the city on September 3, 1958.

Now in the 1980s, the location from which the Bright family fed water to its neighbors is still being used to feed water, but to a much larger group.

After the Warren Avenue Bridge was dedicated on November 25, 1958, the day of the submarine line ended again. A new 20-inch main was laid across the bridge.

MANETTE LIGHTS UP

After many months of laying cables, installing poles, stringing wires and putting up light standards, the Bremerton-Charleston Light and Power Company brought electricity to Manette in March of 1912. Principal streets were then lit up at night and the light bulb gradually displaced oil and gas lamps. The *Bremerton Searchlight* said "...Manette at night looms up like a big city, and while Telegraph Avenue is not so well lighted as the 'Great White Way' the town looks not unlike the lower end of Manhattan Island viewed from the Statue of Liberty."

The next month the *Searchlight* quoted Jack Martin, known as Manette's premier merchant prince, as saying, "These electric lights and other hi-falutin' improvements of modern science have their drawbacks." He said he lost the best lady clerk he ever had because of the lights coming to Manette. The clerk, Loretta Brower, started keeping company with a lineman, Charles Grinnell, who seemed to have had to spend an inordinate amount of time on the wiring around Jack's store. The resulting marriage meant looking for a new clerk.

HOLLER ACROSS?
NO, PHONE

The *Bremerton News* of February 24, 1902, reported that the cable between Seattle and the navy yard had been broken between Decatur and Bremerton, necessitating the use of launches to carry dispatches between these two points. A new cable across Port Washington Narrows was laid, and by May of 1903 it was possible to telephone across—if you happened to miss the last ferry or for some emergency, because that was when a hand-crank telephone was installed (appropriately enough) in a Mrs. Crank's place. By October of that year a dozen phones had been installed and agitation began for the installation of an exchange. To quote the regular Decatur cor-

respondent of the *Bremerton News*, J. W. Martin, "the party line is quite confusing at times." The subscribers of that date and their respective call rings were:

W.S. Crank 1L	S. A. Carlson 1 L and 3 S
J.W.Martin 2L	Mr. Wakeman 2 L and 1 S
Mr. Brewster 3L	Harry Martin Store 2 L and 2 S
W. S. Harris 4L	W.G. Miles 1 L and 1 S and 1L
W. B. Lockwood 1 L and 1S	Harry Fellows 1S and 1 L and 1S

Within a year of the first phone there were 18 phones in Manette. The first interruption of service, according to records, took place a year after that when somebody laid a metal object on the top of a telephone box. (Why this would cause an interruption is not stated.) From there on it was clear sailing and talking until the break-up of A. T. & T. in 1983.

Meanwhile, in the late 1960s, the Bell Telephone Company gave us additional background with this report:

The younger of Bremerton's first two operators, Mable Renn, died several years ago. However, the second, Harriet Holden, is still alive and at 83 can provide a lively account of the telephone business as it was before the turn of the century. As the oldest girl in town at the time, recalled Mrs. Holden, she was a natural choice of the Sunset Telephone Company to be one of its first Bremerton operators. Although she was still in the eighth grade at the time, she went to work to earn money for business college, which she began attending a year later in Seattle. Either she or her co-worker [Mable Renn] was at the switchboard each day for 10 hours to manually connect each call. The two young operators each earned about $15 a week. However, Mrs. Holden added, since only 12 residents could afford the $2.50 installation fee and the monthly payments for a crank telephone, they only had to handle about ten calls a day. Since all 12 phones were on the same line, almost every call turned into a 12-way conversation, said Mrs. Holden. But, she laughed, "Everybody seemed so happy. You could listen in on their conversations and they listened in on yours and nobody minded." There was no telephone service beyond the little settlement's narrow perimeters. The only means of communication across Port Washington Narrows, which separated the town from what is now called East Bremerton, said Mrs. Holden, "was to go down to the shore and holler across."

Telephones came to Manette in 1903. So, therefore, did telephone poles, at right in this picture. View looks south on Winfield Avenue from about East 16th Street.   *- Holden album*

SEWERS REPLACE OUTHOUSES

On November 17, 1936, the Bremerton city council formally passed a resolution accepting an offer of a U. S. Government grant through the Federal Emergency Administration of Public Works for Bremerton sewer additions. The grant was not to exceed $78,225 and represented 45 percent of the cost of the projects.

Jewell Sollie (Tenge) furnished a copy of the minutes of the East Bremerton Improvement Club (EBIC) meeting of Friday, November 13, 1936. (This is a rare document, for all the other records of the EBIC were destroyed by fire.) Miss Palmer appears to have been the secretary, though the copy isn't signed.

Mr. Roy Ellis called the meeting to order. The purpose was "to obtain information in regard to securing sewers in Manette." Attending the meeting from city hall were City Attorney Gorman, Engineer C. C. Casad and Finance Commissioner Carl Halverson.

Those answering questions at the meeting were Mr. Gorman, Mr. Casad and Mr. Halverson. Those asking questions were Mr. Voll, Mr. Losee, Mr. Bright, Mr. Dix, Mr. Jack Martin, Mrs. Burlew, Mrs. Losee, Mr. McDonald, Mr. Hall, Mrs. Martin and Mr. Hook.

Those in favor of the proposed sewer project were Mr. Wheaton, Mr. Brown, Mr. Cowan, Mr. Bubke, Mr. Gillette and Mr. Abbott.

Mr. Gillette stated that the biggest reason it had been so hard to get FHA loans in Manette had been because of the lack of sewers.

Mr. Casad stated that the logical place to start the first sewer project was Manette; that time was short, as bids would have to be called by the first of the year so construction could start by the January 11 deadline set by the Government. He would start on the lateral lines and face the complications of the outfall at a later date. He had petitions for the people of Manette to sign to indicate that they wanted the sewers.

Mr. Halversen encouraged the signing of the petitions. The balance of the money would come from bonds that would be paid from assessments on the improvement district. There should be no trouble selling the bonds as Bremerton improvement districts had good payment records. Mr. Gorman said that it was Mr. Halvorsen who went after the grant. (Nowadays most larger community organizations have in their employment a person skilled in going after Government grants.) Mr. Gorman elaborated on the legalities of which properties would be assessed.

There followed a long session of questions and answers ranging from "How about the outfall?" (As far as they knew it would be located under 20 feet of water at extreme low tide.) to "What is the object of the sewer?" (The object of the sewer is to dispose of sewage.)

As expected, there was some opposition to the sewer, but the general tenor of the meeting seemed to be in favor of going ahead with the project.

December 19, 1936, the city council passed ordinance 1116 for the project, local improvement district 152. Protests were presented by A. L. Stranahan, E. B. Christianson, Mrs. Hagen, Mrs. Meredith, C. E. Barrett, T. G. Pidduck, B. E. Steffens and others, stating basically that the sewer was of no use and the outfall would be a nuisance. The council noted that if it was of no benefit, laws would not permit assessment.

So the trunks and laterals were laid and the streets that had been recently oiled (at the local residents' expense) to keep the dust down were all dug up and the EBIC was at City Hall to get the streets back in shape.

The outfall was finally located at the foot of Trenton Avenue. According to Superintendent McKenzie of the Bremerton wastewater operation the outfall is located some 340 feet out from the low-tide line. The trunkline is now connected to a main trunk which carries the material to the disposal plants. However, during heavy concentrations of downpour the storm water can overload the plants, under which conditions the outfall is put back in use.

Chapter 4

SCHOOLS

BEGINNING AND GROWTH

**By Walt and Mary Fellows
and Eleanor Carlson Harrington**

The first meeting of School District 3 was held in July 1867 at the Colman and Glidden Mill store. The directors were F.M. Guye, D.J. Sackman and N. Hale and the clerk Theodore O. Williams. Instruction began later that year.

"It was resolved that the schoolhouse of said district be located on a tract of land at the mouth of Port Washington Narrows, known by the name of Dyes Inlet, at or adjoining the land of Theodore O. Williams," the minutes state. "It was further resolved that a schoolhouse be built by volunteer subscription, and be 16 by 20 feet with a house or apartment adjoining, sufficient for the accommodation of a teacher and the children who may board with the teacher."

The tract of land was Government Lot 5, Section 13 of the Public Lands, 40 acres bounded by what is now Perry Avenue on the east, East 13th Street on the south, East 16th Street on the north and the water on the west. The school was the first in what is now Bremerton School District 100-C.

The teacher was Warren W. Perrigo, 31, born and educated in New Brunswick, Canada, married to the former Laura M. MacDuff of LaGrange, Maine. They came here from Seattle, where they had arrived in 1866. The Perrigos ran the boarding house at the school.

On May 15, 1869, the Perrigos purchased the 40-acre school property at a base price of $1.25 per acre, and on April 5, 1871, they sold the south 10 acres, on which the school was constructed, to School District 3 for $80.

Perrigo was soon followed by others who taught for short periods. Miss Emma Babbitt, who taught in 1880 for $60 per month for 6 months, remembered the children as having had very little previous opportunity for education but said they were teachable. White children were a minority among Indians and half-whites.

The Port Orchard School, as it was known, was located near the east end of the present Manette Bridge, at the site of today's Sunset Shores Apartments, 1115 Wheaton Way. An old oak tree, thought to have been planted by teacher Miss Lizzie Ordway in 1880, and a marker plate on a granite boulder still stand at the site.

In 1878 a second room, 20 by 22 feet, was added to the school. Another teacher during these early times was Hanna Condon, who was the last teacher at Port Orchard when the school was abandoned in 1885.

A new school was started at Sackman, near Tracyton, in 1886 with Jennie W. Tappan as the first teacher. Joseph Sackman donated an old camp building as the school. Sara Sumner and Cora Finch followed as teachers in a new school built in Tracyton in 1889. There were 19 students in 1890.

District 3 was now designated District 4. As the county population grew, more road districts and voting precincts were needed. School districts at that time were set up on road district boundaries. Transportation limitations of the time made for small school districts, which increased in number rather than size as settlements grew in the county.

Warren W. Perrigo was the first teacher in what is now Manette. The area was then known as Port Orchard. The school opened in 1867 in a building erected by volunteer subscription near the east end of the present Manette Bridge. Perrigo was born in Salisbury, New Brunswick, April 10, 1836. He married Laura M. Macduff of LaGrange, Maine, June 25, 1864. They were at the Port Orchard School 2 years. In 1871 the Perrigos homesteaded as the first pioneers in Redmond, Wash. Laura died in September 1887. Warren died in December 1914. The Perrigos had four children, Laura M., Warren H., Theodore J. and Caroline A.

First Manette (Port Orchard) School. Located at present site of Sunset Shore Apartments, 1115 Wheaton Way, structure was built in 1867. Photo was taken in 1897, after building had been sold to George Fellows and remodeled into a residence. On porch are (from left), George Fellows, Arthur Fellows, Hattie MacIntosh, Thomas Fellows, Renus Bender, Ella Bender and Jessie Williams. In front are Arthur Bender and Lewis Bender (holding young Renus).-Photo from Don and Anna Jo Atkinson

On May 4, 1886, on recommendation of School Superintendent Lizzie M. Ordway, School District 4 was reduced in size. Within the new boundaries were Tracyton, Chico, Silverdale and other settlements along the waterfront and inland. Within this district the new school at Tracyton opened, and the Port Orchard school closed.

On May 8, 1888, School Directors Nathan Cosman, T.O. Williams and David H. Sackman declared the 10-acre Port Orchard school property surplus and sold it to George Fellows, the highest bidder, for $350. Fellows remodeled the school building into a residence for himself and his three sons, Harry, Thomas and Arthur. Lewis A. and wife Ella Fellows Bender later built a new home at this location.

SHIFT TO SHERIDAN

On February 20, 1897, Sheldon Smith offered land he owned near Sheridan Road and Olympus Drive as a school site for a dollar, and the offer was accepted. Until the school could be built, Mrs. Jane Ruley taught the children on a month-to-month basis at $20 a month.

It was a year and a half before the new school was finished. Strout and Peters furnished 10,000 feet of logs, the Bender/Fellows sawmill cut the lumber, R. Ryther, Paul Ruley, Edwin Phillips, Joseph Pitt, John Mikkleson and others contributed the carpenter work and Munro Brewster built the chimney. In February of 1898 Alonzo Coder finished the interior of the school and Mrs. Eva Reeve was hired to teach for a month. In April of 1898 Helen Toles was hired to teach for 4 months in the new school, called "Dewey."

In June 1913 bids were called for a new Sheridan School, and in July H.A. Hatfield was chosen as contractor for the low

Historic site. This oak tree marks the location of Manette's first school. Tree is said to have been planted by teacher Lizzie Ordway in 1880. Site is near east end of Manette Bridge. The tree and a granite marker still stand.   -Photo from Orville Schultz

Early Sheridan School., School district 22 erected this building in 1898 at what is now Sheridan Road and Olympus Drive. Photo was taken in 1907. In back row are (from left), Earl Baker, George Baker, Ralph Ohman, Erik Engstrom, Gertrude Ruley, John Heffner, Velna Farmer, Vera Peckenpaugh, David Stevenson, teacher George Cody Johnson. Front row, Percy Ohman, Vere Farmer, Jack Gordon, Leonard Parker, Theodore Baker, Ethel Baker, Elsie van Nuys, Frances Schlagel, Margaret Young, Eleanor Sampson, Thelma Henderson. George Schlagel, Blanche van Nuys, Loran Avery, Birdie Avery.　　　　　　　-Photo from Hattie Elliott Engstrom

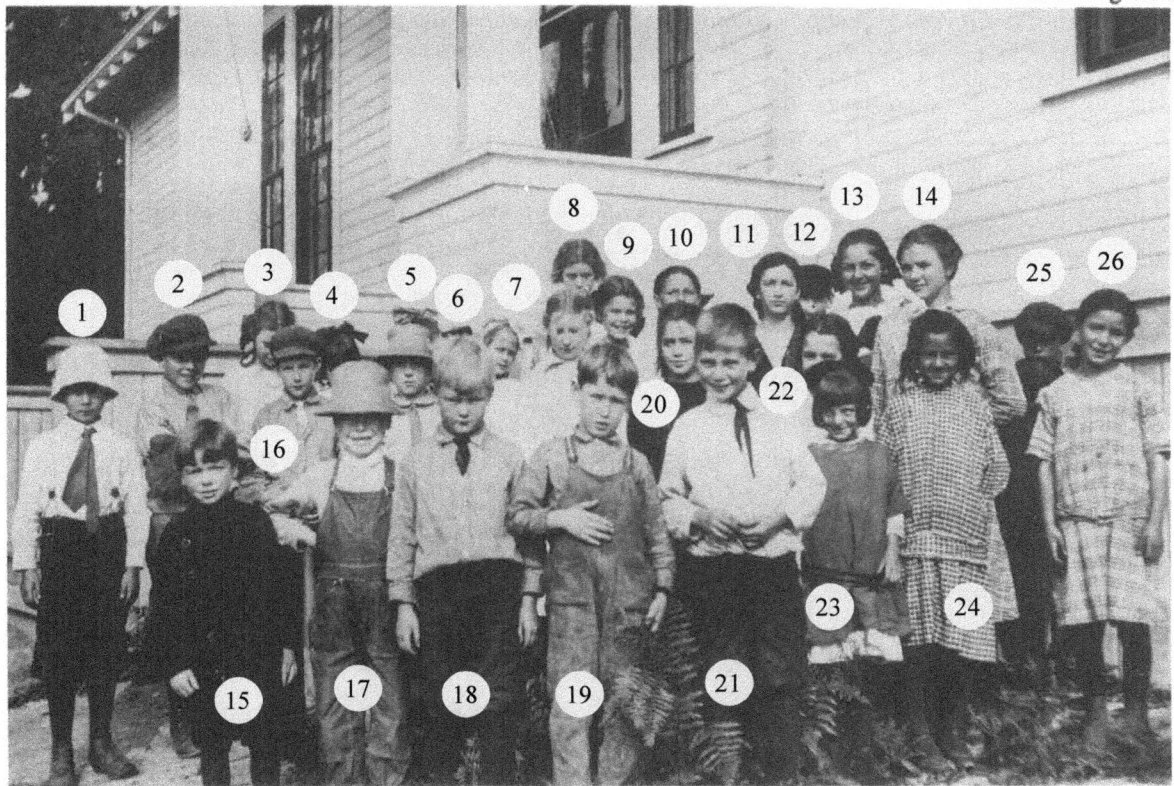

Sheridan School, 1913. 1_____, 2_____, 3_____, 4_____, 5_____, 6 Dora Ohman, 7 Beda Ohman, 8 Eleanor Sampson, 9 Margaret Young, 10 Beatrice Schlagel, 11 Agnes Waltenburg, 12_____, 13 Cornelia Hitt, 14 Catherine Peters, 15_____, 16 Herbert Ballew, 17_____, 18 Frank Ballew, 19 Herman Avery, 20 Violet Waltenburg, 21 Murray Hitt, 22 Mary Hubbell, 23 Mary Schlagel, 24 Emelia Schlagel, 25_____, 26 Erma Avery.

Sheridan School, 1931–1932. Teachers: Mrs. Gladys Theis, grades 1-4, and Mrs. Dorothy Mumford, grades 5-8. Back row (from left), Georgia Moffat, _____ Hepworth, Mrs. Mumford, Robert Quay, Raymond Hepworth. Row 6, Clifford Reanier, _____, David Morris. Row 5, William Johnson, Walter Bertram, Evelyn Pardee, Mary Christianson, Zoe Cowan, Harold Sherman, _____, Dallas Pentz. Row 4, Fred Johnson, Ed Wintermute, Ralph Hart. Row 3, Nancy Christianson, Hazel Hart, Lucy Hepworth, Bernice Clare, _____, Elmer Elliott, James Parr, Harlan Parker, _____. Row 2, Margaret Christianson, Lamar Davis, Ruby Hart, Olwin Christianson, Grace Clare, Mrs. Theis. Front row, Robert Wintermute, Charles Parr, Glen Reanier, James Wintermute, Glenn Cowan, Robert Moffat, Del _____, Kenneth Pardee, _____ Sherman, Virgie Hart, _____, _____ Johnson.   -Photo from Harlan Parker

New Sheridan School, 1932. This school, at the present site of Kono Village Apartments, 1717 Sheridan Road, replaced the one that burned in 1932 on the opposite side of Sheridan Road.   -Photo from Harlan Parker

New—and long-lasting—school location. Occupancy of property at present-day East 13th Street and Ironsides Avenue for school purposes began with erection of this one-room Decatur-Manette School in 1902 and continued into modern times. Photo taken in 1909. In window are Earl Martin and Wesley Hammond. On porch, Troy Hammond, Adam Karst, Teena Clark, Ruth Risser, Vere Farmer, Elva Morris, Anna Casey, Willie Hammond, Len Card, Archie Clark. In front row, Esther Olsen, Hilda Olsen, Lena Miles, Lola Thompson, Fred Bell (behind Lola), _____, _____, Lucille Short, _____, Mercedes Gothright, _____, Florence Clark, _____, _____, _____, _____, Earl Bright, Walt Bell, Dwight Miles, Holt Karst, John McDougal, Len Bright, Frank Clark (5 years old), Art Bright, Walter Fellows, Willia Peters, Morgan Avery, teacher Effie Hester. -Photo from Elva Hibbard

bid of $2,140. R.B. Neff was hired to grade the grounds adjacent to the old school for $15.

This school burned in 1932 and a new two-story school was built across Sheridan Road, where the Kono Village Apartments now stand.

On May 26, 1902, the area known as Decatur was designated as School District 49. Funds were raised locally to purchase an acre at East 13th Street and Ironsides Avenue for a new school. The Decatur Improvement Club helped by sponsoring a social ball, and a contract was soon let to build. Prior to completion of the building, a news item of the time states, "School will be held in the store building upstairs, temporarily, with Miss Ethel Wheeler as teacher." The A.B. Williams store referred to was near the present Edgewater East Apartments at East 10th Street and Lower Shore Drive.

The new school opened in October 1902 and was called the Decatur/Manette School, as a Bremerton News item announced that a new post office would be called Manette. The first mail pouch marked "Manette" was received December 10, 1902.

By 1912 a new two-story four-room school had been built up the hill and adjacent to the old single room school at East

Two-story four-room school, circa 1912. Solid's home behind school to right. -Photo from Marjorie Rea Ray

Two stories, four classrooms. Manette School went comparatively modern with construction of this stately building in 1912-1913. Addition at left came later.

13th Street and Ironsides Avenue. Gideon Hermanson bought the lumber in the old school and used it to build a house on the corner of East 13th Street and Trenton Avenue. This house was later owned by Mr. Kidder, but has since been torn down and a duplex constructed.

In 1918 the Manette and Sheridan Schools, six classrooms in all, were annexed to the Bremerton School District.

By 1948 a new, larger brick and concrete school was built on the lower portion of the East 13th and Ironsides Avenue school grounds. The old building remained on the upper portion. A new kindergarten section with a fireplace was part of the new school. Kindergarten was first offered in Manette by Mrs. Isaac (Amy) Hoopes in her own home. She held these sessions for 11 years beginning in 1921. Then a pre-school organization held kindergarten in a private basement, and later in the basement of the 1912 school. During World War II some kindergarten, first, second and fourth grade classes were held in the basement of the Manette Community Church.

By 1959 the old building was removed and its bell installed in the new building. Its weathervane, built by coppersmith Eric A. Wall, was given to Margaret Elliott, who had taught fourth grade at Manette for 29 years. She later presented it to the Kitsap County Historical Museum at Silverdale.

Consolidation led to the suspension of classes at Manette School in 1974 and children were bused to other schools.

The building was leased to the navy in 1984, closing the book on a much loved school supported by a loyal, dedicated community for over 85 years.

First and second grades, 1916-1917. Back row (from left), teacher Miss Edith May Monk, Carl Lee, Lyle Dillon, Paul Almon, Olav Jacobsen, Orville Paulson, Viggo Jensen. Middle row, Svend Jensen, Harold Lee, _____, Orby Nicolai, Scott Harrington, Fred Howerton, Eugene Parkins, Herbert Solibakke, Emmett Bledsoe. Front row, Mildred Ross, Alice Fellows, Myrtle Hermanson, Elsie Wilsen, Muriel Rodger, Esther Price, Nellie Clark.

-Photo from Alice Fellows Lawson

Third and fourth grades, 1916-1917. Back row (from left), Emery Bales, Jack Bales, Everts Burlew, Gilbert Burk, _____. Third row, Jack Cole, Anchor Hermanson, Kenneth Bales, Wilhelm Larson, Clarence Hook, Harry Cramer, Richard Bledsoe, _____, Claude Cole, Lloyd Price, teacher Miss Agnes Iverson. Second row, Dorothy Bright, Florence Dewar, Esther Wilsen, Dorothy Fellows, Dorothy Price, Ruth Jennings, Geneva Howerton, Helen Pallo, Grace Hook. First row, Charles Fellows, Ellen Jensen, Bessie Clark, Gladys Hermanson, Josephine Lee, Aileen Wolf, Edna Hoopes, Marjorie Bubb, Marjorie Jennings, Vivian Hall, Edith Burlew, Erma Mitty.

-Photo from Ellen Jensen Magnussen

Seventh and eighth grades, 1916-1917. Back row (from left), teacher Miss Vida Cornell, Caroline Lee, Fawn Walsh, Maymie Collins, Lois Casey. Second row, Arthur Pallo, Albert Card, Charles Dewar, Malcolm Meredith, Neal Harrington, Hazel Mitty, Gladys Olsen. Front row, Carter Garthright, Walter Hermanson, Lavern Kirk, Alfred Bright, Charlotte Dumkee, Marguerite Olsen, Mercedes Garthwright, Florence Fellows. -Photo from Gladys Olsen Solid

First and second grades, 1921-1922. Back row (from left), teacher Miss Eldridge Turner, George Personette, Martha Palmer, Dorothy Wall, Harold Christensen, _____, Henry Hunter, _____. Second row, _____, _____, Clyde Nelson, Marjorie Wood, Helga Enkeboll, Barbara Christensen. Front row, _____, Eugene Stone, Bernard McKale, Mary Mattera, Kenneth Hall, _____, _____.   *-Photo from Walter Fellows*

Manette School grades 3-4, 1921-22. Teacher, Miss Livingston. Back row (from left), Charles Mattera, _____, _____, Vernon Sanford, _____, William Schweer. Third row, _____, Spencer Sherman, Elizabeth Midland, Orville Schultz, Harold Reanier, Daisy Thompson. Second row, _____, _____, James Morris, Inza Dean, Lola Masters, Arlene Wilsen. Front row, Edith Jensen, Selma Wilsen, Anita Howerton, Marjorie Adams, Dorothy Sidam, Eleanor Carlson, Lois Brown.

Fifth and sixth grades, 1921-1922. Back row (from left), Ray Nosker, Marion Nelson. Fourth row, Martin Cropp, George Morris, Russell Emerson, Harold Rausch, George Sherman, Richard Davidson, Walter Frodsham, Merrick McHenry, George Grantham, Thomas Clark. Third row, teacher Miss Mentha Crofoot, Margaret Carlson, Alice Fellows, _____, Sylvia Reanier, Eugene Parkins. Second row, Elizabeth von Hoene, Anna Parkins, Evelyn Aldrich, Jessie Crowell, Bertha Primm, Marguerite Purcell, Margaret Frodsham, Alma Matson, Evelyn Holden. Front row, Julia Nelson, Margaret von Hoene, Irene Cole, Mildred Ross, Agnus Paulson, Bertha Williams, Elsie Wilsen, Muriel Rodger.   -Photo from Elizabeth von Hoene Waters

Seventh and eighth grades, 1921-1922. Back row (from left), Clarence Hook, Lyle Dillon, Jack Cole, Clarence Carlson, Claude Cole, Darrell Jones, Leroy Brallier, _____. Third row, Svend Jensen, Fred Howerton, Paul Almon, Oval Martin, _____, Charles Fellows, Lloyd Clark, _____, Glen Wood. Second row, teacher Blanche Copley, Grace Hook, Neva Emmons, Florence Dewar, Grace Wilsen, Muriel Clark, Eleanor Emerson, _____. Front row, Edith Burlew, Marjorie Jennings, Marjorie Bubb, Ellen Jensen, Rejene Croxton, Gladys Marlett, Edna Hoopes, Florence Rice.
-Photo from Ellen Jensen Magnussen

Eighth grade graduation, 1924. Teacher Mrs. Inez Howard was not in photo. Back row (from left), George Grantham, William Shontel, Evelyn Aldrich, Eugene Parkins. Second row, Elizabeth von Hoene, Joe Sullivan, Margaret Frodsham, Marion Nelson, Mamie Elliott. Front row, Alice Fellows, Olav Jacobsen, Virginia Akers.
-Photo from *Hattie Elliott Engstrom.*

First through eighth grade, 1926-1927. 1 Jesse Howerton, 2 Mark Nelson, 3 Leland Kidder, 4 Melvin Renn, 5 Lillian Peterman, 6 Evelyn Waugh, 7 Elizabeth Middleton, 8 Adda Anderson, 9 Ruth Wall, 10 Mae Lawing, 11 Bill Schweer, 12 George Personette, 13 Orville Schultz, 14 Dorothy Crowell, 15 Robert Driscoll, 16 Harold Christensen, 17 Floyd Buchanan, 18 Selma Wilsen, 19 Jaqueline Spitzen, 20 Katherine Clay, 21 Zilda Jones, 22 Laska Clark, 23 Grace Young, 24 Dorothy Wall, 25 Bonnie Booth, 26 Russell Elliott, 27 Glen Harris, 28 Raymond Cole, 29 Dorothy Akers, 30 Katherine Bratt, 31 Edith Jensen, 32 Gertrude Perriman, 33 Stefona Soyat, 34 Anita Howerton, 35 Ruby Keil, 36 Martha Worland, 37 Herman Ditbenner, 38 Raymond Schoonover, 39 Genevieve Nelson, 40 Ward Muller, 41 _____, 42 Murville Osborne, 43 Kenneth Hall, 44 Ervin Jensen, 45 Roger Paquette, 46 Willard Muller, 47 Vera Breed, 48 Lola Course, 49 Bernice Pederson, 50 Dick Feek, 51 Glen Kidder, 52 Howard Larson, 53 _____, 54 Kenneth Muller, 55 Gracie Elliott, 56 Duncan Buchanan, 57 Lois Harrison, 58 Anna Jo Harkins, 59 Arlene Wilsen, 60 Jeane Martin, 61 Dorothy Mey, 62 Vera Workman (Lawrence), 63 Cortis Jones, 64 Marcus Soyat, 65 James Ditbenner, 66 Mary Worland, 67 Betty Bender, 68 Joy Bright, 69 Doris Cowan, 70 Dorothy Cole, 71 Ada Schoonover, 72 Mildred Starevich, 73 Ruth Peters, 74 Helen Akers, 75 Alice Holden, 76 Helga Enkeboll, 77 Eugene Howerton, 78 Lyle Hart, 79 Lyle Womac. 80 Jack Kean, 81 Rachel Peters, 82 Margaret Daley, 83 Eugene Daley, 84 Doris Welborn, 85 Margaret Hoopes, 86 Genevieve Painter, 87 _____, 88 Helen Holden, 89 Marian Akers, 90 Viola Dean, 91 Archel Bouchard, 92 Floyd Taft, 93 John Nelson, 94 Ellsworth Holmes, 95 Kenneth Hendrickson, 96 Wayne Burlew, 97 _____, 98 Kenneth Ziegler, 99 Fred McHenry, 100 George Worland, 101 _____, 102 Thelma Osborne, 103 John Mey, 104 Earl Harrison, 105 Theodore Womac, 106 Winnie Rider, 107 Alvin Rider, 108 Clyde Clark, 109 Robert Starevich, 110 Warren Dean, 111 Robert Davidson, 112 Robert Clay, 113 Charles Hook, 114 Ruth Danel, 115 Mary Jane Ditbenner, 116 Blossom Bright, 117 Ferris Buchanan, 118 Irene Lawing, 119 Georgia May Moffat, 120 Thelma Callison, 121 Corinne Muller, 122 _____, 123 Jean Hendrickson, 124 Elmer Hoffman, 125 _____, 126 Patricia Driscoll, 127 Wilma Taylor, 128 Wayne Muller, 129 Clara McKelvy, 130 June Martin, 131 Helen Starevich, 132 Marjorie Schoonover, 133 Betty Driscoll, 134 Muriel Peterson, 135 Eleanor Pidduck, 136 Virginia Karst, 137 Esther Buchanan, 138 _____, 139 Jane Bender, 140 Genevieve Worland, 141 Louise Parsons, 142 _____, 143 Laura Ellis, 144 Helen Clare, 145 Anna Starevich, 146 Marjorie Kidder, 147 Marcella Walker, 148 Evelyn Pardee, 149 Richard Avery, 150 Robert Bowdy, 151 Robert Lawing, 152. _____, 153 Riley Cole, 154 Leonard Ziegler, 155 Kenneth Karst, 156 _____, 157 Neil Nelson, 158 Harold Lloyd, 159 _____, 160 Alfred Jensen.

Kindergarten, October 1928. Teacher Amy Hoopes behind students (from left), Roy Etten, Louise Hermanson, Charles Kidder, Marion Wall, Katherine Pease, Bernice Jack, Arthur Card, Harold Callison, Joann Tathum, Joyce Walsh, Marjorie Rea, Joe Hall.

-Photo from Marjorie Rea Ray

Kindergarten reunion, December 1940. From left, Roy Etten, Louise Hermanson, Charles Kidder, Katherine Pease, Bernice Jack, Arthur Card, Harold Callison, Joyce Walsh, Joann Tathum, Marjorie Rea, teacher Amy Hoopes, Joe Hall.

Fourth and fifth grades, 1928-1929. Back row (from left), Clyde Clark, Lyle Womac, Kenneth Ziegler, Winnie Rider, Irene Lawing, Thelma Callison, Esther Buchanan, Corinne Muller. Third row, Richard Paquette, Edward Forbes, Robert Bowdy, Clara McKelvy, Howard Harrison, Beryl Ellis, Eleanor Pidduck, Jean Campbell, June Martin. Second row, Elmer Hoffman, Charles Hook, Robert Clay, Mildred Johnson, Margaret Dilks, Howard Lloyd, Alfred Jensen, Warren Dean, Wayne Muller, Richard Avery, teacher Miss Louise Pallas. Front row, William Bubke, Jane Bender, Marjorie Kidder, Laura Ellis, Jewell Tenge, Louise Parsons, Genevieve Worland, Marguerite Bailey, Georgia Breer.

-Photo from Jewell Tenge Sollie

Sixth grade, 1929-1930. Back row (from left), Ted Womac, Clark Isard, Leonard McKelvy, George Worland, Robert Wall, Ellsworth Holmes. Fourth row, Clyde Clark, Robert Brown, Jack Kean, Beecher Walker, Ruth Danel, _____.Martin. Third row, Lyle Womac, Robert Hilstad, Margaret Daley, Thelma Callison, Leoda Senn, Irene Lawing, Clifford Reanier. Second row, Teacher-principal Miss Florence Condy, Ray Donovan, Esther Buchanan, Corinne Muller, Muriel Peterson, Mary Personette, Virginia Karst, Charles Reanier. Front row, Fred Bubke, Wayne Burlew, Howard Harrison, Marjorie Schoonover, Robert Starevich, James Root, Robert Davidson, Robert Carlson.   -Photo from Robert Carlson

Third and fourth grades, 1930-1931. Back row (from left), Lawrence Worland, Donald Brown, Gordon McHenry, Bernice Schoonover, Virginia Galleher, Anna Starevich. Fourth row, Kenneth Tenge, Forrest Millikan, Harold Callison, Joe Hall, Glen Forbes. Third row, James Schultz, Howard Fawcett, Louise Hermanson, Katherine Starevich, Robert Kennedy, Bernice Jack, Roy Etten. Second row, Marjorie Rea, Arthur Card, Emma Belle Harrison, Frank Akers, Lenora Alinder, John Adams, Charles Kidder. Front row, Maryjayne Meredith, Robert Jackson, Albert Barrett, Paul Jones, Kathleen _____, Joyce Walsh, June Womac.   -Photo from Estelle Meredith

Third and fourth grades, 1932-1933. Teacher Miss Dorthea Spencer not in photo. Back row (from left), Joe Fischer, Robert Kennedy, Phyllis Hagan, James Avery, Doris Spencer, Katherine Starevich, Louise Hermanson. Third row, Howard Fawcett, Stephen Hilstad, Ruth Baker, Berenice Bouchard, Arthur Card, Roy Etten, Forrest Millikan, Grant Martin. Second row, Jay Hendricks, John Forbes, Wilbur Tenge, Frances Hall, Joe Hall, June Womac, Joyce Walsh, Gertrude Gaither. Front row, _____, William Chandler, Larry Rea, Kathryn Alinder, Paul Jones, Maryjayne Meredith, Teckla Worland, Iris Senn. -Photo from Maryjayne Meredith Hladky

Third grade, 1933-1934 . Back row (from left), Bill Williams, Joan Lindsey, Robert Ballew, James Penn, James Hermanson, Donald Weedin, _____Williams, Myrtle Forbes, _____. Third row, Ernest Howerton, Douglas Washburn, Ray Hall, Lexine Stranahan, Pauline Pidduck, Wayne Palmer, Doris Houston, Raymond Berglind. Second row, Donald Hart, Burton Brenden, Frances Dick, Walter Clare, Eileen Millikan, Ernest Kimball, Stanley Baselt, Edith Baker, Betty Johanson. Front row, Betty Avery, Donna Pidduck, Esther Dick, Chryselda Meagher, Harold Danel, James Meredith, Enid Booth, Barbara Sigurdson, Leslie Weedin, Hazel Hendrickson, teacher Miss Judith Anderson. -Photo from Harold Danel

Fifth and sixth grades, 1935-1936. Back row (from left), Keith Lyman, Grant Martin, Marilyn Hoffman, Ruth Baker, Robert Kennedy, Doris Spencer, Dolores Bowdy. Fourth row, Larry Rea, Walter Jack, Warren White, Steve Hilstad, Norman Ludvigson, James Avery. Third row, Berenice Bouchard, John Forbes, Jack Bender, John McKelvy, Jean Callison. Second row, Dean Gillette, June Womac, Gertrude Gaither, Kathryn Alinder, Frances Hall, Dolores Flint, Iris Senn, teacher Miss Florence Holman, Joe Hall. First row, Bill Chandler, Betti Shoemaker, Rowena Harkins, Eva Jane Thomas, Harlene Hoffman, Valla Mottner, June Etten, Don Owens. -Photo from Berenice Bouchard Root

Fifth and sixth grades, 1937-1938: Back row (from left), William Card, Joan Lindsey, Lexine Stranahan, Cleo Fellows, Mae McKelvy, Pauline Pidduck, Janis Kerr, Donald Weedin, teacher-principal Miss Florence Holman. Third row, Burton Brenden, James Hermanson, Mary Lou Stranahan, Eileen Millikan, Myrtle Forbes, Edith Baker, Raymond Berglind, Wallace Kean, Ernest Howerton, Ernest Brenden. Second row, Cleo McDonald, Donna Pidduck, Carlton Henning, Hazel Hendrickson, Marie Hardin, Leslie Weedin, Ray Jacobsen, Ray Hall, Robert Ballew, Wayne Palmer. Front row, Fred Bowdy, Benjamin Murray, Roger Henning, Betty Lou Avery, Ruth Howerton, Betty Kidder, Pat Henning, James Meredith, Stanley Baselt, Ernest Kimball, Donald Hart. -Photo from Janis Kerr Arnold

THE P-TA

By Eleanor Carlson Harrington,
Manette P-TA President, 1952 to 1954

The following information about the Manette P-TA was obtained from five notebooks of meeting minutes. These books were rescued by Mary Hulbert, then secretary of the school, just before its closure in 1974. Many other record books had been lost or discarded through the years as changes took place in personnel and in administration.

This material lends itself naturally into three specific periods: just prior to World War I, the pre-Depression and Depression years, and the period right after World War II. Even though first names are often omitted it is a veritable Who's Who of Manette. The account presents a picture of the high personal values and stable background given to the children of Manette.

PRE-WORLD WAR I PERIOD

On October 25, 1916, a group of interested and dedicated parents and teachers were gathered together by a committee composed of Mrs. James W. Martin, chairman pro tem; Mrs. Menth; and secretary pro tem Mrs. Cornell. A constitution and bylaws, prepared by the committee beforehand, was read. It was accepted and an election of officers followed. Mrs. Howard was elected president, Mrs. Menth vice-president, Mrs. Cornell secretary and Miss Pumpelly treasurer. There were 20 members present.

Dues were 25 cents, business meetings were to be held every first and third Wednesday, and a public evening meeting was to be held every third month at which the children would perform. Early committees were basic: program, membership, child-study and publicity. Membership lists were not included but the committees had a fine balance of both parents and teachers. Familiar names in addition to the officers often mentioned were Seifert, Miller, Solibakke, Dewar, Fellows, Miss Iverson and Mrs. Copeland.

One incident occurred which illustrated the effort to promote understanding between the administration and the community. At meetings December 6, 1916, and January 3, 1917, Mr. Elliot, the superintendent of schools, explained a new program called Home Record Work. After the discussion that followed his speech Mr. Elliot agreed to decrease the number of credits required for each student and this satisfied the majority of parents. Programs usually consisted of members reading articles on child welfare.

It was surprising that while this was the period just before our participation in World War I, no reference was made to the war. Special items noted were:

1. The possible use of the acre next to the school for a garden; this was ruled out because the boys played baseball there.

2. A change in program planning to excuse adults from participating because of the long hours in the navy yard.

3. A motion that Manette be represented in the "food preparedness organization" which had started in Bremerton.

4. A canvass of places available for room and board for the many newcomers to the navy yard.

5. A call for parents to write President Wilson to protect the morals of the boys in the army and navy.

Mrs. Jennings read an article from the magazine, "Work of

Women Today." She then described the Washington Women's Legislative Association and urged the unit to support this group. Further requests for support were made later but were voted down.

Much emphasis was placed on health. Doctors assisting in free examination clinics were Dr. Schutt, Dr. Taggert and Dr. Ira Brown. Years later an orthopedic guild was formed in Bremerton and named after Dr. Edward J. Taggert.

The latest minutes available for this period were those of November 1917. Mrs. Howard was reelected president. Meetings may have been curtailed because of the flu epidemic, which was raging worldwide. It was several years before the account was continued.

THE DEPRESSION PERIOD

From 1924 to 1936 the unit flourished in interest and activity. These years were before and during the Depression, and the parents and teachers worked hard to better the school and provide for the children.

Health remained a high priority. The first mention of a baby clinic was in 1926. In 1930 local doctors in conjunction with the Kiwanis Club held a school for parents. A city-wide dental clinic for the school children was explained in a program by Dr. J. B. Bright. Plans were made for the Spring Roundup, a program to prepare children who would be entering school for the first time the following September.

One of the most important projects was the hot lunch program. Good nutrition was a concern, so early in the school year all children were weighed to spot those who were underweight. A committee of three mothers was appointed each month to provide lunches for 3 cents a pupil and provision was made for those who couldn't pay. Hot lunches usually consisted of hot soup cooked at home and brought to school by the mothers, but in 1928 Mrs. Solid was hired at $1 a day to be the cook. From time to time mention was made of plans for holding a cup and plate shower, furnishing oilcloth for the tables and ordering mugs and spoons and a coffee pot for a refreshment hour.

In 1943 lunches were cooked and served in the basement of the school by Laura Newburn, who used a coal and wood stove, a single sink and a small cupboard for dishes to serve 50 to 70 pupils on four long tables with bench seating. (Much later, in 1957, while Goldie Manning was food services supervisor for the district, a packaged lunch program was introduced. Lunches were prepared at a central kitchen, transported to the individual schools and reheated in small electric ovens. This system is still in use in Bremerton.)

The school board was not able to provide much in the way of extras, so the Manette P-TA constantly worked for playground equipment and other school equipment, including a set of Compton's Encyclopedia, a Brayco "stereopticon" that included slides and a book, a ditto machine and a radio. The P-TA also made arrangements to participate in the traveling library, and at times added new books under the direction of one of the teachers.

These projects cost money, so money-raisers were constantly held, including paper drives, candy, donut and coffee sales, donation drives and silver teas. Even a popular play, "Womanless Wedding," was presented, enacted entirely by the men. Holding school carnivals became very popular, too. All this participation stimulated interest and in November of

The Womanless Wedding, April 22, 1925, enacted by Masons from Steadfast Lodge to raise money for school supplies. 1 Thomas Bright, 2 Duncan Buchanan, 3 John "Jack" Martin, 4 H. Richard "Red" Palmer, 5 "Minister" Lendall Hunton, 6 Frank Clay, 7 _____, 8 Ben Kean, 9 Arthur Personette, 10 _____, 11 Mark Nelson, 12 Forrest "Doc" Cole, 13 William Abbott, bride, 14 Clyde Meredith, groom, 15 Harry Martin, 16 William von Hoene, 17 _____, 18 Arthur Holden, 19 George Ross, 20 Clarence Welborn, 21 Bruno Lund, 22 Ferris Buchanan, 23 Bryan Buchanan, 24 _____, 25 _____, 26 Isaac Hoopes, 27 William Schultz, 28 Joseph Hagan, 29 Richard Feek, 30 Jack Kean, 31 James Rodger, 32 Herman Renn. 33, Daisy Schweer, director.

1930 P-TA membership among the 85 families in the school was 72 percent. That year Manette took the prize for the highest percentage of membership in the Bremerton P-TA Council. P-TA members took training seriously, sometimes conducting parliamentary procedure classes before meetings. Twice a year the secretary would read the constitution and bylaws. One of the secretary books contained a copy of these as well as a membership list.

At the yearly observance of Founder's Day for 1932, Manette honored seven former presidents: Mrs. Cora Burlew, Mrs. Amy Hoopes, Mrs. Eugene Schweer, Mrs. Nellie Peterson, Mrs. Ralph Danel, Mrs. Wall (standing in for Mrs. Harrison), and Mrs. Parr. Maryjayne Meredith, Mrs. Gilman, Mrs. Parr and Miss Condy took part in the candle-lighting ceremony.

On the last day of school the P-TA usually had a picnic but in 1935 an ice cream treat was substituted for this event.

POST WORLD WAR II PERIOD

The last period covered by the books was between 1946 and 1948. World War II was over and the school picture had changed during the war years. Bremerton School District 100-C had received extra federal funds to handle children of increased navy yard and armed forces personnel. New schools were built and talk was current of a new building for Manette. The new school was built at East 13th Street and Ironsides Avenue in 1948.

The school district now provided hot lunches, playground

equipment and other equipment for the school. There was a special services department for handicapped and a music department with special personnel, so that each school could have its own orchestra and singing groups. Kindergarten was now part of the established curriculum.

Program emphasis and projects changed, too, seeming to become more community oriented. Programs related to community health problems, to the understanding of the handicapped, and to participation in a tuberculosis X-ray clinic were introduced. New studies included "Recreation for the Group and the Individual." City-wide music meets were held.

Poster contests for the children and hobby shows were some of the activities. Students also worked hard on paper and magazine drives to build up the city swimming pool fund.

Each year two room-mothers were appointed for each home room to assist the teacher in any project or field trip. They also continued a savings bond program, which had been started during the war. One of the changes noted was that the February P-TA meeting was often eliminated in favor of an all-city Founder's Day observance. The unit participated in the all-city school survey held by the district to determine the density of school population, and supported school levies for expansion. The presidents serving at this time were Mrs. Reddick, Mrs. Ada Williams and Mrs. Charles Sidam.

New hope for the future arose as efforts were made to rebuild a war-damaged world. Manette remained strong as it adjusted to new direction in education and community growth until Manette School closed as an elementary school in 1974.

P-TA OFFICERS

YEAR	PRESIDENT	SECRETARY
1916-17	Mrs. Inez Howard	Mrs. Vida Cornell
1924-25	Nellie (Mrs. Nels) Peterson	Dorothy E. Cole
1925-26	Daisy (Mrs. Eugene) Schweer	Dorothy E. Cole
1926-27	Daisy (Mrs. Eugene) Schweer	Mrs. Margaret Mey
1927-28	Elva (Mrs. Ralph) Danel	Mrs. Margaret Mey
1928-30	Vera (Mrs. Lee) Harrison	Theo Parr
1930-31	Mrs. Theo Parr	Alyce(Mrs. Theo) Peterson
1931-32	Mrs. Theo Parr	Grace Hagan
1932-34	Grace, (Mrs. Eugene) Jack	Lenora A. Alinder
1934-35	Dorothy (Mrs. Charles) Sidam	Gladys E. Millikan
1935-36	Mrs. Gladys Millikan	Gertrude, Mrs. Eric Carr
1943-44	Gertrude (Mrs. W.A). Buchanan	Ardis(Mrs. R.) Scribner
1944-45	Helen (Mrs. Renus) Bender	Evelyn(Mrs. G.) Buell
1946-47	Mrs. Reddick	Pauline Duff
1947-48	Dorothy (Mrs. Charles) Sidam	Ann Womac

Recollections Of A Principal

By Florence Condy

[Florence Condy now lives at Lacey, Wash. (Panorama City) She was interviewed there by Ann Baltzo in 1985. Excerpts follow].

I was a teacher and principal for 41 years and principal of Manette School from 1928 until 1939. Besides being principal, I taught the fifth and sixth grades. The principal at the Bremerton High School always appreciated Manette's "trained" students....

This old teacher loves good manners. I once knew a family with four sons. Visiting their house for dinner was always a pleasure. Each son would take turns being the host. He would meet me at the door, take my coat, show me to a chair, and set me at the table. Upon departing, he would get my coat and see me to the door. Not once would the parents indicate such was out of the ordinary. I was happy to be invited and often wonder how well their training held in later years. I like good manners.

One never knows where or how far one's influence reaches. I have a scrapbook filled with Christmas cards—some from former students, especially from the fifth and sixth grades. I can recall exactly where they sat in the classroom.

There never was a year that I didn't enjoy teaching. The greatest compliment I received was from a man over 60— "My most memorable school year was the sixth grade in your class." Another hated the very sight of school but "you made it fun."

A teacher's responsibility is getting the requirements across: Learning can be fun. For arithmetic we used coins and played store. I never lost a coin from our box. It is nice to know it was worthwhile.

For reading—at 1 p.m. the students came in after playing madly. I would read for 15 minutes to calm them. They'd learn by hearing. I remember reading a memorable travel story about the Peruvian Mountains. British explorers built a boat...they had no way to get it to a lake...they took it apart, then reassembled it on Lake Titicaca. The students absorbed the story like a sponge. On another subject one student told me, "I never thought of or about Lewis and Clark 'til you read it."

As a teacher I encountered many personalities. Some students love to tease. A boy sat right in front of me and was particularly obnoxious. "I'll see you after school," I told him, and we proceeded with what we were doing. After lunch he came with a beautiful pot of flowers as a present. The kids hooted. I think he was trying for a lighter term. "Thank you, but we'll talk about it later," I told him. But I really never had a thought of punishment.

A Teacher Thinks Back

By Margaret L. Elliott

It was good fortune that brought me to Manette School in 1943. I had been teaching in a nice little two-room country school in the Poulsbo district, but I wanted to be in the "city." I stayed at Manette School for 29 years.

Because of the crowded conditions caused by World War II my fourth-grade class was in the basement of the old Manette Community Church. A kindergarten class was also there, with only a thin plywood partition between. Of course kindergartners were seldom very quiet. It was good, though, that we were spared the double-shifting required in other schools.

Furnishings were a problem. My desk was a shaky old library table which finally collapsed in a heap. The rickety portable blackboard had a hole in it which would catch the eraser and hurt my hand. One day they brought a makeshift bookshelf which I gladly accepted. It had to be propped against a wall to stay standing. The one new piece of equipment I had was a nice metal filing cabinet. The children's desks were the standard kind of that time with the pretty ornate iron grillwork on the sides, and with seats that turned up when not in use. They were placed in rows on wooden runners. Inkwells in the desks were filled with ink made by the janitor. I liked the antique pump organ which was probably used for Sunday School. The Manette Community Church deserves our heartfelt thanks for having us there.

Margaret Elliott

After half a year my class was moved to the big old Manette School building. To me it was most beautiful and palatial with large rooms and best of all a spectacular view of the Olympic Mountains and the bay. It was a two-story building with a bell tower and a big copper weather vane on top. I loved to hear the bell ringing in the mornings to call the children to school. It must have been nice for them to be walking or running to school while listening to that music.

The school lunchroom was something else! It was in the school basement in a back room by the furnace—no windows and no air-conditioning. Laura Newburn was the cook and she managed to serve delicious hot lunches even though she had only an old wood-and-coal-burning range. She cooked and we all dined in that same small room. She later returned to the schools as a teacher.

On rainy days the children played in the small basement. It was always very noisy as could be expected and I used to wish that children had been born with softer voices. Usually, though, they played on the big hilltop playground, which had plenty of space. One of their favorite games was Boys Chase and Catch Girls and Girls Chase Boys. When the game became too rough it would be outlawed so they would start the game again but with a new name such as Stagecoach or Pirates. The other games were the usual sports such as baseball, football, marbles, and Red Rover. Later, after the new school was built, they used the big city playground on East 13th Street and Nipsic Avenue. The P-TA helped us to have nice playground equipment such as a jungle gym and ladder bars.

NEW SCHOOL

It was so interesting and exciting for us to watch the building of the new Manette School by Keith Branch Construction Company 1948. This building was planned by Branch and Branch Architects, Manette residents. They designed the movable furniture as well. We loved being in the beautiful modern building with pretty colors and all new furniture. It was a pretty building with glass brick walls for good lighting. How we appreciated the large classrooms, a teachers' room and workroom, a nurse's room and a nice office! There was a multipurpose room downstairs which served as the auditorium, the playroom for P.E. activities, and as the lunchroom. Now our cooks had a modern kitchen with good equipment for hot lunches. Later the school lunches were prepared in a central kitchen and were delivered to the schools to be heated in a special oven. These packaged lunches were airline style. I think Bremerton was first in the nation to use this system.

It was fun to produce nice Christmas and spring programs. Of course every child was a performer and I used to like to watch their proud parents and grandparents watching them. We featured plays, pageants, choral and orchestra music, and folk dances. Carnivals were big for fund-raising events by the P-TA. The parents had many clever ideas for such events. The money was used for such things as playground equipment.

The parents helped us in many ways with their volunteering in the classrooms, going with us on excursions and helping on the playground. My students used to go to Fort Nisqually, where they would be Pioneers and Indians for awhile. Once we had a train ride from Tacoma to Seattle with the privilege of riding in the dome car. On the way home the children shopped in the Old Curiosity Shop and showed off their purchases on the ferry back to Bremerton. Another trip took us to Nalley's in Tacoma, where we watched the making of potato chips and mayonnaise. My pupils came home with a pack of 16 snacks, to the envy of the rest of the school children.

We appreciated Manette because it was more established than some of the other schools, such as Westpark, Eastpark and Sheridan Park, which had a lot of military housing. It was nice to have less moving of the students during the year.

During the 1960s when the open concept of teaching became popular a wall was removed between two classrooms and carpeting was installed. Erma Miller and Verda Wilson used that room for team teaching. Team teaching was also done by Bernice Homan and Dorothy Grahn for the primary grades. One year while the new addition was being built Charles Barker and Erma Miller shared the auditorium for their classrooms.

I had classes of various sizes. The largest, 43 students in the old building, was too large for the sake of the children. Of course there were no teacher aides then. The smallest class for me was 21 with a combined third and fourth grade and that was really nice for all of us. My usual class size was about 33 students. In the 29 years at Manette School I probably taught about 900 children. In all my 39 years in Kitsap County the number of my students was probably about 1200.

I taught in two country schools before I came to Manette. The first was Wildwood, a one-room school in South Kitsap, where I taught for 2 years. The second was Pleasant Ridge School in the Poulsbo district. That was a two-room school. I was there for 7 years.

NEW MATH

Many changes in elementary education occurred while I was in Manette. Phonics were out and then came back. Science and math labs were emphasized with the beginning of space exploration. We were suddenly plunged into modern math, which was a foreign language and confusing to many of us who were used to the good old times tables and long division. We were introduced to many helpful visual aids such as movie projectors, television in the classroom and filmstrips. We would listen to the Standard School Broadcast for good music appreciation and stories of the history and cultures of the world. The duplicating machines were wonderful for us. When I first started to teach we used shallow pans of gelatin with messy carbon of purple ditto ink. I was even thrifty enough to melt down the gelatin for re-use the next year. Now since I have retired the computer age is with us.

A lot of special help was available for us. We were helped by teachers for remedial reading and speech therapy and by the school nurse for health instruction. Special teachers came for music, orchestra and chorus. Another frequent visitor was police officer Art Morken, a favorite of the children, who talked to them about safety: "I will look both ways before crossing the street."

My classes had a lot of fun making and working with puppets. Often when I see former students they remember the puppets and remind me of them. They made spool puppets and hand puppets and gave some clever performances. I remember one of the Beatles which was made by some boys. A lot of horse puppets were made by the girls. One year especially, my fourth-grade girls were so intrigued with horses that they ran around the playground galloping and whinnying like horses. One mother was embarrassed when her daughter galloped downtown in Bremerton. For the puppet plays they made some interesting scenes and props. They did some nice creative writing and art work. I wish that I had saved more of those things.

I left Manette Elementary School in 1972, when it closed as an elementary school. I retired in 1973 after a year at Navy Yard City School. Manette School was occupied as a school for one more year after that. The majority of teachers from Manette were transferred to Kegal School on Perry Avenue for the 1972 year, but returned in 1973 to teach one more year before final closure of the school in 1974. The building was vacant for several years and was somewhat vandalized—

especially the glass brick walls. Now it has been completely restored and remodeled for use for offices by the navy. The school district still owns the building and it is leased to the navy.

I now live at 3004 Mountain View Drive. When I meet Manette students and their families I am proud to hear of their many fine accomplishments. I feel happy to have shared a small part of their lives.

My Years At Sheridan School
A DIVERSE CHALLENGE
By Florence Coardy Merriam, Principal, 1925-1927

I remember vividly meeting the Sheridan School Board in Bremerton at a noon luncheon to make a personal application. Mr. Locko Walker was president of the board. The men all worked in the navy yard and would have their lunch hour to talk. The meeting was successfully concluded; I became Sheridan School principal at 19. I remained 2 years. Friendships started that lasted for many years.

Names I recall are Christensen—there were four girls in the school; Lewis—they had four boys in school and lived near Christensens; Ammermans had one boy. Other names have faded in the past 60 years.

I came from Spokane. I had attended Washington Teachers College at Cheney and had been superintendent for primary and intermediate church classes.

BASEBALL CHAMPIONS
I think one thing the upper grade boys had the most pride in was that for those 2 years we had the champion baseball team around our bay area. All the other principals were men, and the natural assumption was that they had the best teams. It fell to me to learn the rules and to coach our team to meet their challenge, so I did. I was fortunate that the boys were good natural players. We practiced every noon and after school until each boy was a solid batter as well as catcher. Manette School waited to be the last to challenge. Their principal, whom I knew, was positive he would win the match. They lost.

After a couple of P-TA meetings and the wet winters, the mothers came to the school and provided hot soup for the children at noon.

In my second year I secured permission to have a bazaar at Halloween. Each area and grade selected a theme. The event was highly successful—costumes and all. Everything from Wishing Well to Bobbing for Apples to Scary Witches provided financial returns for the treasury.

The second year I lived down in Manette with the Ford Dewar family.

For years, when I returned to Bremerton, I would call to see who was around. The reply was "Come on over. I'll call all the rest of the 'Pumpkin Hollow Kids' and we'll have a great evening." So we always did just that. [Pumpkin Hollow was the low-lying area southwest of Perry Avenue and Stone Way.] [Mrs Merriam now lives in Pullman.]

Eight Grades; One Room
By Birdie Mae Avery Hilstad (1899-1979)
[From her recollections]

In 1908 when I started school in Sheridan School there were two other girls in my class, Thelma Henderson and Hazel Hodges, and several boys, Allan Johnson, Percy Ohman, Rudd Hubbell and Jack Gordon. Our first teacher was George Cady Johnson. There were eight grades in one room. The school room was heated by a wood stove. The teacher came early enough to make a fire and have the room warm for us at 8:55, when the last bell rang. The older boys would be sent out for more wood to keep the fire burning. Our water came from a well with a pump beside the playground.

Later a two-room school was built and we had two teachers. T.C. Waldron taught grades five, six, seven and eight. Evelyn Naugle taught the four lower grades. Later Theo Lewis taught the four lower grades.

Mr. Waldron always started the day by having us sing "Work, for the Night is Coming."

Chapter 5

BUSINESS AND INDUSTRY

THE RETAIL STORES
By Roger Paquette

Before the full impact of the automobile was felt, pedestrian traffic dictated the location of Manette's store buildings and public gathering places. So we find early entrepreneurs on the western side of Manette along Shore Drive between East 9th and East 11th Streets, where the ferry landings were located. Later, East 11th Street became the main business district. In 1930, the opening of the bridge expanded the area to include Winfield Avenue (Wheaton Way) and Harkins Street.

The accompanying map and numbered business legend details many of the changes in ownership and types of businesses at the indicated locations, as determined from written records and recalled by present owners, Manette History Club members, and others. Key non-business uses also are shown. The street grid shown on the map has varied somewhat with time. The numbers on the map show localities rather than exact locations. Two businesses listed at the same number may not have been at exactly the same site. Remodeling, re-

placement with apartment and office structures, and complete removal are some of the fates that have fallen upon some of the business buildings in Manette. While the legend reflects many of the uses of the various locations, there also were others. Some of the additional ones are shown in the pages of old advertisements which follow the legend.

It is interesting to look at the comparable durability of institutions and businesses. Although rebuilt after a fire and undergoing a name change, the Manette Community Church, dedicated as Bethany Baptist Church in 1906 and still under a Baptist ministry today, is certainly the senior organization of the community. Next would come the Masonic Temple, dating from the 20s.

Opened after the repeal of the Eighteenth Amendment in 1933, the Maple Leaf Tavern at 1735 Wheaton Way has been serving beer 55 years at the same location under the same name. No other commercial enterprise has ever come close to this record in the history of Manette.

Ad from Manette Gazette, 1940.

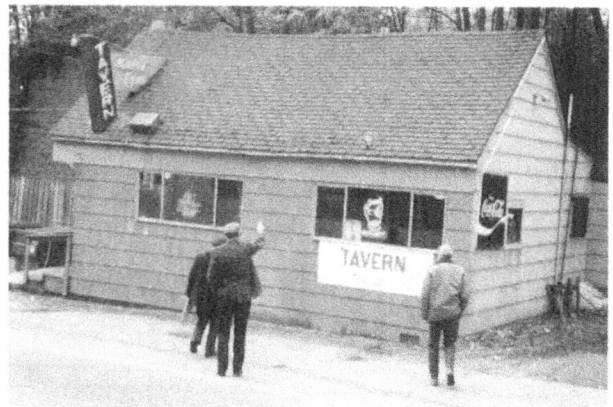

Maple Leaf Tavern today.

ENETAI

N

Jacobsen Blvd.

(Wynard Court)

Shore Drive

Public
Wharf
1907

(E.A. Wall Rd.)   Trenton Ave.   (6th.)

Vandalia Ave.   (5th.)

1

Vandalia

Nipsic
Pl.

(4th.)

2

Nipsic

(Telegraph Ave.)

(Center St.)

(Tunbridge Ave.)

(Perry Ave.)

Nipsic Ave.

Ironsides Ave.   (3rd.)

E. 18th. St.

E. 17th. St.

E. 16th. St.

E. 13th. St.

(Division)

3   4   5

E. 11th. St.

E. 10th. St.

Hayward Ave.   (2nd.)

6

7

8

E. 9th. St.

(Water St.)

(1st.)

(County Rd. #27) (Stringtown) (Main St.) Perry Ave.

9   10   11

Scott
Pl.

12   13

14-15   16

Scott Ave. (Decatur)

E. 15th. St.

E. 14th. St.

E. 13th. St.

18-19   22

Shore Dr. (Winfield)

27

17   21

Pitt

20   26   29 Decatur
28   Improvement
23-24-25   31   Club Wharf
47 34   32   1902
39

Pitt Ave.

30   37
33
35-36 38

Harkins

41
Auto Ferry
Dock 1916

(Mildred)   Decatur Ave.   Winfield Ave.

40

(Hwy. 21-B)

43

1930   42

Wheaton Way   Marlowe Ave.

45-46

44

Bridge

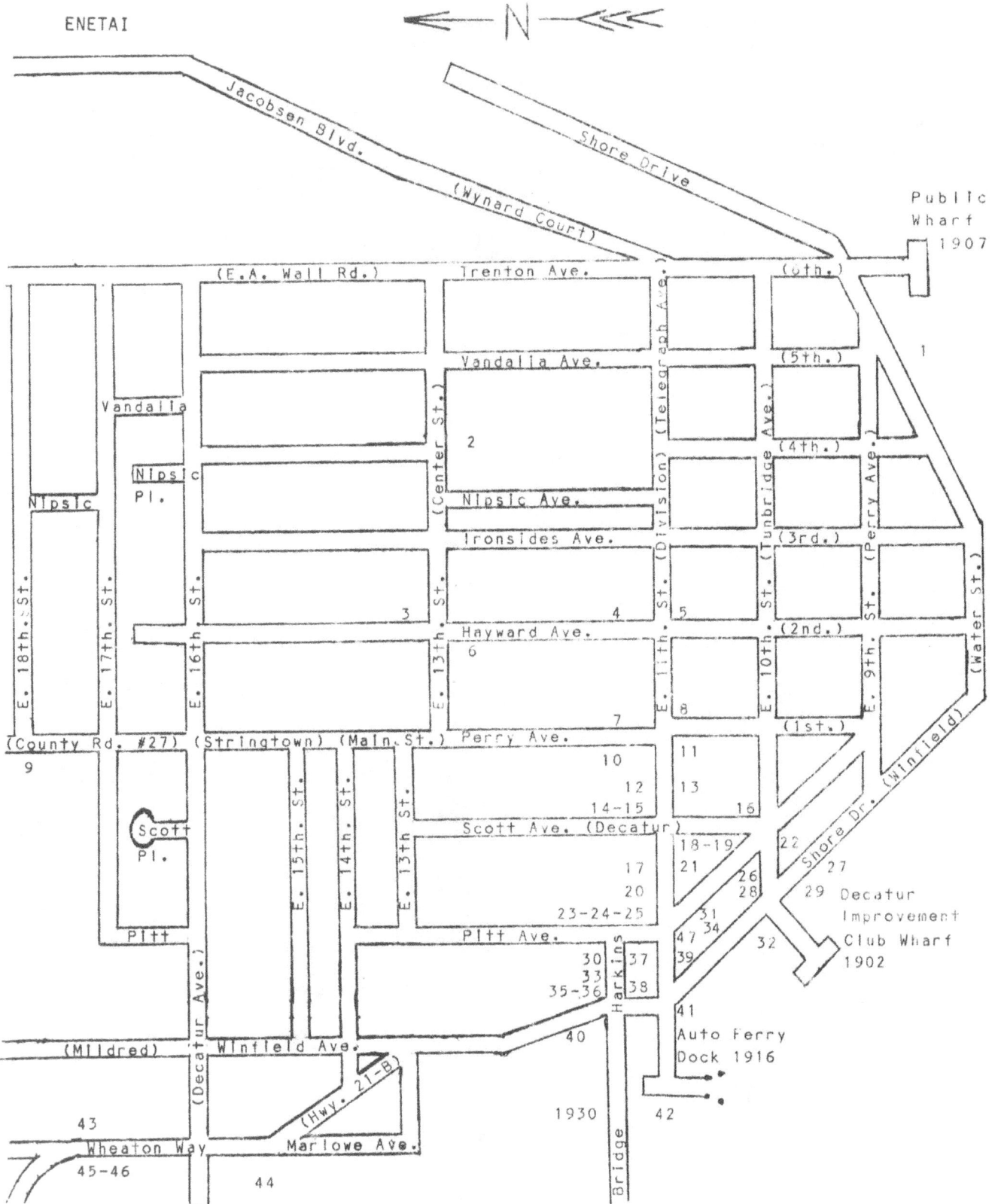

Manette business location map. Legend explaining numbers is on following pages.

Legend

X. Port Orchard Mill at Enetai Beach, 1854-1870.
1. Park and Lockwood Sash and Door Company, 1903 to 1905.
2. Manette Playfield, built 1933.
3. Manette Elementary School: original, 1902-1913; two-story, 1914-1959; brick, 1949-1972. Now leased to the navy.
4. Tom Fellows' greenhouse, built circa 1908. Later tenants were R.H. Higgins and I. Shimasaki.
5. Sara Hawthorne real estate office, 1020 Hayward

T.S. Fellows' Manette Greenhouse, East 11th Street and Ironsides Avenue, built about 1901. Photo taken 1912. People in photo are (back to front), Thomas Fellows (holding Alice), Mary Fellows (holding Charles), Walter Fellows, Leo Miller, Florence Fellows, D. Fujihara, "Shorty" Shimasaki.

Avenue, 1940-1949. Succeeded by Nettie Mahone's beauty parlor.
6. Bethany Baptist Church, built 1905. Now Manette Community Church.
7. I.E. Green and Ted Bertram hardware store;
   • LaVerne Painter and Malcolm Meredith general repair garage, 1927;
   • Axel Jacobsen's General Garage, 1930;
   • Jacobsen's American Motors (Willys dealer), 1941;
   • New salesroom and garage built, 1945. Salesroom featured Kaiser-Frazer automobiles. Old garage became body and fender shop;
   • Building now houses an industrial laundry.
8. Masonic Temple, built 1926-27.
9. Miner's Greenhouse, 1805 Perry Avenue, built 1939.
10. David Brown blacksmith shop, 1121 Perry Avenue, 1908;
    • F.F. Clark new owner, 1920-21;
    • Union Electric Company, 1115 Perry Avenue, started by Ike Parker and Bill Thompson, 1946; later Thompson Pole Line Company.
11. John H. "Jack" Martin two-story building, southwest

Axel Jacobsen's General Garage, northeast corner, East 11th Street and Perry Avenue. Ray Jacobsen's 1940 Lincoln Continental convertible.

- Photo from Ray Jacobsen

John H. "Jack" Martin's Dry Goods Store, southwest corner, East 11th Street and Perry Avenue, built 1912. Photo taken 1916, year of a big snow. Thomas and George Fellows standing near store.

corner of East 11th Street and Perry Avenue, 1912, for dry goods store and post office;
• J.E. Wood's department store, operated by Gene Schweer, 1920;
• Ben A. Townsend a dry goods, notions and drug store, 1921;
• George Mitchell and Mel Solie's Manette Foods, 1930s;
• Post office in annex closed, 1943;

- Post office in annex closed, 1943;
- Lee Harrison's barber shop, 1930;
- Beauty shop operated by Madeline Brown;
- Madsen shoe repair shop;
- Building sublet to Aaron Shifrin, 1937;
- Building sold by John H. "Jack" Martin to Duncan Munro, 1942;
- Now location of Casa Del Sol Apartments.

12. Manette Bakery, J.P. Tennis, 1918.
    In this building and two additional office locations many small businesses followed:
    - Myrtle's Place;
    - French Cleaners;
    - Gerry's Cafe, 1939;
    - Hoyt's Meat Market;
    - Joe Sibon's shoe repair, 1957;
    - Tackle Shack, operated by Richard Rahman, 1955-65;
    - Boat shop;
    - Anthony Guyman's Western Stock and Gun Company
    - Judi's Kitchen;
    - Now Bread Basket Cafe, operated by Rob and Merlaine Seever;
    - All-A-Round Plumbing;
    - Smokoff Printing;
    - Bolton's Saw Shop storage area.

13. Bolton's Saw Shop, Sheldon Bolton, 1948, now owned by Herbert Colburn, seventh owner.

14. Manette's first contract post office, 1943; building was owned by John McDonnell;
    - Now Bruce Construction Company.

15. George Fellows Hall, 1904. Manette's second two-story building.
    FIRST FLOOR:
    - General store, opened by Ben Panchot and James Rodger, 1906;
    - Card brothers purchased, 1907;
    - A.B. Williams and son Nathan purchased and opened hardware store, 1908;
    - J.W. Meredith purchased, 1913, and opened Manette Hardware and later Rochdale cooperative grocery store;
    - Clyde Meredith joined his father in business, 1918, and operated Meredith & Son grocery until 1951;
    - Victor and Velma Casebeer operated grocery store for 3-4 years after Merediths' retirement;
    - Verne Freeman, Union Electric and Hardware Company, 1950s and 1960s;
    - Now the Gamesters, operated by Mike Armbruster.
    SECOND FLOOR:
    - Steadfast Lodge, 1916-1927;
    - East Bremerton Improvement Club (EBIC) and other civic organizations, 1931 through 1940s;
    - Now Far West Sails, owned by Clyde Meredith's grandson, Richard Hladky Jr.

16. Manette Improvement and Investment Company real estate office, 1909.

17. Root's East Side Grocery, 2110 East 11th Street, Lawrence Root, 1941;
    - Glenn Buckner grocery store, 1947-1956;
    - Now Two-Way Talk Shop.

18. Aldrich Building, built 1931 by Duncan and Ethel Aldrich for variety store and since enlarged to extend from 2109 through 2117 East 11th Street;
    - Drug store added, 1934; Raymond Wright hired as druggist;
    - Wright purchased business and it became Wright's Drug Store;
    - Sanford (Raymond Wright's son) had Manette Electric in basement;
    - Roy Brown purchased and it became Brown's Drug, 1951;
    - Clyde Allen purchased and it became Clyde's Pharmacy, 1957-1965.

Aldrich's variety and drug store, 2109 East 11th Street, early 1930s.

The Manette Hotel (arrow), was built about 1908. It burned about 1914. Location was approximately at today's 1007 Scott Avenue. Photo taken in 1909. View is from a point north of today's East 11th Street and Perry Avenue.

- Aldrich's Tavern 1934;
- Eastside Tavern, James Rollins and Art Leroy, 1946-47;
- Clancy Foote owned tavern, about 1953-1970, followed by Jim Trotman, and later Don Vining;
- Harry Jens purchased tavern, 1978;

AUTO PARTS
- Lee Harris' auto parts store, 2109 East 11th, 1953-1970;
- Bess Lombard's variety shop;
- Twyla's Restaurant; Watkins Products; Wright's Manette Radio; Clarice's Apparel, 1959-1965;
- Ward Dance Studio;
- Botokukan Karate Association;
- Now Children's Hair Fair occupies the site.

- (Harold Kemp and Ernest Stingl purchased Aldrich Building in 1956. In 1978 Kemp sold the property to his son and daughter-in-law, Tim and Patty Kemp, the present owners.)

19. Manette Hotel, 1007 Scott Street, 1908; burned about 1914;
   - The 1007 Scott Building, Tim and Patty Kemp, 1985.

20. Herb Akers' Used Furniture, 2102 East 11th Street;
   - Vernon Higbee's Manette Radio;
   - Mary Smith's Poulsbo Bakery;
   - Now Hair Harbor barber.
   - Bobby Austin Real Estate, 2104 East 11th Street;
   - Lawrence Weaver, naval architect;
   - Grams and Linden, contractors;
   - Simmons Construction Company.
   - Post office, 2106 East 11th Street, 1967. Station

James W. Martin's store, 112 Shore Drive, 1904.

James W. Martin store, 112 Shore Drive, 1908. -Photo from Bill Schweer

managers: Mary Wagner, Frances Rickey, Winona Seymour, Delbert Miles, Helen Parker and at present Wesley Langrell.
- Harry Flint barber shop, 2108 East 11th Street;
- Don Smead, barber; Mike Ward, barber;
- Photo Lab;
- Balloon Shop.
21. James W. and Harry Martin moved grocery business from 112 Shore Drive to this location, 2105 East 11th Street, in 1918, and it became Martin's P.S.Q. store;
- Vernon Higbee, Manette Radio and TV, purchased building from Hattie Martin in 1949 and moved his business from across the street;
- Building burned, 1966; rebuilt by Higbee.
- Now Higbee's Manette TV and Electric.
22. William S. Harris real estate office, 1906.
23. Salon Eleven Fourteen beauty shop, by Jean Robards, Johanne Leidy, Virginia Bond.
24. 1104 Pitt Building, Paul Harmer, 1953, now owned by Estelle Meredith;
- Herman Coker's bakery;
- Joe Sibon's shoe repair;
- Rudolph Bernhoft Labratories, owned by William Farrell's Pharmaceutical Manufacturing Company;
- Gene Nelson's Pacific Creative Arts, Kitsap Greeter Service, and Pacific Transit Advertising until 1987.
25. Vernon Powers' Jewelry, 2010 East 11th Street, started 1946; moved to 2100 East 11th Street, 1949.
26. Roy B. Neff Grocery, adjacent to Martin's and facing East 10th Street; burned in 1913.
27. J.F. Bryan Jewelry Repair, in the 200 block Shore Drive, 1939.

28. Hay, grain and feed store, J.W. and Harry Martin, 1904. Location was Tunbridge and Water Streets, now East 10th Street and Shore Drive;
- (Building expanded, 1941, for Standard Plumbing and Heating, owned by Harold Kemp and Jim May, 1941; Ernst Stingl and Harold Mahan later became partners of Kemp; Property now owned by Stingl's daughter and son Ellen Fitz and Don Stingl;)
- Peninsula Fuel, Kemp and James McCallum, part of Standard Plumbing, 1964;
- U.S. Engineering;
- Now Miller Sheet Metal, Inc., 112 Shore Drive.
- Bremerton Billiard Supply, Harry Jens, 2004 East 10th Street;
- Comfort Company, insulation, 111 Shore Drive.
29. Grines Cabinet Shop, 200 block Shore Drive.
30. Safeway grocery store, opened March 1942;
- Roy Etten and Ted Thompson's grocery, 1964;
- Sunshine East grocery;
- Now Thompson's Village Mart and grocery.
31. Oscar Etten's Manette Meat Market, 1011 East 11th Street, previously Stone's, moved from across the street and purchased by Etten, 1927;
- Roy Etten and Glenn Jarstad's market, 1946-1964;
- Barcelon's Radiator Repair and Body Shop. Bob Barcelon;
- Now John Tracy, lawyer, and Evergreen Legal Services.
32. Decatur Wharf built 1902, at end of Tunbridge Street (East 10th Street);
- Thompson building, first two-story building, a general store, built in 1902 by T.N. Thompson, on second lot

Etten's Manette Meat Market truck, about 1930. Driver Archie Bouchard Sr. and daughter Berenice.
-Photo from Berenice Bouchard Root

Oscar Etten in front of his meat market, 1011 East 11th Street, 1937. -Photo from June Etten Jarstad

east of wharf; W.S. Crank, manager, 1902;
• James and Harry Martin purchased Crank's grocery stock and moved to Thompson Building, post office included;
• Crank leased land next to wharf for new store and home, 1903;
• A.B. Williams purchased Thompson Building and opened hardware store, 1906; community hall upstairs;
• Decatur (Manette) Wharf burned, 1917; fire spread from ferry *Swan*;
• Ralph W. Tracy Lumber Company started, 1919;
• Frank Gillette purchased Tracy Lumber Company, 1934;
• William A. Parker and son Albert "Ike" purchased Gil-

lette Lumber Company, 1939; operated until 1971;
• Edgewater Apartments, built by Ike Parker, 1958;
• Narrows Apartments, built by Ike Parker, 1977.
33. William H. Hawkes' real estate office, moved from Manette Dock, 1930.
34. Keith Branch, contractors, early 1950s and 60s;
• Superior Glass Company, 114 Shore Drive, Charles and Keith Passe.
35. James Burns' Winfield Cleaners, 1132 Wheaton Way, established 1942;
• Ted Jones' Ted's Lunch and Manette Dinette were nearby.
36. Union Oil Station, northeast corner Harkins Street and Winfield Avenue, built by Harold H. Newton at end of

Lumber Yard at 201 Shore Drive. Established by Tracy Lumber Company, 1919. Became Gillette Lumber, 1934, and Parker's Manette Lumber, 1939. Photo taken about 1930. -Photo from Berenice Bouchard Root

W.H. Hawkes' real estate office on Harkins Street, 1936. -Photo from Charlotte Hammersburg Forbes

Manette Bridge. Dick Feek opened business April 1938;
- Feek sold business to Ernie Dixon and Billie McKenzie, 1944;
- Dixon retired, 1975;
- Station was removed and a new business complex, Manette Plaza, built in 1987 by Ken Hills.

37. Signal Oil Company under management of Fred Steinhardt built service station, 1942. Henry and Ray Streutker managed. After World War II Signal Oil Company ceased to exist and station was removed;
- Real estate office, 2011 Harkins Street;

Ernie's Union Service, northeast corner Harkins Street and Winfield Avenue, seen from Manette Bridge, late 1940s. Coker's Bakery and Safeway store in background.-Photo from Mable Dickson

Henry and Ray Streutker's Signal Station, second location, southeast corner Harkins Street and Winfield Avenue, 1940.   -Photo from Bill Streutker

Dick Feek's service station, northeast corner East 11th Street and Winfield Avenue, circa 1936.
Later sold to Henry Streutker.   - Photo from Ray Streutker

- Joe Sibon's Shoe Repair Shop, 2009 Harkins Street, 1940s-1950s;
- Bill Berrigan's Manette Drug Company, 1940s;
- Presently Brad Buskirk's Frame Shop and Gallery;
- Dress shops and other small businesses, 2005 Harkins Street.

38. Manette Garage, built by Stone brothers at East 11th Street and Winfield Avenue, 1920;
   - Stone brothers built meat market adjacent to garage on east;
   - Louis Martin leased garage to Jim and Ona Hoonan, 1933;
   - Louis Martin sold business to George and Pearl Weiss, about 1935;
   - Dick Feek purchased business, 1936;
   - Signal Oil Company representative Fred Steinhart

bought property, 1938;
   - Bill Johnson managed business, 1939;
   - Henry Streutker operated business as Manette Signal Service, 1940.

39. Ben Kean's fuel yard and gas station, established 1921;
   - Ada Schoonover Mattson's beauty shop;
   - Stan's Drive-in (Stan Baselt), 1950s;
   - S. and R. Laundromat, owned and operated by Mae Davis, 1960.

40. Port Orchard School, established by School District 3, 1867;
   - Port Orchard Lumber and Transportation Company (Fellows-Bender Mill), 1896-1900;
   - Decatur dance hall and community center, about 1900;
   - Manette Bridge, opened June 1930.

41. Manette Dock, built 1916. Martin Hefner and Harry Hansen operated *Pioneer*, second auto ferry on Puget Sound, from this dock, 1916;

Manette Garage, northeast corner, East 11th Street and Winfield Avenue, 1921. Stone's Manette Meat Market at right.   -Photo from Esther Miner Westover

Fellows-Bender Decatur mill, 1895-1900. Location was near east end of present Manette Bridge.

Manette Dock and business section at foot of East 11th Street, circa 1925.

Monson Boat Rental, 1943.

The Maple Leaf Tavern, at right, during one of road projects carried on since tavern was built in 1933.

- Pioneer Pool Hall and C.M. Crum's barber shop;
- Lee Harrison Barber Shop, 1930;
- Duncan Aldrich purchased pool hall and added cafe, 1919;
- Len Bright's auto repair shop, 1921;
- Tom Bright's foundry, 1921;
- Oscar Hilstad's fuel yard and Lee Harrison's barber shop (Lee took the fuel orders), 107 Shore Drive;
- Monson family boat rental company, 1943;
- Business was sold to Dave Wheaton, 1947;
- Wheaton sold to McCowan;
- Ansel Sawyer purchased and ran business, 1956 to 1975;
- Boat Shed Restaurant, started by Brian Buskirk; owned and operated by Brett Hayfield since 1979.

Lee Harrison outside his barber shop at Manette Dock, 1930.

42. Sam Hall's confectionary, end of Manette Dock;
    - William H. Hawkes' real estate office; later moved to inner end of dock, opposite Pioneer Pool Hall.
43. Herman and Blanche Avery's grocery store and gas station opposite Maple Leaf Tavern, 1930s.
44. Kitsap County Childrens Home, started 1919; closed by county commissioners, 1934.
45. Stiles' Handy Grocery, World War II years.
46. Tom Dixon's Maple Leaf Tavern, started immediately

after prohibition repealed, 1933; still in operation.
47. Parr Electric and Battery Company, between Ben Kean's service station and Oscar Etten's meat market, 1932; moved to 639 Sheridan Road and operated there until 1937.

Manette Improvement and Investment Company
By Orville Schultz

The articles of incorporation of the Manette Improvement and Investment Company were filed with the Kitsap County Auditor's Office on November 22, 1905.

The corporation's objects were "to purchase, let, lease, bargain, sell, mortgage, hold and dispose of lands, real estate, tenements and appurtenances thereto belonging—and to do all things necessary and proper to carry on the business of investment and loaning and to incur an indebtedness not exceeding the paid up stock of $50,000.00."

The corporation officers were Neil McDougall as president, M. R. Brewster vice president, B. S. Wolfe secretary and W. S. Harris treasurer. The original seven trustees were S.W. Gallotte, J.M. Armstrong, H.E. Harrington, T.S. Fellows, E.A. Wall, Charles Martin and George Bachmann.

Among other names appearing in later historical material related to the company are J.A. Gamage, George Fellows, J.B.

Neil McDougall, president of Manette Improvement and Investment Company.- Kitsap County 1909 plat book photo, from E.H. Eskridge

Manette Improvement and Investment Company, near East 10th Street on Scott Avenue, 1909.

Wakeman, O.E. Avery, G.W. McConkey, R.L. Jacobs, S.F. Dewar, William A. Hook, S. Mikkelson and Isaac P. Hoopes.

The undersigned—Neil McDougall, M.R. Brewster, B.S. Wolfe, J.M. Armstrong, J.A. Gammage, S.W. Gallotte, E.A. Wall, H.E. Harrington, George Fellows, W.S. Harris, J.B. Wakeman, George Bachman, T.S. Fellows, Charles Martin, all citizens of and living in Manette on November 22, 1905, have incorporated to form the Manette Improvement and Investment Company.

The corporation founders "saw the need of the navy yard workers with a steady income to invest a small amount of their income, which might otherwise be foolishly spent, in a savings investment," according to one account of the venture. The idea was "to instil in the mind of the wage worker habits of thrift and economy, and the ambition to lay up a competence for old age or misfortune, as well as to acquire, with the individual savings, such property as might be had cheaply and to build thereon a neat comfortable home on terms so easy that there would be no incentive to pay rent. They could purchase a home or acre tract for $25 down and the balance at the rate of $5 per month."

During the first 10 years of existence the Manette Improvement and Investment Company raised among the citizens in the way of collections, subscriptions and donations over $14,000 for help in building a wharf, a ferry, water works and public improvements.

The company was still active in 1918, but no later records have been found.

References: Manette Improvement and Investment Company brochure, published in 1912 by W.S. Harris Port Orchard; Abstract #22678 - compiled for Bremerton Trust and Savings Bank and William H. Schultz, McTeighs Garden Tracts (1700 Jacobsen Boulevard).

Meredith's Store

Meredith's store has played an important role in the history of Manette. It was built originally for George Fellows by Mr. Lehea, a contractor, and was opened with a moving picture entertainment and dance on Saturday, May 14, 1904.

The original plan was "two store rooms on the ground floor with public hall upstairs." An early report states that "it has one of the best dance floors on the bay." Those floors—the solid oak ground floor and fir second floor—are still there.

It was over 2 years before Ben Panchot and James Rodger opened a general store as reported in the *Bremerton News* of June 9, 1906.

Right from that opening night, the papers record a busy and varied schedule of community activities taking place in Fellows Hall. Some of these events were box socials, improvement club meetings, dances, political rallies, W.C.T.U. (Womens' Christian Temperance Union) meetings, Grange meetings. G.A.R. (Grand Army of the Republic), suffragettes, magic lantern shows, church services, weddings, lodges, minstral shows, Girl Scout meetings—on and on.

George Card and his brother took possession of Ben Panchot's store in September 1907 and A.B. Williams and son Nathan purchased George Card's interest in April 1908.

A May 23, 1908, news item states "An explosion occurred in Fellows Hall, Tuesday morning at 7:50, of the gas ap-

paratus of Hummel & Huse's moving picture show. These gentlemen had given a show the night before and were charging the tank with gas for the next entertainment, when by some means the generator exploded. The force of the explosion was terrific, blowing out all but one window in the hall, and shaking the buildings all over town. Mr. Hummel was badly injured, sustaining a comminutive fracture of the right forearm, also severe injuries to the face and head. Mr. Huse was also severely shocked by the explosion.''

George Fellows died May 25, 1910, and Thomas Fellows inherited the property, which he later sold on January 30, 1912, to H.P. Martin. In 1913 Martin traded the property to J.W. Meredith for a store owned by Meredith in Seattle, and it has been in the Meredith family since then. After J. W. Meredith's death in 1927, his son, Clyde, managed the grocery business. Stores were more than just places for buying things; they were information centers that nourished the grapevine and helped keep people in touch. Even in the 1920s the big stove in the back corner of Meredith's provided a spot where people would stand for a few minutes to visit while warming themselves.

When a fire was reported by telephoning 425 for Meredith's store, Clyde ran across East 11th Street and rang the fire bell to alert volunteer firemen.

MILESTONES

1904: Fellows Hall constructed for George Fellows.

1906: Ben Panchot and James Rodger opened a general store.

1907: (September 24) George Card took possession of store.

1908: A.B. Williams sold hardware and general merchandise.

1920: James W. Meredith, Clyde's father, operated Manette-Rochdale Company and sold hardware, feed, general merchandise and groceries.

1922: Clyde Meredith joined his father and the store became known as Meredith & Son. Later, after J. W. Meredith died, Clyde contracted with the Red & White grocery company to provide canned and packaged groceries, which became the store's specialty. When Clyde retired in 1946, the business was sold as a grocery; later the building was rented by Union Electric and Hardware Company. Today, the building is occupied by The Gamesters.

Landmark. This building at 2202 East 11th Street encompasses much of Manette's past. Constructed as Fellows Hall in 1904, it became A.B. Williams store (above, 1908), Manette-Rochdale Company (above right, 1920) and Meredith and Son (right, 1922). Clyde Meredith operated a grocery store in the building until 1946, when he sold the business but kept the building. Of the many subsequent occupants The Gamesters is the latest. Clyde's widow Estelle, 93, still owns the property. Adults (from left) in photo at right are Clyde Meredith, Anna Tennis (Joe's wife), Ruby Tennis (Joe's sister) and Joe Tennis. Five children are unidentified. Leaning against walk is Malcolm Meredith.

Meredith's Red and White Store, 2202 East 11th Street, 1930. From left are clerk Lawrence Root and owners Clyde and Estelle Meredith.

Logging Camp
By Harold Reanier

I recall playing at the logging camp in the mid-1920s. It was north of the end of Perry Avenue. There was a bunk house, a cookhouse and a mess hall large enough for about 20-25 men.

This was a high-lead logging operation. A steam donkey engine provided the power. First a tall fir about 3 to 4 feet in diameter at the butt was selected close to the edge of the area to be logged. A "high climber" climbed to where the first limbs were growing, usually 80 to 100 feet up, and cut the top off. He then rigged a block and tackle to hoist a larger pulley, called a bull-block, with a 2-inch cable running through it. This was known as the main line and was about 2000 feet long.

A smaller cable, about 1 inch thick, known as the haul-back cable, was used to pull the main line back out into the woods so the "choker setter" could attach the logs to it. A "whistle punk" would signal the "donkey engineer" to start pulling the logs out to the loading deck.

In those days the trees measured anywhere from 4 to 8 feet in diameter—and no knots.

When the logs were dragged in to the loading deck they were loaded onto flatcars with large concave steel wheels that ran on round logs about 16 inches in diameter that were used for rails. The logs were hauled about 3 miles down to the bay near Illahee and dumped into the water. A tug would come and tow them to a mill. The flatcars were pulled by a medium-sized steam locomotive.

The donkey engineer's son and I used to go fishing in the creek out there and we would always get out to the camp in time for breakfast. The cook would tell us to pull up to the table. Talk about food! There were hot biscuits, doughnuts, cake, hash-brown potatoes, eggs, toast, gravy, fruit, bacon, ham, sausage, apple pie, mince pie and hotcakes.

One day the engineer, William Buffon, had just hauled in a turn of logs and started the haul-back drum to drag the main line back out to the woods. He gave the all-clear signal and threw the throttle control wide open. He stepped around to pour some oil on the gear and stepped into a loop in the cable. He was wrapped around and around the haul-back drum four or five times before the fireman could get around to stop it. Bill Buffon got hurt critically. Other workers took the door off the bunkhouse to use as a stretcher and laid it across between the front and back seat of a touring car to take Bill to the hospital in Bremerton. Miraculously he survived and came out of it with the only permanent damage being one short leg.

Jake's General Garage
By Ray Jacobsen

Axel or "Jake" Jacobsen as he was known by most, operated The General Garage through the 30s, doing auto repair work only.

In 1940 he became a dealer for Willys automobiles. At that time one could purchase a new Willys speedway coupe (standard model) for $575 at the factory in Toledo, Ohio. The 1941 model was called the "Willys Americar." In keeping with the new name and the spirit of the times, just prior to World War II, Jake changed the name of his business to American Motors. To speed delivery of the first new Americars, Jake, Frank Wing, Harry C. Clark, son Ray and two others he hired drove to Toledo, Ohio, arriving October 11, 1940, Ray's 13th birthday. Jake took delivery of the new cars at the end of the assembly line. The new cars were hooked together in pairs, using tow bars, and driven back to Manette. On the trip home, a stop was made somewhere in Illinois so Jake and Frank could register for the draft.

Shortly thereafter, Jake opened a sales and service for the new Willys at Fourth Street and Naval Avenue in Bremerton and operated this in conjunction with the shop in Manette. The Americar sold well and during the 1941 year, Jake's dealership sold more new Americars than any other Willys dealer in the U.S. Jake was flown back to Toledo and given an award and commendation by Joseph W. Frazer, then president of for Willys and later the Frazer of Kaiser-Frazer Corporation.

The U.S. entry into World War II in December, 1941, signaled the end of U.S. civilian auto manufacturing. When the production of civilian cars was halted in 1942, Jake closed the dealership at Fourth and Naval and handled all repair work at Perry Avenue.

At the close of World War II (1945) he built a new garage and showroom at the corner of East 11th Street and Perry Avenue, adjoining the old garage, which then became the body and fender shop. Herschel Garinger was the contractor for the new building.

Sales and service of the new Willys-Jeep line of cars and trucks was resumed in 1946. In 1947 Jake acquired the Kaiser-Frazer franchise and in 1948 the GMC truck franchise was added. He dropped the K-F line in 1951 but continued with Willys and GMC until closing the garage in 1964 or 65 because of ill health. The GMC franchise was sold to Chuck Haselwood, and Jake worked as a truck salesman for Chuck as much as health permitted until he passed away in 1978.

Maple Leaf Tavern
A Lot for $2
By Harold Reanier

I worked for Oscar Etten at Etten's Meat Market. In 1933 prohibition was repealed and, I believe it was Tom Dixon who propositioned Oscar—he said he knew where he could buy a lot cheap for taxes, if Oscar would supply the money. Oscar gave me $2 to go to the courthouse in Port Orchard and I bought the lot for $1.99. Dixon built and operated the Maple Leaf Tavern on this piece of property at 1735 Wheaton Way.

A Stump For a Site
By Don and Anna Jo Atkinson

Maple Leaf Tavern's present owner is Mr. Ron Ligman. His wife is Esther and they have seven children—five boys and two girls. Mr. Ligman purchased the business from Mr. John Coleman. Coleman owned Maple Leaf for 22 years. Among other owners have been Joe Borgen, Les Robinson, Rob Seever, Jack and Liz Balshum and a Mr. Weber. Tommy Burns, a former world heavyweight boxing champion, was once the bartender.

The only other information the above gentlemen could tell us was that the building was built in 1932. It was originally a house built on a stump. It was one of the first taverns in the area to open after prohibition.

Henry Streutker's Manette Signal Service
By Ray Streutker

The story of Henry Streutker taking over operation of the Manette Signal Service in 1940 is the tale of one Depression-ridden family that emerged from rural poverty. Hank, as he

was known, heard of the station management opportunity through his brother "Hiway John" who had earlier made the transition to Gorst from Whidbey Island. But Hank at first could not bring himself to a move mood after several unsuccessful farm occupancies. And looking at the $600 station inventory to be purchased he was convinced the local banker would not grant a loan, due to the nature of that banker and the times. He clearly had "Depression depression."

But 17-year-old son Ray, fired by the challenge of a car-related business and a life in the city, offered to sell his pigs (an FFA project) and urged his dad to try to mortgage the cows. Hank reluctantly agreed to try for a loan and to his dismay the banker approved one, even without going out to see the cows. He even commended Hank, saying he admired him for venturing out at a time when so many had lost initiative. Then he added another $10 for travel. Hank and Ray left at once for Bremerton, leaving the rest of the family to finish the harvest and have an auction sale.

The father and son team pumped their first gas on July 7, 1940, and that day made a whopping $7 profit. They lived in the station, Hank sleeping on a folding cot on the floor. They cooked on an electric hot plate. Groceries from Clyde Meredith's Red & White store were kept in cabinets among cans of oil. But they were excited. In 6 month's time the loan was paid off according to terms. By now Henry with his family of six had occupied the old residence at the rear of the station property, having been moved by Ollie Avery with Ted Howerton driving. But on the night of November 15 the family was forced to escape for their lives as the old flimsy frame structure was destroyed in a fire. Their concern was that the station too would be consumed by the flames. Kindly Manette neighbors, namely the Millikans and the Langrells, took in the Streutkers, who had lost about all they had.

The business grew rapidly, fed much by the influx of residents due to increased activities at the naval shipyard. The Signal Oil Company under Fred Steinhardt, Perry Avenue resident, demolished the rear part of the car storage area of the station to begin construction of a new station facing Harkins Street. A retaining wall collapsed, destroying more of the old building. Some cars were damaged but no one was injured.

The new station opened in March of 1942 with Hank and Ray as partners. Boxes of chocolates were given out with each full tank of gasoline for the grand opening. But, yes, you had to have those gasoline rationing stamps in those wartime days! Business soon grew to the extent that the station topped all others in the city in gallonage.

In September 1945, Ray left to enroll for the ministry at Seattle Pacific University and Hank continued on until September 1946. In 1986 Ray was pastor of North Kitsap Methodist Church.

The Signal Oil Company has ceased to exist and the station has been torn down. Since the old original Manette Garage—built by the Stone brothers in 1920—went down in 1942, no other building has occupied that site and as far as I know none had ever been there prior to it.

Henry Streutker lived in Manette until he died at 88 in September of 1986.

A Few More Reminders What Discount Will Do

Peas, that melt in your mouth .20¼
Corn, a quality article .15
Tomatoes, standards 11¼
Prunes, a 25c grade .18
Peaches, extra fancy dried .27c
Tomatoe Pulp, a snap 3 cans for .22½
Minced Clams, per can .12

+ + +

(21) AT MARTIN'S

For Sale or Will Trade

For Bremerton Property
Water front home. One acre of ground, 4 room Modern Bunga-low with bath and sleeping porch cabinet kitchen, fire-place. Gar-age, 3 room plastered house in rear with sink. 15 bearing fruit trees choice variety, fine lawn and shrubbery runs to water's edge. Call Phone 430J or address
Box 507 Bremerton

PURE R. I. Red and Plymouth Rock Cockerels
$1.50 and $2.00
Matteson Place
Fruits and Vegetables in Season

(41) Bright's Auto
REPAIR SHOP
Oil, Gas, Assessories.
On The Dock:

(41) W. TOWNSEND
Pioneer Pool Hall
Cigars, Tobacco
Candy Soft Drinks
—STRICTLY CLEAN GAMES—

Agent for the City of New York Insurance Co.
See me about that policy.

LEE TRANSFER & STORAGE CO
Local and Long Distance Hauling
PHONE 273 x   PROMPT SERVICE

EAT
MORE
BREAD
(12) Manette Bakery
J. P. TENNIS, Prop.

FOR SALE
5 Passenger Auto
Furniture   Phonograph
Electric Washer
Row Boat and out board
Engine   Double Camp
Phone 275 L

CORRELL'S
EAST BREMERTON TRANSFER
All Kinds of Hauling. Reasonable Rates
PHONES 344 L   436L

Reduced Prices
On Piece Goods, Hose and Uuderwear

Gingham, old price 40c   now   25c yd
Davenshire, old price 60c   now   45c yd
Romper Cloth, old price 52c now   37c yd

BOTTLED POP and ICE CREAM

(11) B. A. TOWNSEND
DRY GOODS   NOTIONS   DRUGS
Phone 273 J

Ads from East Bremerton Fog-Horn, February 17, 1921. Circled numbers refer to locations on map on page 40.

SPECIALS
THIS WEEK

Cocoa ½ lb Package		20c
Can Beets 15c two for		25c
Prepared Mustard, per bottle		10c
Two cans Libby Pork and Beans		25c
Salt Mackeral		20c
Small Karo, light		20c
Small Karo, dark 18c two for 35c		

(15) **MEREDITH & SON**

GROCERIES, HARDWARE and FEED.

(32) **TRACY LUMBER CO.**

Lumber and Building Material, Concrete Piers.
Chimney Blocks, Bricks and Square
Deal Wall Board.

TRACY LUMBER CO.   PHONE 24 L

(41) **MANETTE
TRANSFER**

Phone 479 R
WOOD, COAL and
GENERAL TRANSFER

Expect a Scow of Mill
Wood Soon.

(41) Manette Barber Shop
Open evenings after 7:30
IN PIONEER POOL HALL
C. M. CRUM, Prop.

Nothing but the Very Best
SELECT MEATS

will be sold at our Market. We cannot handle the cheaper
grades which are being sold at other markets in order to cut
prices grab patronage. A look at OUR QUALITY and
a consideration of OUR PRICES will convince you that we are
DOING THE STRICTLY SQUARE DEAL

Ribs of beef to boil		15c
Pot Roasts from	20 to 25c	
Steaks, All Cuts		38c
Shoulder of Lamb		25c
Leg of Lamb		35c

The wholesale prices for the
class of meats which we are
handling have advanced.

TRY OUR CURED MEATS

(31) **Manette Meat Market**

(10) **East Bremerton Blacksmith Shop**

F. F. CLARK, Successor to David Brown.

Blaksmithing,   Sheet Metal Work, Pipe Fitting
Saw Filing and General Repairing,

Real Estate and Notary Public
See me for Homes, Acreage or Lots
REASONABLE and ON EASY TERMS

(41) **W. H. HAWKES** MANETTE WHARF

Office Phone 104 J   Residence Phone 478 X

If you can use an almost new 7
foot cross cut saw call at the Fog-
Horn office and see the one we
have for sale. It can be bought
cheap.

Ads from **East Bremerton Fog-Horn,** *February 17, 1921. Circled numbers refer to locations on map on page 40.*

31
Manette
Market

QUALITY
MEATS

At Lowest Prices

15
Meredith & Son

GENERAL

MERCHANDISE

Phone 425
                Manette, Wash.

Pierson
Hardware

QUALITY
HARDWARE

513 Pacific   Phone 271

Office Phone 381-J   Res Phone 104-J

39
Manette Fuel
AND
Transfer Co.
BEN KEAN, Propr.

12 Best Fuels—Instant Service

Monroe Dairy

Pure Whole Milk
Delivered Daily

Manette
Ferry System

BEST ON THE BAY

Phone 24-L   R. W. Tracy

32
Tracy Lumber Co.

LUMBER, HAY and GRAIN

East Bremerton   Washington

Go Slow, Mary

A Farce Comedy in Three Acts

Auspices Philathea Chapter No. 174, O. E. S.

NEW MASONIC TEMPLE

FRIDAY, DECEMBER 16th, 1927

CHARACTERS

Billy Abbey .... Theodore Peterson
Mary Abbey .... Bernice Carlow
Mrs. Berdun .... Mrs. Georgia Persunette
Sally Carter .... Mrs. Edna Bailey
Harry Stevens .... Leonard Card
Burt Childs .... Gideon Hermansen
Bobby Berdun .... Floyd Buchanan
Dolly Berdun .... Alice Holden
Katie .... Mrs. Carrie Bright
Danny Grubb .... Wm. Sutherland
Murphy .... Tom Bright

Time—The Present.
Place—Suburb of Philadelphia, Pa.
Time of Playing—About Two Hours.

SYNOPSIS OF ACTS.

ACT I.—Living Room of the Abbey Home in Philadelphia.
ACT II.—The Same: Three Days Later.
ACT III.—The Same: Immediately After Act II.

Directed by Mrs. Lillian Meicho.

Music Furnished by A. R. McCallum and Roy Wood.

REALTY   INSURANCE

41
W. H. Hawkes

Manette, Wash.

Prices Low   Terms Easy

21
Martin & Co.
PIONEER
STORE

GROCERIES,
DRUGS and
FOUNTAIN

7
General
Garage

STORAGE,
REPAIRING,
WRECKER SERVICE

Parr Electric &
Battery Co.

Battery Repairing and
Auto Ignition
A Specialty

The Appropriate Gift
and One He will
Appreciate
MEMBERSHIP FOR 1928
in the
Kitsap Rifle & Revolver Club
Bremerton, Wash.

D. S. Morrison   W. H. Gates, Jr.

Compliments of

U. S. Furniture Co.

Complete Home Furnishers'
Telephone 363-J
719 Pacific Ave.   Bremerton, Wash.

41
Reliable Fuel &
Transfer
We Know the Value of a
Satisfied Customer
Phone 1129-M

Sanitary Barbers

Business support of Eastern Star play, 1927.

IF YOUR [stairs] LOOK LIKE THIS BECAUSE YOUR [house] IS [?]

WE WILL FURNISH [tools] etc. IF YOU CAN AFFORD TO PAY A FEW [coins] A MONTH IN A JIFFY YOUR [stairs] WILL LOOK LIKE THIS

CALL US ANY [clock] FROM [sunrise] to [sunset]

(32) Parker's Manette Lumber Co.

END OF BRIDGE — MANETTE

Phone 463

SHOES

DRESS & WORK

S. F. DEWAR

MANETTE, WN.

PHONE 843-R

AT BOSTON PRICES

MERRITT-MASON

(35) **"TED'S" LUNCH**

FORMERLY
MANETTE DINETTE

Choice Foods Excellently Cooked

Winfield Ave., near Bridge End
MANETTE, WASH.

ANNOUNCING

The opening of the MANETTE SHOE REPAIR SHOP on Perry Avenue, Manette, just opposite the Masonic Temple and just in the rear of the HARRISON BARBER SHOP. Have lived here for past 3 years.

WE DO EXPERT REPAIR WORK ON YOUR SHOES.
Soles and Heels   LACES
Rubber and Leather Top Lifts   Polish of all kinds.

(11) **MANETTE SHOE REPAIR SHOP**

SHOE SHINE!   —Howard Peterson, Prop.

(11) Your Peninsula---- **BARBER SHOP**

LEE R. HARRISON - Barber
"Neighborly and friendly" -Drop in for a rest -fine Opera Chairs. Corner, Masonic Temple, MANETTE.

(17) **ROOT'S**

East Side Grocery

MANETTE   PHONE 2682
(We Have Free Delivery)

OVEN-BAKED BEANS —
2 No. 2 Tall Cans 25c

FANCY RED SALMON —
S & W — Tall No. 1 Can 27c

OYSTERS — Bonnie Best
5-Oz. Can, 2 for 27c

S & W COFFEE — Regular or
Drip, 1-Lb. Can 26c

SUNSWEET PRUNES —
2-Lb. pkg. 14c

CAKE FLOUR — Centennial
2½-Lb. 19c

PANCAKE FLOUR —
Centennial, 2½-Lb. 19c

MILK — Rock Dell
3 Tall Cans 21c

JELLY — Meadowlark
2-Lb. Jar 25c

PEACHES — Fancy Halves
Rock Dell, 2 No. 2½ Cans 39c

CRISCO — 3 Lbs. 52c

KRAUT — Rock Dell
No. 2½ Can 10c

SOAP — Crystal White or
P & G — 4 for 15c

Always Week-End Specials In
FRUITS and VEGETABLES

at

ROOT'S

PHONE 2682

PIANO STUDIO
Mrs. H. T. Topritzhofer
Teacher
Graduate Teacher's Normal
School
Reasonable Rates!
Telephone 2347-J
1129 Pitt St. — Manette

For Mother's Day!
Give Her a Nice Potted Plant
from

(9) **MINER'S**

MANETTE
Half-Mile from Post Office
Telephone 1344-J

TOMATO PLANTS and
ANNUALS Now Available!

Ads from Manette Gazette, *1939-1940. Circled numbers refer to locations on map on page 40.*

NOW you can buy a brand new car of latest design at the same price you'll pay for a good used car.

The most amazing low-price, full family-size car ever built. *First* to reveal the NEW defense-time trend in low-price cars. Powered with the sensational, new, defense-time Willys "GO-DEVIL" Engine. A devil for power—a miser on fuel and oil ... All-steel, weather- and sound-insulated body ... New cross-bar "butcher's grip" steering wheel ... Simple, vertical "H" gear shift on steering column ... Over-size, easy action, super-hydraulic brakes ... Pelican hood—opens wide for quick, money-saving adjustments, lock controlled from inside of car ... Safety glass in all doors and windows.

SAVE up to $20.00 a month

on complete* operating cost, on the average

*When you think what $20 a month will buy in terms of food—shoes—clothing—home conveniences—luxuries—remember the above Willys American saving. It includes payment on the car plus expenses for gas, oil, etc.—the total monthly cost—as compared to average of so-called "low cost" cars.

Willys Pick-Up Trucks Only . . . $710

⑦ GENERAL GARAGE . . . Manette

DISTRIBUTORS

Phone 741-M for Demonstration — A. W. Jacobsen

⑪ HAWTHORNE REALTY CO.

REJOICES that we are to have a FREE BRIDGE and cordially invites you all to come in and see the EXCELLENT REAL ESTATE BUYS we now have listed.

Located: Next to POST OFFICE, Manette, Wash.

Home phone: 1223

PROMPT-COURTEOUS SERVICE

To introduce the first low-price back-to-normal-size

DEFENSE-TIME MOTOR CAR

We Will Actually Allow

$100.00

ON ANY OLD CAR no matter how old

to apply on the purchase of

THE NEW

WILLYS

AMERICAR

This is the *least* we will pay. If your car is worth *more*, we will allow more. But no matter how old we will allow $100.00. JUST DRIVE IT IN.

Prices Start at

$595

All prices F.O.B. Toledo, Ohio. Federal, state and local taxes (if any) and transportation extra. Prices and specifications subject to change without notice.

Wood

Bone Dry .... $8.00 per cord
Pinner Ends .... 7.50 per cord
Dry Forest .... 7.50 per cord

SAND, GRAVEL and GENERAL HAULING

Peat Moss and Fertilizer —
Per yard $2.00

OLLIE AVERY

Manette   Phone 741-M

OTTO VOLL

—Signs—

212 Second St.   Bremerton
Telephones 620 and 1458
"Your Peninsula Sign Man"

㊱ DICK FEEK'S SERVICE

End of the Bridge
                    MANETTE
UNION OIL PRODUCTS
STOP WEAR LUBRICATION
    FIRESTONE TIRES & TUBES
Complete line of Automotive
        Accessories.

Complete Line of Ha-Dees Heaters
$9.95 and up.

Yes, and CLEAN--SANITARY REST
        ROOMS
Drop in at Dick Feek's Service
        Phone 24

FOR A SQUEAK SEE FEEK

        Dick Feek--Prop.

NOW OPEN!

㉟ The Manette Dinette

NEW AND MODERN

Serving You With the Best of Foods for

Breakfast, Lunch and Dinner

State Highway — Near Bridge End — Manette
HOURS: 7 A. M. to 9 P. M.
Friday, Saturday and Sunday to Midnight
GLADYS FEEK, RUTH LARAWAY, Mgrs.

ESTHER WAUGH

TEACHER OF

PIANO

STUDIO— Herman Waugh's Residence.

MANETTE, WN.

Located on WINFIELD AVENUE NORTH AT
Top of Hill —Right.
PHONE ———— 182-J

Ads from Manette Gazette, 1939-1940. Circled numbers refer to locations on map on page 40.

The Economical

WATER PUMP

MANETTE PENINSULA FARMS AND RURAL HOMES ARE TALKING ABOUT

★

'ADVANCE PUMP

FIVE RECENTLY SOLD AND INSTALLED IN THE DISTRICT AROUND THE ILLAHEE-STATE PARK CORNER AND NEIGHBORING DISTRICT

These Guaranteed Water Pumps Sold By

A MESSAGE To the Man Who Wants the Most for His Money

See and Try on ADVANCE PUMP Before You Buy

YOUR LOCAL ADVANCE DEALER WILL DEMONSTRATE THESE ADVANTAGES TO YOU!

1. Highest capacity ejector type pump for either deep or shallow well. Can be offset from over well.

2. Scientifically designed—accurately built. Motors protected from burnout with built-in thermostat.

3. No Belts – Gears – Pulleys – Rods. No Hammering – Oiling – Springs.

4. More gallons per dollar—more gallons per horsepower. Low cost—liberal terms.

(28) STANDARD PLUMBING & HEATING, INC.

Manette, Wash — Across from Manette Lumber Co.

Home of Plumbing — All Standard Brands — Ornamental Iron Railing — Goehler Heating Systems

TELEPHONE 2869　　　HAROLD E. KEMP, Pres.

P. S.—If you have not already done so—be sure to visit our new store and shop here at Manette.

(18) ALDRICH PHARMACY

PHONE 40, MANETTE　　Better Service — Low Prices

HOUSE CLEANING TIME

Clean the Professional Way — Use Chamois and Sponges
CHAMOIS SKINS, Large Size ....69c - $1.19 - $1.59
SPONGES, Four Sizes ....19c - 29c - 39c and 49c
RUBBER GLOVES, Extra Heavy — Small, Medium and Large Sizes 49c
ADHESIVE TAPE, Red Cross — All Sizes 10c - 19c & 33c
ORIGINAL SAN-NAP-PAK, Sanitary Napkins — For Extra Protection, Large Pkg., 50 napkins 39c
VITA-FLOR — Vitamin B-1 for Plants and Garden Use. Large Bottle with dropper 50c
MAZDA LAMP GLOBES — 100-75-60-40-25-Watt Each 15c
THREE WAY I.E.S. LAMPS, Each 60c
FRESH KODAK FILMS — All Sizes at Standard Prices! Printing and Enlarging at New Low Prices

CANDY SPECIALS!

PEANUT BRITTLE — (Made with real butter) Lb. 25c
GUM DROPS, Jumbo — Assorted Flavors, Lb. 15c
CHOCOLATES, Assorted — The Old Fashioned Kind Lb. 15c
DOLLAR MINTS — Each 1c, Lb. 15c

GROCERY SPECIALS

RED & WHITE COFFEE, 2-lb. can 57c
RED & WHITE COFFE, 3-lb. can 89c
CAMPBELL'S TOMATO SOUP, 3 cans 25c
RED & WHITE PEANUT BUTTER, 2-lb. jar 35c
UNDERWOOD'S GENUINE DEVILED HAM—
　2 quarter cans 27c; Table jar 23c
RED & WHITE PANCAKE FLOUR, large package 19c
CANADA DRY GINGER ALE, large bottle 15c
　(plus deposit)
RED & WHITE SWEET DILL PICKLES, large jar 29c
RED & WHITE OLIVES, 9-oz. can 17c
LARGE CAN RED & WHITE GENUINE OVEN BAKED BEANS and LARGE CAN RED & WHITE BROWN BREAD—Both for 33c
FRENCH'S PREPARED MUSTARD, 9-oz. jar 13c
SUNSHINE HYDE PARK FANCY ASSORTED COOKIES, large 1-lb. box 25c
SUNSHINE HI-HO, large 1-lb. pkg. 19c
BARNES' FINEST BREAD, 1-lb. loaf 9c
BARNES' FINEST BREAD, 1½-lb. loaf 13c
RED & WHITE SPECIAL CAKE
MALTED MILK SQUARE (a dark cake) each 25c

(15) MEREDITH'S Red & White Store

2202 EAST 11th　　Manette　　TELEPHONE 425

(31)
MANETTE MEAT MARKET
Telephone 486

Cash Specials — Fri.-Sat., April 5-6

Pay Cash Here and Save Plenty!

★

Pork Sale — Pork Sale — Pork Sale

PORK ROAST, Shoulder (Grain Fed) ....lb. 15c
PORK ROAST, Loin ....lb. 18c
PORK STEAK ....lb. 17c
PORK CHOPS ....lb. 23c
PORK LINK SAUSAGE, Armour Star or Acme ....lb. 23c
BEEF POT ROAST ....lb. 12½c
BEEF STEAK, T-Bone or Rib ....lb. 19c
BEEF STEAK, Round ....lb. 25c
BEEF SHORT RIBS, Meaty ....3 lbs. 25c
HAMBURGER or SAUSAGE ....lb. 17c
BACON, Piece ....lb. 17c
BACON, Sliced ....lb. 20c
PURE LARD ....4 lbs. 29c
FRESH BUTTER ....lb. 30c
HAMS, Skinned, Whole or Half, Premium or Armour's Star ....lb. 22c
HAM SLICES ....ea. 10c

TELEPHONE 486 — OSCAR ETTEN

Ads from Manette Gazette, *1939-1940. Circled numbers refer to locations on map on page 40.*

Chapter 6

POSTAL SERVICE

By Anna Jo Harkins Atkinson

SHAKY BEGINNING

When William R. Renton and Daniel L. Howard established their mill at Port Orchard (now Enetai) early in 1854, there was probably no mail service. In 1857 there was one mail route on Puget Sound, by steamer from Olympia to Whatcom (Bellingham). Ports of call included Seattle and Port Madison. Port Orchard was named as one of several ports that had to provide its own local service.

On March 1 of 1861 the Port Orchard post office was established at the mill, with William Renton as postmaster. This post office was discontinued October 21, 1861, but Port Orchard was still serviced, by a mail contractor.

Service was provided twice a week. The ship left Seattle at 8 a.m. It stopped at Port Blakely and then at Port Orchard, where it remained overnight, sailing for Seattle the next morning at 8.

Pioneer historian Ezra Meeker wrote that by 1870 there was a daily trip via Freeport (now West Seattle) and Port Blakely to Port Orchard and back to Seattle. The mail boats carried not only mail but other supplies needed by the pioneers.

The Port Orchard post office was reestablished October 27, 1868, with Nicholas Hale as postmaster. But it closed again December 29, 1871, after the mill burned.

Activity on our peninsula at this time moved north and west, centering in the Sackman area (now Tracyton) where Daniel Sackman had based his large and growing logging interests. By 1884 there were enough people scattered through the outback for William Abrahamson to lead a successful effort to secure a post office for this area.

NON-MODERN EQUIPMENT

Briefly named Dyes (less than 2 months) then re-named Sackman, the post office was in Abrahamson's home on the land now called Hammargren Point just north of Sulphur Springs. Its most important piece of post office furniture was an apple box partitioned to provide about a dozen pigeon holes for mail.

In a *Bremerton Sun* article of May 19, 1950, the apple box was recalled by Ella Fellows Bender, who came from New York in 1888 to make her home with her father, George Fellows, and her three brothers. They lived in what had been the old Port Orchard schoolhouse. For the *Sun* article Mrs. Bender and her husband Lewis were interviewed in their home on the site of the old schoolhouse by Faye Gaither, who

also tells how Ella would row to Sackman for mail. There was no road.

Abrahamson's daughter Dora was named postmistress when the office opened. She remained in that position until 1890, when the name was changed to Tracyton and John Hansberry was named postmaster.

Dora had changed her own name; she was now Mrs. Hansen. Her sons, Harry and Alvin, would later operate the ferry *Pioneer* between Manette and Bremerton.

Postal service at Sheridan was established May 6, 1901, with Fred G. Reeve as postmaster. Facilities were in a small building on the Sheridan Dock. Sheldon Lewis became postmaster in September of 1908, George Reeve in March of 1909, and Katherine McGauley became postmaster in October of 1912.

Early in 1901, according to W. S. Harris as quoted in Faye Gaither's *Bremerton Sun* article, "there was just one house below Telegraph Avenue" (East 11th Street). Harris was defining the 38.75 acres that had been platted in March of 1891 as the townsite of Decatur (Manette). Now, in 1901, new owners of the townsite were putting the lots on the open market. Other tracts close in had already attracted a few navy yard workers who were willing to row to their jobs every day as well as others who had built up small farms and were producing for the Bremerton market.

LOCAL OFFICE SOUGHT

The year 1902 saw the start of the Decatur Improvement Club, which sought a post office as one of its early goals. The first setback came when it was learned that the name Decatur was already in use in Washington State. There is reason to believe that correspondence with Washington, D. C., involved other delays as well. At any rate, the name Manette (for the steamer *Manette*, which called here) was chosen over a list of other favorites, one of which was Fellows, and in August a new petition for a post office was circulated. Thomas N. Thompson was named as the peoples' choice for postmaster and the whole thing was on its way by the end of the month. Mr. Thompson had just completed a big two-story building in the second lot south of the new dock, and a grocery store on the ground floor was open for business.

The first post office petition had been started in January, so when final approval came through on October 17, 1902, there was no way anyone wanted to start over, even though the new postmaster had sold his building and moved to Poulsbo.

The improvement club appointed Mr. M.R. Brewster as a committee of one to go to Poulsbo and ask Mr. Thompson to take the appointment and to appoint a deputy. This was done. Mr. Thompson is in the books as Manette's first postmaster, and Mr. Crank, the new storekeeper, was the deputy who handled the mail.

FIRST DELIVERY

On December 10, 1902, the first mail pouch marked "Manette" was received.

April 11, 1903, E. Johnson was named postmaster.

August 10, 1903, George Fellows received his appointment.

March 15, 1904, James W. Martin was appointed.

Postmaster James W. Martin-Photo from 1909 plat book via E. H. Eskridge

Martin and Company bought the grocery stock of W. S. Crank in July of 1903 and continued to operate in the Thompson Building until July of 1904, when they moved into their own building on the upper side of Water Street. This same building now forms part of a much larger U. S. Engineering Co. plant on the same corner. When Martin and Company moved across the street, J. W. Martin, postmaster, took his post office and moved, too.

On June 9, 1910, John H.

"Jack" Martin (not related to James or Harry) was appointed postmaster. He moved the operation into a small building he was renting on Water Street just north of the original post office, where he had started a clothing and variety store. In 1912 he moved his business and post office into his new two-story building at East 11th Street and Perry Avenue. (The site today is occupied by the Casa de Sol Apartments).

Jack Martin served as postmaster until 1916.

Postmaster John H. "Jack" Martin, appointed 1910.

ETTA ARRIVES

Etta Rowena Eggleston came to Monroe, Wash., from Michigan. She went to work in Monroe for a Mr. J.E. Wood, who owned stores in Monroe, Everett and Bremerton. Mr. Wood's store was Peoples Store, which was later sold to Mr. Bremer and became Bremers Department Store.

When World War I began, Jack Martin went to work in Puget Sound Navy Yard. At Mr. Wood's recommendation, Etta Eggleston took over Jack Martin's store duties and also

Etta R. Harkins.

served in the postal facility. The post office had 50 boxes for patrons.

In 1918 President Woodrow Wilson gave Etta her first presidential commission as postmistress; subsequent commissions were held by her from Presidents Warren G. Harding, Calvin Coolidge and Herbert Hoover. When Franklin D. Roosevelt became president, he gave Etta a lifetime appointment.

The growing population of the Manette Peninsula demanded larger postal facilities, and an addition was built onto Jack Martin's store. It was the office's fifth location. The addition was small, long and narrow. There were two small grilled windows, one for general delivery and stamp patrons and one for money orders and parcel post service.

Many confidences were shared, sorrows unburdened and joys related through those little grilled windows. Since Etta was a very kind, understanding and sympathetic person who loved people, her patrons knew that anything shared with her would go no further.

ETTA AND EARL

Etta married Earl Henry Harkins June 30, 1921. Earl had a medical retirement from the U.S. Army with the rank of captain. Being physically unable to work, he helped Etta with various postal duties, filling in for her when she wished to get away for a few hours or longer, as when their daughter Rowena was born in 1924.

The Manette post office served the whole Manette Peninsula including Manette, Illahee, Gilberton, Brownsville, Central Valley, Silverdale Corner to Tracyton, and back to Manette. At the time of her marriage, Etta was handling all postal duties with the help of one rural carrier, on a 36-mile route, and one mail handler that hauled the mail from the ferry

Cramped quarters. When the post office needed larger quarters, the addition shown in the foreground was built onto Jack Martin's store. Photo, taken about 1919, looks northeast from below the building. At left are billboards which then occupied the northeast corner of the East 11th Street and Perry Avenue intersection. Behind them is the Fellows water tower.

dock to the post office.

The job of mail handler was no easy chore. The first recorded handler was "Grandpa Hixon," who pushed the mail in a wheelbarrow. He would meet the ferry, *Pioneer* or *Urania*, load the steel-wheeled barrow—no rubber tires those days—and trundle and bump his way over the narrow, uneven boardwalks that graced the main street up the steep hill to the post office.

Grandpa Hixon was a Civil War veteran. In his later years he was unable to walk to the post office to collect his pension check. Earl and Etta would take his check to him each month and witness his signature, which was an "X." They then cashed his check for him. This was just one of the "above and beyond" duties they performed which so endeared them to their patrons.

Bob Fraser, with his big, bushy mustache, also wheeled the mail to and from the post office. Ned Verrell modernized the service with his Model A Ford. That was a big improvement, since by 1934 Manette's population was expanding and a wheelbarrow was not adequate for all the mail, magazines, newspapers and parcel post.

During Etta's tenure as postmistress she saw the area's population grow from a few hundred to 40,000 during World War II.

RURAL SERVICE

As early as April or May, 1912, there was rural delivery up the hill on what is now Perry Avenue. Mail was delivered via horse and buggy. There were no blacktopped roads, just gravel and dirt. The whole peninsula was usually served in one long day. Sometimes a storm and wet, soggy roads would mire down the wagon and it would take 2 or 3 days to complete the trip.

Bill Avery was the first recorded rural carrier. He delivered the mail up Perry Avenue with a well-trained horse named "Old Bill." They zig-zagged back and forth across the street, stopping at each home. Later, when Old Bill was retired from the postal service he became the property of the Howerton

family. When Old Bill was taken to market to haul home the family's supplies, they had a hard time keeping him in the middle of the road. He would still want to zig-zag back and forth across the street and stop at each home.

In Manette Mr. W.T. Johnson (the kids called him "Watertight"—no one knew why) followed Bill Avery. Kids liked

Manette post office cancellation. Note price of stamp.

to jump on and hang onto the back of the wagon. W.T. would grab his whip and, with a flick of the wrist backwards, get the kids off in a hurry.

Gordon Overly was the next rural carrier. He graduated from horse and wagon to a car in the late 1920s.

John Rausa transferred to Manette from a Chicago post office. He had the job of rural carrier until his retirement in 1940. His substitute, Don Atkinson, took over the rural delivery.

Don Atkinson was given a permanent appointment to Route 1, Manette, in 1941. There were 301 boxes when Don took over in 1940 on the route that covered 57 miles.

Just as the population pressure resulting from World War I had put our restless post office in its fifth location, the explosive growth during World War II meant another move, back into the main building, which had been remodeled to handle mail for the 40,000 people that now populated the Manette Peninsula.

OVERLOADS

At that time the Postal Department did not allow money for extra assistants at Christmas. Etta and Earl both worked long, hard hours and paid temporary workers out of their own pockets to get all the mail delivered on time at Christmas. Neither did Don Atkinson have an allowance for Christmas help. He worked from 6 a.m. until midnight many times before Christmas to insure that his patrons received their cards and parcels. He was assisted by his wife, Anna Jo, and he paid young men around town to help during the Christmas rush. Before the size of his route was reduced, the mail was so massive he had to rent two delivery trucks from garage-man Axel Jacobsen to carry the load.

During World War II there were many nights Don's work did not allow him time to go home. He would case the mail, send his subs out on the route, grab a few hours sleep on a pile of mail bags in the back of the office, then start all over again casing the mail.

In 1940 the Manette office was incorporated with the Bremerton office. In 1942 Etta became supervisor of the new sub-station. In 1942, John McDonell built a new post office

World War II quarters. In 1942 the Manette postal station moved into this building at 1104 Scott Avenue.

building to again provide more space for the expanding mail service. The new post office was at 1104 Scott Avenue, north of Meredith's store. By that time the service included 500 postal boxes, two rural routes and three city routes. The Scott Avenue location is occupied today by Bruce Construction Company.

SHERIDAN PARK STATION

Sheridan Park Station was established about 1943, taking much of the load from the Manette Station. Don Atkinson's route was split from Route 1 into Routes 4 and 5.

Route 4 served residents on the Brownsville Highway to Brownsville, over Bucklin Hill Road, through Tracyton and back to Manette. Don carried Route 4 until his retirement in 1969 after 35 years' service.

Route 5 went out Perry Avenue, through Illahee and Gilberton and returned to Manette. Wesley Jones transferred from the Bremerton downtown business route to Route 5. A heart attack forced him into an early retirement. Wes passed away in 1961.

Etta was postmistress and supervisor in Manette for 30 years. She retired in 1948. She and Earl enjoyed only 2 years of retirement together; Earl passed away in 1950.

Postal clerks serving under Etta were Laura Chase in 1918, Grace Carlaw Hoopes, Lois Harrison Williamson, Mildred Stone Muller, Clara Halvorson, Johnny Fortuna, George Atwood, Pearl Welborn, Ralph Whitmer, Elva Danel, Floyd Buchanan, Willard Muller and Etta's husband Earl, and daughter and son-in-law

Don Atkinson in 1969.
- Bremerton Sun Photo

Anna Jo and Don Atkinson. During World War II Gladys Solid, Madeline Brown Walmer, Lucile Olsen Wilcox, Elmine Ricks, Ellen Jensen Magnussen, Christena Buchanan, Julia Sokal and Mae Brenden were postal clerks in 1942. There are others.

CONTRACTORS

After Etta retired, Frank Lockwood served as interim superintendent until Charles Allin was appointed. Allin served until his retirement in 1964. Also in 1964, the station, with its reduced load, became a contract office, operated, in the language of the Post Office Manual, "by persons not in the classified service."

Mrs. Warren (Mary) Wagner of Sheridan Heights received the first contract February 29, 1964. Wagners moved the facility to 2106 East 11th Street on April 1, 1967. The Wagners personally did all the work of relocating.

Winona (Mrs. Arthur) Seymour of East 31st Street had the contract from April of 1971 until May 1974. She was well known for her work with Bremerton Community Theater. Winona died in November 1983.

Delbert L. Miles of Jacobsen Boulevard operated the post office from June 1974 until July 1978. Assisting him were his wife Dorien and son Bob. Del was retired from PSNS.

Francis Rickey, sister of Mrs. Wagner, worked as clerk for all three of the above postmasters.

Helen Parker held the contract for about 6 months until March 2, 1979.

Wesley W. Langrell has had the contract since March 3, 1979. During his years such familiar faces as Winona Seymour, Del and Bob Miles, Mindy Alexander and Marjorie Hendershot have been seen clerking. The station has 100 postal boxes.

In 1987 mail service had again outgrown its facility and a new station was built at 1281 Sylvan Way. Robert Anderson is station manager and Robert Mower Jr. is superintendent of branch operations. There are two full-time window clerks and one distribution clerk. The station has 640 postal boxes. Seven foot carriers and five mounted carriers serve 12 routes within the city limits. Nine rural routes are served on the Manette Peninsula.

After Earl and Etta's deaths in 1950 and 1961, the family home at 1118 Pitt Avenue was rented out. All postal, military and family records were stored and locked in the attic of the home. All were destroyed by a fire. The information presented here comes from memories of my lifetime in a postal family, from the National Archives, and from Geneva Howerton Pickering, Don Atkinson, Lawrence E. Haddon, Mrs. Warren Wagner, Gladys Solid, Ferris Buchanan, Wes Langrell and others.

Latest location. Since 1967 the Manette contract station has been in this building, 2106 East 11th Street. Standing in front of door is the contractor, Wes Langrell.

Chapter 7

CHURCHES

By Orville Schultz and Roger Paquette

The history of churches on the Manette Peninsula is in a large part the history of the Manette Community Church. Under this name and at a single location, East 13th Street and Hayward Avenue, the church has existed since 1916. Under another name it goes back at least 10 years further; unnamed, further yet.

Sources for this chapter include:
1. Edna (Hoopes) Brookman's *A History of the Manette Community Church,* a collection of clippings, programs and pictures.
2. Minutes kept by Sam Gallotte until 1907, then by Jane Card. Others followed until 1927. (This book survived the church fire of 1951 and was unearthed by Justin Kennedy and Katrina Schultz.)
3. Church Brotherhood minutes of 1915-17, and trustees' minutes of 1921-23. S.F. Dewar was secretary for both groups.
4. The minutes of the church business meetings of 1914-24.
5. Microfilm of the *Bremerton News-Searchlight* and *Bremerton Sun.*
6. Material written by Grace Hoopes Wesseler.

Here are key dates and events:

1898
Mrs. Jane Card and Mrs. Mary Brewster held the Manette Peninsula's first Sunday School classes in Sheridan School. Mrs. Paul Ruley, a black woman whose father had been a slave, later joined them and also served as church organist.

1902-1905
Church services were held above what later became the A.B. Williams store at 201 Shore Drive. In the evenings of 1902, a young marine from the naval shipyard held services here. Mr. W.C. Hardin, a Christian businessman from Seattle, was the first to serve as a regular minister on Sunday mornings.

1903-1904
Reverend S. Walter Terry, executive secretary of the Washington Baptist Convention, filled in until D.W. Townsend, a home missionary, arrived in the area to organize a church.

1905
At 2:30 p.m. January 29, 1905, a meeting was held at the home of Mr. Sam Gallotte to discuss the feasibility of organizing a church. Brother Townsend was appointed to visit several interested families and solicit their cooperation.

The following evening a meeting was held at the schoolhouse to listen to a discussion by Brother J.M. Dean of Seattle on how to organize a church. The church was organized by the following statement and signed by the charter members.

"We the undersigned do hereby organize ourselves into a church of Jesus Christ according to the Baptist position. We hold that we are entitled to do this by the authority of the New Testament. We solemnly invoke the blessing of Almighty God upon our action. In the name and to the glory of Jesus we subscribe our names.

"D.W. Townsend, S.B. Nichols, Mrs. E.J. Miles, Charles Wilsen, Julia T. Gallotte, Samuel W. Gallotte, Mrs. Martha Armstrong."

1905
February 12. Mrs. Gallotte reported that a building fund was already started. A committee of three was appointed to find a location for the church.

1905
February 26. It was voted to call the new church the Bethany Baptist and to close the bargain with Mrs. Mikkelson for two lots $100. Brother Townsend and Sam Gallotte went to the Port Gamble sawmill in the gospel boat *Mamie Beale* and towed back a raft of lumber. George Card hauled the load with his team of horses to the church site. Mr. Gallotte, a carpenter by trade, gave up his own business and worked full time on the building with some volunteer help.

1905
August. The foundation was installed for the church building and the cornerstone (southwest corner) laid with appropriate ceremonies. A box containing a church history was deposited in the concrete.

INCORPORATION
1906
January 3. It was voted and carried to incorporate as a Bap-

Julia Gallotte, wife of pioneer Manette churchman Samuel Gallotte, and her Sunday School class, circa 1904. Mrs. Gallotte is at front center. Others who have been identified are: standing, fourth, fifth and sixth from left, Emma Miles, Harry Martin, Walda Wall. Seated at left is Walter Wall.   -Photo from Gertrude Wall Carr

tist church under the laws of the State of Washington and the corporate name was to be "Bethany Baptist Church." The following officers were selected for the first year: Charles Wilsen, deacon; S. W. Gallotte, clerk; Mrs. Martha Armstrong, treasurer. Trustees elected were S.W. Gallotte, Walter Wall, S.B. Nichols, Charles Wilsen, Walter Barren.

1906
February 11. A dedication ceremony was held upon completion of the new building, which was valued at $2000. It had an auditorium, three classrooms and acetylene lighting donated by Walter Wall's father, Mr. E.A. Wall, and Mr. W.S. Harris. Father Cairne of Seattle and Brother Terry of Tacoma delivered morning and afternoon sermons with Judge Green of Seattle offering the dedication prayers.

1906
March 10. A reception was held for Brother W.C. Hardin, who is leaving.

1906
April 18. George and Jane Card were the first people to be baptized in the new church, although Walter Wall, Walter Barren, Marie Miles, Martha Garland, Irving Miles and Mildred and Lyle Wakeman had received their baptism at the Tabernacle Church of Seattle February 26, 1905, by Brother Townsend. Brother Townsend had been called to start a new church in Brownsville and Mr. and Mrs. C. Grahn, Florence and Earl transferred from Bethany Baptist to Brownsville. On April 14, 1907, the Bethany Baptist congregation had gone by boat, the *Mamie Beale*, to participate in the laying of the cornerstone of the new Brownsville Church with Reverend Townsend officiating.

1906
May. The Reverend Inuan Haynes came from the first Church of Seattle and stayed to give his final sermon January 19, 1908.

SALT WATER BAPTISM
1907
April 21. Tom Bright Jr. was baptized in the salt water of Port Washington Narrows.

1908
July. Reverend Archibald MacIntosh with his Scottish brogue became the first resident pastor and remained until December 1909.

Bethany Baptist Church in 1910. In 1916 the church was renamed Manette Community Church.
-Photo from Edna Hoopes Brookman

1908

November 7. A license to preach was presented to Walter Wall.

1910

Reverend S.A. Jensen came from Charleston Baptist Church in March. He departed in September and was followed by Reverend Colgrove, who served from October until

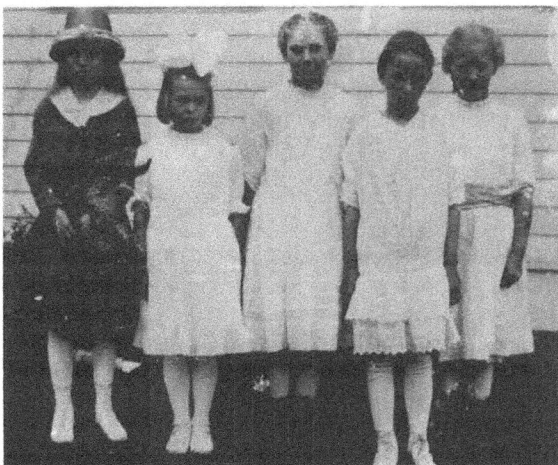

The 1918 Sunday School class. From left are Marjorie Bubb, Gladys Boney, Florence Dewar, Ellen Jensen and Grace Wilsen.   -Photo from Gladys Olsen Solid

Manette Community Church, circa 1920, after remodeling with lumber from unfinished hotel located on the east side of Hayward Avenue.

August 1911.

1911

October 25. Maggie Jane Sidam and Chris Christiansen were the first couple married in the church.

1911

November. Reverend G.A. Nokes, a young bachelor, lived in the church attic. He was especially liked by the young people.

1915

April. Reverend A.D. Carpenter became the minister of the church. He had a flair for science and later left to go into the Chautauqua Circuit. During his term the church was reorganized as Manette Community Church, open to all Protestant Christians, regardless of denomination. A few Catholics also attended. It was stipulated that the church would always have a Baptist pastor and any undesignated money would go to support Baptist missions.

1917

Reverend I.H. Woods came from California and rented a small house in Manette. A few previous pastors had commuted via steamboat to Bremerton and from Bremerton to Manette in small launches. With Reverend Woods' help an addition to the church was built with lumber taken from a partially built and abandoned hotel from the east side of Hayward Avenue. The addition was dedicated December 12, 1920.

1922

Reverend E.A. Earns arrived from Cuba, where he had worked in the YMCA. Reverend Earns, his wife and daughter Geraldine were musically talented and an asset to the church program. They were unable to acclimate themselves to the Northwest and soon moved to warm, sunny California.

1923

Reverend J.H. Walker came and proved to be an excellent builder, for at this time a full concrete foundation was laid and the basement completed, making room for Sunday School and other activities. A new furnace was installed, the

Manette Community Church Vacation Bible School, 1927. Standing on steps, (from left): BACK ROW 1 Isaac Hoopes, 2 Lillian Meicho, 3 Reverend Richmond.   FIFTH ROW 4 _____ 5 Margaret von Hoene, 6 Genevieve Nelson (?), 7 Elsie Wilsen. FOURTH ROW 8 Muriel Rodger, 9 Ruth Wall, 10 _____, 11 Edna Hoopes, 12 Jane Card, 13 Alma Gilman. THIRD ROW 14 _____, 15 _____, 16 _____, 17 _____, 18 _____, 19 _____, 20 _____, 21 SECOND ROW Faith Christensen, 22 _____, 23 Marion Wall, 24 Genevieve Meicho, 25 Christena Buchanan, 26 Josephine Lawrence, 27 _____. FRONT ROW 28 Charles Wall, 29 Howard Ellis, 30 Louise Hermanson, 31 Cherie Bright, 32 Maryjayne Meredith, 33 Theodore Peterson, 34 Arthur Card, 35 Bernice Martin. Left of steps: BACK ROW 1 Arlene Wilsen, 2 Grace Hoopes, 3 Anna Jo Harkins, 4 Louise Waugh, 5 Albert Meicho, 6 _____, 7 Harold Christensen, 8 George Personette, 9 Lois Harrison, 10 Vera Lawrence, 11 Elizabeth von Hoene, 12 Stefona Soyat. FOURTH ROW 13 Carrie Bright, 14 Hulda Wall, 15 Mae Stewart, 16 _____, 17 Duncan Buchanan, 18 Robert Starevich, 19 _____, 20 Fred McHenry, 21 _____, 22 _____, 23 Doris Welborn, 24 Dorothy Wall, 25 Dorothy May. THIRD ROW 26 Amy Hoopes, 27 Earl Harrison, 28 _____, 29 _____, 30 Mildred Starevich, 31 Dorothy Cole, 32 Eleanor McCallum, 33 Margaret Hoopes, 34 Ada Schoonover, 35 _____, 36 _____, 37 Margaret Dilks (?), 38 Muriel Peterson, 39 Mary Jane Didbenner, 40 Laura Ellis, 41 Marjorie Schoonover, 42 Katherine Starevich, 43 Esther Buchanan, 44 Georgia May Moffat, 45 Phyllis Baker, 46 Kenneth Karst, 47 Bernice Schoonover, 48 Helen Starevich. FRONT ROW 49 Riley Cole, 50 Robert Wall, 51 Howard Harrison, 52 _____, 53 Eleanor Pidduck, 54 Jean Harrison, 55 Emmabelle Harrison, 56 Blossom Bright, 57 Virginia Karst, 58 Mary Personette, 59 Ferris Buchanan, 60 Jack Kean, 61 Robert Bowdy.
-Photo from Lois Harrison Williamson

mortgage burned and this new addition dedicated on April 1, 1924.

1925

Reverend V.E. Davis, a Presbyterian minister, arrived. He joined the Baptist Church to comply with the church requirement of 1916 and resigned June 11, 1926.

SCOUTS SPONSORED
1926

Boy Scout Troop 505, sponsored by the church, received a charter January 31, with Albert Meicho as Scoutmaster and Samuel Sigurdson as Assistant Scoutmaster. Reverend Claude Richmond came west to study arts and theology at the University of Washington, and served as pastor until his courses were completed in 1928. A meeting called to order by

Reverend Claude Richmond December 31 referred to the annual meeting of the Bethany Baptist Church of Manette, even though the Manette Community Church had been in existence for 10 years.

1927

February 13. Anna Jo Harkins, Anna Marie Parkins and Margaret von Hoene were baptized.

1929

Reverend Robert Thompson and family were the first to live in the parsonage at 1128 Ironsides Avenue, that had been purchased from Tom Bright. Thompson's younger son drowned in the Pacific Ocean while on an outing from Linfield College.

Painting the parsonage at 1128 Ironsides Avenue, 1929. —Photo from Gladys Olsen Solid

Reverend Robert and Mrs. Mary Thompson, 1935 —Photo from Mrs. Clyde (Estelle) Meredith

Reverend Walter Laetsch (left), wife Marie (right) and children (from left) Bruce, Watson, Margaret. —Photo from Mrs. Clyde (Estelle) Meredith

1936

Reverend Walter Laetsch and family arrived. During his pastorate the church was renovated. He was interested in music and organized a church choir. He occasionally joined the choir in a musical presentation. Because of the influx of people into the Puget Sound Navy Yard during World War II, he requested a home missionary for the Sheridan Park area. Miss Jennie Bewsey came and was soon joined by Lyle Job (Huestis). They set up Sunday School classes for the children and these eventually led to the organization of Sheridan Community Church. Reverend Laetsch preached the first sermon on Easter Sunday 1943, in Lower View Ridge Community Hall. He resigned in June 1943 to enter the U.S. Army Chaplain School.

1943

Reverend Sydney Cooper and wife Verona came with their family. (Their son Clyde remained and is in business here; the Clyde Cooper family is active in the Manette Community Church. Sons David, John and Ben work in its youth programs.)

1944

The cornerstone of the Sheridan Park Community Church was laid at the corner of Wheaton Way and Sheridan Road.

(This church served until July 31, 1966, when it closed. Members transferred to other churches in the area; 15 came to Manette Community Church. Today the former church is a veterinarian clinic.)

1950

Reverend Phillip Graf with wife Helen and family came to serve Manette Community Church.

CHURCH BURNS
1951

January 11. A short circuit in the electrical wiring of the

George Card breaking ground for rebuilding Manette Community Church destroyed by fire in 1951. New church was dedicated in 1955. —Photo from Marjorie Rea Ray

Manette Community Church—1987

baptismal tank caused a fire which destroyed the building. Some furniture and material from the basement were saved. The Bremerton School Board approved the use of the new Manette School auditorium for Sunday morning services, since the church had allowed the schools to use rooms for classes to take care of the many students arriving in Manette during World War II. The Community Hall at Manette Playground had already been approved for Sunday School and evening services, and many homes were opened for classes and meetings.

The church was rebuilt and dedicated April 24, 1955. Pastor Phil Graf stated, "This is the day which the Lord hath made and we should rejoice and be glad in it. By the devotion of your hearts, generosity of your tithes and offerings, and your toil, you, my people, have erected this edifice by the grace of God and to the glory of His son, our Savior."

1957

July 14. Reverend Glen Soule, wife Margaret and children Susan and David came from Liberty Park Baptist Church in Spokane. (After 28 years of ministry in Manette Community Church, Reverend Soule retired as of June 30, 1985.)

LaBEAU HALL
1957

LaBeau Hall.

June 26. The Ironsides Avenue parsonage was sold and the house at 1137 Hayward Avenue was purchased. (The Soules lived there until 1971, when the church bought the Day property at 1135 Hayward Avenue. The house at 1137 Hayward has been renamed LaBeau Hall in memory of William LaBeau. LaBeau actively worked with the Kitsap County Sheriff's Department in rehabilitation of troubled youth. He realized the need for continuous constructive activities for all young people. The hall is also used for Sunday School classes and meetings of all groups.)

1961

Parking space was increased by purchase of two lots off Perry Avenue.

1963

The church gymnasium was remodeled to provide additional classrooms on the second floor and a fellowship hall below.

1969

The first church bus was purchased for use in outlying areas.

1972

Reverend Daniel Franklin and his wife Carolyn came to serve as youth workers and as assistants to the pastor. With regret we saw them leave to accept a pastorate in North Bend Community Church.

1976

The congregation attended services in colonial costume to celebrate the nation's bicentennial and the church's 70th anniversary. A picnic followed at the Joseph Leafs' property at Pearson Point, Scandia.

1978

David and Carol McFarlane arrived to work as assistants to the pastor in Christian education. David was ordained here May 7, 1978.

1979

The McFarlanes returned to California for further education.

1980

The McFarlanes returned to Manette Community Church.

1980

Pastor McFarlane was called to become pastor at the Panther Lake Community Church in Kent, Wash.

1984

Bill and Martha Nelson arrived to work as assistants to the pastor in Christian education.

CHURCH ACTIVITIES

Many church groups have developed over the years:

Endeavor, for young people, was organized in the early 1900s. Later it became the Baptist Young People's Union and

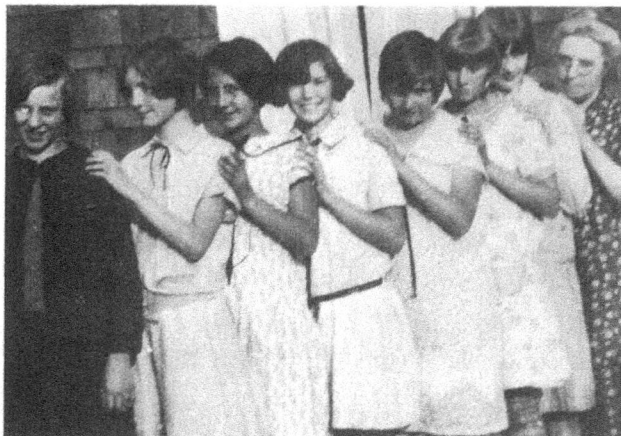

A Christian Endeavor class at Manette Community Church, about 1928. From left, Ada Schoonover, Helen Akers, Mildred Stark, Dorothy Cole, Bernice Pederson, Louise Waugh, Jeane Martin and Mrs. Nichols, the teacher.
-Photo from Dorothy Cole Rogers

now the Youth Fellowship Group.

Mission groups began in the early 1900s and at present there are four mission circles: Fidelis, Ruth, Friendship and Hope, with the Women's Missionary Society as coordinator.

In 1906 Jane Card started the Ladies Aid, which is still active. The Women's Christian Temperance Union was active in early days.

Anna Olsen Anderson, Gladys Solid's sister, started the cradle roll in 1917.

Amy (Mrs. Isaac) Hoopes was one of the early teachers.

The church has sponsored two Girl Scout troops, a Blue Bird group, Ann Judson and Sally Peck Guilds, God's Squad, King's Kids, Crusaders, Disciples and Olympians; also Vacation Bible School and Children's Church. Organized for fun and social life were the 50-50 Club, now called un-club, and adult fellowship for senior citizens. The church has contributed to the Food Bank, YMCA, Red Cross and Servicemen's Center.

Reverend Glen Soule for 28 years led the congregation in singing with his fine voice. Dick Norton since the 1960s has directed the choir for church services and cantatas, assuring music as our heritage of freedom to worship God since the 1960s.

In 1958 Helen Oldham was the first librarian, followed by Mary Fellows, Marie Yoder, and Doreen LeCompte for the last 10 years.

People from the church in Christian service have included Walter Wall, pastor; James Eggleston, YMCA; Benjamin Lawrence, Brazil foreign missionary; Lawrence Rea, pastor in Brazil; Wesley Langrell, pastor; Thomas Meicho, pastor and director of admissions at Linfield College, Oreg.; Dennis Crawford, YMCA; Donald Ricks, music ministry worldwide; Ronald Jensen, School of Theology; Donald Etten, pastor; Robert Miles, pastor and American missionary; Ray Mengel, pastor; Diane Pitke and husband, missionaries in Holland; Kirk Wonderly, discipleship with young people; Douglas Petrowski, the Crista Camps organization.

Reverend Glenn Soule and his wife Margaret.-Photo from Bremerton Sun

MUSIC

In 1936 during Reverend Laetsch's ministry a choir was organized that sang for Sunday morning services.

Gideon Hermanson and Frank Carr were active in forming an orchestra that played at Sunday evening services. Walter Wall played violin and cello; Frank Carr and his student Bill Jenkins (Chandler) played clarinets; Mrs. Walter (Laverne) Ziebell played piano; Gideon Hermanson played violin; Louise Hermanson, baritone saxophone; Bernice Jack, bassoon; June Womac, violin; Grace Jack played a bass viol belonging to Walter Wall; Wallace Brown, trumpet; Maryjayne Meredith, flute. Sailors from the U.S.S. *Pennsylvania* and other ships in the navy yard joined the church orchestra while their ships were stationed in Bremerton.

A quartet consisting of Joanne Gilman, Marion Wall, Grace and Ruth Jack sang for church services.

CHURCHES MULTIPLY

In 1987 there were 16 churches in East Bremerton south of Riddell Road:

Peace Lutheran Church
1234 N.E. Riddell Road

Unitarian Universalist Fellowship
4418 Perry Avenue NE

Bremerton Bible Church
1940 Sylvan Way

Sylvan Way Baptist Church
900 Sylvan Way

Eastgate Assembly of God
1541 Sylvan Way

Grace Pentecostal Church
317 Sheridan Road

Church of Christ Eastside
2381 Perry Avenue

Unity Church
1712 Trenton Avenue

Church of Nazarene First
924 Sheridan Road

St. Luke's United Methodist Church
1547 Sheridan Road

Emmanuel Lutheran Church
2509 Perry Avenue

St. Paul's Episcopal Church
700 Callahan Drive

Church of Jesus Christ
of Latter Day Saints
2225 Perry Avenue

Trenton Avenue Baptist Church
1810 Trenton Avenue

Holy Trinity Catholic Church
4215 Pine Road

Manette Community Church
1314 Hayward Avenue

Here is a list of pastors at Bethany Baptist (Manette Community) Church from 1902 to 1986:

1902 W.A. Hardin; 1906 I. Haynes; 1908 Archibald McIntosh; 1910 S.A. Jensen; 1911 Colgrove; 1911 G.A. Nokes; 1915 Allen; 1915 A.D. Carpenter; 1917 I.H. Woods; 1922 E.A. Earns; 1923 J.H. Walker; 1925 V.E. Davis; 1926 Claude Richmond; 1929 Robert Thompson; 1936 Walter Laetsch; 1943 Sydney Cooper; 1950 Phil Graf; 1957 Glen Soule; 1985 Sam Quirling; 1986 Robert A. Reider.

LOUISE HERMANSON COX'S "DEBT TO THE CHURCH"

[*Louise Hermanson Cox's accomplishments are included in the Hermanson family history. This former Manette girl recalls the influence of church members on her life.*]

HOOPES: Mr. Isaac Hoopes was Manette Community Church's Sunday School superintendent and song leader during opening sessions, and I remember the smile on his face as he sang his testimony. Mrs. Hoopes taught Sunday School classes.

A number of us who lived in Manette attended pre-school kindergarten classes, also conducted by Mrs. Hoopes. It was a foundational experience for me to have a Christian influence in education. Mrs. Hoopes was big of heart and short of stature. A number of us were so fond of her that we returned for visits at her home. About a dozen of us as high school seniors returned for a photo with her, and she was now dwarfed by us.

WALL: Mr. Walter Wall invited the Sunday School class to his home to view the sky through his home-made telescope. Through his teaching we knew of the Creator-God. He also encouraged us in music.

Mrs. Wall as bible expositor was one of the best. Fascination with biblical prophecy came as a result of the thirst she gave me. She instructed in a way that left no margin of error in the Word of God or in the God of the Word.

REA: Mr. and Mrs. Rea became special friends as I saw their Christian life carried into a home and family. Marjorie Rea became my first Christian friend and we had a spiritual bond beyond that which I had with other girls in my age group. I often had Sunday dinner in the Rea home.

Local
News

Chapter 8

NEWSPAPERS

MANETTE GAZETTE

By Willard C. Muller

The *Manette Gazette* had two beginnings. Kenneth "Kink" Muller had a flair for humor from early boyhood. He phrased things in a way that would make his friends laugh. Perhaps because he enjoyed doing this, he started the *Gazette* as a high school junior in 1933. He'd take a piece of typing paper, fold it in two from top to bottom, turn it sidewise so it opened like a book, roll it into the typewriter and type across the top: MANETTE GAZETTE. The "paper's" masthead neatly listed each staff position: Publisher, Editor, News Editor, Sports Editor, Society Editor, Circulation Manager, Janitor. Kink was the entire staff. On the four pages he reported all kinds of Manette community events. Each story had only one purpose: to entertain—bring laughter. In one story he might have Constable Charlie Young engaged in derring-do, tracking Manette's errant youth on Halloween night while they looked for privies to give the heave-ho. Another story might have Captain Hansen or Bob Carter at the helm of the ferry *Pioneer*, completely lost in the fog, making an approach to the middle pier in the navy yard, while the commandant stood ready to order the battleship *California*, at the next pier, to fire all her 16-inch batteries at the foreign intruder. The stories were done in a gentle, respectful way that let the reader clearly understand that this teen-age humor was all in good fun.

Perhaps what gave the *Gazette* respectability and a jump in circulation was that one of its regular readers was Mr. Harry D. Sorensen, principal of Bremerton High School. How he came to know about the *Gazette* was never learned, but regularly he approached the editor in the high school hallways when each new edition appeared and asked if he might read it. Kink never published more than a single copy for each edition. It was circulated from hand to hand at high school and to young friends in Manette. In all, Kink might have put out 20 issues during his junior and senior years.

The second and quite distinctive phase of the *Manette Gazette's* life began in 1934 in Davy Jones' bakery, located on the right-hand side of Meredith's store. It was the middle of the Depression. Money was scarce. A group of boys, all good friends and all but one recent high school graduates, started meeting on summer evenings down at Davy's place.

They sat around a table visiting and eating Davy's doughnuts and drinking his soda pop.

After entertaining each other with stories of their recent working, someone said, "What this town needs is a young men's business association." He looked around the table at his friends: John Nelson, part-time carpenter's helper; Ray Nosker, clerk and delivery man at Meredith's; Kink, clerk-bookkeeper at Parker Lumber Company; August "Gus" Halverson, newly employed in the advertising department of the *Bremerton Searchlight* and Willard Muller, clerk at the Manette post office.

Ed Todd, who had moved to Manette that summer when his father bought what became Todd's Hardware on lower Pacific Avenue in Bremerton, also became one of the YMBA members. Still later, Don McReynolds, who lived in Sheridan, joined the group. "Good idea!" someone else responded. "The Young Men's Business Association of Manette! Has a nice ring to it."

"We ought to have our own stationery," a third person said, falling in with the humor, "with a club motto as part of the letterhead."

"How about: The pen is mightier than the pencil?" still another member offered, catching the complete lack of seriousness in the matter.

They collected a dollar apiece—each dollar in those years being equivalent to 10 1987 dollars—and agreed to allocate 5 dollars for the stationery, complete with the zany slogan.

At a later bull session in Davy's bakery, one YMBA member suggested that since Manette had no newspaper, maybe they ought to start one. That was the beginning of The *Manette Gazette's* second life. They decided to issue it once a month, free, and sell advertising to cover expenses. There never was any formal assignment of duties. All six or seven members pitched in, writing stories, soliciting local merchants for ads at 50 cents apiece for a two-square-inch box ad and $3 for a full-page ad. Others did art work for the cover—printed on heavy art paper and a different color each month—and they took turns mimeographing and stapling. They paid a couple of paper boys to deliver it all over town. Circulation reached virtually the entire community. When people didn't receive their copy, they often asked one of the paper's staff for a copy.

The *Gazette* covered such community stories as new families coming to town, Manette Grade School and Manette

VISION   COURAGE   SINCERITY   FORTITUDE

The Manette Gazette

K. L. MULLER
Editor

Successor to the "FOG - HORN," Official Bulletin E. B. I. C.

$1.00 Per Year
10c Per Copy

Published to assist the Development of the Manette Peninsula—Enetai, Sheridan, Sheridan Heights, Illahee, Gilberton, Brownsville, Central Valley, Fairview, Tracyton, Manette, Territory North and Kitsap County.

Vol. X   MANETTE (East Bremerton), WASHINGTON, MAY 31, 1939   No. 73

ALDRICH'S
Variety Store and Pharmacy
"The Shopping Place of the Peninsula"
PRESCRIPTION DRUGGISTS
SUNDRIES — HOSIERY
NOTIONS
SCHOOL SUPPLIES
Magazines, Fountain, Beverages
2117 E. 11th St.
Manette, Washington
Phone 40
See Our Large Ad, Pages 3-7

"Left Hand Service"
SLIM'S PLACE
State Highway near Brownsville
SHELL GAS & OILS
GROCERIES
Phone Silverdale 15-Y-11

Dick Feek's Service
UNION OIL PRODUCTS
End of Bridge — Manette
BATTERY SERVICE
We Call For & Deliver—Phone 24
See My Large Ad Elsewhere

DRESS AND WORK SHOES
At Boston Prices — Call
S. F. DEWAR
MANETTE
Established Agent For
Merritt, Mason and Doublewear
Shoes . . . "The Nation's Best"
Phone 843-R

For Your
DIESEL AND FUEL OIL
Call
SERVICE FUEL CO.
Just Phone 383
BREMERTON

Every Magazine Published
CLUBBING RATES
Subscribe From
EARL HARKINS
Phone 2315   Manette

Your Peninsula
BEAUTY SHOPPE
1145 Scott Street
MANETTE
Maybelle Langrell   Phone 2406-W

AUTO NEEDS!
General Garage
Manette, Wash.
Phone 741-M — Day or Night
WRECKER SERVICE
See Large Ad Elsewhere

IN MEMORIAM
Sleep on, ye valiant warrior dead,
Where 'ere thy tortured bodies lie,
In rock lined trench, or under sod
Of grave where lillies lift on high,
Their emblems of eternal peace.
Sleep on beneath the rolling wave
Of ocean, or the shifting sands,
That hide a thousand nameless graves,
The world knows thee no more,
Sleep on, and rest.

No more for you the bugle blows,
Nor streaming flags that thrill the eye,
Or thundering guns belch forth their hell,
Or death rain on thee from the sky.
Such trivials cannot wake thee now.
No more the marching to and fro,
The dreaded waiting and the pain,
Or clash of battle with the foe,
You bought release with life,
Sleep on, and rest.

If we who live will keep the light
Of peace for which these honored dead,
Paid supreme sacrifice of life,
To guide us on our way ahead,
They have not died in vain.
God grant we heed their silent plea,
To make the world one brotherhood,
To live our lives in unity,
The world from war forever freed,
Sleep on, ye loved ones, sleep.
                    W. H. von HOENE,
                    Past President, E. B. I. C.

DON BROWN — MANETTE
Farewell, Donald Brown, son of Mr. and Mrs. E. M. Brown, and once a member of Manette's famous "Slickerbill" junior Soft Ball Team. Donald, just speak a good word in Heaven for a lot of us "Slickerbills," and we shall every year see your smilin' face in blossoming Maytime flowers. "Safe, at home, Don."   —Gazette Staff.

5th ANNUAL PENINSULA PLAYFIELD CELEBRATION SATURDAY, JUNE 17, AT MANETTE
The Executive and Advisory committees of E. B. I. C. met Thursday last week and voted to hold another peninsula playfield celebration, the date having been set for Saturday, June 17. So on that day and evening (rain or shine) the Manette peninsula invites the world to its doors and asks for a 100 percent peninsula participation in all of the events. Yep, get in the parade.

MANETTE
French Cleaners
Next to Red & White Store
MANETTE
We Call For and Deliver
Agents for City Hand Laundry
PHONE 156

MEMBERSHIP DRIVE
With this issue of the Gazette the annual membership quest of E.B.I.C. gets under way hoping to to finish it by July 1. W. H. von Hoene is chairman. Elsewhere in this issue you'll find a membership blank—fill it in and mail or turn in today.

When Ordering Specify
PUGET SOUND EXPRESS, Inc.
Bremerton's Own Transportation Co.
FAST AUTO FREIGHT SERVICE
SEATTLE — BREMERTON
PHONE 45
"When You Move — Move By Heck"

FRENCH CLEANERS and DYERS
Phone 861 . . . . 604 Burwell Street

Front page of Manette Gazette *(second version).*

WEEK END
MEAT SPECIALS
MANETTE MEAT MARKET
Phone 486
See Our Large Ad

FRED W. KRAUSE
FIRE & AUTOMOBILE INSURANCE
283 Fourth Street, Bremerton
Phones: Office 817 Home: 1341-J
See Large Ad Elsewhere

REAL ESTATE   INSURANCE
W. H. HAWKES
Manette, Wash. — End of Bridge
See Special Real Estate Buys
Phone 104 or 2425-W

For WOOD and COAL Call
P. O. HILSTAD
Manette   Phone 1129-M
"We Know the Value of a Satisfied Customer"

BANK'S GROCERY
Open Every Day of Week
7 A. M. to 9 P. M.
STAPLE GROCERIES
ICE CREAM — BEVERAGES
ASSOCIATED GAS & OILS
1½ Mi. from Manette State Hiway

USE AIR MAIL
Every Day
U. S. Postoffice and Rural Route,
Manette — Phone 1584

LAWRENCES CASH STORE
MANETTE
Illahee Road 1 Mile from State Park
Complete Line of Groceries
Gilmore Gas and Lion Head Oil
Notions, Films & Sundry Articles

Cold Storage Lockers
Silverdale, Wash.
Buy Your Meats and Vegetables Wholesale and Save by Using One of Our Lockers
Phone Silverdale 49-J
COMFORT & GLIDDEN, Prop.

Your Broken Lenses Replaced Like New — Your Watch Repaired
J. F. Bryan
Diamond Setting a Specialty
All Work Absolutely Guaranteed
615 WINFIELD AVE.
Near Lumber Co. — Manette

Community Church special activities, group-sponsored suppers, weddings, plans for the annual Boy Scouts' summer camping trip, and special achievements by Manette people, like a boy making Eagle Scout or youngsters getting on the honor roll. The *Gazette* carried regular features such as the column "Mirrored In Manette," and "Through The Knothole," both of which carried many local names. Another popular feature was: "Then They Walked Up The Aisle,"—about how different Manette couples met and married. It also had a column, "Around The Cracker Barrel," that tried to both philosophize and editorialize.

Nearly all the merchants and other business people in Manette advertised. These included Oscar "Butch" Etten's meat market, Aldrich's Pharmacy, Meredith's, Martin's and Mitchell's (new in town) grocery stores, Parker Lumber Company, Axel Jacobsen's garage, Lee Harrison's and Harry Flint's barber shops, Jones' Bakery, one or two service stations and Mrs. Hawthorne's yarn shop, around the corner from Lee Harrison's barber shop.

Within 6 months the *Gazette* staff found itself with an embarrassment of riches: more than $100 in its treasury. They decided to purchase their own mimeograph, some styluses and other supplies. Until then, they had been using the East Bremerton Improvement Club's mimeograph, of which Earl Henry Harkins, one of the community's most active and effective civic leaders, was the custodian. The staff assembled one evening each month to drink Mrs. Harkins' milk, eat her cookies, and print the *Gazette*.

Although some of the original *Gazette* staff left after a year or two to take a job on the Coulee Dam construction or start college, the rest of the staff continued to publish it until just before World War II, when many Manette young men left for the war. Thus the second version of the *Gazette* spanned the years 1934-40.

In the spring of 1935, the Boy Scout Troop 505 committeemen asked the Young Men's Business Association (the *Gazette* staff) to put on a fund-raiser for the annual troop summer outing. The YMBA members agreed, and presented a musical show, dripping with nostalgia, built around the theme of the "National Barn Dance," a popular network radio program of that era.

Warren "Whitey" White played the banjo, along with another friend; William "Will" von Hoene, Manette's Edgar A. Guest of that era, wrote and recited a poem for the occasion; some of the town's talented vocalists sang; and the *Gazette* staff did what they billed as a humorous skit. After the show, the Wicklund Brothers' "Cascade Rangers" band played Western music and the community, which had packed the Masonic Temple for the Scout benefit show, danced until after midnight.

MANETTE NEWSLETTER

By Jack Rogers

Earl Harkins originated the *Manette News-Letter*. My wife Dorothy and I paid Earl $100 for it when he tired of producing it during World War II about 1943. We changed the name to *Manette News* and then (probably a fatal error) to the *Kitsap News*, later the *Kitsap County News*, in hopes to represent a larger circulation area than the community of Manette and

to increase advertising and news content to make a commercial venture of the publication.

Dorothy recalls driving out through Tracyton and Silverdale, soliciting stores and gas stations for ads with our first-born daughter Mary in a basket in the back seat.

We published this paper regularly until it eventually was merged into the *Silverdale Breeze*, which Dave and Verda Averill and Dorothy and I purchased from George Harrison. The Averills lived at Poulsbo at that time and published the *Poulsbo Weekly*, which Mrs. Averill still owns, as far as I know. The Averills also acquired the *Bainbridge Review* from Walt and Millie Woodward and the Averills moved to Bainbridge Island for their residence and printing plant.

Dorothy and I acquired the *Port Orchard Independent* in 1947 and we published that newspaper until 1966, when we sold it to Ace Comstock.

When Julius Gius established the *Bremerton Sun*, a Scripps League publication, on July 15, 1935, in Bremerton, he hired me as the first reporter. Alex Ottevaere, another Manette resident, was business manager for the *Sun*, which observed its 50th anniversary on July 15, 1985.

THE NEWS IN 1902

(The flavor of life in Decatur-Manette about the time the name was changed to Manette in 1902 is illustrated by the following items published in the *Bremerton Searchlight* that year.)

Chances on the burnt leather sofa pillow being raffled off for the benefit of the Decatur school site fund will be on sale at the Bremerton Mercantile Company's store until Tuesday noon. Those who bought chances at the dance at Decatur will please leave them at the store before that time.

Mr. and Mrs. Mikkelson were Seattle visitors last Saturday.

The launch for Decatur is in great demand, making three regular trips to Bremerton daily with many extras.

Parties prospecting the mineral spring at the Hansberry place have increased the flow one hundred per cent, and have discovered a vein of coal a foot in thickness.

Edwin Phillips shot at and wounded a bear Sunday. Bruin was feeding on the clover not far from Mr. Phillip's house, but scenting danger, fled before a good shot could be obtained. Moral: When you wish to shoot a bear do not approach from the windward side.

Of the many enjoyable occasions this season on Port Orchard Bay the dance given at the old Decatur Mill last evening will be remembered as one of the most enjoyable in every way. Fully ninety couples were present.... The new pavilion is large and splendidly arranged for dancing parties, with dressing, banquet and smoking rooms, and can comfortably accommodate a much larger number than were present last evening, the floor space of the hall alone being 40 x 111 feet. Under the present management and with the pains being taken to provide a jolly good time and to debar any unpleasant feature the Decatur Pavilion will certainly become exceedingly popular both for dancing parties and theatricals, the hall being provided with a commodious stage and splendid curtains and stage fixtures. The music by Messrs. McClelland and Donovan.

The next event of the Decatur Amusement Club will be a calico ball on Wednesday, August 27, in the old mill pavilion. Every lady is supposed to bring a sample ribbon of the dress or waist she wears. These will be placed together and drawn by the gentlemen, the wearer of the dress matching the sample being the partner.

Decatur now has a store and one of the finest pleasure pavilions on Port Orchard bay, also it possesses as good a location for a hotel as one might wish.

M.R. Brewster and John Mikkelson are clearing their town lots.

A hop was enjoyed by a select few, about ten couples participating, Wednesday evening at the pavilion.

N.E. Ryther met with an accident at the Excelsior mines last week. He escaped with but one broken rib, and is reported as being out of danger.

Mrs. J.W. (Jack) Martin made a recent visit to Seattle.

Mr. and Mrs. Gallotte and daughter spent Tuesday in town.

A meeting of citizens was held at the house of Mr. John Pfenning on Tuesday evening, and a Decatur Improvement Club was formed with Mr. (Tom) Bright as chairman, Mr. J.W. (Jack) Martin, secretary, and Mr. Fellows, treasurer. The question of building a wharf was considered. It was found that the majority of those present favored the vicinity of the old site. Nearly four hundred dollars were pledged by those present, and Mr. Joseph Pitt was chosen to wait upon absent interested parties and receive their subscriptions. A committee of three was appointed, consisting of Mr. John Mikkelson, Mr. M.R. Brewster and Mr. Joseph Pitt to obtain information concerning cost of building a wharf, etc., and to report at next meeting, which will be on Tuesday evening, January 21.

The meeting of the Debating Club was held at Mrs. J.W. (Jack) Martin's on Thursday evening.

Residents of Decatur are complaining, and very justly too, that there is too much promiscuous and reckless shooting along the water front opposite their town on the Bremerton side. The distance across the water is short and several recent cases are mentioned of bullets striking buildings and other objects on the Decatur side, narrowly missing people who were moving about. The authorities should take the matter in hand and see that the practice is stopped before serious damage is done. And it should be attended to at once, for should any one be killed the authorities, as well as the person committing the act, would be held blamable.

Chapter 9

ORGANIZATIONS

SERVICE GROUPS
East Bremerton Improvement Club
By Orville Schultz

Building of the Manette Bridge in 1930 started Manette people thinking of improvements—streets, sidewalks, playfields—for their little town. Dave Wheaton, who supervised construction of the bridge and who had purchased property in Manette, suggested to community booster Earl Harkins that the community needed an improvement club. In the spring of 1931 a meeting resulted at the home of Clyde and Estelle Meredith on Scott Avenue. A mass meeting was called for Monday, June 22, 1931, in the Manette Community Church.

Minutes of the June 22 meeting state, "Mr. Harkins suggested forming a club for looking after the interests of the Manette Peninsula and, meeting a hearty response, asked Mr. R. Higgins to draft a set of by-laws patterned after similar organizations."

The following were named to a temporary executive committee: J.H. Martin, H.P. Martin, Clyde Meredith, Lloyd Solid, Ralph Danel, N.E. Peterson, Thomas Hodges and Arthur Bright.

On July 15, in the J.H. Martin building, East Bremerton Improvement Club held its second meeting, adopting its constitution and by-laws and electing temporary officers: Earl Harkins, president; D.S. Aldrich, vice president; C.E. Meredith, treasurer, and B.J. Kean, secretary. At the third meeting, on July 20, the temporary officers were made permanent for the year.

Most of the minutes of EBIC meetings were destroyed when the Harkins home burned, but some newspaper accounts of the club's progress are available.

The first year found 417 paid-up members. By 1944 membership exceeded 700. The EBIC roster, like that of the P-TA, was a Who's Who of Manette. The second president was Theodore "Theo" Peterson; third, E.W. "Gene" Schweer; fourth, Otto Voll; fifth, W.H. "Bill" von Hoene; sixth, Roy Ellis; seventh, J.H. "Jack" Martin and George Mitchell, who finished Martin's term; eighth, Jack Martin, and ninth, Gideon Hermanson.

Each president had the challenges of a growing community to meet, working for sidewalks, streets, playfields, outlying roads, and most of all, a free bridge.

The free bridge became a reality in 1939 after the state purchased the span from the privately owned Bremerton Bridge Company.

In ensuing years EBIC worked on many other projects, including Illahee State Park, playfields at Manette, Sheridan and Tracyton, and small projects virtually all over the peninsula. EBIC was well-known and respected by legislators at Olympia for its many fine efforts. The club sponsored sports for adults, boys and girls and the annual Peninsula playfield fete for all ages. Because of EBIC sponsorship, Manette is known as the birthplace of softball in Kitsap County, and its teams were top competitors.

In listing the various EBIC committee members in 1944, then president Lee Harrison named the following:

LEGISLATIVE: W.H. von Hoene, chairman; Rose Mitchell, Mrs. L.A. Bender, Theodore Peterson, George Giblett, D.A. Buchanan.

COMMUNITY ACTIVITY: Paul McHenry, chairman; Reverend Sidney Cooper, B.H. Branch, E.C. Childs, William Filion.

EDUCATION: George Giblett, chairman; C.A. Dakan, Mrs. J.A. Hill, W.R. Stiles, Mrs. Gary Mason.

ILLAHEE STATE PARK: H.P. Bubke, chairman; W.H. von Hoene, Ray Nosker, Wayne Muller, Charles Barrett, Dr. Ray Schutt, Rose Mitchell, Ethel von Hoene.

STREETS AND PUBLIC IMPROVEMENTS: Lloyd Solid, chairman; I.C. Williams Jr., Earl D. McNeill, A.S. Wolfe, L.A. Bender, William Filion.

WIN THE WAR: B.H. Murray, chairman; Willard Parker, J.P. Ayres, Mrs. Pearl Murray, Mrs. Ralph Baselt.

NEW BRIDGE: Willard Parker, chairman; E.W. Schweer, Dick Feek, Henry Streutker, Mrs. Ethel Aldrich, D.B. Wheaton.

RECREATION AND PLAYFIELD: Reverend Sidney Cooper, chairman; H.P. Bubke, Gary Mason, Wayne Bonn, J.A. McCallum, Mrs. Robert Losee, Mrs. W.R. Gaither, Howard Root, Mrs. I.C. Williams, E.C. Childs.

RURAL ROADS: Don Atkinson, chairman; E.C. Grahn, Gilberton; John Carlson, Meadowdale; E.E. Riddell, Tracyton; L.A. Magnussen, Trenton Avenue; Louis Martin, Manette.

PUBLIC SAFETY: O.W. Hand, chairman; Ralph Stewart.

MANETTE BUSINESS ASSOCIATION: George Mitchell, chairman; W.R. Stiles, W.C. Thompson.

ENTERTAINMENT: Mrs. Pearl Murray, chairman; Mrs. Kate Bender, Mrs. Roger Paquette, Phyllis Palmer.

AREA CONTACTS: Reverend Sidney Cooper, chairman; William Berrigan, B.H. Branch, Miss Jennie Bewsey, Miss Lyle Job, Mrs. A.E. Gilman.

PUBLICITY: Earl H. Harkins, chairman; George Thomas, George Thompson, Otto Voll.

REMEMBRANCE AND DECORATION: Mrs. H.P. Bubke, chairman; Mrs. Tom Bright, Mrs. Otto Voll, Mrs. A.E. Meicho.

CLUB AFFILIATIONS: G.S. Hermanson, chairman; L.E. Tostenrude, Pliny Allen, L.A. Root, W.H. von Hoene.

FINANCE AND AUDITING: Don Young, chairman; L.A. Root, C.E. Meredith, Al Opsata, Ted Jones.

DISTINGUISHED GUESTS: A.P. Ayres, chairman; Theodore Peterson, C.E. Dixon, Harold E. Kemp, Fred W. Stinehart.

AUXILIARY TO EBIC

Seeing a need for organized social service on the Manette Peninsula, a small group of women met in the J.H. Martin building in 1931 to organize an auxiliary to the EBIC. Mrs. Isadora Beach was elected president, Mrs. Etta Harkins vice president and Mrs. Cora Burlew secretary/treasurer.

Other officers and ardent workers through the years were Mrs. Lillian Voll, Mrs. Ethel von Hoene, Mrs. Rose Mitchell, Mrs. Carolyn Kimball, Mrs. Ethel Root, Mrs. Rose Tracy, Mrs. Ethel Hausdorf, Mrs. Addie Clayton, Mrs. Flora Martin, Mrs. Winnie Ellis, Mrs. Edith Helmerson and Mrs. Nellie Isard.

Many a needy family received a helping hand in the form of food, clothing, bedding and medical relief from the auxiliary.

"There never has been a laggard nor loafer in the entire membership," one observer commented.

The entire peninsula felt these women's helping hand. Calls for aid from other agencies such as the Sunshine Society, Community Fund, Red Cross, Firemen's Christmas Fund, American Legion Ambulance Fund and others were all helped by the auxiliary. Many quilts were made, fresh garden produce given, canned fruit prepared and a few spare dollars made available, collected by solicitation, entertainments, card parties and food sales. Membership included women from the neighboring towns of Illahee, Tracyton, Brownsville, Sheridan, Gilberton and Fairview.

Activites of the growing auxiliary expanded to include drives for better playfields, roads, streets and facilities. To the tireless efforts of the auxiliary must be attributed much of the success of the parent EBIC.

Children's Home
FIFTEEN YEARS OF CHILD RELIEF WORK IN KITSAP COUNTY
By Gladys Solid and Raymond Berglind

In the early 1900s, as Kitsap County was developing beyond a strictly rural community, social problems arose.

One of these was that welfare for children was inadequate. Charitably inclined individuals and organizations were supporting homeless children, but in a hit-and-miss fashion. Organization seemed necessary.

On August 8, 1919, Mrs. W.D. (Florence) Calder, Mrs. L.A. (Ella) Bender, Mrs. C.H. Snyder and Mr. Harry Frost met in the office of H.E. Gorman, an attorney in Bremerton. They decided to form an association of as many members as possible, with a goal of providing a home for the children, and to ask the county commissioners for financial help. (Mrs. Bender was the local representative of the Sunshine Society of New York. See "Sunshine Society" below.)

On August 19, 1919, officers were elected and the organization was named the Children's Relief Association of Kitsap County. Mrs. Calder was elected president, Mrs. Harlow treasurer, Mrs. Snyder secretary and Mrs. Bender, Mr. Cartier, Mr. Gorman and Mr. Frost trustees.

An annual membership plan was chosen. Life memberships were authorized for those contributing $100 or more. Annual election of directors was decided upon.

Fund drives were started throughout the county. Bids were called for supplying a home site.

By October of 1919 the fund drive had the enthusiastic support of churches, fraternal groups, businesses and individuals. For a homesite the board selected the Hugo W. Berglind property along Port Washington Narrows, at what is now 1413 Marlow Avenue. It was close to the main part of Manette and it included a 2 1/2-story house with outbuildings that could be incorporated into the main house if needed. The price was $5000. Adjacent property was available for expansion.

INCORPORATION

Negotiations for the Berglind property were delayed when incorporation action was begun by the association. Funds, however, were still coming in. The International Order of Odd Fellows offered to run the fund drive and the board accepted.

On May 13, 1920, at the annual meeting, a new board was elected: Mrs. Bender president, Dr. LaViolette vice-president, Mrs. Harlow secretary and Mrs. Calder treasurer. The treasurer's report showed, after expenses, $1,138.62 in the bank.

At a special meeting on May 17, 1920, a committee of Mrs. Bender and Mrs. Coder reported that the Berglind property was still available for $5000. The board authorized payment of $100 earnest money.

Financial support was county-wide. There were several life members. Support continued after the home was purchased. Furnishings from light bulbs to stoves were needed, and when a newspaper advertisement listed the items required, most were donated and only a few had to be purchased.

THE CHILDREN COME

On July 17, 1920, the Children's Home opened its doors. The matron was Mrs. Louise O'Donnell, mother of three children—Nan, Jean and Dalith. Her salary was $50 per month. Mrs. King was cook and laundry stewardess.

On July 20 the first child, a boy aged 2 1/2, arrived. The circumstances illustrated the value of the home. With the boy safely cared for, the mother, a chambermaid, was able to work elsewhere and help care for him.

"A child needing relief needs it even though he may have

The Childrens' Home at 1413 Marlow Avenue, circa 1920. Mrs. Louise King, cook, and Mrs. Louise O'Donnell, matron, stand nearby as children slide down fire escape.

two perfectly able though negligent parents," a board member later wrote, noting that the first child was not an orphan. "No distinction has ever been made between children with or without parents. There are many and varying circumstances under which a child may be in need of relief and a review of just a small number of cases which the home management has encountered would make you ashamed of some of the human race. Children with parents living have come to the home with their bodies bruised and swollen from mistreatment. Some of them required a complete scrubbing and their clothes burned before they were fit to play with the other children. While there is no set rule that society is responsible for every other member of society, one thing is certain, children must have livable conditions during the formative period of their lives, or society will pay and pay in later years."

On July 21, 1920, the second child, an orphan only a few weeks old, was taken in.

EXPANSION

By November of 1920 donations had paid for the home. Wood and Parker, contractors, volunteered to put in a full concrete basement and enlarge the front porch. The home now had 11 children. Mrs. Harlow resigned as treasurer and Mrs. Coder was elected to replace her.

By March of 1921 the home had been in operation for 8 months, and 50 children had passed through the doors. By September of 1921 adjacent property was purchased and an eight-room house on it was moved to the home and the two combined into one.

In June, 1921, it was reported that the State Legislature had voted to allow the home $3000 a year, but no records of receipt of this money have been found. The county commissioners voted the home $1500 annually in monthly payments. Records, however, indicate that the amount varied from month to month and from year to year and usually totalled less than $1500 a year. It was nevertheless of great help.

The home was financially healthy. The Bremerton Daily *News-Searchlight* said: "With a cash balance on hand of $664.05 as of July 14, 1922,...financial affairs of the Kitsap Childrens' Home are now in a favorable condition, according to the report of Treasurer Frank Coder."

"Thanks to the wonderful success of the Kiwanis Club May Day Festival, assisted by the ladies of the Sunshine Society," the newspaper quoted Coder, "the Children's home is entirely out of debt.

"It is not possible to mention the host of friends of the Kitsap County Children's Home, with their donations of labor and materials, clothing, fruits, vegetables and provisions, but we especially wish to mention the Doctors Robson, Murphy and Schutt for much free medical attention; to Dr. G.A. Bender for free dental services.

"To the managers of the Rialto and Blue Bird theatres for free entertainment...to the Manette Ferry Company for free transportation; to the Messrs. Urban and Jones of Bremerton Creamery for a continuous supply of fresh milk...to Otto Voll for much volunteer labor."

For the next 12 years the home continued caring for children, with the help of many loyal contributors. Navy per-

Childrens' Home in 1932 showing the 1921 expansion.   - Photo from Bill Schweer

sonnel aboard ships in the navy yard also helped, bringing the children candy and presents, especially at Christmas.

The number of children who passed through the home in its 15 years is not known, but during the winter of 1930 there were as few as three and as many as 40.

THE FINAL DAYS

In 1932 by-laws were amended to provide that any non-profit organization in the county might participate by electing a representative and notifying the association of that election. In May 1932, the first annual meeting of the association under the new setup was attended by some 180 such elected representatives, and a new board of nine directors was elected. The nine were J.A. McGillivray, mayor of Bremerton; L. Graonett of Harper; Mrs. Addie Josephson, housewife and active social worker; Mrs. Zella Heinisch, treasurer of the home board for several years; John Jessup of the *News-Searchlight*; Mrs. Ella Bender, one of the original founders of the home; C. Christensen of Annapolis, navy yard pilot; H.H. Perrin, navy yard worker, and E.W. Schweer, Puget Sound Power and Light Company.

The board took action to:
• Continue operation of the home;
• Amend the by-laws to provide that the chairman of the board of county commissioners, the judge of the superior court and the county sheriff be ex-officio members of the board;
• Request that the county commissioners provide monthly funding for the home.

The county commissioners granted the request, allocating $12 per child per month, but there was a movement within the commissioners to close the home and to send those children who were wards of the court to the Washington Children's Home in Seattle.

In 1933 two new county commissioners were elected who were set on closing the Manette Home and sending the children to Seattle. In December of 1933 the commissioners signed a contract with the Washington Home for a flat fee of $1000 to provide care in 1934 for the children who were wards of the court, and Superior Judge H.G. Sutton ordered their release to the Washington Home.

The children were allowed to stay on long enough to attend a Christmas party aboard the USS *Tennessee* in the navy yard on December 25, but on December 26 Buddy Mowry, Clarence Mann, Fred Hanning, Richard Hanning and Bobby Hanning were taken by Mrs. Arnett, juvenile officer, to the Washington Children's Home in Seattle.

On February 13, 1934, the board called for a special meeting of the association to consider the situation that existed, and on May 1, 1934, the association voted to close the home. Two boys who still lived there would be cared for elsewhere and sent to school until the term ended on June 8.

The last entry in the diary of Mrs. O'Donnell, the matron, was made on May 6, 1934. It says, "Harold went to Sunday School this morning and to Mrs. Koke for the day. Mrs. Dick came to take charge."

Today, more than 50 years later, the exact meaning of Mrs. O'Donnell's words is uncertain, but it is clear that the era of the Manette Children's Home was ending.

Floyd Taft, last resident of the Children's Home.
-Photo from Charlotte Forbes

NEW ROLE

Barracks were built on the property for soldiers assigned to barrage balloon duty in Manette during World War II. These barracks also housed carpenters for the Navy Eastpark housing project.

Phil and Eunice Hudson purchased the property from the Children's Home Society in 1944 and lived in the two-story building while they remodeled it into a home. The present owner is Dr. Dolores DeMier, who has modernized the old home along the waterfront of Port Washington Narrows, 1413 Marlow Avenue.

Recollections

Louise O'Donnell, Children's Home matron (from her diary):

November 23, 1920 [Thanksgiving]. We got a box of supplies from the Hobnob Club to the amount of $16 and about 400 lb. of things from the primary department of the Smith School. Meredith's store sent two dozen oranges and a box of assorted cookies.

Newspaper clipping, 1934: Last resident of Manette Children's Home, Floyd Taft, will graduate an honor student from Bremerton High School this week....

Charlotte Forbes: Floyd Taft lived in the home after its closure. He climbed in and out a window. Mrs. Gene (Daisy) Schweer provided Floyd's meals in return for chores Floyd performed. He did yard work for Schweers and the L.A. Benders.

Alice Bender Davis: There was one of the little boys from the Children's Home whom mother [Ella Bender] kept at our home—she did this very often—until she found a family for him. He had very bowed legs. Mother took him to a Seattle hospital and they put the legs in casts, and in no time he was a couple of inches taller and running around with the other

children. He grew into a very talented young man. He did a very nice painting for Mother. It hung on her living room wall. His last name was Hurlbert, but I've forgotten his first name.

Helen Starevich Cuellar: I really can't tell much about our years in the Children's Home. They were not the years we like to remember. Mrs. King, the cook, was a kind, hard-working woman and we older girls liked to help her run the clothes through the wringer on wash day; that was until I ran my hand through the wringer and we weren't allowed to help any more. All of the clothes were dried above the stove in the kitchen in the wintertime.

One day Mrs. King took all of us on a mushroom hunting trip to a large burned area near Sheridan Road. The mushrooms were brown curly ones. We had them for supper. I don't remember anyone being wild about the mushrooms, but we did enjoy the hunt.

Christmas aboard ship was a strange experience—more like a dream. Every child was assigned to a sailor for the day. We had turkey and everything that went with it. Santa gave every child a gift of clothing and one toy. Some years, children were farmed out for the holidays into private homes. I remember people as being kind, but that too was a strange, frightening experience.

The older children watched the younger children. Everyone who could, made their own beds and did other chores. You had to keep things picked up. If your coat was found on the floor, you held it over your head for one hour.

Dentists donated their skills and I do remember trips to the dentist. Doctors must have done the same as I remember we all had our tonsils out. In and out on the same day. That was one time I remember having ice cream.

In the summertime it was a special treat to have peanut butter and lettuce sandwiches and to eat out on the porch.

Bill Schweer: We lived next door to the home from its beginning to its close. Some of my fondest childhood memories center around the Children's Home. I was an only child. The home was a fountainhead of companionship and enthusiastic support for creative projects, and it provided a ready supply of kids for group games and competitions. I was never lonely.

Metal chutes served as fire escapes from the top floor to the ground. It was a fast ride. When the chute was heated by the sun you went twice as fast and shot off the end like a bullet.

The long summer evenings were game times. Choose the game, draw up sides and it was Hide and Go Seek; Pom Pom Pull Away; Run Sheep Run; Red Light-Cheese It; or Duck on the Rock.

The learning experience of creating things together, cooperating to make them work and giving everyone a chance to "have a turn" and physically compete, is what growing up should be all about.

Memories include making our own kites and actually getting them to fly. Once we had one up so high that when the string broke it fell into a tree clear up at the Nelson's place, nearly 2 miles away.

Making stilts and duck legs or even jamming condensed milk cans onto our shoes and having races also are treasured memories.

The stilts and duck legs competitions deserve a more detailed telling. Duck legs are stilts that are tied to your legs

Sunshine Society's annual lilac tea at the Lewis and Ella Bender home. Seated (at left), Ella Bender; (at right), Lillian Voll. Standing (from left), Daisy Schweer, Nellie White, Rose Mitchell, Joaquina Feek, Rose Tracy, Ethel Root, Marguerite Bright, Grace Jack, Hattie Martin.   - Photo from Bill Schweer.

so your hands are free. In a small gully out beside the home was the ash pile. The best fun was to walk your duck legs out into the ashes where, of course, the "legs" started sinking with each step until there was no pulling them out, and you would fall slowly forward, face down, into the ash pile. Another competition that always ended in disaster was walking your stilts up and then back down the home steps.

The home building was constructed by moving two existing houses together. I remember watching this operation. Mr. Stebbins had lived in one and he told me about digging a hole for a flag pole and finding they were digging into an old Indian grave. My passion at that time was digging Indian graves and this information was music to my ears. Mr. Stebbins came and located the spot. It wasn't 50 feet from the building. I couldn't possibly dig unnoticed. Finally Mrs. Ella Bender, who had charge of all things to do with the home, gave me permission to dig but only if the home kids didn't know about it. Two of my friends and I laid our plans. We would start digging at midnight. Armed with picks, shovels, buckets, and lanterns we arrived at the spot. Keeping the adventure quiet was out of the question - so everyone shared in the digging. Incidentally, only three old bones showed up in the hole.

Sunshine Society
By Alice Bender Davis

My mother, Ella Bender, formed the Sunshine Society in Bremerton in 1909. She was an early-day leader in social service work in the community and served for many years as

juvenile court officer for Kitsap County. She was instrumental in forming and supervising the Kitsap County Children's Home, which was located near her home in Manette.

At the Children's Home she and Mrs. O'Donnell, the matron, tried very hard to make a pleasant home for the many children who, for one reason or another, had no other place to live.

The Sunshine Society was the only organization for many years which cared for the needy. Our spacious home in Manette was the center of many of the large social gatherings of organizations in which she took an active part.

One of the loveliest social events in Manette was the annual Sunshine Society lilac tea which was always held at the Bender home in the spring when the lilac hedge (alternating English and Persian lilacs) was in full bloom. The hedge skirted the path down by the water's edge.

American Legion
By Wells and Alice Ehrhardt

MANETTE POST 68 RECEIVES CHARTER

With veterans from all parts of the district in attendance and a crowd of over 250 viewing the ceremony, Manette Peninsula American Legion Post 68 officially got under way Friday night, January 17, 1936, at East Bremerton Masonic Temple. State Commander Walter S. Talbot presented the charter.

Other distinguished guests were Fred M. Fueker of Seattle, department adjutant and national head of the Forty et Eight; Homer R. Jones, Bremerton past department commander;

Charles Deamer, Bremerton third district commander; Mayor J.A. McGillivray of Bremerton, who delivered an address to the members of the new post; and Reverend Walter Givens, Bremerton, who pronounced the invocation.

The ritualistic team of the Bremerton Forty et Eight voiture gave the ceremonial work.

The post installed the following officers:

Commander Daniel O'Neil, 1st Vice Commander W.P. Byl, 2nd Vice Commander Glenn M. Kelly, 3rd Vice Commander Harry Flint, Finance Officer Albert Chase, Adjutant Donald E. Pitt, Service Officer Frank Gillette, Historian Earl Harkins, Chaplain Cecil Owens and Sergeant-at-Arms Frank D. Lindsey. Trustees were Renus Bender, D.M. Munro, Charles Walsh, Benjamin Murray, Anton Mottner and Hugo Berglind. Color bearers were Robert Losee and E.E. McDowell.

Additional charter members were:

George Alinder, Waldemer Blom, R. Bourgett, O.E. Brenden, Frank Bunker, Herman Bunker, Earl Callison, W.G. Callow, Leonard Card, Peter Carlson, S.M. Clare, J.L. Coleman, M.J. Comer, A.J. Cooper, W.W. Cowan, T. Dickson, Earl Fawcett, Ruth Gillette, A. Gordon, F.J. Hagen, Hummell Hall, H.D. Hanson, W.M. Hennis, E.C. Hoffman, E.C. Hausdorf, George Howard, Oscar Jackson, Fred Jacobsen, Ray Jenkins, John Johanson, Frederick Johnson, S.H. Jones, Howard Juneau, Charles Kimball, Louis Kittock, W.J. Martin, Albert Meicho, Marion Moores, John Peters, T.G. Pidduck, Clarence Rakestraw, W.L. Rea, Alvin Reid, Charles Sanders, Charles Sidam, David Smith, W.M. Smith, A.D. Snyder, Joseph Tatham, Ingvold Tostenrude, Elmer Trask, Carl Wagner, Henry Wintermute and Donald Pitt.

The charter was effective July 6, 1936; the post celebrated its 50th anniversary July 12, 1986.

The legion is a fraternal organization of veterans of all world wars. The legion works for the benefit of widows and orphans of veterans. Manette Peninsula Post meetings are held the second and fourth Thursday evening each month. An annual convention is held in Washington state the third week of July. Each year a different post hosts the convention. The 1986 convention was held in Everett.

Post Commanders

1936 Dan O'Neil	1953 Harley Drake	1970 Adrino Austria
1937 George Baker	1954 R.H. Maulsby	1971 Estel Schooler
1938 Herman Bunker,	1955 Carl Armstrong	1972 James Johnson
Harry Flint	1956 Harry Keegan	1973 Pat Patungan
1939 Lawrence Moses	1957 James White	1974 Paul Young
1940 Cecil Owens	1958 H. Hollingsworth	1975 Mark Schmeller
1941 Ben Murray	1959 Albert Dial	1976 John Butler
1942 Harry Kelly	1960 Ray Spalding	1977 Robert Tomas
1943 William Gaither	1961 Don Ireland	1978 Kenneth Avery
1944 Ralph Baselt	1962 Kenneth Avery	1979 Leroy Hester
1945 O.D. Brenden	1963 Jack Redenbaugh	1980 William Warcup
1946 R.H. Maulsby	1964 Harold Higgins	1981 Phil Davis
1947 Alfred Bechlem	1965 Pearle Hyer	1982 Carl Christensen
1948 Al Opsata	1966 Estel Schooler	1983 John Bollinger
1949 John Swalling	1967 Charles Grimes	1984 Bill Swank
1950 Maurice Scott	1968 Vern Dashel	1985 James Angell
1951 Vernon Powers	1969 Dave Rasmussen	1986 James Angell
1952 W.C. Woodruff		

THE AUXILIARY

Unit 68 of the American Legion Auxiliary was chartered February 19, 1936, with Etta Harkins as its first president.

Other members were Merle Baker, Helen Bender, Edith Blom, Beatrice Callison, Elva Cowan, Leta Fawcett, Lillian Larsen, Rose Lindsey, Helene Losee, Theresa O'Neil, Esther Owens, Marcia Mae Pitt, Dorothy Sidam and Martha Walsh. Other early members were Ella Bender, Clara Bunker, Delia Bunker, Laura Chase, Carolyn Kimball, Alice McDowell, Genevieve Quay, Pearl Wess, Mae Brenden, Myrtle Flint, Elsie Martin, Marie Mottner and Pearl Murray.

Meetings were held in the hall above the Meredith grocery store and later at the East Bremerton Improvement Club. The first year there were 30 members. Today there are 329.

The focus of the unit has been to assist veterans at Retsil. The unit has supplied items needed by residents there, adopted grandparents and provided homecooked meals. It also assists in raising funds for the kidney center, handicapped swim program, K-9 units for the Bremerton police and Kitsap County sheriff's department, and has sponsored a scholarship program. It volunteers services for the YMCA. It also assists its American Legion Post—most recently in the post's building program.

Auxiliary Presidents:

1936 Etta Harkins	1954 Mae Brenden	1973 Rita Petriello
1936 Helen Losee	1955 Mary Sublett	1974 Vivian Proctor
1937 Esther Owens	1956 Joan Armstrong	1975 Kathy Bollinger
1938 Merle Ittner	1957 Joan Armstrong	1976 Vivian Proctor
1939 Virginia Gillard	1958 Vivian Proctor	1977 Marilyn Shearer
1940 Effie Robinson	1959 Carol Rowley	1978 Marilyn Shearer
1941 Marie DeSar	1960 Alice Ehrhardt	1979 Dorothy Johnson
1942 Pearl Murray	1961 Barbara Avery	1980 Laura Hester
1943 Faye Gaither	1962 Barbara Avery	1981 Laura Hester
1944 Ethel Hausdorf	1963 Violet Scott	1982 Shirley Nicholson
1945 Mae Brenden	1964 Violet Higgens	1983 Shirley Nicholson
1946 Mae Brenden	1965 Alice Ehrhardt	1984 Joy Golden
1947 Helen Friend	1966 Rue Tewksbury	1985 Doris Stonecipher
1948 Violet Higgens	1967 Hazel Grass	1986 Mary Angell
1949 Louise Powers	1968 Dorothy Johnson	1987 Ginger Hueske
1950 Mary Norwood	1969 Alice Hyer	
1951 Bonnie Piercy	1970 Ethel Austria	
1952 Kath. Magerstaedt	1971 Barbara Avery	
1953 Isabelle Drake	1972 Barbara Avery	

Volunteer Fire Department

Fire Truck Needed

[A volunteer fire department existed in Manette at least as early as 1924. Following is an item from the *Kitsap American* of April 10, 1924, written by W.H. von Hoene.]

The vital need of proper equipment for fighting fire was forcefully brought home to citizens of this community Saturday night, March 29, when the Dilks residence was totally destroyed by fire, together with the entire contents of the building. The fire is believed to have originated from an overheated stove. No one was home when it started and before it was discovered it had gained such headway that the efforts of the fire department were centered on confining it to the house alone. The difficulty of moving the hose carts by hand over the streets of Manette was emphasized by the darkness of the night and several times the hose cart companies had to call for help to move them. Mr. Dilks is staying with his father at present while his wife and son will continue their visit in California until he can make other arrangements for them. This is the second total loss by fire Manette has experienced within the last two months and the greatest difficulty each time was the moving of the hose carts. If a suitable auto truck for transporting the equipment was available it would materially reduce the fire loss.

Recollections

GEORGE McKEOWN: The fire truck was acquired from Charleston in 1925. I remember Tom Bright was the fire chief. He made a speech every time we had a fire.

Fire bell (arrow) west of post office on East 11th Street near Perry Avenue, circa 1925.
                                                    - Photo from Dorothy Rogers

BILL FILION: I remember some of the members of the volunteer fire department in 1925—Hiram Garrett, Jack Carlaw, Jack Martin, Earl Harkins, Malcolm Meredith and Earl McNeill.

On one call, the truck came up East 11th Street past 1117 Hayward Avenue and Hiram Garrett tried to jump on the truck as it passed. He slipped and the truck ran over him. His pelvis was broken. I took up a collection to pay his hospital bill. He suffered the rest of his life from that accident.

BLOSSOM BRIGHT LANE: When we lived on Ironsides Avenue, I can remember going around with Daddy (Tom Bright) on Saturdays in the fire truck as he went to check on the water hydrants. He was the fire chief.

When houses burned, neighbors often helped rebuild them.

Fire Alarms

There was a fire bell under a tower near the post office on East 11th Street. A phone call to 425, Meredith's store, reporting a fire, would send Clyde Meredith running across the street to ring the fire bell. The Model T Ford fire truck was at one time housed in a lean-to to a barn owned by the Fellows family on Hayward Avenue. Later it was kept alongside Meredith's store.

Fire Department for North Perry Avenue

During World War II Arthur E. Knutson and approximately five other individuals from the Community Club circulated petitions to form a fire department for North Perry Avenue. Art was elected fire chief and served several years. He had come to Manette during World War II, bought a one-acre tract of land between North Perry Avenue and Petersville Road from Herman Waugh and become active in community affairs.

Manette's Model-T fire truck. In driver's seat is Don Young; standing is Charles Fellows. Photo taken 1925. In background is Walter and Hulda Wall's house, 1134 Hayward Avenue.   - Photo from Alice Fellows Lawson

Manette Garden Club

By Orville Schultz

The Manette Garden Club was an outgrowth of the Home and Garden Committee of the East Bremerton Improvement Club. The first meeting was held February 27, 1935, at the home of Mrs. W.L. Rea. Harriet Holden was chosen president. The club goal was to beautify the community.

At the first meeting 17 persons were present as charter members: Mrs. L.A. Bender, Mrs. I.P. Hoopes, Mrs. Lee Harrison, Mrs. H.P. Martin, Mrs. Otto Voll, Mrs. James Hawthorne, Ethel Root, Mrs. W.L. Rea, Mrs. Archie Bouchard, Nancy Thomas, Mrs. William von Hoene, Mrs. E.W. Schweer, Mrs. C.V. Walsh, Mrs. George Mitchell, Ruth Gillette, Gladys Solid and Harriet Holden.

In 1936 with a membership of 30, the club joined the Washington State Federation of Garden Clubs, and the same year won the Best Garden Program award established by *Sunset* magazine for the western states of Washington, Oregon, California, Idaho, Nevada, Utah and Arizona. Mrs. H.P. (Hattie) Martin was then president, and her committee members were Mrs. W.E. White, Mrs. Luther Elmore, Mrs. W.L. Rea and Mrs. George Mitchell.

In April of 1937 the club sponsored its first rhododendron tour, with 34 cars traveling Kitsap Peninsula roads. Mrs. Hattie Martin was president. Her committee included Mrs. Otto Voll, Mrs. E.W. Schweer, Mrs. Ella Bender, Mrs. Lambert Sternbergh and Mrs. P.A. Steiger. By 1947, 700 guests were turning out for the annual tour, which had been extended to 2 days.

Billie Lebo was president in 1937 when a spring flower, bulb and primrose show was held April 6 and 7.

By 1939 the club had been renamed East Bremerton Garden Club. The April flower show became an annual event held at the Masonic Temple and open to the public. The primrose was the club flower and members provided primrose plants as prizes.

During World War II members were trained as Red Cross volunteers at the YMCA and YWCA. They wrapped packages and decorated wards at the Naval Hospital. In 1951 they began wrapping Christmas packages for both servicemen and their families.

During the 1946-47 club year a rhododendron tour was held. Tickets were sold at the Olympic Hotel in Seattle. Buses met the ferry; there were 21 drivers of buses and cars. Sixteen hundred persons attended the 2-day affair.

On July 16, 1950, the garden club received the highest award given garden club flower shows by the State Federation of Garden Clubs. This award was the national purple rib-

bon, for achievement in the 1950 primrose and spring flower show.

Chloe Sutton, president of the Kitsap County Historical Association, was a guest of the East Bremerton Garden Club in October of 1950 and told of the customs of the early Indians as well as the naming of the Douglas Fir in 1895 by David Douglas. She also stated that her father as gardener planted the first rhododendron in the gardens of the shipyard.

In 1953 there were 23 Washington State Federated Garden

Manette Garden Club members, circa 1935. Standing in Lillian Voll's garden are (from left), Alma Gilman, Lillian Voll, Hattie Martin.   -Photo from Jack Voll

Clubs in this area, belonging to the Snoqualmie District. Transportation became a problem and a new district called Cross Sound was formed, with 20 clubs participating. These continued educating people in conservation, ecology and beautification. Locally, club members continued to send fresh flowers every week to the Naval Hospital and the YMCA.

On June 19, 1985, the club—which had been expanded and become the Bremerton Garden Club—celebrated 50 years of enjoyment and community service at the Sheridan Park Community Center. Members celebrated with a tea and their favorite centerpiece flower, a primrose. Adeline Cunningham, 1984 president, and Julia Pickering, 1985 president, served as hostesses. They joined these past presidents:

Harriet Holden	1935	Donna Carlson	1955
Hattie Martin	1936-37	Adele Murphy	1956-57
Myrtle Byl	1938	Lorraine Strachan	1960
Nellie White	1939	Jane Barber	1961-62
Mabel Kilgore	1940-41	Janice Stewart	1963-64
Billie Lebo	1942	Bessie Larson	1965
Daisy Schweer	1943-44	Edna Thompson	1966-67
Ora Hensel	1945-48	Janice Stewart	1968-69
Maurine Shohoney	1949	Ruth Oliver	1970-71
Esther Johnson	1950-51	Gloria Moore	1972-73
Gladys Solid	1951	Ruth Oliver	1974-80
Lillian Larson	1952-53	Adeline Cunningham	1981-84
Ruth Cole	1953	Julia Pickering	1985-86
Edith Klinefelter	1955		

Other early members included Elizabeth Lamson, Mattie Harres, Edith Erwin, Marie Burwig, Flora Martin, Hilaria

"Larry" Tempelmon, Mrs. Paul McHenry, Mrs. L.G. Bright, Calla Henly, Margaret Rice, Emma Welton, Ollie Baselt, Neal Meredith, Vida Grenstad and Mae Tracy.

"I enjoy belonging to the garden club," says long-time member Mae Tracy. "The club has taken flowers into the Navy Yard Hospital twice a month. At Christmas, members make swags and small arrangements for the wards. This was a tradition in the old navy hospital and we continue for the new one. In 1964 or 65 the club put on an Easter show at the old hospital. We also wrapped Christmas packages for the boys at the YMCA - both gifts for the servicemen and packages they wanted to mail."

FRATERNAL ORGANIZATIONS

Steadfast Masonic Lodge 216

By Roy Williamson

On the first day of February, 1916, 11 brethren met in Martin's Hall on East 11th Street to discuss organizing a Masonic Lodge on the Manette Peninsula. They were: Ralph E. Hibbard, Russell H. Hibbard, William J. Abbott, Arthur A. Holden, Theodore Peterson, David Grey Smith, R.O. Hilstad, S.F. Dewar, J.H. Martin, B.E. Stebbins and Nels E. Peterson. Ralph Hibbard was elected chairman and Isaac P. Hoopes secretary. The chairman appointed brothers Dewar, Holden and Hibbard as a committee to estimate expenses to operate a lodge for one year.

After much discussion, it was agreed that a lodge was needed in Manette. It was so moved by Brother Smith, seconded by Brother Abbott and passed.

A meeting of Master Masons was held at Martin's Hall February 24, 1916. Brother Stebbins presided. Ten Master Masons were present. Brothers David Smith and Ralph Hibbard were appointed to get Grand Lecturer Gifford to meet with the brethren.

Steadfast Masonic Temple at East 11th Street and Perry Avenue. Cornerstone laid in 1926.
                                    - Photo from Roy Williamson

DISPENSATION

The next meeting was March 4, 1916. Attendance consisted of 20 local Masons and 15 visitors. Grand Lecturer Gifford assured them he would be glad to recommend a dispensation when they were ready for it. All visitors expressed a willingness to help get a lodge started.

On March 7, 1916, a request for a dispensation was signed, and on March 9 the following names for the lodge were suggested: Mosaic, Trowel, Utopia and Steadfast. Four ballots were spread before Steadfast was adopted.

Officers elected were: Worshipful Master David Grey Smith, Senior Warden S.F. Dewar, Junior Warden B.E. Stebbins, Secretary I.P. Hoopes and Treasurer B.H. Ross.

At the sixth meeting on March 14, 1916, recommendations were received from Bremerton Lodge 117 and William H. Upton Naval and Military Lodge 206.

SWORD DONATIONS

On March 21 Brother Woodbury donated a sword to the lodge. (However, our present sword was presented by Very Worshipful Joseph P. Yank.) Worshipful Master-elect Smith announced appointments as follows: Senior Deacon Ralph E. Hibbard, Junior Deacon Arthur A. Holden, Senior Steward William J. Abbott, Junior Steward R.O. Hilstad, Chaplain A.M. Peterson, Marshall O. Peters, Tiler J.A. Martin, and Librarian N.E. Peterson. On motion of N.E. Peterson, seconded by William J. Abbott, meetings were set for Tuesday nights and stated communications for first Tuesdays.

Our request for dispensation was forwarded to the grand secretary. Signers were David Grey Smith, S.F. Dewar, B.E. Stebbins, I.P. Hoopes, G.H. Ross, R.E. Hibbard, A.A. Holden, William J. Abbott, R.O. Hilstad, A.M. Peterson, O. Peters, J.H. Martin, N.E. Peterson and W.H. Sadler.

The last meeting before dispensation was March 28, 1916, when a letter from the grand secretary was read requiring demits from current lodges of all signers of the request for dispensation for a new lodge.

First meeting of Steadfast Lodge under dispensation was Tuesday, April 4, 1916, in Martin's Hall. Petitions were received from Walter James Peterson, James Peterson, Paul McHenry, Charles Wesley Cropp and Harold Clifford King.

LARGER QUARTERS

As of May 2, 1916, meetings were moved to Meredith's Hall for more room. On May 16 Brother R.E. Hibbard moved that application be made to the June session of Grand Lodge for a charter. The motion was seconded by brother N.E. Peterson and passed.

On May 23 and May 30, degrees were conferred to satisfy requirements of Grand Lodge.

Charter was issued June 14, 1916. A special communication of the Most Worshipful Grand Lodge of Free and Accepted Masons of Washington was convened for the purpose of constituting Steadfast Lodge 216 as a regular lodge on September 9, 1916, in Meredith's Hall, Manette.

Grand Lodge was opened at 4 p.m. on the Third Degree of Masonry in Ample Form by Most Worshipful Grand Master George R. Malcolm—and Steadfast Lodge 216 was duly constituted.

The September 13, 1920, issue of the *Bremerton News* reported that members of Steadfast Lodge celebrated their

STEADFAST LODGE PAST MASTERS

David Gray Smith 1916   Saunders Dewar 1917   Ralph Hibbard 1919   Nels Peterson 1920   John Martin 1921

Paul McHenry 1922   Harold Moodie   1923   George Ross 1924   William Abbott 1925   Alonzo Almon 1926

John McNeill 1927   Henry Strehlau 1928   Albert Chase 1929   Arthur Personette 1930   Hubert Saety 1931

Hugo Berglind 1932   Walter Bruns 1933   Leonard Caro 1934   J. Malcolm Meredith 1935   James Rodger 1936

Jesse Houghton 1937   Walter Fellows 1938   Ord Harris 1939   Albert Meicho 1940   William Glud 1941

STEADFAST PAST MASTERS
(continued)

Webster Taylor 1942   Francis J. Hagan 1943   Frank I. Jackson 1944   Ray Nosker 1945   Earl McNeill 1946

Joseph Yank 1947   Lee Harrison 1948   Carl Hoff 1949   Clyde Dickinson 1950   Milt Schelly 1951

Ray Ball 1952   Raymond Taylor 1953   Rolland Musser 1954   James Kesterson 1955   Pete Hagan 1956

Benjamin Lyons 1957   George Toepel 1958   Ivan Jackson 1959   Hubert Boone 1960   John Murray 1961

Ray Netwig 1962   Ralph Klamm 1963   Lyle Stokesbary 1964   Olav Jacobsen 1965   William Liggett 1966

STEADFAST PAST MASTERS
(continued)

Roger Ewbank 1967

William Card 1968

Gilbert Cox 1969

Charles Johnston 1970

William VanHorn 1971

Rodney Nelson 1972

Eugene Crampton 1973

Ronald Pettygrove 1974

Homer Moody 1975

Gerard Vergeer Jr. 1976

Roy Williamson 1977

Robert Trask 1978

Walter Zwieg 1979

Charles Compton 1980

William Cooper 1981

Charles Johnston 1982

William Megaw 1983

Charles Yoder 1984-85

Clyde E. Meredith
Honorary 1947

Roy Ellis
Honorary 1956

Ross Hepner
Honorary 1982

Carl Mahone
Honorary 1984

fourth anniversary at a splendid session Saturday night. Grand Master James Howard Begg was present and the hall was packed with guests from Bremerton, Charleston and Port Orchard. Speaking was indulged in during the evening and at 11 o'clock a splendid banquet was served. All had a fine time.

TEMPLE PLANNED

On January 20, 1919, Steadfast Masonic Temple Association was organized with D.G. Smith as chairman, Paul McHenry secretary, Charles Cropp treasurer and Ralph Hibbard and Nels Peterson members.

Stock was sold and funds raised, and on May 12, 1925, bids were opened for construction of the temple at East 11th Street and Perry Avenue. William P. White was chosen as architect, Peter Fedt Sr. and Ole O. Dahl were awarded the building contract, and contracts were let for heating and wiring.

Worshipful Brother Alonzo (Pop) Almon was worshipful master when the cornerstone for the building was laid. The Most Worshipful Grand Lodge of Free and Accepted Masons of Washington laid the cornerstone on August 28, 1926. Acting as special deputy for Grand Master Walter F. Meier was Most Worshipful Brother James H. Begg.

Brother D. A. Buchanan built the altar and officers' stations. Brother Nels Peterson presented the lesser lights, and the records show that Worshipful Brother William Glud gave ashlers, as did Bremerton Lodge 117.

RENOVATIONS

In 1953, under the leadership of Worshipful Brother Ray Taylor, the temple was repaired, with much new plaster and redecorating. This same year Steadfast was honored by the appointment of Very Worshipful Brother Joseph P. Yank as deputy of the grand master, the first for Steadfast. Later the lodge was honored with appointments of three other deputies: Very Worshipful Brother L.C. Stokesbury, Very Worshipful Brother William C. van Horn and Very Worshipful Brother E.F. Crampton.

In 1963 the stage was removed and the kitchen was enlarged, greatly improving the cooking and serving facilities.

The building has long been a center for community activities.

In 1967 extensive repairs were made to the south wall. The foundation was raised, many studs were replaced and extensive replastering done.

In 1976 the Steadfast Masonic Temple Association established a savings account for the building fund, financed by $2 per member annually and various donations and bequests. The funds may be used only for building replacement or extensive repairs.

The year 1984 found Steadfast Lodge 68 years old and remodeling again. Deteriorating west-end windows were replaced or blanked off.

Also in June, 1984, Worshipful Brother Charles Johnston was appointed grand historian of the Grand Lodge of Washington.

Philathea Chapter 174

(Condensed from a history written in 1950 by Lillie Card and Alma Gilman)

On September 17, 1920, in Steadfast Lodge Hall (over Meredith's grocery store at East 11th Street and Scott Avenue), formation of an Eastern Star chapter in Manette began. Mrs. Amy C. Hoopes, associate conductress of Reliance Chapter 70, was elected chairman. A petition to grand chapter for dispensation was requested.

A meeting to adopt by-laws followed on December 8. January 12 was set as the date to institute the new chapter. Alma Gilman suggested the name "Philathea," meaning "love of truth."

January 12, 1921, Brother Anthony J. Swindle, grand patron of Washington, presided over the instituting of Philathea Chapter. Sister Ella Strickland, worthy matron of Reliance Chapter 70, assisted as grand marshall; Brother Walter Meir of Seattle, grand sentinel; Sister Minnie McCall, grand conductress; Sister Anna Hagan, grand associate conductress; Sister Goldsworthy, grand warden; Sister Nellie Wagner, grand organist (all of Reliance Chapter), and Sister Ella M. Rossman of Doric Chapter 69, grand secretary pro tem. Illness prevented Grand Secretary Vesta A. Schoff from being present.

Amy C. Hoopes was installed worthy matron; Len E. Hunton, worthy patron; Nellie Peterson, associate matron; Alma Gilman, secretary; Lena Rodger, treasurer; Jean Abbott, conductress, and Mary Kean, associate conductress. Thirty-nine members knelt behind the altar to take the obligation and hold the "love of truth" as the star to guide the destiny of this new chapter. They were William J. Abbott, Jean Abbott, Pearl Almon, Verga Brown, I.L. Brown, Maude Bright, Carrie Bright, Lillian Card, Irene E. Correll, R.H. Correll, Alma P. Gilman, Albert B. Gilman, Anna R. Green, Enos I. Green, Bertha L. Hall, Elmer C. Hall, Margaret P. Hawkes, Amy C. Hoopes, Isaac P. Hoopes, Hulda Hunton, Len E. Hunton, Margaret P. Irey, W.E. Irey, Mary L. Kean, Adella Martin, Margaret Martin, J.H. Martin, Edith McNeill, Margaret Neill, Alyce Peterson, Nellie Peterson, Nels Peterson, Carrie Price, Mabel L. Rea, Lena Rodger, James Rodger, Mamie B. Snyder, Joy M. Wood and W.E. Wood. Reliance Chapter 70 exemplified the degrees, using two of their own candidates, Charles and Addie Morrison.

Ten dollars was the original initiation fee. This has remained the same. Annual dues were $3. By 1984 they were $10.

On September 9, 1921, Philathea Chapter was constituted with Sister Edith E. Gattis, grand matron; Walter F. Meir, associate grand patron; Mabel C. Gundlach, grand secretary, and Lovelia K. West, grand marshal. Our charter was granted and Philathea Chapter No. 174, Order of Eastern Star, was dedicated to the work of charity, truth, love and benevolence.

Members at the institution, together with the following new members, signed the charter: Elizabeth Bonney, Thomas Bright, Leonard D. Card, Grace Carlaw, Marguerite Clark, Ethel B. Collins, Neal Harrington, Ralph E. Hibbard, Hannah Hibbard, Gladys Hilstad, Harriet Holden, Arthur Holden, Lenore W. Hogue, Mark Isbill, Olive Isbill, Ardo Jones, Harvey Jones, Thomas Klepper, Gine Klepper, Halvor Kravick, Clyde E. Meredith, John McNeill, Gladys H. Olsen, Adeline V. Perry, Mabel L. Renn, S.B. Sigurdson and Alta Strehlau; a total of 67 names on our charter. At the close of the first year, membership was 79.

Our first Matron's Ball was in 1922. The first moneymaking event was a farce play titled "Female Masons," which netted $82.50.

Philathea Past Matrons, at Theo and Alyce Peterson's place on Hood Canal, 1933. Back row (from left), Carrie Bright, Esther Sigurdson, Grace Carlaw, Maude Bright, Nellie Peterson, Gladys Solid, Alyce Peterson, Mabel Renn, Myrtle Oliver. Front row, Lillian Card, May Hammargren, Amy Hoopes, Theo Parr, Edith McNeill, Lena Rodger, Estelle Meredith, Minnie Jeffs (visitor from Suquamish), Edna Bailey.

In 1923 Philathea Chapter was honored by having as our installing matron Sister Emma P. Chadwick, right worthy grand conductress of the world.

Construction of Steadfast Masonic Temple in Manette started in 1926. Philathea Chapter purchased $550 of temple stock.

Here are some other important dates:

January, 1925: the death of Sister Myrtle Burton was the first broken link in our chain.

March, 1925: a group of our members attended a meeting in Bremerton Masonic Temple and heard their first radio broadcast. The subject: "Free Masonry and America."

1926: Past Matrons and Past Patrons Night was observed. Philathea and Reliance Chapters became co-sponsors for Rainbow Assembly 12 of Bremerton.

1927: In December we moved to Steadfast Masonic Temple and gave a New Year's Eve dance.

January 13, 1928: Alma Gilman and Theodore Peterson were installed matron and patron. Miss Edna Hoopes was the first candidate initiated in our new home. Her mother, Amy C. Hoopes, our first worthy matron, presided in the East during the initiation.

1929: Our first annual Christmas dinner and party was held.

1935: Past Matron Lillie Card was appointed mother advisor of Rainbow Assembly 12.

1936: Past Matron Estelle Meredith was appointed grand representative of Kentucky and a reception was given in her honor.

February 1941: We lost Sister Amy C. Hoopes, the first worthy matron and mother-of-our-chapter, one loved and revered by all who knew her.

1942: Worthy Matron Neal Meredith was installed by her parents Nellie and Nels E. Peterson.

1943-1944: We contributed $189 to emergency war relief, sent baked foods to soldiers and gave $60 to the polio fund. We sewed for the Red Cross. Jobs Daughters Bethel 21 was organized. Past matron Lela Sutherland was the first guardian and Cleo Fellows the first queen.

1945: Rainbow Assembly 94 was instituted.

1946: Philathiette Club was organized. Life membership was presented to Nellie Peterson.

1948: We observed our 25th anniversary. Reliance Chapter presented a new memorial cloth and two veils for Adah. Our sister Marjorie Hammargren (matron of 1943) was appointed Grand Adah, and a reception was given for her.

1949: Worthy Matron and Worthy Patron Leta and Joe Yank presented our chapter a new Eastern Star banner made by Sister Leta Mae Sutherland.

BENEVOLENCES

During our first 10 years we contributed to the Washington Childrens' Home, Salvation Army, Flood Relief, Near East Relief and a few needy chapter members. Later we contributed funds to the Rose Mundt Education Fund, Masonic Home at Zenith and Christmas gifts to individual members.

Christmas dinners with a tree became an annual event. Gifts for members' children were provided.

Members' new babies received cups or baby spoons.

During our first several years we raised money through food sales, fairs, bazaars, raffles, card parties, dances, plays and musical entertainments.

Membership in 1984 was 206.

SOCIAL ORGANIZATIONS

The 500 Club
By Madora Hicks and Estelle Meredith

Manette's 500 Club— "500" was a variation of the card game bridge—was organized in 1920 with the following members: Tate and Alyce Peterson, Welby and Mabel Rea, Warren "Whitey" and Nellie White, Leonard and Lillie Card, Tom and Carrie Bright, Bernie and Myrtle Oliver, Hugo and Carrie Berglind and Fred and Madora Hicks. In 1921 Frank and Margaret Neill and then Clyde Meredith and Estelle Outland, Clyde's bride-to-be, became members. Later, George and Esther Frederickson and Ken and Dorothy Perry joined the club. Vic and Ruth (Margaret Neill's sister) Linstedt were substitutes. The group met monthly for 48 years.

Besides playing cards, the group celebrated milestones in the lives of its members.

When Clyde and Estelle Meredith returned from their honeymoon May 17, 1922, the club held a shivaree, centered at the home of James and Marinda Meredith, Clyde's parents. Dad Meredith brought about half a barrel of hard candy from his grocery store and placed it on the porch for the guests. Children beating on tin pans came to welcome the couple. The Abbotts, the Jack Martins, Keans, Huntons, Carlaws, Hoopeses, Nels Petersons, Malcolm Meredith and Neal Harrington were there. Scott Harrington handled the tin pans and serenading instruments up the street. Marinda Meredith and Nellie Peterson made punch. Clyde's cousin Joe Tennis, who had a bakery next to the grocery store, made pastries, cooking them in his brick fireplace.

Twenty-fifth wedding anniversaries were celebrated by the 500 Club. The town was made aware of Tate and Alyce Peterson's 25th anniversary in August of 1942 when they were brought across the Manette Bridge in a police motorcycle sidecar. Alyce had a lace-curtain cape streaming behind the vehicle. Appropriate siren sounds announced the event. Dinner was served later.

When a couple's first grandchild was born, "Grandfather's Day" became a ritual. The first grandfather of the group was Theo Peterson when Muriel and Edward Anthony presented him with a grandchild Edward Jr. in December of 1942. Fred Hicks was grandfather of the day when Madora Jane and Jerome Doherty gave him a granddaughter, Madora Jane II, born June 13, 1945, in Montclair, N.J. Clyde Meredith was honored when Richard Hladky Jr., son of Dick and Maryjayne Hladky, arrived in Bremerton in November of 1945.

Welby and Mabel Rea's cabin on Mount Rainier was the site for one party in August of 1922. The 500 Club stayed two nights, visited a glacier and enjoyed the mountain.

Fred and Madora Hicks invited the club to their home to celebrate New Year's Eve annually.

Masquerade dances were held in Martin's old store building on Shore Drive.

In the summer of 1927, Berglinds, Whites and Petersons hosted picnics at their summer cabins near Seabeck on Hood Canal. Hugo Berglind had a boat and took members cruising on the canal.

Meetings for the card parties were held in individual homes and in the hall—at one time known as Fellows' Hall—over Meredith's grocery store.

Madora Hicks was the only woman with a driver's license during the early years of the organization in the 1930s. She frequently provided transportation for other women. This was a period when most of the couples were starting their families. There was a particularly rough portion of road that became known as "miscarriage bump." Since Madora was a conservative driver there were never any problems when one of the expecting members was taken over this section of road.

Ken and Dorothy Perry joined the group in 1965. With a final meeting on New Year's Eve 1969 at Madora and Fred Hicks' home the 500 Club disbanded.

The 500 Club at Theo and Alyce Peterson's place on Hood Canal, circa 1927. Back row (from left), Bernie Oliver, Fred Hicks, Clyde Meredith, Frank Neill, Leonard Card. Front row, Madora Hicks, Alyce Peterson, Grace Carlaw, Estelle Meredith, Myrtle Oliver, Lillie Card, Margaret Neill. Theo Peterson took picture.
- Photo from Estelle Meredith

Star and Compass Bridge Club
By Estelle Meredith

The Star and Compass Bridge Club, another social organization that brought community members closer together, was formed by members of Steadfast Masonic Lodge and Philathea Chapter. This group met monthly.

Members included Bill and Jean Abbott, Louis and Edna Bailey, Lewis and Ella Bender, John and Grace Carlaw, Albert and Alma Gilman, Len and Hulda Hunton, Jack and Margaret Martin, Clyde and Estelle Meredith, Fred and Maria Paquette, Arthur and Georgia Personette and Nels and Nellie Peterson.

Manette Home Economics Club

Manette Home Economics Club members, pictured at Harriet Holden's home, May 1948. Back row (from left), _____, _____, Vera Hermanson, Gladys Solid, Edith Womac, Stella Fuller, Hazel Landon, Bertha Karst, Lillie Card. Front row, Grace Carlaw Hoopes, Ethel von Hoene.
-Photo from Grace Carlaw Hoopes' sister Wanda Holladay

YOUTH GROUPS

Boy Scouts
By Orville Schultz

Tillicum Troop 1
The minutes of the Bethany Baptist Church (which became the Manette Community Church) state that on February 10, 1915, Pastor Carpenter started a men's brotherhood in connection with the church work. The brotherhood voted to endorse and carry out a Boy Scout program.

According to the minutes, George Bledsoe was Scoutmaster and David Smith and Paul McHenry assistant Scoutmasters, and the troop was named Tillicum Troop 1. An entry of June 8, 1916, indicates that an effort was begun to raise money for camping equipment and uniforms. But no other reference appears until November 1925.

Troop 505

On November 18, 1925, the Manette Community Church applied for a charter to sponsor a Boy Scout troop. The application was signed by S.F. Dewar, D.A. Buchanan and James Rodger. The troop came into existence in 1926 with Albert O. Meicho as Scoutmaster and Samuel Sigurdsen Assistant Scoutmaster. They served in these postiions for the next 6 years.

Mr. Meicho was a conscientious Scoutmaster and a serious Sunday School teacher. He encouraged the Scouts to attend Sunday School classes.

Many of the meetings were held in an old shack at 1122 Perry Avenue, called Kravick Lodge, complete with a large yard and flag pole. Mr. Sigurdsen later purchased the proper-

AN EMINENT RECORD

During the years the troop has served over 600 boys for a total of over 1600 Scout years. Sixty boys of Troop 505 have become Eagle Scouts.

In 1938 Mr. Henry Hitt, the second Scoutmaster of Troop 505, trying to whet the appetites of his boys for a winter hike, told them that the troop had its first hike on New Year's Day of 1926. He invited them all to retrace it on New Year's Day of 1932, hoping it could become an annual affair. He referred to Scoutmaster Meicho's account of the 1926 trip:

It was a great day for us that New Year's Day, January 1, 1926, the day picked for our first hike. The sun was warm but still there was a tinge of coolness in the air to be just right for a stiff hike.

The boys assembled at the home of the Scoutmaster about 8 o'clock in the morning and our first hike began a short time later.

Striking out the county road [now Perry Avenue] going north we proceeded a few short blocks when Raymond Schoonover wished to go back and get his camera to take a few pictures. About another half mile

Manette Boy Scout Troop 505, March 17, 1928. Back row (from left), Assistant Scoutmaster Sam Sigurdson, Scoutmaster Albert Meicho. Third row, Elton Pentz, William Ziegler, Russell Elliott, Murville ""Bud'' Osborne, Howard Larson, Bruce Walker. Second row, Bill Schweer, Floyd Buchanan, Orville Schultz, Melvin Renn, George McKeown, Raymond Nosker. Front row, Raymond Cole, Glen Kidder, Ward Muller, James McCallum, George Personette, Roger Paquette, David Ammerman, William Enkeboll..
                                                                                                    - Photo from Orville Schultz

ty and built a home there.

The Scout Hall on East 14th Street was purchased in November of 1929. A stone fireplace was added in November 1931. The first fire in the fireplace was started by fire by friction on April 8, 1932, by Scout Clyde Nelson. Clyde was killed in World War II.

In 1950 men who were Troop 505 Scouts in 1935 held a reunion and opened a brass brick which they had imbedded in the Scout Hall fireplace. The mementos and pictures from it are in the church archives.

On February 8, 1976, George LeCompte, Scoutmaster, shared many of his troop experiences with members of Manette Community Church as the troop celebrated its golden anniversary: 1926-1976. Mr. Duncan Buchanan, the only living member of the original signers of the troop charter for the church, was present to be honored for his years of service to the troop and to the church.

July 31, 1976, a picnic was held at Jarstad Park at Gorst. Mr. Meicho, the first Scoutmaster, was present.

Manette Boy Scout hall west of 2130 East 14th Street, built in 1929. (1986 Photo).

out he caught up with us, and another half mile or so we turned to the east travelling for 6 or 7 blocks before going north again. We followed this road which led us into a patch of timber that shut out most all the sunlight.

For 15 or 20 minutes we stayed on the road, then came to a trail that some of the boys knew; therefore we took it until we came to a large rock, on the side of which we could climb, but on the other side was a drop of about 20 or 30 feet.

The boys began to gather wood and soon had a fire going full blast on the top of the rock where potatoes were roasted and weiners, bacon, eggs and meat were fast getting in the eatable stage.

After the rest of the meal of sandwiches, the boys began to gather licorice root that grew on the side of the rock, knocking it down with long sticks.

Raymond Schoonover got the idea of passing a rope around his body and having someone lower him over the side of the rock, but he was doomed to disappointment for Assistant Scoutmaster Sigurdson, who was on top at the time, refused to allow him to do so.

After a time the newness of gathering licorice root began to wear off and the day being still young we struck out on an exploring hike, retracing our steps back to the County Road. Once more we were going north, passing, at times, puddles of water that was frozen over. A skid road was left behind and at last we came to Johnson's ranch where we all enjoyed a big drink of well water.

The boys made lances out of straight branches of trees and amused themselves by throwing at targets.

Following another highway to the west they went over hill and dale, gulley and woods until the Silverdale road started them back to Manette. Along the road the different trees were named, until Mr. Sigurdson spotted an elder bush and he gave instructions in making pop guns. A half hour later all boys had pop guns of a variety of sizes and we proceeded east again.

It was getting late so when a half mile from home Mr. Waltenberg came along with his truck, all piled in.

Listed below are citizens who have helped support the troop for its 60 years. A roster of the boys who were members between 1926 and 1975 may be found in the Manette Community Church library.

CHURCH REPRESENTATIVE		SCOUTMASTER	
1926-36	John Carlaw	1926-29	Albert Meicho
1937-38	Paul McHenry	1932-34	Henry Hitt
1938-41	Leonard Card	1934-35	Richard Davidson
1942-44	Welby L. Rea	1935-36	Ward Muller
1945-46	William Filion	1936-37	K.L. Brookman
1947	L.W. Germaine	1938	Ward Muller
1948-49	Eugene Parkins	1940	Gideon Hermanson
1950	John Murray	1941-43	Kenneth Branch
1951-52	Lee Tennison	1944	Wayne Muller
1953	Irving C. Williams	1945-48	Howard Harrison
1954-57	Lee Tennison	1949	Norman Spruce
1958-59	Delbert Miles	1950	B.R. Middleton
1960	Harold Alfred	1951	W.H. Lester
1961	Delbert Miles	1952	William Junell
1962-64	Roy Etten	1953	Harvey Richstein
1965-66	Berger Jacobson	1954	William Junell
1967	George LeCompte	1955	Gene Davis
1968	Delbert Miles	1956	Dick Feek
1969-70	Monty Johnson	1957-58	Bruce Towne
1971	Herbert Alfred	1959	Palmer Hanson
1972-73	Clyde Cooper	1960-62	Orville Schultz
1974	George LeCompte	1963	Earl Schmauck
1975	Jack Hensley	1964-66	George LeCompte
1976	Joe Leaf	1967	George Yount
1977-82	Mary Hensley	1968-69	George LeCompte
1983-86	Jack Hensley	1970-74	Bernie Berkimer
1987	Steve Schultz	1975-79	George LeCompte
		1980-82	Jack Hensley
		1983	Doug Coglizer
		1984-86	William Schmitt
		1987	Ronald Langstaff

In 1986, three generations were registered with Troop 505: Orville Schultz, grandfather, Steven Schultz, father, and Kevin Schultz, son.

Explorer Scouts 505

Sponsor: American Legion Post 68
  Advisor: 1948-49 H.C. Corbin
  (In 1950 The Legion stopped sponsoring the program and the Explorer Scouts transferred to Troop 505.)

Sponsor: Manette Community Church
Advisor:

1952	Norman Bowers		
1953	Roy Williamson	1968-69	George LeCompte
1954-56	Carl Chamberlin	1970-74	Bernie Berkimer
1957-59	Don McCloud	1975-79	George LeCompte
1960	Norman Bowers	1980-82	Jack Hensley
1961-62	Jim Pruitt	1983	Doug Coglizer
1963-66	Orville Schultz	1984-86	William Schmitt
1967	Roy Etten	1987	Ronald Langstaff

Cub Scouts

(From the *Manette News-Letter* May 11, 1944.)
  NEW CUB PACK IS ORGANIZED FOR SHERIDAN PARK - VIEW RIDGE AREAS...Pack 518-C has just been organized under the sponsorship of the Sheridan Park Community Church.... Mr. Jacobson was elected chairman of the committee...J.B. Childress was chosen acting Cubmaster....

May 11, 1944, *Manette News-Letter* also reported:
  TWO NEW MANETTE CUBS RECEIVE BOBCAT PINS. Charter was presented to the Manette Cub pack last Friday.... Merle Frank, Cub commissioner for the Bremerton district, presented the charter to William Gaither, chairman of the pack's committee....

Two new Cubs received their Bobcat pins. They were Raymond Senn, son of Mr. and Mrs. Bud Senn, and Frank Jacobs, son of Mr. and Mrs. Frank Jacobs.

Eight boys received their Wolf badges,...James Callison, Lewis Morris, Robert Reddick, Richard Miller, Douglas Dakin, Lee Germaine, Mike Siegner and Monty Johnson.

Cubmaster [is] I.C. Williams.

Girl Scouts

Trillium Troop 1
By Anna Jo Harkins Atkinson

The first Girl Scout troop in the Manette area was Trillium Troop 1, and was started by Mrs. Clarence (Pearl) Welborn in 1924. I could hardly wait for my 10th birthday so I could join the "big girls." In the troop when I joined in 1926 were Betty Bender, Alice Fellows, Julia Nelson, Anna Parkins, Muriel Rodger, Mary Soyat, Elizabeth and Margaret von Hoene, Jewell Welborn, Doris Welborn and others. I was thrilled to have so many beautiful big sisters.

There was one other troop on the Bremerton side of the bay.

Our troop met in the basement of Lewis and Ella Bender's beautiful waterfront home. They graciously hosted many special fun parties for us. Kate Bender helped the girls learn knot tying.

As our troop grew we moved our meetings to the social hall above Clyde and Estelle Meredith's grocery store. Girls of my age I remember in our troop were Helen Akers, Dorothy Cole, Helga Enkeboll, Lois Harrison, Alice Holden, Helen Holden, Margaret Hoopes, Ruby Keil, Vera Lawrence, Jeane Martin, Dorothy Mey, Genevieve Nelson, Genevieve Painter, Bernice Pederson, Mary Personette, Mildred Ross, Ada and

Margie Schoonover, Tonie Soyat, Mildred Starevich, Dorothy Wall, Evelyn Waugh and Elsie Wilsen. There were others but 60 years later it's hard to remember.

Scouting taught us many things: reverence for God, country and flag; honesty, loyalty, truthfulness; a variety of home-making, home improvement and handcraft skills; gardening; knot-tying, hiking, fire-building, camping and swimming.

We enjoyed many nature hikes, beach parties and picnics. We camped at Island Lake, at Tracy's beach cabin on Hood Canal and on Sandy Point, next to the present Illahee State Park.

A CHOICE PLACE

Our favorite spot was Sandy Point, but we didn't reach it by the highway of today. We struggled over a trail through dense forest and undergrowth of salal, huckleberry, blackberry, nettles and devil's club. But the prize at the end was worth it.

There was a fresh-water spring that bubbled and gurgled all the time. This supplied us with ice-cold, pure drinking water.

Bedtime was always a hilarious time - invariably a giggling session. One night after we had sung "Taps" and Mom Welborn had finally quieted us down for the night, Julia Nelson, feigning sleep, said in a loud, drowsy voice, "Dad, turn the water off, it's keeping me awake." Of course that started the giggles all over again.

Camp food was always simple but abundant. A real treat around the campfire at night was "S'mores." We toasted marshmallows, put a square of Hershey bar on a graham cracker, the toasted marshmallow on top, another cracker, and m-m-good.

Mom Welborn was an excellent leader. She was patient, kind, loving and understanding, a real friend to every girl. We later elected to call her "Robin," but she and Mr. Welborn were always "Mom and Pop" to me, as their daughter Doris and I were real close friends.

Pop had a Model-T touring car to take us long distances to camp. How he crammed so many girls and all our camping gear in that old Ford I'll never know. He always had a cheery smile and many humorous stories and remarks to keep us laughing. He was never too busy to pack up and take a load of girls somewhere.

SERVICE

Our troop took part in community service projects. We would wait tables and wash dishes at church dinners, which were the focal points of social activity. We helped in area clean-ups and community celebrations. We took turns baby-sitting the Meicho children, Genevieve and Tom, so their parents could take part in Boy Scout and church choir activities.

My dad, Earl Harkins, trained our troop in marching - squads left, squads right - for weeks on Mother Bender's lawn. He shouted orders at us as if he were back in the army. We marched at the dedication of Camp Wesley Harris, and his weeks of threatening, shouting, and yes, cussing a little, paid off. We were a good-looking group of girls in our snappy green uniforms. He was proud of us.

I cannot remember the year our troop disbanded, but it was before we went into high school. With funds left over from our weekly dues, we purchased a pulpit Bible for Manette Community Church. That Bible was destroyed when the church burned in 1951. It was later replaced by all the former Girl Scouts that could be contacted after the new church was built.

I believe the next leader to form a troop was Mrs. Renus (Helen) Bender. For awhile I assisted her with the girls. That was a different side of the coin for me. It was then that I truly realized and appreciated what a tremendous gift Mom Welborn had given us in her time and leadership, along with three other dear ladies whom I remember helping us at various times: Mrs. William (Ethel) von Hoene, Mrs. Forrest (Dorothy) Cole and Mrs. Carl Pederson.

Before I married, the girls of the troop had a home-canned goods shower for me. No gifts were ever more appreciated. With all the canned fruit, vegetables, pickles, jams and jellies Helen and the girls brought, apples from two trees in the yard of the house on Sheridan Heights that we rented for $5 per month and ten 50-pound sacks of potatoes purchased for 29 cents a sack, we managed to survive our first winter. Those were Depression days, 1934, with not much cash or any jobs available.

Guess you'd say Girl Scouting got in my blood. When our little daughter came along, her first-grade teacher formed a Brownie troop and asked me to assist. As soon as she found out I was interested she promptly turned 27 little Brownies over to me. I had the troop for 3 years, then "flew" up with

Trillium Troop 1. Back row (from left), Vera Lawrence, Helga Enkeboll, Dorothy Mey, Toni Soyat, Ada Schoonover, Dorothy Cole, Mary Soyat, Martha Palmer, Anna Jo Harkins, Pearl Welborn (leader) and Jeane Martin. Front row, Lois Harrison, Doris Welborn, Betty Bender, Margaret Hoopes, Bernice Pederson, Mildred Starevich and Genevieve Painter.

my girls to Girl Scouting for 2 more years. Many were the headaches and problems, but fun too, as well as much satisfaction.

My girls also camped at Illahee State Park, but they missed half the fun. They slept in double bunks in a little cabin, cooked over a camp stove, took well-maintained trails to the beach, and had outhouses for rest stations.

When I was a girl we rolled up in blanket rolls under the trees—no sleeping bags then—built fires in pits on the beach to cook over, scrambled up and down the banks with never a trail, and hit the bushes for bathroom facilities.

It was a real joy to me to see a group of mischievous, giggling girls grow and mature with a promise of developing into fine young ladies. Having the troop was well worth the time and effort.

Troop 3
By Grace Jack Barlow

In 1933 our troop was started as one patrol of a Bremerton troop. We went to Bremerton once a month for the full troop meeting, but met in Manette the other weeks.

Soon there were enough girls for a full Manette troop and some Bremerton girls joined us. We became Troop 3 and met in Rea's recreation room. Christena Buchanan, later Mrs. Robert George, was elected scribe in April of 1938, shortly before the troop disbanded. Her secretary book with court of honor meetings—March 1936 to April 1938—is signed by secretaries Frances McKelvy, Frances Rea, Marion Wall and Christena Buchanan.

Members included June Martin, now Schweer; Jane Bender, now Heffner; Cherie Bright, now Baker; Jean Harrison, now Glude; Faith Christensen, now Glud; Frances Rea, now Weber. Anna Jo Harkins, now Atkinson; Betty Bender,

now Bounds; and Lois Harrison, now Williamson, helped with our troop hikes and at other times.

Our leaders were my mother, Grace Jack; Carrie Bright; Helen Bender; Mary Fellows; Mrs. Clyde.

Troop 4
By Maryjayne Meredith Hladky

Girl Scout Troop 4 was organized in 1935. Neal Meredith was leader and Hazel Callison was her assistant. Troop meetings were held weekly in the hall over Meredith's grocery store. Later Estelle Meredith became leader and Grace McNeill was assistant.

The troop enjoyed many camp-outs on Hood Canal, first at Malcolm and Neal Meredith's Hood Canal summer camp. There was a swimming area outlined with logs which Malcolm had installed and chained together for safety. Later the troop went to Mable Renn's camp on the north shore of Hood Canal.

Members included Bernice Jack, Marjorie Rea, Louise Hermanson, June Womac, Emmabelle Harrison, Genevieve Meicho, Goldie Lindsey, Doris Spencer, Lenora Alinder, Joyce Walsh, Peggy Bourgette, Mary Moses, Rowena Harkins, Jean Callison, Janis Kerr, Frances Hall, Joan Lindsey, Ruth Baker, Kathryn Alinder and Maryjayne Meredith.

Members of the troop still meet.

Several members of Girl Scout Troop 4 became members of a Girl Mariners' group in 1939. Marjorie Hammargren was leader and Edythe Renn was her assistant. Their activities were similar to those of the boy Sea Scouts. The mariners met at Clyde and Estelle Meredith's home and enjoyed outings at Renn's Hood Canal summer camp and on the Sea Scouts' boat.

Girl Scout Troop 3, 1934. Back row (standing, from left) Anna Starevich, Margaret Isard. Second row, Elsie Wheaton, Jane Bender, Clara McKelvey, Aletha Millikan, Evelyn Alinder, Eleanor Pidduck, Jewell Tenge, Jean Harrison, Faith Christensen, Joanne Gilman, June Martin. Front row, Grace Jack, Cherie Bright, Dora Myers, Jean Hendrickson, Elizabeth Myers, Frances Rea. Standing, Anna Jo Harkins, Betty Bender.

Manette Girl Scout Troop 4, 1935. Back row (from left), Hazel Callison (assistant Scout leader), Louise Hermanson, Neal Meredith (Scout leader), Genevieve Meicho, Doris Spencer. Second row, Jean Callison, Marjorie Rea, Ruth Baker, Emma Belle Harrison, Lenora Alinder. Front row, Joyce Walsh, Maryjayne Meredith, Kathryn Alinder, June Womac, Frances Hall, Goldie Lindsey.
                    - Photo from Jean Callison Jones

Chapter 10

RECREATION

ILLAHEE STATE PARK

Park Carved from Wilderness

(From the *Bremerton Sun*, January 27, 1939)

The Illahee State Park, number 53 in the state's fine parks system, was never dreamed, thought of or even considered a little more than five years ago. It just happened.

It came about from an area rugged in contour, with much of its original first-growth timber still standing and was turned from 13-1/2 acres of timber, undergrowth, vines, etc., that for years made most of the area hard for a person to travel through.

Fifty some years ago, this area was first logged by a pioneer in Kitsap County, August, the father of Nels Peterson, a retired navy yard workman and for years active in the affairs of EBIC.

Nels Peterson as a young man helped his dad with oxen log this rugged terrain—now developed into one of the state's prettiest parks.

A recent letter from W.S. Weigle, superintendent of state parks, commended EBIC, stating that it deserved all the credit for this beautiful park and its development the past year. However, EBIC would have never known of the area had it not been called to its attention by Walter J. Rue, former county commissioner of the district. He urged that the club appoint a committee to look the area over and suggested that if they thought such suitable for park purposes, he would lend his effort in having it made a county park—or that we might go farther and have the state purchase the area and make it a state park. He further advised, that the area had reverted to the county for back taxes and that it was soon to be sold, and if EBIC was interested in the purchase of the area to file a bid.

EBIC lost no time in appointing a committee to inspect the

Logging with oxen. Land that was to become Illahee State Park was logged this way in the late 1880s. This photograph was a possession of Nels Peterson [see PETERSON, NELS, family history], one of the loggers, and he is the man seated behind the oxteam. The driver is Peterson's brother-in-law, Alex Watt. Peterson logged at various locations in the county. Where this picture was taken is not certain, but it does represent an "Illahee-type" operation.

area and report favorably back to the club, asking that the committee be enlarged and that the state's park board be invited here to look over the area. The board came here, and soon afterward accepted the area into the state park system.

That was the start of the now beautiful Illahee State Park, which unofficially opened to public use last year—unofficial to the extent that after more development is made there, EBIC, through the state parks committee, plans a fitting dedication ceremony.

The First Caretakers

By Anna Jo Harkins Atkinson

Illahee State Park was opened in 1938. My father, Earl Henry Harkins, who had spearheaded the efforts of the East Bremerton Improvement Club (EBIC) to establish the park, set about to find a caretaker. No one was interested in the round-the-clock, 7-day-a-week job, 5 months of the year at $80 per month.

In 1942 Dad persuaded my husband Don Atkinson to take the job, suggesting he would be able to handle it since I could take charge during the day until Don could get there after serving his postal rural route.

We accepted reluctantly in 1942, more to please my dad than anything else, as we had just moved into the Womac house on Perry Avenue. We were in the process of getting a new household established and raising our family of three young children, one little Boston bull pup, Tippy, and one boarder—a young navy wife.

The park boasted one community kitchen, a few camping spaces with little individual fireplaces, one water-well with a creaking pump that you had to prime to get started, a few picnic tables and two outdoor privies—all of which had been built by the Work Progress Administration (WPA).

Living facilities consisted of a small one-room cabin with two built-in bunks and an old wood range, plus a large sleeping tent pitched on a wooden floor.

Our wages were paid from May 1 through September 30. Beginning May 1, as soon as I sent our two older children Bob and Frances off to school, I'd leave our baby David with Bernice, our boarder, and head for the park to cut grass, pile up brush and debris and burn it, clean the toilets and start to work on the trails to the beach.

Don came after finishing his mail route and we would cut wood from downed timber for the camp stoves. We didn't use

Illahee State Park entrance, 1938.
-Photo from Ed Fischer

high-powered chain saws but a 7-foot two-man cross-cut saw, only the man on the other end was a girl—me. That 7-foot saw now graces the wall of our family room as a reminder that it wasn't always so easy.

TRAILBUILDING

The trails to the beach had been there for sometime, but were in such bad shape they were nearly impassable. We dug them out with pick, shovel and lots of elbow grease, widened the trail and put in log steps wherever feasible. We bridged gullies and ravines so that access to the beach was a little easier. It was never easy at any time as the bank was very steep and it was a long way down to the beach, but a much longer way back to the top.

As soon as school was out in June, we packed up our family, our pup and our boarder and moved to the park for the summer months. The boarder, Bernice, slept in the cabin with our little son David. Don and I, Bob, Frances and the little pup Tippy slept in the tent. One night Tippy started to growl, then dashed outside barking savagely. All of a sudden the barking turned to ki-yiing and whimpering and the most atrocious odor pervaded the air. A skunk had gotten poor little Tip right between the eyes.

We had taken an old Hoosier kitchen cabinet out to store supplies in. There was not enough room in the cabin so we put it just outside the door. It was full of packaged beans, rice and macaroni in cellophane, packaged crackers and cookies, all of which we had to throw away. That cabinet was right in the line of fire and the varnish was peeled off from one side. Anything that was not sealed in tin or glass had to be disposed of. Our little dog that we loved so much just could not understand why no one wanted anything to do with him.

We built the first baseball field across the ravine from the kitchen that first summer. By main strength and awkwardness we erected some big logs to make the backstop. Lots of lively games were played there. That ball diamond is now a parking lot.

Wesley Jones was given a contract to build new picnic tables for $10 apiece. They were heavy, sturdy tables that could not easily be thrown over the cliff as several rowdy picnickers tried to do.

The camping spots were on the bank overlooking the water, just below the kitchen. One summer two companies of marines had training sessions there, each a week at a time.

The park hosted many picnics for various organizations, schools, churches, Sunday schools, military personnel, the sheriff's department, Camp Fire Girls and Girl and Boy Scouts. The Girl Scouts held day camp there during the summer months.

ROWDIES SUBDUED

A few patrons gave us problems. One Sunday three sailors and three girls arrived with beer. Don told them beer was illegal in state parks, but if they'd keep it out of sight he would let them keep it. After two or three beers they became a little noisy. Don told them to quiet down, but they just became progressively noisier. Don walked up to them and told them to leave. I had followed Don and as I passed the wood pile I picked up a double-bitted axe to take back to the cabin for the night.

One big, burly sailor said to Don, "You've bugged us all

Gunmounts at Illahee State Park entrance. The guns are a monument both by and to Earl H. Harkins, park founder, who died in 1950 while working to obtain them for the park. The plaque says: "Dedicated by a grateful community to the memory of EARL HENRY HARKINS, founder of Illahee State Park, in recognition of his constant labor in the preservation of American ideals." In photo (from left) are Frances, Robert and David Atkinson, children of Don and Anna Jo Atkinson and grandchildren of Earl and Etta Harkins.

day long and we've had enough. I'm going to take you apart." As he started for Don I stepped up beside Don and said, "Sailor, take one more step toward my husband and I'll split your head right down the middle!" I was swinging the axe back and forth. Needless to say, the sailor stopped in his tracks and said, "Lady, I'm leaving." And they did.

Don hired a bulldozer to come in and clean the beach. The big rocks were all scraped and piled together and we burned lots of brush, logs and trash on the beach. The dozer cost all of $100.

The second summer we were there the state paid me $2 a day to patrol the beach and watch the swimmers. Several times I had to haul children out that would slip and lose their footing and come up crying and gulping salt water, then go into a coughing spasm, but I never had to go after anyone who was in serious trouble.

It was hard work, but happy, healthful work. We enjoyed the summers we spent there, meeting and talking with people from all over the states and a good many foreign countries. At the end of the summer we always looked forward to our return home to Perry Avenue, especially the luxury of indoor plumbing, a bathtub and hot running water.

After 3 years at the park we could see that a full time caretaker was needed, because of the influx of people during World War II. There were no camping or usage fees then, and each summer, like Topsy, the park patronage "just growed," by leaps and bounds.

TRIBUTE TO EARL HARKINS

When I think of the hours, days and months Dad spent acquiring the park property, the endless trips he made to Olympia to work on legislators to provide funds for improvements to the park, the hours and hours of phone calls, the sleepless nights he spent worrying over some project or needed im-

provements, it makes me very proud, happy and humble to think we had a small part in the beginning of our beautiful Illahee State Park, now one of the more widely used parks in the state.

At the time of Dad's death in 1950 he had seen the road to the beach put in and blacktopped, a beach parking lot created and a few picnic spots with tables installed. He was working on obtaining a fishing pier. Dad never saw that dream realized, but he had put the wheels in motion. The pier stands there today, and the vast number of fishermen and boaters that use it are a great tribute to his efforts.

Dad was also working on a memorial at the entrance of the park commemorating the war efforts of our citizens and military personnel. He had acquired two big guns from the navy to be placed at the memorial. After his death the memorial was completed, and a community-wide memorial service was held at the park to dedicate his monument to the people, also a monument dedicated to him, Earl Henry Harkins, my father and founder of Illahee Park.

Love isn't love until it's given away, and give away Dad did. He loved his community, friends, neighbors and family and he worked endlessly and tirelessly without remuneration or any thought of thanks for the many improvements that made our little community of Manette such a special place. He would be happy indeed to see today the beautiful facility of Illahee Park and the endless streams of people that pass through its gates to camp, picnic, swim, greet friends and family or just sit and contemplate the beauty of the majestic trees that keep watch over Dad's labor of love.

PARK PERSONNEL

(The park's rangers are listed below. The names from 1942 to 1955 are from local sources; those after 1955 are from state records. A *Bremerton Sun* item of January 27, 1939, identifies

E.W. Granger as caretaker at that time, but no record that Granger was paid has been found. A number of EBIC members worked as volunteers in the park, clearing brush and building trails.)

Don and Anna Jo Atkinson	1942 to 1945
Elmer Ford	1945 to 1955
Leonard van Dolay	9-8-55 to 4-30-63
Bob Ensworth	5-6-63 to 9-9-63
Verne McCormick	9-10-63 to 5-19-64
Joe Anderson	6-15-64 to 12-31-66
Joe Skipper	3-21-67 to 10-09-67
Don Stalter	11-1-67 to 5-21-68
Bob Shiveley	6-1-68 to 9-30-68
Wallace Girton	10-1-68 to 6-15-71
Robert McCoy	6-28-71 to 4-25-75
Monty Fields	5-1-75 to 7-8-76
Richard Torset	8-3-76 to 7-29-77
Brian Carter	8-1-77 to 9-11-78
David Barton	12-1-78 to 6-18-80
Gailen Troxel	7-16-80 to 10-18-81
Norman Rockett	1981 ----

Elmer Ford, ranger at Illahee State Park from 1945 until 1955. Elmer's 10-year stint is the longest of any ranger to date.

STEPS IN PARK ACQUISITION

GRANTORS	DATE	ACRES
Kitsap County	6-13-34	13.32
John G. Fischer	3-21-45	45
Fred Jurges	2-25-46	11.25
Louisa Wagner	11-14-49	4.75
Allan W. Foss 1	1-27-51	.01
Louisa Wagner	1-15-52	.21
Dept. Pub. Lands	6-28-54	

SPORTS
By Berenice Bouchard Root

Baseball

During the early decades of the 20th century, interest in baseball was keen in Manette. The players, according to old-timers, "were better than the facilities."

The "ball park" was a weedy field at the northwest corner of today's Cascade Trail and Nipsic Avenue. Left field was fairly level but center and right fields sloped away so sharply that, as one infielder put it, "if the batter hit a long fly you couldn't see whether the outfielder caught it."

Various comments about baseball as played here in the 1920s have been heard in recent years from people who as children watched the contests in those days. Among the

Manette Baseball Team, 1920-1924. Back row, (from left), Richard "Red" Palmer, Ralph Baselt, Melvin "Babe" Johnson, Arne "Swede" Lee, _____, Bob Callison. Front row, Frank Ross, Earl Callison, _____, _____, _____, Pete Garinger, manager Sam Hall.

remarks have been these:

The games were played on Sunday afternoons.... The fans were numerous and vociferous. The plank seats would hold maybe 150, and were regularly well filled—men, wives and children.... They rooted loudly for the home team.... Fred Howerton [see HOWERTON, FREDERICK family history] added to the din by jangling a cowbell....

Balls fouled into the nearby woods were eagerly searched out by youngsters, who were rewarded for returning them. The reward was an ice cream cone, donated by Duncan S. "Slim" Aldrich, Manette businessman who had a tiny concessions stand alongside the backstop....

A batsman who could drive a ball across Cascade Trail in far left field was considered a slugger indeed.... First baseman Pete Garinger is said to have put one through a window in Constable A.C. Isard's house, nearly 100 feet beyond the playing field....

Garinger's fans included the numerous offspring of Mark and Grace Nelson, these children being nieces and nephews of his. They rooted for him with loud, plaintive calls of "C'mon, Uncle Pete!"—and Pete became "Uncle Pete" to all.

Expanding population eventually claimed the ball park for residential development, and today nice homes occupy the old playing field. Meanwhile, in the early 1930s, softball—a game that could be played in the comparatively small park available at the Manette Playfield—came to the community.

Softball

Softball was one of America's fastest growing amateur sports in the 1930s. The residents of Manette embraced the sport. The community became known as the birthplace of softball in Kitsap County.

The City of Bremerton purchased an acre from J.H. Martin in 1933 for a playfield and other recreational facilities after the purchase had been advocated by the EBIC. A Works Progress Administration (WPA) grant was obtained and the city supplied matching funds.

The EBIC sponsored teams for adults and young boys and girls alike.

Manette Playfield in the making, March 5, 1933.

Playfield backers. EBIC members who worked to develop the Manette Playfield are: Back row, (from left), Lloyd Solid, Henry Bubke, Ethel von Hoene, Isadora Beach, Frank Gillette, Flora Martin, Eugene Schweer. Front row, Earl Harkins, George Mitchell, Clyde Meredith, William von Hoene.

The EBIC men's softball team was organized in 1935 from players taken from four community league teams, Meredith's Red & White, Mitchell's Manette Foods, Martin's Price-Rite and Axel Jacobsen's General Garage. R.L. Callison, "father of softball in Kitsap County" managed the team for two seasons; then Axel Jacobsen became its engineer. The team had a long and glorious record, defeating teams in Bremerton, Kitsap County, the Olympic Peninsula and most of the State of Washington. In 1942 the team won the state championship, defeating Spokane in the final game, 3-2. This team was made up of players from Manette, Tracyton and Bremerton. Manette boys on this championship team were Erv, Alf and Svend Jensen, George Personette, Ray Forbes, Mack Brown, Earl Callison, Benny Murray Jr. and Archie Bouchard Jr., who captained the team.

GIRLS' TEAM

In 1938 Norman Noble and Sid Brune, WPA Manette Playfield instructors and coaches, organized a girls' softball team of girls living in the Manette area.

Games were played with other girls' teams from Bremerton (the Warren Avenue girls and Bremerton YMCA), Tracyton, Silverdale and Port Orchard.

The Manette girls developed into a strong team, beating all the local competition. Because of the team's successful winning season they entered the fourth annual Washington State Softball Championship Tournament at Sick's Stadium in Seattle August 26, 27, and 28 in 1938, staged by the *Seattle Post Intelligencer*.

Andrew G. Nelson, candidate for Kitsap County commissioner, financed the girls, paid the entry fee and provided uniforms. The team was made up of many fine local girls. However, one reason the team was so successful was the fine pitching of Opal Barrios, a recruit from Bremerton.

The Manette girls' softball team came through the tournament with the second place title.

In 1939 Norman Nobel and Glenn Kidder coached the girls, now not all from the Manette area. On their second trip to the state tournament, Mack Brown was the coach.

The Manette Lumber Company sponsored the team in

Manette Womens' Softball Team, 1938. Back row, from left, Opal Barrios, Alice Henning, Thelma Johnson, Dorothy Myers, coach Norman Noble, Marion Wall, coach Sidney Brune, Berenice Bouchard, Etta Kidder. Front row, Peggy Duddleston, Edith Henning, Polly Welch, Anna Starevich, Myrtle Forbes, Iris Senn.

Softball game at Manette Playfield, East 13th Street and Nipsic Avenue, mid-1930s.

1940. Again the team ended the season by entering the state tournament in Seattle. The team was co-managed by Ike Parker, Kink Muller and Sunny Simons.

As the community entered World War II, the girls' softball team developed into a Bremerton-based regional team, acquiring players from throughout Kitsap County.

BOYS' TEAMS

Manette also had two junior teams, the Slickerbills and the Hillbillies.

Ted Peterson recalls that the first meeting was held above Meredith's store and the teams were organized by the EBIC under the direction of Earl Harkins. Members of the Slickerbills lived near the water and those of the Hillbillies lived up the hill north of downtown.

The Hillbillies' team managers were Earl Callison, coach; Barrie Branch, manager, and Butch Hoffman, captain. The Slickerbills' coach was Bob Callison. Ed Forbes was manager

East Bremerton Improvement Club (EBIC) state champion softball team, 1942. Back row, (from left), Ben Murray, Mack Brown, Alfred Jensen, Erv Jensen, Svend Jensen, Dick Frees, Andy Forbes. Front row, Manager Axel "Jake" Jacobsen, Earl Callison, Archie Bouchard, John Pederson, Ray Forbes, Fred Wing.

and Jack Walsh captain. A flyer dated July 19, 1935, states that the Hillbillies flattened the Slickerbills in the last two games. Alfred Jensen of the Hillbillies was called "King of Swat." Other members were Riley Cole, Don Hilstad, Bob Baselt, D. Mottner, Jim Karst, W. Waltenburg, Jack Walsh, Bill Hall, B. Hoffman, J. Martin, B. Branch, Don Brown, D. Avery, Ed Forbes and Jim Avery. Members of the Slickerbills were Bill Bubke, Tom Pidduck, Douglas Brown, D. Johnson, Bud Senn, Glenn Forbes, Stan Solid, Bob Kennedy, Ted Peterson, J. Helmerson, Forrest Millikan, Wilbur Tenge, Kenneth Tenge, Ervin Nestor and Richard Paquette.

Four Stars

The Manette area produced many fine athletes over the years, men and women, who excelled in sports in high school and college and then continued on o be active in sports. Special mention should be made of Harold (Hal) Lee, Myrtle Forbes Kressin, Erv Jensen, and George Personette.

HAROLD "Hal" LEE was an outstanding basketball player at the University of Washington, three times earning All-Coast honors. In 1934 he won a place on the college All-America team. Harold played baseball at the U. of W. under Tubby Graves and was signed by the Yankees in 1937. When Pearl Harbor Day came he was playing AAA baseball in the Texas League. He spent 4 years in the army. After the war he became a prominent basketball referee in the Pacific Coast Conference and officiated at college games. He was inducted into Washington State's Basketball Hall of Fame in 1974.

Harold Lee.

MYRTLE FORBES KRESSIN was named to the Amateur Softball Association Northwest Region Hall of Fame in 1976. Myrtle began it all on Manette Playfield in the late 1930s. At age 11 in 1938 she appeared in her first state softball tournament.

She was active in softball and other women's athletics, including bowling and golf, in the Bremerton area for more than 30 years. When not playing softball she played AAU (Amateur Athletics Union) basketball and volleyball. For many years she also was a playfield instructor for the Bremerton Parks and Recreation Department. She was named "Man of the Year" by Kitsap Quarterbacks Club in 1956.

ERV JENSEN played softball from the years 1935 to 1954 and was an intimidating pitcher and hitter. He was named to the Amateur Softball Association Northwest Region Hall of

Myrtle.

Fame on Friday, July 29, 1983. Jensen started his softball career on the Manette playfield in the mid 1930s, playing for Manette Community League and East Bremerton Improvement Club (EBIC) teams.

Jensen made the all-regional team in 1944 as a pitcher for Bremerton's Tony's, the Washington State champs, who finished third in the regionals at Sick's Seattle Stadium that year. He also made the all-regional team as an outfielder in 1950, playing for Spokane's Orphans. Jensen was a pickup player that year.

A player must have achieved all-regional honors in at least two tournaments to be considered for election to the Hall of Fame.

GEORGE PERSONETTE was one of Manette's outstanding athletes during the 30s.

A swimming club was formed in Bremerton early in 1931. By June of that year, George had established himself as the outstanding junior boy swimmer in the Puget Sound area after meets with Seattle's Washington Athletic Club and Crystal Pool Club. The _Bremerton News-Searchlight_ of June 17, 1931, stated, "As usual George Personette stole the

George Personette,

lion's share of the thunder as far as Bremerton was concerned. George is just about the sweetest junior freestyle performer you will find in the state—and he's getting better all the time...first place in the junior boys 50 and 100...directly responsible for the junior boys relay victory, starting on the last lap with about a six foot handicap and passing his man to beat him by about two feet. It was a chills and fever exhibition." And he did get better. This was the first of many similar write-ups which saw him swimming sprints and anchoring the relay teams for the Bremerton Club and later Crystal Pool Club.

Summers he competed in water carnivals in the Northwest and Canada, collecting innumerable ribbons, medals, and trophies.

George was a very strong swimmer who went on to become a member of University of Washington swim team and do very well.

His career culminated in the free style championship of the northern division of the Pacific Coast Conference in the late 1930s while attending the University of Washington.

FOOTBALL TEAM TO HAWAII

Several members of the Bremerton High School Washington Cross-State League football champions of 1935 were from Manette and accompanied the team on a memorable trip to Honolulu, Hawaii, in late 1936 to play McKinley High School. (McKinley won, 14 to 13.)

The Last Swim
By Roger Paquette

It was a hot July day in 1931. A Bremerton city policeman had climbed about half way down the steep bank to the bay at a location which, in today's addressing system, would be about 1931 Wheaton Way. He watched a dozen or so nude teen and pre-teen boys swimming or cavorting on the beach or basking in the sun. Then he yelled out, "That's it! You're all under arrest! Get your clothes on and get up this bank! You're going to jail!"

We were startled, but he didn't have to tell us what the charge was. (He didn't read us our rights.)

We knew there had been complaints lately. One man had come and told us how we disgusted him - he'd brought his

family down to the Sandbanks for a day's picnic and we'd spoiled their whole day. The story was often told (and still is) of the complaint by the woman across the bay from our swimming hole about our dishabille. When asked how she could identify our apparel from such a distance, she brought out her husband's telescope.

Once we had thrown a scare into the people at the city park. It was a slack low tide and we had a rowboat. Three or four of the boys decided it would be a good time to swim across the bay. When they got back one of the boys, George Personette, said "The people at the park had a worried look on their faces when we walked out of the water over there." No problem - the boys had modestly worn swim suits on that occasion. (George later went on to be the sprint swim champ of the Pacific Northwest and won letters at the University of Washington.)

And Charlie Young, the local marshal, had pleaded with us in a very reasonable way to wear something, anything.

Today, looking at the high-bank waterfront below Bremerton Gardens and on north, it is not easy to understand the nomenclature, "Sandbanks". But before the massive deposit of riprap below the banks up and down the beach, each winter's storm resulted in the sloughing off of large amounts of sand from the banks onto the beach. This resulted in areas of nice tan-colored sand beaches that on a hot summer day provided surcease from the icy waters of Washington Narrows. You could roll around in it and be warm and dry in seconds. Rolling around on hot sand in a bathing suit is a comparatively messy proposition, but in the buff you don't have that darn wet sandy suit to contend with.

The riprap served the purpose of the owners of the property by slowing down the sloughing which had made them understandably nervous. But it did ruin the beaches, and the subsequent growth, planted or natural, has covered the banks with a green coat and the "Sandbanks" have virtually disappeared.

I guess the uniformed officer awed us because we all dressed and scrambled up the bank to the top. Construction on the link between the Manette Bridge and the Brownsville Highway (now Wheaton Way) was in progress, so we were all herded onto a dump truck and taken across the bridge to the jailhouse. (Not all. One of the boys, who was nicknamed "Fat," was late making the climb, not an easy one, and missed

Sandbanks, 1941. Eastpark and Bremerton Gardens are visible.

connection with the truck. We hollered, but the driver wouldn't stop. I can still see Fat running futilely behind us.) We were booked and locked up for a half hour or so, then given a lecture by the sergeant.

George Baker was at the toll booth when I came back. I told him I was on city business and didn't have to pay toll. "You dumbhead," he said, "You were outside the city limits. He had no right to arrest you." He was right, of course, and I've often wondered what the marshal would have done if we had refused to come up the bank. I don't think he wanted to come the rest of the way down. It was steep and tricky.

That was the last swim. The bridge and the highway and the development hastened the demise of the swimming hole anyway.

My first swim was in the latter part of May in 1926 on a nice day after school. Somebody said, "Come on, we're going down to the Sandbanks." I didn't know what he was talking about but I wasn't going to miss out. I found out we were going swimming. "But I don't have a suit." They all laughed. It was a delightful place for me for five summers.

Ferris Buchanan took me down there the other day and showed me the rock we used to dive off at high tide. Somebody had put some kind of a survey marker on it. It was a distinctive rock. Three of us could stand on it at once. But the beach had risen since then, and where the beach had been about 4 feet below the top of the rock on the water side, it is now barely a foot below it.

There IS a small patch of sand near it. Maybe I'll give it a try this summer.

DANCING

(Excerpts from the *Bremerton Searchlight*, 1902.)

The dance given in the old mill at Decatur Thursday evening by the Decatur Amusement Club was a complete success. Large numbers attended from Charleston, Bremerton and Tracyton, about 75 couples in all being in attendance. The club will begin work at once laying a matched floor over the entire floor space with a banquet room in connection and will give regular by-weekly dances which will undoubtedly prove very popular.

Of the many enjoyable occasions this season on Port Orchard Bay the dance given at the old Decatur mill last evening will be rememebered as one of the most successful and enjoyable in every way. Fully ninety couples were present from the three navy yard towns, Decatur and Tracyton. The new pavilion is large and splendidly arranged for dancing parties, with dressing, banquet and smoking rooms, and can comfortably accommodate a much larger number than were present last evening, the floor space of the hall alone being 40x111 feet. Under the present management and with the pains being taken to provide a jolly time and to debar any unpleasant feature the Decatur pavilion will certainly become exceedingly popular both for dancing parties and theatricals, the hall being provided with a commodious stage and splendid curtains and stage fixtures. The music by Messrs. McClelland and Donovan.

The next event of the Decatur Amusement Club will be a calico ball on Wednesday, August 27, in the old mill pavilion. Every lady is supposed to bring a sample ribbon of the dress or waist she wears. These will be placed together and drawn by the gentlemen, the wearer of the dress matching the sample being the partner.

Chapter 11

NEIGHBORHOODS

ENETAI BEACH

By Eleanor Carlson Harrington

[Manette's history is closely tied to its wealth of waterfront. In every stretch of shoreline rests some old-timer's nostalgia. Here is one sample.]

It was a privilege to grow up on Enetai Beach, that portion of waterfront from Bremerton city limits to Enetai Point. Platted in 1892 as McTeigh's Garden Tracts, it was first settled by Jens and Minnie Jacobsen in 1899, John and Ellen Carlson in 1902 and Chris and Valborg Jensen in 1907.

Enetai proper, which extended from Hazel Gillespie's north to the Manson Backus property, was a fascinating "off limits" area to ordinary beachcombers, since it was owned by several well-to-do families of Seattle for their summer homes. South of Hazel Gillespie's was the Enetai gate, which separated the "off limits" area from the rest of the beach.

My acquaintance with Enetai was limited to accompanying my aunt and brothers when they walked to the Enetai dock on a Sunday night to take the *F.G. Reeve* back to Seattle. The trail passed the imposing houses of the Keils and Croxtons and crossed over McMicken Creek bridge past the little golf course and tennis court. When wild roses were in bloom the fragrance was unforgettable. The dock itself was fascinating with a little waiting room at the end and an attached open boat house on the beach in which were stored canoes, supplies and Ruth Wagner's rowboat. We admired the bravery and fortitude of Miss Wagner, for she usually stayed alone in a little tent house on Sandy Point, getting there by rowboat.

Of a more exciting nature were the visits to Enetai of the yacht *Lotus*, which belonged to Maurice McMicken. Rumor had it that its luxurious furnishings included a piano, and since Mr. McMicken was partial to Enetai water he had a pipe run the length of the dock with which to fill the water tanks.

Mr. Croxton, in knickers, lent atmosphere to the five-hole golf course. The Croxtons had a beautiful daughter, Rejene, and a son Ken. Ken had sailed in the merchant marine and his language would sometimes get very salty. He was a dedicated one-man patrol who would challenge anyone who approached, especially at night, much to my surprise once when I took a stroll with a friend.

Ray Palmer Tracy was a colorful, unforgettable character who lived in the Hawley house in the winters. He had been a major in the army in World War I. A prolific pulp writer, he was very proud of having had some of his work published in the Saturday Evening Post. He had a wonderful sense of

Lotus. -Photo from Curtiss Gruye

humor and often spoke of a fiancee back east but he remained a bachelor as long as we knew him.

My brother Clarence Carlson must have been one of the original joggers, for he made so many trips back and forth to Enetai while doing odd jobs and caretaking that he ran rather than walked to save time. One winter he worked for Miss Catherine Winn at the Deep Forest Inn. Since she planned to spend the Christmas season in Seattle she let "Clare" take her radio for a couple of weeks. We didn't have a radio at that time and we made the wonderful discovery of the Hit Parade, Comedy Hours, Opera at the Met and Midnight Mass on Christmas Eve.

In a letter about Enetai John Rupp tells of a barge full of firewood overturning and everyone scrambling to pick the wood up. Drifts of wood were high priority. After a drift on a high tide, whatever else you were doing was postponed until every piece of wood on your beach had been retrieved. Even for those who had other means of heating, driftwood meant beach fires on a summer's night.

A favorite walk was to Enetai Point, where there was the mouth of the creek to explore, and clams to dig when the tide was out. You could see the huge pile of rocks which as unwanted ballast had been thrown off the sailing ships that came to the Port Orchard mill years before. They were visible at low tide. Further offshore, a big kelp bed that had formed around more of the ballast made for wonderful rock-cod fishing.

Years ago smelt fishermen would set their nets along the water's edge. It wasn't long before neighbors were there with pails and dishpans. You couldn't get fish fresher than that, and the fishermen were generous.

Pods of blackfish or killer whales would occasionally come through the narrows and follow the ferry lanes. In the daytime you would wait for the huge dorsal fins to show out of the water, and at night you could tell their presence by the sound of their blowing. Once in a while one would jump completely out of the water and come down with a loud splash. The whales did not always follow the same course. Once some girls were swimming when a pod appeared suddenly about 200 yards from shore. When the girls saw those fins their swim became the fastest one on record.

Sailing ships' ballast. Still to be seen on the beach at Enetai are these rocks dumped from ships calling at the Port Orchard Mill for lumber. Today's homes in background are those (from left) of Sumner Orr Jr., Glen Jurges and Julius Templeton.

Memories of many kinds of boats come to mind. During World War II the battleships and destroyers were painted in mottled patterns designed to make them disappear into the horizon. There were little steam launches that went back and forth between Keyport and the navy yard, and often big open boats, rowed by young sailors, would go by. An officer sat in the stern.

The ferries most remembered were the *F.G. Reeve*, which made stops at Enetai and at Waterman across the bay; the *Chickaree*, a long, narrow boat which went past morning and night from Bainbridge Island to Bremerton; the *Chippewa*, infamous for its big waves which washed out bulkheads and set rowboats adrift, and of course the *Kalakala*, with its unusual shape and silver color, a unique tourist attraction.

Freight boats and tugboats plied the Sound and a sight to see were the Navy's ocean-going tugboats the *Pawtucket* and the *Sodeoma* with "bones in their teeth" a term to describe the wall of white foam made as their bows pushed through the water.

Not all tugs stayed on course, either. Early one morning my husband Scott woke to the labored sound of a boat engine going into forward and then into reverse gear. When he went to check out the situation he saw a tow tug stuck on the beach just past our dock. He shouted inquiries to the man on board. He was ignored, however, while the powerful propeller continued to dig deeper and deeper into the beach around the piling. It took a lot of convincing with the tug company to come to terms on repairs. The pilot had not entered his mishap into the log book.

CHANGING SCENE

Reminiscing about the location of different houses reminds one of many incidents concerning the different people who have lived in them. It covers a lot of time periods, too, World War I, the Depression and World War II up to the present.

South of Hazel Gillespie's where the Enetai gate was located was a little cabin high on the hill which belonged to people from Seattle named Brandt. On their beach was an old gnarled madrona tree with some big limbs which hung over the beach and over the water at high tide. Once Mildred Ross, who lived in Manette, and my sister Margaret Carlson climbed the tree late in the afternoon and didn't check the tide. Milly was frozen to the spot when she looked down into the water. The man delivering groceries came along at the right time and came to their rescue.

In the late 30s Mrs. Aldrich bought the Owens house and lived there until her daughter Evelyn's family, the Walkers, came during World War II. When it came time for them to move they had all their belongings carried up the steep trail but were at an impasse about the piano. My husband Scott came up with a solution. He had a 13-1/2 foot boat in which he had every confidence. Much to everyone's amazement the piano made the trip on the bow of the boat to our place, where it was loaded on a truck to go up the road. Several bets had been placed that night, waiting to see a piano plunge into the bay. The Owens/Aldrich house is now owned by Van Zantens.

Next in line was the summer house which belonged to the Wall family of Manette. Gertrude Wall Carr and Frank Carr lived there before moving to Seattle. Hap and Don Edson lived there during World War II. The next owners, Bruce and Beverly Connally, made an unsuccessful attempt to put a road down the hill. The cottage burned not long ago, after having been rented periodically. The original house had a pump in the sink of the kitchen. The beach house remains unique today for the two big rocks perched high there, as though mysteriously placed by some giant of long ago.

The Solibakke house was long and slender and changed hands many times. The Gallehers enlarged it, followed by the Robisons, who were a vital part of beach activities, then Tom Rupp, who once spent summers at Enetai. He pursued his dream of building a sailboat until his untimely death. Now the Fred Smiths are the owners.

For a long time the Frank Wolfrom land remained vacant except for summer tents. Around 1930 it was bought by George Frederickson and George Giblett and each built a house. The Fredericksons had no children but were loved by the Gallehers and Gibletts. Esther Frederickson was famous for her cookies, cakes, you name it! George Giblett served on the Bremerton school board for many years. A man of strong opinions, he often stated that the day his wife Bea got a job was the day he was quitting. Bea was a capable and witty match for him. Today these houses are owned by two good friends, the Mike McKnights and the Ted Berneys.

Before the McKnights had the Frederickson house, a renter decided to anchor a buoy out front for his boat. On a hot summer day when all the neighbors were out in force watching him, he loaded anchor and buoy in a rowboat, and chose an appropriate spot. Much to his chagrin and the neighbors' amusement, anchor, buoy, boat and occupant plunged into several feet of water. Brock Robison rowed to his rescue. The boat had swamped when the gear was unloaded.

My grandfather, O.E. Cooley, was one of the earliest residents of the beach and he shared his place with his daughter Ellen and her husband John Carlson and their children. After grandpa's death the Carlsons moved from Tacoma and lived in the beach home during the Depression. It was known as "Sunshine Beach."

Later the Duffs bought it, sight unseen, while still in Texas. The Duffs came from Texas and were not used to the ferries or prepared for the waves they made. Their little girl was floating face down out in the water when Bea Giblett jumped in and pulled her out. After the war the "Sunshine Beach" house sold to Henry and Reta Short. The Shorts fit into the beach scene with informal grace, turned their big yard into a playfield, over which Reta watched with a careful eye. Sometimes the relaxed atmosphere left situations that were difficult to explain, such as the time a young naval officer and his wife came to call and found the next-door neighbor asleep on the couch. He got up with a stretch and a "see you tomorrow," but no explanation. Reta didn't offer one either.

Bruno and Pearl Lund owned the next piece of property. Their friends and neighbors helped them build a little house on the north side for Pearl's Grandma and Grandpa Walker. Part of it was a little store in which the Walkers carried a few staples, pop and candy. Clyde Meredith sold him groceries at cost. It proved to be popular that far from town. Pearl and Bruno had no children but were friends to young and old. Later they sold the Walker house to my husband Scott Harrington and me. Not long afterwards we built a road down the hill, making the beach more accessible for light and phone service, moving and other emergencies. Our son Scotty Jr. was an avid beachcomber and in his teen years, with the help of some of his friends, built a dock out front. Marge and Don Reese own the Lund house now and have made it much bigger.

The Schultzes came around the first World War. Bea was a lovely, gracious lady and Bill had a quiet twinkle in his eye that made you check twice to see if he was laughing with you. In 1940 they built a new house on the hill. Today his son Orville with his wife Virginia live in the original beach home. The Schultz property has the distinction of remaining in one family.

The Dan Salt house of 1918 was one to be remembered for its French doors and long open pillared porch. The Roche Davisons and "Grandpa" Thermon occupied it after the Salts and in the 1920s the Akers family moved there. They had several very pretty girls and two boys. They also had a dory in which the kids spent hours at a time on the water. Frank, the youngest, gave my brother Bob some banty chickens but kept two white leghorn hens and a rooster for himself. Since they were not fenced they sometimes wandered back and forth. Once one of the white hens stayed too long with the banties and when she went home the rooster thrashed her soundly for her philandering and wouldn't take her back.

When Edith Gideon bought the property in 1950 she replaced the old house with a modern one.

Bob and Ethel Lowden had come from Alaska. They had no children of their own but had a lot of rapport with the children on the beach. Bob had the welcome habit of producing candy bars out of nowhere and Ethel had much tact with teenagers. Their house passed to Charles Passe, the Al Petersons, and now Jim Streutker.

The Emil Olsens were next in line with two girls, Bonnie and Billie. Cecil and Esther Owens then lived there and were both active in Veterans' affairs. No Memorial Day went by without Esther making her rounds with an abundance of the familiar poppies. Today the property is owned by Bud and Kathleen Fisher.

While the Jensens lived on the beach our families became fast friends, for the Jensens and Carlsons had children of the same ages for a "one on one" contact. When the Jensens moved up to Trenton Avenue the Charles Fredericksons moved into the house and raised beans and strawberries for market. When the picking was done "Aunt" Emma Fredrickson would serve the pickers sandwiches, lemonade and chocolate cake. This area was known as the "Cherry Hill Poultry Farm" when owned by Chris Jensen. Don Young owned this home for many years and completely remodeled it; it is now owned by James Burns.

Walter and Elsie LeCompte bought the next home—the Dan O'Neil house—and have lived there for many years. On the other side was the McGovern house; the Tom Rosebraughs live there now. Next came the Jacobsen property. South of the Jacobsen home Len and Hulda Hunton lived with sons Dick and Lendall Jr., who recalls finding Indian beads that had been washed out of the ground by the little creek coming down from Jacobsen's Canyon. This house was owned by two generations of Womacs, Jethro and Ted. Neil Harrington Fort is the current owner.

Jacobsen Boulevard was named for Jens Jacobsen, one of the original pioneers, well known for his wonderful garden produce. Fred, the oldest boy, had a disability from the first World War. He loved classical music, was very knowledgeable about it and had a large library of records. Son Axel owned the General Garage in Manette, and Olav, the youngest son, had a career in the navy yard. The Jacobsens had a milk cow which played a major part in my first day at school. Excited and eager I went with my brothers and sister to school. The first grade got out early so I confidently started home. Halfway down the trail through Jacobsen's canyon I saw this monster. The cow had moved up close to the fence. Its eyes were as big as saucers. Somehow I never noticed the fence but ran screaming back toward school. Soon heads were popping out of doors to see what murder was being committed.

Neighbors were relieved but not too sympathetic and while I tried to figure out what to do next, Orville Schultz came down the road. It was his first day at school, too. Unperturbed, he took me home by another route. His scouting tendencies of looking out for others had already begun to surface. He later became leader of a Boy Scout troop and worked in scouting for many years.

When circumstances have made it necessary to leave the beach there is always a tug pulling you back, a feeling shared by many. One day this feeling expressed itself in the following poem:

THE BEACH AND I

I walk the shores of the sea
and tales of the past echo to me.
Have you heard the songs of the waves
as they lightly tap the shore?
Like murmuring voices they rise and fall,
relating forever in dulcet tones
all that took place and more.
I often seek solace of the beach,
restlessly, crunching rocks rolled smooth
by the rhythm of many tides.
As footsteps harmonize with ebb and flow
all restless feelings gradually subside.
My eyes are fascinated once again
with medley of colors, of stones
sparkling when wet by water's edge
muted in shade on higher ground.
Gulls circle overhead watching intently
for gestures of proffered fare.
Their plaintive cries and raucous calls
Lend strange comfort to one in need.
Memories of loved ones and days long ago
rise to be sorted and blended
with beach, sea and sky--
once again, happy am I!

ENETAI

By Eleanor Carlson Harrington
and Orville Schultz

In 1876 the Port Blakely Mill Company purchased Government Lots 3 and 4, Section 7, of Colman and Glidden mill town at what today is called Enetai.

[Enetai was originally called "Enetai Beach." Today "Enetai Beach" generally means the stretch of waterfront running from Enetai Point south to approximately the Bremerton city limits, and Enetai lies north of Enetai Beach.]

The Territory of Washington gave a tax deed to Joseph McCarroghee on August 16, 1884, for Government Lots 3 and 4. The Port Orchard mill site had been on Lot 4 on the north side of Enetai Creek, also known as McMicken Creek.

This area extended from the "Enetai gate" south of Hazel Gillespie's home at 1926 Jacobsen Boulevard north to the Manson Backus property.

On April 3, 1895, Maurice McMicken, acting in the name of himself, Abraham Engle, Alexander Stewart and Herbert McMicken, purchased Lots 3 and 4 from McCarroghee for $500, a considerable amount at the time, since money was not available following the Panic of 1893. It was at this time that they named this property "Enetai."

In 1906, April 17, Maurice McMicken sold the land south of the creek to Thomas M. Green. Green built a house for himself on the northern half around 1910. He then sold the south half to Edward Garrett, who built a house similar in style and size. Green lived there until 1918, when he sold to Alvyn Croxton, who was Bremerton's first mayor. Garrett sold to

Ernie Keil. In December of 1953, Al and Lucille Love purchased the Garrett-Keil house.

The four original owners were left with the remainder of Lots 3 and 4. A deed registered September 25, 1907, showed that they had it surveyed and subdivided. They kept in common all the back property, the Port Orchard mill site just north of the creek, the golf course and the tennis court. The rest they divided into four tracts, each one over 400 feet. Number 1 on the north went to Engle, and 3 and 2 in the middle were shared by the McMickens.

A dock was built by 1906 on the McMicken tract, and this brought steamboat services to Enetai, notably the *F.G. Reeve* with one round trip each day.

Thus Enetai became the background for an era of gracious living for these families and their guests. Maurice McMicken was the spearhead for the community but he was not there as often as the others. He chose rather to steam into Enetai waters on his yacht *Lotus*. On the other hand, Herbert McMicken retired and lived in Enetai permanently. Their grandchildren Loman Tibbals and his sister Nannette still own a portion of the original tract. They have early pictures of the tent houses in which the families lived before homes were built.

With the exception of Croxtons and Keils who were just south of the creek, the residents of Enetai remained by themselves with little contact with local people. They did hire Mr. Creiger and Clarence Carlson for work to be done and bought fresh vegetables from J.P. Jacobsen.

Over the years they established traditions such as opening the season each spring. Rejene Croxton and Hazel Gillespie observed this ritual as long as Rejene lived there. They would decorate their canoes with crepe paper, flowers and lights and paddle along the shore.

The first tract to be divided was Lot 4, belonging to Stewart. He sold to a Seattle lawyer, James A. Kerr. Prior to 1919 he had sold the north part to A.L. Hawley. Mrs. Hawley was Mrs. Ostrander's sister, and the Ostranders, as early as 1915, had been given permission to place a summer house on the tract belonging to Maurice McMicken. The Hawley house was a big green one with two stories which could accommodate many guests.

When this house was inherited in later years, their son, Dr. Sydney Hawley, sold it to the Ostrander children, who replaced it with a modern house designed to be shared by all four with an individual wing for each family. It is referred to as the House of BLOW, each letter for the last names of Ballinger, Langdon, Ostrander and Wright.

On the south side of Tract 4, Kerr built a new home which he sold to Ella Newton. She never became very active in the community. In 1929 she divided her portion again, selling the part adjacent to the tennis court to Harry L. Adams. By 1930, Alfred J. Schweppe had bought the Kerr house and 145 feet of property from Mrs. Newton. Kerr sold to Howard Bechtel, who was there in the late 1930s. Bechtel's son George, being an entrepreneur, brought several rental houses in by barge.

In 1919 Tract 1 had two houses. The Engles lived in the bigger one on the south. In the late 1920s they sold it to a Miss Catherine Winn, who converted it to the "Deep Forest Inn" and opened it to paying guests. Today it is owned by Hank and Marie Blass. Hank is a retired art teacher from Olympic College. The smaller house was sold to Harry Peterson some time around World War II.

The two McMicken tracts, 2 and 3, did not change hands

until April 5, 1925, when Maurice McMicken sold Tract 3 to Otto Rupp. When the property was owned jointly by the two Mc-Micken brothers it is presumed that there was one tax statement. By some arrangement Rupp continued to pay the taxes. When Maud Tibbals inherited Tract 2 she reimbursed Otto Rupp by deeding him 30 feet of property. She sold 100 feet to a Mr. Courtright. This 100 feet later became the Lowell Dixon place. By 1943, Maud sold another 117 feet to George Morton. Loman Tibbals and his sister still own the remaining 190 feet.

Just north of Tract 1, now owned by Petersons, is the 300 feet called the Manson Backus place. It had no house, but there was an old or-

Home occupied by the Engles in 1919. In 1920 Engles sold to Catherine Winn, who converted it to "Deep Forest Inn." Occupied today by Henry Blass and his wife Maria.

chard, and a bulkhead on the beach. Backus' son, Leroy Backus, owned property just north of it. He had a house as well as an overflow creek from the Enetai water system. When the house burned between 1928 and 1930, Leroy Backus sold to Mr. Sutton, a grain merchant of Seattle. He barged in a home for himself and his son.

North of Leroy Backus was located the William Bremer property. This house was set back about 150 feet on a gentle slope. It contained the spring of the water supply for Enetai. John and Ed Bremer lived there as small boys. This property was sold to Leisers and then to Ben Cheney of Tacoma.

The Collins place was next and then Ruth Wagner's at Sandy Point. The only access she had was by rowboat. Her property abuts Illahee State Park.

For many years transportation to Enetai was either by the *F.G. Reeve*, which made a round trip daily from Silverdale to Seattle, making one of its stops at Enetai dock; or if passengers came by ferry to Bremerton and were there by 5:15 p.m., they could take the *Chickaree*, which would stop at the dock. Otherwise they would walk from Manette along the road following the waterfront that at that time was open as far as the Enetai gate. A number of residents began to block access to this road for a number of reasons—such as wishing to preserve their lawns. In the early 1930s the city and county were forced to put in a road along the top of the hill which went as far as today's Cascade Trail. This is Jacobsen Boulevard, named for the early settler, Jens P. Jacobsen, who settled along the beach around 1899. The Enetai community then continued this road on a private basis across the Keil and Croxton properties and some land which Schweppe bought from Jensen in order to cross the creek. They extended this road through the back country and it is still a private road.

The dock was dismantled in the 1960s for safety reasons. The gate which protected the privacy of the area is gone. The community still functions as a unit in many ways, to maintain the road and for adequate water service.

The property held in common has all been traded or sold to accommodate the influx of new people during World War II

and the years following. Enetai proper now remains mostly in the memory of those still residing on Enetai Beach—a continuation of the beach story.

EXCERPTS FROM MEMORIES OF JOHN N. RUPP

Dad and Mother bought...property from Mr. McMicken on April 25, 1925.... the house was there before that. I know it was there in 1919, the first summer that we went to Enetai and rented the "red-roof" cottage.

Herbert McMicken...was a full-time Enetai resident. I think...he had been in the real estate business in Seattle, but he was retired by the time we started going to Enetai. He couldn't have been much over 60 years old when I first saw him, but to me he always seemed older.... Perhaps it was because he had a great white beard, trimmed in the style known as a "spade beard."

We did know his wife, Helen. She was a cheerful lady who liked little kids and dogs and birds. She talked to the birds—"tweety, tweety," she would say....

The Herbert McMickens had two daughters, Maud and Kate. Kate married Edwin Ivey, a Seattle architect....

Maud...married Maurice Tibbals, a member of an old Port Townsend family....

I was once told that Mrs. Croxton was the daughter of H.B. Kennedy. Kennedy was an early-day steamship man on Puget Sound. When we first started going to Enetai...there was passenger steamship service between Seattle and Bremerton, rendered by the stern-wheeler *Bailey Gatzert* and the propeller steamer *H. B. Kennedy*....

In the 1920s there were no roads into Enetai. One got there in two ways. One was by water to the Enetai dock. From Seattle one took the steamer *F.G. Reeve* which made one round trip per day between Seattle and Silverdale. If you were in Bremerton at 5:15 p.m., you could go to Enetai on the gasoline launch *Chickaree*. But if you wanted to get to Enetai by land, you started at Manette and proceeded along a road at the top of the beach until you got to the Enetai Gate. There the road stopped. Thence you proceeded on foot to your house.

SHERIDAN
By Dorothy Peckenpaugh McAlinden

My memories of Sheridan have a dream-like quality because it is a world that no longer exists. It slowly disappeared through progress and development. During the years 1915-1936, when I lived in Sheridan, our good friends of the neighborhood were the following families: Gordon, Van Stralen, Hubbell, Parker, Morton, Greenstreet, Pitt, Glaser, Kanthack, Voight, Heffner, Lewis, Schlagel, Ammerman, Dickerson, Champlin, Billings, Copley, Carter and Atkinson. Some of my very special friends were Louise Parker, Virgie Greenstreet, Louise Morton, Elsie Kanthack, Addie Mae Atkinson and Phyllis Copley.

The *F.G. Reeve* steamship made regular stops at the Sheridan dock on its daily round trip to Seattle. It was a big event to ride that steamer to Bremerton or to Seattle. We used to play on the dock and fish from it to catch pogies and perch and watch the dogfish. In the summer we would jump off the dock and swim. But swimming in the bay was hazardous because of the fast tides, the barnacles and the cold water.

On the Fourth of July our father would help us set off our fireworks from the end of the dock.

There was a creek and bridge south of the dock below Grandpa Morton's house. Under the bridge there was a pond where we would often swim on a warm summer day. In the spring we would walk in the nearby woods to pick the first trilliums and lamb's tongues. In season we would go to the beach and dig clams and geoducks. There was always plenty to do to keep the children busy.

We were up early each morning to do our chores before leaving for school. When I was in the second grade (1922) the first school bus went into service. I recall that the body of the bus was made of wood. It was very exciting to ride the bus and not have to walk to school. The Atkinson family provided the school bus drivers. I remember Frances, Don and Dick Atkinson as bus drivers. I learned to drive by watching how they drove the bus.

On returning from school we changed our clothes. We had three sets of clothes: school, work/play and Sunday clothes.

During the summer vacations Burt Carter, Rudd Hubbell and Harlan Parker would hire the neighbor children to pick peas, beans, strawberries and cherries. Burt Carter ran a successful produce ranch for many years. I recall being paid 2 cents per pound to pick peas. One summer I made $73 and I was very proud because that was big money in 1927. I used the money to buy school clothes for my brother and sister and me.

Most homes were run on a weekly schedule: Monday, wash clothes; Tuesday, iron clothes; Wednesday, sew and mend; Thursday, bake bread; Friday, clean house; Saturday, shop in Manette or Bremerton; Sunday, attend Sunday School and church and enjoy a company dinner. We would have some friends to our house or we would drive to a neighbor or relative's home for the day.

I remember the sounds of Sheridan: In the early morning we would wake up to the roosters crowing, the birds chirping and singing, the whistles of the *F.G. Reeve* and the Puget Sound Navy Yard, the deep bellows of the battleships returning to port, the sounds of the bay and the occasional thumping of the piledriver repairing the dock pilings. Best of all I remember the view from our kitchen window of the tides moving in the bay and the flocks of seabirds flying and diving in the water. And in the distance the Olympic Mountains. These are a part of my beautiful memories of Sheridan.

LINCOLN HEIGHTS
The Progressive League
By Elva Hibbard

In 1911 the settlers who lived over a mile from Manette, out the County Road now known as Perry Avenue, formed Lincoln Heights Progressive League. Ralph Hibbard was the first secretary. His son Russell became secretary later. Ralph's friend, George Hastings, who worked with him in the navy yard, was elected president of the league.

Excerpts from Lincoln Heights Progressive League secretary's notes:

DECEMBER 6, 1911. The first meeting of the Lincoln Heights Progressive League met in the building known as the Bachman House [now 2541 Perry Avenue] at 8 p.m.... Officers elected were: Mr. George Hastings, president; Mr. R.E. Hibbard, secretary; Mr. Morrison, Mr. George Phillips and Mr. Hatch, trustees. Henry C. Hoffman was on the board of directors.

DECEMBER 14, 1911. The following committees were appointed:
Road Committee: Puterbaugh, Mr. Hibbard, Mr. Morrison and Mr. Robinson.
Country Life Committee: James Rodger, Archie Ruley, E. Irons.
Building and Grounds Committee: O. Avery, Mr. Hughes, Mr. Peters, Mr. Stebbins.
Library Committee: Mr. Morrison, Russell Hibbard, Ray Philips, Mr. Kelso, Mr. Michner.
Reception Committee: Mr. Hastings, Mr. Hoffman, Mr. George Seaford.

DECEMBER 20, 1911. A committee on sports was appointed: Mr. E. Engstrom, Archie Ruley, Ray Phillips, Russell Hibbard, E.E. Kelsoe.

JANUARY 3, 1912. Mr. Hastings explained...the plans of the League were...the first and third Thursday of each month would be for both ladies and gentlemen and...social. The other nights are given up for the gentlemen for athletics, sports, etc.
The rural free delivery was discussed explaining how essential it is that every one should sign stating they would put out a box so as to be sure to get the required number of signatures.
Mr. and Mrs. Morrison entertained with some singing. Mr. Fellows recited.

JANUARY 16, 1912. Mr. H. Harrington...gave some very progressive suggestions. Mr. Card was called upon and responded by singing which was enjoyed very much. Mr. Hastings...read the Ballad of Blasphemus Bill.

MARCH 22, 1912. The Sports Committee reported that work on the tennis court would begin soon.
Mr. Hastings appointed a Committee on Country Life or Agriculture: George Phillips, Henry McKelvy, Erik Engstrom and Russell Hibbard. Mr. Hatch gave a talk on agriculture and fertilization.

FEBRUARY 18, 1913. The following officers were elected: President, Mr. Hughes; Secretary Evelyn Naugle; Treasurer, Mr. Renner; Trustees, Mr. Hibbard, Mr. Avery.

APRIL 22, 1913. Meeting opened by song, "What A Friend We Have In Jesus." Collection for refreshment $2.35; Expense .25; Balance $2.10. Bill for lights $1.00. Meeting closed by song "God Be With You."

MAY 27, 1913. Motion made by Mr. Smith that we organize a fire department.

JANUARY 21, 1914. Discussion on new hall, committee appointed to solicit funds to build new hall: Mrs. C.C. Collins, Mrs. Irons, Mrs. Hoffman.

FEBRUARY 25, 1914. Building committee: O.E. Avery, C. Collins, G. Shoure, E. Engstrom, G. Seifort.

MARCH 4, 1914. Motion seconded that new building be placed in front of old building.

APRIL 8, 1914. Bill of $139.20 for lumber paid...bill for scow and towing $5.00 paid...go ahead and buy shingles.

JULY 23, 1914. Piano man from George P. Bent Piano House came...agreed to place a piano in the hall...at $25 down and allowing $25 for the old organ. The piano to cost $475.

Neighbors building Lincoln Heights Community Center, circa 1912. Far right, standing, are William and Josie Avery; in front in shawl is 10-year-old Birdie May Avery.   -Photo from Doris Houston

AUGUST 11, 1914. Rules to be carried out by the club:
  1. Dancing to begin at 8 p.m.
  2. Refreshments to be served at 11 p.m.
  3. No suggestive dancing or ragging will be allowed.
  4. Parents with children are welcome and children old enough to dance...are entitled to the floor.
  5. Extra ladies to be charged 10 cents admission after August 15.
  6. No swearing, no smoking.

Lincoln Heights Progressive League charter members listed: E.F. Irons, A. Harris, J. McNeill, A.E. Kelso, H.G. Smith, Archie Ruley, George Philips, C.S. Morrison, Peter Sillestol, Erik Engstrom, Ray Philips, R.W. Hatch, C.R. Peters, W.S. Harris, S.S. Hughes, I.M. Robinson, H. Harrington, R.E. Hibbard, J. Greenhow, George Hastings, Bert Saunders, W.S. Wolliver, George Bachman, Thomas Fellows, Russell Hibbard, George Seifert, Mr. Michner, Walter Davis, James Rodger, O. Avery, H.C. Hoffman, Puterbaugh, Parker, Sansome, Clarence Woods, Dan Burlew, G.E. Stebbins, Jay Burlew.

Recollections of Lincoln Heights
By Elgie J. Hoffman

In 1911, a group was formed by the name of Lincoln Heights. Ralph Hibbard, master of the Puget Sound Navy Yard sheet metal shop, was elected secretary. George Hastings, head of drafting, building 78, was elected president. My father, Henry C. Hoffman, acting yard master of PSNY public works department, was on the board of directors.

A small building on the property [at about what is today 2541 Perry Avenue] was used as the clubhouse for meetings and social gatherings. The little clubhouse became too small—especially for dancing—so Mr. Parker suggested the use of "The General Store" on his property. That building had been erected by the promoter of Hillman City, but was never occupied. Willing hands cleared the building of stored hay, grain, etc., and dances were held there until the group could get their own dance hall and recreation building.

Bazaars, cake sales and raffles were held and donations collected to raise money to build a dance hall adjacent to the clubhouse. Lumber was purchased from the Port Orchard Mill at Smith Cove and floated across the bay to Manette. George Card, with his huge draft horse (originally a fire horse) and his wagon, hauled the lumber to the Lincoln Heights property, where eager hands—large and small—men, women and children—went to work as constructors. They were well fed and the building project was like a big party.

After completion of the building, the group had enough money to purchase a piano. Charles Collins was the caller for the square dances. There was enough room for two squares. The kids—Maymie Collins, Helen Siefert and Elgie Hoffman, to name a few—had a big time in one of the corners.

The big snow of 1916 collapsed the building, thus ending the activities of Lincoln Heights, the boundaries of which were never established.

THE FIELD
By Berenice Bouchard Root

Everyone who was fortunate enough to grow up in Manette probably feels that their own little neighborhood was unique.

Our neighborhood playfield was three cleared lots at East 18th Street and Winfield Avenue, next to property we had moved to in 1926.

Children of the following families who played in "the field" were: Forbes, Bouchard, Clare, Avery, Dean, Kimball and Weedin, to name a few. However, it was primarily the domain of the Forbeses and Bouchards.

Myrtle Forbes Kressin and I learned our softball skills there playing scrub-baseball or work-up with the boys. They reluctantly let us play.

Third base was a hazel-nut tree and a ball hit over the fence into Bouchards' vegetable garden was "out."

Summer evenings we played Kick-the-Can, Run Sheep Run, Hide and Seek and other group games. Fall was touch-football time. Snowy winters brought out home-made sleds. March was for kite-flying. We often lost our kites to the power lines and trees. Soon the marbles would appear and prized "aggies" would change hands.

Hopscotch diagrams were scratched in the dirt. Jump-ropes swished and thumped. Cans in the ground were golf cups.

I can still see George McKeown hitting long baseballs, Wendell Mawson and Archie Bouchard wrestling and Archie trying to perfect his high-jump and pole-vaulting skills out there in our field.

Those of us who remained in the neighborhood to raise our own families often reminisced about The Field and regretted that our own children weren't able to enjoy it the way we did.

By this time the blackberry vines were very thick and im-

Improvised playground. Three vacant lots known as "The Field" at East 18th Street and Winfield Avenue provided hours of recreation for neighborhood youngsters in the 1920s. From left—next to Walter Clare's dog—are John Forbes, Walter Clare Jr., Danny Burton, Berenice Bouchard and Myrtle Forbes.   - Photo from Berenice Bouchard Root

penetrable. However, we did pick the berries for pies and jam.

In the 1970s the property was sold to developers and three duplexes were built on it.

On a clear summer's night, if you listen very carefully, you just might hear children laughing and the cry of "Run Sheep Run."

Chapter 12

FAMILY HISTORIES

This chapter reviews the lives and activities of many Manette Pioneers and traces their descendants to modern times, often to persons well known in the community today. The chapter, like the rest of the book, is the work of volunteers; individuals who responded to published requests for contributions. It thus represents a sampling of families with roots in Manette. It is not a directory of all.

The authors in most instances are family members. Responsibility for accuracy and completeness lies solely with them.

Length of the histories is no measure of their importance. The authors said what they wished to say. Some said much and others little.

Editing has generally been limited to minor changes intended to improve readability. The style of individual authors has been largely preserved. Most of the original manuscripts submitted are on file at the Kitsap County Historical Museum in Silverdale.

Some contributors may find that part of the material they submitted for this chapter appears instead in the TREASURY OF MEMORIES, and vice versa.

A few persons offered manuscripts too late for inclusion in the book. Others have said they submitted nothing "because no one asked me." They apparently did not realize that published invitations to contribute applied to them as individuals.

Because their stories are no less worthy than those here presented, publication of a supplement is under consideration. Material may be sent to the Kitsap County Historical Society at 3343 NW Byron Street, Silverdale, WA 98383. It willl be filed in the museum for possible future use.

ABERNATHY, GEORGE W.
By Wendell Abernathy

THE ABERNATHYS AND THE HUFFS

George Washington Abernathy, my father, was born on a farm in Davis County, Iowa, October 28, 1864. When he was 20 he and a friend went to Kansas in a covered wagon. George claimed a parcel of land and built a sod shanty. George remained there one year until he could sell the land. From Kansas he went to Denver, then Idaho, where he entered the sewing machine business in Boise.

Allie M. Huff was born in Warrensburg, Mo., April 29, 1880. When she was 3 the family migrated to Idaho. On April 30, 1884, her sister Bertha was the first white girl born in Caldwell, Idaho, which was Indian territory then. When Allie was 18 she was employed by George to take care of the books, make collections and sell sewing machines while he was away from Boise. A year later, January 3, 1900, they were married.

My two brothers were born in the living quarters of the Singer Sewing machine store in Boise. Elton was born in 1900, and Earl in 1902. I was born in July of 1915, 2 months before expected, in Ontario, Oreg., just over the Snake River from Idaho. I was named Wendell after a Marshall-Wendell piano my parents owned.

LOCAL ATTRACTIONS

We came to Manette in 1919. Elton was 18, Earl 16 and I 3. My father was one of the first Singer agents in Idaho, and the Singer Company offered him the Bremerton area. He became the Singer agent in Bremerton when Mr. Perry retired in 1920, 21 or 22.

My parents had visited the Seattle Exposition in 1912 and the beauty of the Puget Sound area got to them. They were eager to move here. The Singer Sewing Machine Company provided the opportunity.

Our family bought the Showers' house on what is now Perry Avenue, and I remember, like yesterday, Mrs. Showers baking gooseberry pies the day my folks signed the papers at the kitchen table. I had to wait for the pies to cool before I

George and Allie Abernathy's sons, Earl, Wendell and Elton in front of the Abernathy home about 1920.
- Photo from Wendell Abernathy

could have a piece. The gooseberry bush was at the corner of the back porch near the well.

Our new home was a mile from the *Pioneer* ferry dock. Our neighbors were the George Cards on one side and the Jim Rodgers on the other [Now 2224 Perry Avenue]. Mrs. Harrison/Brewster lived across the road where the Latter Day Saints Church now stands.

SIDEWALKS AND PRINCE

Wooden planks were the sidewalks on the west side of the road. I can hear Aunt Marie Huff's heels clicking yet on those planks when she was on her way to a dance in Bremerton. Anita Howerton was probably 12 years old when she came to our house my first year of school—1921-1922—to watch over me.

We thought nothing of walking in those days. I walked to Manette School every day.

My dog Prince had perfect timing. He would walk me to school, go home and guard the chickens and our 5-acre farm,

The Abernathy brothers, Earl, Wendell and Elton, with the family's Marshall-Wendell piano, about 1920. Wendell was named for the piano.
- Photo from Wendell Abernathy

be back for my lunch time at school, then return home until it was time for me to get out of school at 3 o'clock. I don't know how he learned to do this or how long it took but he was a remarkable dog. Animals don't have pockets for watches and no one ever heard of one wearing a wristwatch.

MUSIC

Vera C. Schroeder lived in Bremerton and taught piano lessons in Manette. She came over on the *Pioneer* and walked all over Manette giving piano lessons. She started me on my lifetime and lifelong work playing the keyboard. I was 7 but should have started at 5 or 6. Vera married John Day and became Vera Day, a well known piano teacher in Bremerton.

FAMILY

My brother Earl was engaged to Dorothy Walker but her father, Reverend Walker, was the pastor of the Manette Community Church, and he didn't approve, as Earl went to dances—and I know for a fact that Earl played the punchboard for boxes of candy at the dock where the *Pioneer* docked—that was gambling. My mother was very active in the Manette Community Church and we all attended.

In 1921 my grandfather, Archibald Thistle Huff, who was then 77, bought a 5-acre tract farther out on Perry Avenue, where Wyoming Street now ends, from Christopher Nicholas Richter. This "Huff Ranch" became our home in 1933-34, the last year I was in high school in Bremerton.

We lived there until Mother had to be moved back into town for cancer radiation treatment in Seattle. After Mother's death on October 18, 1934, Elton and my father lived on this Huff Ranch.

When Elton married Grace DeVore in 1942 I insisted my father live with me in Hollywood, so in 1944 until his death in 1948 I was fortunate in having him live with me. After Hollywood we moved to San Francisco, then to Waikiki. Dad is buried at Diamond Head Cemetery in Hawaii.

In 1923 Dr. John Schutt of Bremerton asked Elton to buy a new car and start a taxi business in Manette, since one was needed. Elton bought a new 1923 Ford touring car and to my knowledge this was the first taxicab in Manette. I remember this Ford at the dock meeting the auto ferry *Pioneer* and the passenger boat *Urania*. A terrible thing that I remember—Mrs. Armstrong lost her life as the float to board this boat capsized when too many people got on one side of it. [For an account of this tragedy see Chapter 2.]

At times, Elton would meet Dr. John or Ray Schutt, take them to someone's house to deliver a baby, wait, and take them back to the ferry dock.

SCHOOL, FRIENDS AND NEIGHBORS

I have a school picture of Dorothy Cole, Dick Feek, one of the Nelson boys, Ada Schoonover and other classmates, but I was sick the day they took the picture and was not photographed. Miss Turner was our first-grade teacher at the Manette School, 1921-22.

Across the street from the school and next to the church was the foundation of a building—a hotel that was never completed. Many frogs that lived there became the pets of the school kids.

Our home was moved and it now has an address, 2230 Perry Avenue.

Archibald Thistle Huff, 77, (center) and his grandchildren in front of the log cabin on 5 acres he purchased from Nicholas Lichter in 1920. The grandchildren are (from left) Janet Huff, 12; Wendell Abernathy, 6; Howard Huff, 14; Josephine Huff, 7; and Helen Huff, 5. Grace Abernathy Rodgers now lives on the property, 1945 East Wyoming.

RECOLLECTIONS

I recall the Worlands. Mary was in my classes all through school until our 1934 graduation from Bremerton High School. Among others I remember are Fred McHenry, Kenneth Purcell, Ada Schoonover.

Our family became friends with the DeVores when they rented the Huff ranch from us in the summer of 1934. In 1942 my brother Elton married Grace DeVore.

GENEALOGY

GEORGE WASHINGTON ABERNATHY (1864-1948) was born in Davis County, Iowa. In 1900 George married ALLIE M. HUFF (1880-1934), born in Warrensberg, Mo. They had three sons.

1. ELTON RAYMOND ABERNATHY, born in Boise, Idaho, December 12, 1900. Elton worked in the sewing machine business with his father, then in the navy yard as an electrician. Elton married GRACE I. DEVORE in 1942. They had no children. Elton died December 29, 1968, in Manette.

2. EARL HUFF ABERNATHY, born in Boise, Idaho, August 7, 1902. Earl worked in the Mare Island Navy Yard in Vallejo, Calif. He married SOPHIE KURPRESKIE September 15, 1929. Earl died May 15, 1967. Earl and Sophie had three sons: DARREL, born in 1936, STANLEY, born in 1938 and GARY, born about 1942.

3. WENDELL ABERNATHY, born in Ontario, Oreg., July 21, 1915. Wendell has not married. He lives part of the year in Union City, Calif., in the San Francisco Bay area, and part of the year in Honolulu, Hawaii. He teaches organ class lessons in both places.

[Additions by Grace DeVore Abernathy Rodgers.]

AKERS, MELVIN
By Helen Akers Oldham
1986

My parents, Melvin Akers and Charlotte Corder Akers, came to Manette during World War I from Montana.

News from Bremerton that the navy yard was hiring workers brought my father to Bremerton. He found a house to rent in Brownsville—no housing in Bremerton was available—and my mother traveled to Washington from Montana with their five small children on a very crowded train. The

children were Howard, Virginia, Dorothy, Helen and Marian. We stayed in Brownsville for a short time until my parents found a home in Illahee and after a few years we bought a home in Manette on Enetai Beach. This was our family home for many years. It was here that Frank was born in 1923.

I have wonderful memories of the very special years of being raised on the Enetai waterfront, watching ferries crossing to Seattle and activities on the water...growing up, playing on the beach, exploring for starfish and sea shells during minus tides, roasting wieners on our beach with neighbors.

The neighbor children all earned money picking green beans at our neighbors Mr. and Mrs. Fredericksons', where we earned one cent a pound. To earn one dollar we worked hard on a sunny day but loved the chance to earn the dollar for spending money. We also enjoyed our chance to pick strawberries at the Jensen family's strawberry fields.

We attended Manette Grade School, went to Lincoln Junior High by ferry and to high school after the bridge was built.

We joined the Manette Community Church at a young age and especially remember Reverend Robert Thompson and his family.

Our Girl Scout troop, with our very special leader, Mrs. Pearl Welborn, was a fun time in our life.

The neighbor kids were all fun too: Bonnie and Billie Olsen, Orville Schultz, Ruby Keil (later Grantham), Eleanor Carlson (now Harrington), Dorothy Cole (now Rogers) from up on East 13th Street would come down to our beach many summer days.

Fond memories remain of Mrs. Jens (Minnie) Jacobsen, our neighbor. Jacobsen Boulevard was named for her family.

My parents' vegetable garden up on our hill was a place I would enjoy at the end of a summer day when they watered their garden.

We had many apples on this same hill in an orchard that gave us apples enough for our family and lots to share. We made delicious apple cider on a cider press our good Swedish neighbors, Mr. and Mrs. Fredrickson, had. This we also shared with friends.

This hill was divided in 1933 when Jacobsen Boulevard was cut through as a road. Many times we hiked to Sandy Point north of our home and took our lunch. The point was next to what has since become Illahee State Park.

I belonged to Women of Rotary, P.E.O. and Delta Chi Sigma Sorority

THE AKERS FAMILY

MELVIN H. AKERS (born July 4, 1871, in Virginia, died in 1952 in Bremerton) and his wife CHARLOTTE CORDER AKERS (born March 1, 1884, in Virginia, died December 12, 1949, in Bremerton) had six children.

1. HOWARD AKERS, born December 2, 1907, in Virginia. Howard died in Seattle in 1969. He and his wife MABEL had no children.

2. VIRGINIA AKERS, born February 5, 1909, in Virginia. Virginia married BUDD KELLEY. Virginia died June 3, 1985, in Seattle. Virginia and Budd had two children who were born in Bremerton: ROLAND and RICK.

3. DOROTHY AKERS, born July 14, 1913, in Montana. Dorothy married FRED MARTIN in 1937. Dorothy died March 19, 1980, in Seattle. Dorothy and Fred had three children born in Centralia: GARY, DOUGLAS, and LYNN.

4. HELEN AKERS, born December 12, 1915, in Montana. Helen married GENE OLDHAM in 1940. Gene was born in Bremerton December 19, 1913. His father, C.E.B. Oldham, was mayor of Bremerton from November

1925 until 1930. Gene died April 8, 1956. Helen and Gene had two children.

4A. TOM C. OLDHAM, born November 27, 1942, in Bremerton. Tom and his wife SHARON BURBACH of Portland, Oreg., live in Seattle. They have two children.
4A1. RYAN OLDHAM, born April 8, 1973, in Portland, Oreg.
4A2. BRYN OLDHAM, born August 2, 1977, in Seattle.
4B. BETH GENE OLDHAM, born January 25, 1946, in Bremerton. Beth married TOM J. JOHNSTON and they live on Bainbridge Island. Beth and Tom have three children.
4B1. DARAH JOHNSTON, born September 13, 1973, in Seattle.
4B2.. GARRETT JOHNSTON, born January 26, 1977, in Seattle.
4B3. TYLER JOHNSTON, born May 16, 1985, in Seattle.

5. MARIAN AKERS, born September 23, 1917, in Montana. Marian married BOB BOUDREAUX in 1942. They had no children.

6. FRANK AKERS, born August 14, 1923, in Illahee. Frank married VIRGINIA OTT of Montana. They had a daughter. Frank died in Honolulu in 1967.

ALDRICH, DUNCAN S.
By Evelyn Aldrich Walker (1910-1987)

My father and mother, Duncan S. and Ethel M. (Davis) Aldrich, moved from Tacoma to Bremerton in 1916, bringing me with them. I was 7. We lived with one of the Lent brothers until we found a home in Manette in the spring of 1917. We lived on East 15th Street between Perry and Winfield Avenues. My dad went to work in the navy yard as a plumber and pipefitter.

After a couple of years he quit work in the navy yard and bought a small store on the Manette Dock. The store had two pool tables and three card tables in the back part, a barber chair and sundries such as candy bars and tobacco in the front. Dad later took out the card tables and put in a lunch counter.

While the Manette Bridge was being built in 1929-30, my mother cooked big dinners and baked pies every day at home, brought them to the store in the car and served hot meals to the bridge workers. All this cooking and baking was done on a wood stove. Many a time I saw Mother make as many as 15 pies for various affairs being held that evening.

How I used to love to go down to the Children's Home and play. We would race through the house and up the stairs, climb out the window and slide down the big slide that was the fire escape. The Children's Home was down close to Schweers' home, a converted houseboat that we all admired.

BOARDWALKS
I don't recall street names. There was the upper road [now Perry Avenue] which went past the Jimmy Rodger home and the lower road [now Winfield Avenue] that went past the Dewar home. On the upper road was a plank sidewalk that people walked on to keep out of the mud. One Halloween the kids pulled all those boards up and threw them off to one side.

Many a Sunday a bunch of us would all go on a hike, take our lunch and go out to Big Rock above Illahee. Licorice root grew on the rock. We had a lot of fun that children miss today.

How I remember the ferry *Pioneer* that plied between Manette and Bremerton. It carried five cars but if a sixth one came along Bob Carter would jiggle the last car over and make room. How he lifted those cars I will never know.

I left Manette in 1930 and went to Boise to work as a secretary for the Veterans Administration. Soon after that my parents built a variety store on the corner of East 11th Street and Scott Avenue. They also purchased a home at 1014 Scott Avenue, across the street from the store. Several years later they added two new stores to the old building, one a drug store and the other a tavern.

In 1941 my parents added three more stores to their original building. The new large basement was used by Nalleys as a depot.

Dad passed away on December 28, 1941. He was only 52 years old. My mother ran the business and soon took me in as a partner. After the war she sold the tavern, retaining the other two businesses for several more years. When my dad died, my husband, Charles Walker, and I were living in New Jersey. We came back to Manette and bought a place on Enetai Beach (1910 Jacobsen Boulevard), where we lived for 3 years. Then my husband, a federal liquor inspector, was transferred to Bellingham.

My mother, Ethel Aldrich, died in 1962; my husband, Charles Walker, died in 1983. I now live in Petaluma, Calif.

GENEALOGY
DUNCAN S. ALDRICH was born in April 1889, in Rhode Island. He married ETHEL M. DAVIS, who was born in October 1889 in Massachusetts. Duncan and Ethel had one daughter.

1. EVELYN ALDRICH, born July 1, 1910, in Tacoma. I attended school in Manette. On March 19, 1934, CHARLES WALKER and I were married in Vail, Oreg. Charles, known as Jimmy, was born in Alexandria, Va., in 1896. Charles and I had three children.
1A. BARBARA WALKER, born in February 1935. Barbara married JOE SHAHAN in July 1953. They divorced in 1980. They had four children.
1A1. VALERIE SHAHAN, born in December 1954. Valerie married CHARLES GABLE in 1979.
1A2. JONI SHAHAN, born in October 1955. Joni married CHARLES SHERMAN in 1976. They had one child: ADRIAN, born in 1977. In 1980 Joni and Charles divorced. Joni married BILL DUPAY in 1983. Joni and Bill have one child: ERIN, born in 1983.
1A3. BETH SHAHAN, born in October 1958. Beth married ROGER THOMPSON in 1975. They have one daughter: JENNY, born in 1976.
1A4. JOE SHAHAN, born in December 1962.
1B. BEVERLY WALKER, born in July 1936. Beverly married WALLY CLARKE in May 1955. They were divorced in 1980. They had three children.
1B1. MIKE CLARKE, born in 1959.
1B2. KRISTI CLARKE, born in 1961. Kristi married BRAD MOHAR in 1982. Kristi and Brad have one son: DUSTIN, born in 1984.
1B3. WALLY CLARKE, born in 1963.
1C. BILL WALKER, born in August 1938. Bill married SHARON SOMMERVILLE in 1959. Bill and Sharon have one son.
1C1. KENNETH WALKER, born in 1967.

[Evelyn died March 26, 1987]

ALINDER, GEORGE
By Lenora Alinder Yeager
1985

The Alinders came to Manette in 1929. The family included George Alinder, his wife Lenora and their daughters Evelyn, Lenora, Kathryn and Virginia. They lived in the big old house of Lillivicks at first, then moved to a house at 1153 Scott Avenue.

After Mother died in 1935, Virginia, who was 7, moved to live with an aunt in Seattle.

Shortly afterward Evelyn also moved to Seattle. George Alinder worked as a machinist in the navy yard. He died in September of 1937. Kathryn went to Aberdeen to live with an aunt. I lived with the Meichos, then with another family, then with the Trasks, who considered me their eldest daughter.

After my freshman year at Bremerton High School I lived with an aunt in Seattle.

OUR FAMILY

GEORGE and LENORA ALINDER had four daughters.

1. EVELYN ALINDER. Evelyn married HENRY MILLER. She is now divorced and lives in San Francisco.

2. LENORA ALINDER. Lenora married JACK YEAGER (now deceased), and lives in Seattle. Lenora and Jack had four children.
2A. JOHN F. YEAGER. He lives in Los Angeles.
2B. DAVID ALLEN YEAGER. He died when he was 2.
2C. CAROL A. YEAGER. She lives in Reno.
2D. RICHARD L. YEAGER. Richard married BONNIE HARTMAN. Richard and Bonnie had one son, CHRISTOPHER.

3. KATHRYN ALINDER. Kathryn married HUGO MEYER (now deceased) and lives in Oshkosh, Wis. Kathryn and Hugo had four children: KATHRYN, CHARLES, MAXINE AND JEFF. They all live around Oshkosh.

4. VIRGINIA ALINDER. Virginia married HAROLD L."Frosty" FOWLER and they have two children.
4A. JEFF FOWLER. Jeff and his wife CAROL have two sons, TODD and COLBY.
4B. TOBIE FOWLER. Tobie married JAMES STEPHENSON and they have one son, AARON.

ANDERSON, MARY
By Ralph D. Smith
1985

Mary Roberts Anderson, my grandmother, arrived in Manette some time around 1905. She was born Mary Roberts Kingdon, in Mount Holly, N.J., about 1846. She married Matthew Anderson, a printer, who had emigrated from Scotland. Their daughter Susan was my mother. Matthew died when Susan was in her teens.

Around the turn of the century my grandmother, a widow then, sold her house in Somerville, Mass., and bought a place in Corning, Calif. After a very few years, she decided she would not live long enough to see an olive grove mature, so she sold that place and moved to Manette. I believe her son Malcolm and younger daughter Emily were with her or joined her soon.

The Anderson property in Manette was on what I knew as the county road, now Perry Avenue. Her neighbors on the downhill side were the Bubb family and on the uphill side a Mr. Pfenning. Grandma sometimes complained that Pfenning's cow got into her pasture.

EARLY DAYS IN MANETTE

I have pleasant memories of my grandmother's little farm. She lived a Spartan life, which was just what she wanted. She grew a huge garden, well fertilized by the manure from Jetty, her cow. She saved her own seed. I remember fine ears of corn hanging from a shelf above the kitchen stove. Her chickens produced some income. She traded some of the eggs and chickens for staples at the store. In the summer she sold fruit, mainly cherries, from her many trees on a "you pick" basis. In spite of the efforts of her son, Malcolm Anderson, to help, she insisted on doing her own maintenance. That included not allowing any extravagances like putting in running water or electric lights.

My early memories of Manette included the steamer ride on the *H.B. Kennedy*, the *Bailey Gatzert* or the *Tourist* from Seattle to Bremerton. Then there was a launch trip, from a float at the Bremerton pier to one on the Manette side of the inlet. The road up the hill to Grandma's had a planked sidewalk—two 12-inch boards with a 6-inch plank in the middle. Grandmother died in 1922. My uncle, Malcolm Anderson, and his family moved into the house after her death.

THE ANDERSON FAMILY

MARY ROBERTS ANDERSON and MATTHEW ANDERSON had four children.

1. ROBERT ANDERSON, probably born in Boston. He was an associate librarian in Harvard Law Library.

2. MALCOLM ANDERSON, born in Boston. He graduated from Tufts University. Malcolm married FLORENCE CROSBY. Malcolm taught French and Latin at Bremerton High School and later worked for the postal service. He was an able amateur scientist and had a butterfly collection at least equal to the university's. After he retired he went to Mexico to add to his collection. He died there in Vera Cruz. Malcolm and Florence had three children.
2A. ADDA MARY ANDERSON, born November 2, 1914, in West Seattle. Adda married SVEND JENSEN and they lived in Poulsbo. Svend died in 1984. Adda lives in Poulsbo.
2B. SAMUEL KINGDON ANDERSON, born May 17, 1921. He became a professor of history in Monmouth, Oreg. [Sam died in 1987].
2C. FRANCES MAY ANDERSON, born May 24, 1932, in Manette.

3. SUSAN MORFORD ANDERSON, my mother, was born in Cambridge, Mass., October 31, 1878. Susan married CHARLES M. SMITH. They had two children.
3A. MARIAN KINGDON SMITH, born June 20, 1905, in Fitchburg, Mass. One of her former playmates in Manette was Marjorie Bubb. Marian married MALCOLM RIGBY and now lives in Arlington, Va.
3B. RALPH DREW SMITH, born January 11, 1909, in Manette. Ralph graduated from the University of Washington School of Journalism in 1932. He worked on newspapers in Puyallup, Hoodsport — *Hood Canal Courier* —, Bothell, LaConner, Spokane, Tacoma, Albuquerque, N. Mex., and San Bernardino, Calif., until 1952 when he joined the University of California staff. He retired in 1974 and lives in Hawaii.

4. EMILY BATES ANDERSON, born in Massachusetts. Emily married ARTHUR HARLOW. They had two daughters who spent a great deal of time in Manette.
4A. SUE HARLOW, now retired from counsular service, lives in Sun City, Ariz.
4B. MARGARET HARLOW, now Mrs. COCHRANE, lives in Tacoma.

ARMSTRONG, JAMES
By Doris Harkness

James M. Armstrong and his wife Martha Jane, known as Matt, arrived in Manette on January 1, 1901, with Matt's sister and brother-in-law Josie and Bill Avery, who brought

James and Martha Jane Armstrong in the garden of their home at 2513 East 16th Street in the 1920s.

their infant daughter Birdie.

James and Matt were born in Williams County, Ill.—James in 1856 and Matt on October 5, 1862. James died in Manette in 1935 and Matt in 1959.

Uncle Jim was a very active participant in state fairs, where he won many a blue ribbon for his displays. He and Aunt Matt had an orchard with fruit trees and a very large garden. Uncle Jim was the beloved janitor at Manette School in the 1920s.

They lived one block away from the school on a couple of acres that had a full view of the ships and boats that came to the navy yard. However, their house faced away from the view, the front facing on an old dusty road. I guess these midwesterners were more interested in tilling the soil than in enjoying the view. The address was 2513 East 16th Street.

My mother, Erma Avery Houston, and step-dad, Edward Houston, bought the old homestead in 1939 from Aunt Matt and we lived there until 1948.

ATKINSON, DeMACK
By Anna Jo Harkins Atkinson
1986

DeMack and Susan Atkinson, with three of their children, Frances, Sarah and Don, migrated to Montana from their native Tennessee in 1914. Eldest daughter Ruth stayed in Tennessee with relatives to attend school. DeMack's mother, one brother and one sister, along with six other relatives and families, joined them to homestead near Jordan to establish what was called the Tennessee Settlement. They travelled with a trainload of new farming equipment. They soon found out all the land would grow was sage brush and cactus. It was ranch land. After struggling against winter storms, summer droughts and countless misfortunes for 5 years, they all gave up and went their various ways.

In January 1919, DeMack came to Bremerton to work in the navy yard. He rode the train to Washington but not as a paying guest. He clung to the cow-catcher in front of the engine all the way in bitter below-freezing temperatures.

Susan and her growing family of youngsters, Dick and twins Olla and Addie Mae, who had been born on the homestead, arrived in August 1919, after DeMack had found a place for his family. He purchased a 5-acre plot in Sheridan Heights with a magnificent view of the Sound, Mount Rainier and the City of Bremerton. This land is now premium building sites in East Bremerton. The land was purchased from people by the name of Tucker and a Mrs. Gibson. Mrs. Gibson had originally homesteaded the whole Sheridan Heights area.

The family was transported from the Manette ferry to their new home by Jake Williams and his team of mules.

Three more children were born to DeMack and Susan at Sheridan Heights: Anne, DeMack Jr. and Charles Rooke. Dr. Ray Schutt rowed across the bay to climb the hill to the Atkinson home to deliver the babies.

The eldest daughter, Ruth, came from Tennessee to rejoin her family at Sheridan Heights when she was 11.

The children all attended grade school in Tracyton and graduated from high school in Silverdale. Four of the older children, Frances, Sarah, Don and Dick all drove school buses. The school board obtained a special license for Don when he was 14 so he could drive the bus. DeMack and Susan both served alternately on the school board for 30 years. They were active in the Grange and the Tracyton church. Susan par-

ticipated in all ladies' organizations, the Sunshine Society, Get-to-Gether Club and Homemakers Club.

Susan passed away in 1952 after a 10-year illness. DeMack continued to live in the family home, still cooking huge family meals for his children, now all married with families of their own, who frequently came to visit.

DeMack took great delight in having lunch ready for his son Don daily when Don stopped there with the mail while serving his postal rural route. DeMack passed away in 1961.

While the Atkinsons' school and church activities were centered in Tracyton, Manette was the center of their business transactions. Frank Stevens weekly traversed Sheridan Heights for Martin's store. Archie Bouchard Sr. also came weekly for meat orders. Each week when meat and grocery orders were delivered the order for the next week would be picked up.

Mail delivery was out of the Manette post office and the family went to Bremerton via the Manette ferry *Pioneer*. Many staunch citizens of our present day city were reared on Sheridan Heights. The Frank Champlin family lived next door. Two Champlin daughters, Blanche Copley and Inez Howard Solie, were teachers in Bremerton and Manette schools. On Sheridan Heights there were also the Dickersons, George Martin, Burt Carter, James Peckenpaugh, Chad Parr, W.I. Jones, Burt Billings, Charles Schlagel, Harlan Parker, John Hodges, George Sunich, A.M. Larson, the William Irish and Brautigan and Greenstreet families, and many other fine families. (The Irish family had Irish's Dairy and delivered milk all over the Manette Peninsula.)

All family members are interested in boating, camping, traveling and staying together as a family. Several head south with RVs in the winter. In Susan and DeMack's family there were 10 children. Nine are still living, seven in the Puget Sound area. There are 29 grandchildren, 68 great grandchildren and 32 great-great grandchildren. The Atkinson families are among those of Sheridan Heights who have contributed greatly to the Manette Peninsula; many descendants are staunch citizens of Bremerton and Kitsap County.

DeMACK AND SUSAN'S CHILDREN
DeMack and Susan had ten children.

1. RUTH ATKINSON married a marine, HENRY STREET, stationed in Bremerton. They returned to his home town, Hoboken, N.J., to live.

2.. FRANCES ATKINSON married HUBERT KOSKEY of Poulsbo, a commercial fisherman. They built their home in Silverdale. Frances worked in PSNS until her retirement.

3. SARAH ATKINSON returned to Tennessee to attend college. She married JOHN STAMPS, of the Nashville Transit System. Sarah retired from teaching in Nashville schools.

4. DON ATKINSON married ANNA JO HARKINS of Manette. He retired after 35 years of U.S. Postal Service. They live at Tiger Lake. (see Harkins history and Postal Service history).

5. DICK ATKINSON was an apprentice in PSNS. He became Pipe and Copper Shop master at Pearl Harbor Navy Yard; group master at Brooklyn Navy Yard; administrative officer at Subic Bay; then back to PSNS to retire. Dick and his wife MARGARET "Molly" MORGAN have homes on Hood Canal's North Shore and at Waianae, Hawaii, between which they divide their time.

6. OLLA ATKINSON married EERO WAALI of Poulsbo. She helped her husband with his store, Waali Grocery, and continued to operate it after his death. Olla later moved to Seattle and married JOHN RADOVICH. She worked for and retired from Safeco, and still resides in Seattle winters and at her home on North Shore in the summertime.

The DeMack and Susan Atkinson family, 1946. Back row (from left), Sarah, Dick, Olla, DeMack Jr., Anne, Charles. Front row, Frances, DeMack Sr., Susan and Donald.   - Photo from Don Atkinson.

7. ADDIE MAE ATKINSON, twin to Olla, died during surgery at age 14.

8. ANNE ATKINSON married BURT CARTER Jr., another neighbor of De-Mack and Susan. Burt was in the sheet metal business. Anne worked for many years as a secretary in Bremerton schools and the school board office. Burt and Anne built a home overlooking Dyes Inlet on property adjacent to Burt's family home. Burt's father had the Carter farm and raised fruit, berries and garden produce, which he sold at the Old Farmers Market on Burwell and to many customers on the Manette peninsula. Burt also provided many young people with summertime jobs picking fruit and produce.

9. DeMACK ATKINSON Jr.,"Bud," married IRENE SUDER of Omak. After serving in World War II he was employed at Boeing, retiring as a supervisor. Their home is on Vashon Island.

10. CHARLES ROOKE ATKINSON married ROSIE BRUDER of Silverdale. He served his apprenticeship at PSNS and now works at Boeing, where he is supervisor of the print shop. Their home is at South Colby near the Southworth ferry.

AVERY, WILLIAM WEBSTER
By Carol Hilstad Schwabe
1985

With exerpts from Reflections by Birdie May Avery Hilstad (1899-1979).

William Webster Avery was born in 1875 in Johnson City, Ill. On August 9, 1896, he married Josie May Sharp, who was born November 1, 1877, in Benton, Ill. Their first child, Birdie May Avery, was born December 11, 1899, in Owensville, Ind. They came from Logan, Ind., to Seattle by train, arriving January 1, 1900. Coming with them from Indiana were James and Martha Armstrong. Martha was Josie's sister. From Seattle they probably took the ferry *Mary Perley*, which made one

trip daily to Bremerton. The *Mary Perley* retired from that run in 1900.

Birdie May Avery recalls later ferries such as the *Yosemite, Athlon, Norwood, Inland Flyer, City of Seattle, Bailey Gatzert, H. B. Kennedy* and *F. G. Reeve.*

On New Year's day of January 1900, John Mikkelson took the Averys across to Manette in his rowboat. There were no passenger boats running between Manette and Bremerton then.

Soon, William started to work in a sawmill on the Bremerton side of Dyes Inlet and crossed by rowboat each day. That was easy when the weather was good but there were dark mornings, rain, wind and swift tides that made the passage difficult and dangerous. This was also a time when men worked 10-hour days.

Birdie May's memories: In about 1907 or 1908 passenger boat service began. As I recall the first ferry was *Bern II*, later *Swan* and *Urania*, then about 1917 or 1918 the *Pioneer*, which could carry several cars. Boatmen's names I remember were Clarence Lampman, Joe Nagarr, Bert Iverson, Harry Hanson, Martin Heffner, John Heffner and William W. "Bill" Jones.

In 1908 Averys lived in the house that William built on the northwest corner of Perry Avenue a block past what is now Warner Avenue. Herman was born there. William died in 1944 and Josie died in 1956.

DESCENDANTS

1. BIRDIE MAY AVERY was born December 11, 1899, in Owensville, Ind. She married CHRISTIAN STENER HILSTAD (1884-1950) of Manette March 17, 1918. They lived in Manette until August 1925, when they moved

to 1419 31st Avenue, Seattle. In 1931 they moved to Fairview, Wash. Birdie May died in 1978. Birdie May and Christian's children are:

1A. EVELYN SHARP HILSTAD, born March 9, 1919, in Manette. Evelyn became deaf from measles at a few months of age. She died of Bright's disease in 1934 when she was 15.

1B. JEAN VIRGINIA HILSTAD, born September 22, 1920, in Manette. Jean recalls attending Mrs. Hoopes' kindergarten with Jean's sister Evelyn. Their great aunt and uncle Martha and James Armstrong lived just across the street. Jean attended fifth grade in Manette School in 1930. She married JOSEPH KUKULAN of Tacoma. Their children are:

1B1. JOHN CHRISTIAN "Jack" KUKULAN, born August 28, 1946. John died August 1, 1986.

1B2. NICHOLAS KUKULAN, born July 8, 1950. Joe Kukulan died in 1979 and Jean has since married LEONARD REILLY of Toronto, Canada. They live in Berkley, California.

1C. CAROL LILA HILSTAD, born April 5, 1928. She married EDWARD LAURIER SCHWABE. They live in Anacortes. Their children are:

1C1. KAREN ADAIR SCHWABE, born November 15, 1949, in Seattle. She married NELS LUNDE. They had one daughter, KRISTIN. Karen is now divorced and lives in Mukilteo.

1C2. MITCHELL EDWARD SCHWABE, born March 12, 1952, in Oakland. He married TERESA ANN BASH and they live in Anacortes. Mitchell and Teresa have three daughters, MARISA, MICHELLE and SARA.

1C3. JEFFREY LAURIER SCHWABE, born January 17, 1955, in Seattle. Jeffry married KAREN LYNN VAGUE and they live in Anacortes. Jeffrey and Karen have three children, PHILLIP, JUSTIN and BREANNE.

2.. LORAN EMIL AVERY was born in Manette October 19, 1904, and died in 1984. He married EDITH BUSHBY. Their children are: THOMAS, PATRICIA and EDITH.

3. ERMA FAY AVERY was born June 27, 1906, and died in 1984. She married STANLEY BAILEY [see Bailey family history]. Erma and Stanley had one daughter.

3A. DORIS MAY BAILEY, born February 9, 1926. Doris lives at 12230 Ashworth, in Seattle. Doris married HARRY HARKNESS in 1947. Doris and Harry divorced. They have three children, EDWARD, born in 1948, RANDALL, born in 1950 and CYNTHIA, born in 1955. Erma and Stanley divorced. In 1934, Erma married EDWARD W. HOUSTON, USN. Erma and Edward had one daughter.

3B. ADELAID FAY HOUSTON, born in 1936. Adelaid is unmarried.

4. HERMAN LEE AVERY, born May, 23, 1908, at the family home on Perry Avenue in Manette. He married BLANCHE FISHER June 11, 1926, the day Blanche graduated from Union High School in Bremerton. Blanche was born March 13, 1909, and grew up in Manette. Herman died September 5, 1972. Blanche died January 12, 1982. Herman and Blanche's children are:

4A. BETTY LOU AVERY, born February 12, 1927. Betty was married to C. J. LIBBY in 1945 and was divorced in 1946. She married Navy Captain DANIEL L. BANKS Jr., on February 27, 1947, and they live in McLean, Va. Betty's children are:

4A1. LINDA LEE LIBBY, born April 16, 1946, in Bremerton. She married WILLIAM C. THAMES in 1965.

4A2.. DIANA LEWIS BANKS, born December 13, 1947, in Bremerton. She married PETER C. SOUTHARD in 1971.

4A3. THERESA LESLIE BANKS, born November 1, 1954, in San Diego. She married PHILIP C. GAMLIN in 1982.

4A4. DANIEL LOUIS BANKS II, born July 15, 1956, in San Diego. He married KATHERINE E. SABRI in 1984.

4B. ROBERT EUGENE AVERY " Bob/Socko", born September 3, 1928. He married DONNA JEAN IRVINE of Spokane. Robert is a sheet metal worker. Robert and Donna's children are:

4B1. KATHERINE MARIE AVERY, born April 7, 1950, in Spokane. She married TERRY REDDICK August 24, 1968.

4B2. JAMES ROBERT AVERY, born May 5, 1951, in Spokane. He married ROXANNE BRANNON in 1969, then DIANE MORLEY KNAPP, March 4, 1978.

William and Josie Avery at their home on County Road, now Perry Avenue, about 1913. From left, Birdie May, Erma Fay, Josie May, Beatrice, Viola, William, Herman and Loran.

4B3. TERRY LEE AVERY, born October 1, 1953, in Bremerton. He married DIANE DEBARD in 1973, then MARCIA HART WOODBERRY in 1980.

4B4. LARRY GENE AVERY, born October 1, 1953, in Bremerton. He married JACKIE ROTT November 10, 1972.

4C. DONNA LEE AVERY, born April 24, 1936. She married WILLIAM PRITCHARD, then RICHARD CARDINAL of Port Orchard. Donna and Richard's children are:

4C1. WILLIAM PRITCHARD, born August 6, 1955, in Bremerton.

4C2.. KIMBERLY PRITCHARD, born February 10, 1957, in Bremerton.

4C3. ROBERT PRITCHARD, born May 1, 1959, in Bremerton.

4C4. TAMERA CARDINAL, born March 23, 1962, in Bremerton.

5. BEATRICE VIOLA (Pod) AVERY, born March 6, 1911, in Manette. She married HALLIE DEAN CARNES. They had no children. Beatrice died in January, 1982.

HERMAN AVERY FAMILY

Herman and Blanche Avery's children, Betty, Bob and Donna, attended Manette grade schools and Manette Community Church and Bible school on East 13th Street. Betty still has the Bible she received for faithful attendance. Betty and Bob went to Lincoln Junior High and Bremerton High Schools. Betty and Bob took tap dancing in the Masonic Temple at East 11th Street and Perry Avenue, 1933-34. Betty played softball for Manette Lumber Company from 1939 to 1943. Herman and Blanche both played softball for East Bremerton Improvement Club in the early thirties. Betty remembers dancing the Maypole dance and being a senorita in a "Ferdinand the Bull" skit at Manette School.

Herman's wife Blanche was from a pioneer family. Her parents, Mr. and Mrs. George A. Fisher, owned 12 acres known as Hal's Corner and their old farm house was used as an office building for years.

In 1932 Herman built a home for himself and his family on Marlow Avenue. In 1935 he built a grocery store next door to the family home. He also had a fleet of trucks in the 1930s and 1940s that delivered for Bremerton stores and florists. Prior to this, he worked for Martin's Price Rite on East 11th Street. By 1942 he had sold the property on Marlow Avenue, bought a home on Stone Way, and gone to work for Sexton's Auto Freight. He also worked as a warehouseman for Lents.

[Additional information from Doris and Jean Reilly.]

BAILEY, SOPHIA AND FRANK
By Doris Bailey Harkness
1986

Frank Bailey was born in Michigan in 1873. He married Sophia Graf Rumble, who was born in Seattle. They moved to Charleston in 1907 with Stanley and Vena, Sophia's two children by a previous marriage to Thomas Rumble. Frank worked in the navy yard. Sophia was a midwife and nurse and worked for Drs. Schutt. Frank and Sophia had two more children.

Frank and Sophia bought a house for $2200 at the present location of 2531 Perry Avenue. They became very active in the community. Sophia belonged to Philathea Chapter of Eastern Star. We grandchildren attended Masonic dances along with our parents or grandparents. Between dances we sat on straight-backed chairs around the edge of the dance floor.

In about 1917, after Frank and Sophia divorced, Sophia married Archie R. Bailey, not related to Frank. Archie worked in the navy yard as a machinist. He also took a flyer at several businesses, such as dealing in real estate and propagating

Frank and Sophia Bailey family at 2531 Perry Avenue home, 1910. From left, Adlore Bailey, Grandma Edwitch Bailey, Sadie Johnson (neighbor), Isadore (Frank's brother), Vena, Frank, Warren Bailey, Charles Johnson (neighbor), Sophia Bailey (Frank's wife).

trees. Archie and Sophia became active in the East Bremerton Improvement Club, the Masons and Eastern Star.

I remember Grandma Bailey, (her maiden name was Sophia Graf. She was Stanley, Katherine (Vena), Warren and Adlore Bailey's mother) ordering groceries from Meredith's store. They were delivered to her door. She actually had a telephone in those very early days.

Their neighbors were the Pentzes, Reaniers, Lynches, Hoffmans, Christiansens, Waltenburgs, Morrises and the Hermansons, who lived down the road. Uncle Warren said the area where they lived, southwest of the present Perry Avenue and Stone Way, was called "Pumpkin Center."

It was in Grandma Bailey's kitchen that I first discovered my love for cooking. She let my two cousins, Jean and Phyllis, and me make cookies and pies. She made sure we rolled the crust "out from the middle." She also let us sip her homemade blackberry wine. One of my vivid memories was watching her singe the pin feathers off a freshly killed chicken. I'll never forget that odd odor.

SOPHIA BAILEY'S FAMILY

1. STANLEY BAILEY was born in Seattle in 1895. Stanley married ERMA AVERY, daughter of Bill and Josie Avery of Manette, in 1925. Stanley died in 1956. Stanley and Erma had one daughter.

1A. DORIS BAILEY, born in 1926 in Bremerton. Doris married HARRY HARKNESS of Bremerton in 1946. They have three children: EDWARD, born in 1948, RANDALL, born in 1950 and CYNTHIA, born in 1955.

2. KATHERINE LA VENA BAILEY was born in Seattle in 1902. She married JOHN SHAW. They had two daughters.

2A. JEAN SHAW, born in 1920. Jean married EULAS JOHNSON in 1942. They live in Manette and have two children.

2A1. SHERRY JOHNSON, born in 1943. Sherry is married and lives in Olalla. She has two sons, KEVIN and ERIC.

2A2. GARY JOHNSON, born in 1948. He lives in Manette. Gary married LINDA JOHNSTON and they have two sons, BLAINE and GRANT.

2B. PHYLLIS SHAW, born in 1923. Phyllis married AL CHESTNUT in 1947. They have two children: STEVE, born in 1949 and CAROL, born in 1953. La Vena and John Shaw divorced. La Vena married GEORGE STEAD November 19, 1925. They celebrated their 60th anniversary in 1985. La Vena and George live in Tacoma. They have a son.

2C. MICHAEL STEAD, born May 24, 1944. Michael and his wife HEIDE live in Puyallup. They have Michael's three sons by previous marriages: MICHAEL Jr., born in 1967, PATRICK, born in 1968, and SEAN, born in 1970.

Bailey family at the 2531 Perry Avenue home in 1939. Standing are (from left) Vena Bailey Rumble Stead, Doris Bailey Harkness (Stanley Bailey's daughter), George Stead, Florence (Stanley's stepdaughter), Adlore Bailey, Jean Stead, Warren Bailey, Hazel Bailey (Stanley's second wife), Phyllis Stead, Stanley Bailey and Arling Bailey. Seated are Archie Bailey and Sophia Bailey.

3. ADLORE BAILEY was born in Seattle in 1906. Adlore married ENZYNE COTTEEN. They had no children. Adlore died in Seattle in 1965.

4. WARREN BAILEY was born in Charleston in 1908. He married JUANITA VALDEZ in Mazatlan, Mexico, in 1964. Their child from a previous marriage is:
4A. MARIE BAILEY, born in 1961. Marie married ALEX TROYER. Marie and Alex have two sons.
4A1. ANDY TROYER, born in 1982 in Yuma, Ariz.
4A2. JOHN TROYER, born in 1984 in Palmyra, Pa.
5. ARLING BAILEY was adopted by Sophia and Archie. Arling married MARY O'RIAN. They had no children. Arling died in Poulsbo in 1963.

BAKER, WALTER

Walter and Leona Baker family. From left, Wayne, Ethel, Edith, Leona and Walter Baker.
-Photo from Anna Starevich Hepworth

BALLEW, CHARLES W.
By Robert A. "Buster" Ballew
1985

CHARLIE AND WIFE

Charles Walker "Charlie" Ballew was born in Jerome, Ind., December 28, 1887. He joined the navy in 1906 and set forth to see the world, never to return to his home state except for one or two visits. In 1910 at age 22 he was honorably discharged. Charles worked in Nevada and western Washington, then went to work in the Puget Sound Naval Shipyard July 18, 1911, as a rigger helper. In 1913 he made rigger. He lived with the Elgie Hoffman family in Manette.

Charlotte E. Dilks came to Manette with her family early in 1915 and soon caught the eye of Charlie. They married July 27, 1915. They established their home at Hayward Avenue and Upper Shore Drive.

HELPFUL PEOPLE

Manette was covered with fields, trees, paths, wild blackberries, flowers and good people. Everyone was friendly and

Ballew home at 812 Hayward Avenue.

Charles Ballew, circa 1925, and Vera Ballew, circa 1927.

helped one another—like a large family. It was a good place to settle, make a home and raise a family, despite the inconvienence of having to take a ferry to go anywhere.

Another couple from Indiana, Sam and Agnes Hall, moved next door on Hayward Avenue. Hershel "Hash" Hall, Sam's brother, moved into the house across the alley behind the Ballews on Upper Shore Drive and Ironsides Avenue. Behind them were madrona trees, huckleberry, Oregon grape, greasewood, salal and scotchbroom. Paths wound through the greenery to neighbors' homes. There were only four houses on Hayward Avenue between Upper Shore Drive and East 9th Street.

Charlie and Charlotte Ballew had a daughter, Maysie, and a son, Charles, "Buddie," both born in Manette.

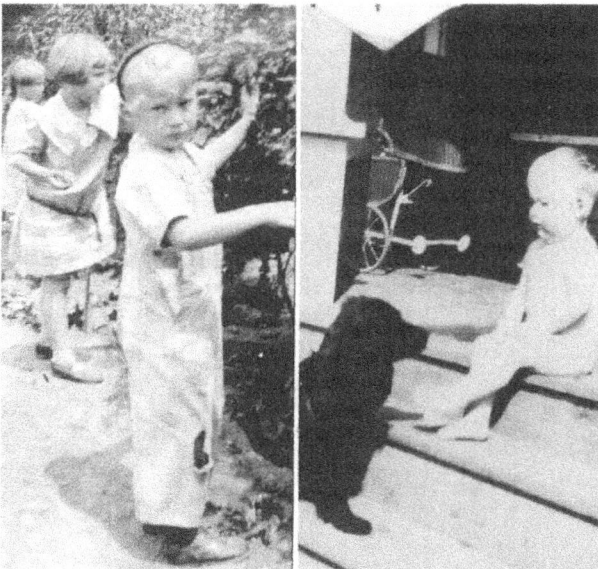

Left photo: Charlie "Buddie" Ballew and Maysie Ballew with Edna Mae Rath in background. 1920.
Right photo: Bob Ballew with dog Speed,1925.

In 1920 Charlie made quarterman rigger, earning the grand sum of $7.52 a day. In 1923 Charlotte and Charlie divorced.

ANOTHER FAMILY

Their neighbor, Vera Washburn, had baby-sat Maysie and Charles. Maysie and Vera's sister Edna Mae Rath were playmates. In 1925 Vera and Charlie married. They had two sons. Robert "Buster," and William. During the 20s many were laid off in the naval shipyard. Charlie was one of the fortunate ones who was kept on, although in 1927 he was "broke back" to leadingman rigger.

The family moved to 812 Hayward Avenue, between the Sam Halls and the Raths. Charlie and Vera lived there the rest of their lives.

Vera became well known for her ability to grow things and soon the small house was surrounded by flowers, shrubs, trees, pets and ducks. Their home attracted neighbors to many happy times.

FREE MANETTE

Freedom seemed to be the key word for all who lived in Manette—freedom to run, play, explore, visit, get into mischief—to be and do. There was always the beach, the Sandbanks, the woods and fields to explore and enjoy. As parents gathered and visited, their youngsters banded together to have fun.

When I was about 6 I had just acquired logger boots that reached just below the knees and had a side pocket for a jack-knife. I went exploring down the beach and was soon on the raft in front of the Wall home. I went past the boards onto the algae-covered logs that supported the raft. My feet went out from under me and I fell. The water was deep and cold and the current was strong. Mrs. Troop dove in, pulled me to safety and took me home to my parents.

Another time, March 18, 1943, the ferry *Malahat* caught fire in Bremerton. It was towed away and beached on Point Herron beyond Hayward Avenue. It was repaired and returned to service.

Even as a toddler, I seemed to have a need to be rescued. Manette's original "streaker," I was rescued by Hazel Hendrickson, who covered me and returned me home.

Once, when I was about 3, I was left with Grandpa Pete Rath. He was working on his automobile and since I was playing quietly he didn't notice I drank a bottle of gasoline. When my parents returned they noted that my coloring was blotchy and I was becoming ill. They detected the odor of gasoline and rushed me to the ferry *Pioneer*. Mother stood on the running boards between two cars and held me by my feet when my color darkened. She was screaming in the terror that overwhelmed her, I was told. The doctor pumped my stomach but I didn't completely recover until I was about 18.

Charlie Ballew was broken back once more to rigger but he was thankful to have a job. He was a "high climber," in demand at places like Tatoosh Island, off the northwest tip of Washington, to install communication antennas for the navy. Despite hard times for many, he was kept busy.

NEIGHBORHOOD ATTRACTIONS

The Otto Volls lived up the street at East 9th Street and Hayward Avenue. In the center of a vacant lot they owned, between their home and ours, was a huge granite boulder covered with scotchbroom and bushes. Mrs. Voll, who was quite a gardener, worked hard to landscape their home and it became a showplace. The granite rockery that surrounded it was from the boulder. About 1931-32, Otto circled the boulder with rubber tires and set fire to them. After a time he threw water on the huge rock to break off large chunks that he carried across the road to use in the yard. The process was an attraction to the kids.

Once, while the tires were burning, I was playing with Don Waltenberg and Frances and Ray Hall. We were running around the fire when I tripped and fell into a burning tire. My face and arms were badly burned. Screaming, I raced for home across the road. My parents smeared a thick coating of Unguentine over the burns. In time they healed.

There were many reasons that Manette was one of the better places to live. One was the deer that wandered about without fear. One deer became so friendly he paid daily visits in some neighborhoods. We told people we could set our clocks by the time of his arrival at our back gate.

Jake Williams lived at the site of the present Dairy Queen. His barns and other out-buildings were across the road. He hired out to plow for others and could be seen riding into town driving his wagon pulled by two mules. He invited some of the kids to hop on to ride along the way. This was a big deal.

Children could play safely after dark or explore anywhere in Manette. We gathered about dusk at 9th Street and Hayward Avenue to play games like kick-the-can.

The Howertons lived on what is now Trenton Avenue and just beyond was the Burton A. Reanier family. They were our friends. We enjoyed Beatrice Reanier, the second oldest daughter, and when she married Bob Greenamyer and moved to a little house at Harkins Street and Pitt Avenue, we visited back and forth. The Greenamyers had a baby boy they named Robin. He was less than a year old when their house caught fire. Robin was lost, along with all else. It stunned all who knew them.

There were ice-skating parties out at Clare's Marsh; visits to a bootlegger out in that same area and parties there; dances at the 2X4 Inn beyond Tracyton; picnics in many places; Barker's Creek was a favorite.

The Fellows family had a large orchard and garden area on the north side of what is now East 11th Street between Hayward and Ironsides Avenues. The Shimasakis leased part of the land with greenhouses there. Their grandchildren, Heyday and Hatsu Yamasaki, came to visit. They were taken into my group of friends that included John McKelvy, Ray Hall and Don Waltenberg. Heyday and Hatsu were sent back to Japan. Prior to December 7, 1941—Pearl Harbor Day—the Shimasakis closed the greenhouses and left for Japan.

In 1937 another son, William Taylor Ballew, joined our family. Now I had a little brother who later became a small fry to keep an eye on. In 1940 Dad made leadingman and in 1943 quarterman.

PEARL HARBOR

Maysie was in Honolulu December 7, 1941. Dad spent hours leaning toward the radio, straining to hear a single word that might give him a clue to his daughter's safety.

Work in the navy yard exploded to three shifts and Charlie worked 10-12 hour shifts, 7 days a week, with the phone ringing in the night calling him back or asking him to resolve a problem. Hearing that Maysie was alive and well gave him relief and when she phoned to tell him she had returned safely to California, it was one of the brighter spots in those terrible days for him.

The Volls' vacant lot had a shed for Otto's work as a sign painter and for building a boat for their son, Jack. The army set up a barrage balloon, and the shed was turned into a barracks. A couple of soldiers overflowed into the small house in our back yard. The soldiers were taken to the hearts of those around them and some married Manette girls.

For an Armed Forces Day display in Bremerton Charlie made a large board with a display of knots. Soon a sailing ship, masted and rigged by Charlie and Mr. Rasmussen, was added. Both are on display in the local naval museum.

In 1943 I signed up for the army air force but did not leave for active duty until 1944. While waiting for active duty, I met Bonnie Brown, who was working at Eva's Malt Shop on Harkins Street. Bonnie attended Tracyton, Bremerton and Silverdale schools and lived up on what is now Pine Road with her parents, Murle and Bessie Brown, and brothers and sisters in their large farm house with its orchards that ran along the old skid road to Tracyton. This is where the Catholic church now stands. Bonnie and I were married in 1944.

In 1945 my sister Maysie married a navy man, Ellis W. Lord, who reminded her of her father. They have one child and two grandchildren. Ellis died August 31, 1982. Maysie worked as assistant manager at Dorr-Oliver Inport Export in San Francisco. She is retired and lives in Escondido.

After 39 years, 5 months and 22 days of service Charlie Ballew left the navy yard. It was 1946. He had received more than 10 outstanding acheivement certificates. On February 24, 1947, he folded into the arms of his wife, Vera, and died of a brain hemorrhage.

My brother Charles "Bud" graduated from the Pacific School of Banking. He returned for a visit in 1943 with his bride Sue McKennon Ballew. They moved to Elko, Nev., in 1944. He managed the First National Bank of Elko, worked in Reno, then returned to Nevada Bank of Commerce in Elko. He retired in 1984.

My mother Vera continued to live at 812 Hayward Avenue with Bill, the youngest son. Bill attended Manette Grade School, then Bremerton High School. He married Marguerite Daugherty in 1959. He is senior drafting engineer at Lambs Grays Harbor Company in Hoquiam. Bill and Marguerite have five children and two grandchildren.

I, Robert A, worked for Bremerton Parks and Recreation Department and as a welder in the navy yard. Mother lived with Bonnie and me her last few years. She missed the faces that once brightened her life. I retired from my job as welder at PSNS in July 1981.

Mother died April 7, 1984. Her home of 55 years at 812 Hayward Avenue was bought by Terry Giesel, grandchild of Harry Flint, a Manette pioneer.

Another Charles Ballew, my son, serves his country in the air force. He's the first grandchild Charles Walker Ballew cradled to his heart. He has a heritage to be proud of.

GENEALOGY
CHARLES BALLEW and CHARLOTTE DILKS BALLEW had two children.

1. MAYSIE E. BALLEW, born May 7, 1916, in Manette. Maysie married ELLIS W. LORD February 9, 1945. They had one son.

1A. DEAN LORD, born June 18, 1940, in Colorado. He married
  JOANNE CANEPA August 7, 1960. They live in Carson City, Nev.
  They have two children:
1A1. DAVID A. LORD, born October 27, 1961.
1A2. TINA E. LORD, born December 6, 1963.

2. CHARLES JOSEPH BALLEW, born June 3, 1919, in Manette. Charles
  married SUE McKENNON May 16, 1943. Charles died October 17, 1985.
  Charles and Sue had three children.
2A. THOMAS C. BALLEW, born March 12, 1953. Thomas married
  SUZI BRIDGE. They have two sons.
2A1. JAMES THOMAS BALLEW, born October 28, 1979, in Elko, Nev.
2A2. JOSEPH SUTTON BALLEW, born July 6, 1982, in Elko, Nev.
2B. KENNETH T. BALLEW, born October 6, 1954. Kenneth married
  LORRAINE DODD and they have two girls. Kenneth and Lorraine
  divorced. Kenneth later married DEBBIE BUSCHELMAN and they
  have one girl.
2B1. SHAWNA RAE BALLEW, born February 25, 1974, in Reno.
2B2. JENNIFER ANN BALLEW, born April 12, 1976, in Reno.
2B3. APRIL SUE BALLEW, born September 12, 1978, in Reno.
2C. LAURIE M. BALLEW, born February 10, 1961. Laurie married
  MARK ANDERSON.
CHARLES BALLEW married VERA FERN WASHBURN in 1925. They
  had two children.

3. ROBERT A. "Buster" BALLEW, born March 30, 1926, in Manette. Robert
  married BONNIE J. BROWN in 1944. They have three children.
3A. CHARLES A. BALLEW, born February 19, 1945. Charles is a
  master sergeant in the U.S. Air Force, stationed in Scotland. Charles
  married VIRGINIA GARZA and they have one daughter.
3A1. THERESA VICTORIA MARIA BALLEW, born December 8, 1980,
  in England.
3B. LINDA L. BALLEW, born August 22, 1946. Linda married CHAR-
  LES HART. They have two girls.
3B1. BELYNDA BONNIE HART, born September 15, 1965, in Bremerton.
3B2. DUSTINA MARIE HART, born June 6, 1974, in Bremerton.
3C. LYLE W. BALLEW, born October 27, 1948. Lyle married SHARON
  FORAKER. Lyle is a teacher and coach at South Kitsap High School.
  Lyle and Sharon have one son.
3C1. BRETT WALKER BALLEW, born November 24, 1970, in Seattle.

4. WILLIAM T. BALLEW, born November 21, 1936, in Bremerton. William married MARGUERITE DAUGHERTY in 1959. They have five
  children.
4A. MICHAEL W. BALLEW, born April 24, 1961. Michael married
  ELIZABETH ANGELES. Michael is a sergeant in the army. Michael
  and Elizabeth have one daughter.
4A1. CRISTINA BALLEW, born April 28, 1985, in Okinawa.
4B. CARL L. BALLEW, born March 5, 1964. Carl married VANESSA
  FOSTER. They live in Montesano, Wash., with their son.
4B1. TODD FOSTER, born January 10, 1985, in Aberdeen.
4C. JEANETTE L. BALLEW, born March 5, 1964. Jeanette married
  RICHARD PENNINGTON and they live in Alaska.
4D. GREGORY R. BALLEW, born November 11, 1966. He attends
  Grays Harbor Community College.
4E. STEVEN P. BALLEW, born June 11, 1971.

BASELT, RALPH
By Bob Baselt
1987

Ralph Baselt was born September 14, 1894, in Little Falls,
Minn. Olive Weldfelt was born October 29, 1898, in Topeka,
Kans. Their families moved to Bainbridge Island when they
were 7 and 3 years old. They were raised on the island.

Ralph went to work as an apprentice in PSNS in 1917. Later
that year he went into the army. After the war he returned to
PSNS.

Ralph married Olive Weldfelt in 1917 and they rented a
house at Trenton Avenue and Shore Drive. In 1932 they built
their new home that is still standing at 1151 Shore Drive.

THE FAMILY
RALPH and OLIVE BASELT had three sons, all of whom attended
Manette School.

1. ROBERT BASELT, born July 22, 1921. Bob worked in PSNS until World
  War II, when he joined the navy. After the war he returned to the machine

*Ralph Baselt family. Back row, from left, Robert, Olive
and Ralph Baselt and neighbor Pearl Lund. Front row,
Wallace and Stanley Baselt. At right, Olive*
— Photo from Bob Baselt

shop at PSNS. He is now retired and lives at Tiger Lake. He has two children.
1A. RICHARD CHARLES BASELT, born July 27, 1945.
1B. CAROL LaPREAL BASELT, born November 20, 1948. Carol has
  two children: TROY JOHNSON and JANICE BROWN.

2. STANLEY BASELT, born March 19, 1925. Stan was on an army transport
  during World War II. After the war he operated Stan's Drive-In on East 11th
  Street in Manette. He is now retired and lives in Manette. Stanley has two
  children.
2A. JAMES BASELT, born July 8, 1946. Jim has two children: KRIS-
  TINE, born February 13, 1969 and WILLIAM, born May 31, 1972.
2B. ANNE BASELT, born June 27, 1947.

3. WALLACE BASELT, born November 4, 1929. Wally retired from the
  pipe shop in PSNS and lives in Belfair. Wallace has four children.
3A. NANCY LATHAM, born May 4, 1951.
3B. CONNIE ROLLINS, born April 16, 1953. Connie has two children:
  KYLE BASELT, born August 26, 1981 and KELLY DAWN ROL-
  LINS, born February 25, 1987.
3C. ALAN BASELT, born September 28, 1954. Alan is deceased. He had
  a daughter: RIO, born April 1, 1985.
3D. BRAD BASELT, born February 8, 1956.

BENDER, LEWIS
By Renus and Helen Bender
Alice Bender Davis and Jack Bender
1983

Lewis A. Bender was born in Wisconsin. He came to
Mitchell's Point near present day Port Orchard in 1891.

Soon afterward he bought a general store at Mitchell's
Point with a friend, Mr. Thompson. Thompson decided it was
too rainy for him and he moved back East. Lewis used to tell
stories about the Indians paddling down the bay to buy sugar
from his store. He sacked it in little striped bags and the Indians considered it something very special.

In 1888 Ella Fellows, at age 17, came west to join her father
and three brothers who had preceded her to Decatur
(Manette), following their mother's death in New York. Ella

crossed the continent from New York to Tacoma on one of
the first trains to travel through the newly cut Cascade Tun-
nel. Ella's father was George Fellows and her three brothers
were Harry, Arthur and Thomas "Tommy". The Fellows
home in Manette had been built in 1867 as a school and boarding house for students. George Fellows purchased it and 10
acres from School District 4 in 1886 and converted it to a
family residence. The site was at the present location of Sunset Shores Apartments, 1113 Winfield Avenue.

The Fellows family used to talk about the days of the week
—Friday, Saturday, and Bender-day, because Sunday was the
day Lewis would row across from Manchester to court Ella.
Ella and Lewis were married in 1893 and lived in Sidney (Port
Orchard). Their first son, George Arthur, was born there May
5, 1894.

PUBLIC SERVICE

Lewis was elected the first county auditor in 1893 and
helped move the courthouse equipment and records from the
county seat at Port Madison on Bainbridge Island to Sidney.
They used a flat-bottomed boat, a stern-wheeler, to bring the
safe and other equipment over. They had a horrible time getting up the hill in Port Orchard. It was too steep a hill—that's
why it's called Profanity Hill—but they managed to get the
equipment up.

Lewis established a Port Orchard post office. He also was
postmaster in Charleston, now West Bremerton. Since the
boat that delivered mail did not dock at Charleston, Lewis accepted mail from Captain Seymore of the *S.S. Grace* at
Mitchell's Point and rowed it across the bay to the Charleston post office. Lewis was one of the incorporators of the Port
Orchard Lumber and Transportation Company. In 1894, he
was one of the three directors of School District 22. He was
defeated the second time he ran for county auditor so he took
a job in Seattle with Pliny Allen's printing plant, and the family moved to Seattle.

SAWMILL

In 1895, Lewis moved from Seattle to Decatur with his
family and worked with his father-in-law, George Fellows, in
the Fellows saw mill. The mill operated in Decatur until 1900.
They used to store logs in what they called log booms. They
would drill holes in the ends of cedar or fir logs, join them
with chains and use this to encircle logs for the mill. These
log booms would withstand ordinary winds and tides but high
winds and high tides would move them out and the logs would
drift down the bay. New homesteaders would saw up the logs

*The Lewis and Ella Bender home, 1123 Winfield
Avenue, winter of 1929.* - Photo from Toni Allen

*The L.A. Bender family, circa 1911. Back row (from
left), Arthur, Alice and Renus. Front row, Lewis and
Ella.* - Photo from Toni Allen

and use them for firewood. In 1896, when it was time for
Lewis and Ella's second child to be born, two of Lewis'
brothers rowed across in high winds to Port Orchard to get
Dr. Breidenstein. The baby, Renus, was born February 29, a
leap year baby and the first white child born in Decatur.

In 1898, when the gold rush fever hit in Alaska, Lewis, his
brother Cyrenus, and two brothers-in-law, Arthur and
Thomas Fellows, went to Alaska, not seeking gold, but to
build boats to rent or sell to the men going down the Yukon.
They first went to Seattle and found a steam schooner that
would take their logs and lumber and allow the four of them
to be the crew. They loaded the logs and lumber on the deck
of the schooner in Ballard. Upon arriving at Dyea, near Skagway, they threw the lumber off the side of the boat, towed it
ashore, hauled it up Chilcoot Pass and set up business at Lake
Bennett in Canada's Yukon Territory.

SMITH COVE MOVE

When they returned from Alaska in 1899, Lewis, Arthur
and Tommy decided to move the mill from Decatur because
swift tides and high winds often disrupted work. They bought
land at Smith's Cove on the Bremerton side, where now
stands the Standard Oil dock. Here they built the new mill and
a ramp from the water. Wooden crossbars formed a base for
the ramp. Logs were fed into two wheel-saws each 6 feet in
diameter. Everything was quiet until the saws hit the log; then
they really howled. You could hear them across the bay.

Lewis built the family home in Bremerton on the high bank
near the mill. Here a daughter Alice was born October 4,
1900. Dr. Harlow was the family doctor but he was busy elsewhere, so as in many other cases the baby came without the
doctor's help. Commuters from Manette to Bremerton would
row across in their rowboats and leave them on the beach until
they wanted to return. These boats were seldom stolen.

One time the navy asked several mills to submit bids for
timbers 60 feet long that were 3 or 4 feet square. No one would
bid. Lewis was asked if he would bid. He did and was the only
bidder. He got the contract. Dad later heard that those
premium beams were used for fenders on a navy barge. In

1902 Lewis was one of the petitioners in Bremerton who applied to the Masonic Lodge to establish a Royal Arch Chapter in their city. Through the years he served in all the offices: in the mid-1930s he was elected grand high priest of the state.

POWER PLANT

The Manette Improvement and Investment Club formed and built a wharf at the end of East 10th Street in 1902.

In 1903 Lewis and the Fellows brothers were instrumental in establishing an electric light and power plant which furnished electricity to Bremerton and Charleston, and was a forerunner of the Puget Sound Power and Light Company. They used the slabs and other sawmill refuse to furnish the steam power. In 1908 there were only about eight houses on the East side of Perry Avenue in Manette.

RENUS BENDER recalls: *(Following are excerpts from an interview with Renus Bender April 28, 1984, shortly before his death June 28, 1984.)*

I used to have a paper route in Bremerton when I was a kid. We used to wait for "that boat" to come around the point. The *Tourist* or the *Bailey Gatzert* were stern-wheelers that brought the *Seattle Times*. They'd throw the big bundle of papers off and it would hit the wharf. Us kids who delivered papers would each pick out our own number of papers and take off to deliver them. I had a route that went down Washington Avenue , down behind the city park and over there on that side. I was about 8 years old.

SKID ROADS

There used to be a skid road up from the mill, near where the Manette end of the bridge is now, towards where the Dewey school is. They made skids out of logs cut wide enough so they could walk on top of them. They'd dig this log down partly with a shovel so it would just barely stick out of the ground. They used oxen for power to move the logs along the skid-road down to the mill. The woods were full of those skid roads when they were logging heavily.

The *Happy Jack*, was a boat about 28 feet long. It had an old thrashing machine steam engine for power. When it was built it was the only boat around here. After that there was the *Dandy*. It used slab wood for fuel. A slab was the bark and edge of a log that was cut off and discarded when they were preparing timber for the mill. Once some of the top brass railroad officials were coming out to Seattle from the East. They decided that they would like to get over to see the Olympics. There were no small

boats in Seattle that would go that way. My dad said he had a boat. The officials looked it over and agreed to use it. My dad took the three executives around Point No Point into Hood Canal. The three men aboard became aware of what Dad was doing — about every 5 miles he'd pull into the beach to saw up some wood. Soon they all pitched in to help saw up wood for fuel for the boiler so they could get some steam up. The boat didn't go very fast but it got them there.

I remember the Rythers were neighbors here in Manette. They left here and started a children's home in Seattle. Later, Tom Bright, Scott Wetzel and some more old timers used to get together to discuss things that had happened around Manette.

I remember that down along the beach, now Enetai, there were six or eight beautiful big old houses built by a Seattle timber firm for their executives. In 1909 Dad sold the mill and moved his family to Mead, Wash., a small town north of Spokane, where he operated a general merchandise store. A disastrous fire struck, burning our store and home but the most tragic thing of all was the loss of all the letters my Dad had written while in Alaska and also my mother's wedding gown.

Dad rebuilt a fine new store and a new home in Mead, then sold out and in 1916 we returned to Manette to live in our new home, built on the exact spot where the old school had stood which George Fellows had made into a home for himself and his four children in 1886. Later in 1916 while we were living in this house [site of Sunset Shores Apartment] near the bridge approach, a couple of young ladies called and wanted to rent the house. Dad figured they were wealthy California people, and their husbands were naval officers who had been sent up here. Dad thought his price of $750 a month would scare them off. They took it and enjoyed living in a waterfront home for about 3 months. In the meantime, we went to Enetai and rented one of those big old homes there. We had to walk along the road that followed the beach to get home from the ferry.

Art, Lewis' eldest son, graduated from dental college, married Kate Watson of Platte, S. Dak., and opened his dental office in Bremerton all in the month of June 1916. They had three children; Betty, Jane and Jack.

I went to the same dental school in Portland. The school is part of the University of Oregon now. That was where I met Helen Thomas. She lived next door to me in Portland; she was the only one in the neighborhood who could play the piano, and about 20 of us in the fraternity house would invite her and her mother to come over and play the piano for us. Helen and I were married in 1923, the same year I graduated. Our children are Nancy Ellen, born December 14, 1932, and Barbara Jean, born September 25, 1937. I joined Arthur in his dental practice in Bremerton. Helen's mother Nancy Thomas came from her home in Portland and lived with us in Manette for several years. She joined Manette Community Church and Women's Christian Temperance Union.

ALICE BENDER DAVIS recalls

When I was a junior in high school [1916], all things had settled down after our move into our new home in Manette. Dad (Lewis Bender) was not ready to retire, so he and his old friend Roy S. Hayward opened a real

Ella and Lewis Bender in their home in 1950.   -Photo from Toni Allen

estate office on Washington Avenue in about 1916. Later, Dad and Bill Parker opened a lumber yard. Dad retired in 1935 after a very worthwhile active life.

I studied music (voice) at Cornish School in Seattle with Klabansky from New York. In 1921 I went to Rochester, N. Y., and studied at Eastman School of Music. Later I returned to the west coast and in 1926 married Marsh Davis. We had two daughters, Pamela and Marsha. I live in Tacoma. My mother, Ella, was a member of Chapter AH, PEO, and a member of Reliance Chapter, Eastern Star. She was founder and very active in the Sunshine Society chapter formed in Bremerton in 1909 and which in later years was active in helping finance the Children's Home, located up the beach in Manette. She was appointed by the Sunshine Society of New York to lead all groups in Washington State, but she assumed responsibility for the Bremerton chapter only. My mother was 82 when she died in 1954. My father (Lewis) lived with us the last 2 years of his life. He died here in Tacoma in 1960 at age 93.

I am the last living member of my generation of the Bender family. My husband Marsh is also gone but I am still living in my big old home in Tacoma.

As of now, April 1986, Renus is gone; his wife Helen lives in Panorama City, a retirement home near Lacey. Their daughter Barbara Tyler has two children and lives in Oregon and their eldest daughter, Nancy Filler, has three children, owns and operates a book store in Bremerton, and is the last one of the Bender family still living in the area. Although the old Bender property no longer belongs to the family, two markers remain. An oak tree planted by the teacher in the original Perrigo school still stands. A rock marking this as the location of an Indian fort bears an engraving that tells of its significance.

ARTHUR BENDER *(as told by son Jack)*

My father, Arthur Bender, was Ella and Lewis Bender's first child. He lived only 38 years.

In 1916, he married my mother, Kate Watson from Platte, S. Dak. He practiced dentistry in Bremerton until his death in 1932. I have two older sisters, Betty and Jane. After my father's death, my mother took Betty with her and went back to college to renew her teaching certificate, and Jane and I lived with Grandma and Grandpa Bender.

Mother taught in the Bremerton school system for many years and was principal of the Navy Yard City School, retiring there. My career was army. After being drafted in 1943 I was fortunate enough to be selected to attend West Point, where I graduated in 1949. I married Charlotte Gilliam in 1950 and of course travelled the world over through my various assignments. I attained the rank of colonel.

After retirement in 1977 I built a home overlooking the water on South Puget Sound between Tacoma and Olympia. It reminds me very much of our old homestead in Manette. Betty, my older sister, married an army man, Lt. James G. Bounds, in 1942. He brought in the first coast artillery unit which constructed the barrage balloon facility surrounding the city of Bremerton (to protect the shipyard from an air attack) during the second world war. He resigned from the army after the war and went back to his old job with Fluor Construction Company, which is involved with oil production. They lived abroad in Beirut and other cities.

My sister Jane married her college sweetheart after her University of Washington days. She was very active in the music and drama departments while there. Her husband, Chet Heffner, joined the navy before they were married in 1942 and rose to the rank of Rear Admiral at the time of his retirement. They live in Columbus, Ohio, and love it. Jane is busy on the opera and philharmonic boards, while Chet is still involved with Batelle and other city projects. They have two children; a daughter Jann, who with her husband and child live in Columbus, and a son Grayson, who is married and living in California.

THE BENDER FAMILY

LEWIS ALBERT BENDER, born in Oconomowac, Wis., November 19, 1866, married ELLA FELLOWS. Ella died in 1954 at age 82 and Lewis died in 1960 at age 93. Lewis and Ella had three children:

1. GEORGE ARTHUR BENDER, born in Sidney, now Port Orchard in 1894. Arthur married KATHRYN "Kate" WATSON. Arthur died in 1932. They had three children:
1A. BETTY BENDER, born December 12, 1917, in Manette. Betty married JAMES BOUNDS. James is now deceased. Betty lives in Newport Beach, Calif. Betty and James had one daughter.
1A1. REBECCA BOUNDS, born October 8, 1943, in Bremerton. Rebecca lives in New York City.
1B. JANE BENDER, born September 22, 1920, in Bremerton. She married CHET HEFFNER. They have two children.
1B1. JANN HEFFNER, born August 25, 1948, in Oakland, Calif. Jann married KEVIN OSTERKAMP. They have one child, a daughter.
1B1a. CASEY OSTERKAMP, born in 1982 in Columbus, Ohio.
1B2. GRAYSON HEFFNER, born August 25, 1952, in Arlington, Va. Grayson married ANN CLAYTON. Grayson and Ann live in Walnut Creek, Calif.

1C. JACK BENDER, born April 20, 1925, in Manette. Jack married CHARLOTTE GILLIAM in 1950. Jack and Charlotte have four children.
1C1. JOHN BENDER, born August 11, 1953, at Rome Air Force Base. John married DEBORAH TAYLOR. They live in Roswell, Ga.
1C2. MARK BENDER, born October 7, 1955, in Heidelberg, Germany. He now lives in Olympia.
1C3. WENDY BENDER, born February 20, 1960, in Fort Belvoir, Va. She now lives in Seattle.
1C4. MATTHEW BENDER, born February 27, 1961, in Naples, Italy. He now lives in Seattle.

2. RENUS BENDER, born February 29, 1896, in Manette. Renus married HELEN THOMAS in 1923. Renus and Helen had a daughter and adopted a second daughter.
2A. NANCY ELLEN BENDER, born December 14, 1932, in Bremerton. Nancy married LEWIS FILLER. They have three children.
2A1. LESLIE JANN FILLER, born June 30, 1955, in New York. She married GEOFFREY GRAVES. They live in Seattle. They have two children, TIMOTHY and HELEN KATHRYN.
2A2. MARY ELIZABETH FILLER, born March 8, 1957, in New York. She married ROBERT A. BALLARD. They live in Pleasant Hill, Calif.
2A3. BRIAN LEWIS FILLER, born May 9, 1959, in New York.
2B. BARBARA JEAN BENDER, born September 25, 1937. Barbara married JOHN TYLER. She lives in Monmouth, Oreg. Barbara has two children.
2B1. JOHN TYLER, born May 13, 1968, in Salem, Oreg.
2B2. TAMARA TYLER, born January 8, 1970, in Salem.

3. ALICE BENDER, born in Bremerton October 4, 1900. Alice married MARSH DAVIS. Alice and Marsh had two daughters.
3A. PAMELA DAVIS, born May 11, 1929, in Aberdeen, Wash. Pam married HAROLD PRESCOTT. They have three daughters.
3A1. ALICIA ANN PRESCOTT, born December 14, 1952, in Tacoma. She married RAY LANGBERG and they live in Marysville.
3A2. CONSTANCE BROOKS PRESCOTT, born April 16, 1956, in Tacoma. She married TED WERNER. They live in Tacoma. They have a son.
3A2a. BROOKS WERNER, born April 5, 1979.
3A3. MARSHA ROBIN PRESCOTT, born April 6, 1958, in Tacoma. She married DENNIS BRADY. They live in Tacoma. They have a daughter.
3A3a. BRIANA COLLEEN BRADY, born August 6, 1986, in Tacoma.
3B. MARSHA DAVIS, born September 1, 1934, in Seattle. Marsha married JACK DAVIS; Jack retired from the air force as a lieutenant colonel. He and Marsha have one son.
3B1. GREGORY BENDER DAVIS, born September 17, 1959, in Biloxi, Miss. He now lives in Seattle.

[For more about the Benders read Kitsap County History *and* The Year of the Child *by the Kitsap County Historical Society.*]

BERGLIND, CARL
By Raymond Berglind
1985

SWEDEN TO OREGON

Carl Gustov Berglind was born in Stockholm, Sweden, September 7, 1858. Alma Walfreda Segerholm was born in Stockholm April 4, 1861. They married in 1883. A daughter, Elsa, born in 1884, died at 5 months of measles. A son, Rudolf, was born in 1886.

Carl was a clipper-ship sailor and had been to Portland, Oreg. He liked the area and decided in 1888 to bring his family to the United States. Alma kept a very brief diary of the trip, saying much with very few words. She and 2-year-old Rudolf sailed from Stockholm September 26, 1888, made one brief stop in Goteborg, then sailed to Hull, England, arriving on the 30th. They continued by train to Liverpool, where they stayed in a hotel until October 5, when they boarded the *British Princess*. Sailing was delayed 12 hours by a broken propeller.

Alma's poignant entry in the diary, dated October 11 at 5 a.m., says simply, "Rudolf quiet and still on board...."

The ship doctor's certificate states that Rudolf Berglin (misspelled) died of meningitis on October 11. We have no record of burial at sea. Carl knew nothing of Rudolph's death until Alma's arrival in the U.S. The next entry, on October 14, says, "On deck, Hedvig sang songs for us and the moonlight was the most beautiful any person can imagine." Steerage passage from Liverpool to Fremont, Nebr. was $62.75 for one adult and one child.

Alma arrived by train at Philadelphia on the 15th of October. She then boarded the immigrant train for Chicago, where she arrived October 19. She arrived in Fremont, Ohio, January 1, 1889. Alma's last entry says, "Left for Oregon and arrived there Feb. 4th happy and well."

Hugo Waldemar Berglind, Carl and Alma's third child, was born in Oswego on May 22, 1892.

OREGON TO BREMERTON

Carl came to Bremerton in 1893. His family came in February of 1894. Carl was naturalized at Sidney (now Port Orchard) February 7, 1894. The house in Bremerton is still standing near 4th Street and Park Avenue; a picture of it is in *A History of Kitsap County*. Carl and Alma's fourth child, Rosa, was born in Bremerton May 29, 1895. She was the second white child born in Bremerton.

MANETTE, A JOB AND A FAMILY

Carl and Alma moved to Manette with their family some time after 1905. Hugo said they needed more land and a larger house.

Many family stories depict Carl as being fascinated by anything mechanical. He is supposed to have had the first outboard motor in the area, as well as the first phonograph. We still have the phonograph.

Alma played jokes on her children, hiding and surprising them. She enjoyed dressing up like W.C. Fields.

They enjoyed local social activities. Carl was a member of the Odd Fellows Lodge.

Alma and a neighbor, Hannah Peterson, were the very best of friends. Alma's son Hugo married Hannah's daughter Carrie in 1917. Alma and Hannah made a pact early in their friendship that they would be buried with their spouses next

The Carl and Alma Berglind family (from left), Hugo, Carl, Alma and Rosa. - Photo from Raymond Berglind

to one another. Their children honored this request and they rest side by side at Forest Lawn Cemetery.

HUGO

Hugo joined the U.S. Revenue Service at 17, served in the U.S. Navy in World War I and then worked as a machinist in Puget Sound Navy Yard. He was a unit commander for a naval reserve group from 1934 to 1938. At that time he became a civilian inspector for the navy, remaining in that position until his death in 1952. He was a member of Steadfast Masonic Lodge and served as its master in 1932. Hugo and his family lived in Manette until 1942, when they moved to Portland. Hugo died January 21, 1952.

RAYMOND AND ANOTHER GENERATION

Hugo and Carrie's son Raymond attended school in Bremerton until 1942 and later served an apprenticeship as a marine electrician in the navy yard. He served in the army of occupation in Japan in 1947-48.

Raymond married Barbara B. Needham of Portland, Oreg., in 1948. Upon graduation from Portland University in 1953 he returned to Bremerton and worked in the navy yard design department for 2 years. In 1955 they returned to Portland, where he worked for Bonneville Power Administration.

RETIRED IN KITSAP COUNTY

Raymond and Barbara now reside in Seabeck, where his parents had a summer cottage. Raymond is retired. Barbara is a teacher for the Central Kitsap School District.

Carl and Alma Berglind's home at 1413 Marlow Avenue.   - Photo from Raymond Berglind

CARL AND ALMA BERGLIND'S FAMILY

1. ELSA BERGLIND, born in 1884 in Sweden, died at 5 months of measles.

2. RUDOLF BERGLIND, born in 1886 in Sweden, died on a ship out of England in 1888.

3. HUGO WALDEMAR BERGLIND, born May 22, 1892, in Oswego, Oreg., married CARRIE PETERSON in 1917. They had one son.
3A. RAYMOND BERGLIND, born in Bremerton December 17, 1926. Raymond married BARBARA B. NEEDHAM of Portland in 1948.

They have two children.
3A1. SIGNE ANN BERGLIND, born March 21, 1954, in Bremerton. She married WESLEY L. HILL in 1976. They live in Bellingham, where Wesley is a civil engineer for Whatcom County. Signe is a commercial artist. They have two children, DEVON, born September 29, 1978, and ANDREW, born December 20, 1983.
3A2. JON ERIC BERGLIND, born December 17, 1957, in Portland. Jon is a 1980 graduate of the University of Washington. He attended Navy Officers' candidate School in Newport, R.I., and was commissioned in November, 1980. He served 3 years aboard the nuclear submarine USS *Swordfish*, and is now stationed at the Trident training facility at Bangor.

4. ROSA BERGLIND, born May 29, 1895, in Bremerton. Rosa married LIONEL W. POTTER. Rosa died in San Marino, Calif., November 12, 1966. Rosa and Lionel had two children.
4A. LIONEL BERGLIND POTTER was born September 22, 1917, in Seattle. He married JANICE WILLIAMS in 1942.
4B. ROSELLA POTTER was born June 8, 1921, in Seattle. She married JACK REESLUND in 1947.

BOUCHARD, ARCHEL
By Berenice Bouchard Root
1984

Archel "Archie" J. Bouchard Sr. was born in Saginaw, Mich., April 24, 1893, to Joseph and Anna Bouchard, who had immigrated from Quebec, Canada. They lived in Duluth, Minn., They came to Ballard when Archie was 14. Archie found work as a shingle-weaver.

This line of work eventually took him to Tenino, where he met his future wife, Novella Mawson, at a local dance. After a 6-month courtship they were married in Centralia in 1915. They moved to Seattle, where their first child, Archel "Archie" Joseph Jr., was born June 25, 1916.

About the end of 1917, Archie Sr. and Uncle Wendell Mawson moved to Bremerton and went to work in the Bremerton navy yard, Archie as a driller and Wendell as a helper welder. They rode the small commuter passenger ferry *Chickaree* from Brownsville to Bremerton. If they missed the return ferry they had to walk the 5 miles home. Often the water would be over the roadway at Clare's Marsh (which was a favorite ice skating spot until the 1960s, when it was filled in to make the Value Giant shopping area). Archie often talked about having to remove his shoes and socks and wade

Bouchard, Mawson, Stevens family, circa 1919. Back row (from left), Wendell Mawson, Edith Mawson, Jack Stevens, Mildred Mawson Stevens, Archel Bouchard Sr., Novella Mawson Bouchard. Front row, John Stevens, Louise Stevens, Archel Bouchard Jr.

Archel and Novella Bouchard's home at 1819 Winfield Avenue, circa 1930. - Photo from Berenice Bouchard Root

through the cold water. Sometimes he and Uncle Wendell would ride their bicycles the 10-mile round trip to work.

When World War I was over, Archie Sr. quit working in the navy yard since the noise bothered him and he preferred to work outdoors. The Bouchard and Stevens families (Mrs. Stevens, Mildred, was my mother's sister) tried sheep farming in Scio, Oreg. My father decided he wasn't cut out to be a farmer, so the Bouchards moved to Kalama, Wash., where Archie again found work as a shingle-weaver.

I was born in Kalama on January 20, 1924. When I was about 2 1/2 we moved to Manette, probably in the fall of 1926. We rented a small house near East 16th Street on Wheaton Way for a few months. Then we moved to another rental at East 17th Street and Winfield Avenue, where I celebrated my third birthday.

In September 1926 Grandmother Edith purchased two lots at 1819 Winfield Avenue, which my parents afterward bought from her. They had a house built and we moved into it in 1927. I have lived at this address through my childhood and most of my married life.

MEAT ROUTE

My father worked for a short time at road construction when Wheaton Way was built at its present location. A fill was put in across the canyon between East 18th Street and Mountain View Drive, doing away with an old wooden bridge that crossed the canyon from Marlowe Avenue.

About the end of 1926 Archie went to work for Oscar Etten, who owned the Manette Meat Market. Archie drove a delivery truck out in the country, where he sold meat from the back of the truck. This truck was equipped with an icebox, a display case for the meat, a scale, a cutting board, knife and sharpener. Archie in his white butcher's apron, served three routes, each twice a week. His territory included Perry Avenue, Illahee, Gilberton, Brownsville, Keyport, Central Valley, Clear Creek Road, Chico, Erland's Point, Tracyton and also the Fletcher's Bay, Eagledale and Battle Point areas on Bainbridge Island.

In the 1920s and 30s there were no supermarkets and most people didn't have cars or refrigerators, so rural families were very happy to have fresh meat delivered twice a week.

Mawson, Bouchard, Stevens family, circa 1937. Back row (from left), Leo Meadows, Louise Stevens Meadows, Archel Bouchard Sr., Novella Bouchard, Berenice Bouchard, John Stevens, Archel Bouchard Jr., Grace Broderson Bouchard, Edith Mawson, Wendell Mawson, Theresa Mawson. Front row, Novella Meadows, Charles Meadows, Roberta Stevens, Arlene Wilsen Stevens.

Archie loved children and I've been told how they would wait anxiously by the roadside for his arrival to receive the wieners he would hand out to them. He was affectionately known as "Butch" and "The Wienie Man."

The shortage of meat during World War II brought an end to my father's job after 17 years. The job had provided him with many fond memories and many friends.

In 1940 Archie and Novella purchased Grandmother's property at 1821 Winfield Avenue. Her little cabin was torn down and replaced by a new small house on the back of the lot for her, and a new two-bedroom home was built by George McKeown in front for the Bouchards.

NOVELLA BOUCHARD

Novella loved to do water-color paintings and started taking art lessons from a teacher, Miss Mint, who stayed in our home for several weeks and for board and room gave lessons to Archie and me also. She stayed with us when I was about 4 or 5.

Novella also studied art at Olympic College, and took from private teachers. She was a charter member of Bremerton Art Guild. She won ribbons at the Kitsap County Fair for her water colors and her oil and acrylic paintings. Her paintings were displayed at Bremerton City Hall, in Kitsap Regional Library and in many one-artist exhibits. She was also proficient in clay sculpturing and painting on ceramics. Her other hobbies included volleyball, gardening and antique doll collecting.

Novella was a sensitive, caring person who has been greatly missed by her family and friends since her death in Manette in 1975 at 76 years from cancer. Archie and Novella enjoyed 59 happy years of marriage.

ARCHIE SR.

In 1943 Archie went to work for Lofthus Oil Company delivering oil to many of the same country customers he sold meat to.

After pumping oil for 19 years, he retired in 1962 at age 69 to a life of gardening, furniture refinishing, horseshoe playing, shooting pool and dancing at Senior Citizens' Center on Nipsic Avenue. He drove his brown 1953 Chevy until his 88th birthday in 1981.

Archie entered Belmont Terrace Nursing Home in November 1982. He died March 24, 1987, at age 93.

ARCHIE JR.

My brother, Archie J. Bouchard Jr., started his elementary schooling in Kalama, Wash., then continued in Manette School when our family moved back to Kitsap County in 1926. He attended Lincoln Junior High School and in 1936 graduated from Bremerton High School.

Archie was a natural athlete and excelled in sports. In high school he won letters in baseball, basketball, football and track. He was a halfback on the Bremerton High School team which won the Cross State Football Championship in 1935. He attended Washington State College for one semester on a football scholarship.

He was the catcher for the East Bremerton Improvement Club (EBIC) Softball team, managed by Axel Jacobsen, and he played semi-pro baseball with the Bremerton Cruisers.

One of the highlights of his athletic career was when a Tacoma softball team selected him as an alternate player for the national softball playoffs in Detroit, Mich.

Archie spent many years as umpire and referee of athletic events in Bremerton.

On August 11, 1939, Archie and Grace Broderson from

Crosby were married at home plate at Roosevelt Field by the Reverend Walter Wall of Manette. Archie and Grace made their first home in Manette. They were the parents of two daughters, Archelle, born in 1944, and Kathie, born in 1945.

Archie continued to be active in sports; football with the Bremerton Destroyers, basketball, softball and bowling.

Archie worked in Puget Sound Naval Shipyard and on the Bremerton Fire Department, serving 10 years as a fireman. At one time he also owned the White Pig Tavern in West Bremerton and the Star Tavern in Port Orchard. In the early 1960s he spent several years working at Kwajalein in the Marshall Islands.

THE DAUGHTERS MARRY

Archie returned to the states to attend his daughters' weddings in 1965.

Archelle married Larry Reynolds from Bellingham and they live in Gig Harbor. They have two teen-age daughters, Noelle and Robin.

Kathie married Lauren Stoner of Bremerton and they live in Silverdale. They have two teen-age sons, Richard and Shain.

In 1966 Archie Jr. was employed by Boeing and lived in Tacoma, where he died suddenly of a heart attack at age 50.

Grace has remarried and lives in Rosedale, Pierce County.

I came to Manette from Kalama with my parents and brother around the end of 1926. I attended Mrs. Hoopes' kindergarten class in her home on East 16th Street and received elementary schooling at Manette School, went on to Lincoln Junior High and graduated from Bremerton High School in 1942.

My interests when I was young were art, ballet and softball. I played softball on the Manette Playfield with the Manette girl's softball team.

After high school graduation in 1942 I worked in the office at Bremer's Department Store. After World War II I was employed by Lofthus Oil Company for several months.

My husband, Dale E. Root, was born in Hope, Kans., in 1918. He joined the navy in 1940. He was aboard the USS *Maryland* in Bremerton and we met at a dance at Perl Maurer's Pavilion in 1941. Dale was at Pearl Harbor on December 7, 1941, when the Japanese attacked. His tour of duty kept him in the South Pacific during the remainder of the war. We were married in November 1945.

Dale was discharged from the navy in 1946 and we lived in Long Beach, Calif., then Bremerton before moving to Manette and Winfield Avenue in 1947.

I worked at Lents', Inc., from 1946 until our only child, a son, William Dale, was born in 1950.

Dale commuted for 6 years to work at Bethlehem Steel in Seattle, then worked at the old Naval Ammunition Depot in Bremerton. He transferred to the Naval Torpedo Station at Keyport in 1954, retiring as a planner and estimator in 1980. He worked part-time for Honeywell for 2 years and now works on our places in Manette and our summer home on Hood Canal.

When our son Bill was young, Dale worked with Manette Cub Scout Webeloes and helped coach the Peewee A squad baseball team. I was den mother with Cub Scouts.

Bill attended Manette and Kegel Schools, Dewey Junior High and East High School. He was active in Cub Scouts and Boy Scouts and played on the Manette Peewee baseball team.

Bill married Phyllis Day in 1970 and they have a son, William Dale Jr., and a daughter Jessica. Bill, Phyllis and the children now reside in Spokane.

BRANCH, BERTRAM H.
By Ken Branch
1985

In 1910, Bertram Henry Branch, having completed his architect's apprenticeship with his uncle and finished night school at the University of London, received membership in the Royal Academy of Architects in London. The same year he and Amy Frances Moore immigrated to Wallaceburg, Ontario, Canada, where they were married.

In September, 1914, their first son, Kenneth Gordon, was born in Vernon, B.C.

From Vernon the family moved to Vancouver, B.C., where their second son, Keith Overton, was born in July 1919.

After World War I the Branches came to Charleston (West Bremerton) to visit Mrs. Branch's parents, and decided to settle here. B.H. Branch designed the Silverdale bank built in 1919 that is now the Kitsap County Historical Museum. Their third son, Barry Dale, was born in Charleston in 1921.

When fire destroyed Astoria, Oreg., in 1923, architects and contractors were needed to rebuild it, and we moved there.

When the work in Astoria was completed we moved to Multnomah, a smaller town outside Portland. Seven or eight years later, work was again scarce and we moved to Seattle. I graduated from Roosevelt High School there in June 1931. My father worked in the Bremerton area and commuted.

SETTLING IN MANETTE

In the summer of 1931 we found a place in Manette. My father set up his own architectural office in the Wallace Building in Bremerton. The Manette Bridge had been opened in 1930, so Manette was now available directly to Bremerton by car or truck, or on foot.

Our property was an acre of land at 2616 East 11th Sreet, with an old farmhouse and outbuildings. The yard had beautiful big cherry trees that must have been started in the early 1900s.

It didn't take my father long to start remodeling the house. When we tore the wallpaper off, we found newspapers dating to the early 1900s.

The house was constructed of rough sawn lumber. The exterior walls were of 1-by-12 inch vertical boards fastened either side of 2-by-4 inch plates at the floor, ceiling and midway between. Old newspapers were glued on the inside, over which wallpaper was pasted.

This was in 1931, soon after the stock market crash, and there was very little employment. But Bremerton was the home of the navy yard and was hit economically much less than other parts of the country.

I got a job as a carpenter's apprentice with a contractor working on the Golden Apartments on Burwell Street. This meant I had to get to Bremerton from Manette, and the Manette Bridge had a 5-cent toll for pedestrians or car passengers. I wasn't making more than $12 a week, so I wasn't about to pay 10 cents a day to walk back and forth to Bremerton. I acquired a 7-foot punt with a pair of oars and rowed to a float near the Bremerton ferry dock, a block from work.

One day my father came with me. He sat on the stern and he could hardly get his legs out of the way of the oars. I think he held his breath most of the way.

I became a journeyman carpenter and worked summers while attending the University of Washington, graduating as an architect.

Going back to our early days in Manette, I joined Boy Scout Troop 505. Later I was its Scoutmaster.

Manette in those days was just a one-street town a few blocks long. All the business activity was on this street, East 11th, leading up from the ferry landing.

I had a wooden, steel-wheeled wheelbarrow that I would take downtown each morning to Mitchell's Manette Foods at East 11th Street and Perry Avenue. Vegetables came to the store from the farm untrimmed, so a lot of green leaves, etc., were thrown aside in crates. The grocer was happy for me to load these crates on my wheelbarrow and push them up the hill to our house, where my mother and I would remove the edible goodies. The rest I would feed to my rabbits. I had converted some outbuildings to rabbit hutches.

My mother adapted to this more-or-less frontier life. It was the first time she had been free to have her own garden and access to so many sources of food. Her background was working with her father in London as a wholesale meat merchant, so she knew various cuts of meat, and she sent me to Oscar Etten's meat market for "skirt" (the underside of the animal). My mother removed the fascia from it, leaving some very tender pieces of meat from a very low-priced cut. In those days, meat didn't cost much anyway, but this was almost throw-away material.

William Enkeboll, member of a Manette pioneer family, preceded me at the University of Washington and sponsored me when I applied to his fraternity, Beta Kappa. Through this fraternity I met Genevieve Kohler from Seattle. In June of 1939 we were married. We moved back to the old homestead and I built a house on the back of the acre.

Both Keith and Barry Branch attended Manette grade school and Bremerton High School.

GENEALOGY

BERTRAM HENRY BRANCH, born in London, England, in 1887 married AMY FRANCES MOORE, born in London in 1882. Bertram and Amy had three children.

1. KENNETH GORDON BRANCH, born February 9, 1914, in Vernon, B.C. Kenneth married GENEVIEVE M. KOHLER in 1939. Kenneth and Genevieve have a daughter and two sons.
1A. BEATRICE DALE BRANCH, born in July 1940 in Bremerton. Beatrice married ROBERT R. GRIFFITH in 1961. Beatrice and Robert have two children.
1A1. ERINN GRIFFITH, born in June 1969 in Seattle.
1A2. ALEC HART GRIFFITH, born in June 1971 in Tacoma.
1B. QUENTIN MARR BRANCH, born in May 1942 in Bremerton. Quentin married DONNA KAE ROSS in 1962. Quentin and Donna have two children.
1B1. TOBY MARR BRANCH, born in January 1967 in Tucson, Ariz.
1B2. MICHELLE KARMA BRANCH, born in March 1969 in Tucson.
1C. COURTNEY CHARLES BRANCH, born in January 1944 in Seattle. Courtney married HEATHER WARREN in 1985.

2. KEITH OVERTON BRANCH, born in July 1919 in Vancouver, B.C. Keith became a construction contractor. He married BETTY ROLLER in 1940. Keith retired and lives at 700 Northeast McWilliams Road, Bremerton. Keith and Betty have two children.
2A. KEITH WILLIAM BRANCH, born in September 1941 in Bremerton. Keith married SHARON ROBARDS in 1962. Keith and Sharon had three children.
2A1. DARRIN KEITH BRANCH, born in February 1965 in Bremerton.
2A2. KEITH WILLIAM BRANCH, born in August 1967 in Bremerton. Keith died in April of 1984 in Bremerton.
2A3. CINDY BRANCH, born in August of 1970 in Bremerton.
2B. BEVERLY BRANCH, born in July 1948 in Bremerton. Beverly married DICK ROTHROCK.

3. BARRY DALE BRANCH, born October 18, 1921, in Charleston. He is an architect. Barry married PHYLLIS PRUITT of Bremerton in 1941. They live at Sahali Drive in Bremerton. Barry and Phyllis have three children.
3A. GREGORY WAYNE BRANCH, born in 1947 in Bremerton. Gregory married JOAN QUIMBY in 1969.
3B. RODNEY PAUL BRANCH, born in 1951 in Bremerton. Rodney married CYNTHIA COBBLER in 1977.
3C. MARK EDWARD BRANCH, born in 1951 in Bremerton. Mark married SUSAN in 1981.

BRIGHT, THOMAS
By Cherie Bright Baker
1984

Thomas Bright (Astrup was originally his last name) of Stavanger, Norway (born 1865, died May 24, 1938), and Dora Dahm of Klausdorf Holstein, Germany (born 1867, died February 3, 1947), were married November 6, 1889, in Portland. They came to Manette in 1900 when Thomas was recruited from San Francisco to work in the naval shipyard as a master painter, a position he held until his retirement.

When Leise Robbins interviewed Bright's son Tom for Kitsap County Historical Society Tom recalled his father chartering a boat in Seattle to move the family and their belongings to Bremerton.

"The trip took eight hours. It was a two-man affair, just an engineer and captain...on the way over they got into a fight, the engineer quit at Pleasant Beach and Dad had to steer the boat the remainder of the trip, while the captain fired the boiler."

On November 28, 1900, Bright purchased 10 acres from A.H. Coder between Perry Avenue and Trenton Avenue, property now divided by East 17th Street. The home the Brights built still stands on the property, although it has been moved north and east and remodeled. The lumber for the house was all cut at Bender's Mill and was cut to the size of the building.

Thomas and Dora had eight children: Stanley William, Thomas Astrup, Arthur Benjamin, Jacob Bartineus, Lennox Goldborough, Earl William, Alfred Joachim, and Dorothea May.

Dora Bright operated Bremerton Bottling Works Company for many years, and the boys delivered the soda syrup by rowboat to all the stores on the docks of the area.

The Brights also furnished water to many homes in the Manette area from their two wells, which were only 18 feet deep. They did this until the late 30s.

TOM BRIGHT

Thomas A. Bright went to work in the shipyard as an apprentice molder at the age of 14. He and Carrie Seifried were married June 6, 1917. He built a brick home on Ironsides Avenue. Later it was sold to the church for a parsonage. The bricks were hauled by barge from a brick kiln in Harper. During the 20s Thomas ran a small foundry on the beach south of the Manette ferry dock. He also operated the store on the dock, which his mother owned for a short time. Several times he went commercial fishing in Alaska in his boat, the *Seabird*, with Elmer Waltenburg and Roland Elliott.

In 1932 the Thomas A. Brights purchased and moved onto

Thomas and Dora Bright home as shown in 1909 plat book. Location was between today's Perry and Trenton Avenues on East 17th Street.

the original 10 acres.

In December of 1941 Tom laid the keel of a 50-foot steel troller he planned to build for commercial fishing after his retirement from the shipyard. His plans were delayed by World War II. When he finally retired in 1947 after 35 years' service in the navy yard, he completed his troller, the *Dora B*, and he and Carrie fished out of Neah Bay.

They moved to Fletcher Bay on Bainbridge Island in 1947, and moved back to Manette in 1969.

ARTHUR BRIGHT

Arthur Bright worked in the sheetmetal shop in the shipyard for 38 years, retiring as a chief quarterman. He and his wife Maud built a home at East 16th Street and Winfield Avenue.

JACOB BRIGHT

Jacob "Jake" Bright, apron and all, circa 1910. Jake delivered soda syrup for the Bremerton Bottling Works, owned by his mother. Later he became a Bremerton dentist.

Thomas Sr. and Dora Bright family, circa 1920. Back row (from left), Thomas Jr., Dora, Thomas Sr., Arthur. Front row, Lennox, Alfred, Dorothea, Jacob, Earl..

Jacob Bright attended dental school in Portland and he had a dental practice in Bremerton until his retirement. He and his wife Harriet settled on Gregory Way in Bremerton.

LENNOX BRIGHT

Lennox Bright and his wife Marguerite lived in Bremerton, and he worked in the machine shop in the shipyard.

EARL BRIGHT

Earl went to work for the U.S. Fish and Wildlife Service (after an apprenticeship in the navy yard machine shop) and spent most of his time between Alaska and Seattle.

ALFRED BRIGHT

Alfred attended dental school in Portland and went into practice in Seattle.

DORTHEA BRIGHT

Dorthea lived in Bremerton and Seattle. She married Robert Ewing. Later she married Earl Rieck.

THE FAMILY OF THOMAS AND DORA BRIGHT

1. STANLY WILLIAM BRIGHT, born June 15, 1890. Stanly died April 10, 1983.

2. THOMAS ASTRUP BRIGHT, born May 13, 1892, in San Francisco. He married CARRIE SEIFRIED of Seattle on June 6, 1917. Thomas died May 10, 1974. Carrie died in Ellsworth, Maine, September 25, 1979. Tom and Carrie had two daughters.
2A. BLOSSOM BRIGHT, born May 4, 1919, in Bremerton. Blossom married REYFORD LANE of Essex, Mass., and they lived in Maine. Blossom died March 2, 1987. Blossom and Reyford had four children.
2A1. DIANA BLOSSOM LANE (now Mrs. YOUNG), born May 23, 1945, in Bremerton.
2A2. THOMAS BRIGHT LANE, born May 4, 1948, in Washington, D.C.
2A3. STEPHEN LANE, born September 16, 1951, in Winter Harbor, Maine.
2A4. ROGER LANE, born January 27, 1953, in Winter Harbor.
2B. CHERIE BRIGHT, born July 7, 1922, in Seattle. Cherie married JOHN G. BAKER of Brownsville and they live in Port Orchard. They have three children, all born in Bremerton: DANIEL THOMAS, born April 4, 1946; TIMOTHY JOHN, born July 30, 1948, and SHERYL LEE, born November 4, 1949.

3. ARTHUR BENJAMIN BRIGHT, born October 10, 1894, in San Francisco. Arthur married MAUD WOOD. Arthur died December 20, 1965. MAUD died December 21, 1970. Arthur and Maud had two daughters.
3A. JOY BRIGHT, born January 4, 1918, in Bremerton. Joy married RAY NOSKER and they had a daughter. After Ray died Joy married HARRY JOHNSTON and they had a son. Joy is the widow of JOSEPH CARRIA and she lives on a portion of her folks' property. Joy's two children were born in Bremerton: MARY NOSKER, now Mrs. HARVEY. Mary's son BEN BOZICK has a daughter, TAMARA. Joy's son AARON JOHNSTON has a son JAMES JOHNSTON.
3B. SHIRLEY BRIGHT, born June 1, 1922, in Bremerton. Shirley married STANLEY TAYLOR and lives in Tuscon, Ariz. Shirley has a daughter and a son: BECKY VATNE, born August 5, 1946, and THOMAS GRIFFORD, born November 27, 1956.

4. JACOB BARTINEUS BRIGHT, born October 16, 1896. Jacob married HARRIET EMDE of Portland. Jacob died February 18, 1961. Harriet died December 14, 1969. Jacob and Harriet had two sons.
4A. ROBERT B. BRIGHT, born June 2, 1921, in Bremerton. Robert married JACKIE PARKER of Bremerton and they live in Bremerton, where Robert, a medical doctor, has a practice. Robert and Jackie have four children, all born in Bremerton: MARSHA, born October 22, 1950; ROGER, born January 9, 1954; ROBERT B. Jr., born February 20, 1957, and KEVIN, born March 29, 1962. Robert married MARSHA MALLAY, grandniece of Lulu Haddon.
4B. RONALD BRIGHT, born August 5, 1936, in Bremerton. Ronald married JOCELYN ATTRIDGE of Bremerton. They live in Bremerton and have three children.
4B1. GREGORY BRIGHT, born June 26, 1956, in Seattle.
4B2. RICHARD BRIGHT, born April 11, 1960, in St. Louis Park, Minn.
4B3. DONALD BRIGHT, born February 23, 1964, in Bremerton.

5. LENNOX GOLDBOROUGH BRIGHT, born October 20, 1899. Lennox married MARGUERITE OLSEN. Lennox died February 29, 1968. Marguerite resides in Bremerton. Lennox and Marguerite had a son and a daughter.
5A. LENNOX BRIGHT Jr., born September 28, 1925, in Bremerton. Lennox married RUTH BURROUGHS and they have four children, all born in Bremerton: GREGORY, born May 16, 1954; KATHLEEN, born August 30, 1956; STEPHEN, born November 4, 1958, and CAROLINE, born May 5, 1960.
5B. GLORIA BRIGHT, born December 20, 1929, in Bremerton. Gloria married ELVIN LEONARD of Port Orchard. Gloria lives in Port Orchard and has four children, all born in Bremerton: THOMAS, born May 27, 1956; PAUL, born June 6, 1958; KAREN, born April 27, 1961, and BETTY, born October 15, 1962.

6. EARL WILLIAM BRIGHT, born March 13, 1902. Earl married CLARA BACH of Seattle. Earl died February 17, 1972. Clara died March 23, 1963. Earl and Clara had a son and a daughter.
6A. WILLIAM BRIGHT, born September 7, 1935, in Seattle. He resides between Alaska and Seattle.
6B. BARBARA JOANNA BRIGHT, born January 8, 1943, in Seattle. Barbara married KENNETH H. GEHRING of New Orleans and they live in Douglas, Alaska. Barbara and Kenneth have two children, both born in Juneau: BILLIE JOANNA, born July 14, 1966, and LOREN, born June 23, 1968.

7. ALFRED JOACHIM BRIGHT Sr., born July 7, 1904, in Manette. Alfred died March 4, 1963. He and his wife LYDIA had a daughter.
7A. MIRIAM BRIGHT, born December 31, 1927, in Seattle. Miriam married WILLIAM LOHSE and has three children: PATRICIA ANN, born December 24, 1949; KENNETH, born March 21, 1954, and SUSAN, born December 11, 1956.
Alfred Sr. and his wife CLOVER had a son.
7B. ALFRED BRIGHT Jr., born December 2, 1935. Alfred Jr. lives in Richland and has seven children. Six were born in Seattle: DEBORAH, (now Mrs. LOHSE) born June 26, 1955; GAIL, born August 18, 1956; STEVEN, born March 20, 1958; JEFFRY, born June 2, 1959; ANTHONY, born June 17, 1964; EDWARD, born June 21, 1967, and a daughter born in Richland.
Alfred Sr. and his wife BARBARA had three children.
7C. THOMAS BRIGHT, born September 23, 1941, in Seattle.
7D. STAR BRIGHT, born January 6, 1949, in Seattle.
7E. LAURIE BRIGHT, born March 28, 1953, in Seattle.

8. DORTHEA MAY BRIGHT, born September 1, 1907. Dorthea married ROBERT EWING. Dorthea died March 9, 1976. Dorthea and Robert had a daughter.
8A. CHARLOTTE EWING, born April 27, 1928. Charlotte married WARREN PATRICK of Montana and they have two children: SANDRA LEE, born April 23, 1953, and GARY, born April 24, 1955. Dorthea married EARL RIECK and they lived in Seattle and Bremerton. Dorthea and Earl had a son.
8B. GERALD THOMAS RIECK, born February 10, 1938. Gerald has two daughters born in Seattle: LAURA LYNN, born July 19, 1961, and DEANNA LEE, born June 19, 1963.

BUBKE, HENRY
By Fred Bubke
1984

Henry Bubke was born in Iowa in 1881, grew up on an Iowa farm and received an engineering degree from Iowa State College, Ames. He moved to Spokane, where he worked for the Washington Water Power Company. While in Spokane he met Margaret Thompson, a nurse. Margaret was born in 1891 in Thornton, Wash. They were married in Spokane in 1917.

They established their home in Bremerton in 1917. The same year Henry entered employment in the Puget Sound Navy Yard as an electrical engineer.

I, Fred, was born in September 1918; William "Bill" was born in 1920, and Gerald in 1924. Gerald was stricken with encephalitis in 1927 and was a helpless invalid at the family home until his death in 1977.

Our family moved to 1348 Ironsides Avenue in Manette in 1927. The five-lot site provided space for gardening, which

William (left) and Henry Bubke, circa 1946; at right, Margaret Bubke, circa 1950.   - Photos from Fred Bubke.

Henry Bubke(left), son Fred and Fred's son David, 1953.   -Photo from Fred Bubke

my dad loved and worked at almost constantly in his spare time. My mother loved raising flowers, and during the 1930s was a member of the Kitsap County Dahlia Society. She won the sweepstakes prize at one of the society's shows and often provided flowers for church services and other occasions.

My father was interested in recreational activities and served in an advisory capacity under Bremerton Mayor H.A. Bruenn in developing playfields and other recreational facilities. Father was also an elder of the First Presbyterian Church for many years. Both my parents were active in the East Bremerton Improvement Club during the 1930s.

I graduated from high school in 1936. While in high school I was a member of the band, playing a clarinet and saxophone. Bill was also in the band, playing a trumpet and french horn. He still is active musically, playing a french horn in the Huntsville, Ala., civic orchestra.

In 1939 I moved to Portland, Oreg., for employment in the Bonneville Power Administration. During 1942-46 I saw service in the US Army. Overseas service included New Guinea, the Philippines and Japan. I returned to Portland and Bonneville Power in 1946, then attended the University of Washington in Seattle in 1950. In 1954 I received a degree in economics. During 1954-57 I worked at the Seattle army terminal. In 1957 I moved to San Bernardino, Calif. for employment at Norton Air Force Base. I transferred to San Diego in 1965, working in the navy manpower and material analysis command as management analyst. I retired from government employment in 1981 and continue to reside in San Diego.

THE FAMILY
HENRY AND MARGARET BUBKE'S descendants include:

1. FRED BUBKE, born in 1918 in Bremerton. Fred married GRACE BOERNER in Portland in June, 1947. We have three children:
1A. DAVID BUBKE, born in 1948 in Vancouver, Wash. He is now an electrical engineer. David married MARGARET KROETSCH, and they live in Canoga Park, Calif. They have no children.
1B. SHARON BUBKE, born in 1954 in Seattle. Sharon married C.A. JONES and is now divorced.
1C. DANIEL BUBKE, born in 1960 in Fontana, Calif. He works in audio-visual technology in San Diego.

2. WILLIAM BUBKE, born in 1920 in Seattle. William served in the 41st division of the army during World War II. He was assigned to a headquarters band and still attends its annual reunions. Overseas service included Australia, New Guinea and the Philippines. Bill studied liberal arts at Stanford from 1946 to 1949. Following college he was employed by Transamerica Corporation in Portland, Oreg., Birmingham and St. Louis. He is employed as a computer programmer at the NASA facility in Huntsville, Ala. Bill married LAURICE DENNIS in 1951. They have two daughters.

2A. ANNA BUBKE, born in 1952. Anna married HERBERT BAILEY and they live in Marietta, Ga.
2B. ERICA BUBKE, born in 1954. Erica married JIM KEVER and they live in Nashville, Tenn. They have two daughters.
2B1. LINDSEY KEVER, born in Nashville in 1983.
2B2. BROOKE KEVER, born in Nashville in 1985.

3. GERALD BUBKE, born in 1924, in Seattle. Gerald died in Bremerton in 1977.

To me, an 8-year old, Manette seemed "back-woodsy" when we moved there in 1927—unpaved streets, outdoor plumbing and water piped to the back porch. But over the years I saw it develop into one of Bremerton's finest areas. I shall never forget the magnificent setting—great water vistas, Mount Rainier (weather permitting), and most of all, the great sawtooth profile of the Olympics. I have always enjoyed the many visits back home since my first departure in 1939. My father died in 1964. It was my rather sad lot to have to sell the family home in Manette following my mother's death in 1980, thus severing the last tangible tie there. But we shall return from time to time to visit friends and enjoy the Great Northwest "fatherland." It's in our blood.

BUCHANAN, DUNCAN A. Sr.
By Christena Buchanan George (1921-1986)
1985

My father, Duncan A. Buchanan, was born January 25, 1892, in Bad Axe, Mich. His father was sheriff of Huron County. Dad grew up on the family farm near Bad Axe and attended the local school. He continued his schooling at Ferris Institute in Big Rapids, Mich. It was here he met Phoebe Fuller, who would later become his wife. She was born July 14, 1891, in Otisville, Mich., where her father published the *Otisville Bee*, a weekly newspaper.

After leaving Ferris Institute Phoebe taught school in Kansas. She also attended school in Emporia, Kans., where she earned an additional teaching certificate. She first taught at a country school. Her next school was a one-room school in Dunn County on the edge of the North Dakota Badlands.

Dad taught school in Michigan and then traveled for a year

before following Phoebe to North Dakota. They were married in Dickinson, N.Dak., September 3, 1913.

Early in 1918, Dad, now the principal of the new two-story school in Dunn Center, left Mom and my three brothers, Floyd, 3 1/2, Duncan, 1 1/2, and Ferris, the baby, to answer the call for workers at the navy yard in Bremerton. Mom and the boys followed as soon as a home could be found for the family. This proved to be a tent house erected on a wooden platform on Charleston Beach. The family spent 10 months there.

The move to Manette was made early in 1919 to a house on the corner of East 10th Street and Ironsides Avenue. Here Esther was born August 18, 1919. My folks bought the house from Charlie Cropp and later sold it to John McDonnel. Mr. and Mrs. Cropp, and their only daughter, Charlotte, lived in the house on the beach at the end of Trenton Avenue, where the Von Hoenes later lived. Our family visited the Cropps in that home many times. Charlotte taught in a one-room school in Illahee. Our family remembers attending a Christmas program at her school.

Dad and Mom next moved our family one street over and up one block to a yellow house on the corner of East 11th Street and Hayward Avenue. It was here that I was born October 14, 1921. The Fellows' house was up on a hill and across East 11th Street from us. Mrs. Fellows and her children were very good to us. Mr. and Mrs. Ed Mey and their children, Jack and Dorothy, lived on Hayward Avenue down the street from us. I remember playing at their house.

Dad was a Manette volunteer fireman. Once when a fire siren was being installed on the pole in front of the yellow house, it was first tested in our living room. Mom wasn't too thrilled about that. Prior to the siren, Manette had a bell in a tower next to the post office. This tower was put up by the volunteer firemen under the supervision of my dad. He had had considerable experience in that type of work.

We moved again in 1925, this time to a two-story brown shingled house on Ironsides Avenue across from the old Manette School.

I remember going to kindergarten, taught by Mrs. Amy Hoopes in her home. I didn't get to finish the year because I came down with scarlet fever. Dad and Floyd rented a house down on Perry Avenue so they could continue going to work

Duncan and Phoebe Buchanan, 1942

and to school, since our house was quarantined.

In the spring of 1930 we moved to the O. Lillevick house at 1617 Wheaton Way. In the fall of the same year we moved to 908 Winfield Avenue, now 220 Shore Drive, and still the Buchanan family home. Our next-door neighbors for many years were the Eric Walls.

Dad was very active in Scouting and was one of the signers of the Charter of Boy Scout Troop 505, Manette. Along with Warren White and several other men, he also started the Kitsap Rifle and Revolver Club.

Mom was very active in the P-TA. and will also be remembered for her many years of service on election boards.

After leaving his job as shipwright at the navy yard in 1929, Dad sold New York Life Insurance. Then, in 1933, he began working as a field deputy for the State Department of Labor and Industries. He retired as district supervisor after 27 years.

He was a craftsman in woodworking and made many beautifully inlaid tables, lamps, picture frames, bowls, plates and trinket boxes. There are pieces of his work in many states and several foreign countries.

Duncan A. Buchanan, Sr., died at home December 23, 1978. His beloved wife, Phoebe, followed him on April 3, 1979.

DESCENDANTS

1. FLOYD ARCHIBALD BUCHANAN, born July 6, 1914, in Hierschville, N.Dak. He married FRANCES VIRGINIA PETERSON (born November 2, 1913, in Port Orchard) in Port Orchard in 1937 and lives in Seattle. Floyd and Frances' four children are:
1A. VICTORIA MARY BUCHANAN, born January 16, 1941, in Seattle. She married RICHARD GEDDES and had two children.
1A1. MARIAN GEDDES, born October 7, 1960, in Seattle.
1A2. WILLIAM EDWARD GEDDES, born July 26, 1962, in Seattle. Victoria Mary married MARVIN OLSON in 1968.
1B. FRANCES MERRIEL BUCHANAN, born May 27, 1946, in Seattle. She married JACOB STEFAN in 1964. They have a daughter.
1B1. TRACY RENEI STEFAN, born April 18, 1965, in Seattle.
1C. F. ARCHIE BUCHANAN, born August 20, 1948, in Seattle. He married AMY HOWAGE in 1984. They have a son.
1C1. ALEXANDER BUCHANAN, born July 10, 1985, in Nehalem, Oreg.
1D. JAMES DOUGLAS BUCHANAN, born September 8, 1956, in Seattle.

2. DUNCAN ARCHIBALD BUCHANAN Jr., born June 1, 1916, in Dunn Center, N.Dak. He married OLIVE ANITA PLANTE (born June 13, 1914, in Pawtucket, R.I.) on December 12, 1945. They live in Bremerton. They have a daughter.
2A. SANDRA ANN BUCHANAN, born March 20, 1953. She married SCOTT BULLOUGH and they have a daughter.
2A1. SHELBY FRANCESCA BULLOUGH, born December 27, 1973, in Bremerton. Sandra married DEAN BOYD in Port Angeles. They have two children.
2A2. AMBER CHRISTINE BOYD, born October 6, 1983, in Port Angeles.
2A3. JOSHUA FRANCIS BOYD, born October 5, 1984, in Port Angeles.

3. FERRIS BUCHANAN, born in North Dakota in 1918. He lives in the family home in Manette and is not married.

4. ROWENA ESTHER BUCHANAN, born in Manette August 19, 1919. She married FRED W. SHEPHERD (born January 31, 1919, in Wichita, Kans.) in Bremerton October 12, 1941. Fred died August 28, 1977, in Tacoma. Fred and Esther had three children.
4A. WILLIAM DUNCAN SHEPHERD, born September 15, 1945, in Camp Shoemaker, Calif.
4B. RONALD EARLE SHEPHERD, born January 2, 1947. He married SHERRIE ARMSTRONG in Tacoma. They have three children.
4B1. JEANETTE LAVONNE SHEPHERD, born May 12, 1974, in Tacoma.
4B2. KENNETH EARL SHEPHERD, born August 13, 1975, in Tacoma.
4B3. REBECCA RENEA SHEPHERD, born April 10, 1977, in Tacoma.
4C. JAMES EOIN SHEPHERD, born August 22, 1956, in Tacoma.

5. CHRISTENA MARY BUCHANAN, born in Manette October 14, 1921. She married ROBERT WILLIAM GEORGE (born March 24, 1921, in Dawson, N.Dak.) in 1947 in Bremerton. Christena died in August of 1986. She and Robert had five children.

5A. MICHAEL JOSEPH GEORGE, born January 30, 1948, in
   Wenatchee. He died April 25, 1968, in Miami, Fla. He is buried at Ivy
   Green Cemetery in Bremerton.
5B. DAVID BRYAN GEORGE, born July 3, 1950, in Bremerton. David
   married DIANNE THORSON April 19, 1986, in Stanwood. They live in
   Marysville.
5C. STEPHEN ARTHUR GEORGE, born December 26, 1951, in Bremer
   ton. He lives in Centralia.
5D. KATHLEEN LOUISE GEORGE, born October 12, 1953, in Bremer
   ton. She married DALE THOMAS GIBSON (born March 27, 1950, in
   Bremerton) on September 13, 1973. Kathleen lives in Red Bluff, Calif.
5E. RICHARD FERRIS GEORGE, born June 3, 1956, in Bremerton. He
   married MARY ELLEN WILKIN (born November 9, 1957, in Port Or
   chard) on June 19, 1982. They have a son and live in Seattle.
5E1. WILLIAM MICHAEL GEORGE, born October 10, 1983, in Seattle.

BURLEW, CHARLES
By Everts P. Burlew
1984

Charles B. Burlew and Cora Palmer Burlew came to
Bremerton prior to World War I, in about 1912. They lived
in a home rented from the Mitcheners in Manette from about
1914 until 1921. They built their own home at 1322 Trenton
Avenue in approximately 1921.

Charles B. Burlew was a graduate of Grinnell College,
Iowa, class of 1892. In Bremerton he was in the accounting
department of the navy yard. When he retired from the navy
yard October 31, 1939, he was senior property and supply
clerk. After retiring he moved to southern California, where
he lived until his death November 28, 1947.

Cora Palmer Burlew grew up in Iowa and graduated from
Capitol City Commercial College of Des Moines, Iowa, in
1903. She was a Sunday school teacher and organist for the
Manette Community Church for many years. She also worked
for the Children's Home. She was a member of Philathea
Chapter, Order of the Eastern Star. Cora died May 18, 1977,
at the home of her son Everts in Charlo, Mont., where she had
spent her last few years.

Due to a problem about my age I attended private school
for the first 3 years—first year of public schools (Manette)
was the fourth grade. The year must have been 1917. In 1920
my mother and I spent the winter in Spencer, Iowa, taking
care of my grandfather. I had my seventh grade there. I
graduated from Manette Grade School in 1921. The only
teacher I remember was Mrs. Kallander, who taught seventh

Charles B. and Cora P. Burlew.

and eighth grades and was principal.

I had 2 years of high school at Union High in Bremerton.
In 1923 I went to live with my uncle, Dr. J.M. Burlew, in Santa
Ana, Calif. I graduated from high school in Santa Ana in
1925.

I entered the University of Washington in mechanical en
gineering in 1925 and graduated in 1929. I did not spend very
much time at home during the school year. In the summer I
usually worked. One summer I drove a fuel truck—wood and
coal—and tended service station for Ben Kean. The service
station was located just up the hill from the ferry dock. For
two summers I worked in the navy yard as a laborer and
machinist helper.

During the last quarter at college I worked half-days for
Continental Can Company in Seattle, and after graduation I
worked full time for them in Seattle, San Francisco, Stock
ton, Chicago, Milwaukee and Los Angeles. I left Continental
Can in 1954 to work for the can division of Campbell Soup
Company in Camden, N.J. In 1960 I went to work for
Reynolds Metals Company in Richmond, Va., to put the
aluminum beer can into production. I retired in 1968 and
moved to Charlo, Mont.

THE FAMILY

CHARLES B. BURLEW was born October 1, 1869, in Grinnell, Iowa.
CORA PALMER was born September 15, 1880, in Bluffton, Minn. Charles
and Cora married August 8, 1906, in Spencer, Iowa. They had one son.

1. EVERTS P. BURLEW was born in Grinnell, Iowa, June 15, 1908. Everts
   married MARGARET KENYON (born March 23, 1908), daughter of a
   well-known Bremertonian J.S. Kenyon, on June 21, 1931. Margaret
   graduated from Bremerton Union High School in 1926, and earned a
   bachelor of science degree from the University of Washington in 1930.
   Everts retired from Reynolds Metals Company and has a home in Charlo,
   Mont. Margaret teaches weaving. Everts and Margaret had one son.
1A. CHARLES K. BURLEW was born in San Francisco May 4, 1944.
   He lives in North Carolina after serving in the army in Germany. He has
   two children:
1A1. ELIZABETH PALMER BURLEW, born October 21, 1972, in Rich
   mond, Va.
1A2. CHARLES K. BURLEW Jr., born September 10, 1977, in Richmond,
   Va.

Charles and Cora Burlew home, 1322 Trenton Avenue, 1923

BURLEW, JAY
By Alfred Wayne Burlew (1918-1985)
1983

My parents, Jay and Alice Burlew, came to Manette from Iowa. Father worked at Puget Sound Navy Yard.

My sister Edith was born in 1908. I was born in Manette June 30, 1918. Our old house is still there at East 16th Street and Wheaton Way.

My father died in 1923 when I was 5. I stayed in the Children's Home during the day while my mother worked at a laundry. Later my mother married Wladislaus Bednawski.

I got pretty well acquainted with the town because I delivered milk here for years, first for Pahrman's Dairy and then for Kitsap Dairy. My fondest memory of Manette is just being here. I went to Manette School. I relate to Manette...sitting in the sun with my back up against one of the stores, watching people go by.

I was in the army during World War II, then in the National Guard for 6 years. I worked in the navy yard as a rigger for 26 years until I retired in 1976. I enjoyed fishing and I belonged to the Pacers CB Club.

In 1937 I married Margaret Irish of Manette. Margaret and I enjoy square dancing. We have five children.

Mother died in San Diego in 1976.

THE FAMILY OF JAY AND ALICE BURLEW

1. EDITH BURLEW. Edith married CHARLES WEIST from Colorado. Charles died and Edith lives in San Diego.
2. ALFRED WAYNE BURLEW, known as Wayne. Wayne married MARGARET IRISH and they had five children.
2A. MARY BURLEW, born January 31, 1940, in Bremerton. She went to school in Mossy Rock, Wash. Mary married ROSCOE KINYON. They divorced and Mary married ERNIE GRAYSON. Mary and Ernie live in Manchester and she works in Poulsbo. Mary has three children: ALICE, ROSS and AMY KINYON.
2B. JAY WILLIAM BURLEW, born April 15, 1943, in Bremerton. He went to school in Mossy Rock. Jay married JOANNA HENKLE. They live in Tracyton and Jay works at Puget Sound Naval Shipyard. Jay and Joanna had five children: ROSE, deceased, STEFEN, TONY, SAMANTHA AND JASON.
2C. NITA BURLEW, born June 23, 1947, in Morton, Wash. She attended Bremerton schools. Nita married JOE LESH. They divorced. She married ED STEWART. They divorced. Nita lives in Bremerton and has two children: PATRICK and MICHAEL LESH.
2D. NIKKI BURLEW, born June 23, 1947, in Morton. She went to school in Bremerton. Nikki married DICK LARSON. They divorced. She married, then divorced, JIM FLOOD. She married RON LINDSEY and they live in Bremerton. They have a daughter, JENNIFER FLOOD.
2E. SALLY BURLEW, born July 26, 1961, in Bremerton. She went to Bremerton schools. Sally married JORGE SALGADO and they live in Virginia. They have two children, JOEL SALGADO and MICHELLE.

Jay and Alice Burlew home, East 16th Street and Wheaton Way

BURTON-FORBES
By Charlotte Hammersburg Forbes

NEW ZEALAND TO THE WEST COAST, U.S.

Arthur Burton was born in New Zealand May 1, 1880. In 1898, when he was 18, Arthur left New Zealand on a three-masted schooner. He arrived in Victoria, B.C., Canada. He traveled around and worked at several different trades such as sheepherder, miner and carpenter.

FAMILIES and HOME

Arthur married his first wife, Tillie Myrtle (April 12, 1882-January 21, 1925), in Cody, Wyo., in 1906. They moved out west and settled in Manette in 1916. Burton built his home at 1816 North Marlow Avenue, the present home of Edward Forbes. Winfield Avenue was the main road out of Manette and it came up by Burtons' and crossed the canyon on a wooden bridge. There was no lower road in those days.

In 1925 Arthur Burton's first wife passed away. In 1928 he married Hazel Burlew Forbes, a widow with seven children. Some of her children were staying in the Sunshine Orphanage (Children's Home) in Manette. More bedrooms were built at the Burton house and they all moved home. Hazel Forbes' children were Raymond Douglas, Donald Robert, Benjamin Addison, Edward Burel, Glen Murray, John Keeford and Myrtle Mae, all born in Bremerton. In 1929, a son, Daniel Burlew Burton, was born to Arthur and Hazel. Arthur died in 1951. Hazel died in 1953.

BUSINESS and RECREATION

Arthur Burton and Robert Moffatt were partners as building contractors in Manette. The Forbes boys were helpers. They built such homes as the Gideon Hermanson home, the Rea home, the Mottner home and many others in Manette. They did reconstruction work on Harry Martin's grocery store and Oscar Etten's meat market on East 11th Street.

At one time Burton was in partnership with Oscar Etten in the meat market. Stone, a previous owner of the meat market, made a violin which he sold to Burton. Ben played it at square dances when he was a square dance teacher and caller in the 1950 and 1960s. He is still playing that violin. He now belongs to the Washington Old Time Fiddlers Association.

Frank and Anna Hawley, who were pioneers in Manette, lived next door to the Burtons. Hawley was a very active politician.

The six Forbes boys, sister Myrtle and Dan Burton were active in many sports. They were all known for their softball playing. Ray and Donald played on the East Bremerton Improvement Club team which was about the first softball team around. They went on to play on teams that twice won state softball tournaments. Sister Myrtle excelled in many sports. She pitched in world tournaments for a Portland softball team. She is in the Northwest Regional Softball Hall of Fame. See "Four Stars" in Chapter 10, RECREATION.

DESCENDANTS

1. RAYMOND DOUGLAS FORBES was born November 22, 1913. On October 28, 1939, he married CHARLOTTE HAMMERSBURG, who was born in Turlock, Calif., June 23, 1920. They had a home wedding in the Manette Children's Home. Mrs. Ben Murray Sr. was the photographer. She wanted experience in taking wedding pictures for the *Bremerton Searchlight* newspaper. Ray and Charlotte have three children.

1A. REBECCA LUCIA FORBES, born March 16, 1941, in Tacoma. She was cared for by Raymond and Charlotte from birth and adopted by them in 1945. Rebecca married ALFRED KILBURG in 1962. In 1970 Rebecca married STEPHEN HOPKINS II. Rebecca and Alfred had one child. Rebecca and Stephen had two children.

1A1. NICOLE KILBURG, born August 7, 1964, in Seattle.

1A2. MEGAN HOPKINS, born September 12, 1972, in Bloomsburg, Pa.

1A3. STEPHEN HOPKINS III, born September 1, 1974, in Bloomsburg, Pa.

1B. DAVID DANIEL FORBES, born November 23, 1942, in Bremerton. David married ADRIANA RODRIEGUEZ (born in Chili, S.A., April 19, 1939) in 1976. They have no children. David is a shipwright foreman at PSNS.

1C. ROBERT GARY FORBES, born January 19, 1944, in Bremerton. He married MARSHA DUNLAP of Sequim. They have three children.

1C1. ROBERT MATHEW FORBES, born February 21, 1969, in Port Angeles.

1C2. KARA ELIZABETH FORBES, born November 3, 1974, in Juneau, Alaska.

1C3. KELCIE ANN FORBES, born January 23, 1983, in Mt. Vernon, Wash.

2. DONALD ROBERT FORBES, born January 30, 1915, in Bremerton. He married JUANITA HENDRY, born July 1, 1921. They have one son.

2A. FARREL FORBES, born August 4, 1941, in Bremerton. Farrel and his wife ANN of Gresham, Oreg., have two children.

2A1. MONIQUE FORBES, born December 16, 1974, in Portland.

2A2. BRADLEY FORBES, born in April 1982 in Portland.

3. BENJAMIN ADDISON FORBES, born July 9, 1917, in Bremerton. He married LEOTA IRISH August 4, 1945.

4. EDWARD BUREL FORBES, born April 15, 1919, in Bremerton. He was married for a few years to EVA, whom he met when he was in the army in Missouri. Ed married DOROTHY AUTREY HALL December 16, 1955. They have five children.

4A. DORIS FORBES, born June 28, 1947. She married BRENT LIPPARD. They have three children.

4A1. TRACI LIPPARD, born November 3, 1965. Traci married RANDY LAKIN. They have one child, RACHEL, born August 20, 1985.

4A2. WILLIAM LIPPARD, born March 27, 1967.

4A3. BRANDI LIPPARD, born July 5, 1973.

4B. SHERWOOD FORBES, born December 6, 1950. He and his wife CINDY have three children, NATHAN, born in 1975, JACOB, born February 28, 1977, and SHELBY, born in 1979. Later Sherwood married DONNA CASTER.

4C. CHARLES RAY FORBES, born August 12, 1953. Charles married BARBARA SANTOS June 26, 1982. They have two children, AUDREY MARIE, born May 17, 1983, and ERICK, born July 16, 1984.

4D. RHONDA MAY FORBES, born August 24, 1956. She married CHAD WINGER. Theyhave two children, SARAH, born April 10, 1981, and ADAM, born July 24, 1984.

4E. TIMOTHY FORBES, born October 26, 1957. Timothy is employed at Bangor as a tile setter.

Burton-Forbes home at 1816 Marlow Avenue, 1987

Arthur Burton and Hazel Forbes Burton family, early 1940s. Back row (from left), Benjamin, John, Raymond, Edward Forbes. Front row, Daniel Burton, Donald, Myrtle and Glen Forbes.

5. GLEN MURRAY FORBES, born October 10, 1920. Glen married VIOLET GOIN December 16, 1943. Glen died May 7, 1977, in Port Orchard. Glen and Violet had three children.

5A. RONALD FORBES, born January 30, 1947, in Bremerton. Ronald and his wives had six children, JOANNA, DANIEL, BRENDA, GLEN, HEATHER and MICHELL. Joanna and Daniel died in early childhood.

5B. FLOYD FORBES, born November 3, 1949, in Bremerton. Floyd and his wife LINDA have one child, ISAAC.

5C. GLENNA FORBES, born August 29, 1964, in Bremerton. Glenna is employed at PSNS as a technician instructor.

6. JOHN KEEFORD FORBES, born February 5, 1923, in Bremerton. He married DOROTHY WHIELDON June 10, 1950. Dorothy died June 6, 1981. John married LOIS BRIGGS KNOTT February 19, 1983. John and Dorothy have two children.

6A. LAURA FORBES, born July 4, 1954. Laura married HARRY GUERRA October 25, 1975. They have three children, KATHLEEN, born July 31, 1979; GEOFFREY, born February 12, 1982, and ANDREW, born December 18, 1983.

6B. LYNN FORBES, born June 11, 1957. Lynn married SOREN NIELSON in July 1975 in Seattle. Lynn and Soren have one child.

6B1. SOREN NIELSON, born June 28, 1978, in Seattle.

7. MYRTLE MAE FORBES, born September 1, 1925, in Bremerton. Myrtle married GARY PIERCE August 18, 1945. Myrtle and Gary had two children. They divorced and Myrtle married RALPH KRESSIN November 13, 1970. Ralph died in 1986. Myrtle lives in Bremerton.

7A. GERALD PIERCE, born May 31, 1948, in Bremerton. Gerald died October 11, 1976, of a heart attack.

7B. KELLY ALLEN PIERCE, born May 31, 1955. Kelly married CORLISS STITH of Woodland, Wash., June 11, 1983. They have one daughter, ASHLEE, born February 2, 1985.

8. DANIEL BURLEW BURTON, born December 24, 1929, in Bremerton. He married MARILYN BURGESS March 9, 1957, in Bremerton. They have two children.

8A. DANIEL ARTHUR BURTON, born December 16, 1957. Daniel married APRIL MAHONEY July 2, 1983, in Bellevue. Daniel and April have a son DANIEL RICHARD, born March 16, 1987.

8B. TERI LYNN BURTON, born May 27, 1965. She is employed as a checker at a Thriftway store in west Bremerton.

CALLISON, ROBERT
By Hazel Callison
1985

Robert and Hazel Callison came from Missouri to Manette in January of 1918. We stayed with Jesse and Sarah Farmer at what is 2802 Perry Avenue today. Farmers had two sons, Dick and Carl, and a daughter, Velna.

I was one of the first to develop flu in Manette during the national epidemic. I remember Mrs. Farmer sent food upstairs for me to eat in the room where I was isolated. I recovered.

Soon we moved into a small house of Farmers' on property near their home. Bob bought the house from Farmers for $1000.

Later we moved to 1123 Pitt Avenue and then to 1514 Perry Avenue.

Bob and Malcolm Meredith formed an early softball team in Manette. They studied the game, which had originated on the East Coast. When Bob's brother Earl came to Manette he joined the team.

In 1935 Girl Scout Troop 4 was formed. Neal Meredith was troop leader and I was her assistant.

OUR FAMILY
ROBERT and HAZEL CALLISON had three children.

1. THELMA CALLISON was born in Manette. She attended Manette School and graduated from Bremerton High School.

2. HAROLD CALLISON was born in Manette January 30, 1923. He attended Manette School and graduated from Bremerton High School in 1940. He is now deceased.

Jean Callison Jones and Vern Jones with two of their three sons. From left, Jean holding Stevie, Jimmy Lee and Vern.   -Photo from June Womac Wilmot

3. JEAN CALLISON was born in Manette in December 1924. Jean married VERNON JONES. Vernon and Jean operated Ted's Lunch on Park Avenue in Bremerton. Vernon died in 1985. Jean lives in Bremerton. Jean and Ted had three sons: RANDY, who lives in Port Orchard; JIMMY, who is a trooper with the Washington State Patrol in Seattle, and STEVEN, who is with the armed services in Washington, D.C.

CARD, GEORGE
By Arthur Card [1923-1986]
1984

George Card was born February 23, 1861, in Tunbridge Wells, County of Kent, England, where he was raised and educated. He taught school and did some private tutoring before leaving England for Canada in 1882. From Winnipeg he traveled across Canada and the northern part of the United States. He returned to England in 1886 and went to work assisting in a prosperous hauling and livery stable business owned by his father, Ephraim Card, which was well serviced by George's five brothers and three sisters. A return to teaching was quickly rejected, and George Card again left England for the United States, landing in New York in 1887. He crossed the United States to Seattle, where he purchased a farm. The farm proved profitable enough to support a family, and on July 30, 1891, George Card and his childhood sweetheart, Jane Elizabeth Batson of Tunbridge Wells, were married in Trinity Parish House in Seattle.

FAMILY AND FARM

Farming gradually took a back seat to child rearing with the arrival of Alyce Mary, born July 21, 1892; Ethel Harriet, October 2, 1893, and Leonard David, September 26, 1895. Another son, Harry Albert "Bert" was born in Manette February 3, 1903.

The farm on the outskirts of Seattle was sold and the family moved to Manette in March 1898. The closest that boat transportation could come to their new home was the dock at Tracyton. With three small children, a wife, livestock and all their possessions, they made the short but very difficult jour-

George Card home at 2450 Perry Avenue.
-Photo from Kitsap County plat book, 1909

ney through the heavily wooded area from Tracyton to the 40 acres they had purchased. The location by present landmarks would be on Perry Avenue between Holman Road and Stone Way, encompassing the area occupied by the Bremerton School District.

George farmed this land until his retirement in 1925, but maintained a garden plot for 28 years after that.

Until the appearance in sufficient numbers of that new invention, the automobile, along with roads, George realized an additional source of income by putting to use his experiences in his father's hauling and livery business. With large wagons pulled by two or four horses he delivered stacks of lumber from the Fellows-Bender sawmill. Later he delivered items of every description dumped by the ferries at the Tracyton, Brownsville and Manette Docks.

In the 1930s a large apple orchard George had planted and protected from the deer led to a brisk business in cider and vinegar. Cider making was a 4-week "outing" staunchly supported by George's son Leonard and grandsons and all the children in the area. They gathered and washed the apples, fed and cranked the grinder and turned the screw press with

Jane and George Card in the mid-1920s.
-Photo from William Card

its heavy oak bar. The jugs of cider were then delivered at 25 cents a gallon. Volunteers for cleanup were harder to find.

The first Sunday School in the area was started by Jane and George Card in the Sheridan School in 1899. They also were the first people baptized into membership in the Manette Community Church in 1906. They remained active throughout their lives in church and community affairs. For many years their home was used as the area polling location for the community.

Through the years the Card family visited back and forth with George's brothers and sisters who had also left England and lived in Cardston, Alberta, Canada.

George Card was a dapper little man with a full, well-trimmed Van Dyke beard, a cigar and a cane or umbrella. He was a familiar figure walking around the community. In 1952 at the age of 91, George turned the first shovelful of dirt in ground-breaking ceremonies for the rebuilding of the Manette Community Church after the original church burned.

The George Card family, 1914. Top row, (from left), Alyce and Harry. Middle row, George and Jane. Front row, Leonard and Ethel.   -Photo from Ted Peterson

George Card and his wife Jane often spent summers with George Card's brother's family in Cardston.

George and Jane celebrated their 60th wedding anniversary July 30, 1951. After 58 years in Manette, at the age of 95, George Card died June 10, 1956, to be followed a few months later by his wife and childhood sweetheart, Jane, November 2, 1956.

THE CARD FAMILY
George and Jane Card had four children.

1. ALYCE MARY CARD, born in Seattle July 21, 1892, attended Sheridan School and Bremerton High School. Alyce married THEODORE PETERSON. [see PETERSON history].

2. ETHEL HARRIET CARD, born in Seattle, October 2, 1893, attended Sheridan School and Bremerton High School. Ethel married ELVIN CLARENCE HAUSDORF [see HAUSDORF history].

3. LEONARD DAVID CARD, born in Seattle September 16, 1895, was only 3 1/2 when the family moved from Seattle to Manette. His chores eventually embraced all the various activities of farming and livestock maintenance. In his early teens he drove the team of horses, making deliveries throughout the area. He completed Sheridan School but the time-consuming ferry service to Bremerton made high school impractical. He worked on the farm and picked up hauling jobs for about 2 years before going to work in shipyards in Seattle. On February 3, 1913, he entered Puget Sound Navy

Leonard and Lillie Card's home at 1145 Wheaton Way, built in 1925 - Photo from William Card

Yard as an apprentice sheetmetal worker.

During World War I while serving in naval aviation, Leonard saw action in France at Dunkirk, Polliac and Bordeaux among other places during his 16 months of overseas duty. He returned home to resume his career in the sheetmetal shop in PSNY and to marry LILLIE WRIGHT of Sumner, on September 11, 1920.

They lived in Sheridan until their home at what is now 1145 Wheaton Way was built.

Leonard and Lillie participated in most of the community activities, but with special long-term commitment to the Manette Community Church, Steadfast Masonic Lodge 216, Order of Eastern Star's Philathea Chapter 174, American Legion Post 68, The Boy Scouts, and The Kitsap County Historical Society. They were also avid gardeners.

During World War II, Leonard and Lillie's activities centered on the war effort. Sheetmetal quarterman Leonard Card devoted many long hours toward the excellent record achieved by the Puget Sound Naval Shipyard for the quick repair and building of ships. Lillie assisted in the USO, Red Cross and the church.

After almost 41 years of government service Leonard retired as a quarterman from Puget Sound Naval Shipyard's sheetmetal shop on October 1, 1955. He continued his fraternal and civic activities along with a part-time pick-up and delivery job for Bolton's saw shop. Leonard was a friendly, happy and respected individual. The delivery job was ideal, because it gave him an opportunity to see and talk with old friends. On March 4, 1960, on his way home from delivering saws, he was stricken with a heart attack and died at the age of 64.

Lillie turned her attention to her home, gardening, grandchildren and the managing of the wedding/reception service for the Manette Community Church. She had a heart attack on October 10, 1972, and passed away at the age of 76.

Leonard and Lillie had three sons.

3A. LEONARD DAVID CARD Jr. was born in Harrison Memorial Hospital in Bremerton on August 20, 1921. He died 3 months later.

3B. ARTHUR CARD was born in Bremerton August 9, 1923. He was active in the Manette Community Church, Boy Scout Troop 505, and the high school football team. He attended Manette School, Lincoln Junior High and Bremerton High Schools. He left Washington State College at Pullman after Pearl Harbor to enlist in the navy. He received radio operator training at the University of Colorado in Boulder. He worked in ship repair at San Diego, Calif., and Norfolk, Va., then served at Port Moresby, New Guinea, before being sent to Hollandia, where he installed antennas and transmission lines through an unfriendly jungle. He next volunteered for duty with a mobile communications unit and was in the initial landings at Morotai, Halmahera Islands, and at San Narciso and Subic Bay in the Philippines. He completed his 6-year enlistment as an electronics instructor in the Electronic Materiel School at Treasure Island, Calif. Arthur was recalled to active duty October 13, 1950, and was assigned to the USS Essex (CV-9) at PSNS, where the aircraft carrier was being readied for duty off the coast of Korea with the Seventh Fleet. Before Arthur left for Korea, he and NORMA L. PETERSON, Bremerton High School class of 1946 and Pacific Lutheran College graduate, were married on February 23, 1951. After serving 16 months, Arthur returned home to re-enroll in Olympic Junior College, and then the University of Washington, where he earned an electrical engineering degree in March 1955.

Norma resigned her teaching position with the Bremerton School District and Arthur, Norma, and a son, WILLIAM ARTHUR, born October 2, 1953, moved to Mountain View, Calif. A daughter, MICHELE

YVONNE, was born in Palo Alto, October 21, 1956. Arthur went to work as a design engineer with Sylvania Electronic Defense Laboratory at Mountain View, Calif. Arthur retired as program manager for GTE-Sylvania on June 30, 1983. He and Norma lived at 838 Cathedral Drive, Sunnyvale.

Arthur and Norma's son William is a marine major in Quantico, Va. William and his wife KAREN LEA (POWELL) live in Stafford, Va. He has two step-daughters, VALERIE and DEANNA, and a son WILLIAM PATRICK. Arthur and Norma's daughter MICHELE is married to THEODORE VIVEIROS, a police officer in Sunnyvale. Michele and Theodore have two daughters SARAH and DEBRA, and a son DAVID. [Arthur died September 16, 1986.]

3C. WILLIAM GEORGE CARD was born in Bremerton June 21, 1925. He attended Manette and Lincoln Schools and Bremerton High School and was active in Manette Community Church, Boy Scout Troop 505 and the high school football team. He left school early to enlist in the US Navy. He was granted his diploma by Bremerton High School in 1944, since he had attained the rating of EM 3/c. After brief instruction at a training facility in Idaho, Bill was assigned to the new destroyer U.S.S. *Sullivans* as an electrician. Bill was with the ship for the remainder of the war. The *Sullivans* became one of the famous ships of World War II and took part in major sea battles. The ship is now at Buffalo, N.Y., in the Naval and Servicemen's Park Museum.

After separation from the navy Bill became a central office repairman for Pacific Northwest Bell, working in Seattle, San Jose, Bremerton and Port Angeles. He later worked as an equipment evaluator in the Washington, Idaho and Oregon areas, retiring in February 1981 as a telephone engineer. Bill is single; he enjoys travelling and cruising. He lives on Sunset Lane, near Seabeck.

4. HARRY ALBERT "BERT" CARD was born in Manette February 3, 1903. He attended high school in Bremerton and then the Merchant Marine Academy. Bert went to sea in almost every type of ship. Sea duty was compatible with his bachelor life. He worked in almost every deck capacity from seaman to master. He served with the Matson Shipping Line on several of the President liners, which made routine trips between Seattle or San Francisco and the Orient. He was also employed as a deck hand for the Black Ball ferries on the Bremerton-to-Seattle run.

During World War II Bert served on several merchant ships as first mate. He survived the torpedoing and sinking of his disabled liberty ship while awaiting a seagoing tug when they were about 3 days out of Australia. While waiting for the loading of his ship in Seattle, Bert was killed in an automobile accident in September 1947.

CARLAW, JACK
By Wanda McLeod Holladay
1985

Jack and Grace Carlaw, with their 9-year-old daughter Bernice, came from Nampa, Idaho, to Manette in 1915. Jack worked in the blacksmith shop in the navy yard. Their home was at 1147 Perry Avenue. Grace's mother, Mrs. McLeod, lived with them in Manette.

Grace was born in Lead, S. Dak., July 15, 1886. I believe Jack was born in Idaho in about 1883. Daughter Bernice was born in Nampa, Idaho, August 4, 1907. A son, Billie Jack, was born in Bremerton. He died in 1918.

CHURCH AND RECREATION

Grace belonged to the Manette Community Church, taught Sunday School and was active in the Ladies Aid for 52 years. Grace was a member of Philathea Chapter of Eastern Star and was its matron one year. She also belonged to Rebekahs, Homemakers Club and the Red Cross. Jack belonged to Steadfast Lodge of the Masons, enjoyed hunting deer and was a volunteer fireman.

BERNICE

Bernice was born August 4, 1907. She attended Manette and Bremerton schools and Washington State College. In 1929 she married "Butch" Meeker, a famous Washington State College football player. They adopted a daughter, Adele. Bernice and Butch divorced and Bernice worked in Meredith's store. Bernice died in Bremerton August 4, 1941.

John "Jack" and Grace Carlaw's home at 1147 Perry Avenue.   -Photo from Wanda Holladay

Grace adopted Adele.

The Carlaws' neighbors were the Sidams, Whites, Filions, Tracys, Egglestons, Dewars, McHenrys and Hoopeses.

Jack died in approximately 1942. On April 8, 1944, Grace married Isaac Hoopes, whose wife Amy had died in 1941. Grace died at age 94 in 1980.

WANDA MCLEOD HOLLADAY

I am Grace's sister Wanda. I lived with Grace and Jack at 1147 Perry Avenue when I came to Manette in 1921. I remember going back and forth to high school on the ferry *Pioneer* and the building of the bridge.

I recall rowboat rides across the bay after ferry hours. I remember the Masonic dances at the Bremerton Masonic Temple and at Island Lake. What fun we had.

I now live at Panorama City in Lacey.

CARLSON, JOHN AARON
By Robert and Violet Carlson
1983

John and Ellen Carlson's wedding picture, October 1895

John Aaron Carlson, his wife Ellen Eliza (Cooley) Carlson and their first four children, Dorothy, Oliver, Raymond and Dean, moved from Batavia, Ill., to the Enetai Beach area of Manette in 1902.

They owned 180 feet of waterfront property, from what is now the north edge of the Scott Harrington property (1710 Jacobsen Boulevard) to 180 feet south. Part of the original house which John built has been incorporated into what is now the Donald Reese residence (1706 Jacobsen Boulevard). Reese bought the property from Pearl and Bruno Lund. The Carlson family lived there until 1910, when they moved to a homestead in eastern Washington.

John Jr. was born in 1903 and died 6 weeks later. Three more children, Kenneth, Clarence and Margaret, also were born while they lived on Enetai Beach.

John Sr., a patternmaker, worked in Puget Sound Navy Yard. He had to row to work in a rowboat when the family first came.

They used to buy fish from the Indians who fished the local waters.

The family lived in Seattle for a time, during which two more children, Eleanor and Robert, were born.

About 1903 Mrs. Carlson's parents, Oliver Emerson Cooley and his wife Mary Margaret, bought the property now owned by Henry Short (1716 Jacobsen Boulevard), adjoining the Carlsons to the north.

In late 1917 or early 1918 the Carlsons moved to a house on the Cooley property and lived there until 1922, when they moved to Tacoma. After 6 years they returned, remaining until 1937. The property then was owned by the Cooleys' other daughter, Sarah Haase, after the death of the Cooleys. Sarah sold it in 1939.

EARLY NEIGHBORS

The Chris Jensens moved to the property south of Carlsons in 1905. The Jensens sold to Charles and Emma Fredrickson around 1919. Emma Fredrickson was a sister of John Carlson.

There has been some member of the Carlson family living on this area of Enetai Beach from 1902. Today, Scott and Eleanor (Carlson) Harrington reside at 1710 Jacobsen Boulevard. They have been there since 1934. The home of Scott and Eleanor Harrington is a former home of Grandpa Walker, who ran a little neighborhood grocery store in his front room in the 1920s. Estelle Meredith states that her husband, grocer Clyde Meredith, kept Walker supplied with staple groceries so he (Clyde) would not have to make so many deliveries to the people on Enetai Beach. Bruno Lund, Bill Schultz and John Carlson built the little home-store for Grandpa Walker, who was Pearl Lund's step-grandfather.

The above properties are all part of McTeigh's Garden Tracts. They were platted in 1892.

GENEALOGY
JOHN AARON CARLSON (born in Sweden August 25, 1865, died in Tacoma August 22, 1939) and ELLEN COOLEY (born in Batavia, Ill. July 6, 1873, died in Bremerton October 20, 1952) were married October 30, 1895, in Batavia. John and Ellen had 10 children.

1. DOROTHY BEATRICE CARLSON, born in Batavia, August 16, 1896. Dorothy married ERNEST T. LINDGREN. Dorothy died in Bremerton February 7, 1980. Dorothy and Ernest had a son.
1A. ERNEST H. LINDGREN, born in Seattle May 14, 1916. Ernest died in Seattle September 1966.

Ellen Carlson and her children Oliver, Dorothy, Dean and Raymond in front of the John Carlson home on Enetai Beach in 1905. The house, extensively remodeled, now belongs to Donald Reese, 1706 Jacobsen Boulevard.

2. OLIVER EMERSON CARLSON, born in Ottawa, Ill., April 8, 1898. Oliver married ADELE BAZANT. Oliver was a patternmaker. Oliver and Adele owned the property at 1711 Jacobsen Boulevard from 1945 until 1956. Oliver died in Nevada in 1965.

3. RAYMOND MAURICE CARLSON, born in Batavia June 22, 1899. Raymond married CAROL HAGER. Raymond retired as a navy captain. Raymond died in Bremerton October 7, 1981.

4. WILLIAM DEAN CARLSON, born in Batavia September 6, 1901. Dean was a patternmaker and married HELEN. Dean died in Alhambra, Calif., May 11, 1969.

5. JOHN AARON CARLSON Jr., born in Manette August 5, 1903. John died September 9, 1903.

6. KENNETH BRETT CARLSON, born in Bremerton June 17, 1905. Kenneth married MILDRED WEINRICH. Kenneth and Mildred had four children.
6A. KENNETH WAYNE CARLSON, born in Tacoma August 2, 1931.
6B. ETHEL MILDRED CARLSON, born in Tacoma May 4, 1939.
6C. JEANNINE DALE CARLSON, born in Tacoma August 30, 1946.
6D. ROBERT BRUCE CARLSON, born in Tacoma November 30, 1948.

7. CLARENCE EDWIN CARLSON, born in Manette January 26, 1908. Clarence married BEATRICE ULVESTED. They lived at 1903 Jacobsen Boulevard from 1937 to 1939. Clarence was a cabinetmaker. He attended the University of Washington and lived in Seattle from 1948 until 1984, when he returned to Bremerton. Clarence died in Manette April 2, 1985. Clarence and Beatrice had two children.
7A. NICOLA INGRED CARLSON, born in Tacoma July 11, 1940.
7B. CHRISTINA VICTORIA CARLSON, born in Seattle May 9, 1942.

8. MARGARET LUCILE CARLSON, born in Manette July 22, 1909. Margaret married GEORGE S. O'LEARY. Margaret and George had one son.
8A. GEORGE KENNETH O'LEARY, born June 21, 1929. He died August 19, 1929.

9. ELEANOR ELIZABETH CARLSON, born in Seattle August 20, 1913. She married SCOTT HARRINGTON. [See HARRINGTON, HERBERT.] Eleanor and Scott have three children: SCOTT Jr., ROBERTA and NEAL.

10. ROBERT A. CARLSON, born in Seattle May 31, 1917. Robert married VIOLET ELLEN TANNAHILL. The Robert Carlsons moved to their property at 1820 Marlowe Avenue in November 1948 and still live there. This property is part of Ryther's First Addition to Decatur. Robert retired from the electronic shop in PSNS. Robert and Violet had two children.
10A. SANDRA LOUISE CARLSON, born May 6, 1947, in Bremerton. Sandra is a supervisor at Kitsap Regional Library.
10B. DONNA LUCILLE CARLSON, born November 17, 1949, in Bremerton. Donna married ROBERT J. OVERLY September 11, 1971, in Bremerton. Donna and Robert have two children.
10B1. JOHN JOSEPH OVERLY, born July 14, 1977, in Kirkland.
10B2. ANNE ELIZABETH OVERLY, born March 14, 1980, in Kirkland.

O.E. Cooley property with the two waterfront houses, 1920. Property is now owned by Henry and Reta Short, 1716 Jacobsen Boulevard. The white house is now part of the Short house. The shake house was torn down by Robert Carlson in 1938.

CARTER, JOHN
By members of the Carter family
1986

John and Cora Carter left Louisiana and moved to Kansas. They lived there a few years, then moved to Seattle. They had 12 children. They purchased a home and 20 acres in Sheridan in 1906 from Fred Reeve, who had built the house in 1901. The acreage was situated on a hillside with a panoramic view of the Olympic Mountains, Port Washington Narrows and the Bremerton area and included the waterfront and tidelands.

John Carter was killed in 1907 while he and his sons were pulling stumps to clear the hillside for a farm. The place was passed on to his wife Cora. Their son Van Burton "Bert" became responsible for running the ranch at the age of 18. All of the family had to pitch in and help.

Seven years later Cora Carter died, leaving the property to the 12 children: Bob, Bert, Earle, Ross, Sewell, Lola, Stella, Coral, Deanne, Hazel, Dora and Belle.

Belle was responsible for clearing title to the ranch by getting the brothers and sisters to deed their shares of the property to Bert.

The Carter farm, like the Jensen farm, was a well known established business on the Manette Peninsula. The farms provided employment for many peninsula young people during the summers. Don and Dick Atkinson both started at the age of 6 picking berries, weeding gardens and running errands. Don continued working all through his school years and even after marriage. That was during the Depression and the only job he had. He earned $1 a day and all the produce he could carry home.

When Bert Carter died in 1950 the property was left to his wife Grace. The waterfront lots on the northwest of the estate had been deeded earlier to son Burt and Anne Carter and daughter Lorraine and Ralph Reed. Grace sold one parcel, including waterfront (below the house) to Dwight and Mildred Scheyer. They still live there. Roy Mottner purchased a section of waterfront, which he later sold to Pat Beatty.

At the death of Grace Carter in 1975, the house and the remainder of the property was left to their children, Van Burton Jr. and Lorraine (Carter) Reed.

The house, with an acre of land, was sold to Alfred "Duffy" and Francy Fouch, who restored it, then to Dick and Pat Miller, who finished the remodeling. It is now owned by George and Doreen LeCompte. Two waterfront lots had been sold to the Strandbergs. The LeComptes purchased those lots

John and Cora Carter's family, about 1918. Back row, (from left), Van Burton "Bert," Snowy Nyberg, Deanne, Earl, Stella, Ross, Lola, Sewell, Al Norman. Middle row, Grace (holding Burt Jr.), Viola (holding Jack), Leslie Reeve, Coral, Mabel (holding Bob Jr.). Front row, May, Belle, Hazel, Dora. - Photo from Lorraine Carter Reed

The John and Cora Carter home in the early years, with the barn in the left foreground. To the right is the home of George and Jessie Morton; Thomas Stockley's home is on the hillside.

from them, also.

The remaining 13 acres are now owned by Burt and Anne Carter and Lorraine and Ralph Reed.

The Carter home still stands, a beautifully restored piece of pioneer history with one of the most magnificent views in Kitsap County.

THE JOHN AND CORA CARTER FAMILY
John and Cora had five sons and seven daughters.

1. ROBERT "BOB" CARTER, born April 11, 1888, eldest son of John and Cora, married MABEL HANSEN, from a pioneer Tracyton family. He worked on the *Pioneer* and *Urania* ferries. He was beloved by every person that rode the ferries, a soft-spoken, kindly man with a ready smile and twinkling eyes. Bob had a heart attack and died while helping lift a car to get it off the ferry. Bob and Mabel had two children:
1A. ROBERT "Bob" CARTER Jr. was born in Bremerton April 11, 1918. He married JOYCE HAMMARGREN and they live on the waterfront near Tracyton. He worked at the Bremerton navy yard and is now retired.
1B. JUNE CARTER was born in Bremerton June 13, 1925. She married SI "Mac" MACDONALD and they live in Orient in eastern Washington. They owned a ranch there, and are now retired.

2. VAN BURTON "Bert" CARTER was born January 11, 1890. He married GRACE RITTER, from a pioneer Tracyton family. As the brothers and sisters moved out, Bert and Grace stayed to run the ranch. They raised grapes, cherries, strawberries, peaches, peas, tomatoes and other vegetables and berries. They sold the fruit and produce to the stores in Bremerton and at the Farmer's Market. Bert hired the neighborhood boys and his son to help him. Children from around the area — Manette and the whole peninsula — came to pick peas and strawberries. Bert's judgment as to how, when and what to plant for successful results in Kitsap County was rated as gospel. Bert and Grace had two children:
2A. VAN BURTON "Burt" CARTER, born in Sheridan July 1, 1918, married ANNE ATKINSON and they live on the waterfront north of the ranch. Burt was in the sheet metal business in Bremerton until retirement. Anne worked for the Bremerton schools and is now retired.
2B. LORRAINE CARTER was born in Sheridan November 18, 1921. She married RALPH REED and they live at Martha Lake near Lynnwood. Ralph has been in the automobile business in Port Angeles and Seattle, and is now retired.

3. EARLE CARTER was born May 7, 1891. He operated a gas station at 6th Street and Naval Avenue. He also started Carter Nursery on Kitsap Way near Kitsap Lake. Earle married VIOLA "Vi" RIECK. Viola died in 1962 and Earle died in 1963. They had two children.

3A. MAE CARTER was born in Alberta, Canada, December 3, 1913. Mae married LOREN GRAHAM and they operated restaurants in Bremerton and at Kitsap Lake.
3B. JACK CARTER was born in Sheridan August 6, 1917. After his father's death, Jack continued to operate the nursery business. Jack also played and his wife NORMA "Sue" sang with a country western band until Jack's death.

4. ROSS CARTER worked on the farm with Bert. He was interested in music, astronomy and good books. A head injury suffered in an automobile accident left him impaired. He never married.

5. SEWELL CARTER was a well-known and popular Bremerton businessman. He operated a gas station and garage at 6th Street and Pacific Avenue until his death. He never married.

The seven daughters of John and Cora Carter lived in Bremerton after leaving home. Each eventually moved to Seattle.

6. LOLA CARTER, the eldest daughter, was born October 17, 1892. She married AL NORMAN. He worked at the Bremerton navy yard until retirement. They had one daughter.
6A. CHERIE NORMAN, born in Seattle June 28, 1927. She married JIM GIBBS, author of books on marine history and shipwrecks. They live near Yachats, on the Oregon Coast.

7. STELLA CARTER, born March 3, 1894, was in charge of the household after their mother died. She married CLIFFORD RIECK. He worked at Sand Point in Seattle. They had one son.
7A. AL RIECK was born in Bremerton March 18, 1921. He married LILLIAN "Lil" VUKELICH. They both worked at Sand Point. They have retired and live in Juanita, Wash.

8. CORAL "Tiny" CARTER was born April 6, 1895. She married LESLIE REEVE, who worked as a bookkeeper and accountant for Cudahy and other Seattle firms. They had no children.

9. DEANNE "Daisy" CARTER was married to SNOWY NYBERG and then was divorced. She later married JOSHUA FALK; his family was part owner of Black Ball Lines. Deanne and her sister Belle owned a grocery store near downtown Seattle in the 1940s. Deanne had no children.

10. HAZEL CARTER was born January 28, 1904. She married WILLIAM SEIDLE. He worked in the Federal Building, and later owned the Cherry Street Garage and surplus stores in Seattle and Pasco. Hazel married JERRY VROOM after Bill's death, and they lived in Kennewick. Hazel and Bill had one son.
10A. WILLIAM SEIDLE Jr. was born in Seattle May 26, 1929. He mar-

ried VIVIAN ZEMAN and they live in Arlington, Tex.

11. DORA CARTER was born August 2, 1905. She married KENNETH
BATES. He worked for United Air Lines. They lived in Seattle, Ohio and
California and then retired and moved to Kansas City, Kans. They had no
children.

12. BELLE CARTER, the youngest sister, was born March 25, 1907. She
married EDWIN O'HARE; they were both accountants and lived in Seattle, Oregon and California. They have retired and live in Kansas City, Kans.
They have one daughter.
12A. JAQUELLINE O'HARE was born in Seattle May 25, 1930. She married MICHAEL KLAMANN, a commercial artist. They live in Kansas
City, Kans. Jackie works for the city.

CHRISTENSEN, CHRIS
By Harold Christensen and
Faith Christensen Glud
1985

The first member of the Christensen family to arrive in
Manette came here as Maggie Jane Sidam. She arrived in July
1906 by train from Billings, Mont. She spent her 21st birthday
on the train.

After arrival she wrote articles of her trip for a Billings
newspaper.

Maggie's parents [see SIDAM, ALFRED, history] were
caretakers for summer homes of Seattle residents at Enetai
and Maggie, while also working there, met Chris Christensen, captain on the yacht *Lotus*. The *Lotus* would be anchored
offshore or at the dock at Enetai during the summer when her
owners, the McMickens, were at their summer home there.

Captain Christensen had sailed from Denmark as a lad of
14 and worked on ships for several years. He became an
American citizen April 1, 1907, in Seattle. While captain of
the *Lotus* he spent winters in harbor at Port Madison on the
boat and summers plying the waters of Puget Sound and the
inland passage to Alaska. He also skippered other boats to
California and Mexico.

Captain Christensen and Maggie were married October 25,
1911, at Bethany Baptist Church, now Manette Community
Church, by Reverend J.H. Wood. Maggie was the first bride
married in that church. In a newspaper interview December
17, 1964, Maggie recounted the event.

"I'd worked days making the wedding cakes at our home
in Enetai. The day of the wedding Mother, Father and I
walked the full distance from our home to the church, lugging
the cake and all the other paraphernalia we needed."

Maggie was attired in a tan suit with lace collar and tan hat
with a huge ostrich feather. After the wedding, Maggie's
mother warned Chris that some of the men intended to take
him for a mule ride, and fearing Chris' bad temper and strong
arm might best the fun loving guests, she shoved him out the
back door, so he could return to the yacht.

Maggie stayed on at the church entertaining the guests, then
walked back to Enetai to spend the night. When the neighbors
saw her arrive alone that night, her ostrich feather blowing in
the wind, they got together with buckets of rice and sprayed
her.

Maggie also recalled that one of the summer homes her
father took care of was that of Mr. and Mrs. William Bremer.
She had a fondness and great admiration for that family. "William would stop his launch en route to Bremerton and pick up
friends and neighbors who wanted to go to town."

In the summer when the yacht was in use, Maggie lived in

a tent at Enetai. In the winter she lived aboard the yacht. Maggie and Chris painted, varnished and cleaned to prepare the
boat for summer travels. After their son Harold was born in
1914 Maggie feared he might fall overboard and they moved
to what is now 1147 Perry Avenue. They also owned a home
in the early days at what is now 1300-1304 Ironsides Avenue,
across from the Manette School. In about 1920 they bought a
house and 4 acres at what is now 2702 East 16th Street. Their
daughter Faith was born in 1921 and lived in that house until
she married in 1940.

During World War II Maggie rented rooms to people who
had come to work in the navy yard. If you had an empty bed
they pleaded with you to let someone sleep in it.

Although Chris after skippering the *Lotus* worked in Seattle at Pioneer Sand and Gravel until retirement in 1951, Maggie had the kids in school and was staying in Manette.

HAROLD CHRISTENSEN

I was known as "Chris" like my father. I attended school in
Manette and graduated from Bremerton High School. My
hobbies included music, amateur radio and boats.

I remember sitting in the cabin of the *Pioneer* waiting for
the boat from Seattle to bring the *Post-Intelligencer* papers so
I could get them and do my paper route in the evening instead
of getting up at 6 in the morning to do it before school.

After high school I went to Vancouver, B.C., and signed on
as engine room junior on the Danish motor ship *Stjerneborg*.
We made port in Australia, South Africa, Canary Islands,
Ireland, England, Holland, Panama Canal, and then
Longview.

I was at my aunt's in San Francisco when a friend notified
me that the army transport *Republic* was short an oiler. Grab-
bing my sea bag and hailing a taxi, I made a "pier head jump"
just as they were pulling up the gangplank. I went to New
York, where I signed off the *Republic* in 1937.

I came back to Seattle and worked out of the Inland
Boatmen's Union. I worked on the *Bainbridge* in 1937. She
ran from Port Blakley to Seattle with a passenger stop at
Country Club, a small peninsula south of Port Blakely on
Bainbridge Island. In 1937 and 1938 I made the run from
Seattle to Bremerton on the motor vessels *Klahanie* and
Keloken. I worked at one time or another on every run on
Puget Sound covered by the Black Ball Line except the
Fletcher Bay to Brownsville run.

FAITH CHRISTENSEN GLUD

Our 4-acre property on East 16th Street was bounded on
the west by Isaac Hoopes' property, on the north by Tom
Bright's and on the east by Trenton Avenue. The E.E.
Schoonovers and the Jim Armstrongs lived across East 16th
street from us. Vandalia and Nipsic Avenues were not cut
through.

Margaret Hoopes and I had tents on each side of the property line and we slept there and played in our tents during the
summer. Margaret, the Schoonover girls and I packed lunches
and went to the Sandbanks to swim during the summer. The
water was cold and we got barnacle cuts on our feet but we
would get wet and yell out, "How warm it is today."

We attended Sunday School and Vacation Bible School
and remember the Sunday School picnics at Island Lake or at
Ammermans' and Stevensons'. They were related and lived

in the same house. It was a big thing to get together and play games, eat and just visit.

Maggie and Chris sold the East 16th Street home about 1945. Maggie went to Winthrop to help my husband Clarence and me on our farm for a while. She then returned to her brother William's in Bremerton to help his wife with his care.

About 1950 Maggie and Chris bought a place at what is now 3415 Forest Drive next to the old Sylvan Way Baptist Church (now Bremerton Bible Church). Chris retired in 1951 and came home to live. He passed away in 1953.

Maggie stayed on until August 1970, when she sold her home and came to Aberdeen to live with us. She died in 1977.

GENEALOGY

CHRISTIAN EDVARD CHRISTENSEN was born in Hjorring, Denmark, April 14, 1878. He married MAGGIE JANE SIDAM, born in 1885. Chris died in 1953; Maggie died in 1977. Chris and Maggie had two children.

1. HAROLD CHRISTENSEN, born in 1914 in Bremerton. Harold married ANN BOTTEM from Port Orchard and they live in Council, Idaho. They have three children.
1A. HAZEL JEAN CHRISTENSEN, born in 1941 in Bremerton. Hazel married DAVID K. OESTREICH and they live in Richland.
1B. GEORGE EDWARD CHRISTENSEN, born in 1945 in Bremerton. George is single. He lives in Bremerton.
1C. BETH ELLEN CHRISTENSEN, born in 1951 in Bremerton. Beth married RICK MALLORY and they live in Donnely, Idaho.

2. FAITH CHRISTENSEN, born in 1921 in Manette. Faith attended school in Manette and graduated from Bremerton High School. Her interests during school were swimming, skating and youth group activities at Manette Community Church. Faith married CLARENCE W. GLUD of a Kitsap pioneer family and they live on the old Glud homestead in a home they had built and moved into in 1985. Faith and Clarence have four children.
2A. CAROLE ANN GLUD, born in 1941 in Bremerton. Carole married N. AHLFS. They divorced and Carole now lives in Poulsbo.
2B. LINDSEY JANE GLUD, born in 1944 in Bremerton. Lindsey married PAT McCAULEY. They divorced and she now lives in Bend, Oreg.
2C. DONALD WALTER GLUD, born in 1952 in Bremerton. Donald is single and lives in Hoquiam.
2D. ROBIN MAY GLUD, born in 1955 in Bremerton. Robin married MIKE STENBERG and now lives in Yakima.

CLARE, CHESTER

[The following information about Chester Clare came from the *Bremerton Sun* of June 29, 1962. Chester Clare was one of eight sons and five daughters of Samuel Norval Clare and Josephine Ellen Clare, but no information on the others was submitted. In 1904 Samuel purchased a ranch off Brownsville Highway, in the area subsequently known as "Clare's Marsh."

Newlyweds, Chester and Nina Clare, 1912.
-Photo from Bremerton Sun.

Clare Avenue also was named for the Clare family.]

Chester Clare was born in Winnipeg, Manitoba, April 1, 1886. He married Nina Walker, born in Mound, Minn., March 24, 1890. Chester worked at PSNS as a pipefitter and pipe coverer for 25 years. He transferred to Keyport in 1944 and retired in 1946. Chester and Nina had five children, Mrs. J.V. (Helen) Prather, Mrs. E.C. (Ruth) Otto, Mrs. Bernice Jackson, Mrs. Robert (Grace) Lawing and Douglas Clare.

After retiring, Chester enjoyed hunting, fishing, gardening and working in his workshop, where he made rolling pins and walking canes. He was a member of Masonic Lodge 218 of Manette.

Nina was noted for her handiwork, particularly her wool shirred rugs. She was an active member of the Home Economics Club and served as president of Kitsap County Homemakers Council. She was also a member of Bremerton Court 9, Order of Amaranth.

CLAY, GEORGE
By Kathryn Clay Dickerson
1984

George and Mary Clay left Cedar County, Miss., in 1889. They and their four children, Frank, Clarissa, Nettie and Ollie, arrived at Tracyton. They had friends near there who had come west several years before. These friends, the Peckenpaughs, made them welcome. Soon George built a home for his family. The Clays were the first white family to settle on the Tracyton township. They had a hard time as someone had stolen George's purse with all their money while they were on the train.

Eight-year-old Frank helped his family in any way he could. He picked tomatoes for the Moshers for 25 cents a day plus lunch—always stewed tomatoes.

In 1897 the family moved to Bremerton. The same year, another son, Leland, was born. He was a dependable young man like his brother Frank. He died tragically on Halloween Eve, 1911. A group of young men were following some marines that had been dumping over outhouses and doing other mischief. A man on the corner of 8th Street and Chester Avenue was so angry that he shot into the group of boys. They had a count and found Leland missing so they backtracked and found Leland dead on the street. The man people suspected left town. Years later the Clays learned that this man had moved to Canada and before he died had confessed to the killing.

In 1900 Frank got work at the shipyard. Mary's sister and her husband, Mr. and Mrs. George Benskin, came to Bremerton about this time.

George Clay went to work for the city of Bremerton. With Frank's help they bought a home at 8th Street and Boston Avenue. Now Boston is called Veneta.

FRANK CLAY WEDS

On June 1, 1912, Frank Clay and Katherine Syversen were married on Bainbridge Island. Frank and a friend, Jim Boe, built a home at 10th Street and Vandalia Avenue. The newly married Clays moved into this new home on October 1, 1912. The following April 5, Kathryn Louise Clay was born.

About 1917 Frank had a duplex built next to their home on

East 10th Street. There was such a shortage of homes in Bremerton during the first world war that every available bedroom was rented out. During that time there were people living in tent houses. There were tent houses on Shore Drive. Government houses were built in Bremerton.

On February 5, 1920, Robert F. Clay was born in a Seattle hospital. This was during the horrible flu epidemic. Katherine was taken to the hospital in a hearse instead of an ambulance because there were so many people sick at the time. It was unusual for both the mother and child to live when the mother had the flu, but both did.

During these years we all had to go to Bremerton by boat to see the doctor and the dentist. Mr. Fetterman, the druggist, prescribed medicine to many people. He had a drug store close to the shipyard gate where McDonald's restaurant is now.

To go to Bremerton, we rode the auto ferry *Pioneer* or its passengers-only substitute, the *Urania*. The *Pioneer* carried about six cars. The boats to Manette tried to connect with the schedule of the Seattle boats.

In 1937 Frank and Katherine sold their home on East 10th Street, as Katherine had inherited 82 feet of waterfront property at Crystal Springs on Bainbridge Island. The seven daughters of Katherine's parents, Captain and Mrs. Charles Syversen, returned to the family property. They lived in a row, the oldest at one end of the tract and the youngest at the other end. Five of the sisters lived to be over 91. They all lived there the rest of their lives except the Clays, who moved in with daughter Kathryn and her husband George Dickerson in 1961.

Frank and Katherine Clay and daughter Kathryn at their home at 2704 East 10th Street, about 1917.
- Photo from Kathryn Clay Dickerson

Frank Clay passed away on November 14, 1963, and Katherine Clay on October 2, 1974. She was the last of the seven Syversen sisters from Bainbridge Island.

KATHRYN

In 1932 Kathryn commuted to the University District in Seattle to a business school. In 1934 she went to work for the telephone company.

In 1938 Kathryn married George Dickerson, a childhood

sweetheart. They had three children, two girls and a son. The son, Clay M. Dickerson, served his apprenticeship in the shipyrd. He works there as a supervisory nuclear pipefitter. He and his wife Patti have a son and a daughter.

The older girl, Claudia Johnson, lives near Nashville. Her husband is a vice chancellor for the Universities of Tennessee. They have three children.

Kay Derkland, the younger girl, is a beautician in Bremerton. She and her daughter, Sheree, the Dickerson's first grandchild, live at 2010 2nd Avenue SW in Bremerton, next door to Kay's parents.

In 1943 George and Kathryn moved back to Manette and lived on some of the Chris Jensen property at Cascade View and Trenton Avenue until 1950. They then moved to East 11th Street and Veneta Avenue. They stayed there until George retired from Puget Power as a line foreman in 1973. Then they bought a mobile home and moved it to their own lot above the highway to Gorst. George passed away May 24, 1983.

The Frank Clay family. From left are Bob, Frank, Katherine and Kathryn. The car is a 1923 Buick.
-Photo from Kathryn Clay Dickerson

ROBERT

Robert graduated from Washington State University in 1941 and in 1942 got a degree in education for a teaching certificate. He was teaching in Winlock, Wash., when he enlisted in the air corps during World War II.

He and Maxine Rattan were married in Denver in September 1943. Bob went from a private to a captain in 4 years. He spent another 2 years during the Korean War in North Africa.

As a civilian at Tinker Air Force Base in Oklahoma he headed one of the largest computer data-processing complexes in the United States for 13 years before he retired in 1973. He was also chairman of one of the 10 largest credit unions in the world with assets of over $200 million.

Bob and Maxine have a son and a daughter and three grandchildren. They spend their winters in the Rio Grande Valley in Texas and travel during the summer in their motor home. In the summer of 1984 they went to Alaska, met Kathryn in Juneau and they all came back to Seattle on the ferry *Columbia*. The rest of the summer they stayed near Bremerton.

DESCENDANTS OF GEORGE AND MARY CLAY

1. FRANK CLAY was born in Missouri October 29, 1881. In 1912 Frank married KATHERINE SYVERSEN. Frank and Katherine had two children.

1A. KATHRYN LOUISE CLAY, born in Bremerton April 5, 1913. In 1938, Kathryn married GEORGE DICKERSON. Kathryn and George have three children.

1A1. CLAY M. DICKERSON, born in Bremerton in 1950. Clay married PATTI MORSE. Clay and Patty have a son and a daughter, JOSHUA and KARA.

1A2. CLAUDIA DICKERSON, born in Bremerton. Claudia married KARL N. JOHNSON and lives near Nashville. They have three children, KARY L., JOHN and DOROTHY OLGA "Dodie."

1A3. KAY DICKERSON, born in Bremerton. She lives in Bremerton. Kay married WILLIAM DERKLAND. They have a daughter, SHEREE, born in Bremerton in 1967.

1B. ROBERT F. CLAY, born in Seattle February 5, 1920. He married MAXINE RATTAN. They have a son and a daughter, MICHAEL and KAREN.

2. CLARISSA CLAY.

3. NETTIE CLAY.

4. OLLIE CLAY.

5. LELAND CLAY, born in 1897 in Tracyton. Leland died in Bremerton in 1911.

COLE, FORREST JOSEPH
By Dorothy Cole Rogers
1986

Mr. and Mrs. Forrest Joseph Cole lived many years at 2706 East 13th Street. They came to Manette from Spokane in 1917 to take work at the Puget Sound Navy Yard, as many others did at that period in World War I.

Mr. Cole, known as "Doc," worked to retirement at the shipyard in the shipfitter shop. He served as a quarterman during World War II.

"Doc" Cole's first home was a tent near the beach on the Marlett property at the north end of Lower Shore Drive. He was soon able to rent a home on the beach in the vicinity of the Marletts' property, and brought his wife Dorothy, a son Raymond, and a daughter Dorothy to Manette. A second son Riley was born in a Bremerton hospital, where Mrs. Cole was taken by rowboat for the birth. They had no car.

I, Dorothy, and my two brothers attended Manette School and the Manette Community Church. Mr. and Mrs. Cole were active in the church and sang in the choir.

I was married February 5, 1937, to Jack Rogers. Jack's parents were Mr. and Mrs. J.F. Rogers, who came to Manette during World War I and later moved to Bremerton.

After our marriage, I worked with Jack in our newspaper businesses in Manette, Port Orchard and Silverdale. I also helped to open the Treasure Chest gift shop in Bremerton, which we owned with the Wendell Arnolds. I also worked with Jack in operating the Bremerton Printing Company for several years.

Jack and I paid Earl Harkins $100 for his *Manette News-Letter* and this paper eventually became the *Kitsap County News*, published on the Manette Peninsula until it was ultimately combined with the *Silverdale Breeze* which Jack Rogers and Dave Averill purchased from George Harrison. Jack and I purchased the Arnolds' interest in The Treasure Chest and operated it until 1956, when it was sold.

After Jack and I moved from Chico to Olympia in 1969, I operated Fernbrook Herbs, a wholesale herb-growing nursery, and joined Karman McReynolds in writing a cookbook of favorite recipes featuring home-grown herbs. Karman and her husband Donald operate Cederbrook Herb Farm at Se-

Forrest and Dorothy Cole and son Raymond (seated on porch) at Cole home, circa 1918. Photo from Dorothy Cole Rogers.

quim. They formerly operated The Melody Lane restaurant in Bremerton. They lived in Tracyton at the time.

I have been very active in volunteer work, both in Bremerton and Olympia. I have been chairman of the Herb Garden Committee at the Washington State Capitol Museum and also have given many volunteer hours to the St. Peter Hospital Auxiliary and the Puget Sound Blood Bank. I was a docent, guiding tours through the Governor's Mansion in Olympia.

My mother worked as a clerk at Harry Martin's grocery store when there were boardwalks along East 11th Street. Brother Raymond delivered groceries from Martin's grocery store by wheelbarrow to the summer residents along Enetai Beach, where wealthy Seattle folks lived in their vacation homes. I also remember delivering the *Post-Intelligencer* newspaper by bicycle along what is now Shore Drive. I particularly recall driving my bicycle off the path near the Parkins house and landing in a heap 'neath the window of Eugene Parkins' bedroom. Another fond memory from those days at 2706 East 13th Street was the joyful sound of Mrs. Art (Georgia) Personette singing lustily and playing her piano at their home nearby. Art and Georgia Personette were the parents of George and Mary Personette.

In 1986 Jack and I moved from Olympia back to our home on Chico Way near Silverdale, where we had lived for 25

The Cole home at 2706 East 13th Street. 1987 Photo

years while raising our family. We have two daughters, Mary Rogers Smith, who resides in Connecticut, and Cathy Rogers, who resides in Seattle.

THE FAMILY
FORREST JOSEPH COLE was born October 4, 1888, in Grafton, Nebr. He married DOROTHY EVA WELLER, born March 22, 1896, in Broadstairs, England. Forrest died in 1960. Dorothy died in 1970. They had three children.

1. RAYMOND F. COLE, born July 29, 1915, in Spokane. He graduated from Bremerton High School in 1933. He enlisted in the U.S. Army Air Force in 1941 and served as radar mechanic. Later he was stationed with a unit that worked on the Alaska Highway. After the war Raymond operated an appliance sales business in Manette. Raymond died February 19, 1986, in Veterans Hospital near Tacoma, where he had been a patient for 25 years.

2. DOROTHY GRACE COLE, born November 7, 1916, in Spokane. Dorothy married JACK ROGERS February 5, 1937. They have two children.
2A. MARY ROGERS, born June 3, 1940, in Bremerton. Mary married DAVID SMITH and they live in Connecticut. They have two children.
2A1. ANN SMITH, born January 21, 1967, in Middletown, Conn.
2A2. SARAH SMITH, born October 8, 1968, in Middletown, Conn.
2B. CATHY ROGERS, born November 14, 1942, in Bremerton. Cathy lives in Seattle and has one son, Noah. Noah uses his mother's name. His father is James Tapley.
2B1. NOAH ROGERS, born October 31, 1970.

3. RILEY WALTER COLE, born in Bremerton June 6, 1920. He graduated from Bremerton High School in 1938. Riley married PAULINE MULVANEY of Bremerton. He worked as an electrician in the Bremerton and Vancouver, Washington, areas. He also worked in San Francisco, where he was an electrical supervisor on the Bay Area Rapid Transit system. He served in the Seabees during World War II. Riley died in Oakland in 1971. Riley and Pauline had a son and a daughter.
3A. RILEY DENNIS COLE, born June 29, 1946. Riley lives in California.
3B. LYNN COLE, born March 8, 1949. She married CHARLES McCONVEY. They live in California, and have two children, JAMIE and SHAWN.

CROWELL, CONNIE
By Dorothy Crowell Germaine
1985

FROM UTAH TO MONTANA TO MANETTE
Mother, Connie Carter Crowell, was born in Ogden, Utah, in 1893. She came to Kitsap County from Montana with a friend, Helene Calhoun, in 1919. My sister Jessie was born in Helena, Mont., in 1912. When I was born in Great Falls, Mont., April 18, 1914, Dad claimed he wired his Irish relatives and they celebrated so loudly that Kaiser Bill thought his cousin, George of England, was shooting at him so he started to shoot back and that was the beginning of World War I. Dad, Obei Crowell (1890-1948), entered military service in 1916 and mother went to work for the post office in Helena. When Dad returned in 1919, mother decided she didn't want to return to being a housewife but wanted to remain liberated. My parents separated. Mother applied for a position in Puget Sound Navy Yard. She was hired in the fiscal office, where she worked for 30 years and was promoted to fiscal supervisor.

A NEW FAMILY IN A NEW TOWN
In June, 1920, Helene came back to Helena to get us girls.
I remember traveling with my sister Jessie and Mother's friend Helene to Seattle in a train. How well I remember our first ferryboat ride from Seattle. I was sure the ferry would sink before we got to Bremerton. We moved into a little house on 5th Street. The house has since burned down.
Mother earned enough money in the accounting department at the navy yard for us to live on, $30 a month, and

Helene kept house. Helene was 15 years old when I was born, and virtually adopted me.

In 1920 Mother met and married Ben Robins, a mechanic for Stubbs Studebaker Company on 4th Street near Washington Avenue in Bremerton. We moved to a larger house on Park Avenue across from the Park Avenue Dairy. Mom and Ben bought a little old house in Manette. They spent all their spare moments over there making it livable. On Memorial Day of 1921 we were packed into a borrowed truck with our household goods and our cat, Tommy. Instead of going on that terrifying big boat that brought us from Seattle to Bremerton, we drove onto the safe little *Pioneer*. Bob Carter, who worked on the *Pioneer*, looked at me and smiled, "So you are the new little girl moving to Manette!" I knew I was moving to the most wonderful place in the whole world — Manette. It never let me down in the 30 years I lived there.

Our little house was at what is now 1117 Hayward Avenue, across from Fellows' farm with its big water tower. We kids would climb the steep steps to the top where we could see a "million miles" away. There we would tell each other our special dreams of what we would do when we grew up. I shared my dreams with Roger Paquette. Dreams were never repeated off the water tower.

The Wall family lived next to the water tower. I remember Ruth, Dorothy, Charlie, Bob and Marion. What happy times I had with them. Next to our house lived the Bubb family.

My stepdad built me a 4-foot high doll house and the furniture for it. Mom and Helene Calhoun made curtains and bedspreads. Then Mom admonished me not to mess it up or get it dirty. I was afraid to play with it. Later she decided,

The Crowell sisters—Jessie, 8, and Dorothy, 6, in 1920.
-Photo from Dorothy Crowell Germaine Fiallo.

The Ben and Connie Crowell Robbins home at 1117 Hayward Avenue in 1930.
-Photo from Dorothy Crowell Germaine Fiallo

since I never played with my doll house, she would give it to the Childrens' Home. I went down to the home, and what fun I had playing and sharing it with everyone else!

In 1924, when I was 10, Helene went back to Helena to care for her dad. Four years later she came back to take care of mother after mother had gall bladder surgery, a very serious operation in 1928. Mother was in the hospital for almost a month.

Mother was divorced from Ben Robins and in 1926 married Merville Osburn. Mother died in 1982 at age 89. She is buried at Poulsbo Mountain View Cemetery. Beside her is Helene, who died in 1958 at age 59.

EARLY BUILDINGS

On the corner of East 11th Street and Perry Avenue, construction of the Masonic Temple was started with the laying of a cornerstone in 1926. I was a Rainbow girl in the Bremerton lodge. What dances we would have at Manette's new Masonic Temple after its completion the end of 1927! At intermission we would cross the street to an old building where the Eastern Star ladies sold sandwiches, homemade pies and cakes.

Down what was later Hayward Avenue and across 9th Street was a little shack of a house that the Chases owned. It had two small rooms, a pantry and a bathroom. During the Depression they tried to sell the house and lot for $100, but had no takers. It was my first dream home. When George Mitchell "Mitch" Sherman and I were married June 3, 1931, we paid $900 for the place. Mother said I could have $100 for a church wedding or $100 for a down payment on the house. I chose the house. Helene came from Montana to prepare everything for my wedding at home.

Mitch took an apprenticeship as a machinist in the navy yard. Later he transferred to electronics. He was the designer of the Sherman Sleeve, better known as the nose cone on our rockets in space.

I worked a couple of years in Bremerton in Sears' credit department, then I worked in the accounting department in Puget Sound Navy Yard in 1941-1942. Mitch Sherman and I divorced in 1939. We had three sons, Charles, Lee and Jerry.

I met William George Germaine Jr. when World War II

started and the army moved into the abandoned Children's Home. The army piled great heaps of coal on the playgrounds. George was caught sneaking back into camp after curfew and had to put in a week of hard work on that coal pile. Then I had to sneak in to visit him. The sarge was always nice and looked the other way, particularly if I brought along some extra homemade cookies.

George was born in Jersey City, N.J., September 3, 1915. He retired from the Naval Torpedo Station at Keyport in 1972. He died in 1978 and is buried in Poulsbo.

George and I were married April 18, 1942. We had four sons, George III, Frank, Tom and Tim.

I am a resident manager of the Pointe East Apartment Complex in Enumclaw.

I married Oswaldo Mario Fiallo in 1987.

THE FAMILY
Connie and Obei Crowell's descendants include:

1. JESSIE ELIZABETH CROWELL, born in Helena, Mont., in 1912. She married ELMER EDWARD "Ed" DODSON of Nelscott, Oreg. They met at McMinnville College. Ed was a policeman in Detroit, Mich. Jessie died in 1980. Ed and Jessie had five children:
1A. ARLEIGH RUSSELL DODSON, born in Bremerton in December 1932. He is a professor at Lewis and Clark College in Portland. Arleigh has four sons.
1B. JAMES "Jim" DODSON, born in July of 1934 in Detroit. He lives with his wife FRANCIS in Bremerton. James is a postman in Poulsbo.
1C. LESLIE EDWARD DODSON, born in Detroit in 1936. Leslie lives in Kalamazoo and is a tennis pro. He has two sons.
1D. RALPH OBADIAH DODSON, born in 1943. Ralph lives in California.
1E. CONNIE DODSON, born in 1945. Connie lives in California.

2. DOROTHY IRENE CROWELL, born April 18, 1914, in Great Falls. I married GEORGE MITCHELL "Mitch" SHERMAN in Manette on June 3, 1931, at the pastor's parsonage. We divorced in 1939. Mitch died in 1964. Mitch and I had three sons:
2A. CHARLES MITCHELL SHERMAN Sr., born May 20, 1932. Charles became a computer scientist for the government. He is now retired and lives in Pennsylvania. In 1951 he married MYRA CURTIS of Bremerton. They were divorced in 1962 and he married LEORA STARKS of Bremerton, who had three sons, SKIP, VERN and EDDIE AHLF. Charles and Myra had four children:
2A1. CHARLES M. SHERMAN Jr., born in Bremerton June 28, 1952. He lives near Chico and works for PSNY.
2A2. STEVEN CURTIS SHERMAN, born in Bremerton October 31, 1956. He attended college in Dillsburg, Pa. Steven has two children.
2A3. SCOTT O'RILEY SHERMAN, born in Bremerton December 21, 1957. He died from an accidental gunshot wound in 1985. Scott had two children.
2A3a. CHARLIE SHERMAN, born in Bremerton in 1980.
2A3b. RANI LYN SHERMAN, born in Bremerton in 1983.
2A4. KIMBERLY LAINE SHERMAN, born in Bremerton July 19, 1959. She now lives in Bremerton.
2B. LEE ALLEN SHERMAN Sr., born April 21, 1934, in Manette at his grandmother Connie's house. He married VIRGINIA CLIATT in Augusta, Ga., in 1954. They were divorced in 1956. Lee is retired and lives in Sulphur, La. Lee and Virginia have one son.
2B1. LEE ALLEN SHERMAN Jr., born July 14, 1955, in Bremerton. Lee lives in Bremerton and works at Bangor.
2C. JERRY DALE SHERMAN Sr., born June 23, 1936. He married PATRICIA CURTIS June 7, 1958, in Bremerton. They divorced in 1976. Jerry lives in Bremerton and works at PSNS. Jerry and Patricia had three children.
2C1. KELLY LYNN SHERMAN, born August 12, 1959. Kelly married CHRIS PETTY in Bremerton in 1982. They divorced in 1986. Kelly and Chris had one daughter.
2C1a. ASHLEY CARRIN PETTY, born July 20, 1983, in Bremerton.
2C2. JERRY DALE SHERMAN Jr., born July 1, 1963. He lives in Bremerton and works for Firestone.
2C3. TIFFANY SHERMAN, born December 6, 1971, in Bremerton. She lives in Bremerton with her father.

I married GEORGE GERMAINE April 18, 1942. He was employed at Keyport Torpedo Station. George died July 24, 1978. George and I had four sons:

2D. GEORGE WILLIAM GERMAINE III, born August 17, 1943. He married CHERYL KAAS in Seattle June 7, 1969. George is a teacher and lives in Bonny Lake, Wash. George and Cheryl have two children.
2D1. AMY COLLEEN GERMAINE, born July 3, 1976, in Seattle.
2D2. COLIN MATTHEW GERMAINE, born August 29, 1980, in Wenatchee.
2E. FRANCIS DERMOTT GERMAINE, born September 14, 1945, in Bremerton. He married PATRICIA THOMPSON June 8, 1968, in Poulsbo. They have two daughters.
2E1. MOVAE GERMAINE, born May 15, 1969, in Bremerton. She lives in Poulsbo and works at Keyport.
2E2. ANGELA GERMAINE, born October 22, 1975, in Bremerton.
2F. THOMAS CARTER GERMAINE, born August 2, 1949. He married ARDITH WALKER in Poulsbo in 1970. He works at Bangor and lives in Poulsbo. Thomas and Ardith have two children.
2F1. SHELA RENEE GERMAINE, born September 21, 1974, in Bremerton.
2F2. SHELLY LYN GERMAINE, born January 28, 1979, in Bremerton.
2G. TIMOTHY JOHN GERMAINE, born May 26, 1956. He married KARRIE MURKER in Manette in 1976. They divorced and in 1986 he married SALLY MARTIN. Timothy has four children.
2G1. SARAH ANN GERMAINE, born June 15, 1977, in Bremerton.
2G2. TIMOTHY JOHN GERMAINE Jr, born August 24, 1980, in Bremerton.
2G3. KATIE ADELL GERMAINE, born September 10, 1981, in Bremerton.
2G4. DUSTIN DANIEL (OLSEN) GERMAINE, born April 9, 1987.

I married OSWALDO MARIO FIALLO August 7, 1987, and we live in Enumclaw.

CROXTON, ALVYN L.
By Orville Schultz

Alvyn Littler Croxton was born August 5, 1869, in Palestine, Ind. He studied electricity at the University of Indiana and then worked for Standard Electric Company of Chicago, remaining with the firm from 1890 to 1896. He then moved to California and was employed at Mare Island Navy Shipyard before coming to Puget Sound Navy Yard in 1898. Here he was master electrician in the yards and docks department and later master of the power plant. After 34 years, 10 months and 23 days of Government service he retired in 1934.

He lived in Manette at Enetai Beach during most of his time in Kitsap County.

In 1901 Croxton was instrumental in the establishment of a volunteer fire department in Bremerton.

With the incorporation of Bremerton on October 16, 1901, Croxton was elected the first mayor at the age of 32. He remained in office until January 12, 1904.

In an interview by Patricia Granger of Manette on September 7, 1936, Croxton, in recalling his service to the city of Bremerton as its first mayor, said, "I should say that being mayor during my term of office was a much tougher job than it is now. Now it is pretty much a matter of routine, while in my time, there were laws but no precedents.

"There were 17 saloons in Bremerton when I took office and we put them all out of commission. The country was full of gamblers, but we cleaned them up and moved them out. They didn't want to go, but we made them. The Secretary of Navy ordered it. It was fight your way through then. People thought Bremerton was a wild town and that they could do as they pleased. It took some work to curb them. But we did it."

In an interview with Willard Muller, Croxton said he took office as mayor without ceremony. His office was a small, unfinished shack on a vacant lot.

One night not long after his election—he had retired for the night in his home, which was located on the water side of Washington Avenue at Burwell Street—there was a knock on his door. The marshal entered. "Mr. Mayor," the marshal

panted, "they is six Marines on a rampage an' I don't think I can handle 'em alone." Mr. Croxton assisted.

After his retirement as mayor he served on the local school board and aided in the selection of sites for the Central, Smith and Bremerton Union High Schools.

A front page article in a Bremerton newspaper of April 21, 1941, states, "A prominent figure in Kitsap County history was removed today with the death of A.L. Croxton, 71, first mayor of Bremerton. He had resided with his family at their home on Enetai Beach."

Always active in community organizations, Croxton was past master of Manette Masonic Lodge 117, a member of Nile Temple of Shrine, the Masters Association of Puget Sound Navy Yard and Electricians Association, and a graduate of the University of Indiana.

Croxton and his wife Chloa had a son, Kenneth, and a daughter, Rejene, both now deceased.

Rejene became well known in Manette and Bremerton. She graduated from Union High School in Bremerton and earned a bachelor of arts degree in music at the University of Washington.

Rejene married Gray Beck. The outdoor wedding ceremony and reception at the Croxton home in Enetai ended as a seaplane landed at the beach and took the couple on their honeymoon. They divorced later.

Alvyn Littler Croxton.
-old Bremerton Sun photo

She taught music in an evening school program in Bremerton in the 1930s. She also taught ballet lessons in a class above Meredith's store. She was employed in the Puget Sound Naval Shipyard public works department from 1941 until 1946.

Rejene joined the Bremerton School District in 1947 and served as secretary to the director of instruction. Later she was secretary to three successive superintendents — Armin Jahr, Dr. James Hoffner and Dr. Orin B. Fjeran. She retired in 1973.

Rejene was a soloist at the Christian Science Church and sang for many community groups. She belonged to Philathea Chapter, Order of Eastern Star, and CM Chapter, PEO Sisterhood. Rejene died in 1980.

Marie Galleher recalled that Chloa Croxton's father was Mr. Canady, a cook on sailing ships. He had been all over the world and was a widower when Marie knew him. Canady owned 5 acres on Enetai Beach and had a fine apple orchard. He died of pneumonia in a veterans' hospital in about 1920.

Rejene Croxton.
-Photo from Bremerton Sun

DANEL-HOLMES
By Ruth Danel Blasberg
1984

RALPH FRANCIS DANEL 1888-1941

Ralph Francis Danel was born August 31, 1888, in Winnipeg, Canada. His parents migrated to Seattle by wagon when he was a very small boy. He was one of five boys and two girls. His father became a tailor on Madison Avenue in Seattle.

VERA BELLE NOBLE 1890-1922

Vera Belle Noble Danel, my mother, was born in Snohomish in 1890. She was raised on her parents' homestead in Granite Falls. This later was known as Canyon Creek Lodge, popular in the late 30s and 40s. Eleanor Roosevelt stayed there when visiting her daughter, Anna Roosevelt Boetteger, and son-in-law. The lodge burned in the early 50s,I believe, and was never rebuilt. Later I browsed through the cabins remaining and viewed a cedar barn my grandfather Charles Noble built over 100 years ago. Grandpa Noble was a timber cruiser for many years at Jordan, Wash. Later he became quite a well-known character on Seattle's waterfront as night watchman for Alaska Steamship Company. So while one of my grandfathers sewed vestments for priests, the other I'm sure tried the patience of many a priest.

Ralph Danel married Vera Belle Noble in Seattle August 18, 1916.

Ralph Danel purchased our home at 1105 Perry Avenue from Linn R. Totten in April 1926. Early pictures indicate Dad had lived there for some time. I arrived there when my mother and I were released, 2 weeks after my birth, from Columbus Sanitarium, the Seattle hospital where I was born.

The home was remodeled two or three times during the years we resided there.

Ralph and Elva Danel's home at 1105 Perry Avenue.
                    -Photo from Ruth Danel Blasberg

CONSOLIDATED FAMILY

My mother passed away before I was 3 years old. My father, Ralph Danel, married Elva Holmes, a widow with a son John Holmes, later called Ellsworth Danel or Al. All of our school years I was "Al Holmes' sis" and he was "Ruth Danel's brud." This mixed family got a little brother, Harold, 5 years later. Now we were "your kid, my kid and our kid."

OTHER MEMORIES

We all attended Mrs. Hoopes' kindergarten classes. We loved living across the street from the post office, since Mrs. Etta Harkins, the postmistress, would call to one of us when a special delivery letter was to be delivered. We earned 5 cents, 9 cents, maybe more as the postal rates increased. We watched the Masonic Temple being built in 1926-27. The huge lilac trees are still in our yard. The flowers supplied many a May basket. The baskets were always made from wallpaper sample books.

My brothers and I recall the fire bell across the street by the alley of Aldrich's yard and the fire engine next to our second garage.

In about 1932 we had a fawn in a pen next to the fire hall. He had been rescued from a pack of dogs near "Dewar's Creek." We got to feed him and give him salt lick. The fawn later went on to Woodland Park Zoo. They named him Manette. Our dad never did hunt, nor did my brothers.

Dad worked in the navy yard as a leadingman in the pipe shop and in new construction. Dad was a volunteer fireman and his other claim to civic fame was driving the first car across the Manette Bridge during the dedication in 1930. Among other passengers were Jack Martin, Manette's honorary mayor, and Jane Garrison, a 106-year-old Indian woman from Tracyton.

CAMPING

We camped almost every weekend during summer. I would slide down in the back seat and pretend I wasn't along as we drove through town. We had a million-dollar childhood. We frequented Eglon, Hansville, Joe's Place on Hood Canal, Hoodsport, Anderson's Landing, Barker Creek, Kingston, Port Gamble and Brownsville.

Dad always brought a lot of queries from other campers.

Harold and Ruth Danel standing while John Ellsworth "Al" Holmes plays the accordion—in 1935. Old store and post office building, East 11th Street and Perry Avenue, in background.   -Photo from Harold Danel.

Ralph Danel and his camping rig, a Buick touring car, in 1928.   - Photo from Ruth Danel Blasberg

He was a very clever, ingenious man. We had everything attached to our touring sedan including a two-piece wooden boat on a rack with rollers. The boat was Number One with Dad. His love of water, fishing and camping carried over to his children and theirs. The boat was named "Misfit," being parts of two boats racked together. Dad took each part to the beach and bolted them together.

We remember swimming off Grandpa (August) Wall's float and from Eleanor Pidduck's house; our 4-H meetings at Mrs. Worland's; ice-cream floats, the makings bought at Meredith's for us by Bonnie Olsen, who had credit there; sitting on our front porch to drink them; Mrs. Wall making my birthday cakes; Esther Buchanan's and my May-Day costumes of crepe-paper; dancing the May pole ceremony; Ellsworth's paper route, his convertible, his Essex; roller skating on the bridge with Dot Myers; my brother Harold and his friend Jimmy Meredith borrowing Jimmy's father's car to drive along Shore Drive — neither of them was 10 years old. One operated the steering wheel and gearshift and the other the starter, gas, clutch and brake.

We lost our dad in January 1941. Mom sold the big house and moved up to East 16th Street. She died in March of 1974.

I am a recent widow and live in Manette. My career serviceman husband, Marlow Blasberg, died in 1982. I met Marlow at Perl Maurer's dance pavilion in October 1940 and we were married in Hollywood, Calif., in 1944. He survived the Pearl Harbor attack while in the navy aboard the USS *Whitney*, AD4. He later served in the army and air force. Two of our children were born in Carmel, Calif., and two in Germany. They are "Navy, Army, Air Force and an adopted brat." We have six grandsons and one step-grandchild.

THE DANEL-HOLMES DESCENDANTS

1. JOHN ELLSWORTH HOLMES, also known as Al, was born in Seattle February 23, 1917. He married BESSIE ELIZABETH VALES at Star of the Sea Rectory in Bremerton August 24, 1940. They have no children. Al went to Fort Bliss, Tex., in 1945-46, then back to the shipyard; he was an outside machinist. He is retired and enjoys boating, gardening and flowers. He and Bessie have a home adjacent to Long Lake Park, which is part of Bessie's family homestead. Al spends a great deal of time playing his accordian at rest homes and other functions. He manages the farmer's market on Bay Street in Port Orchard; the farmer's market consists of local farmers who rent stall space to sell their produce. Al collects the fees and oversees the operation. He is also active in the Port Orchard Yacht club.

2.. RUTH MARIE DANEL, born in Seattle July 27, 1919. She married MARLOW FREDERICK BLASBERG at Immaculate Heart of Mary Rectory in Hollywood, Calif., August 28, 1944. Their children are:
2A. MARLOW F. BLASBERG Jr., "Skip", born August 3, 1945, in Carmel, Calif. Marlow married LORETTA LELAND SPATZ in 1968.

They live on Nokomis Road, Southworth. Skip has Bob Fogle & Son septic tank service and is a heavy equipment operator for private contracting. He is very involved with a Seabees Mobile Construction Unit, USN, which volunteers many hours to community projects. Loretta works for the shipyard. They enjoy bowling, travel and being parents. Their children are:
2A1. MARLOW F. BLASBERG III, born June 20, 1980.
2A2.. BRANDON MICHAEL BLASBERG, born July 21, 1983.
2B. MARLYS MARIE BLASBERG, born in Carmel, Calif., April 27, 1953. She married EDWARD JAMES RECKNAGLE in Port Orchard February 19, 1972. They live in Port Orchard, where Ed owns Puget Sound Paving. Marlys owns Genesis II hair design of Port Orchard. Ed enjoys dirt-bike riding with his sons, traveling by motor home, fishing, cross-country skiing and most of all parenting three active boys: ERIK, born May 13, 1974, JEREMY JAMES, born February 25, 1975, and RYAN MICHAEL, born July 28, 1977.
2C. DANEL ANN BLASBERG, born in Furstenfeldbruck, Germany, March 14, 1956. She married PAUL DONALD OBERHOLTZER in Port Orchard, August 1, 1981. They live in Port Orchard and work in PSNS, Paul as a control systems technician and Danel as a motor vehicle operator. Paul is an avid gardener, restores cars, attends swap meets, gathers antiques in their trailer and works on their acreage at Lake Symington, where he plans to build their log home. Danel is an avid skier — both snow and water — and plays softball. They both enjoy dancing and now they also enjoy their son:
2C1. ANDREW ALAN OBERHOLTZER, who was born February 23, 1985.
2D. PERRY MICHAEL BLASBERG was born in Landshut, Germany, April 17, 1949. We adopted him August 17, 1956. Perry married TRINA PARKHURST ALLEN in Port Orchard July 30, 1982. They live in Bremerton. Perry is manager of Lumbermen's on Bainbridge Island. Trina is assistant manager of the Sheridan branch of American Marine Bank. They both enjoy water and snow skiing. Perry plays golf and has a pilot's license. Trina has a daughter, Christy Allen, born March 8, 1972.

3. HAROLD FRANCIS DANEL was born in Bremerton November 30, 1925. He married HAZEL JOY VANT in Our Lady Star of the Sea Rectory in Bremerton December 6, 1947. Harold spent part of his army time during World War II on the Azores. He kept Mom busy mailing him cheese, flashlights, lunch boxes and head scarves for the natives. He is retired from Darigold. Boating and trailering occupy his and Hazel's time. Their home in Manchester is a bit of history. It was built by Carleton Fitchett, author and writer for the Seattle Post-Intelligencer in the 30s and 40s. Harold is active with the Port Orchard Yacht Club, Helpline, and in St. Gabriel Church. Harold and Hazel have three daughters.
3A. KATHLEEN MARIE DANEL, born April 9, 1949, married WILLIAM M. DUFFY Jr. at St. Gabriel Catholic Church in Port Orchard June 22, 1968. They live in Bremerton, where Bill is superintendent of the Bremerton Water Department. Kathy is talented with creating doll clothes. They both enjoy camping, backpacking, traveling and boating. Their two daughters attend Our Lady Star of the Sea School. They are: ELIZABETH, born March 3, 1971, and REBECCA, born February 17, 1977.
3B. SUSAN ANN DANEL, born September 2, 1951, married THOMAS K. NEILL Jr. October 22, 1972. They separated and Susan lives in Port Orchard with their children. She enjoys handcrafts, gardening and her animals. She works with Bremerton School District food services. Their children are: KRISTEN, born May 20, 1973, SARAH, born November 21, 1974, and MELISSA, born April 7, 1977.
3C. MARSHA RENEE DANEL, born December 27, 1954. Marsha married Lt. STEVEN C. PFEIFER, USN, July 13, 1985, at St. Gabriel Church in Port Orchard. Marsha just returned from Whidbey Island and works as recreation director of Claremont East Retirement Home. She enjoys all sports. Lieutenant Pfeifer is serving in the South Pacific.

DEAN, NED
By Theron "Tad" and Teresa Dean

Ned and Mary Dean moved to Manette in the early 1920s. Ned was a machinist in the shipyard. On arriving in Manette they bought a home on East 18th Street. There were four children, Inza, Viola, Warren and Theron "Tad." All attended Manette School.

Mary was active in community work. One year in the early 30s she and some of the other women made sleeping bags for the Boy Scouts so the boys could go camping. Mary was president of the Bremerton High School P-TA in about 1935-36. She also belonged to the garden club, and sold Avon products.

Ned and Mary lived here until 1942, when they moved to Bangor. After a year in Bangor they moved to Seattle, where Ned worked for the Seattle-Tacoma Shipyard until he retired in 1945. He was also retired from the shipyard in Bremerton. Ned passed away in 1960. Mary continued living in Seattle until 1973, when she moved to Bremerton. Mary passed away in August 1986. Warren passed away in June of 1986.

FAMILY OF NED AND MARY DEAN

1. INZA DEAN. Inza married and had three sons and a daughter. Inza passed away in 1970. Her children are: JOHN, who lives in Portland; WILLIAM "Bill," who lives near Mukilteo; JAMES "Jim," who lives in Bremerton, and OLIVIA, who lives near Mukilteo.

2. VIOLA DEAN. Viola and her husband HENRY SMITH live near Vancouver, Wash. They have two sons: MIKE, who lives in Camas, and MARTY, who lives in Vancouver.

3. WARREN DEAN. Warren married and has two children: MORRIS and GAIL. Gail married and lives near Monroe, Wash.

4. THERON "TAD" DEAN. Tad married and has two sons: NORMAN, who lives in California, and DENNIS, a step-son who was raised in Silverdale and lives in Salt Lake City.

DEWAR, SAUNDERS FORD
By Anna Jo Atkinson
from information by Florence Dewar Moore
1987

The S. Ford Dewar home is located at 1702 Winfield Avenue. Ford and Mary Elizabeth Dewar were born, raised and married in Canada. Their eldest son William was born in Canada in 1901. Ford was a graduate of Woodstock College in Canada. He became a pattern maker and machinist by trade.

In 1902 the family moved to North Dakota, where relatives had homesteaded. Ford read of jobs available at Todd's shipyard in Seattle, so the little family of three migrated to the Northwest.

After seeing the beautiful countryside he decided any house he bought had to have a view. They found a house at what is now the Mount Baker area of Seattle. The house commanded a view of both Puget Sound and the beautiful Olympics. There the rest of the Dewar children were born, Charles in 1903, Warren in 1905 and Florence in 1907.

After several years as a pattern maker at Todd's, Ford was hired at Puget Sound Navy Yard at a higher wage than Todd paid. He commuted to Bremerton for several months, but the many delays, ferry break-downs and the tedious rides back and forth each day made him know they had to move again.

The family started searching. Bremerton was too flat and didn't offer the view they wanted, so they turned to Manette. They rented a small summer cottage from the Stebbens family. It was on East 16th Street near the beach across from property owned by Neil McDougall.

The family rented out their Seattle home and lived through two summers in the little cabin. The children loved it but Mother Dewar worried terribly that one would get hurt climbing around or falling in the water.

Again, when looking for property on which to build, they required a view. They chose the property at 1702 Winfield Avenue. There was a magnificent view of Puget Sound, Bremerton, Port Orchard, Mount Rainier and the Olympics. There was nothing across the street to hamper their view. They could look over the forest and brush that covered the

The Dewar home at 1702 Winfield Avenue, 1983.
-Photo from Berenice Bouchard Root

hillside.

At first the family lived in a large double tent. There was a stove, table and chairs and two double beds. The boys—all three—slept in one bed, with little sister Florence sleeping crosswise across the foot of the bed. Mother and Father slept in the other bed.

The tent was erected over wooden floor and walls. The big wood range kept them cozy and warm throughout the winter.

In 1910 Ford engaged Mr. Andre Lofthus, owner of Lofthus Lumber, to draw plans and build a house for the family. The kitchen, pantry and dining room were the first rooms constructed. The Dewars lived this way for months, still sleeping in the tent.

With the advent of World War I, materials were hard or impossible to obtain. As materials became available, the rest of the house very gradually took shape. A living room, upstairs bath and bedrooms were added.

Before the house was completed, a knock on the door brought a young girl seeking a place to board and room. Mother Dewar said, "No, we're in such a mess." The girl replied she didn't mind, she would even help clean up the sawdust and chips made by the carpenters.

In the course of conversation, Mother Dewar found the girl had come from the same area of North Dakota as the Dewars, and that the girl's father was a mutual friend of Dewar relatives. That decided the issue and Margery Hannah, first and second grade teacher at Manette School, came to be part of the Dewar family. Florence had to give up her new bedroom and sleep on a couch in the dining room to accommodate the teacher.

Margery was just the first of boarders Mother Dewar took in. When Margery left teaching to marry, Eldridge

Florence Dewar at about age 3, circa 1910.
-Photo from Evelyn Holden Newkirk.

Turner took her position and her room as well. Eldridge was a member of the Dewar family for many years.

The Dewar boys spent their summers picking berries, peas and beans at the Jensen farm. Florence helped her mother with household chores and gardening. Free time was spent roaming the beaches and hills, rowing, and swimming at the Sandbanks. One of Florence's happiest memories is of climbing up and down the steep cliffs in steps carved in the sand, and of swimming in the clear cool water.

The Dewar children all attended Manette Grade School and graduated from Union High School in Bremerton.

William graduated from the University of Washington. He became a certified life insurance underwriter. He married Gertrude Standard. One daughter was born to them. They lived in Seattle.

Warren graduated from the University of Washington and became an attorney. He married Esther Mehner of Bremerton. They had three sons. The family also resided in Seattle, at Fauntleroy Beach.

Florence worked as a receptionist for several Bremerton doctors until her marriage to William Moore, an officer of the U.S. Navy. They had one son. Their home is on Marine Drive in Bremerton.

Charles took an apprenticeship in PSNY and remained there until ill health forced retirement. Charles married Marian Berlien. They had no children.

The Dewar family was a very vital part of the early years of Manette. Ford was active in Boy Scouts and the Masonic Lodge and was a staunch pillar of Manette Community Church as a deacon. He also taught a Sunday School class.

Mother Dewar also taught Sunday School as well as being very active in the Ladies Aid Society, the WCTU, and the White Shield Home for unwed mothers. She was instrumental in helping childless Manette couples adopt babies. She was never too busy to keep her cookie jar full for the many frequent visitors to her home.

Mother Dewar's Cookies
1 cup shortening, 2 cups sugar, 2 eggs, 1 cup sweet milk, 1 t soda, 1 t baking powder, 1 t salt, sifted with sufficient flour (I find 4 cups about right) to roll out soft dough. Cream shortening, sugar and eggs. Sift in dry ingredients and mix together with milk with 1 teaspoon of vanilla or lemon flavoring. Roll out 1/4 inch, bake on greased pan at 350 degrees 8-10 minutes. Raisins, nuts, coconut or mixed spices may be added for variety.

Mother Dewar loved flowers and planted a large rose garden. Much to her dismay, Ford planted beans between the rows of roses—just couldn't waste the space.

There were large bay windows in the dining room, always full of blooming geraniums. Visitors always took away slips of plants to start their own.

To make more room for plants, the Dewars added a large front porch, and glassed in part of it. There was also enough room for a bed so Florence could move out of the dining room.

Mother Dewar passed away in 1946, Father Ford passed away in 1958. The boys have since all joined their parents in death—Florence alone remains of the original family.

The family home has passed into other hands, but it still stands atop the hill, a stately reminder of the family that built it and did so much living and loving in it.

DILKS, JOSEPH
By Margaret Dilks Munson
1985

Joseph W. Dilks, born August 2, 1847, in Philadelphia, Pa., came from Colorado to Port Orchard in 1904 with his wife Elizabeth and their three children: Ann, age 11; Joseph N., age 8; and Charlotte, age 6. Dilks, who had worked as a miner, went to work at Puget Sound Navy Yard as a boilermaker. The Dilkses lived in Annapolis and Waterman before moving across the bay to their first home in Manette on Shore Drive. Later they moved to 1104 Scott Avenue.

THE FAMILY
JOSEPH W. DILKS married ELIZABETH MASON. Elizabeth died January 28, 1920. Joseph died in Seattle February 24, 1926. Joseph and Elizabeth had three children.

1. ANN DILKS, born December 28, 1893, in Leadville, Colo. Ann married DALLAS COWAN in 1911. Dallas worked in the navy yard as a welder. They lived on Perry Avenue, then built a home known as Colleen's Garden at the northeast corner of Perry Avenue and Sylvan Way. Ann died in Bremerton in July 1969. Ann and Dallas had six children.
1A. MARGUERITE COWAN, born in Manette, now lives in California.
1B. LAUREL COWAN, born in Manette, lives in Port Orchard.
1C. OPAL COWAN, born in Manette, lives in California.
1D. ZOE COWAN, born in Manette, married Robert Heath. They lived in Port Orchard. Zoe died in 1986.
1E. GLENN COWAN, born in Manette, lives in Las Vegas, Nev.
1F. ANN DALLAS COWAN, born April 5, 1927, in Manette, lives in Port Orchard.

2. JOSEPH NATHAN DILKS, born September 10, 1896, in Leadville, Colo. Joseph attended school in Waterman. As a boy, Joseph was an apprentice and then pipefitter in the shipyard until his medical retirement in 1949. Joseph married MILDRED STEVEN in 1916. Mildred had arrived in Manette in 1915 from Idaho Falls. Joseph was a World War I veteran. He worked from 1942 to 1944 in Pearl Harbor. Joseph died in Bremerton December 10, 1969. Mildred died March 2, 1986. Joseph and Mildred had two children:
2A. MARGARET ELIZABETH DILKS, born March 7, 1920, in Manette. Margaret went to Mrs. Hoopes' kindergarten, Manette School, Sheridan School and Manette Community Church. Margaret married ALLAN MUNSON in 1941. Margaret worked as a housewife and as a licensed practical nurse at Harrison Memorial Hospital. Allan worked in the navy yard, retiring in August of 1970. They lived at 2501 East Phinney Bay Place, Bremerton. Allan died September 27, 1986. Margaret and Allan had two children.
2A1. ALLAN JOSEPH MUNSON, born December 5, 1942, in Bremerton. Allan is an engineer at Puget Sound Naval Shipyard. He lives in Port Orchard.
2A2. HOLLY MUNSON, born November 30, 1946, in Bremerton. Holly married DICK NESS and they had a son. They divorced. Holly married HARRY FARTHING. Holly and Harry have a daughter.
2A2a. STEVEN ALLAN NESS, born in Aberdeen May 31, 1966.
2A2b. MEGAN ELIZABETH FARTHING, born in Seattle January 12, 1984.
2B. GLORIA LEE DILKS, born April 3, 1927, in Manette. Gloria married FRED LARSEN in 1945. They live in Eugene, Oreg. Fred worked in logging and retired 8 years ago. Gloria and Fred have five children.
2B1. JOANN LARSEN, born August 4, 1946, in Astoria. JoAnn married WILL PERKINS and they live in Greenwood, Ariz.
2B2. FRAN LARSEN, born January 19, 1948, in Ilwaco, Oreg. Fran married DAN RINEY and they live in Fort Lewis.
2B3. KRIS LARSEN, born September 19, 1950, in Bremerton. Kris married BRUCE SHELQUIST and they live in The Dalles.
2B4. FRED LARSEN, born September 15, 1961, in Florence, Oreg. Fred lives in Mapleton, Oreg.
2B5. MARTIN LARSEN, born February 3, 1963, in Florence. He lives in Eugene.

3. CHARLOTTE DILKS, born December 11, 1898, in Leadville, Colo. She went to school in Colby, Wash. Charlotte married CHARLES BALLEW. Charlotte and Charles had two children. They divorced. Charlotte married T.J. NIEWODOWSKI in 1932. They lived in Alameda. Charlotte died in

Nevada in 1976.
3A. MAYSIE BALLEW, born May 7, 1917. Maysie is Mrs. LORD, and
now a widow living in Escondido.
3B. CHARLES JOSEPH BALLEW, known as "Buddie," born in Manette
June 3, 1919. Charles died in December 1985. His widow SUE lives in
Elko, Nev.

DIXON, CHARLES
By Jane Ellen Dixon Quinn
1984

Charles E. Dixon was born in Nebraska December 31, 1895. At age 17 he bicycled from Nebraska to Coos Bay, Oreg. On September 24, 1915, he married Myrtle V. Swisher in Portland, where he was a letter carrier. Myrtle was born in Kansas October 22, 1898.

A son, Lowell Russell, was born in 1918.

Myrtle Swisher and Charles E. Dixon
were married in 1916 in Portland.

In 1919 the family moved to Manette, where their daughter Jane Ellen was born. Charley worked as a purser on the Manette ferry *Pioneer*, owned by his brother-in-law, Harry Hansen. Myrtle and Harry's wife Ellen were sisters.

Southern Oregon gold fields drew the family in 1922 to Murphy, Oreg. where they bought and farmed 100 acres; farming proved more profitable than gold mining for them. They were active in the social and civic life of the Murphy community and Charley was the justice of the peace, presiding over trials held in the front room of his home.

In the fall of 1929 they moved back to Manette. Charley worked on the ferry again and after the bridge was completed in 1930 he drove the Manette-Bremerton bus on the night shift for many years.

During World War II he worked at Puget Sound Navy Yard as a shipfitter, retiring as a general helper at age 70.

In 1935 the Dixons bought the Brewster house and 5-acre farm on Perry Avenue where Latter Day Saints Church now stands. During World War II they converted the big house into apartments and opened a trailer park on the property. Myrtle taught sewing during the Depression and worked at

Puget Sound Navy Yard during World War II. She was a member of the Daughters of the American Revolution, Agate Club and Women's Benefit Association.

Charley was a rock-hound. He wrote stories and articles for gem magazines and had a beautiful collection of agates, most of which he found himself. He belonged to the Agate Club and was past president of the East Bremerton Improvement Club. Charley was a frequent contributor to the letters section of the *Bremerton Sun*, maintaining an interest in legislative affairs all his life. He was also interested in music, having played the French horn in the navy band in World War I.

In 1938 he was justice of the peace in Manette. Charley died of a heart attack April 11, 1975, at the age of 89; Myrtle lived to be 94. She died of a heart attack June 6, 1983.

Lowell attended Bremerton High School for 4 years with perfect attendance. He received a music scholarship from the University of Washington and attended the University for a short time in the premed program. He became the first nuclear inspector supervisor at Puget Sound Naval Shipyard. He lived at 2354 Enetai Beach.

DESCENDANTS OF CHARLES AND MYRTLE DIXON

1. LOWELL RUSSELL DIXON was born January 17, 1918. In 1940 Lowell
married ALICE SEQUIN of Dawson City, Yukon Territory. They were later
divorced. They had three children.
1A. SHARON LEE DIXON, born September 14, 1940. Sharon is married
to NORMAN NICOLAS "Nick" HURD, a pharmacist, and lives in Belfair. Sharon and Nick have three chldren.
1A1. ERIC ANTHONY HURD, born September 20, 1960. Eric is a logger
in the Belfair-Shelton area. He married AMY JEAN LINCOLN.
1A2.. DANE CHRISTOPHER HURD, born October 27, 1961. Dane is a high
school music teacher in Lyle, Wash.
1A3. DAWN MARIE HURD, born October 6, 1965. She is a Central
Washington University student.
1B. RUSSELL RICHARD "Dick" DIXON, born December 1, 1941. Dick
is divorced and lives in Bremerton. His two children, RUSSELL and
CONNIE SUE, live in Texas.
1C. VAUGHN CHARLES DIXON, born October 16, 1943. Vaughn married PATRICIA REDDIN of Bremerton. They were later divorced. They
had two sons, THOMAS and PAUL, who live in Bremerton. Vaughn
died of a heart attack in 1982.

Lowell married JOYCE PETERSON; they divorced. In 1971 Lowell married HELEN ANDERSON ADAMS. Lowell lived to be 65. He suffered a
major heart attack and stroke almost a year previous to his death. He never
recovered. He died January 31, 1983. Helen lives in Seattle.

2.. JANE ELLEN DIXON was born June 22, 1919, in Bremerton. She
graduated from Bremerton High School in 1937. Jane married EARL J.
QUINN, since deceased. She moved to El Cajon, Calif., where she still lives
with her only son, JOHN QUINN.

ELLIOTT, RALPH
By Hattie Elliott Engstrom
1984

MIGRATION TO MANETTE
Ralph Elliott and his wife Abbie were living in Nebraska. Ralph was born in Hastings, Nebr., September 23, 1888. Abbie was born in Oxford, Nebr., March 21, 1884. Papa (Ralph) had diphtheria and several bouts with typhoid fever. Doctors told him he should go West, go to the mountains or cross them. Since he had an uncle out here he came on to the Seattle area with his family. This was in 1913. Two children came with them: my sister Mamie and I, Hattie.

In 1914 we moved via a scow—livestock and all—to what

Abbie, Hattie, Gracie and Mamie Elliott in about 1922 at their home in what is today the 2500 area of Greenwood Drive NE. This home was destroyed by fire. -Photo from a glass negative from Hattie Elliott Engstrom.

was called Ingraham Place in Illahee; in later years it became the Rue home. My sister Gracie was born there in 1915.

Mamie and I loved the beach. To get to our mail box we had to hike a trail through a neighbor's up to what is now Perry Avenue. I didn't get to see the town of Manette because we lived so far out.

I remember a heavy snowstorm in 1916. Lincoln Hall, on County Road (Perry Avenue), collapsed.

In 1917 Ralph moved his family closer to town. The new location was west and north of what is now Trenton Avenue and Stone Way. The house was on the bank of the creek that ran through the woods of the Howerton and Jensen properties to Enetai Beach, about a mile away.

I enjoyed sports in school and got a letter and a silver pin in competition.

Papa cleared land and made roads all over the county with a team of mules. He made the road into Illahee that went down the hill from the south past the Tom Peterson place. In 1933 he cleared the way for Jacobsen Boulevard to its north end.

He was a great "powder man" and did lots of blasting around the area. He was recognized in a *Daily News Searchlight* article in the 1930s as one of the best powder men in the county. He also did odd jobs around Manette and Bremerton and worked in the navy yard.

We moved to the Vancouver, Wash., area for a time and our brother Elmer was born at Salmon Creek, not far from Vancouver, in 1923.

When we returned I worked for Mrs. Hattie Martin. I bought my first piano from Mrs. Joaquina Feek.

Mother and Papa remained in the Trenton Avenue home until 1947, when they were divorced.

Mother passed away in 1966 and Papa in 1969.

ENGSTROM

During the early years we spent at Illahee, Ralph and Hannah Hibbard and their son Russell were neighbors. Living with them was Erik Engstrom, who had come from Boras, Sweden, in 1904—and who was to become my husband. The Hibbards treated Erik like a son.

Erik rowed across the bay to school at Crystal Springs on Bainbridge Island.

Ralph Hibbard was the master in the sheet metal shop in the navy yard; later his son Russell succeeded him in this job. Erik worked under both of them.

LOW POWER TO ALASKA

In 1914, Erik Engstrom and a friend, Ralph Ohman, left

The Elliott home in 1934 in the 2500 area of today's Greenwood Drive NE. From left, Elmer, Ralph, Gracie and Abbie Elliott.

Gracia's wedding day, May 4, 1941. Back row (from left), Mamie Elliott Henderson, Gracia Elliott Schapsmeier, Hattie Elliott Engstrom. Front row, Abbie, Ralph and Elmer Elliott.   - Photo by Prints of Wales

from in front of our place on a trip to Alaska in a rowboat with a 3-horsepower Coban motor on it.

They landed in Ketchikan and went to work in a sawmill. Erik suffered a smashed thumb in an accident and returned home. Ralph remained, to become an employee of the U.S. Fish and Wildlife Service.

In 1956 Erik and I took a trip to Ketchikan, and Erik and Ralph enjoyed a reunion after 42 years.

Erik's role in the history of the Manette area dates in a sense to 1885, when William Christianson took up the first homestead at the present townsite of Illahee. Before proving up on the property Christianson relinquished his right to his nephew, Samuel Anderson, who proved up on it in 1895. This is now the Palbitska home. Samuel sold this property in 1903 to Mrs. Ellen M. Munro and went to Sweden. He returned a year later with Erik, who was his nephew, and bought the property Walter J. Rue later purchased. Samuel sold that property and bought 10 acres at the head of Illahee Creek, now 4230 Perry Avenue. Erik bought this from Samuel and added to it after we were married in 1927. This is where I still live. Erik's uncle returned to Sweden when Erik was 19.

A NEW FAMILY

Erik Engstrom and I were married July 10, 1927. Hattie

Hattie, Doretta and Erik Engstrom in 1933.
- Photo from Hattie Elliott Engstrom

Martin, wife of Manette grocer Harry Martin, made our wedding cake.

RALPH AND ABBIE ELLIOTT'S DESCENDANTS

1. MAMIE MARIE ELLIOTT was born in Prosser, Nebr., July 29, 1908. She married ARCH OTIS HENDERSON, born at Mossy Rock, Wash., November 18, 1892. The wedding was in the Elliott home in Manette. Archie died April 28, 1958. Mamie lives in Puyallup. They had four children.
1A. MARIE LUELLA HENDERSON, born at Kennewick, Wash., November 26, 1926. She married ROBERT LEONARD RODGERS, born at Fort Wayne, Ind., September 23, 1926. They now live in San Jose, Calif. They have three children.
1A1. STEVEN ROBERT RODGERS, born in Compton, Calif., November 4, 1950. He married JUDITH MARIE EHNAT. Judith was born in Tacoma December 3, 1949. They now live in Federal Way, Wash. They have three children.
1A1a. SHEILA MYJO RODGERS, born in Tacoma March 25, 1974.
1A1b. AARON DANIEL RODGERS, born in Tacoma August 26, 1976.
1A1c. JOSHUA CALEB RODGERS, born in Tacoma December 30, 1979.
1A2. VALERIE LYNN RODGERS, born in Compton, Calif., June 6, 1956. She married DALE ALFRED HALVORSON, born March 31, 1954. They live in San Jose. They have one daughter.
1A2a. SHAUNA MARIE HALVORSON, born in San Jose April 5, 1983.
1A3. CRAIG LESLIE RODGERS, Valerie's twin, born in Compton June 6, 1956. He married THERESA DARLENE WALLER, born August 13, 1958. They live in Bessemer, Ala. They have one daughter.
1A3a. TIFFANY MARIE RODGERS, born September 14, 1982.
1B. LESLIE BENJAMIN HENDERSON, born in Seattle December 31, 1927. He died in Seattle May 16, 1929.
1C. REA NARISSA HENDERSON, born in Kennydale, Wash., August 26, 1930. A wedding took place in the Engstrom home when Rea married JOHN POPE YOUNGBLOOD, born in Augusta, Ga., July 18, 1928. John died in Augusta January 18, 1973. Rea is now living with her mother, Mamie, in Puyallup. Rea and John had one daughter.
1C1. ALICE LEANORA YOUNGBLOOD, born in Augusta April 12, 1950. She married VERLIN PRESTON CRANK, born at Rainier, Oreg., March 21, 1934. They were married in Springfield, Oreg. Alice and Verlin live in Puyallup.
1D. CHANE ALLEN HENDERSON, born in the Engstrom home August 11, 1931. He married DORIS LOREETA EASLEY, born in Memphis, Tex., November 27, 1931. They live in Puyallup. They had two children.
1D1. BABY BOY HENDERSON, born in Inglewood, Calif., November 16, 1951; died at birth.
1D2. CARY SUE HENDERSON, born in Inglewood, Calif., September 10, 1955. She married ARLIN KAY LIDSTROM and they live in Puyallup. Cary and Arlin have one son.
1D2a. CHAD ALLEN LIDSTROM, born in Puyallup August 12, 1976.

2. HATTIE LUELLA ELLIOTT was born at Grand Island, Nebr., October 18, 1910. She married ERIK GOTTFRID ENGSTROM, born at Bredared, Sweden, February 21, 1892. He had a heart attack and died November 21, 1965, on the same property he came to in 1904. Hattie and Erik have one daughter.
2A. DORETTA ESTHER ENGSTROM, born in Bremerton October 25, 1929. She was married in the Engstrom home to DONALD DEAN KELLOGG. Donald was born in Troy, Kans., April 10, 1926. They live on the original homestead property at Illahee. Doretta and Donald had two children.
2A1. LLOYD DEAN KELLOGG, born in 1948 in Bremerton. He died June 20, 1957, in a drowning accident when he fell from the dock on the homestead property in Illahee.
2A2. LINDA LOU KELLOGG, born in Bremerton June 5, 1950. She lives at Suisun, Calif.

3. GRACIA MEDORA ELLIOTT was born at Illahee May 29, 1915. She married HERMAN CARL SCHAPSMEIER in the Engstrom home. Herman was born in Minnesota August 29, 1915. After 40 years in San Diego they are now retired and live in Bremerton.

4. ELMER OSCAR ELLIOTT was born at Salmon Creek, Wash., March 21, 1923. He married ELIZABETH ALDA SUTHERLAND, born in Avoca, Pa., January 17, 1923. They live on the southwest corner of Erik and Hattie's original Perry Avenue property. They have three children.
4A. RONALD DOUGLAS ELLIOTT, born in Bremerton May 16, 1947. He lives in his parents' home.
4B. JANICE LORRAINE ELLIOTT, born in Bremerton November 29, 1948. She married WAYNE HARVEY GIBSON, born in Marion, Ind., August 18, 1944. They live in Seattle. They have two children.
4B1. NOELLE CHRISTINE GIBSON, born in Baldwin Park, Calif., May 9, 1971.
4B2. JUSTIN MARK GIBSON, born in Seattle June 5, 1975.
4C. DIANA LYNN ELLIOTT, born in Bremerton March 12, 1951. She

married DAVID ALLEN VAN ROSSUM. David was born in Bremerton April 3, 1951. They live in Renton with their two children.
4C1. JEREMY DAVID VAN ROSSUM, born in Renton January 28, 1979.
4C2. TANYA LYNNE VAN ROSSUM, born in Renton September 22, 1983.

ELLIOTT, ROLAND
By Russ Elliott
1984

My father, Roland Corthell Elliott, came to Manette with his wife, Julia Mae, and me in 1917.

Dad was born in Kipp, Kans., January 11, 1892. He came to Puyallup and then to a farm east of Auburn in the Green River Valley. He became a deliveryman for the Auburn Ice Company, owned by my grandfather, Alval T. Elliott.

Mother was born in Perry, Mich., September 26, 1892. She grew up in Perry where, I was told, she was the belle of the town. She was from Dutch stock by the name of Boardman and she had, I was told, direct lineage to Lord and Lady Lytle of Holland.

Now, this link to royalty never seemed to show up much in my present or past. My connection is with a little point of land called Manette, to me my true native land.

Roland and Julia Mae were married in Auburn, Wash. I was born March 28, 1915, in a little tar-paper shack near the present railroad tracks of southeast Auburn. The doctor came from Kent via horse and buggy and delivered me for a fee of $50.

My grandfather had the second car in Auburn, an Everett, Metsker and Flanders—E.M.F.—"Every Morning Fixit." That was some car, windshield was extra, and when they went to get the license, a number was given to them and they came home, painted it on a board, and hung it on the front of the car! For night driving, Dad lit the headlights with a match. Them was the good old days!

Dad, Mom, and I migrated to Manette during World War I. We lived in a tent house down by the beach across the street from where Dad later bought our old house on Shore Drive. That house, built in 1908, was torn down in 1986.

Our immediate neighbors were the Von Hoenes on the south and the Zieglers on the north. The Palmers were neighbors of the Zieglers. To the south of the Von Hoene house is the present Bachman Park on Shore Drive. The Pidducks lived across the street and later bought Palmers' place.

Dad worked all through World War I in the navy yard. At the end of the war he bought a surplus navy gig. He built a cabin on it and installed a little N. & S. single-cylinder engine produced in Seattle. The old N. & S. foundry building can still be seen on Elliott Avenue.

That was the first of a series of boats Dad bought, rebuilt and sold. We went clear to Neah Bay in that first boat. Came then the *Siona* and then the *Doris G.* which Dad rebuilt, I don't remember how many times. Tom Bright had acquired the *Sea Bird* along there in the late 20s. He and Dad traveled together to Alaska one season and fished.

Dad went a total of three seasons. Mom and I went north one season, met him and stayed on the boat the rest of the summer. I went up and met him the next season as Mom couldn't stand the boat life.

We spent 11 years on the beach at Manette. Those were the happiest years of my life.

In 1929 we moved to Seattle and as far as I was concerned

that was a major tragedy of my life. You might move a kid out of Manette but you can't move Manette out of the kid.

Dad died in Seattle February 16, 1953. Mother died in Kent December 31, 1967. I now live alone in Auburn. I have four children and seven grandchildren.

ELLIS, ROY
By Laura Ellis Hedgecock
1985

Roy Ellis was born in Evart, Mich., February 26, 1884. He arrived in Bremerton about 1910 and moved to Manette in 1917. Roy worked in the navy yard machine shop and was a supervisor when he retired after 36 years. He was active in civic activities and over the years was involved in the East Bremerton Improvement Club, Machinists Nipsic Lodge 282, Steadfast Masonic Lodge, Manette Community Church, Bremerton School Board and American Association of Retired Persons.

Winnie Salvo was born in Ashland, Wis., August 8, 1886. She came to Manette in 1919. Winnie was a teacher in the Bremerton school system for many years. Roy and Winnie married in 1916. Winnie was active in the Manette Community Church, Philathea Chapter of Eastern Star and AARP.

DESCENDANTS
Roy and Winnie had two children.

1. LAURA ELLIS was born in Bremerton October 2, 1919. I attended Manette School and Bremerton High School. I married RUSSELL HEDGECOCK, a naval officer, in 1945. Russell retired as a captain from the navy after 29 years and was employed by an oil company. We lived in Australia, Japan, Singapore, Yugoslavia and Holland. I have been active in international clubs. We moved to Florida in 1980. We have a son and a daughter.
1A. GREGORY HEDGECOCK was born in California January 9, 1948. Gregory married HIDEKO SATO in 1979.
1B. KIMBERLY HEDGECOCK was born in California July 5, 1950. Kimberly married THOMAS LAUERMAN in 1976. Kimberly and Thomas have three children.
1B1. MARGARET LAUERMAN, born in Atlanta, Ga., August 29, 1980.
1B2. ANDREA LAUERMAN, born in Washington, D.C., January 30, 1984.
1B3. PAUL LAUERMAN.

2. HOWARD ELLIS was born in Bremerton February 27, 1921. He attended Manette School and Bremerton High School. Howard worked as a driller and in tools at PSNS and is retired. He never married and is now living in Manette.

EMERSON
By Russell Emerson

My parents arrived in Manette in 1916 with my sister Eleanor and me. We came from Seattle. My sister and I had already started school in Seattle—I was in the first grade—and we transferred to Manette School.

Mother was very thrifty. Father got a job as an electric plater in the navy yard. He did buffing and plating. We lived with another family in a house we rented from Coles on Perry Avenue.

We bought an acre of land covered with stumps and trees and built a house on it.

When I was between 11 and 13 I used to climb young 30-foot fir trees that were to be felled near our house. Someone chopped until the tree was ready to fall and I would ride the tree down to the ground. When we started blasting the stumps to clear the land one stump flew 200 feet into the air, went through Karst's roof and landed a few feet from where Holt Karst was sitting. We repaired the roof and there were no hard feelings.

We bought our water from Tom Bright for a dollar a month. We had two cows and I delivered milk to six customers every day. I had two canvas bags that criss-crossed over my shoulders that I used to carry the milk. I recall that one of our customers was the Buchanan family. I earned one penny per quart for delivering the milk.

One of my friends was Charlie Hook. One day Mother discovered that we had taken cookies from the cookie barrel in Meredith's store. She made us take them back. Charlie had two brothers and two sisters, Lillian and Grace.

Books about Tarzan were among my favorites.

One December day Charlie and I took our traditional cold-weather ride in a rowboat. The boat overturned and I remember how cold the water was when I swam back to shore with Charlie.

Others I remember were Joe Sullivan, who became a pitcher for the Detroit Tigers, and Harold Lee, who became a basketball star at the University of Washington. Another recollection was the night in 1919 when the float at the ferry dock tipped. One person drowned and Mother came home with her clothes wet from falling into the water.

ENKEBOLL, HALFDAN
By Helga Enkeboll Behr and William Enkeboll
1984

ARRIVAL IN AMERICA

Mama and Papa were born in Denmark—Mama at Rosenborg, daughter of a "skovrider" or forest supervisor, and Papa at Toksvaerd, son of a Lutheran minister. They met and married in the United States.

Mama, Anna Schou, came to her brother Laurence, a taxidermist, in Omaha, Nebr. Papa, Halfdan Enkeboll, came to his brother John, an artist, also living in Omaha. Anna and Halfdan met in Omaha at a social function. They were married in May 1907, and settled in San Francisco. There William was born February 2, 1913, and I, Helga Emilie, was born February 14, 1915.

Papa received a degree in law at the University of Copenhagen. However, after coming to America he took a correspondence course in drafting, and in March 1917 was employed as an engineering draftsman at the Puget Sound Navy Yard. He was permanently appointed by Franklin D. Roosevelt, assistant secretary of the navy, in April of 1917.

HOME AND GARDEN

The Enkeboll home was at 324 Shore Drive on four lots. There were beautiful flower and vegetable gardens, developed by hard work and care. Papa tended the vegetable garden and fruit trees. Once he found an arrowhead while cultivating. Mama created flower beds. It was her desire to have every garden variety flowering plant. She probably did, for that time. Her plants ranged from the common yellow California poppy to an unique blue Tibetan poppy. She raised most of her plants from seeds, started in flats and later transplanted. She won many awards at flower shows.

There were many fruit trees—apple, pear, plum, cherry. The cherry tree became outstanding, towering above the

The Enkeboll home at 324 (upper) Shore Drive

house. An apple tree was grafted with shoots sent by relatives from Denmark. The grafting was done by Mr. Edward Olson, a neighbor who was an expert on roses and the grafting of them. We added an apple, an apricot and a fig tree to the existing orchard.

We enjoyed the back yard while eating meals at a picnic table under the big cherry tree. William built the table when in his teens. Sometimes Mama would say, "Why should we go to another place for picnics, we have it so nice here?"

OUTINGS

Nevertheless, we did picnic at the Sandbanks below the present Bremerton Gardens. We went there in Pal, our round-bottomed rowboat with outboard motor. Occasionally we traveled in the boat to Oyster Bay to visit friends.

We had a pleasant place to relax on the beach below our home. Some evenings we would have a bonfire to roast weiners and marshmallows. Many times the Fourth of July was celebrated this way, and with skyrockets, Roman candles and firecrackers.

Special outings were to the Woodland Park Zoo in Seattle. We took the ferry from Bremerton to Seattle and a streetcar to the park. We were fascinated by the animals, and once we

Halfdan and Anna Enkeboll in 1932.
-Photos from Helga Enkeboll Behr

William and Helga Enkeboll, about 1920

children had a ride on an elephant.

In 1930, William bought a 1922 Overland roadster. (It was not a Willys Overland. Willys and Overland combined about 1925.) William used the car for trips, such as to Camp Parsons, when he was in the Boy Scouts.

When we got our first family car, a 1932 Plymouth, we went to Twanoh State Park on Hood Canal to picnic and swim. Another favorite trip was to Paradise Park on Mount Rainier, where we would picnic and hike on the nature trails. Eventually we took longer trips to many national parks.

DO-IT-YOURSELF

Mama and papa were "do-it-yourself" people. Papa constructed a concrete lily pond and stepping stones in the front lawn as well as concrete sidewalks around the house. For these walks he sifted beach sand. (White specks of crushed clam shells may still be visible.) He erected a flagpole in the front yard, and the American flag flew on Sundays and holidays. The pole became a special landmark. Also, he built a small greenhouse. Indoors he put up sheetrock and painted all the rooms; and for our bathroom, did the plumbing and installations.

Mama canned our fruit, made many of our clothes and was a wonderful cook. To be remembered were her cinnamon rolls and whole-wheat bread, as well as birthday cakes and cookies she made for our parties.

Mama and Papa taught us: 1.responsibility for tasks through chores we were assigned; 2. economy and savings through careful shopping and by having us save our money to pay cash; 3. value of education through encouragement to be good students and higher education at the University of Washington; 4. to speak the Danish language by using it in the home, and by reading it to us in the fairy tales of Hans Christian Andersen. Also, we learned that anything worth doing is worth doing well; and that we should be seen and not heard.

Papa retired in 1948, and in that year, with Mama, took a trip to Denmark.

Papa died January 28, 1950, and Mama died July 30, 1965. They are at rest in Forest Lawn Cemetery, Bremerton.

WILLIAM ENKEBOLL

I graduated from Bremerton High School in 1930. I entered the University of Washington and in 1935 received a bachelor of science degree in civil engineering. I went to Massachusetts Institute of Technology, Cambridge, Mass. for graduate study and in 1947 received a doctor of science degree there.

Among my various jobs I designed for the City of Seattle; laid out and designed earth-moving equipment, railroad cars and manufacturing facilities at Pacific Car and Foundry Company in Renton; instructed in general engineering at UW; surveyed headquarters site for Olympic National Park in Port Angeles; taught soil mechanics at Massachusetts Institute of Technology and designed military aircraft at Chance Vought Aircraft Company in Stratford, Conn.

In 1947 I opened the Seattle office of the engineering consulting firm of Dames and Moore, and in 1951 became a partner. In 1959 I was transferred to the firm's San Francisco office and was in charge of it until 1969. Since then I have been a consultant working out of that office. I am a registered engineer in seven states and have worked on projects in many states and foreign countries.

HELGA ENKEBOLL BEHR

I graduated from Bremerton High School in 1933. I studied dancing at the Novikoff School of Russian American Ballet before attending the University of Washington. At the university I studied art and in 1939 received a bachelor of arts degree. In 1942 I earned a teaching certificate with a major in painting and design and a minor in clothing and textiles. I taught art and home economics in secondary schools in Washington and Oregon.

William and I, during World War II, were employed at Chance Vought Aircraft Company , Stratford, Conn. His job was military aircraft design and mine was drafting isometric views of aircraft parts for manuals.

William married June Scherer December 17, 1947, in the St. Pauls Evangelical Lutheran Church, San Francisco.

I married Richard Behr July 10, 1943, in the Little Church of the Flowers, Glendale, Calif.

GENEALOGY

HALFDAN ENKEBOLL was born in Toksvaerd, Denmark, August 26, 1879. He married ANNA SCHOU, who was born in Rosenborg, Denmark, June 3, 1877. Halfdan died in 1950, Anna in 1965. Their children:

1. WILLIAM ENKEBOLL was born February 2, 1913, in San Franscisco. William married JUNE ALMA SCHERER. They have two sons.
1A. WILLIAM JOHN ENKEBOLL, born August 29, 1950, in Seattle. Bill lives in Seattle.
1B. ROBERT HALFDAN ENKEBOLL, born February 6, 1952, in Seattle. Bob lives in San Francisco.

2. HELGA EMILIE ENKEBOLL was born February 14, 1915, in San Francisco. Helga married RICHARD BEHR. They live in Salem. They have two children.
2A. CHARLES "Chuck" BEHR, born October 29, 1948, in Eugene. Chuck married CHO KYONG CHA and lives in Hamburg, Iowa. They have two children:
2A1. JOHN EDWARD BEHR, born June 14, 1980, in Chicago.
2A2. JULIE ANN BEHR, born August 28, 1984, in Marion, N.C.
2B. DIANA EMILIA BEHR, born May 12, 1953, in Eugene. She lives in Salem.

ETTEN, OSCAR
By June Etten Jarstad
1983

Adeline J. "Addie" (Rice) Etten was born December 29, 1898, and was raised in Santa Maria, Calif., on the Rice Ranch. She came to Bremerton when she was 18 to visit relatives for a month. During that time she went to work for the telephone company. She later worked in the shipyard running a crane in the shipfitter building for about 2 years.

In 1919 she met a handsome man, Oscar Etten. Oscar was born in Tacoma December 6, 1896; his father was a civil engineer, and did a lot of work around the Grays Harbor area building bridges. Oscar was working as a meat cutter at Carstens' meat market on Pacific Avenue in Bremerton. He had learned to be a meat cutter while working on a ship going to Nome. He and Addie courted for about a year and were married in 1920.

They purchased a home in Manette on Water Street, now 609 Shore Drive. Addie quit her job at the shipyard because it just wasn't "right" for a married woman to work at that time.

The home in Manette had one bedroom, a basement, a coal furnace and cooking stove, and no refrigerator; instead it was equipped with a cooler (a sort of box set into the kitchen wall and open to the outside covered with heavy screen). They also had an ice chest. Ice was delivered twice a week. The home was quite comfortable with a nice waterfront view and access to the beach.

In 1922 a son was born, Roy Kenneth. By this time Oscar had his own meat market in Manette, the Manette Meat Market. He had a contract to deliver meat in the shipyard, and had a meat route throughout the county. All this required the addition of extra help. Archie Bouchard, who was raised in Manette also, drove the truck for the meat route. Business was good enough to make a good living for the Etten family.

In 1925 a daughter was born, June Lorraine. In 1933 another son was born, Keith Wayne. The one-bedroom home

The Etten family, about 1930 (before the birth of Keith in 1933). From left are Addie, June, Oscar and Roy.
- Photo from June Etten Jarstad

became inadequate, so the Ettens had two bedrooms added.

Those were the days when the mother in the family did not have to wonder what to do with her time. Mother Etten was no exception. Each day of the week was unofficially designated for different chores. For example, on Monday one usually did the family wash. This took a great deal of time because Mother did not have a washing machine, just a scrub board. The clothes were hung in the basement in the winter time, or outside on lines in the summer. Another day would be for ironing the clothes; everything we wore had to be ironed, and some things were starched.

Addie packed a hot lunch every day for Oscar, as there were no restaurants close by and she felt that he needed a hot lunch. She usually walked to the market with the lunch, since Oscar was alone most of the time at the market and could not leave. When the children were older they would sometimes deliver the lunch, usually on their bicycles.

Addie and Oscar used to go to dances at the Masonic Temple in Manette. Sometimes Addie played the piano for those dances (this was good fun). Raymond "Coony" Schoonover played the saxophone, and someone played a banjo. Addie was also quite proficient as a ragtime pianist.

All three of the Etten children attended the old Manette School [1920s-1930s]. It had four rooms and a large basement for play in the winter. Later another room was added to accommodate a kindergarten class. Florence Condy was the principal. She was a taskmaster, insisting on everyone working hard and doing the best they could.

After grade school, all three of the Etten children attended Lincoln Junior High School in Bremerton. Sometimes when they missed the school bus, June and Roy would ride their bicycles to school.

In 1939 or 1940 Oscar Etten converted the meat market into a grocery store, added to the building and named it Etten's Super Market. It was a large store by those day's standards, and it flourished through World War II.

With the war years came the barrage balloons and the soldiers assigned to them. Some of the local girls met and married these young men. There was a barrage balloon unit stationed above our house on Shore Drive. One day the balloon broke loose and came over our house. Its cable touched the house next door, evidently disturbing some wires, and it set fire to their porch roof. It was promptly put out, but caused a lot of excitement for awhile.

When June was 4 years old she sang over Seattle radio station KJR on a weekly program called "Uncle Frank's Children's Hour." She was sponsored by two dentists and accompanied on the piano by mother Addie.

All three Etten children graduated from Bremerton High School at 5th Street and High Avenue in Bremerton. During the war years the school went on double shift. June spent her last 2 years on this double shift. There were more than 75,000 people in Bremerton at that time.

ROY MARRIES

After graduating from high school Roy enrolled in the University of Washington, as did his high-school sweetheart, Ruth Johnson. They were there only a couple of months when World War II broke out and they came home and got married.

Roy entered the Naval Torpedo Station at Keyport as an apprentice machinist and Ruth went to work at the Sears, Roebuck store in Bremerton. After finishing the 4-year apprenticeship Roy enlisted in the army. By this time they had one daughter, and they all stayed together in different parts of the country, wherever the army decided to send Roy (mostly Florida).

After Roy's return, he and Ruth lived on Perry Avenue. They had another daughter and two sons. The four children all attended Manette School, Dewey Junior High and East High School.

JUNE AND GLENN

When June graduated from Bremerton High School she worked for a few months at Puget Sound Power and Light Company and then married her sweetheart of 2 years, Glenn Jarstad, who would later become mayor of Bremerton. They met at Perl Maurer's Dance Pavilion when June was a junior in high school and Glenn was an apprentice at the Naval Torpedo Station, Keyport.

A year or so later Glenn entered the army and June stayed home to take care of their daughter, Janice, the first of their four children.

June worked as a secretary at Naval Undersea Warfare Engineering Station, formerly Naval Torpedo Station, at Keyport. She retired in 1987.

ROY AND GLENN'S MARKET

When Glenn and Roy returned from the army they were offered the Etten grocery store to operate as partners. Neither man wished to return to work as a machinist, so they took over the store. This allowed Oscar to be free to operate his drug store, which he had purchased some months earlier. It was near the entrance to Westpark.

Roy and Glenn's business was profitable and supported both families during the postwar years. Ruth and June both worked part time at the store.

GLENN ELECTED

After 17 years at the grocery store, Glenn was asked to campaign for mayor of Bremerton. He did and subsequently served 18 years in this capacity. June took a refresher course at Olympic College, brushing up on her secretarial skills, and went to work for the federal government. She is a purchasing agent at the Naval Supply Center in Bremerton. [She retired in 1988].

When Glenn became mayor Roy continued to operate the grocery store for a short time and then went into a partnership with Ted Thompson at the Manette IGA, in a building on Harkins Street formerly occupied by Safeway. He then went to work for the federal government and subsequently retired from the Sand Point Naval Supply Station in Seattle as a contract specialist.

KEITH ETTEN

Keith graduated from Washington State University as a second lieutenant in the ROTC program and served 4 years with the air force, completing his tour with a rating of captain. He married Diane Dibble from Spokane. They have two sons. They reside in Sunnyvale, Calif., where Keith is a supervisory electronics engineer working for Lockheed.

RETIREMENT

After Oscar and Addie retired from the store business, they moved to South Laguna Beach, Calif., where they purchased a new home. They lived there for about 5 years, and later moved to Santa Cruz to be with Addie's mother, who passed away at the age of 91.

Oscar passed away in 1962 while they were living in Santa Cruz, and Addie moved back to Bremerton to be near the family. She moved into the Thunderbird Apartments in Manette when they first opened in 1963, and still lives there.

Glenn and June own and operate the 46-foot charter boat *Joker* out of Westport in the summer time, and at present (1987) are running charters out of Kingston for a special services contract at Bangor submarine base. In their spare time they enjoy hunting, fishing, and taking short automobile trips to the mountains. June keeps active with her singing in the Manette Community Church choir.

Roy and Ruth are ardent mountaineers, climbing, skiing and hiking. Roy is a dedicated tennis player, participating in tournaments whenever possible.

Keith and Diane are square dancers and enjoy the area they live in, in Sunnyvale.

Mother Addie is busy with a multitude of friends, enjoying being a senior citizen with all the advantages it offers, such as bus passes, discounted meals, and other things. She enjoys her great-grandchildren, grandchildren, and her own children; she takes frequent trips to Sunnyvale to visit her son.

OSCAR AND ADELINE ETTEN'S FAMILY

1. ROY KENNETH ETTEN, born December 14, 1922, in Manette. Roy married RUTH JOHNSON of Bremerton. They now live in Seattle. They have four children.
1A. DIANE RUTH ETTEN, born March 17, 1945. Diane married WILLIAM SISSON. They live in Bellevue. They have two sons, SCOTT and DANIEL.
1B. LINDA ETTEN, born November 4, 1946. Linda married TOM THOMPSON and they live in Belfair. They have two daughters, BRENDA and LORI.
1C. DONALD ETTEN, born April 17, 1950. Don married MARY LOU WITHERS of San Jose, Calif. They have one son, MATHEW ROY.
1D. JOHN ETTEN, born December 26, 1953. John and his wife CINDY have two children, LEE and DANIELLE, and three step-children, DAVID, AARON AND AMANDA MARIE.

2. JUNE LORRAINE ETTEN, born June 2, 1925, in Manette. June married GLENN JARSTAD of Bremerton. June and Glenn have four children.
2A. JANICE JARSTAD, born September 11, 1945. Janice married ROBERT GRIMM. Janice works at Naval Supply Center in Bremerton as a small purchase supervisor. Janice lives in Bremerton. Janice and Robert have two sons, BRET and BRIAN.
2B. SUSAN JARSTAD, born July 28, 1949. Susan married RICHARD LEAVELL and they live in Silverdale. Susan is a secretary at Central Kitsap High School. Susan and Richard have two children, AARON and MELISSA.
2C. GLENN "Gene" JARSTAD, born November 1, 1951. Gene graduated cum laude from Washington State University with a master's degree in wildlife biology and range management. He is a pharmaceutical representative for Wyeth Laboratories. He skippers his father's charter boat in the summer on weekends.
2D. KAY JARSTAD, born February 15, 1956. Kay married MICHAEL DENNY and they live in Port Orchard. Kay and Michael have two daughters, MELONIE and TAMI. Kay also has two stepchildren, SCOTT and STACEE.

3. KEITH WAYNE ETTEN, born March 15, 1933, in Manette. Keith married DIANE DIBBLE and they live in San Jose. Keith and Diane have two sons, STEPHEN and KERRY.

FARMER, JESSE
By Fredi Perry

Jesse Edgar Farmer (born November 1, 1861, Fairfield, Iowa; died November 24, 1948, Seattle) was a restless young man. Disliking Missouri, where he had settled with his wife, the former Sarah Frances Ayers (born August 5, 1863, Powersville, Mo.; died June 6, 1934, Manette), he went west on a railroad excursion with his brother-in-law Charlie Ayers and settled on property in Meridian, Idaho. After a year there, he again uprooted his family to join Charlie in the Lone Tree district near Nampa, Idaho.

The young Farmer children loved the Lone Tree area. Vere Loy (born January 20, 1897, Lucerne, Mo.) and Velna Leeta (born February 14, 1895, Powersville; died March 4, 1984, San Diego) rode ponies to their school about 2 miles from home until they were discovered using the ponies to chase jackrabbits. Jesse reprimanded them by insisting that they thereafter ride the old mare.

Jesse suffered a heart attack and his doctor prescribed a change of climate. Jesse thought of the fertile Willamette Valley and in 1904 sold the family farm and loaded the family possessions in a covered wagon, dragging a buggy behind. With the help of a team of bays and a team of greys, the family traveled to Everett to visit Jesse's sister Olie, her husband Noel Caywood and their two children.

While visiting Everett, Jesse read about C.D. Hillman and took the free excursion to Manette, where he and Fletcher Powers bought 5-acre parcels side by side. Again the children were uprooted from school and moved to Manette, where they attended the Sheridan School. The 5-acre tract proved unsuited for farming, even though Hillman had assured the farming Farmers that this was ideal farm land. In 1912 Jesse purchased a parcel of land from C.E. Eastman and built a barn and home at the corner of Sheridan Road and Perry Avenue. The house still stands at 2802 Perry Avenue, an endorsement of Jesse's skill as a carpenter. The original 5-acre tract reverted back to the county for taxes.

Jesse worked at Braman Lumber as a cabinet maker. His eldest son, Carl Rosen Farmer (born May 24, 1888, Powersville; died April 14, 1972, San Jacinto, Calif.) was Clyde Meredith's partner in a grocery store, but soon Carl

The Jesse and Sarah Farmer home built in 1912 and still standing at what is now 2802 Perry Avenue. 1987 photo.

quit, moving to Richvale, Calif., to go into the hardware business with Fred Ayers and then to Chico, Calif., where he worked for the Diamond Match Company. The rest of the family went to visit Carl in Chico, and Velna and Vere decided to stay while their parents returned to Manette. Velna found employment as a telephone operator and Vere (long known by close friends and family by his nickname "Dick") delivered the Chico newspaper on horseback and the *Sacramento Bee* on bicycle. During this time he attended Chico Training School, graduating from the eighth grade in 1912. Dick and Velna then returned to Manette, where Velna secured a job in the navy yard as a telephone operator and Dick entered Union High School. He completed his 4-year manual training course in one year, graduating in 1917 with 31 classmates.

Having learned carpentry skills from his father and through his manual training course, Dick built a dresser of birds-eye maple for himself and a mahogany lamp which he presented to his favorite teacher. As well, he built a 16-foot clinker-built boat with a 12-foot sail which he sailed back and forth between Manette and Bremerton. Once the boom hit his dad, throwing him into the water. They waited for a tow ashore and appeased Mrs. Farmer later with a story that it had rained. It wasn't until later that a friend who had witnessed the accident told her the true story.

One of Dick's Union High School teachers insisted that all students study typing and take the civil service test. Dick preferred the cooking class, but it was not an option for a male student.

Dick worked in the navy yard during summer vacations. After graduation he got a job in the yard's carpenter shop and, shortly after qualifying as a helper, received notice from Civil Service that the Coast Artillery Headquarters, Seattle, wanted him as a clerk typist. He quit his job and moved to Seattle and after a few months talked his mother into giving her permission for him to join the army. He enlisted in a unit that was scheduled to go directly to Europe, but when he got to Newport News he was sent to Washington, D.C., then to Baltimore for duty with the Motor Transport Corps, Camp Holabird. There he spent the rest of the war in the personnel office making up units to go overseas. He came home a sergeant, senior grade, which today is equivalent to master sergeant.

Carl was drafted and sent to France as a sergeant in charge of a sheet metal shop. After World War I he returned to California and had his own sheet metal shop in Corona.

Velna worked as an operator at PSNS during that war. All the operators were made Yeomanettes. Velna met and married a marine, Frank McReynolds. They had two children, Donald Eugene and Betty. After the war they moved to Grants Pass and later to Eugene.

In 1919 Dick took his parents to Orange to visit Carl and Mary van Buskirk, Sarah's sister. That trip took more than 30 days as all the roads were gravel and a rainstorm at Tillamook caused delays, as the roads were washed out and the ruts were deep. It took four horses to pull the car up the Grants Pass mountain and two to pull it down the other side, as the mud was deep in the ruts. While the family was visiting, Mary decided that Carl should get together with Daisy Bridges, who lived with a Mrs. Lacey and her family in San Dimas. Dick had to drive to San Dimas to get Daisy to come to Orange for weekends. Daisy, a prim old maid, took Grace Lacey with her, as she did not want to be with Dick alone. The two couples double-dated and Dick even attended Grace's high school graduation. They also stood up as attendants at Carl and Daisy's wedding in Santa Ana.

In 1938 Carl and Daisy were the attendants at Dick and Grace's wedding in Las Vegas.

Dick worked in the supply department at PSNS from 1922 to 1941. On January 1, 1941, he was called into active duty for a year's service. He took over the Seattle Army Procurement Office as the procurement officer with the rank of captain. The office was uptown at that time, but soon expanded and moved to the port. It wasn't long until the army took over the old Ford plant near Spokane Street. Headquarters, Procurement and Storage, expanded fast. Dick's office was responsible for supplying Washington, Oregon, Idaho, Utah and Montana as well as Alaska. War was declared and jobs were frozen until it was over. Dick was a major by then with the title of director of procurement and was responsible for all procurement and inspection of army quartermaster supplies required for the northwest area. He was then promoted to lieutenant colonel and held the job for 4 years. He was sent to Manila as procurement officer, Base X. In addition, he was to get as much local industry back in operation as possible. After a year, the war was over and he returned to his job in the supply department, PSNS, serving as supervisor, traffic branch, until retirement February 1, 1957. He retired as Colonel Vere L. Farmer, United States Army. He and Grace retired to Pomona, Calif., in 1957 and still live there.

FEEK/BACIGALUPI
By Joaquina Feek and Dick Feek

It was the summer of 1920. Richard "Dick" Feek, his mother Joaquina C. (Bacigalupi) Feek, and Aunt Joaquina Higgins arrived in Manette from Los Angeles to visit Aunt Emelita (nee Bacigalupi, Joaquina's aunt) Walsh and her son, Charles Walsh. They were renting a house called the "Little Green House" at 1115 Scott Avenue, next door to the present Estelle Meredith home.

JOAQUINA FEEK'S RECOLLECTIONS

I remember we had to come from Seattle on the *H.B. Kennedy*—I thought it was the most beautiful ride over here. I loved every minute of it and I always have enjoyed that ride. We had to take a little launch across to Manette. Manette had no paved streets—nothing but dirt roads with mud and rocks in the middle of them. There were a few boardwalks on what is now East 11th Street. The stores here included a drug and variety store, a post office on the corner of East 11th Street and Perry Avenue, two grocery stores—Meredith's and Martin's—and a garage at the foot of East 11th Street near the ferry landing.

The first big house I saw was the Bender house. I walked down there and knocked, and a young girl came to the door. I believe it was Alice Bender. I

Emelita Walsh, circa 1918.   -Photo from Joaquina Feek.

"The little green house." 1115 Scott Avenue, where Joaquina Feek, her son Richard and her aunt Joaquina Higgins lived when they arrived in Manette in 1920. Photo taken 1987.

asked if she knew where the Walshes lived. No, she had never heard of them. We hiked up and found Meredith's store. I asked, by any chance, did they know where Mrs. Walsh lived. Mr. Meredith directed us.

The first person I was introduced to in Manette was Hattie Martin. She took me under her wing and from then on I lived in Manette.

I think Manette is a wonderful place. I'm not sorry I came! It was a wonderful place to raise children. The activities were just great for young people here—scouting and all. Young people of Manette did well scholastically. And they had opportunities. The boys had their bikes and rowboats, they had access to the water and they had access to the YMCA and could learn to swim.

DICK'S MEMORIES

When we first came to Manette in 1920 there were few houses in the area; none had private telephones, and fewer still had indoor plumbing. But the little community of Manette slowly filled with friendly, family-oriented people.

It was here that I had my third birthday party, and here that my cousin, Emelita Walsh (Joaquina's Aunt Emelita's daughter), celebrated her wedding to Joe Newman with Dr. La Violet of the Bremerton Methodist Church officiating.

In 1922 my aunt, Joaquina Higgins, Mother and I moved into the Carrie Cain home near East 11th Street and Pitt Avenue. This place had electric lights, indoor plumbing and all the modern conveniences of the day—a wood-burning kitchen stove, custom-built kitchen cabinets and counters, a back porch pantry, and hot and cold running water. In 1924 my mother's father, Frank Bacigalupi, came to live with us, remaining until his death. Joaquina Feek still resides here at

The Feek and Bacigalupi home at 1110 Pitt Avenue. Photo taken in 1987.

1110 Pitt Avenue.

My earliest recollections of Manette were attending kindergarten at Mrs. Isaac Hoopes' home. As I grew older I attended Manette School on Ironsides Avenue, which housed four large classrooms with cloak rooms for grades 1 to 8. Mr. Cash was the principal.

I left Manette School with the first seventh-grade class to attend Lincoln Junior High School at 11th Street and Ohio Avenue in Bremerton. Commuting to class every day on the car ferry *Pioneer* across Port Washington Narrows proved quite an adventure for a young boy. I graduated from Bremerton High School in 1934, with many others who have remained friends.

Some of my friends included Eugene Stone, Al Danel, Clyde Clark, Glenn Kidder, Ray Cole, Bud Osborne, George and Larry Worland. Some of the girls were Thelma Osborne, Jeane Martin, Dorothy Cole, Bernice Pederson, Helga Enkeboll, Laura Ellis, Rowena Harkins and Jane Bender.

Boy Scout Troop 505 was an important part of my life. I obtained the rank of Eagle Scout in June of 1932. Troop 505 still exists in Manette. I

Frank E. Bacigalupi and daughter Joaquina Feek, circa 1925.

was also a member of the Bremerton Chapter of DeMolay and reached the level of master councilor in 1936 and majority in 1938 at age 21.

In my late teens I followed my first love of cars and worked in the old Manette Garage at the west end of East 11th Street for Jim Hoonan in 1933-34. Jim sold the business to George

and Pearl Wiss. I bought their business in 1936. In March 1938, I opened the first modern gas and service station on the east side at what is now Wheaton Way and Harkins Street. I had an array of tools and a pick-up truck for hauling tires. The slogan was "If you've got a squeak, see Feek." John Nelson was station assistant.

In 1940 I met a Central Valley girl, Gladys A. Anderson, and we married that September. Our first child, Jim, was born in 1942. A year later I joined the Army Transport Service and shortly after sold the service station. I headed home after the war and worked briefly for Willard Parker at Parker Hardware at 7th Street and Pacific Avenue in Bremerton.

In 1946 I opened a new service station in Navy Yard City. That year our second child, Ann, was born. We moved our home from downtown Manette, which was bustling with cars and businesses, to the more residential area of Ironsides Avenue, closer to the Manette School our children attended.

In 1950 I ventured into the home heating and fuel oil business, calling it Feek's Service, with the slogan, "The hottest oil in town!"

I belonged to the Active Club, Bremerton Rotary Club, Bremerton Planning Council, Elk's Club, Chamber of Commerce, Bremerton Yacht Club and Our Saviour's Lutheran Church Council. I was Scoutmaster of Troop 505, and pursued my hobbies of boating and fishing.

In 1958 Carl Aaberg and I opened Aaberg & Feek Auto Parts in Navy Yard City. I retired in 1979.

Gladys and I moved to a home on the waterfront of Oyster Bay during this time. We enjoy good health and remain civically involved in the life of Bremerton. In 1987 I was elected to the Bremerton Port Commission.

DESCENDANTS
Thumbnail sketches of our children follow.

1. JAMES FEEK, born December 23, 1942, in Bremerton. He married KATHY PAIGE on August 23, 1969. They live in Seattle, where Jim has his own insurance firm. They have three sons, all born in Seattle: RHETT, born August 24, 1974, GAVIN, born December 8, 1976, and GRANT, born May 6, 1981.

2. ANN FEEK, born January 16, 1945, in Bremerton. Ann married TIM OLSON, who now owns and manages Aaberg and Feek Auto Parts. Ann is a counselor with the Peninsula School District. Ann and Tim have a son and a daughter, both born in Bremerton: TY, born April 19, 1972, and BETH, born March 17, 1975.

FELLOWS, GEORGE
By Walt and Mary Fellows
and Alice Fellows Lawson

George Fellows was born December 23, 1832, in Penfield, N.Y. He died May 10, 1910, in Manette. George came west in 1856. He started west with a group heading for California but he split off with a few others and came down the Columbia River on a raft to Portland, Oregon Territory.

On the way down the river they came to The Dalles, where they couldn't get past some rocks, so they abandoned the raft, portaged around the rocks, built a new raft and started on their way again. Before they got to Portland they met a wind coming upstream that blew them back as fast as the river pushed them downstream. They rigged an underwater sail with two poles and a blanket under the raft and were able to proceed down the river.

PORTLAND STOPOVER

At Portland George had a tinker's shop. He bought his sheet metal from ships that came to port. During his stay in Portland he met a man named Joe Meek, with whom he was to have several experiences fighting Indians in eastern Oregon. He sold his tinker shop and started for a gold field in Canada with Meek. They got as far as eastern Washington, gave up and returned to Portland.

George Fellows went to Seattle from Portland by sailing ship. At that time it was common in what is now downtown Seattle to get a lot in payment for clearing the brush off another lot for the owner. George, who did not like the rainy weather, passed up the opportunity. He went back to New York and married Alice Ann Stevenson in Rochester in 1865. They had three sons and a daughter: Arthur, Thomas, Harry and Ellen "Ella." Alice died at age 40 in 1885.

The Dandy. *Built by George Fellows and his sons after their arrival in Manette in 1886. It was used for towing and chartering.*
                        - Photo from Don and Anna Jo Atkinson.

George (left) and Alice Fellows (right) and their children (back, from left), Thomas and Harry, and (front), Ella and Arthur. Photo taken about 1878.
                    -Photo from Alice Fellows Lawson

In 1886 George and the boys came west to Portland by train and then by sailing ship to Seattle. While in Seattle they heard of School District 4 property for sale at Decatur. They came here and bought the schoolhouse and 10 acres of land adjoining it. This land was to become the George Fellows Addition to Decatur. George and his sons remodeled the schoolhouse to suit their needs. They built a sawmill on the beach north of the east end of the present Manette Bridge.

They built a steam launch named *Dandy* and used it as an excursion boat to take groups to dances and for other charters. They also used it to do light towing jobs.

Ella, George's daughter, came here in 1889 at age 17. She had been staying with relatives in Michigan. Ella was met in Seattle by a minister who made it a practice to look after single girls.

Ella came to Decatur on the steamer *Grace.* Captain Seymore blew the whistle to notify her family ashore there was a passenger to be picked up by rowboat. No one came out to meet her, so the captain took her to Tracyton, where she stayed with a family for a week until her father and

brothers got back from a hunting trip.

Ella met Lewis Bender, who had a grocery store in the Sidney area, now Port Orchard. They married in 1893. Lewis joined the Fellows mill partnership.

In 1898 the Fellows boys, Art, Tom and Harry, Lewis Bender, and two or three others went to Alaska as crew on a sailing ship to pay the freight for a load of cedar lumber that had been cut at the Fellows-Bender mill. They dumped the lumber overboard just north of Skagway, towed it to shore with a skiff and hauled it over the cliff by cable. They took the lumber to Lake Lindeman, where they built cedar boats which they sold to prospectors going down the Yukon River to the gold fields.

Arthur Fellows.
-From 1909 plat book.

On their return from Alaska the sawmill partnership ended. Arthur Fellows and Lewis Bender moved the mill across the bay to Smith Cove, where the tide was not such a problem. Lumber was sawed there for many of the first homes in Bremerton.

THOMAS STAYS IN MANETTE

Of George and Alice Fellows' three sons, Tom was the only one to remain permanently in Manette. Harry had a chicken ranch here for several years but then, with his wife Carrie and two daughters, Ellen and Dorothy, moved to Puyallup. Arthur stayed in the sawmill business for awhile and then with his wife Belva and two daughters, Lois and Frances, moved to Salem, Oreg. Ella and Lewis Bender built a home on the site of the old schoolhouse. [see Bender history.]

Tom went to work as a machinist in Puget Sound Navy Yard. He later became the first saw-filer there.

Tom married Mary Ellen Cline of Port Orchard, then Sidney, in 1899. Mary Ellen was born in Kansas and came to the northwest at the age of 6, over the Oregon Trail with her family. Her mother was a midwife in Port Orchard. Thomas and Mary Ellen, known as "Mellie" by her relatives, lived in the remodeled schoolhouse. There their first son, George William, was born. They moved into a house they owned on what is now Hayward Avenue between East 10th and East 11th

*Thomas and Mary Ellen Fellows' family, about 1915.
From left are Florence, George, Clifford, Mary Ellen,
Alice, Walter, Thomas and Charles.*
- Photo from Walter Fellows

Streets, where son Walter Thomas was born. This house was later owned by the Dillon family, in about 1915 to 1923.

DIVERSE ACTIVITIES

On Telegraph Avenue, now East 11th Street, between Hayward and Ironsides Avenues, Thomas and Mary Fellows built a two-story, four-bedroom house, very modern at that time since it had hot and cold running water, a bathtub and carbide gas lights. Here Florence Mary, Clifford Henry, Charles and Alice Jane were born.

Until his death in 1910, George, Tom's father, lived with them.

On that 3-acre piece of land Thomas also built a two-story barn, a two-story woodshed, a chicken house, a 50-foot water tower with a garage underneath, three-quarters of an acre of greenhouses, and later a small house for the Japanese caretakers. After several trials with hiring local gardeners

*Thomas and Mary Fellows' children (from left),
Charles, Florence, Alice and Walter in front of their
home at 2410 East 11th Street, about 1915.*
- Photo from Walter Fellows

(Fred Jacobsen was one), the greenhouses were rented to Mr. Fujihara, who raised lettuce, cucumbers, tomatoes and flowers for local and Seattle markets. Tom kept one greenhouse for himself to grow and experiment with flowers. He sold these flowers in a shop in Bremerton for awhile.

There was a furnace that burned cordwood that kept the greenhouses warm. Later the greenhouses were leased (Japanese could not own property) to "Shorty" Shimasaki. The greenhouses were torn down about 1932. Water for the greenhouses and irrigation was stored in the water tower. When a flag showed at the top, it meant water was coming into the tank and the pump was working. The well was south and west of East 11th Street and Scott Avenue.

The Fellows place was called "Fairview." It had a marvelous view of the bay and the Olympic Mountains. We always knew when a ship was coming into the navy yard because we could hear the gun salutes. It was exciting to see the flash and hear the "BOOM."

Tom continued to work as a saw filer in the navy yard 6 days a week. On Sunday he worked on his place while the rest of his family went to Sunday School, only a block away. He planted fruit trees, berries and vegetables. He kept chickens and pigeons, a cow, a horse, a burro and rabbits. He rented stalls in the barn to local teamsters and sold hay and grain.

On Tom's day off from work, neighbors would come to have saws sharpened, since many families were clearing land. Tom would hand the neighbor his shovel, or whatever tool he was using, and put the man to work while Tom sharpened the saw.

The well for household water was on the home place. The tank for this water was in the two-story woodshed. A noisy gas engine pumped water into the tank. It was cool in this tank room. The equipment for the gas lights was also in this shed. On top of the shed was a bell. I'm not sure why it was put there, but all the kids used it for a BB-gun target, to hear it ping.

Thomas died of pneumonia in May 1916 at age 48.

MARY ELLEN

Mary Ellen Cline Fellows, widow of Thomas, was an unsung heroine. Raising six children, ages 5 to 16, she went to work as a seamstress in the linen room at the naval hospital. She got the job when Mrs. Nellie Harrington quit to marry Nels Peterson. Mary Ellen was laid off in about 1922 and worked at the Children's Home in Manette. Her daughter, Alice, was envious of the children at the home since they saw her mother more than Alice did. Later Mrs. Fellows went back to the naval hospital to work. She lived a busy life. She caught the 7 a.m. ferry and walked up the hill to work, then got the 4:15 p.m. ferry home at night. Son Charles always met her in case she had groceries to carry. Then came a busy evening at home, washing, ironing (everything needed ironing then), sewing and generally keeping the home fires burning.

Mary Ellen died March 27, 1970, at age 92.

ELLA

Ella and Lewis Bender built a new home on the site of the old schoolhouse and lived there many years as very active members of the community. [see Bender history].

GEORGE FELLOWS FAMILY

GEORGE AND ALICE FELLOWS had three sons and a daughter.

1. HARRY FELLOWS was born March 13, 1866, in Penfield, N.Y. He married CARRIE MILLS in 1900. Harry died in 1934.

2. THOMAS S. FELLOWS was born August 24, 1867, in Penfield. He married MARY ELLEN CLINE February 8, 1899. Tom died May 30, 1916, in Manette. Tom and Mary Ellen "Mellie" had six children.
2A. GEORGE WILLIAM FELLOWS, named for his two grandfathers, was born December 1, 1899. As a boy, he loved to play baseball and was always on a team. He began working in the navy yard as an apprentice in about 1915. In 1917 he went to California to join the navy for 4 years. George married MARIE D'ALEO on July 6, 1921. Marie died December 15, 1942. George married EVA BURBRIDGE in 1943. George died in California in June 1981. George and Marie had two sons.
2A1. GEORGE WILLIAM FELLOWS Jr., born in April of 1923.
2A2. CLIFFORD WALTER FELLOWS, born in November 1925. Clifford had three daughters and a son. Clifford died in January 1983.
2B. WALTER THOMAS FELLOWS was born August 27, 1901. As a boy he dug clams, gathered Dungeness crabs and fished. He and his brother George delivered milk from the family cows for 5 cents a quart. When a cow was butchered they took orders for meat and would deliver immediately since there was no refrigeration.
The boys all had slings, not slingshots. One day Walt was down on the beach near the end of Trenton Avenue and the *Chickaree* was going by. To test his skill, he put a rock in the sling and to his surprise, he put it through a window on the *Chickaree*.
In 1916 Walter worked in the navy yard as a messenger boy at $1.04 a day and worked up to $4.16 a day as a machinist helper, then was laid off. He farmed in Iowa and South Dakota from about 1919 until 1925, when he returned to Bremerton.
Walter married MARY ELLEN BOICE LaPLANTE December 31, 1935. Walter worked in the navy yard in the sheet metal shop until his retirement in 1960. During times when he was laid off at the navy yard, he worked on the dredge *Calabra* in Aberdeen, had a donut shop here and in Los Angeles and raised cranberries in Grayland, Wash.
Mary Ellen taught in Bremerton schools from 1952 until retirement in 1966. She was classroom teacher, then taught remedial and developmental reading, and later was elementary librarian. She was honored in 1965 as teacher-of-the-year by the Bremerton Education Association and received life membership in Washington Congress of Parents and Teachers in 1949. Walt and Mary now live at Norseland Mobile Estates on the Belfair Highway. Walt and Mary have three children:
2B1. MARY CLEO LaPLANTE FELLOWS, Mary Ellen's daughter, whom Walt adopted. Mary Cleo grew up in Manette and attended Manette School. She married KENNETH MAGELLSEN. Kenneth died in a diving accident. Mary and Kenneth had two daughters and two sons.
2B1a. TONI MAGELLSEN. Toni married FRANKLIN LISTZ. They live in Tacoma and have two children, DEBORAH ANNE and DAVID CHRISTOPHER.
2B1b. LOIS ANNE MAGELLSEN. Lois married WILLIAM ARCHER. They live in Shelton and have two sons, DANIEL WILLIAM and GABRIEL PAUL.
2B1c. WALTER KENNETH MAGELLSEN. Walter lives in Tacoma.
2B1d. DONALD RALPH MAGELLSEN. Donald lives in California and has one son, JAMES DONALD.
2B2. BENJAMIN THOMAS FELLOWS, born in Manette November 9, 1940. Benjamin married MARGIE ANN SCHULTHEIS. They live in Minnesota. Benjamin and Margie have two children, MARILYN KAY and KENNETH THOMAS.
2B3. RUTH SHARON FELLOWS, born in Manette July 28, 1942. Ruth married JOHN LEAR. They divorced and Ruth married THOMAS MASTERS. Ruth is divorced and lives in the Port Orchard area with her daughter, MARY ELLEN LEAR MASTERS.
2C. FLORENCE MARY FELLOWS was born March 28, 1904. Her first 4 years at school were in the two-room school in Manette. After a year of business college, commuting to Seattle, she worked 3 years in the navy yard pay office, where William von Hoene was her supervisor. There were no pay checks — all cash.
Florence married ROY JENNINGS LEVIN of Silverdale in 1925. Roy started as an apprentice electrician in the navy yard, where he worked until his retirement. Florence quit her job in the navy yard when their daughter Alice was born. After a year at home, she went back to the pay office and stayed for another 3 years until their son Roy was born in 1931.
Florence was active in Campfire Girls and Cub Scouts during her children's growing years. She worked as a volunteer at the Horton Nursing home for 15 years. Florence belongs to Eastern Star, Daughters of the Civil War and Daughters of the American Revolution. Roy died in 1987. Roy and Florence had three children.
2C1. ALICE JANE LEVIN, born April 21, 1926. Alice Jane married JOHN BEGG of Seattle. Alice and John have four children.
2C1a. JOHN A. BEGG, III.

2C1b. BARBARA BEGG. Barbara married CHARLES WOLFRED. Barbara and Charles have one son, JOHN.
2C1c. ROBERT BEGG.
2C1d. JAN BEGG.
2C2. ROY ROBERT LEVIN, born March 8, 1931. Roy married JANICEAN WILSON from California. They have three sons.
2C2a. DONALD G. LEVIN. Donald has one son, SPENCER.
2C2b. ROBERT LEVIN.
2C2c. THOMAS LEVIN.
2C3. CHARLES RICHARD "Dick" LEVIN, born July 24, 1942. Charles married JOYCE BENDICKSON. Charles and Joyce have two sons.
2C3a. MONTE LEVIN. Monte has one son, TODD.
2C3b. KJELL LEVIN.
Dick and Joyce divorced. Dick married JUDITH. Dick and Judith have two daughters, JADE and AJA.
2D. CLIFFORD HENRY FELLOWS was born May 1, 1906. During the summers, he worked at Jacobsen's on Jacobsen Boulevard picking beans. He had a paper route. He skinny dipped at the Sandbanks with all the boys and loved playing baseball. He learned telegraph as a messenger and clerk at Western Union in Bremerton.
Clifford joined the army in 1925 when it was recruiting telegraphers and radio operators worldwide. He became a civilian in 1928 and went to sea as a radio operator for a year, then back to the army until 1950, when he retired with a disability as a captain. He worked for Boeing and Great Northern Railroad and retired in 1969. He lives on Bainbridge Island. Clifford and his wife VIENNA had one daughter.
2D1. BARBARA MARY FELLOWS, born December 15, 1930.
Clifford and Vienna were divorced. Barbara lived with her Grandma Fellows for a few years in Manette.
In 1938 Clifford married GENEVA "Geri" S. SWANSON. They adopted a daughter.
2D2. WENDY ANN FELLOWS, born in 1950. Wendy died in 1967 of a brain tumor.
Cliff and Geneva now live on Bainbridge Island for 6 months and in Mesa, Ariz. for 6 months each year.
2E. CHARLES FELLOWS was born July 15, 1908. Growing up in Manette, he had many friends — he was seldom seen alone.
In 1923 he went to South Dakota to join his brother Walter, who was farming. Charles returned to Manette in about 1925. He worked on the dredge boat *Calabra* and then for Coast and Geodetic Survey. The Great Depression hit and he could find no work. He finally went to Detroit to work in a gas station for the father of Jessie Crowell of Manette. He went to other jobs from there.
Charles married CHRISTINE WESLEY March 13, 1937. They live at Fife Lakes, Mich. Charles and Christine had two children:
2E1. THOMAS EDWARD FELLOWS, born August 28, 1938.
2E2. BONNIE FELLOWS, born September 30, 1945.
2F. ALICE JANE FELLOWS, named for her two grandmothers, was born September 16, 1910. When her brother Walter saw her for the first time, his mother said, "Walter, she looks just like you." His response — "Ain't she cute!" Margaret Hixon, age 6, whose grandfather brought the mail from the boat dock to the post office, thought it very unfair that the Fellows had a new baby and she, an only child, wanted one.
Alice was a tomboy and during high school years she turned out for every sport. She was a charter member of the Rainbow Girls in Bremerton. Her dearest friends were Elizabeth and Margaret von Hoene and Evelyn Aldrich. Alice and Margaret spent many summer hours in that icy water at the end of Trenton Avenue.
Alice took training in the Laboratory of Clinical Medicine for about a year and worked at Virginia Mason Laboratory for a few months. September 16, 1930, she married WALTER LAWSON, a navy machinist from Worcester, Mass. He remained in the navy until 1936. Alice retired from Puget Sound Naval Shipyard in 1972 after 18 years of working with IBM and key-punch machines, the last years in tape and card communication.
Lawsons now live at Hansville. Alice and Walter have two daughters.
2F1. KAY ELIZABETH LAWSON, born May 19, 1932. Kay married MARVIN ADAMS in 1950. Kay and Marvin have a daughter and a son.
2F1a. MICHELE RENE ADAMS, born in 1951. Michele married BILL ROBINSON in 1968. Michele and Bill have a son, JEFFREY DEAN, born in 1969, and a daughter, GAYLE, born in 1971.
2F1b. KERRY BRENT ADAMS, born in 1952. Kerry married MAY BROOKS. Kerry and May have a son, JOHN, born in 1977.
2F2. CHRISTINE NOEL LAWSON, born November 27, 1940, in California. She married MICHAEL McINTYRE in 1965. They have two sons.
2F2a. SCOTT PATRICK McINTYRE, born in 1966. Scott married JENIFER ANN JOHNSON March 21, 1987.
2F2b. SEAN MICHAEL McINTYRE, born in 1967.

3. ARTHUR FELLOWS was born August 8, 1869, in New York. He married BELVA SHELLY June 10, 1903. Arthur died in July 1954 in Oregon.

4. SARAH ELLEN "Ella" FELLOWS, was born September 3, 1871, in Grand Blanc, Mich. She married LEWIS ALBERT BENDER June 21,

1893. Ella died June 26, 1954, in Manette. [See BENDER family history.]

BREMERTON SEARCHLIGHT, May 21, 1910: George Fellows, who died at his home in Manette Sunday night, was a pioneer of Kitsap County and known to all the old timers of this region. Mr. Fellows' homestead is the old Decatur fort, afterwards the Indian school facing Port Washington at Manette, and which he had occupied since 1889. Mr. Fellows was born in Penfield, N.Y., in 1832, moved to Michigan in 1852, and fought his way across the plains to Oregon in 1854. During the Fraser River excitement he traveled 1700 miles on horseback fighting the Indians, and in one of the skirmishes lost twenty-five men of whom he was in charge. After his return from British Columbia, he returned to Oregon by way of Whatcom, now Bellingham, and Seattle, refusing an attractive offer of Yesler to settle in Seattle, he fought his way back over the trail to Omaha, Neb., and from there he remained in the East, during that time he married a Miss Stevenson of his old home. On the death of his wife in 1885, Mr. Fellows returned west, bringing with him his three sons, Harry, Arthur and Thomas S. Fellows, and his daughter Ellen, now Mrs. L.A. Bender, all of whom survive him. In 1888 he settled in Manette, then an outpost of civilization where he lived at the old homestead the rest of his life. Mr. Fellows, by geniality and good will, endeared himself to every acquaintance; his thorough acquaintance with hardship and toil in his younger days made him a friend to those who toil, and his active and reminiscent mind, full of tales of frontier life, enlivened by the power of an acute descriptive vocabulary, endeared him to a host of admiring friends of the younger generation. Mr. Fellows was one of the progressive men of that bustling village of Decatur, now called Manette, and much of its growth and activity was due to his generosity and vigor. His death is a great loss to the entire community.

FISCHER, JOHN GEORGE
By Ed Fischer

My dad, John George Fischer, was born in Holland. He moved at about age 4 in 1892 with his parents to St. Louis, Mo., where his father worked as a streetcar conductor. When Dad was 19 he joined the army and served in Alaska for 3 years.

Dad had been home on leave and, while returning to Alaska, met Mom. Mom's family was headed west from South Dakota, leaving the dry lands, seeking "God's Country" in Kitsap County that a friend, John Emel of Silverdale, had written them about. Dad was discharged from the army and returned to Bremerton, and he and Mom were married in May of 1912.

They first lived in Manette at Cascade Trail and Perry Avenue. My older brother, George, was born there January 19, 1913. He was a premature baby so tiny that my grandmother placed him on a warm hot water bottle to keep him alive.

A year later, on a Sunday afternoon, the folks went on a hike north, mostly through the woods and trails. They came across a partially built cabin—logs laid up in a square—on land across Sylvan Way from the southwest corner of what is now Illahee State Park. After some searching they were able to buy the property, 5 acres, from the owner. The unfinished cabin was on this property. Within a year they had completed the cabin floor, windows and roof.

Obtaining drinking water was a problem but Dad went down into the canyon across the road and dammed a trickle of water from a spring. He built steps down and cleared a path some 150 yards uphill to the cabin. The spring was on what is now the southwest corner of Illahee Park.

Two of the seven of us children were born in this log cabin: I, Jacob Edward Fischer, June 27, 1914, and James Robert Fischer October 13, 1916. Each time Dr. John Schutt was rowed across the Sound to be in attendance.

An early recollection of my surroundings was standing on the bed in the cabin looking out the window. The snow was so deep it partially covered the window. [This was probably the "big snow" of 1916.]

My grandad, Jake Waltenburg, used to visit us quite often; he was a very good hunter and lived about a mile and a half away by trail. I recall one of his first visits. My mom called me to the north window, and I climbed up on the woodbox to see out. There was Grandad coming up the hill with his two hunting hounds, a gun over one shoulder and a bobcat over the other.

My father worked in the navy yard and he also cleared some of the 5 acres and planted fruit trees and a garden. At that time, about 1918, he got to the navy yard in the winter by walking the 2 1/2 miles to Manette and taking a boat to Bremerton. In the summertime he rode in Nels Peterson's boat. Nels lived on the waterfront next to what is now the northeast corner of Illahee Park. Neighbors called their home "Grandma Peterson's." Nels sold produce at the Farmers' Market in Bremerton, taking it there in his launch, the *Gussie*. Dad rode with him.

I remember Peterson's cold storage house; cool creek water was circulated by means of a trough. Butter, milk and cream were kept cool there. Shelves were built on the sidewalls for storing apples, prunes and vegetables.

We had a one-horse buggy. It was quite small. My older brother George and I sat in the small box behind the driver's seat with our legs hanging over the back edge. Sylvan Way to Perry Avenue, at that time, was quite crooked as it wound in and out around the large stumps cut high up by springboard tree fellers.

Some of World War I sticks in my mind, for I remember Dad carrying home some of our rations on his shoulders—one large wooden box each day—of canned goods, dried prunes or raisins, sometimes a sack of flour or sugar.

In the summer a few times the cabin roof would catch fire. Sparks from the chimney would start a blaze on the dry cedar shakes. That was always an exciting time, for water was passed up to the roof to extinguish the flames. Two wooden barrels were kept at the corner of the cabin to catch rainwater for this purpose. The shakes were replaced from a never-ending supply cut from the large cedar tree that lay in the canyon beyond the spring.

In 1919 my father purchased the 80 acres across Sylvan Way from our log house. The land was bounded by Sylvan Way on the south, Trenton Avenue on the west, a canyon and creek on the north and what was to be the entrance to Illahee Park on the east. A portion of an old skid road runs diagonally to the east 45 acres and is now used as a park trail. This skid road also ran southwest through the northeast corner of Ralph Hibbard's ranch, across the Bill Avery place at Perry Avenue and Wyoming Sreet and past Sheridan School — now the Kona Village Apartments—through the Harrison Memorial Hospital grounds, and ended up a little west of the Bay Bowl. Logs had been drawn by oxen and dumped in the bay, some of them off Illahee near the Nels Peterson place and some in the Bay Bowl area, downhill from the old Sheridan School.

The log cabin was our home for some time yet; my brother George and I started to Sheridan School from there. We had a very good teacher for the first 4 years, Miss Clements. At that time a teacher taught four grades with 25 to 27 pupils.

For 8 years we used the old skid road for a shortcut to Sheridan School.

About the time I was 6, neighbors, the Nashans, built a

The George and Kathryn Fischer home, 3020 Sylvan Way, built in 1922, photographed in 1986.
                                    -Photo by Orville Schultz

house and moved in west of us. The two boys were 6 and 7 years older than me and my brother George. About twice a year the four of us would make a trip to Lamotts' Creek at Illahee, where Frank, the older boy, would jump into the creek and scoop a salmon to the bank for the rest of us to hold. We would carry them home and my mother would smoke and can fish for the winter.

During the next several years Dad and friends cleared some of the land on the 80 acres, built a barn and dug a well. The family cow was moved to the new barn along with a new team of horses purchased from Fry and Company of Seattle. A great deal of extra time was required going the quarter of a mile to feed the animals and milk the cow. The horses were used to clear land for a new house and grain fields.

For 2 months we moved closer into town, off Perry Avenue and Sunset Lane near my grandmother's. During this time my brother Henry was born on December 4, 1920. This time Dr. John Schutt came across the bay on the regular boat service provided between Bremerton and Manette.

It was about 1922 when we moved from the cabin to our ranch house across the road (still standing on the north side of Sylvan Way near the west end of Illahee Park).

We had not been in our new house long. It was summer and a very hot day. The back door was open for ventilation; we were all seated at the table eating our evening meal when all of a sudden

George shouted, "What is that?" His eyes were nearly leaving the sockets. We all looked out, and there high on a log about 100 yards away lay a large cougar getting ready to attack the cow, which was a few feet away, grazing and unaware of danger so near. Dad took one gun and Mom the other, each circling toward opposite ends of the log; but when they were halfway there, the cougar jumped off and ran away into the woods.

Brother Joe Fischer was the first one of us born in our new home. This was on September 17, 1923. I recall Dr. John Schutt requesting a place to nap and be awakened in half an hour. Then away he went to visit another patient on his way home.

How well I remember my first hay ride, with Dad driving the team. We had gone to Illahee by a road off the north end of Perry Avenue, past the Johnson ranch, then east past the Illahee School and on to Illahee. Just south of the boat landing Dad had cut and stacked a field of hay. I rode home on the stack. At this time this roundabout route was the only way into Illahee except by trail or boat. We could make only one trip a day because of the long distance.

Another well-remembered wagon ride was to Manette with my great-uncle Bill Waltenburg, to deliver loads of small cut wood to the baker. The baker was Don Serry. This trip always turned up some goodies. And about every 6 months or a year we made a trip by wagon to Silverdale to John Emel's blacksmith shop to get the horses shod. We would take along oats and hay for the horses as our trip began at 5 a.m. and lasted well into the night. We carried two lanterns on the wagon, one dangling on a rope at the back for a tail light and the other held by hand on the driver's seat.

The George and Kathryn Fischer family, 1933. Standing, (from left), George Jr., Edward, Robert. Seated, Joseph, George Sr., Annie, Kathryn and Henry (Jerry not present).
                                    -Photo from Ed Fischer

We boys spent a great deal of time burning brush and stump piles—even at night. We enjoyed roasting potatoes, clams or oysters in the hot coals. In the fall we would make our annual trip in the woods southwest of Sheridan School to gather a flour sack of hazelnuts for winter enjoyment. Each year, near home, we picked blackberries and huckleberries for canning. After we had enough berries for ourselves, we would pick and sell them to the ships' cooks in the navy yard.

George and I began high school in 1928, sometimes walking and once in awhile getting a ride the 2 1/2 miles to the Manette ferry, crossing and walking up 4th Street to the school above Veneta Avenue.

Our only sister, Annie, was born New Year's Day in 1929, the first baby of the year. Gifts were presented by several area businesses. Among the gifts was a year's supply of milk. We thought this quite humorous as we had our own daily milk route.

It was a great relief to us when the Manette Bridge opened in 1930, for then we could get to and from high school in the family car. The opening of the bridge also increased the size of our evening milk delivery route.

The youngest brother, Jerry W. Fischer, was born July 12, 1934. This time Dr. Ray Schutt attended, coming from his home in nearby Illahee.

In the following years, all of us worked in the ship yards of Bremerton or Seattle or at the Boeing Company.

GENEALOGY

JOHN GEORGE FISCHER was born in Holland July 24, 1888. He married KATHRYN MAE WALTENBURG, who was born in Balsom Lake, Wis., February 25, 1894. They had seven children. Kathryn died in 1955; John died in 1959. Their children are:

1. GEORGE FISCHER Jr., born January 19, 1913, in Manette. George married MARTINA P. SLOANE in 1940. Martina was born July 12, 1911, and died March 28, 1974. George retired from Todd Shipyard. He lives in Seattle. George and Martina had no children.

2. EDWARD FISCHER, born June 27, 1914, in Manette. Ed married KATHRYN F. LAING of Seattle in 1937. Ed was a shipfitter at PSNS for 22 years. He retired in 1971 from A.I.M. (Assistant Industrial Management) Government Service, Sand Point, where he had worked 10 years. Ed and Kathryn live in East Bremerton. They have four children.
2A. JUDITH K. FISCHER, born July 16, 1939. Judy married C. E. DRAKE of Denver, Colo., in 1956. He is a detective in the Denver police force. Judy is a para-legal with the Mansville Corp. They live in Littleton, Colo. They have five children.
2A1. STEPHEN C. DRAKE, born April 2, 1957, in Kodiak, Alaska. Steve is a policeman on the Commerce City, Colo., police force. Steve married KATHY LANGE of Denver in 1982. They have one child.
2A1a. KIMBERLY DRAKE, born February 8, 1983, in Denver.
2A2. KAREN D. DRAKE, born March 15, 1958, in Denver. Karen married JIM BRODERICK of Littleton, Colo., in 1979. Jim is a detective on the Fort Collins, Colo., police force. Karen sells real estate. They live in Fort Collins. They have two children.
2A2a. BRIAN P. BRODERICK, born September 30, 1979, in Denver.
2A2b. MATTHEW J. BRODERICK, born October 13, 1980, in Fort Collins.
2A3. RICK E. DRAKE, born December 8, 1959, in Denver. Rick married KELLY PINNEY of Littleton in 1980. Rick is a cement worker and Kelly is a dental assistant. They have two children.
2A3a. CRYSTAL DRAKE, born July 2, 1982, in Littleton.
2A3b. ZACKARY D. DRAKE, born January 25, 1984, in Littleton.
2A4. DAWN D. DRAKE, born January 29, 1961, in Denver. Dawn married DALE SCHMICKLAS of Denver in 1980. Dale is a professional polo player. They have no children.
2A5. WENDY L. DRAKE, born October 23, 1962, in Denver. Wendy married DANIEL DENTON of Castle Rock, Colo., in 1982. Danny is an electrician. They have one child.
2A5a. MONIQUE D. DENTON, born August 27, 1983, in Littleton.
2B. MARY L. FISCHER, born January 10, 1942, in Bremerton. Mary married CHARLES MILLSPAUGH in December 1968. Charlie was a shipfitter at PSNS and later an inspector for A.I.M. Government Service at Sand Point and Tacoma Boat. He retired in 1982. He and Mary live in Bremerton. They have no children.

2C. EDWARD G. FISCHER, born October 2, 1945, in Bremerton. Ed married SUSAN A. McVEIGH of Bremerton in 1967. Sue and Ed own Arctic Radiator Shop in East Bremerton, where they both work. They live in Bremerton. They have three children.
2C1. AMY E. FISCHER, born December 17, 1970, in Bremerton.
2C2. BRIAN E. FISCHER, born June 1, 1974, in Bremerton.
2C3. MARY KATHLEEN FISCHER, born November 11, 1979, in Bremerton.
2D. IRENE L. FISCHER, born September 20, 1951, in Bremerton. Irene married JACK D. AYLWARD in Bremerton in 1971. Jack is a sheet metal worker at PSNS. Irene worked in the auditor's office in the Kitsap County Courthouse. They live in Port Orchard. They have two children.
2D1. ANGELA I. AYLWARD, born March 4, 1978, in Bremerton.
2D2. MICHELLE J. AYLWARD, born January 27, 1982, in Bremerton.

3. JAMES ROBERT FISCHER, born October 13, 1916, in Manette. Bob married SHERLY DAVIS of Bremerton in 1940. He worked at PSNS as a shipfitter. In 1973 he retired from A.I.M. Government Service at Sand Point, Seattle, where he had worked for about 12 years. Bob and Sherly lived in Bremerton, Seattle, and George, Wash., and Quartzite, Ariz. Bob died August 24, 1984. Bob and Sherly had two children.
3A. JANICE R. FISCHER, born September 17, 1941, in Bremerton. Jan lives in San Diego and is a clinical psychologist.
3B. JOHN S. FISCHER, born November 24, 1943, in Bremerton. John married CARLA BELL of East Bremerton in 1964. John is a bricklayer and union business agent. Carla is a receiving clerk. They live in Seattle and have two children.
3B1. JOHN C. FISCHER, born November 4, 1964, in Seattle. John lives in Seattle and is a tilesetter.
3B2. WHITNEY K. FISCHER, born May 9, 1967, in Seattle. Whitney attends college in Cheney, Wash.

4. JUDSON HENRY FISCHER, known as Henry, born December 4, 1920, in Manette. Henry married VIOLET G. BRUEMMER in 1941. Henry was a welder at PSNS. He died July 30, 1971. Violet lives in Kitsap County. They had three children.
4A. CAROL D. FISCHER, born March 7, 1948, in Bremerton. Carol married STEVE CHAFFEE of Bremerton in 1978. Steve is an electronics engineer working out of Keyport. Carol and Steve live in Kitsap County. They have one child.
4A1. AARON C. CHAFFEE, born May 25, 1983, in Bremerton.
4B. SIDNEY DALLAS MARTINA FISCHER, born November 6, 1951, in Bremerton. Dallas married BUD HOLLER in 1970. They had one child, SHANNON, born March 24, 1971, in Bremerton. In 1985, Dallas married MIKE FOLEY. Mike is a drill sergeant in the marine corps. Dallas and Mike live in San Diego.
4C. DEBBIE L. FISCHER, born January 29, 1959, in Bremerton. Debbie married JIM DUMONT in September 1982. They were divorced. They had no children. Debbie is a secretary in the Fisheries Department at Sand Point, Seattle. She lives in Kirkland.

5. JOSEPH O. FISCHER, born September 17, 1923, in Kitsap County. Joe married BETTY J. GATESON of Colville in 1942. Joe worked at PSNS and retired as a leadingman shipfitter in 1976. Joe and Betty live in Kitsap County. They had one child.
5A. DANNY JOE FISCHER, born April 27, 1944, in Colville, Wash. Danny married CAROLYN SMITH of East Bremerton in 1966. Danny is a sheet metal worker in the Seattle area. Carolyn is a teller in a bank in Snoqualmie. Danny and Carolyn live in Snoqualmie and have three children.
5A1. DANNY JOE FISCHER, born October 24, 1967, in Seattle.
5A2. KRISTINA MAE FISCHER, born June 13, 1969, in Seattle.
5A3. KARI LOUISE FISCHER, born December 30, 1980, in Bellevue.

6. ANNA MAE FISCHER, born January 1, 1929, in Manette. Ann married HOWARD HULBURT in 1947. Later she married JACK LAWTER. She worked in the Seattle post office. Ann died June 12, 1983. Ann and Howard had two children.
6A. DAVID W. HULBURT, born July 27, 1948, in Vancouver, Wash. Dave married CELIA CLANCY in 1968. Dave and Celia live in Maple Valley. They have two children.
6A1. SEAN E. HULBURT, born February 10, 1966. Sean is in the U.S.Navy. He married TERESA M. DOUTHITT in 1986. They live in San Diego.
6A2. SHANNON M. HULBURT, born March 1, 1971, in Seattle.
6B. KATHY G. HULBURT, born January 12, 1955, in Vancouver, Wash. Kathy married STEVE EARLE of Montana in 1976. Steve manages a Chevron gas station in Missoula. Kathy is assistant vice president of the Missoula Bank of Montana. They live in Missoula and have no children.

7. JERRY W. FISCHER, born July 12, 1934. Jerry married GERRI TIENHAARA of East Bremerton in 1957. Jerry works in the sheet metal building trades in the Seattle area. Jerry and Gerri live in Redmond, Wash., and have three children.
7A. JACQUELINE K. FISCHER, born January 21, 1959, in Seattle.

Jackie lives in Seattle and has a pet grooming business.

7B. CINDY A. FISCHER, born March 10, 1961, in Seattle. Cindy married WILL GYSELINCK in 1981. Cindy and Will both work at the Rocket Research Corporation in Redmond. They live in Redmond and have one child.

7B1. CRAIG T. GYSELINCK, born September 28, 1985.

7C. JODI L. FISCHER, born February 8, 1971, in Hawaii. Jodi lives in Redmond.

GALLEHER, RICHARD LEWIS
By Richard F. Galleher
and Virginia Galleher George
1985

Richard Lewis Galleher (1891-1965) was born to a farm family in Scammon, Kans., October 19, 1891. Little is known of his early years until 1918, when he met and married Marie Karoline Soll. Marie (1895-1986) was born to Lutheran Pastor H.K. Soll and his wife Karoline on May 22, 1895, in Monroe, Mich., the third of eight children. Shortly before World War I the family moved to Yakima, where her father had accepted the call as pastor of the Grace Evangelical Lutheran Church. Marie worked in a fruit-packing house. It was in Yakima that Marie met Richard.

The Manette chapter of the Galleher family history began at the end of World War I when Richard and Marie were married in Illahee and moved to a remote home a few hundred yards southwest of Sandy Point near what is now Illahee State Park. It was here that Marie learned that there is no way to satisfactorily cook a cormorant and Richard learned that if you missed the *Chickaree* it's a long walk home. It was a primitive and remote lifestyle poorly suited for a man trying to raise a family, so a move to Yakima was made. While

Marie Galleher.
-Bremerton Sun photo

there, a daughter, Virginia, and a son, Richard, were born. In 1928 the family returned to Manette (Enetai), buying a piece of waterfront property from "Papa" Wall. They lived in a tiny cabin on the lot until a home was completed in the mid-30s. Richard was a boilermaker and steel worker in the navy yard, and on various bridge building jobs, and was known to enjoy the gaming tables, of which there was no shortage in Bremerton. Marie learned to love the tranquil glen in this primitive area where they established their home.

THE GALLEHER DESCENDANTS

1. ELIZABETH PAULINE GALLEHER, born and died in 1919.

2. DOROTHY ANN GALLEHER, born and died in 1920.

3. VIRGINIA ROSE GALLEHER, born in Yakima in 1922. Virginia attended Manette School and graduated from Bremerton High School in 1940. She married DAVID L. GEORGE in 1946 and they lived in Bremerton. They divorced and in 1957 Virginia moved to Treasure Island, where her mother lived with her until Marie's death in 1986. Virginia was employed in the legal field for more than 25 years. David died in 1981. Virginia and

David had one son.

3A. DAVID L. GEORGE Jr., born April 5, 1947. David attended Grapeview Grade School and was in the first graduating class of North Mason High School, June 1965. David married SUSAN HORN DYER in 1971. They divorced. David resides in Reno and is employed by Hugg School District as an air-conditioning and boiler specialist. David and Susan had one son, TYLER DAVID, born May 6, 1972. Tyler lives with his mother in Olalla.

4. RICHARD F. GALLEHER, born in Yakima March 30, 1923. He attended Manette School and Bremerton High School. He was in the army air corps during World War II from 1943 to 1946. In 1951 he married JOYCE PETERSON from North Dakota. They moved to Alaska, where Dick became a bush pilot; he was owner and manager of the largest bush airline in Alaska, Munz Northern Airline, until he sold it in 1983. Dick and Joyce divide their time between homes in Nome, Honolulu and Poulsbo. Dick and Joyce had four children.

4A. ROSS MICHAEL GALLEHER, born in Anchorage August 25, 1954. Ross died at birth.

4B. GAIL LEANNE GALLEHER, born in Nome September 19, 1957. She graduated valedictorian from Nome High School. She graduated from Stanford University in 1979.

4C. BRIAN GARETH GALLEHER, born in Nome March 22, 1960. He graduated from Nome High School in 1978, then served on the 80-foot schooner *Machias* throughout the South Pacific before completing his flight training in Hawaii. He became a bush pilot in Alaska and was lost in a plane crash near Siberia in November 1981.

4D. BLAINE GREGORY GALLEHER, born in Nome January 22, 1963. He graduated salutatorian from Nome High School in 1981. He spent 2 years as crewman aboard *Machias* in the Central and South Pacific. Blaine entered the University of Northern Colorado and now attends the University of Southern California.

5. JERRY MARION GALLEHER, born in Yakima September 5, 1928. He attended Manette School. The family moved to Seattle and Jerry graduated from Roosevelt High School in 1946. He is an accomplished artist and jewelry designer and was associated with a Seattle jewelry manufacturer before moving back to Bremerton and then to Ocean Shores. Jerry married DOROTHY POUNTAIN in 1954. They are owners of Tom & Jerrys' Lumber & Hardware in Ocean Shores. Jerry and Dorothy had two daughters.

5A. CHERYL LYNN POUNTAIN, born July 9, 1948. Cheryl graduated from Shoreline High School in Seattle in 1966 and completed nurses training at Wenatchee Junior College in 1968. Cheryl was killed in an automobile accident July 6, 1968.

5B. JENNIFER JOLYNN GALLEHER, born in Seattle April 26, 1970. Jennifer is an honor student at North Beach High School, Moclips, Wash.

6. LOUIS LEE GALLEHER, born and died in 1932.

GILMAN, ALBERT
By Joanne Gilman Snyder
1985

Albert B. Gilman was born in Seattle March 4, 1884. He went to sea in his early teens. Albert was from a pioneer Seattle family. He was born and reared on Queen Anne Hill. Many places in and around Seattle, such as Gilman Village and Gilman Trail, are named for his uncles.

Albert became an engineer for a steamship company. In 1916 he married Alma Hart, a secretary for the Ford Motor Company in Seattle. On their honeymoon to Bremerton, Albert applied for and received employment at the naval shipyard as a machinist.

Alma insisted that he settle down when they married. Their first home was on the beach in a wood-and-tent structure while they built their home at 908 Hayward Avenue. They lived there until the early 1950s, when they moved to Seabeck on Hood Canal.

Both Alma and Albert were active in Manette Community Church, Masons, Eastern Star and the East Bremerton Improvement Club. Alma was active in the Garden Club. Alma (born January 17, 1888), died in 1962. Albert died in 1964.

DESCENDANTS

1. JOANNE GILMAN was born December 19, 1921, in Auburn. She attended Manette School and Manette Community Church, where she sang in a quartet. Joanne graduated from Bremerton High School. Joanne married

Albert and Alma Gilman with their daughter Joanne, about 1925. -Photo from Joanne Gilman

Samuel and Agnes Hall's home at 808 Hayward Avenue, circa 1920. Standing on porch are Kenneth Hall and Maysie Ballew. - Photo from Kenneth Hall

EARL SNYDER in 1943. Earl is a retired Clover Park teacher. Joanne and Earl have two daughters and two sons.
1A. JUDITH ANN SNYDER, born in Bremerton December 8, 1945. Judith married LEE FUNDENBERGER in 1976. Lee is a fireman and a paramedic. They live in Ocean Shores, Wash., and have two children.
1A1. JUNIE LYNN FUNDENBERGER, born in Ocean Shores in 1978.
1A2. STACY JEAN FUNDENBERGER, born in Ocean Shores in 1979.
1B. ROBERT GILMAN SNYDER, born in Tacoma April 5, 1948. Robert married ALICIA BOJORQUEZ. They live in Oceanside, Calif. Bob is an electronic engineer and Alicia is a homemaker. They have two children.
1B1. PATRICIA B. SNYDER, born in Mexico in 1970.
1B2. LINDA ANN SNYDER, born in Mexico in 1974.
1C. NORMA JEAN SNYDER, born in Tacoma March 23, 1951. Norma married Dr. D. W."Chip" PETTIGREW III in 1975. They lived in Tacoma while Chip worked at Madigan Hospital. He is stationed at new locations regularly. Norma and Chip have three children.
1C1. NATHAN DANIEL PETTIGREW, born in Little Rock, Ark., in 1979.
1C2. JOEL DAVID PETTIGREW, born in Savannah, Ga., in 1981.
1C3. ADAM JOSEPH PETTIGREW, born in Tacoma in 1983.
1D. TIMOTHY PAUL SNYDER, born in Tacoma October 26, 1956. Timothy married KAREN KNAPP in 1978 and they live in Clackamas. Tim is a professional stenographer and Karen is a banker.

HALL, SAM
By Kenneth Hall
1985

INDIANA TO BREMERTON

Samuel A. Hall was born in Indiana in 1892. When Sam's brother Hershel visited Bremerton during his navy enlistment he told Sam of opportunities in the shipyard. Sam moved to Bremerton from Anderson, Ind., in 1917. His wife, Agnes, with their two children, Mary Elizabeth and Kenneth, joined him a few months later.

They first lived in Bremerton, but in February of 1918 bought a house from Thomas F. Cashill for $950—$200 down and $20 per month. The house was on Lot Nine, Block 20, of the plat of Decatur. This became the Halls' home, 808 Hayward Avenue.

In 1922 Sam organized the Manette baseball team and became its manager. For several years the team played teams from neighboring communities. Tracyton was the chief rival. Home games were played in an area now bounded by Nipsic Avenue, East 23rd Street, Brashem Avenue and Cascade Trail.

In 1924 Sam opened a lunch counter and confectionery store on the ferry dock. Mrs. Hall managed this enterprise during the day and Sam, after working days at the shipyard, took over in the evening. The store was open for only 3 years because Mrs. Hall had to return to Indiana to care for her ailing mother and there was no one to run the business during the day.

The house, with modifications, at 808 Hayward Avenue remained the Hall family home until Sam's retirement in 1950.

DESCENDANTS
SAM and AGNES HALL had two children.

1. MARY ELIZABETH HALL, born in Anderson, Ind., September 15, 1913. Mary died February 8, 1918.

2. KENNETH FRANCIS HALL, born in Anderson, Ind., May 7, 1915. Kenneth married MILDRED M. ARNOLD in Anderson. Ken with his wife returned to Manette in November 1940; at that time he started working in the sheet metal shop at PSNS. He worked there for 34 years. Ken and Mildred have three sons and nine grandchildren.
2A. JOHN A. HALL, born in November 1941.
2B. JAMES E. HALL, born in December 1942.
2C. GEROLD M. HALL, born in September 1945.

HARKINS, EARL
By Anna Jo Harkins Atkinson

Etta Rowena Eggleston Harkins was born Etta Hewitt November 15, 1887, in West Monterey, Mich. She passed away July 16, 1961, in a rest home in Topeka, Kans. She was visiting her son James in Kansas when she had a crippling stroke. She was bedfast for 4 years prior to her death.

Earl Harkins and Etta Eggleston on their wedding day,
June 30, 1921. Anna Jo Harkins is flower girl.
- Photo from Anna Jo Harkins Atkinson

Etta's first husband was James Max Eggleston, who passed away when their son James was only 9 months old. Etta came west for a variety of reasons: to seek more gainful employment, to escape the severe Michigan winters and to see her two brothers, Ernest and Claude Hewitt, who had moved to Monroe, Wash., years before with their families.

To quote from a letter I received from James Eggleston, "Mother and I came west via the Great Northern Railroad - not the covered wagon type, but just slightly removed from it. I was then 10 years old so the year was 1915...Mother went to work in a department store in Monroe for Mr. J.E. Wood. He liked her work and soon moved her to his store in Everett. She had a much bigger job there, was a good and popular store clerk and assistant manager. We moved to Manette in 1916 and she managed Mr. Wood's new store and post office there. This was the old building on the corner of Perry Avenue and East 11th Street which has been torn down. We lived in an apartment over the store."

Later the Manette post office was moved into a small structure added to the side of the store building. When Herbert Hoover became president he appointed Etta Eggleston postmistress. This position she handled well and efficiently until her retirement in June 1948.

Etta married my Dad, Earl Henry Harkins, June 30, 1921. My mother, Maude Mae Thayer Harkins, had passed away during the flu epidemic of 1918. My little brother was stillborn at that time. My father was overseas during World War I and didn't hear of my mother's death for 3 months. My grandparents, Charles and Sarah Thayer, kept me until my dad remarried.

Earl and Etta became acquainted when he came to Bremerton after the war to visit his sister and her husband, Hazel and

Milton Hamilton. He started calling for his mail at the Manette post office and was soon smitten by the beautiful young postmistress.

I can remember their wedding—I was then 5 years old. It was performed in the parlor of the old Methodist parsonage on 5th Street. As the flower-girl, I held a bouquet of sweet peas and baby breath with the wedding ring perched on top. There were just the three of us and the minister and his wife in attendance.

After the ceremony, Etta's neighbors, the Arthur Fentons, had lunch for the newlyweds and their daughter. I have a picture of the three of us taken in Fenton's front yard. I'm still holding the sweet peas.

Fentons lived next door to Etta's little bungalow on Wheaton Way, then Winfield Avenue. The present Thunderbird Apartments were built on Etta's property, adjoining Fenton property on the south side and the Ross property on the north. I've forgotten Mrs. Fenton's first name, but to me she was the "goat lady." She and her husband raised goats and who can forget that? At times the area was quite aromatic.

One Halloween Mrs. Fenton, who had long black hair, dressed herself in a long black skirt and cape, with a witch's hat atop her long flowing hair and thoroughly bewitched all the neighborhood kids.

My birthday falls on November 1, so my dad and my new mom gave me a birthday party and Dad did some bewitching himself. He arranged a big pumpkin jack-o-lantern on the table by the window. He ran a tube from outside into the house into the back of the pumpkin. When he spoke through the tube, he thoroughly frightened all the little girls and Dick Feek, who had gathered for my birthday party.

Poor Dick—he really suffered. Every year when I'd have a party there would be all girls—and Dick. I'm sure Joaquina, his mother, and an auntie made him attend.

My Dad's little prank backfired on him. After scaring us he started into the house and in the blackness of night ran into a big tree and came into the kitchen with blood streaming down his face. We were sure the goblins got him.

Etta soon became mother to me. Never did a girl have a better stepmother. I felt so lucky to have such a nice mother and such a handsome big brother, James.

A HOME, A FIRE, AND HELPFUL NEIGHBORS

Mother's bungalow was a small one-bedroom house situated among tall fir trees. Of course it was much too small for the growing family, so Dad built two bedrooms on the rear of the house for James and me. The entrance to these rooms was through Mother and Dad's bedroom.

One evening in 1923 James had been out on a date. I was sleeping in my new bedroom, and Dad and Mom were in bed. When James came home, he turned their light on so he could talk to them. Smoke was curling around the light globe. They dashed into the new bedrooms to find Jim's room completely consumed and mine burning furiously. Dad got me to the front room. I was bleary-eyed with sleep. Someone turned the hose on me and told me to get outside.

What a terrible night that was! The whole community turned out to help but there was no stopping that fire. The house and all its contents burned completely. We escaped with our lives and night clothes. The only thing saved was a basket of baby clothes.

Mother was pregnant with my sister Rowena at the time. The ladies of Manette had given Mother a baby shower. All the gifts were placed in a baby basket ready to receive the new one. The basket was beneath a front window. Dad smashed the glass and pulled the basket and its contents to safety.

Manette had a fire department, but it was not the most efficient. There was a wooden bell tower on East 11th Street next to the post office. The fire truck with its hose was parked beneath the bell tower. More times than not the truck had to be pushed down the hill to get it started.

Lewis and Ella Bender, affectionately known as Mother and Dad Bender, took my folks in for the remainder of the night and until housing was found for our family. The Carlaws—Jack, Grace and Bernice, took me in. Brother Jim went to the Dewar family since he was a friend of Warren, Charlie, Bill and Florence Dewar.

We moved into a little house on Pitt Avenue across from Joaquina Feek's until Mom and Dad purchased a home. They bought a house from the Peppards at 1118 Pitt Avenue just two houses up from Joaquina's. There the family lived until the kids married and left, and death took our parents.

ROWENA HARKINS

My sister, Rowena Mae, was born March 14, 1924. There was no bridge across the Narrows to the hospital and the ferry service stopped at midnight. Shortly after midnight, my sister decided to make her debut. My Dad had to borrow a rowboat from Ed Olson, row Mother across the bay and phone for a taxi to take her to Harrison Memorial Hospital, then located on Chester Avenue.

A letter from Rowena: "Mother told me that it was a little past midnight on a stormy rain-lashed Puget Sound. Big, gruff ex-army captain [Father], recently home from fighting World War I and in command of every situation, shouted at his 98-pound pregnant wife that her pains were imaginary, that she wasn't going to give birth until the next day when the ferry boat began its hourly runs again. Why? Because he said it was so. After what seemed like an eternity of stifled pain she tried to keep within herself, the big man realized the inevitable and fell apart. Marshalling her courage, the tiny mother-to-be lifted the big man's head from his shaking hands, kissed and comforted him and sent him down to the wave-buffeted beach where a Swedish fisherman lived and kept his boats. One of his tiny rowboats carried the couple across the waters on a ride of life. It took them 45 minutes to land in the strong winds. They took a taxi to Harrison Memorial Hospital just in time for Dr. Ray Schutt to deliver me. What a great way to come into this world."

POST OFFICE

Mother continued as postmistress after my sister's birth. [see POSTAL SERVICE] Dad helped out in the post office. Between the two of them and an assortment of housekeepers and part-time postal clerks, they managed to run a home and the post office and raise a family.

EARL HARKINS

Dad's health was always poor due to shell shock and injuries suffered during World War I. He retired as captain from the U.S. Army. He was never gainfully employed, but devoted his energies to community projects and affairs.

He was involved in getting American Legion posts started in Charleston and Manette. He helped organize the East Bremerton Improvement Club, an organization highly responsible for the growth and development of Manette. EBIC was organized in 1929 and Dad was its first president.

Dad was active in the softball league of Manette and served as its secretary and scorekeeper. He helped spearhead the campaign to get our first bridge across Port Washington Narrows. I have a silver trophy presented to him for his tireless efforts for the bridge. The names engraved there are:

Division A Manager: W.J. Abbott
Group #2 Manager: Earl Harkins
Co-workers: W.H. Hawkes, George Hoberecht, H.P. Martin, R.O. Hilstad, B.J. Kean, J.H. Martin, Dr. H.W. Lindblad, E. Waltenburg, F.L. Hawley, R.L. Davidson and Frank Clay.

Later, Earl headed another campaign that resulted in the tolls being lifted.

Our dad was practically the founding father of Illahee State Park and the supporting Illahee State Park Association of Bremerton.

When Father died, The Bremerton *Sun* of January 18, 1950, reported the following:

Two guns from a naval ship will be mounted in Illahee State Park as a memorial to all Navy men who served in World War II, and a plaque will be established there in recognition of the outstanding volunteer work contributed by Earl Harkins.

The Illahee Park association has worked nearly two years to obtain a pair of guns as a memorial and the Navy department has now sanctioned the gift.

Dedication of the plaque to Earl Harkins will be at the request of the State Parks and Recreation commission, and marks an unprecedented move on the part of the commission.

Three generations. Earl and Etta Harkins seated, daughter Rowena and granddaughter Carolynn standing, in yard of Harkins home, 1118 Pitt Avenue, 1949.
- Photo from Rowena Harkins Hinshaw

Earl was secretary of the Kitsap Rifle and Revolver Club for many years. He was instrumental in securing Camp Wesley Harris rifle range. He was active in the Veterans of Foreign Wars and the Disabled American Veterans. At one time he printed the little town newspaper, *The Manette Gazette*. At the time of his death he was helping secure a fishing dock at Illahee State Park.

Dad passed away quietly in his sleep January 17, 1950, 2 days after the big blizzard that virtually immobilized Bremerton and the surrounding communities.

The Manette area and city of Bremerton is a much better place today because of the efforts of my mom and dad. The Bremerton *Sun* published this editorial January 18, 1950:.

A TRUE CIVIC LEADER

Ofttimes the term "civic leader" is used loosely. But when applied in the case of Earl Harkins, it has full meaning.

In the generous effort which he expended to make Bremerton a better home community, Mr. Harkins sought neither personal recognition nor reward. His tremendous vitality, steered into channels of business or industry, might have brought him an abundance of worldly goods; yet he was satisfied to live modestly, and to undertake the type of work which brought comfort, convenience and pleasure to his neighbors and friends. He found his ample reward in their expressed appreciation, and in seeing his beloved Manette peninsula area grow more populous.

Sometimes Dad was quite unorthodox in the method of getting things done, but once he started something he bulldozed it through to the finish.

Mother and Dad, both being in the public eye, had a wealth of friends, true friends of the good old American caliber. They carried many burdens, shared many griefs, sorrows and joys, had many agonizing worries poured out to them because people knew they could be trusted and be true confidants. Through them I learned to know some of the most wonderful people a girl was ever privileged to know. The older I grow the more I value the influence these dear people had on my life. To name a very few:

Clarence and Pearl Welborn, who devoted untold hours and energies to the first Girl Scout troop, Trillium Troop 1, in Manette; Al and Lillian Meicho, who contributed their time to Boy Scouting; Lee Harrison, the town barber, and wife Vera, and parents of one of my dearest friends, Lois Williamson; the Clyde Meredith and Harry Martin families, who operated the local grocery stores; the Bender family, Lewis and Ella, Renus and Helen, Art and Kate, Marsh and Alice Bender Davis; the Schweers; the Jacks; the Ellises; the Reas; the Hugo Berglinds; Carl Pedersons; William Abbotts; Jack Martins; Marion Martins; Ed Olsons; Hawthornes; Waughs; Schoonovers; Hoopeses; Carlaws; Dewars; Wheatons; Mullers; Hagens; Von Hoenes; Akerses; Forrest Coles; Worlands; Ettens; Hermansons; Walter Walls; Fellowses; Nels Petersons; Solids; Alonzo Almons; and our dear friends and neighbors, Joaquina Feek and son Dick. So many more names could be added.

I learned something from each of these families, important things that have been of value to me in rearing our own two sons and one daughter, plus numerous foster children.

Few children today know the privilege of growing up in a small community, where everyone is called by name and

Anna Jo Harkins Atkinson and Don Atkinson, 1946.

where the whole population shares everyone's joys, sorrows and troubles as in little old Manette. Thank God I was privileged to grow up in Manette.

EGGLESTON/HARKINS DESCENDANTS

1. JAMES EGGLESTON, born October 20, 1905, in Monterey, Mich. He graduated from the old Union High School in Bremerton in 1924. He worked one year at the Bremerton YMCA under Herbert Holiday and Ed Cooper. In 1925 he enrolled in George William College, one of three professional YMCA colleges at the time, located in Chicago. He graduated in 1929.

His first job was at the Elgin, Ill., YMCA, where he remained until September 1936. Jim met his wife JOAN while a senior in college. They were married October 5, 1929.

James remained in YMCA work until his retirement in 1970. He also served at the YMCA in Akron, Ohio, 1936-1941; Pacific Southwest area YMCA, San Francisco, 1941-1945; State YMCA, New Haven, Conn., 1945-1949; then on to become executive of West Central area of the YMCA at Topeka, Kans., until his retirement. In the summers he was associated with the YMCA Camp of the Rockies at Estes Park, Colo.

James and Joan moved in 1970 to Daytona Beach, Fla., where he manages the insurance office for YMCA employees. This is a part-time, semi-retirement job, but as with everything Jim does, he puts his whole heart and soul into it, turning it into a full-time job.

Jim and Joan still spend occasional summers at the YMCA camp in Estes, returning to their home on the peninsula midway between the Halifax River waterway and the sandy stretch of Daytona Beach, just a nice walk in either direction. Jim and Joan celebrated their 50th wedding anniversary in 1979. Jim and Joan have one daughter.

1A. JANET EGGLESTON, born October 9, 1938, in Akron. Janet and her husband live in St. Petersburg, Fla. Janet works for Merrill Lynch and her husband is retired from the army. Janet has two sons by a former marriage: JAMES and JON DAVIS.

2. ANNA JO HARKINS, born November 1, 1916. She married DON ATKINSON of Sheridan Heights in 1934. Those were Depression years and not too many jobs were available. Don helped out occasionally when Mother or Dad was ill, eventually becoming her postal clerk. Some days when John Rousa was unable to work, Don would take his route. When John retired, Don was appointed to his route. He served that rural route for 35 years.

It's often been said a fellow would do anything during Depression years to land a job, so Don married the postmistress' daughter. However, that marriage is in its 55th year. Anna Jo and Don have three children.

2A. ROBERT ATKINSON, born December 9, 1937, in Bremerton. ROBERT is regional director of Indian affairs in Prince Rupert, B.C., Canada. Robert married DELIGHT JACKSON and they have three daughters: TAMARA JO, DANA MARIE and ROBYN DEE. Robert and Delight divorced.

2B. FRAN ATKINSON, born May 13, 1939, in Bremerton. Fran and her husband, LARRY THORNTON, have recently moved to Tucson, Ariz. She is part of the emergency medical squad for Rural Metro Fire Department. Fran has five children by a former marriage: PATRICIA RAYE SCHOOLEY, now Mrs. JOHN GUERRERO, DAVID RICHARD SCHOOLEY, ELISABETH CHRISTINA SCHOOLEY, LEANNA JEAN SCHOOLEY and ROBERT GEORGE SCHOOLEY ATKINSON. Larry has two sons and a daughter by a former marriage: LARRY JR., DAVID and PAM.

2C. DAVID ATKINSON, born March 30, 1942, in Bremerton. David married DIXIE MILLER. David is dean of social sciences at Pacific Lutheran University in Tacoma. David and Dixie have a son and a daughter: DONALD MATTHEW and WENDY LEE.

3. ROWENA HARKINS, born March 14 1924, in Bremerton. She married GEORGE HINSHAW while he was stationed at Bremerton Naval Hospital during World War II. Rowena was also working in the hospital. They lived in Seattle while George completed his study of pharmacy at the University of Washington, graduating in 1948.
George died in 1982. Rowena now works for the navy post exchange in San Diego.
Rowena and George had two daughters and a son.

3A. CAROLYNN ANN HINSHAW. She is a property and real estate manager in San Diego. Carolynn Ann married Major ROLF LEWIS SPICER, USMC. He passed away in 1983. She is now married to DEXTER CARLTON LaPIERRE, an advertising director in San Diego.

3B. NANCY ROWENA ELIZABETH HINSHAW. Nancy married GARY MORISHITA and they live in the San Diego area. Nancy is a recreational activities director and an accredited teacher of natural childbirth and midwifery. Nancy and Gary have had four children: MISCHA MAKOTO ROBERT, born August 14, 1979; KAZUMI, born August 5, 1983, died January 23, 1984; and twins TADASHI THOMAS and MALLORY OMITSU, born August 1, 1985.

3C. GREGORY HINSHAW. Gregory is a cosmotologist and hair stylist. He and his wife CELIA (nee DeMARCO) have one daughter, JESSICA ELIZABETH ANN LORRAINE.

HARRINGTON, HERBERT
By Eleanor Carlson Harrington
1985

In 1903 Herbert Harrington, his wife Nellie and baby daughter Neal came to Manette from Roundlake, Minn., accompanied by his parents, Captain Scott W. Harrington and his wife Sarah.

They made their first home on Perry Avenue just south of East 11th Street while waiting for their home to be built at 1123 Scott Avenue—a home both families occupied in harmony while sharing mutual benefits and responsibilities.

Herbert Harrington worked in the sheet metal shop in the navy yard. Scott Harrington was on a disability pension. He

The Herbert and Nellie Harrington home at 1123 Scott Avenue. In 1916 this became the Nels and Nellie Peterson home. - Photo from 1909 plat book

had been commissioned a captain in the Civil War and was referred to by family and friends as "Captain."

All the family members participated in community activities and civic groups as well as being active members of the Masons and Eastern Star.

One of Herbert Harrington's main interests was the Manette Improvement and Investment Company, of which he was a director. In a little book promoting the area, he wrote, "What more could one wish for, a climate with just enough variety to relieve the monotony, everything green, trees, no bad storms, no industrial disturbances...We built our house for around $800 and it is now worth $4,500 but not for sale at any price."

Sarah Harrington, "Muffie" to the family, was not only a wonderful live-in grandmother but she also took an active part in shaping the community. When it was being decided how much land to allow for Manette School she held out for setting aside at least 2 acres, which by present-day standards is far too small for an elementary schoolground.

Later when Nellie Harrington was serving as president of Manette P-TA, a hot lunch program was started by the mothers, who volunteered to prepare and serve lunches to the children. She told of Mrs. Howerton, who willingly took her turn even though the Howertons lived on the outskirts of town and she had to bring her youngest in a baby buggy.

Scott W. Harrington passed on in 1909 and the following year a son was born to Nellie and Herbert. They named him Scott W. Harrington the second, in honor of his grandfather.

On September 18, 1913, there was an explosion in the sheet metal shop in the navy yard. One of the workers was killed and Herbert Harrington's left leg was severely injured and was amputated. He passed on 2 months later of pneumonia.

The Harringtons had served their country well: Scott Harrington in the Civil War, and Herbert Harrington as a corporal in the Spanish American War. Sarah Harrington had lost a father, a brother and an uncle. When the Grand Army of the Republic Encampment was held on May 30, 1913, in Bremerton, the *Bremerton News* printed in full the moving speech given by Sarah Harrington of her life as a young girl during the years 1861—1865.

By the next summer Grandma Harrington also passed on and these sad times left young Scott lonely and eager for a new father. He would greet any man who came to the home with the query, "Are you going to be my new daddy?"

In 1916 Nellie Harrington and Nels E. Peterson were married. Nels had come with his family as an early pioneer in 1888, and was one of the participants in raising the first flag over the navy yard on September 16, 1891. After a first marriage he went back to Minnesota but had returned in 1909 and settled in Manette. He worked as a crane operator in the navy yard until his retirement [See PETERSON, NELS history].

In September 1922 Neal Harrington married Malcolm Meredith, a childhood sweetheart whose family owned one of the grocery stores in Manette. Neal and Malcolm took an active part in the Masons, Eastern Star and the Eagles as well as civic groups. Neal was a leader of Girl Scout Troop 4.

Nellie Peterson died in 1958. The house at 1123 Scott Avenue subsequently passed into other hands.

Malcolm passed on in 1970. Neal is currently living at Resthaven Convalescent Center.

Scott and Eleanor live at 1710 Jacobsen Boulevard in Manette.

Neal Harrington Meredith, Malcolm Meredith, Nellie Harrington Peterson, Nels Peterson, Eleanor Carlson Harrington, Scott Harrington, 1932.
- Photo from Neal Harrington Meredith

THE FAMILY OF SCOTT W. HARRINGTON II

SCOTT WINFIELD HARRINGTON II married ELEANOR CARLSON (see CARLSON, JOHN, history) in 1932 and they have three children.

1. SCOTT WINFIELD HARRINGTON Jr., born June 27, 1939. Scott married SANDRA JEAN MacARTHUR. Scott works out of the University of Washington as a Sea Grant agent assisting commercial fishermen. Scott and Sandra live in Gig Harbor. Their two children were born in Bremerton: BRENDA MARIE January 9, 1973, and ERIC NELS February 8, 1976.

2. ROBERTA EILEEN HARRINGTON, born October 11, 1944. Roberta married TIMOTHY DAVID PASCHAL. They are now divorced. Roberta, a teacher, lives in Central Kitsap County. Roberta and Timothy had two children born in Bremerton: DAVID SCOTT June 27, 1973, and NICOLE MARIE October 7, 1975.

3. NEAL ELIZABETH HARRINGTON, born April 6, 1946. Neal married MICHAEL DAVID FORT. They spent several years in England and Singapore. Neal owns a home on the waterfront of her old neighborhood along Jacobsen Boulevard. Neal and Michael have two children: ADRIENNE ELLEN, born March 13, 1968, in New Orleans, and JAMES MICHAEL, born May 14, 1971, in England.

HARRISON, LEE R.
By Lois Harrison Williamson
and Jean Harrison Glude
1985

Lee Roy Harrison came to Bremerton in 1924 after a navy friend suggested that Lee work in Puget Sound Navy Yard. Lee lived with his friend while he worked for 6 months. He then felt that his job was secure and moved his family to Manette.

The family arrived the spring of 1925. When they disembarked from the Seattle ferry, they found the moving van with their belongings too tall to get on the ferry *Pioneer* that would take them to Manette, so all had to be unloaded and put on a smaller van. Several trips were required.

The first night in Manette was spent at the Brewster home, which is the present site of the Church of Jesus Christ of Latter-Day Saints. Mrs. Mary Brewster was married for a time to Frank Harrison, a third cousin of Lee Harrison.

The Harrison family's first home was the top floor of the building across Perry Avenue from the Masonic Temple. The building housed the post office and later Manette Foods.

After a few years in Manette, Lee Harrison bought lots 3,4 and 5 in the Second Brewster addition for $500 from Mrs. Brewster. Here Lee built a home for his family in what is now the East 16th Street and Hayward Avenue area. Lots are valued at $8000 each today.

BARBER TRAINING

After another 6 months the yard had a reduction-in-force and Lee lost his job. He then decided to go to a barber school in Seattle.

Lee Harrison's first barber shop was at the west end of the Manette dock. The building belonged to Oscar Hilstad, who had a coal dock nearby and a wood yard about where East 16th Street and Winfield Avenue are today. Lee Harrison worked in his barber shop and took orders for coal and wood for Hilstad.

Lee and Vera Harrison family, 1939. Back row (from left), Earl, Howard and Jean. Front row, Lois, Lee, Vera and Emma Belle.
- Photo from Lois Harrison Williamson

After the Manette Bridge opened in 1930, Harrison moved his barber shop to the building at East 11th Street and Perry Avenue. He added a second chair in 1945-46, when Julian Mathiason became a partner. Harrison worked there until he retired in 1957. Julian continued on as barber following Harrison's retirement.

A HOME WITHOUT A CAR

When the Harrisons arrived in Manette they had a Model-T Ford. The only road suitable for a drive at that time was the narrow Tracyton road, which was full of curves as it followed along the water. Mrs. Harrison was so frightened by this drive that she said they must get rid of the car. Oscar Hilstad bought the Ford and used the engine in his work at the wood yard.

During World War II, Manette really grew. Many streets were widened and given names. The street where the Harrison family grew up became Hayward Avenue.

GROWING UP IN MANETTE

The Harrison children attended Manette School at East 13th Street and Ironsides Avenue. They all attended Manette Community Church, where they were active members. Lois, Jean and Emmabelle were Girl Scouts and Earl and Howard were Boy Scouts. Howard was Scoutmaster of troop 505 for several years. Both Howard and Earl were Eagle Scouts.

Earl attended the University of Washington. Howard went to Washington State College at Pullman and was away for 2 years. He then served an apprenticeship as a tool and die maker at Keyport, where he worked until after World War II.

Lee died in 1962 and Vera died in 1963.

I, Lois, have enjoyed growing up and growing older in Manette, where families don't seem to change residences too often, and neighbors and friends have remained the same for many years.

GENEALOGY

LEE ROY HARRISON was born in Eastsound, San Juan County, Wash., February 28, 1890. He married VERA EMMA BUFFUM, born January 25, 1892, in Olinda, Shasta County, Calif. They had five children.

1. LOIS VERA HARRISON, born November 27, 1914, in Seattle. Lois married CLARENCE SYMON in 1933. They had two daughters. They were later divorced. Lois married ROY WILLIAMSON in 1941. He adopted the two daughters and he and Lois had one more daughter. Lois and Roy raised the three daughters at 1611 Hayward Avenue and still live there. Roy and Lois have been active in the Manette Community Church and Philathea Chapter, Order of Eastern Star, where they have served as worthy matron and worthy patron. Roy is active in the Masonic Lodge, where he is a past master. Their three daughters are:

1A. BETTY JEAN (SYMON) WILLIAMSON, born April 1, 1934. Betty married ALLEN V. ARCHER in 1953. In 1962 Betty divorced Allen and in 1965 she married IRVIN LEISS. Betty and Allen had four children, and adopted a fifth.

1A1. RONALD ALLEN ARCHER, born January 16, 1955. Ronald later took his stepfather's name, Leiss. Ronald married JODENE GAIL WALKER January 1, 1976. They have two children: MELLONIE MAE, born August 17, 1977 and JUSTIN ALLEN, born July 30, 1978.

1A2. CATHERINE MARIE ARCHER, born July 15, 1957. Catherine took her stepfather's name, Leiss.
1A3. STEPHEN MICHAEL ARCHER, born December 5, 1959. Stephen took his stepfather's name, Leiss. Stephen married TAMIE RAYE DAUGHTY. They have one son: STEVEN SCOTT, born January 12, 1977.
1A4. ANTHONY SCOTT ARCHER, born March 7, 1962. Anthony took his stepfather's name, Leiss.
1A5. VALERIE ANN LEISS, born April 27, 1977.
1B. ANNABELLE LOIS (SYMON) WILLIAMSON, born June 8, 1935. Annabelle married RICHARD E. THEIS. They have one son.
1B1. GERALD LYNN THEIS, (later BOYD), born May 12, 1953. Gerald married CATHLEEN JOAN O'HARA September 27, 1980. They have a son.
1B1a. RICHARD ALAN BOYD, born February 11, 1982.
Annabelle and Richard divorced and on August 16, 1959, Annabelle married MICHAEL McMURRY BOYD. They have two children.
1B2. DIANIA LEE BOYD, born January 22, 1963, was adopted by Annabelle and Michael.
1B3. MICHAEL McMURRY BOYD, born September 3, 1972.
Annabelle and Michael divorced.
1C. PAMELA LEE WILLIAMSON, born to Roy and Lois May 10, 1954. Pamela married BILLY RAY LEE August 3, 1974. They have two children.
1C1. TAMARA NICOLE LEE, born March 4, 1977.
1C2. BRANDON MICHAEL LEE, born February 14, 1980.

2. EARL LEE HARRISON, born April 10, 1917, in Bellingham. Earl married LEONA DAY in 1939. They were later divorced. Earl lives in Seattle. Earl and Leona had one son.
2A. EARL HARRISON, born May 7, 1940. He later took the name KRUSE, for his stepfather. He married LINDA MEREDITH STEVENSON May 19, 1973.
Earl Sr. married MARGARET JOHNSON in 1948. They have two children.
2B. LEE ANN HARRISON, born December 22, 1951. Lee Ann married OWEN CURT LYSON August 5, 1972. They have one daughter.
2B1. DENA LOUISE LYSON, born November 12, 1973.
Lee Ann and Owen divorced in 1980. Lee Ann married MICHAEL RODDY in 1982.
2C. SCOTT DOUGLAS HARRISON, born October 16, 1953.

3. HOWARD WESLEY HARRISON, born February 28, 1919, in Bellingham. Howard married LOLA CAVIN in 1942. They were divorced. In 1967, Howard married FLORA NELL WAGNER. They live in Slidell, La. Howard and Lola had four children.
3A. MARCIA JEANNE HARRISON, born June 6, 1945. Marcia married LOREN A. BUSCH April 3, 1965. They divorced in 1967. Marcia married MORRIS JEROME ROSS November 25, 1967. Morris died in Vietnam October 9, 1968. Marcia married LARRY FRITCH. Marcia passed away at age 40 October 4, 1985. Marcia and Larry had one child.
3A1. ROCHELLE ALENKA FRITCH, born December 18, 1981.
3B. HOWARD WESLEY HARRISON Jr., born February 9, 1947. He married BARBARA KRISTINE GREGORICH August 24, 1975. They have one child, RYAN GARDNER, born June 20, 1976.
3C. LARRY CAVIN HARRISON, born September 14, 1948. Larry married SUZANNE LYNN PURKAPILE December 16, 1968. They have two daughters, CARIN SUZANNE, born June 16, 1971, and NIKOL JOSEPHINE, born November 6, 1974.
3D. DEBORAH ROSE HARRISON, born September 7, 1950, was adopted by Howard and Lola in 1959. Deborah married HENRY ERNEST ARCE December 30, 1978. They have one daughter, LISA MARIE, born August 13, 1979.

4. EVELINE JEAN HARRISON, born January 15, 1921, in Eastsound. Jean married JOHN BRYCE GLUD (later changed to GLUDE) in 1940. Jean and John live in Seattle. They have one daughter and two sons.
4A. NANCY JEAN GLUDE, born September 5, 1942. Nancy married WILLIAM DIMSDALE in 1960. Nancy and William divorced in 1973. Nancy married FREDERICKS LINES KELLY in 1975. Nancy and William adopted two babies.
4A1. JOHN LAWRENCE DIMSDALE, born November 11, 1965, in Jacksonville, Fla.
4A2. REBECCA DIANNE DIMSDALE, born April 6, 1968, in Seattle. Rebecca married RONALD DONOWAY and they live in South Carolina. They have one son.
4A2a. BRANDON CHARLES DONOWAY, born September 5, 1985, in Sumter, S.C.
4B. TERRY LEE GLUDE, born August 30, 1945. Terry married NANCY ELLEN BROWN in 1964. They have three children.
4B1. KELLY SUZANNE GLUDE, born September 13, 1964, in Seattle.
4B2. KRISTIN LEIGH GLUDE, born June 1, 1967, in Seattle.
4B3. STEVEN JOHN GLUDE, born September 8, 1970, in Lynchburg, Va.
4C. WILLIAM JOHN GLUDE, born September 22, 1951. The John Glud family changed the spelling of its name from Glud to Glude at this time.

William married GAYLE MARIE HAMPTON in 1979. They have one daughter.
4C1. HEATHER ELRA GLUDE, born in 1979 in Anchorage, Alaska.

5. HELLEN EMMABELLE HARRISON (called Emmabelle), born August 30, 1922, in Bellingham. Emmabelle married RICHARD N. STEELE in 1948. Emmabelle died of cancer in 1980. She and Richard had two sons.
5A. EARL NEWELL STEELE, born December 3, 1949. Earl married CHARLOTTE JACOBS RUDOLPH DECAMDOA. They have two children.
5A1. CHRISTOPHER MORRIS RUDOLPH (Charlotte's from a former marriage), born September 7, 1970.
5A2. ANGELA MARIE DECANDIA (Charlotte's from a former marriage), born June 22, 1976.
5B. DAVID LEE STEELE, born September 9, 1951. David married CAIRN PAULINE CARLETON September 4, 1971. They have two children, APRIL MARIE, born April 9, 1975, and LEE CARLETON, born July 24, 1976.

HAUSDORF, ELVIN CLARENCE
By Arthur Card (1923-1986)
and James Hausdorf
1986

Elvin Clarence Hausdorf was born in Saint Paul, Minn., November 4, 1886. In 1923 Elvin married Ethel Harriet Card, of the pioneer Manette family. [For photo see CARD, GEORGE, family.] Ethel and Elvin lived in Seattle for many years before moving to Manette in August 1934.

Elvin worked in maintenance for the Bremerton School District. Later he worked in the Public Works Department in PSNS. Elvin died in June 1970. Ethel lives at Ridgemont Terrace Convalescent Center in Port Orchard.

DESCENDANTS
Ethel and Elvin Hausdorf had one son.

1. JAMES E. HAUSDORF, born January 10, 1928, in Seattle. He attended Manette School, Lincoln Junior High School and Bremerton High School. James was a sheetmetal worker in PSNS until he retired in 1985. James married SHIRLEY ARMSTRONG of Port Orchard in 1955. They live at 5610 Fern Avenue NE, Bremerton. James and Shirley are active in the Kingston Cove Yachting Club, the Eagles, the American Legion and the V.F.W. James and Shirley have two sons and a daughter.
1A. RICHARD HAUSDORF, born September 19, 1955. Richard married LEE ANNE KITTS. Richard works for the Washington State ferry system and lives on Old Military Road. Richard and Lee Anne have one son.
1A1. JONATHAN MICHAEL HAUSDORF, born August 7, 1984, in Bremerton.
1B. KOREEN HAUSDORF, born July 10, 1958, in Manette. Koreen married CLINT WILLIAMS. They divorced. Later Koreen married RICHARD BURLINGAME, an apprentice shipfitter in PSNS. They live on Aegean Avenue. Koreen has two sons.
1B1. JASON WILLIAMS, born January 14, 1979, in Bremerton.
1B2. SCOTT BURLINGAME, born October 11, 1982, in Bremerton.
1C. DENNIS HAUSDORF, born April 25, 1963. He works at Eastside Shell. He is unmarried.

HENDRICKSON, HENRY
By Hazel "Tootie" Hendrickson Nagle

My dad, Henry Hendrickson, was born in 1892 in Tacoma. He married Hazel Siegrist, born in 1895 in Gardena, Calif. They had five children and many grandchildren.

Dad started working as a machinist in the navy yard in 1924. We lived in Seattle near Woodland Park and Dad commuted until February 1926, when he decided it would be much easier to move. So we came to Manette. Mom and Dad rented a little house on Perry Avenue until we found a bigger house on Ironsides Avenue. Ken and Jean, my older brother and sister, went to Manette School.

In 1927 we moved to Johnson's Corner to the Borgen house near where the Bay Bowl stands now, and Ken and Jean transferred to Sheridan School. Our neighbors were Mae and Ed Brenden, who lived across a small gulley. Another neighbor, an old farmer, Mr. Jake Williams, had a house on the north side of the road and his barn on the south side.

There was a lot of wilderness there. I remember Dad telling of the cougar that frequented our area and followed the kids to school, but never really bothered anything.

On Sundays we went to the Manette Community Church in our 1925 Model-T truck.

Dad was laid off for about 6 months in 1928, so he drove from Johnson's Corner to Wildcat Lake, where he logged. He was then re-hired at the navy yard. He retired in 1951 because of illness.

In 1929 we moved to Manette—2026 East 15th Street. I started school at Manette School and Ken and Jean went on to Lincoln Junior High and Bremerton High Schools. My sister Ruth went to kindergarten in Manette.

When I was old enough I belonged to the Girl Scouts in Manette. Mary Fellows was our leader. Ken belonged to Boy Scout Troop 505. Henry Hitt was Scoutmaster.

We moved from Manette to Bremerton in the summer of 1939, and in 1940 we moved to Belfair on Hood Canal.

Dad died in 1974 in Bremerton. Mother died in 1983.

DESCENDANTS
Henry and Hazel Hendrickson had five children.

1. KENNETH HENDRICKSON, born May 12, 1918, in Seattle. Kenneth married GOLDIE ANDERSON in 1938.

2. JEAN HENDRICKSON, born October 3, 1919, in Seattle. Jean married CHARLES PRESCOTT in 1939.

3. HAZEL "Tootie" HENDRICKSON, born September 25, 1925, in Seattle. Hazel married LOUIS NAGLE in 1944.

4. RUTH HENDRICKSON, born December 18, 1932, in Manette. Ruth married CECIL SMITH in 1951. Ruth died in Seattle in 1962.

5. ROBERT "Bob" HENDRICKSON, born May 21, 1934, in Manette. Bob married VIVIAN OLSEN in 1970. Bob died in Bremerton in 1980.

HERMANSON, GIDEON
By Gideon Hermanson
1986

I started to work in the machine shop in the Puget Sound Navy Yard September 6, 1916, just 12 days after I returned home from spending the summer on the codfish schooner *Charles Wilson* in the Bering Sea.

Three of us fellows rented a house at East 14th Street and Perry Avenue in Manette. The house is still there. The rent was $1.75 a month for each of us. The sad part was that it was the winter of 1917 and we were not able to get the house warm by day or night. We were burning wood.

In the evening after we came home from work, the school children kept us awake with their playing and coasting in the snow outside our bedroom windows. One of them was Gladys Olsen, now Gladys Solid. She is still living in Manette and is a long-time friend and neighbor.

After 3 or 4 months we moved into a hotel in Bremerton.

In 1917 when World War I was declared, the navy yard started to hire women in various departments—office workers, electric-truck drivers, tool-room attendants and shop's crane operators. Vera Evans was one of the shop tool-

room attendants and one of the early women workers in the yard.

MARRIAGE

I became acquainted with Vera and her family, who had moved to Bremerton from Medford. On November 6, 1920, we were married by Reverend Dr. LaViolette of the Bremerton First Methodist Church, then located at 6th Street and Pacific Avenue.

In the summer of 1921 we bought our first property in

Gideon Hermanson in 1986. - Photo from Bremerton Sun.

James, Vera and Louise Hermanson., circa 1940.
-Photo from June Womac Wilmot

The Hermanson home at 2003 Perry Avenue, built in 1936. Photo taken 1987.

Manette. The house and the four 25-foot-wide lots in the Hillman Addition, in what is now Eastpark, cost $600 cash, which we had saved during our first 6 months of marriage. We now had our first real estate. When we moved in, together we had a little over $2.

Vera quit working in the navy yard but I continued.

Bob Moffitt and his family were our closest neighbors and each day he and I walked down to the Manette Dock to take the ferry *Pioneer* to Bremerton to work in the yard. On my way home I used to shop at Harry Martin's grocery store on Shore Drive just up the hill from where we got off the ferry.

When our daughter Louise was due in 1923 there was no bridge and the *Pioneer* didn't run at night. If we had to go to the hospital at night, I'd have to drive the car all the way around through Silverdale. So we rented a place just above the old hospital.

The day before Vera had to go to the hospital I got laid off from the navy yard for lack of work. That used to happen quite often. Vera was ready to go to the hospital and I didn't have a job. I prayed. Next morning I took my tool box and went to the Ford agency. I put down my tool box and knocked on the door. The fellow said, "Hey, you want a job?" and I said, "That's exactly what I'm coming for." That afternoon I had that job and I also drove for Merchants Parcel Delivery. Every time I would have a delivery near the hospital I would stop in to see Vera. Still in labor; still in labor; still in labor. Towards evening Louise was born.

TWO CHILDREN

Our daughter Louise and our son James were both born while we lived in our first house, which we enlarged and modernized. We had the first electrical extension and hook-up in Hillman Addition. Before long we had the first and only water in a house there. Our fresh-water supply was from a well on the Brewster place. It was pumped to a high water tank behind our house by a hydraulic ram I installed in a creek in the gulch near what is now Evans Boulevard.

We got word that Mrs. Morris had her house and 5 acres for sale on Perry Avenue. I went to the Manette realtor, Mr. Hawkes, who had the farm listed, and made the down payment. The contract was signed in 1929.

I remember the old ivy-covered log house on the property and a barn complete with tools, many of which I still have.

Now we had a new home and a 5-acre farm, a cow, a horse and chickens. Whatever more could a family desire?

In 1936 Vera suggested we build a new and modern house with all the latest facilities.

I drew a house plan and when Vera approved we built our new house. In my opinion it is still the nicest house in Manette —2003 Perry Avenue.

My father was a blacksmith and machinist and lived in Olalla with my stepmother, Louise, for about 15 years until 1930, when they moved to Manette. I bought a house and lot for them close to where Vera and I had lived. My father died in 1932 soon after they moved. I built a small house behind our home at 2003 Perry Avenue, where my stepmother lived until she died in 1941.

COMMUNITY SPIRIT

Citizens of Manette had organized the East Bremerton Improvement Club (EBIC). One main ambition was to get a bridge built from Manette to Bremerton. In 1930 the dream became a reality so instead of taking a boat we could walk across in a very few minutes or drive a car.

Also prominent in recollection is the Manette Community Church, which was established in 1904 and is an important part of the foundation of Manette. A church orchestra was formed about 1938. Frank Carr, who lived on Enetai Beach, became the conductor and gave clarinet lessons to Bill Jenkins, a neighbor boy of ours. Jim Hermanson and Margaret Laetsch, daughter of Rev. Walter Laetsch, played clarinet in the church orchestra. I played the violin and Louise played the baritone saxophone. The Manette church is still spoken of and advertised as a friendly church in a friendly community.

Vera died in 1975, five days after our 55th anniversary.

I still live in Manette.

THE HERMANSON FAMILY

GIDEON HERMANSON was born February 26, 1896, in Hopkins, Minn. Gideon married VERA EVANS, born June 20, 1901, in Delmond, S.Dak. They had a daughter and a son.

1. LOUISE HERMANSON was born February 2, 1923, in Bremerton. She attended Manette School and graduated from Bremerton High School. She married CHARLES COX, a chemical engineer with the government, now retired. Louise and Charles bought 250 acres, retired to Hampshire County, W.Va., and incorporated Sideling-View Farm Bible Camp, a camp for families, children and church groups.
Louise and her husband were founders of Pre-Harvest Ministries, a Christian literature ministry in Maryland. Louise has managed Mustard Seed Bookstore, a Christian bookstore, for 16 years, and has just opened a second bookstore called "The Elim Encounter" in Winchester, Va. She and Charles also operate Bethany Shelter Ministries, Inc., an organization dedicated to helping women 18-65 who ask for assistance in recovering from problems.
Louise and Charles live in Capon Bridge, W.Va. They have two children. They have also taken in more than a dozen foster children. Their own two are:

1A. BARTON COX, born August 7, 1947, in Tacoma. Bart married BEVERLEY LYON. Bart and Beverley live in South Carolina. They have three children: DAVID AARON, MATTHEW WILLIAM and CHRISTINA MARIE.
1B. RUTH COX, born January 12, 1949, in Bremerton. Ruth married DAVE KNAPP, who is president of New Tribes Bible Institute in Jackson, Mich. Ruth and David have four children: KEITH, KATHLEEN, AMY LOUISE and AARON DUAINE.

2. JAMES HERMANSON was born October 19, 1925, in Bremerton. He attended Manette School and Bremerton High School. He married ELIZABETH MEIS. James, a dental technician, retired October 19, 1985. He and his wife live in Gig Harbor. They have two children, who have not married: JAN ELIZABETH and JAMES Jr.

[Gideon Hermanson has been honored by a gallery in his name at Kitsap County Historical Museum.]

HIBBARD , RALPH
and
MORRIS, JOHN
By Elva Morris Hibbard
1985

RALPH HIBBARD

Ralph Hibbard was born in New York and arrived in Manette in 1908 with his wife, Hannah, born Hannah Graham, and their 16-year-old son, Russel J. Hibbard. They lived on acreage at what is now Trenton Avenue and Sylvan Way. Ralph worked in the Bremerton navy yard, where he became sheet-metal shop master [superintendent, by today's titles].

Ralph was the first secretary of the Lincoln Heights Progressive League, a club formed in 1911 of settlers living over a mile from Manette. There were 38 members. The last meeting recorded was January 6, 1915.

Ralph belonged to Steadfast Masonic Lodge, was high potentate of the Nile Temple for two seasons and was a 32nd-degree Mason. He was past patron of Philathea Chapter, Order of Eastern Star. He also belonged to the Kiwanis Club.

Hannah belonged to Philathea Chapter, Daughters of the Nile, the Methodist Church and Ladies Aid.

Ralph died in 1935. Hannah died in 1962.

Ralph Hibbard, 1936- -Photo from Hattie Engstrom

JOHN MORRIS

John Morris was born in Zanesville, Ohio, and arrived in Manette in 1908 with his wife, Aurilla, born in Wisconsin in 1869, and me, their adopted daughter, Elva. I was 11 years old. John worked in real estate and on his small farm.

Both John Morris, my stepfather, and Ralph Hibbard, who

Ralph and Hannah Hibbard's home at 2851 N.E. Sylvan Way. Photo taken taken in 1986.

Ralph and Hannah Hibbard's living room, circa 1920. From left are Elva with Rover, Hannah, a friend holding Verna, Ralph in chair, and a friend standing.

would become my father-in-law, had been in Alaska during the gold rush—Morris in Nome and Hibbard in Fairbanks. Neither, however, stayed in Alaska long.

John died in 1931. His wife Aurilla died in 1939.

ELVA MORRIS

I was born Elva Brazelton in Arlington in 1896. I was the youngest of three children. My parents were deaf, having lost their hearing to a severe illness. My mother died when I was 4. It was then that Aurilla Morris, my father's sister, adopted me. We lived in Ballard.

During an epidemic of scarlet fever and typhoid there I contracted the disease, and the doctor advised that I be taken to the country. My uncle Morris traded his four houses for a 72-acre dairy farm in Bothell.

This farm became too much work. Uncle looked for a smaller place, and in 1907 or 1908 bought, from the Mikkelsons, a house and 5 acres about a mile from Manette on the west side of what is now Perry Avenue. Mrs. Brewster lived north of us. The Mikkelsons built a big house west of the Manette church on the present East 13th Street and Perry Avenue.

I have early memories of Mr. MacIntosh, the minister of the Manette Baptist Church, of which I became a member. Mr. MacIntosh was a warmhearted evangelist type whose rich tenor voice rolled out over the congregation. He made one want to be a part of the music. There were songs like "When the Roll Is Called Up Yonder I'll Be There."

I was worthy matron of Eastern Star Olympic Chapter 216 in 1942. The years I spent in Eastern Star were extremely happy and I found the organization beneficial personally.

SCHOOL DAYS

I attended the two-room Manette School with my lifelong friend Ruth Risser (Layman). Mrs. Short taught the upper four grades and Miss Hester the lower grades.

In the summer of 1909 the school was enlarged but remained a two-room school. Mrs. Maybell of Bremerton replaced Miss Hester and Mr. G. Wolfe replaced Mrs. Short. Mr. Wolfe was my seventh-grade teacher. My eighth-grade teacher was Mrs. Mallory, who taught us how to breathe and enunciate properly. I went to Union High School in Bremerton. It served Charleston and Bremerton, towns that joined. I then attended Wilson's Business College in Seattle.

RUSSEL HIBBARD

Russel Hibbard and I were married in Seattle in 1917.

When Russel was in Union High School in Bremerton in 1913 the Daughters of the American Revolution offered to give a flag to the school for the best essay on the flag. He won the contest and

Russel J. Hibbard in 1953. -Bremerton Sun photo

Aurilla, Elva and John Morris and their home in the 2200 block of Perry Avenue, circa 1907. Elva later married Russel Hibbard.
- Photo from Elva Hibbard

received the flag for the school.

Russel attended the University of Washington for 2 years.

Russel worked in the Bremerton navy yard and in 1935 became master of the sheet-metal shop, the position previously held by his father.

Russel belonged to the Masonic Lodge and Eastern Star. He was president of the Kiwanis Club, belonged to the Bremerton Yacht Club, was a director of the YMCA and was president and founder of the Supervisors' Club of the navy yard.

Russel belonged to the Naval Reserve during World War I. There were soldiers and anti-aircraft guns stationed on our grounds during World War II.

Four years before he retired Russel built a 34-foot motor-sailer, the *Sea Otter*. In 1950 we cruised as far as Sitka and Juneau and around the outside of Vancouver Island.

Russel had always wanted to be an artist, although his father said artists didn't make any money and lived in garrets. Russel took up painting again when he retired and his pictures hang in every room of the home of our daughter Verna May (Mrs. Warren Powell) and family in Kirkland.

Russel died in 1965. I have since lived in Kirkland with my daughter and her family.

THE FAMILY

RALPH HIBBARD was born in New York. He married HANNAH GRAHAM, who was born in 1859 in Pennsylvania. Hannah died in 1962. Ralph died in 1935. Ralph and Hannah had one child.

1. RUSSEL J. HIBBARD, born in New Jersey in 1892. He married ELVA MORRIS in 1917. They had a daughter.
1A. VERNA MAY HIBBARD was born in Bremerton in 1919. Verna married WARREN POWELL in 1954. Warren works for a telephone company. Verna is a violin teacher and also plays the piano. She has a studio in Seattle, where she teaches all string instruments. Verna and Warren live in Kirkland and have five children.
1A1. WARREN H. POWELL, born in Seattle in 1955. He has been a violist with Canary Island Symphony Orchestra, Puerto Rico Symphony, and now with the Tampa Symphony in Florida.
1A2. MARIE ANNA POWELL, born in Seattle in 1958. She lives in Kirkland, teaches and studies the piano and singing.
1A3. GEORGE N. POWELL, born in Seattle in 1959. He is an accountant and ex-baseball player. He played through grade school, high school and college. George now works for General Motors.
1A4. DAVID B. POWELL, born in Seattle in 1960. He is a concert violinist living in Kirkland.
1A5. JOHN R. POWELL, born in Kirkland in 1965. He graduated from Seattle University in May, 1985, and plans to be an astronaut and write science-fiction stories.

HICKS, FRED
By Madora Hicks
1985

We moved to Manette in 1920. My husband, Fred Hicks, and I rented a house at what is now Lower Shore Drive. One of the first people I met was Mother (Ella) Bender. This was fortunate for me, because she took me under her wing. Through her I was introduced to Manette.

One of my early impressions of Manette was my meeting with Joaquina "Quina" Feek. She had black hair and I thought she was the most beautiful, attractive woman in Manette. I always looked forward to seeing her because she was an inspiration.

One of the first things we did was to organize a 500 card club and we played 500 for over 40 years—before most of our husbands, Tate Peterson, Clyde Meredith, Leonard Card, and mine, Fred Hicks—passed away. We had a lot of fun.

One of the best things that happened was the neighborly response I got when Fred was seriously injured in the navy yard. He worked in the inside machine shop, of which he eventually became superintendent.

He was operating a large crane and his helper pulled the wrong lever. Fred's left leg was caught between two gears and was cut off except for a small piece of flesh. The chief surgeon, Dr. Robnett at the Naval Hospital, said to me, "He is t o young to lose a leg and I am going to do something I have never done before." He reattached Fred's leg and put a huge cast on it. He watched it faithfully. After 2 months an order came through to move civilian patients to Seattle. Dr. Robnett obtained special permission to keep Fred. He was not only a fine surgeon but a wonderful man. Between his constant care, Fred's determination and my prayers he had a good leg after about 2 years. It was a miracle.

We were trading at Clyde Meredith's grocery store and when Clyde learned of the accident and that Fred would be in the hospital for a long time, he came to see me and said, "Now, I know you're young, and if you need groceries or money, or whatever you need, don't hesitate to come to me." It always impressed me as a young woman that someone had that much faith in me.

I have a lot of happy memories from Manette. But after Fred had this bad accident, he wasn't able to commute on the little launch that ran to Bremerton so we had to move there.

Our daughter Madora Jane was born in Bremerton August 16, 1919. Madora Jane graduated from Union High School and from the University of Washington. She went to George Washington University in Washington, D.C., for 2 years and earned her law degree from New York University. A New Jersey governor appointed her the first woman judge in a superior court in New Jersey. She now has her own law firm.

I remember when the bridge was being built Bill Abbott pressured everyone to contribute to it. We donated $200, which was a lot of money for us in those days, but it has been a good sturdy bridge.

Fred was a volunteer services chairman during World War II.

Fred died July 31, 1972. I live at Wesley Garden, a Methodist retirement complex in Des Moines, Wash.

THE FAMILY:
FRED HICKS was born October 22, 1897, in Tacoma. MADORA was born July 27, 1898, in Anderson, Ind. They married in Tacoma on March 4, 1918. Fred and Madora had one daughter.

1. MADORA JANE HICKS, born August 16, 1919, in Bremerton. Madora Jane married JEROME DOHERTY. They have a daughter and three sons.
1A. MADORA JANE DOHERTY, born June 13, 1944, in Montclaire, N.J. She is now Mrs. P. BIANCO.
1B. JEROME DOHERTY, born May 19, 1947, in Seaside Heights, N.J.
1C. MATHEW DOHERTY, born November 27, 1952, in Point Pleasant, N.J.
1D. DANIEL DOHERTY, born December 17, 1957, in Point Pleasant, N.J.

HILSTAD, GULDBRAND OSCAR
By Carol Hilstad Schwabe
1985

Guldbrand Oscar Hilstad was born November 21, 1854, in Guldbrandsdalen, Lom, Norway. His family came to the United States when Guldbrand was 14. Anne Peterson was born May 15, 1861, in Guldbrandsdalen, Vaage, Norway. She came with her family to the United States at age 9.

Guldbrand and Anne were married in January of 1881 in Minnesota. They moved to Poulsbo in 1885. Guldbrand, also known as Gilbert or G.O., was elected Kitsap County assessor in 1904 and served until 1908. He did not run for re-election.

THE FAMILY
GULDBRAND and ANNE HILSTAD had nine children.

1. ROBERT OSCAR HILSTAD, known as Oscar, born in Minnesota December 28, 1881. He married GLADYS VICTOR. Oscar died in 1954. Oscar and Gladys had five sons born in Manette: DAVID, ROBERT, STEVEN, DONALD and RICHARD.

2. CHRISTIAN STENER HILSTAD, born in Minnesota February 26, 1884. He married BIRDIE MAY AVERY March 17, 1918, in the family home on Clear Creek, Silverdale [see AVERY family history]. Christian built a little bungalow two doors south of the post office on Perry Avenue. Their first two daughters were born in the bungalow.
Chris built the *Evelyn Sharp*, called the *Eleven Sharp* according to Steve Hilstad, in 1918-1919. It was used as a pleasure boat until 1925, when it was sold to and operated by Lee Beck and Lyn Hetrick as a passenger ferryboat between Pleasant Beach on Bainbridge Island and Bremerton until it burned at the dock in Bremerton in 1930. Chris was on a ferry and saw the fire.
Chris and Birdie's neighbors were the Painters, who lived next to the post office. Dave and Pauline Miner, Manette pioneers, were family friends. Christian died April 5, 1950. Christian and Birdie had three daughters.
2A. EVELYN SHARP HILSTAD, born March 9, 1919, in Manette. Evelyn died of Bright's disease in 1935 at 15 years.
2B. JEAN VIRGINIA HILSTAD, born September 22, 1920. Jean married JOSEPH KUKULAN. Jean (now Mrs. REILLY) lives in Berkeley, Calif. Jean and Joseph had two sons: JOHN CHRISTIAN and NICKOLAS.
2C. CAROL LILA HILSTAD, born April 5, 1928, in Seattle. Carol married EDWARD SCHWABE. They live in Anacortes. Carol and Edward have three children and seven grandchildren.
2C1. KAREN ADAIR SCHWABE, born November 15, 1949.
2C2. MITCHELL EDWARD SCHWABE, born March 12, 1952.
2C3. JEFFREY LAURIER SCHWABE, born January 17, 1955.

3. GINA AMANDA HILSTAD, born April 25, 1886. Gina married JERRY ARTHUR BEHRENS. Gina and Jerry had three children: ARTHUR, HOWARD and MARGIE.

4. THEODORE BENJAMIN HILSTAD, born December 9, 1888. He married MAY VIOLA WALTON. They had no children. Theodore died in April of 1970.

5. PETER GEORGE HILSTAD, born May 19, 1891. He married SIGRID HOLM. Peter and Sigrid had two children: LOUISE and JOHN.

6. ELMER PALMER HILSTAD, born March 16, 1894. He married RACHEL MILLER. Elmer and Rachel had two children: RACHEL and ROLAND.

Guldbrand Oscar and Anne Hilstad family, 1904. Back row (from left), children Elmer Palmer, Peter George, Theodore Benjamin; adults Ragna Howen (relative of Anne's from Norway), Robert Oscar, Christian Stener, Gina Amanda. Front row, Guldbrand Oscar holding Carrie Marie, Anne Pederson Hilstad holding Rodger Martin, Ruth Anna.
                                                                                        - Photo from Stephen Hilstad

7. CARRIE MARIE HILSTAD, born September 25, 1896. She married EARL GRAHN. Carrie died November 23, 1954. Carrie and Earl had four children: LEAH, GILBERT, RODGER CARL and PETER.

8. RUTH ANNA HILSTAD, born June 20, 1899. She married HARRY N. JOHNSON. Ruth and Harry had three children: INEZ, NANCY and HARRY.

9. RODGER MARTIN HILSTAD, born June 13, 1902. He married LINNIA NELSON. Rodger and Linnia had two children.

HOFFMAN, HENRY
By Elgie J. Hoffman
1985

It was on a cold November day in 1910 just after Thanksgiving that my mother, Rosalla A. Hoffman, and I left our home in Ballard and took a boat from there to Bremerton. As we disembarked from the boat onto the floating wharf, we must have looked like two immigrants from the "old country." Helping hands aided us to pile our boxes, suitcases and our two pet geese onto the wharf.

The crate in which the geese were confined most certainly was a picture—two long necks, each topped by a wild-eyed goose head, were stretched through the bars of the crate, high into the air, and their excited honking outsounded the boat's whistle.

We had to wait until my father, Henry Hoffman, came from his job in the Transportation Department in the navy yard to help us find housing. My father was rooming at Peter Heinrick's rooming house—the building still stands on Warren Avenue. We were thankful to find an apartment on Pleasant Avenue, but we didn't stay there long, because two

drummers had the apartment directly above us, and you can imagine how that was.

In a few months my father and mother purchased property in Manette. It was an acre of ground with a house on it at what is now Perry Avenue and Magnuson Way. A board sidewalk led from "downtown" Manette to the driveway of our property—there the sidewalk ended—the present site of Emmanuel Lutheran Church.

I began my first year of school at the one-room Sheridan School in 1911. The teacher, Professor Waldron, short and pleasingly plump, was a strict teacher of the old school. One thing I remember was the way he once disciplined me and Kenneth Hodges. Professor Waldron had us go to the blackboard and trace a large circle—around and around—for an endless period of time.

We sat at double desks. My desk partner was Frances Schlagel. The older student of the two helped keep the younger one in line. The older boys rustled wood for the hungry cordwood stove, which was centrally located near the front of the schoolroom. How friendly and comforting the fire felt after tramping through deep snow on a cold winter day.

The "Big Snow" was in 1916. To see the road, I had to stand on top of our

Elgie Hoffman, 1904.

covered well.

As a special treat, if behavior merited, a young pupil could accompany an older boy to get a couple of buckets of water from the Ohman farm, which was about a quarter-mile away. Everyone drank from the same dipper, and the day's water supply seemed to satisfy the thirst of all present.

The one-room Sheridan School building was moved back to make way for a new two-room school. I attended that school until the fourth grade. I attended the Manette School one year, then graduated from the Bremerton schools. I commuted to Bremerton by boat.

The Manette Community Church holds precious memories of the time I was growing up in Manette. Reverend Woods baptized my father, my mother and me, by immersion. My father became one of the ruling elders of the church. My Sunday School teacher was kindly Mr. [Ford] Dewar. He would start with the third graders and move right along with them until that class was past the teens. Mr. Dewar made Christian Endeavor interesting by taking us on field trips, taffy pulls and parties, as well as giving spiritual knowledge so necessary to us.

Before 1910 a Seattle real estate promoter, Mr. Hillman, came to Manette. He staked out lots and had elaborate plans for "Hillman City." People purchased lots enthusiastically. Hillman had a dock built (It was never used) and a general store. It too, was never used for that purpose, but the community held dances there. The dreams for the city faded. The lot owners received nothing for their investment except the land.

Mr. Harris, a Manette realtor, spearheaded a gala celebration intended to incorporate Manette. This was held July 4th, 1911. A platform was built near Bender's home just north of the present Manette bridge approach. Japanese lanterns hung from the rafters; multi-colored streamers and flags were everywhere. My mother made an Uncle Sam suit and hat for me. For days, she had coached me to speak a lengthy piece, composed by Mr. Harris. I bravely climbed up on the platform and gave it my all. I still remember that recitation:

"The days that I was hard up,
I never shall forget;
But I wouldn't have been hard up
If I had come to Manette.

"I have traveled the country over,
I have gone without a meal.
But I was young, tough and hearty
And I would never squeal.

"Years ago I started,
That day I'll never regret;
I found the land of plenty,
Now the city of Manette.

"Soon after came some Kickers,
And Kickers still they are,
But better had they drowned
And never got so far.

"We can call a meeting,
But the Kickers never go.
If they do, it is through suspicion;
They're afraid the town will grow.

"We would like to have some sidewalks,
And good streets wouldn't hurt a bit;
If we could just incorporate
And let the Kickers pay part of it.

"We would pay our pro rata.
We have been progressive men;
But our town is not progressing
Just on account of them.

"Some people have some foresight,
And some have not a bit.
Let's start today and work one way,
And incorporate Manette.

"The money the Kickers have been making
Was not made by their good brain.
The other side has done the work,
And the Kickers have the gain!"

The celebration included races of every description and a spirited contest to see who could catch, and keep for the catching, a lively greased pig. One of the Lee sisters was the successful winner. I could not participate in the events because of my fancy suit.

Mother had a beauty parlor in the family home. Neighbors came to get their hair done. They brought their hair combings to her to be made into switches and hair pieces called "bobbies." She cut both men's and women's hair.

When Charlie Young resigned as deputy sheriff of the Manette area, Sheriff Stanioch appointed my dad, Henry C. Hoffman, to fill the vacancy.

The last home we had in Manette was on a 23-acre plot. The Perry Avenue Emmanuel Lutheran Church now stands in the vicinity of our house. The government took most of our property and built houses for government workers during WW II. Gone is our orchard and the barns. Gone is our little babbling brook, the lush watercress, the tall fir trees, and the old Model-T. Such is the way of modern progress—country into city. If my folks could only see Manette, now.

I worked as a painter in the navy yard. I was Kitsap County Museum Director for 14 years.

OUR FAMILY
HENRY C. HOFFMAN was born March 10, 1880, in Sioux City, Iowa. His wife ROSALLA was born March 14, 1887, in St. Cloud, Minn. Henry died December 16, 1964. Rosalla died May 7, 1969. Henry and Rosalla had one son.

1. ELGIE HOFFMAN, born February 28, 1904, in San Francisco. Elgie married MARJORIE STEVENSON, born in 1907 in Bremerton. Marjorie's father, Thomas Stevenson, was a lawyer in Bremerton. Elgie and Marjorie have one son.
1A. JOHN THOMAS HOFFMAN, born June 18, 1938, in Bremerton. John has three children.
1A1. KURTIS JOHN HOFFMAN, born May 2, 1966, in Bremerton.
1A2. HEIDI LUISE HOFFMAN, born September 11, 1967, in Bremerton.
1A3. KRISTIN ANN HOFFMAN, born July 3, 1970, in Bremerton.

HOLDEN, ARTHUR
By Evelyn Holden Newkirk

Grandmother and Grandfather, Lizzie and Albert Williams, [see also WILLIAMS, Albert] had five children: Nathan; Theodore; Harriet, who was our mother; Theresa, and Ella. Their first home in Kitsap County was at Phinney Bay. Grandmother took her kids from Phinney Bay to Tracyton School by boat. There were no roads.

Later, when they lived on Highland Avenue in Bremerton, my mom, (Harriet) went to the Fourth Street School in Bremerton.

They moved to Manette in about 1904.

My grandfather owned the A.B. Williams Hardware store at the base of East 10th Street. Later it became Williams & Son. In 1908 they moved their business to the building at 1102

The home of Arthur and Harriet Holden at 1602 Marlow Avenue, now Wheaton Way. Photo taken 1931.

East 11th Street. In 1913 J.W. Meredith bought this building.

My grandmother's maiden name was Smith—her family had come to Kitsap County, too.

My uncle Nathan ran the ferry *City of Manette.*

Mother married Arthur Holden in 1907. They had three daughters: Evelyn, Alice and Helen. One daughter was the first baby born in the Bremerton hospital, on Pacific Avenue across from Penney's.

My father, Arthur Holden, bought material for his house from the Fellows sawmill.

Out in Sheridan was a big hall called Lincoln Hall. It even had bunks for the kids since there were no baby sitters. It took the ladies hours to make the coffee. They had square dancing there. Wayne Burlew's father was the caller. I remember when I was a little kid we would go home from Lincoln Hall at 3 or 4 o'clock in the morning. Father carried my little sister Alice and a lantern.

In 1916 or 17 there was a record snowfall and Lincoln Hall collapsed.

My father, Arthur Holden, was the first boy apprentice in the Bremerton navy yard. His parents died in Seattle when Dad was 6. Dad sold newspapers and finished grammar school. He was recommended for a job as a "minor under instruction" and became the first official apprentice. He told about the navy yard when there was only a wooden drydock and a storage shed, no piers, no electricity, no light. By 1905 he had finished his training and became an assistant ship draftsman. He designed the first cold storage unit for the battleship *Oregon.* After further training he became a supervisor of new construction in 1921. He retired in 1943.

He was a Bremerton city councilman for awhile.

Dad was one of the 16 charter members of Steadfast Masonic Lodge of Manette.

Dad died at 98 in 1981.

Mother worked as the first telephone operator in

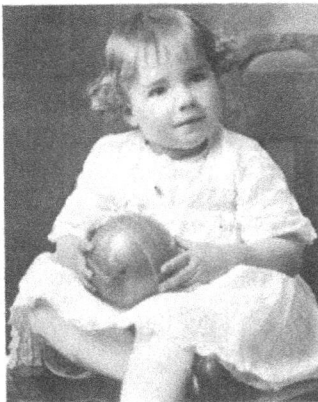

Helen Holden, circa 1919

Harriet and Arthur Holden with Alice, held by Arthur, and Evelyn, behind Arthur, 1912.

1904 for $1 a week. She was a professional photographer and worked for Prints of Wales photo shop in Bremerton.

She started the first garden club in Manette, and was a matron of Philathea Chapter, Order of Eastern Star.

GENEALOGY
ARTHUR HOLDEN was born in September 1883. In 1907 he married HARRIET WILLIAMS, born June 26, 1884. They had three daughters.

1. EVELYN HOLDEN, born June 17, 1909. Evelyn married HARRY HILL in 1936 and he passed away in 1976. Evelyn married MARION NEWKIRK of Belfair January 4, 1981, and he passed away in 1986. Evelyn lives in Bremerton. Evelyn and Harry had four children: JOAN, now Mrs. LUCKHURST, born September 7, 1935; RICHARD, born August 9, 1935; DAN, born January 4, 1941; and MARGERY, now Mrs. TODD, born December 23, 1944.

2. ALICE HOLDEN, born in Bremerton April 11, 1912. She married CLYDE W. SMITH May 16, 1941. Alice lives in Tracyton. Alice and Clyde have two children. [Alice died in 1988].
2A. CAROL LEE SMITH, who became Mrs. DELAURENTI, was born February 24, 1943. She lives in Bremerton and is now divorced. Carol has three children, all born in Puyallup: DERON, born April 10, 1972; DANA, born February 11, 1974, and DERIK, born July 12, 1976.
2B. CRAIG ROBERT SMITH was born in Bremerton in 1945. He graduated from high school in Hawaii and married STARLA TEMPLETON in Bremerton. He graduated from Central Washington State College with a master's degree and is now working on his doctorate. He teaches at Bremerton Middle School in Manette. Craig and Starla live at 2746 Hefner Avenue. They have four children: STEPHANIE, born in 1970; HEATHER, born in 1972; CHRISTOPHER, born in 1974, and LEYNE, born in 1979.

3. HELEN HOLDEN, born in Seattle September 8, 1917. She married GORDON LILLEY and they had two daughters, DIANE and SHARON. Sharon is now Mrs. PITTS. Helen and Gordon are divorced. Helen lives in Bremerton.

HOOPES, ISAAC
By Grace Hoopes Wesseler and Edna Hoopes Brookman
1984

WEST FROM PENNSYLVANIA
Isaac Pennock Hoopes and his bride Amy Wilson Craven Hoopes came west from Pennsylvania for their honeymoon

in 1905. They liked it here so much they remained, living in West Seattle. There they had a family. A daughter, Grace Craven, was the first born, arriving June 29, 1906. Then in 18 months a little sister, Edna Thatcher, came along on December 17, 1907.

Isaac worked in the Bremerton navy yard as a stenographer. Commuting from West Seattle was tiring and kept him away

First home of Isaac and Amy Hoopes, 1348 Ironsides Avenue, circa 1913. In 1927 this became the Bubke home. - Photo from Edna Hoopes Brookman

Isaac and Amy Hoopes family in 1917. Back row (from left), Amy and Isaac. Front row, Grace, Edna holding Margaret. - Photo from Edna Hoopes Brookman

Second home of Isaac and Amy Hoopes, 2516 East 16th Street, 1929.- Photo from Edna Hoopes Brookman

from his family for long hours, so the Hoopeses moved to Bremerton. This was in January 1911. A year or so later they moved to Manette. They bought a home on the hill north of the Manette School at 16th Street and Ironsides (Lockwood) Avenue. Here they raised the girls with another daughter, Margaret Mathews, born at home in Manette January 9, 1917.

In 1919 they moved across the street into a house built by the Lockwoods.

SCHOOL AND CHURCH

The girls all went to the Manette Grade School and then crossed the water on the old ferry *Pioneer* to walk another mile to high school.

During this time Isaac was advancing in the navy yard and was also becoming involved in the community. The Hoopeses were church people and very interested in the young people. Isaac was elected superintendent of the Sunday School in the Manette Community Church, a job he held for 25 years. He became a lifetime deacon and was treasurer for several years among his other duties. He taught a Sunday School class for college-age students, and supervised the Baptist Young Peoples' Union.

While raising the family, Amy Hoopes kept busy teaching in the junior department of the Sunday School for several years; worked during the summers in Vacation Bible School; she then taught junior and senior high school students' Sunday School class until her death. Amy was active in the Ladies Aid and the Women's Christian Temperance Union, in which she held offices. She was also active in P-TA and was secretary, then president, of both grade school and high school P-TA's while her girls were in school. She was president of the Kitsap County Tuberculosis League for 3 years, and of the Missionary Society. Amy belonged to the History Club and took an active part in the P.E.O Sisterhood. She taught summer school for students needing extra help.

AMY'S KINDERGARTEN

Amy Hoopes tried to talk the school board into starting a

4. FLORENCE DESCO HUBBELL, born in August 1893. Florence married GEORGE HAUSAUER. She and George had one child, GEORGE Jr. Florence died in Redmond in April 1985.

5. JAY HAROLD HUBBELL, born in August 1895. He worked at the Park Avenue Grocery. Jay died in February 1938 in Bremerton.

6. RUDD O'DELL HUBBELL, born in April 1898. Rudd and his wife VIOLET had one child, RUDD Jr.

7. HALLIE GLO HUBBELL, born in November 1900. Hallie married DONALD PITT. They had one child, GLORIA. Later she married PAUL CUMMINS. Hallie died in Bremerton in 1939.

8. ALICE ELIZABETH HUBBELL, born in July 1903. Alice married DORCEY T. LAQUEE. They had no children. Dorcey passed away in 1957. Alice lives at Kitsap Lake.

9. MARY LEONA HUBBELL, born in April 1906. Mary married MELVIN HADFORD; they lived in Port Orchard and Seattle. They both worked at PSNS. They had two sons, RONALD and RAYMOND, both born in Port Orchard. Mary died in Bothell in February 1984.

HUDSON, HARRY
By Augustus H. "Gus" Hudson
1985

FROM MAINE TO KITSAP COUNTY

Reverend Harry Hudson and his wife Elizabeth were both born in England in 1865. Their three children, Claude, Augustus and Margaret, were born in Maine.

In 1901 we moved from Maine to Tacoma; then, in 1904, to West Seattle. The Hudson family settled in Kitsap County in 1905. We lived in Bremerton and occupied a summer place between Point Herron and Enetai Beach, probably on what is now Jacobsen Boulevard, from 1908 to 1916.

There was a small well where we used to get our fresh water. My father carried two buckets and I two small ones a distance of probably a fourth mile to our house.

FAMILY AND NEIGHBORS

Father had a 20-foot launch which I used to carry passengers to Bremerton. Among my passengers were C.P. Kimball, Edwin Keith and John Hull, son-in-law of well-known Bremertonian E.J. McCall. McCall had an insurance business in Bremerton, was city clerk for many years and was mayor from 1921 until 1924. Hull had married McCall's daughter Lillian. John and Lillian rented a summer place on Enetai Beach from Keith.

Eddie Bremer's father had a launch similar to ours. Bremers made frequent trips to Bremerton in their launch. Eddie and I became quite well acquainted while waiting for our parents at the Hefner floats in Bremerton.

My father, Reverend Harry Hudson, was pastor of St. Paul's Episcopal Church in Bremerton, where we attended Sunday School and church services. Father had been ordained in Maine before we came to Tacoma.

EARLY DAYS

We bought groceries from Harry Martin's store at the foot of the Manette Dock. Martin made deliveries by horse and wagon and sometimes by launch to beach dwellers. At the price of 10 cents per week, my sister and I carried milk in pails from the home of Walt Fellows' father Thomas to people along the beach.

We bought vegetables from the gardens of Chris Jensen and Jens Jacobsen.

Harry Hansen operated a ferry, the *Bern II*, that carried passengers between Manette and Bremerton. The ship *H.B. Kennedy* came to Bremerton in 1909, the year of the Alaska-Yukon-Pacific Exposition in Seattle. The *Kennedy* carried passengers and freight between Bremerton and Seattle. The last trip from Seattle each day was at 5:30 p.m., except on Saturdays, when trips at 9:30 and 11:30 were added.

Harry and Elizabeth Hudson family at their summer home at Enetai, about 1909. From left, Claude, Harry, Elizabeth, Margaret and Agustus H. "Gus" Hudson.   - Photo from Gus Hudson

trail that the team made to bring in the lumber and later our furniture. Now that trail is Trenton Avenue. Rural mail was delivered a quarter of a mile away on the County Road, now Perry Avenue. We lived across Collins' cow pasture from the County Road. Later, our father felled the trees and blasted the stumps for the road that is now Stone Way.

Jesse was born on Christmas Eve, 1912. Santa Claus came early that year but Fred and I didn't know the difference.

Country living was a change for us, after living in town—San Pedro—on a concrete street with sidewalks and a grocery store one block away.

I attended kindergarten in San Pedro but I didn't go to school in Manette until September 1913, a year later, when I attended the two-room school. After Union High School in Bremerton, I graduated from Bellingham Normal School and taught school for several years.

BLACKSMITH TO RIGGER

Dad worked as a blacksmith in the navy yard and later as a rigger until he retired. While waiting for the transfer from San Pedro to come through, he laid bricks on the streets of Bremerton at Second Street and Washington Avenue.

WATER AND WOOD

While our well was being dug, we carried water a quarter of a mile from Collins', our closest neighbor's, and we caught

Lora and Fred Howerton, wedding picture, 1906.

The Howerton family, 1967. Standing (from left), Fred, Anita, Jesse, Lora, Ruth and Albert (Eugene). Seated, Geneva, Ernie and Ted.
                                                                        - Photo by Bremerton Sun

rainwater. The well was 72 feet deep and we hauled the water up with a rope on a windlass until we got an iron pump. After that we had a hydraulic ram in Enetai Creek. It put water into a tank on the bank. Then the water was gravity-piped to the house. This system was special because it operated on water and required no electricity. Many people used rams in those days.

We had plenty of firewood for our cookstove and heater.

Father had a wholesale wood business at the homesite. A wooden track was built from pasture level some hundreds of feet down into Enetai Creek canyon. A wooden roller car was used to pull wood from the canyon by means of a horse hitched to a pole attached to a capstan. The horse stepped over the capstan rope at each revolution. Wood dealers would buy the wood. The trees used for firewood were huge old-growth fir, vertical grain, now priceless wood. Dad also made cedar kindling and sold it in bundles for 25 cents.

We picked huckleberries for jelly and pies until we got crops of loganberries, gooseberries and blackberries. We raised vegetables and had a cow for milk.

After walking everywhere for years, we got a horse and buggy. The horse plowed the garden, pulled stumps, cleared land, hauled our wood and took us to town for groceries. We surely were happy when we got a Model-T Ford car.

My sister Anita was born in 1914, Eugene in 1916, Ted in 1921, Ernest in 1925 and Ruth in 1927.

We didn't have much money but we never felt poor. We were happy and worked hard. All of us worked in the garden and the orchard and all cut firewood. We went to the Manette Community Church. All eight of us attended Manette School and then Union High in Bremerton, re-named Bremerton High meanwhile.

Father Fred Howerton died January 1, 1941; Mother Lora died November 26, 1971; brother Fred March 5, 1968, and Ted, January 4, 1985.

During World War II Jesse, Eugene and Ernest served in the army, Ted was in the Seabees.

DIVERSE RECOLLECTIONS
By Jesse Howerton
TRAGIC FOREST FIRE

In approximately 1927 there was a forest fire in our canyon, east of Trenton Avenue, beyond the east end of Stone Way. One neighbor, one fire warden, my father, brother Gene, brother Ted and I were fighting the fire, which was out of control. We were gaining on it, but we could not leave to eat dinner. Mother put everything in two baskets and proceeded to the fire site. As we were eating, fire burned off a huge cedar and it crashed into a maple with huge limbs, falling into the dining area. The fire warden had gone to attend to a worse fire so was gone during the accident.

It was such a terrible mess - it was everyone for themselves. Dad hollered, "Everyone. Run like H---." If everyone had gone north, no one would have been injured. Dad, brother Gene and I ran north but the neighbor, brother Ted and Mother ran west. Mother was hit by huge falling tree limbs. She had a most terrible mangled and crippled arm the rest of her life. The neighbor, Oliver Nelson, had several bones broken and died in the hospital 5 hours later.

THE BOYS AND ME

Brother Fred was older, he went to sea, and later, after getting out of the merchant marine and working on government dredges, he went to work in the navy yard.

Brother Gene was in the old Civilian Conservation Corps (CCC) for a long time and then went to work in the navy yard.

Brother Ted went to work in the yard shortly after graduation from high school in 1940.

Brother Ernie, the youngest of us, took to working in bakeries and also is a gifted musician. He plays organ and accordian and gives lessons. He does a lot of volunteer work with music.

And me. I could outwork the proverbial ox, but I had no trade. (Oxen were smarter than me.) I learned how to be a woodcutter and powder monkey, a nickname and trade name for a person skilled in handling explosives. Years ago powder monkeys were in demand to dynamite stumps so horses and mules could pull them out, as there were no bulldozers then.

In 1935 I got my golden opportunity to work as low man on the totem pole in a big logging camp and stayed in the woods many years. I'd come home periodically to visit family and friends, always good to come home to Manette.

I tried a hand at many things and liked falling or bucking timber best, but it was all piece work. The more you cut, the more money you made. Then in late 1942, time out for the army for 3 years, and then back in the woods for a few years. Then to land-fill business, better known as a garbage dump. Said dump was at Silverdale and operated from early 1955 to May 31, 1980.

Politics closed me.

Then retirement. I didn't care much for it and went into the junk business in Snohomish County for 3 years in the Everett area. I hauled junk and junk cars, plus old logging machinery, out of the San Juan Islands to Tacoma.

I finally got tired and said enough for a couple of years. Then I bought some big old bulldozers and now sell them for a pastime. I am active with ancient one-cylinder engines and stump pullers.

I believe if I had my life to live over I would do the same thing.

THE GENERATIONS
FREDERICK FRANKLYN HOWERTON (1873-1941) was born in Malden, Mo. He was a longshoreman in San Pedro when he was transferred to the Bremerton navy yard.
LORA KNUPPENBURG (1887-1971) was born in Milner, Dakota Territory. Lora arrived in Washington in 1888. She spent much of her life in California, caring for her mother, until 1912. Lora and Fred married in 1906. They had eight children.

1. GENEVA M. HOWERTON, born January 30, 1907, in San Pedro. She married EARL J. PICKERING in 1936. The younger children from Earl's previous marriage became part of Earl and Geneva's family. They were CHARLES PICKERING, who was born November 19, 1923, and now lives on Rocky Point, and JEAN PICKERING, born February 22, 1925.
Earl was born April 1, 1895 in Spencer, Iowa. His family came to Sedro Woolley in 1909. Earl came to Manette in 1932. He was a moulder and worked in the navy yard. In 1932 he bought 5 acres in Manette for $140. He felled trees and built a house of fir poles from the land. Earl died in March 1979. Geneva still lives on Pickering Avenue, named for the family. Geneva and Earl had one son.
1A. FREDRICK EARL PICKERING, born December 3, 1939, in Bremerton. Fredrick married LINDA FISKE November 21, 1964. They live in Yacolt, Wash. Fredrick and Linda have three children.
1A1. WILLIAM EARL PICKERING, born March 31, 1968, in Vancouver,

Wash.

1A2. NOEL ARTHUR PICKERING, born December 14, 1973, in Vancouver.

1A3. ELIZABETH JO PICKERING, born August 3, 1977, in Portland.

2. FREDERICK RAYMOND HOWERTON, born August 2, 1909, in San Pedro. Fred married LORENE in 1941. Frederick died in 1968 in Poulsbo.

3. JESSE LOUIS HOWERTON, born December 24, 1912, in Manette. He married THELMA SNYDER in 1943. In 1949 Jesse married GLADYS CHAMBERLAIN of Silverdale. They divorced. Jesse now lives at Timber Lakes near Shelton.

4. ANITA M. HOWERTON, born April 18, 1914, in Manette. Anita married WILLIAM MILLER. Anita and William had a daughter.

4A. LORA MADGE MILLER, born in May 16, 1932 in Seattle. Lora married RAY F. WILLIAMS July 15, 1950, and they live in Pleasant Grove, Ala. Lora and Ray have four children and seven grandchildren. The four children are RAY FRANCIS Jr., born July 5, 1951, LORAY ANN, born December 7, 1954, JENETTA LYNN, born May 28, 1957, and ANN LEA, born June 16, 1961.

In 1945 Anita married EDWARD SCHNECKLOTH from Boise, Idaho. Edward came to Kitsap County from San Pedro in 1942. He worked as a welder in Puget Sound Navy Yard almost 30 years before retiring in 1973. He then built a large shop, where he welded and rebuilt cars. He retired from that business in 1980. They live in Belfair. Anita and Ed adopted a son.

4B. RANDALL CARL SCHNECKLOTH. Randy married BERNADINE MARTIN July 7, 1973, on the island of Crete. They were both in the air force. Randy and Bernie live in Limerick, Maine. They have three children, ROBIN CARL, born March 1, 1978, BRANDON, born November 12, 1981, and AARON, twin to Brandon.

5. ALBERT EUGENE HOWERTON, born December 28, 1916, in Manette. He married JESSIE CHARLES in 1944. In 1949 he married HELEN COBURN, now deceased. Eugene lived in Everett until his death February 1, 1988. Eugene and Helen had one son.

5A. ALLEN EUGENE HOWERTON, born in 1951. Allen married CHARLENE CURRY. Allen and Charlene divorced. Allen and Charlene had two children, DAWN MARIE, born June 17, 1971, and AARON EUGENE, born June 20, 1975.

6. HAROLD THEODORE HOWERTON, known as Ted, born January 18, 1921, in Manette. Ted married GLADYS CORBETT in 1960. He worked in the navy yard as a welder. His hobby was restoring tractors. In 1963 he married EDITH MOYER. In 1967 Ted married BARBARA CARLSEN. In 1972 he married ELIZABETH "Bette" HARRIS. He lived on the Old Belfair Highway. Ted died January 4, 1985.

7. ERNEST FRANKLYN HOWERTON, born April 18, 1925, in Manette.

He married GRACE WILLIAMS in 1963. In 1981 he married DOROTHY PASCHAL GUIDRY. Ernest is the musician in the family. For more than 50 years he has taught and played the accordian professionally.

8. RUTH MARIE HOWERTON, born September 3, 1927, in Manette. She married LESLIE RICHARD "Dick" SMITH in 1947 and moved to Kansas. Ruth and Dick have three children.

8A. CONNIE RUTH SMITH, born February 19, 1949. Connie married JOHN CLARKSON May 11, 1968. Connie and John have two children, COBEY JOHN, born June 20, 1971, and MITZI DANAE, born January 13, 1973.

8B. PAUL DWIGHT SMITH, born February 25, 1953. Paul married LORRAINE SMITH in 1972. They have two sons, LESLIE ALLEN, born April 28, 1973, and DWIGHT RICHARD, born August 10, 1976.

8C. PEGGY FAYE SMITH, born February 14, 1956.

HUBBELL, BARTEL
By Irene Parker (Mrs. Harlan Parker Jr.)
1984

Bartel Dolphes Hubbell was born in 1861. He came to Manette and worked as a truck gardener in the Sheridan area. He also harvested sea cucumbers and took them to Seattle to the Jackson and Main Fish Company.

Bartel married Eliza Elizabeth Shank in Ohio. Eliza was born in January 1864. Eliza died in May 1921 and is buried in Tracyton.

Eliza and Bartel had nine children. The children went to school in Sheridan and attended church in Tracyton. They enjoyed dances in Tracyton. Often they had picnics at Hansens'.

DESCENDANTS
BARTEL and ELIZA HUBBELL had nine children.

1. RULO EDGAR HUBBELL, born in July 1887.

2. EMMA DEANE HUBBELL, born in November 1888. Emma married HARLAN EDWIN PARKER. Emma and Harlan had three children: LOUISE, EILEEN and HARLAN [see PARKER history]. Emma died in 1973 in Seattle.

3. DOT OLGA HUBBELL, born in September 1891. Dot died in June 1982 in Olympia.

Bartel Hubbell family, circa 1910. Back row (from left), Florence, Jay, Dot, Emma. Second row, Rulo, Hallie, Eliza, Mary, Bartel, Rudd. Front, Alice.

kindergarten but to no avail. She started one in her home. This was a great success, and after several years the school system acknowledged the need she had seen. Now all the schools have kindergartens.

Isaac served as president of the Kitsap County Sunday School Association, was a member of the YMCA board and served as its secretary for 3 years. He had a project or hobby during World War II writing letters to 165 servicemen overseas. Many were from the Manette church.

Isaac Hoopes was a member of the Masons' Steadfast Lodge and served as secretary for a few years. He and Amy were both Eastern Star members. Amy was the first matron of Philathea Chapter when it was organized in 1921, later serving as secretary for several years.

Amy Hoopes, Hulda Wall and Cora Burlew met at the Hoopes home once a week for many years for Bible study.

The Hoopeses were ready and willing to help anyone whenever asked. Isaac with his smile and Amy with her quiet understanding way were much loved. Isaac was a jolly person, a "cut-up" at social events and at times a real clown at home. The family often remarked he missed his calling and should have been a clown in the circus.

Seriously, Isaac and Amy, too, met their calling in the church, where they were considered pillars of the church. Both left sweet memories to those who knew them.

Amy C. Hoopes died February 2, 1941. She is buried at Forest Lawn Cemetery.

Isaac married Grace Carlaw April 8, 1944. Isaac died November 28, 1953. He is buried at Forest Lawn Cemetery.

Grace died at 94 in 1980.

GENEALOGY

ISAAC PENNOCK HOOPES (born July 27, 1875; died November 28, 1953) married AMY CRAVEN (born June 23, 1879; died February 2, 1941). They had three daughters.

1. GRACE HOOPES was born June 29, 1906, in Seattle. Grace married WILLIAM ORVILLE WESSELER (son of Orville Wesseler) of Seattle in 1927. William retired in 1963 as PSNS electric shop group master. He died in 1977. Grace lives at 1015 Perry Avenue. Grace and William adopted a son.
1A. DAVID ALBERT WESSELER. David retired from the PSNS Fire Department, after which William and David became two of the partners in Busby's Marina in Bremerton. David married ROSE MARIE SUDDS. They live at 2603 Holman Street in Bremerton. They have two daughters and two sons.
1A1. KAREN LOUISE WESSELER was born September 4, 1951. She married CHARLES RUTTER in 1970. They divorced. Karen married MICHAEL O'NEAL in 1984. They live in New Iberia, La. They have a daughter.
1A1a. HEATHER KAY O'NEAL, born September 4, 1977.
1A2. JOAN MARIE WESSELER was born December 30, 1954. She married MARK M. SCHEMERRAWER in 1974. They divorced. On July 18, 1984, Joan married JAMES PREWITT, a PSNS inspector. They live at Lake Symington. They have two children.
1A2a. KRISTIN MARIE PREWITT was born December 2, 1975.
1A2b. WESLEY JOHN PREWITT was born February 23, 1977.
1A3. WILLIAM EDWARD WESSELER was born August 14, 1959. He lives at Illahee.
1A4. STEVEN DAVID WESSELER was born May 7, 1964. He is a hair stylist and lives at the family home at 2603 Holman Street.

2. EDNA THATCHER HOOPES was born December 17, 1907, in Seattle. She married KENNETH LEONARD BROOKMAN, a PSNS electrician from Charleston (West Bremerton), in 1929. He died of cancer in 1953. Edna lives in Bremerton Gardens. Edna and Kenneth had one daughter and three sons.
2A. DOROTHY GRACE BROOKMAN was born September 11, 1930. In 1950 Dorothy married LaVERNE INMAN, a PSNS coppersmith. He died in 1977. Dorothy lives in Honolulu. She has two stepsons, LaVERNE and STEVEN, and a son.
2A1. JAY RUSSEL INMAN, born December 6, 1953. Jay married KAREN RYAN of Bremerton March 23, 1973. They live in Port Orchard and have

five children, born in Bremerton.
2A1a. STEPHEN MATHEWS INMAN, born September 17, 1976.
2A1b. JOSHUA DAVID INMAN, Stephen's twin, born September 17, 1976.
2A1c. MICHAEL JAMES INMAN, born January 5, 1978.
2A1d. JOSIAH BENJAMIN INMAN, born June 7, 1979.
2A1e. LEAH ELIZABETH INMAN, born February 6, 1981.
2B. JACK RAYMOND BROOKMAN, born March 28, 1935. He died May 2, 1938, at age 3.
2C. ARTHUR WILLIAM BROOKMAN, born January 15, 1939. He married MARION JOY PETERS of Whidbey Island May 19, 1962. They live in Salona Beach, Calif. They have an adopted son and a son.
2C1. TORY KENNETH BROOKMAN, born October 16, 1966, in San Diego.
2C2. DARBY PETER BROOKMAN, born June 20, 1968, in La Jolla, Calif.
2D. JAMES ROBERT BROOKMAN, born April 26, 1946. He is a welder in PSNS. He married BARBARA DAVIS of Bremerton June 26, 1964. They have three daughters.
2D1. DEBRA BROOKMAN, born October 24, 1967, in Landstuhl, Rheinfaltz, West Germany.
2D2. GRACE BROOKMAN, born August 28, 1970, in Bremerton.
2D3. MARY ROBIN BROOKMAN, born December 27, 1976, in Bremerton.

3. MARGARET MATHEWS HOOPES was born January 9, 1917, in Manette. She married HENRY B. MOLLGAARD October 30, 1938. Henry was born in Kiel, West Germany, February 20, 1908. He came to the U.S. at age 20, became a naturalized citizen, and during World War II became a leadingman electrician in PSNS. In 1946 the Mollgaards moved to Snohomish, where they established a wholesale flower-growing business. Henry died November 19, 1984, and their son Bob carries on that business. They had two sons.
3A. HARRY DETLEF MOLLGAARD, born in Bremerton September 8, 1939. He married KARYL KERCHEN of Marysville. They have three children.
3A1. CINDY ANN MOLLGAARD, born in San Louis Obispo October 26, 1960.
3A2. MICHAEL ALLEN MOLLGAARD, born in Everett August 7, 1962.
3A3. MARK STEVEN MOLLGAARD, born in Everett February 28, 1964. Harry and Karyl divorced. Harry, who is in the flower industry and lives in Carlsbad, Calif., married THEO McCOMBS KEENAN of San Diego August 4, 1973. She had two sons, SEAN KEENAN, born May 1, 1967 (adopted) and TROY KEENAN, born February 18, 1968.
3B. ROBERT JOHN MOLLGAARD, born in Bremerton October 25, 1940. He married LINDA HATLEY. They have two daughters.
3B1. TAMARA LEE MOLLGAARD, born in Seattle January 11, 1962.
3B2. TARRILL LYNN MOLLGAARD, born May 28, 1964, in Everett. Robert and Linda divorced. On August 2, 1974, Robert married DONNA LIZOTTE of Yakima. They have two children.
3B3. TRAVIS JOHN MOLLGAARD, born in Everett November 16, 1975.
3B4. NICK LE ANN MOLLGAARD, born in Everett May 29, 1980.
Amy and Isaac cared for a foster daughter, Enid Booth, for several years before Amy's death in 1941.

HOWERTON, FREDERICK
By Geneva Howerton Pickering
1984

SAN PEDRO TO MANETTE

The Howerton family came to Manette in August 1912. My dad, Frederick Franklyn Howerton, was transferred from a government dredge in San Pedro harbor to the Bremerton navy yard.

My parents sold their house and lot in San Pedro and bought 10 acres in Manette. Dad came up to Washington, cleared some land and made arrangements to build a house. It was to be 24 feet square with four rooms.

While Dad was in Washington, Mama, brother Fred and I had whooping cough and were quarantined for 6 weeks. Then Dad returned to San Pedro and brought us, our household goods and our cat on the S.S. *Governor* to Seattle. We took the *H.B. Kennedy* to Bremerton and the *Bern* to Manette. Mama was disappointed at the primitive conditions, the rainy weather and the lack of neighbors.

COUNTRY LIVING

We really roughed it—out in the country—no road, just a

TODAY

My wife Helen and I have been very active in the United States Power Squadrons—an educational boating organization. I was district (Washington and Oregon) commander in 1965 and served on several national committees—nominating, flag and etiquette, and legislative, and on the governing Board.

Elizabeth Hudson died in 1934. Harry Hudson died in 1941.

DESCENDANTS
HARRY and ELIZABETH HUDSON had three children.

1. CLAUDE HUDSON, born February 28, 1894, in Winn, Maine. Claude married MAUDE JONES in 1916. Claude died in 1981. Claude and Maude had four children.
1A. CLAUDE HUDSON Jr., born in 1917. He lives in Everett.
1B. HERBERT HUDSON, born about 1921. He lives on Hood Canal.
1C. BETTY HUDSON, born about 1923. She lives in North Carolina.
1D. LORAINE HUDSON, now Mrs. FILLMAN. She lives in Bremerton.

2. AUGUSTUS H. "Gus" HUDSON, born July 19, 1898. He married HELEN NEWCOMB in 1934. They have no children.

3. MARGARET HUDSON, born October 31, 1899. Margaret married JOHN MANCHINE. Their daughter MARGARET, born about 1931, is now Mrs. VANLUE and lives in California.

HUFF, MARIE
By Wendell Abernathy

Marie Huff, my mother's sister, was born August 7, 1897, in Nampa, Idaho. She lived with us in Manette a great deal of the time and was baptized in the Manette Community Church by Reverend Walker. She was active with the young people of the church. She married Cecil Keeney of Seattle. They were divorced in 1940.

During World War II, Marie worked in the navy yard, where she met Frank Blair Sr., telegrapher. Marie and Frank married. Frank's son from a previous marriage, Frank Blair Jr., was in 1951 to become a newscaster and then a host on the TV Show "Today."

Marie and Cecil had one child, Joan Myrtle Keeney, born in 1927. Joan lives in Moore Park, Fla.

Marie died in Florida in 1978. Frank Blair Sr. lives in California.

HUNTON, LENDALL E.
By Lendall Gilbert Hunton
1985

NORTH TO THE NAVY YARD

My parents, Lendall E. and Hulda G. (Ehlinger) Hunton, were married in 1904 in Portland, Oreg. In 1905 they came to Charleston, where Father built a new home and their first son, Richard, was born. Lendall was employed at Puget Sound Navy Yard as a leadingman and quarterman machinist and later as a planner/estimator. He retired in 1935.

HOMES, SCHOOLS AND NEIGHBORS

I, Lendall Gilbert Hunton, was born in 1906. During 1907 we moved to a new home at 1313 Warren Avenue. My sister Mildred was born in 1908. She died in 1912 in Bremerton. In 1911 my parents purchased the Oxford Hotel on Pacific Avenue, which they operated for several years. During this time my brother Richard, 6, and I, 5, attended Central School first and second grades.

My parents sold the hotel in 1913 and we moved back to Warren Avenue. My brother and I attended Smith School in the third and fourth grades. In 1915 my folks purchased 10 acres of land with a small home in Sheridan, upon which Bremerton High School later was located. Our next-door neighbors were the Charlie Young family. Margaret Young, their oldest daughter, later married Dormie Braman, who was to become Seattle mayor.

My brother and I attended Sheridan School in the fourth and sixth grades and had Miss McLean as a teacher. She later married William Glud.

In 1919 my folks purchased 4-1/2 acres of waterfront property adjacent to the Boe and Jacobsen property in the 1300 block of Jacobsen Boulevard. We moved there because it was more convenient than Sheridan to Bremerton and the navy yard and because we had friends living in the area.

Dick and I attended the seventh and eighth grades in Manette School. Miss Claussen and Mrs. Kallander were the seventh- and eighth-grade teachers, respectively. Mrs. Kallander wrote and played the Manette School Song "Manette Rah Rah Manette" when we were in the eighth grade.

Father operated a dance club in the new Masonic Temple in Bremerton in 1921. It was called the Cinosam Club (Masonic spelled backward). My brother Dick and I were hatcheck clerks for his dances.

My brother Dick and I attended Union High School in Bremerton and graduated together in June 1924. He had lost a year of schooling due to illness. He and I were charter members and officers of the Order of DeMolay in 1922.

We both also have many fond memories of our life on the Manette beach.

After Dick and I left Manette in 1925 my folks sold our place and bought the Boe property next door. They also built new homes on Hood Canal and on Nipsic Avenue in Manette. In 1965 my father died. Mother died in 1971. My brother Dick now resides at Skyline Marina, Anacortes. I live with my wife Carol in Port Ludlow.

Dick owned and operated the West Coast Plumbing and Heating Company in Seattle, then the Western Boat Company in Marysville.

I was employed by Seattle First National Bank for 47 years, 35 of them as branch manager in various Seattle and Western Washington branches.

GENEALOGY
LENDALL and HULDA HUNTON's descendants include:

1. RICHARD HUNTON, born July 28, 1905, in Charleston, Wash. Richard married FAYE PANGBORN in 1930. Richard married OPAL DIETZ in 1965. Richard died November 15, 1987. Richard and Opal had one daughter.
1A. KAYE HUNTON. Kaye married LOUIS WASHBURN and now lives near Everett. They have two sons: LANCE and LOREN, both born in Seattle.

2. LENDALL GILBERT HUNTON, born October 28, 1906, in Portland. Lendall married CAROL SEAMAN in 1942. They live at Port Ludlow. Lendall and Carol have one daughter.
2A. PATRICIA LOUISE HUNTON, born March 16, 1935, in Seattle. Patricia married KENNETH DONOVAN and she now lives in Sacramento. They have three children: TIMOTHY, SHAWN and GREGORY.

3. MILDRED GERTRUDE HUNTON, born March 21, 1908, in Bremerton. Mildred died in 1912.

IRISH, WILLIAM
By Margaret Irish Burlew
1983

My parents, William and Blanche Irish, came to Sheridan Heights in 1924 from Montana. My dad, Bill Irish, had a dairy and he delivered milk around Manette to many people and I heard all the names.

Mom and Dad belonged to the Tracyton P-TA. Dad was a Boy Scoutmaster for several years. He enjoyed raising flowers and any new variety of vegetable.

Mom belonged to the Tracyton Ladies Aid and Sheridan Heights Homemakers Club. She did a lot of embroidering and crocheting.

I went to grade school in Tracyton and high school at Silverdale. Teachers I remember in Tracyton are Gladys (Jones) Theis, Palma (Johnson) Hammargren, Margaret Carlson, Agnes Sund and Svea Opdahl.

DESCENDANTS
WILLIAM and BLANCHE IRISH had four children.

1. WILSON EARL IRISH, born September 6, 1914, in Silverdale. Earl went to school in Tracyton and Silverdale. He married MARY OVERBECK. They had seven children. Wilson worked as a blacksmith at PSNS. He retired and lives in Manchester. Mary died in 1977.

2. LEOTA ESTHER IRISH, born February 2, 1916, in Silverdale. Leota married BEN FORBES. Leota is a retired beauty operator and lives in Long Lake, Wash. [See BURTON/FORBES history]

3. MARGARET LEONA IRISH, born January 20, 1920, in Free Soil, Mich. She attended schools in Tracyton and Silverdale. Margaret married ALFRED WAYNE BURLEW and they had five children. Alfred Wayne died August 17, 1985. Margaret lives in Bremerton. [See BURLEW, JAY, history]

4. LESLIE ALFRED IRISH, born November 28, 1928, in Tracyton. He attended schools in Tracyton, Shelton, Mossy Rock and Centralia and then attended Massachusetts Institute of Technology. He married ANN BAHNSEN. He retired from his engineering job at Boeing and lives on Vashon Island. Leslie and Ann have four children.

JACK, EUGENE C.
By Bernice Jack Thompson
and Grace Jack Barlow
1986

EUROPEAN ROOTS
Our father, Eugene C. Jack, was born September 1, 1886, in Minneapolis and died December 13, 1948, in Bremerton. He came to Bremerton in 1916 to work in Puget Sound Navy Yard as a civil engineer. Eugene's mother, Zeddie Chute, was born in Nova Scotia in 1864. She died in 1945. Eugene's father, William Jack, was born in Frankfort, Germany, in 1861.

PROFESSIONAL ENGINEER
Eugene had studied civil engineering at the University of Washington until 1907, when he went to work for his father, William Jack, in William's construction firm in Seattle.

Eugene was engineer in charge of construction of several railroad bridges in the state. From 1905 until 1916 he worked for different engineering firms in Seattle involved in design, inspection and construction of bridges, drawspans, dredges, piers and caissons around Seattle, Skagit and Vancouver, B.C., and in Oregon. He also worked as supervisor of government construction in Alaska while employed as a civil engineer in the Public Works Department of Puget Sound Navy Yard.

He entered the navy yard in 1916 at a starting salary of $5.52 a day.

He was responsible for the construction of two 400-foot steel radio towers at Keyport; two 300-foot radio towers in Cordova, Alaska; two 200-foot towers at Seward, Alaska, and a 110-foot-diameter steel water tank in New York, and was inspector for a fuel-oil storage plant. He was also in charge of the entire preparation and construction of an Alaska radio station and of the erection of the Lakeview dirigible mooring mast in 1924-25.

He was involved in repairs to waterfront structures, water systems, piers and extensions to dry dock 2 in the shipyard. He returned to college and received his degree in 1928. His thesis, *Repairs to Reinforced Concrete in Forty Feet of Sea Water,* described the deterioration of concrete under salt water.

In 1931 he became chief of the inspection division for shipbuilding and repair in Puget Sound Navy Yard. In 1936-38 he prepared for and supervised a fact-finding expedition to Kodiak, Alaska, for the naval air base there.

He was a lieutenant commander in the navy reserve from 1929 to 1940, when he took an honorable discharge because of illness. He had had a stroke.

MARRIAGE
Eugene Jack married Hazel Grace MacKechnie—Grace, as she was called—in 1918. Grace was born March 24, 1889, in Carrington, N.Dak. She was working in the navy yard as a yeoman F. Their honeymoon was a trip by motorboat from Bremerton up the Sound and into Hood Canal to a campsite in Pleasant Harbor. Their first home was a tent-house in Bremerton.

Grace and Eugene Jack, 1920.

MOTHER'S PROFESSION
Mother had gone to Bellingham Normal School—now Western Washington University. She received her teacher's certificate in 1911. She taught at Chimacum before moving to Bremerton, where she taught at Smith School. She boarded with her pupils' families as part of her salary. Sometimes she had to share a bed with one of the children.

She had botany classes at Bellingham and maintained a lifelong interest in wildflowers, trees and gardening.

She joined the navy during World War I as a yeoman and worked in the Puget Sound Navy Yard pay office, where she met Dad.

FAMILY

Twin girls, Grace Joan and Ruth Eugenie, were born in 1921; Bernice Gail was born in 1923; Walter Quinten was born in 1925.

The Jacks moved to 1135 Winfield Avenue in Manette in about 1925. It was a lovely site on the water and a good place to raise four children.

Ruth and Grace Jack, 1939, high-school graduation.

The Eugene and Grace Jack home, 1135 Winfield Avenue, about 1940.

Father was an early feminist. He believed girls should be encouraged to do anything they made up their minds to do. He also believed girls should have enough education to support themselves. Ruth and Grace were given a bag of nails and a hammer on their 7th birthday. Father always had some kind of project going in the basement workshop that we could help with. He built our oak furniture and our rowboat. We girls worked at the bench and on the wood lathe, making many craft projects for school and Girl Scouts and as gifts.

Dad was an amateur photographer, a dedicated one. We still have some of his plates of Alaska and British Columbia scenery. We also have albums filled with prints and enlargements developed in our basement darkroom of family and friends in natural and posed pictures taken during picnics and trips. Ruth was the only one of the children who developed an interest in photography.

Mother was active in several organizations: East Bremerton Garden Club, East Bremerton Improvement Club, History Club, Eastern Star, Girl Scout Council, Yeoman F. Post 4, and P.E.O. Chapter C.G. (a secret organization). Father belonged to the Kiwanis Club, Bremerton School Board and the Boy Scout Council.

When Dad was president of the Kiwanians, they built the fieldhouse at Warren Avenue Playfield for the use of various youth groups. I think Dad designed it, and at one time his name was above the door.

He was engineer in charge of building the largest crane in the navy yard in 1933. We always called it "Daddy's crane." He went to Kodiak Island in the '30s to help build the naval facility at Women's Bay.

Father died in 1948 in Bremerton of a heart attack at age 62. Mother died in 1969 at Longview. Mother and Father are buried in Forest Lawn Cemetery in Bremerton.

DESCENDANTS

EUGENE JACK and his wife GRACE had three daughters and a son.

1. GRACE JOAN JACK, born in 1921 in Bremerton. Grace attended Manette School and graduated from Bremerton High School and the University of Washington. She became a bacteriologist and served in the WAC during World War II. Grace was chief bacteriologist at Providence Hospital in Seattle in 1948. In 1951 Grace married JOHN F. BARLOW, born in 1921. They live at Lake Cushman. John is retired after working as a chemist for Longview Fiber for 28 years. Grace and John have three children:
1A. TERRI LYNN BARLOW, born in 1952 in Longview. Terri married ROBERT MAJOR in 1972. They live in Federal Way. Terri and Robert have three children.
1A1. IAN ROBERT MAJOR, born in 1976 in Tacoma.
1A2. JESSICA RUTH MAJOR, born in 1978 in Tacoma.
1A3. PHILIP CHARLES MAJOR, born in 1980 in Tacoma.
1B. LAURA JEAN BARLOW, born in 1954 in Longview.
1C. JOHN STEPHEN BARLOW, born in 1955 in Longview. John married KERRY STITHEM in 1980.

2. RUTH EUGENIE JACK, Grace's twin, born in 1921 in Bremerton. Ruth attended Manette School, Bremerton High School and the University of Washington. Ruth became a physiotherapist. She also served in the WAC during World War II. Ruth married JERRY B. ANDERSON in 1953. Jerry died in 1973. They had no children. Ruth lives in Vista, Calif.

3. BERNICE GAIL JACK, born in 1923 in Bremerton. Bernice attended Manette School and Bremerton High School, graduating in 1941. Bernice entered the college of nursing at University of Washington. She married JAMES M. THOMPSON (born in Bremerton in 1922) in 1946. Jim has an accounting firm in Seattle. They have an apartment in Seattle and a beach home near Hansville. Bernice and Jim have two children.
3A. JAMES EUGENE THOMPSON, born in 1950 in Seattle. James married MAUREEN ROHRVICK in 1970. They divorced in 1981. James and Maureen had two daughters.
3A1. DIONE ANGELIQUE THOMPSON, born in 1970 in Seattle.
3A2. SARAH CAROLE THOMPSON, born in 1974 in Seattle.
In 1982 James married BETTY HOOD, who has two daughters, Shelley and Jennifer. James and Betty have one daughter.
3A3. ELIZABETH ROSE THOMPSON, born June 28, 1986, in Bellevue.
3B. PAUL MICHAEL THOMPSON, born in 1954 in Seattle. He married PAMELA HUBBELL in Seattle in 1975. They have two children.
3B1. JASON PAUL THOMPSON, born in 1980 in Seattle.
3B2. KRISTA MICHELLE THOMPSON, born in 1984 in Tigard, Oreg.

4. WALTER Q. JACK, born in 1925 in Bremerton. Walter attended Manette School, Bremerton High School and the University of Washington. Walter became a chemical engineer. He served in the U.S. paratroops during World War II. Walter married GERALDINE VANDERPOOL in 1949. They were divorced and in 1972 Walter married VETA CAMERON and they live in Tacoma. Veta has a daughter, Mary, and two sons, Frank and Gary. Walter

and Geraldine had four children.
4A. JANET LEE JACK, born in 1951 in Tacoma.
4B. DAVID BRUCE JACK, born in 1953 in Tacoma. David married AN-
    NETTE LaVALLE in 1979. They have a son and a daughter.
4B1. RYAN DAVID JACK, born in 1984.
4B2. ALLISON TIARE JACK, born in 1986.
4C. STEPHEN HAROLD JACK, born in 1955 in Tacoma. Stephen mar-
    ried JANET LOUISE LAZENBY in 1979. They have two daughters and
    a son.
4C1. DEANA LOUISE JACK, born in 1983 in Tacoma.
4C2. HILARY GRACE JACK, born in 1985 in Tacoma.
4C3. BRIAN STEPHEN JACK, born in 1987 in Tacoma.
4D. KATHLEEN GAIL JACK, born in 1957 in Tacoma.

JACOBSEN, JENS P.
By Anne Jacobsen, Dolores Jacobsen
and Ray Jacobsen

IMMIGRATION FROM DENMARK AND NORWAY

Jens Peter "J.P."Jacobsen (1866-1946) was born in Vegle, Denmark. He came to the U.S. during the late 1880s with his two brothers, Nils and Maas. J.P. and Nils, with their wives, settled in Minnesota while Maas moved to Chicago, later to become a policeman. A son, Fred, was born to J.P. and his first wife in Minnesota on July 3, 1893.

A short time later J.P., Nils and their families moved to Cape Scott, the northern tip of Vancouver Island. Mrs. Jacobsen contracted tuberculosis and succumbed in 1897. Little is known about her as J.P. never discussed the tragedy at Cape Scott.

J.P. and Fred left Cape Scott to settle in Kirkland, while Nils and family went south to Palo Alto, Calif. In 1897, shortly after his arrival in Kirkland, J.P. acquired 15 acres in Manette near what would later be called Enetai Beach. He and Fred moved here in 1899. J.P. farmed both the Kirkland and Manette properties for some years. He also worked 2 years as a riveter in Puget Sound Navy Yard.

J.P. built a small house near the shore on the south end of the Manette property. Later he constructed a larger residence at what was to become 1358 Jacobsen Boulevard. Both houses are now gone.

Jacobsen Boulevard was named for J.P.

Mrs. Jacobsen (1874-1966), "Minnie" as she was known by many for the 62 years she lived in the family home at 1358 Jacobsen Boulevard, was born Rasmine Jakobina Pilskog December 21, 1874, in Hjorungavag, Norway. She and her

Jens and Minnie Jacobsen and sons Olav (in Jens' lap) and Axel, 1912.

sister Gina immigrated to the U.S. in 1902, coming directly to the Seattle area.

Minnie first worked in a logging camp cook-shack near Preston in King County and then moved to Bremerton to take a position as housekeeper for a Mrs. Anderson. While working there she met J.P. They were married the following year, 1903.

They had two sons, Axel and Olav.

CULTURE

Although J.P. never received a higher education and worked as a farmer most of his life, he was no stranger to knowledge. His interests were many and varied and included literature, astronomy, history and geography, philosophy, political science, economics and poetry. He was an avid reader and writer and translated a number of books—stories and poetry—from Danish. He loved to write poetry and made a custom of writing poems to his children and grandchildren to honor birthdays and graduations. Often he wrote verses on Christmas cards. Many of his relatives and close friends were included in the poetry custom, particularly at Christmas time.

To Ray Jacobsen at 6

Hello you big and smart boy, Ray
Who can offhand without delay
Inform us of all things you know
And that you can the farthest throw.

Who can up to one thousand count
And can with other wisdom flount.
Who knows a lot and strives for more
Of worldly wisdom up to store.

Jacobsen home, 1358 Jacobsen Boulevard.
-Photo from 1909 Kitsap County Plat Book

I hope your mind and body grow
So you will always fill your row
Have power to perform the stunt
To keep yourself up to the front.

May Santa or his substitutes
Remember you upon their routes
Abundant presents leave with you
So that you get a Christmas true.

THE COWS ARRIVE

In 1905 J.P. bought a cow in Seattle and brought it over on the ferry *Atlantic*. When the ferry arrived in front of his home on the beach, deckhands and J.P. shoved the cow into the water. She swam safely to shore and was found enjoying the grass by their house.

In 1925 J.P. bought another cow in Seattle to bring to Manette on the ferry *City of Bremerton*. The cow would not go down the Seattle ferry ramp. Bill Klepper, chief of police in Bremerton, was in his new Dort car behind the cow on the ramp. He gave the cow a nudge with his bumper—and the cow raised her back legs and kicked the headlights out of the new car.

FRED JACOBSEN (1893-1977)

Fred remained in Manette all his life except for U.S. Army service as a private during World War I and several protracted periods in a military hospital. He never married. Fred lived in the family home at 1358 Jacobsen Boulevard prior to military service and, after his return, built a small cottage across the street and on the hillside west of the family home. Although receiving a disability pension from the military, he helped his father, J.P., working on the family farm. Fred also worked on farms near Woodinville, Wash., and at Brier, Wash., traveling from Manette or Bremerton by ferry to Tacoma and to Brier or Woodinville by train. He also worked on his uncle Peter Thompson's wheat farm at Waterville in Eastern Washington.

Fred did much of his traveling by bicycle, once cycling to Palo Alto, Calif., to visit J.P.'s brother Nils and his family.

Another interest was boating. In his early years he saw most of the Puget Sound area via his rowboat. In about 1948 Fred's brother Axel got him a Mercury outboard and a Norseman boat and he was able to retrace many of his early travels with considerably less effort.

He was also very fond of classical music.

Fred on his bicycle was a familiar figure for years to many as he pedaled to Manette for groceries or on across the bridge to Bremerton. He loved to talk and was always willing to stop and pass the time of day with friend or stranger alike.

In his later years Fred was afflicted with arthritis which severely limited his mobility. The last several years of his life were spent in a rest home, where he died May 27, 1977, at age 85.

AXEL JACOBSEN

Son Axel was born to Jens and Minnie Jacobsen June 11, 1905. As a young boy, he would take the first fresh peas to Bremerton by rowboat from his dad's farm to the open air markets. In his early teens he and his friend, Don Young, had the first surf board to be seen around the Sound and had a great time flying over the waves.

Axel attended school in Manette and left high school after the ninth grade to attend an auto mechanic school in Seattle. After graduating he worked for "Slats" Stebeck, for one, in Bremerton. Then he returned to Seattle to work at the Second Avenue Garage, where he became shop foreman.

During a visit to Minnie's sister Gina in Vancouver, B.C., Axel met Dorothy Brown (1907-1955), then living with her parents a few blocks from Gina. A number of harrowing trips by Axel in his bright red Model-T speedster resulted in matrimony in 1926.

Dorothy was born in Hull, England, March 8, 1907, to George M. and Annie Eliza Brown (1879-1942). She arrived in the U.S. July 26, 1923, having moved with her parents and her brother Mack from England to India, then to Australia and later to Prince Rupert and Vancouver, B.C., before marrying Axel and moving to the U.S. Dorothy became a naturalized citizen February 4, 1943.

In 1930 Axel opened his own auto repair business, The General Garage, at 1100 Perry Avenue in a large wooden building previously owned by Tom Bright.

When Axel and Dorothy moved from Seattle to Manette in 1930, they lived in a small house on Shore Drive while having a new home built at 1372 Jacobsen Boulevard, next to the original family home. The new home was built by William "Whitey" Hepworth.

Among Axel's favorite interests, besides his business, were boats and softball. He owned a number of boats, including the 13-foot speedboat *Miss Pat*, named after his daughter. Today, a small speedboat is hardly noteworthy. But during the early 30s, the noise of the over-revved 1926, 4-cylinder Star auto engine and the sight of the *Miss Pat* skipping along at 50+ miles per hour was difficult to forget. For Axel's son Ray, memories of rides in the *Miss Pat*, sitting beside his dad, sometimes on his lap to steer, with a white-knuckled grip on the wheel, eyes streaming with water from the force of the wind and teeth chattering from the clapping of the water against the hull, are among his most treasured.

Axel sponsored and managed softball teams in the 1940s.

Axel earned two commendations during his years in business, the first in 1941 from Americars for selling more Americars than any Willys dealer in the United States. In 1973 he received the outstanding sales performance honor for the Northwest G.M.C. Professional Truck Salesman's Club.

Axel's wife Dorothy worked part-time as a clerk at Root's grocery store on East 11th Street through the 40s and early 50s. After Root sold the store to Glenn Buckner, Dorothy continued to work until about 1954. Her health failed and she passed away December 26, 1955, at age 48.

In 1956 Axel married Dolores Chapman.

Axel and Dolores' son Patrick Jacobsen attended Star of the Sea Catholic School, then graduated from East High School in 1975. He became an apprentice carpenter and in 1979 he followed in his dad's footsteps and formed his own business, Pat Jacobsen Construction, designing and building homes.

In 1966, Axel sold his G.M.C. dealership to Chuck Haselwood and went to work for him as his sales manager. He then leased his building to Interstate Industrial Laundries and later sold the building to them.

Axel died in 1978. Dolores continues to live in the Jacobsen home at 1372 Jacobsen Boulevard.

"Axel was a man of many virtues," Dolores said. "He was

a hard worker, always willing to help his fellow man with a kind and loving heart. He will be remembered for all time for these qualities."

OLAV B. JACOBSEN

Olav, J.P. and Minnie's second son, was born in 1910 in Bremerton.

Olav recalled riding on his dad's shoulders on their way home from a play in which J.P. played the part of a Viking in Viking costume.

He attended Manette School and Union High School. He played on local softball teams. Olav married Anne W. Arklie. Anne was from Winnipeg, Manitoba, Canada, born to William and Rebecca Arklie, who were of Scottish descent. Olav and Anne met in 1933 in Vancouver, B.C., where Anne was visiting her brother and Olav was visiting his cousin, Kris Orskog. Kris introduced them. After Olav made several more trips to Vancouver, he and Anne were married in 1934. Olav and Anne lived in the top story of the family home for a year while they built their home at 1364 Jacobsen Boulevard. Anne became a U.S. citizen in 1940.

Olav worked in Puget Sound Naval Shipyard for 40 1/2 years, retiring as a mechanical estimator in the Public Works Department in November 1969. Anne worked for 9 1/2 years at J.C. Penney Company and later in PSNS shop 17 and the Comptroller Department for a total of 13 1/2 years, retiring in May 1970.

The Jacobsens enjoyed camping, fishing, hunting, trailering and boating in the Pacific Northwest. Anne belonged to Philathea Chapter of the Eastern Star, White Shrine, Hatasu Club and the Sons of Norway. Olav belonged to Steadfast Lodge, Scottish Rite, Philathea Chapter, White Shrine, Fraternal Order of Eagles, Sons of Norway, and the Wally Byum Airstream Club.

Olav died in July 1984. Anne still lives in their 1364 Jacobsen Boulevard home.

RAY JACOBSEN

Axel and Dorothy's son Ray attended Manette School and Lincoln Junior High and graduated from Bremerton High School in 1945. Because of the dramatic population increase in Bremerton during World War II, classes were conducted in half-day shifts. Ray attended the morning shift and after he got his driver's license in 1943, he delivered groceries for Root's Grocery on East 11th Street during the afternoons. He also drove a truck part-time for Ollie Avery, who operated a general hauling service from his home on East 11th Street. Ollie would haul anything that would fit on his 1938 Ford 1-1/2 ton truck. Cargoes included lumber, rock, gravel, household furniture, cow manure for fertilizer, just plain junk and cordwood, usually cut by John Foster in the Central Valley area.

After a brief encounter with the army, Ray went to work for his dad in the garage as an apprentice.

In 1952 Ray took a job with Coast and Geodetic Survey at Pitt Point, 100 miles east of Point Barrow. A job offer from Northern Consolidated Airlines as aircraft mechanic was accepted and Ray's wife Ruth joined him in Dillingham, Alaska, where Dick Galleher, from Manette, was station manager.

In 1957, Ray, Ruth and their daughter Kari moved to An-

gola, Ind. Ray graduated from Tri-State College in Indiana in 1962. He returned to Seattle and worked for Boeing.

GENEALOGY

JENS PETER JACOBSEN was born in Vegle, Denmark, in 1866. He died in Manette in 1946. His wife, RASMINE JACOBINA "Minnie" was born in 1874 in Horungavag, Norway. She died in Manette in 1966. J.P. had one child by a previous wife and he and Minnie had two. The three are:

1. FRED JACOBSEN, born July 3, 1893, in Minnesota. He went with his parents to Cape Scott on Vancouver Island, where his mother died. He came to Manette in 1899. He was fond of classical music. Fred never married. He died in 1977.

2. AXEL JACOBSEN, born June 11, 1905, in Manette. Axel married DOROTHY BROWN in 1926. Dorothy died in 1955. In 1956 Axel married DOLORES CHAPMAN. Axel died in 1978. Axel and Dorothy had two children, Axel and Dolores had a child. The three children are:
2A. RAY ALLAN JACOBSEN, born October 11, 1927, in Seattle. Ray married CLARA NELSON, nee Winkel, in 1947. Ray and Clara had one child.
2A1. RAYE LYNN JACOBSEN, born in 1948. Raye Lynn lives in California with her mother.
Ray and Clara divorced in 1949. In 1952 Ray married RUTH DORSEY. Ray and Ruth have two children.
2A2. KARI JACOBSEN, born May 5, 1954, in Anchorage.
2A3. KAL JACOBSEN, born October 7, 1963, in Seattle.
2B. PATRICIA NANCE JACOBSEN, born August 23, 1930, in Bremerton. Patricia married CARROLL EDWARD SHARP November 17, 1949. They live in Arkansas. They have three children.
2B1. DENNIS EDWARD SHARP, born August 20, 1950, in Bremerton. Dennis is a forester. Dennis and his wife, ELAINE, also a forester, live in Little Rock.
2B2. FAYE NANCE SHARP, born March 13, 1953, in Bremerton. Faye recently married and lives in Texas.
2B3. LEE ANN SHARP, born December 27, 1960, in San Diego.
2C. PATRICK JACOBSEN, born March 5, 1957.

3. OLAV B. JACOBSEN, born July 15, 1910, in Bremerton. He married ANNE W. ARKLIE. Olav died in 1984. Olav and Anne had two children:
3A. WILLIAM J. JACOBSEN, born in May 1935 in Bremerton. William graduated from the University of Washington as a mechanical engineer. He played on the University tennis team, participated in various tennis tournaments and won several trophies. He works for the Boeing Company. He married LORNA JOHNSON in 1957. They live in Seattle. William and Lorna have three children:
3A1. BRENDA JACOBSEN, born August 11, 1960, in Seattle. She graduated from Washington State University in business administration. She played on University of Washington and Washington State tennis teams and in 1977 was appointed to High School All-Americans organization. In 1984 Brenda married JEFF SULLIVAN, a pharmacist.
3A2. BILLY JACOBSEN, born October 15, 1962, in Seattle. In 1980 he was appointed to The Society of Distinguished American High School Students. Billy attended the University of Washington, where he studied psychology and computers. He played on the U of W tennis team.
3A3. ERIK JACOBSEN, born in November 1965 in Seattle. He graduated from high school in 1984. While attending West Valley Junior College in California he played on the college tennis team.
3B. MARILYNN A. JACOBSEN, born in Bremerton April 28, 1939. She is a registered nurse, a graduate of the University of Washington. In 1960 she married RICHARD MOGG. Richard is a history instructor in a community college in Tacoma. Richard and Marilynn have three children:
3B1. BRIAN MOGG, born July 12, 1961, in Bremerton. Brian married VINA BERMUDEZ in 1982. Brian and Vina graduated from Ohio State University in 1983, Brian in political science, Vina in education. Brian is a professional golfer.
3B2. GARY MOGG, born February 20, 1963, in Bremerton. He graduated in 1987 from Washington State University, where he majored in psychology and political science.
3B3. ANNE MOGG, born June 3, 1967, in Seattle. Anne attends Biola University in LaMirada, Calif. She is majoring in education and intercultural studies.

JENSEN, CHRIS
By Ellen Jensen Magnussen and Erv Jensen

IMMIGRATION

Jens Christian Jensen, later to be known as Chris Jensen—and to his six children as "Papa" or "Pop"—came to America from Denmark in 1900, a strapping, 6-foot-4, 220-pound man who had been a member of the king's guard. Arriving in this country in the prime of life at 29, he was prepared to work prodigiously to earn a living in this new land. And work he did.

He was one of two men from separate parts of the Old Country who, by no pre-arrangement that we know of, settled here together. The other was Jens Peter Jacobsen. They bought adjoining waterfront properties stretching between the 1300 and 1700 blocks of today's Jacobsen Boulevard.

Before settling here permanently Papa spent time in Minnesota, at Cape Scott on Vancouver Island and in Alaska. He mined gold for wages near Nome and he fished commercially for salmon out of Ketchikan. To his family he told big-fish tales, such as this: his pay for his catch was a penny a fish, and when he caught a 100-pound king salmon he refused to market such a specimen for one cent. He threw it back.

MARRIAGE

In 1905 Mr. Jensen returned to Denmark to claim his bride, a beautiful, delicate lady, Valborg Petrine Pedersen. They were married in Tyler, Minn.

Valborg and Chris Jensen on wedding day, 1905.
- Photo from Ellen Jensen Magnussen

Valborg was born in Jutland February 24, 1880. Chris was born near Copenhagen May 30, 1871.

The newlyweds' first home here still stands, remodeled, as the James A. Burns residence, 1618 Jacobsen Boulevard.

From 1905 until 1919 Chris and Valborg and their growing family lived in the original home. Livelihood came from a truck farm hewed from the forest and from a milk cow or two. Chris, strong, stern and honest, did indeed work hard. But indeed, so did delicate Valborg, with a procession of babies and without modern conveniences: no electric range, no vacuum cleaner, no electric washing machine and certain-

Chris and Valborg Jensen home, 1816 Jacobsen Boulevard. Photo taken about 1908. House, remodeled, still stands.

ly no disposable diapers.

Papa delivered vegetables by rowboat to "downtown" Manette and to Bremerton. Son Svend, by 1916 at age 7, was carrying milk over a trail to affluent Seattleites enjoying remote summer retreats along northern Enetai Beach. Ellen and Svend rowed out from our beach to buy salmon from commercial net fishermen then working these waters. A fish cost a dime.

CHILDREN

Five of Chris and Valborg's six children were born in the original waterfront home. The first, Viggo, arrived June 20, 1906. Papa rowed to Bremerton to get the doctor and rowed him back again afterwards.

Viggo was so frail he was not even given a middle name. But he survived. In boyhood he adopted the middle name Douglas—he was a fan of movie actor Douglas Fairbanks Sr.

Additional children arrived as follows:
February 25, 1908, Ellen Marie;
August 1, 1909, Svend Tirkild;
January 24, 1914, Edith Margaret;
September 26, 1916, Ervin Harold;
September 2, 1920, Alfred Martin.

SECOND BEGINNING

In 1919 we began an involved process of relocation. Papa sold the original home to Charles and Emma Frederickson and purchased an unimproved 40-acre parcel climbing back on the hillside behind. Before developing a farm there he constructed an interim residence at what is now 906 Ironsides Avenue, and we lived in it until the two-story, five-bedroom home on our 40-acre "homestead" could be completed. We moved to it in 1920.

The property, 1/4 mile square, reached from Trenton Avenue to Jacobsen Boulevard. The farmhouse was near the southwest corner, now 1948 Trenton Avenue. Old-time carpenter Charles Martin helped Papa build.

ABUNDANT NATURE

Our land was a fascinating world, especially for the boys. While some huge stumps marked the days of the Enetai Mill, the forest was solid with remaining trees and new growth. The topography was varied and mysterious, with hills and vales everywhere to be explored. Through the lowlands to the northeast an unspoiled creek sighed and murmured.

High adventure thus awaited us on our own land. Grouse

and quail abounded and the creek was a place for day-long fishing trips, complete with lunches of cheese on home-made sourdough rye bread, mama's superior forerunner to today's store-bought pumpernickel.

In plat books the creek was "unnamed." To us it was "Enetai Creek." To some others it was "Jensen's;" and to still others, "McMicken's." It was also called "Micam Creek." It may also have been "Howerton's" and "Croxton's" for residents upstream and down. By any name it was the stuff of memories. Stingnettles, sword ferns and aromatic salmonberry bushes lined its winding course, and under its green banks lurked trout to 12 inches and more. In the autumn, spawning salmon also came.

MORE WORK

Back up in the "high country" around Trenton Avenue, Papa for the second time set about carving farm from forest. He made firewood of the trees, split the stumps with dynamite, muscled out the sections with a hand-cranked stump-puller and burned the roots in great bonfires.

Stump-blasting was exciting. A few sticks of dynamite dislodged most stumps, but one 5-foot fir was an unprecedented "40-sticker." This was a two-step job; Papa used a half-stick charge to blow a hole for the 40. We children excitedly discussed this record-setting, earth-shaking blast.

"Now we want a 41-sticker," we told Papa. And when the next 5-foot fir was encountered, he obliged.

The stump puller was a crude monster 5 feet high, of wooden timbers, great metal gears and detachable steel cranks 18 inches long, bent from one-inch steel bars. Atop one gear a curved dog bounced, designed to drop between teeth and hold the strain when the operator rested. Dog-on-gear played a clanking melody which, echoing through the forest and across the fields, proclaimed that Papa was pulling stumps today.

Taut cables made stump-pulling hazardous. The cable might snap and whip about. And a greater menace lurked in the dog. If it were not firmly seated, the crank when released became a whirling widow-maker. Papa lived dangerously with the stump puller for many winters. He had some close calls but never a serious mishap until, one day in the early 30s, averages prevailed. The strain was great. The dog slipped.

The unleashed crank felled him with a vicious wallop to the face. Head-on, the blow could have dealt death. But it glanced, ripping his upper lip apart from nose to mouth and scattering his upper denture in pieces on the ground. Papa never had been much of a fan of his false teeth. "But I guess they saved my jaw that time," he said later.

DIVERSITY

As if hand farming was not work enough—or perhaps because its financial rewards were meager—Papa in 1920 or 1921 got $300 on the side from the county for constructing about 1/4 mile of Trenton Avenue.

As another source of supplementary money—and of milk

Chris Jensen family (after the death of Valborg), 1926. Back row (from left), Edith, Svend, Ellen, Viggo. Front row, Alfred, Chris, Ervin.

for his children and fertilizer for his vegetables—Papa kept up to four cows. He fenced the 40 acres and the cows roamed most of it. They were curious about Papa's land clearing. Usually they only stood noncommittally to watch and chew, but one time they ate his dynamite. Another time they ate his pipe tobacco. They also ate his straw hat.

The cows shared the pasture with one horse, acquired for plowing, cultivating and delivering produce. The farming otherwise remained a hand operation although, to break some new ground, Papa once hired "Jake" Williams with his team of mules. Jake lived in the woods near the present Harrison Memorial hospital.

In the early 1930s Papa bought a 1923 Jewett touring car, which he made into a flatbed delivery wagon. Learning to drive was not easy for him. He never yelled "Whoa!" to the Jewett, but neither did he quite master simultaneous operation of clutch, brake and accelerator. His strategy: advance the hand throttle to a set position and manipulate only the clutch and brake. The idea worked, but also attracted audiences, the motor not being particularly quiet.

Papa became well-known for his Marshall strawberries. He also raised peas, beans, tomatoes, corn and other produce. Mostly he sold to stores, including Martin's and Meredith's in Manette and Orchard's, on Pacific Avenue near First Street in Bremerton. In the 1930s he retailed at the Farmers' Market, first on Burwell Street and later on 4th Street, where the Value Giant now is.

SORROW

On the evening of February 13, 1926, Mama became gravely ill. She suffered from asthma and she was never very strong. Life had been demanding. And now, rather old at 45, she was expecting her seventh child.

She was taken to the hospital in Bremerton via dirt roads and the ferry *Pioneer* on a cot placed inside a Model-T Ford delivery truck furnished by Harry Martin, grocer. Papa held the head of the cot off the floor to reduce shocks.

The following morning—Valentine's Day, 1926—Papa gave his children the simple, somber news: "Mama is gone." The baby also had died.

Ellen was then 17, in her senior year of high school. The youngest child, Alfred, was 5. Mama's work would now fall to Ellen, but Papa also wanted her to finish the school year. They managed, and Ellen graduated.

Papa, perhaps, worked harder than before. He became badly stooped with advancing years.

With the influx of defense workers at Kitsap County federal installations in the early 1940s, Chris Jensen retired from farming and platted his land. Today, residences dot the farm on the hill.

In 1941 Papa married Naomi Emerson, whom he had hired as housekeeper. On November 7, 1945, while attending an old-timers' get together in Seattle, Papa suffered a sudden heart attack and died, perhaps never knowing that his time had come. He was 74.

NEXT GENERATION

Chris and Valborg Jensen's six children all attended Manette Grade School. Edith Mae Monk was Ellen's first teacher. All except Viggo went through Union High School— or Bremerton High, as it became in 1927.

Viggo attended Manette School for 2 years, but his hearing failed and he was sent to the State School for the Deaf in Vancouver. He attended there until age 21.

He farmed with Papa, worked as a yardman for Manette Lumber Company and finally was employed as a laborer and helper in shop 72 (riggers and laborers) in the shipyard, until retirement. He never married. Now 81, partially disabled by a stroke, he lives at Martha and Mary Nursing Home in Poulsbo.

Ellen graduated from high school in 1926, then attended Bremerton Business College. On October 24, 1928, she married Elmer John Hike, a navy enlisted man completing a hitch aboard the battleship U.S.S. *Tennessee*. They had a son and a daughter, both of whom died in infancy. Ellen and Elmer were divorced in 1934.

On October 30, 1936, Ellen married Lloyd Axel Magnussen. Lloyd died January 19, 1960. Ellen still lives in their home on part of the farm on the hill, at 2008 Trenton Avenue.

Svend completed high school in 1927, one of only two boys from Manette to graduate that year, the other being Oval Martin. Svend worked on freight boats on Puget Sound, then became a shipyard employee, retiring as a leadingman rigger, shop 72. On February 9, 1935, Svend married Adda Mary Anderson, member of another pioneer family. Svend died in 1984. Adda still lives in Poulsbo. Svend and Adda had three children. The eldest of these, Allan, married Norma Bays. They divorced. They had a daughter, Mary, now married to John Slate. Svend and Adda's second child, Edith, married John Schwartz. They divorced. They had two sons, Douglas and Andrew, and they adopted a daughter, Elizabeth. Elizabeth has a daughter, Stephanie. Svend and Adda's third child, Mary, married Patrick Harrington. They had four children, Teresa, Julie, Amy and Timothy. Teresa married Franklin Schmuck.

Chris and Valborg Jensen's fourth child, Edith, graduated in 1932 and attended business college. She married Milton McInnis but they separated and she was living at home when, on August 7, 1939, at age 25, she died in a fire of undetermined origin that consumed the farmhouse. She was alone in her upstairs bedroom at the time.

Ervin graduated in 1933, became an auto mechanic in Axel Jacobsen's General Garage in Manette and a machinist in shop 31 of the shipyard, and then returned to college. He graduated from the University of Washington school of journalism in 1951. For 12 years he was a reporter and columnist for the Bremerton *Sun* and for 12 more a technical publications editor at the Naval Torpedo Station/Underwater Warfare Engineering Station at Keyport. He retired in 1978.

Ervin married Donna Deane Flaugher September 21, 1956. They live near Silverdale. They have twin daughters, Valerie and Joy. Valerie married Paul Otheim in 1981 and they have a son, Aaron. Joy married Stephen Pope in 1986.

Alfred graduated in 1938. He served an apprenticeship in shipfitters shop 11 in the shipyard. He entered the navy during World War II and was a fireman aboard the troop ship U.S.S. *Braxton* in Tokyo Bay when the Japanese surrendered. He worked at several jobs before returning to the shipyard as a shipfitter. He retired in 1980.

Alfred married Harriet Eloise Anderson June 30, 1953. They were divorced in 1955. Alfred now lives with Ellen on Trenton Avenue. Alfred and Harriet had one daughter, Chrisanne. Chrisanne married James McCabe and had three children, Jason, Daniel and Joseph. Chrisanne and James Mc-Cabe were divorced and Chrisanne now is married to James McCrae.

ATHLETICS

All the children have been sports-minded. All four boys played fastpitch softball. A four-team league in this sport, perhaps the first in the county, was started in Manette about 1933. By 1935 a team sponsored by the East Bremerton Improvement Club was good enough to play in a state tournament in Seattle, and Svend and Ervin were chosen to the all-state team. Alfred achieved similar status several times thereafter. Ervin was twice named a Northwest regional all-star. In 1983 he was elected to the Amateur Softball Association's Northwest hall of fame.

Alfred was the most versatile athlete, accomplished at basketball, tennis and baseball as well as softball. He was the cleanup hitter on the Bremerton Bees semi-pro baseball team in the 1950s.

The four boys also have been bowlers, as has Ellen.

Papa enjoyed watching his sons in athletic contests, although he protested when Ervin and Alfred practiced softball pitching with the Jewett's garage as a backstop. They splintered all the boards on one side.

In 1942 the team won its first state championship and, at a resulting celebration banquet, Papa announced his forgiveness. "I guess it was worth it," he said.

For several years while Ervin was employed at the Bremerton *Sun*, he and Svend made fishing trips to the Ketchikan area of which Papa had told his tales, and Ervin wrote columns for the *Sun* of their adventures, including his own tales of salmon exceeding 50 pounds, taken on sports gear.

WINDING DOWN

Looking back now on the events and developments we have recounted here we are impressed that the Jensen name has been well represented in the history of Manette. It appears, however, that this family name will not continue in history. Although Chris and Valborg had four sons, five of the six children born to the sons were daughters, the only son being Svend's son Allan, now 50 years old. And Allan's only child is a girl.

JOHNSON, HENRY
By Henry Johnson (1896-1986)
1986

I was born in Manette in 1896 on property my father, Fred Johnson, had purchased on Perry Avenue. He bought 40 acres across from Farmer's [at Sheridan Road] for $500. Later he sold 20 acres. He gave me, "Heinie," the first 5 acres across from Farmer's.

Dad was born in Denmark. His father taught him how to be a blacksmith. At the age of 14 he went to London with his uncle and never returned to Denmark.

Dad was 6 feet tall. He built a log cabin on our ranch in Manette. He worked as a blacksmith in the navy yard. During the gold rush he went to Alaska and made his money carrying packs up the trails for men who were searching for gold.

My mother Josephine loved to dance. After she and Dad married he learned to dance and they danced in the hall over Meredith's store every Saturday night. One man played the piano and one the violin. I remember sleeping at Clare's, at Clare's Marsh, after the dances.

Once Dad said, "Heinie, you're going to be a violinist." He bought me a violin—I still have it—and I took lessons from Mrs. Burgess in Bremerton. The violin has the name Stradivarius inside but when I took it in for appraisal I was told it was not authentic.

I had two younger brothers, Melvin, known as Babe, and Allen. Allen became an electric welder.

After Dad and Mother divorced, mother lived at 221 5th Street in Bremerton.

I worked at Todd's. Later I took a job in Alaska on a boat that was a lighthouse tender going to Seward. Now I live at Claremont East in Manette.

KANTHACK,ROBERT G.
By Marlene Kanthack Lindstrom
1985

Robert G. Kanthack was born February 22, 1873, in Germany. He ran away from home to keep out of the German army; he got on a ship as a cabin boy, went to Canada, jumped ship, got on a French ship and landed on Whidbey Island. There he left the ship to go to Bremerton.

Robert settled in Kitsap County in about 1895, and worked as a rigger at Puget Sound Navy Yard. He sent for Martha Paulina (born in Germany June 9, 1879) to join him. Martha could not speak English but came to Bremerton on her own. A Mrs. Kahn helped teach her to speak English. Robert and Martha were married in 1898. They made their home in Sheridan above where the Lebo dock is now located.

DESCENDANTS
Robert and Martha had six children.

1. ROBERT KANTHACK was born in Bremerton in 1906. He died in California.

2. FRANK J. KANTHACK was born in Bremerton June 19, 1907. He went to local schools and graduated from Bremerton Union High School. He graduated from Puget Sound Naval Shipyard apprentice school as a machinist and worked there until he retired in 1960. He was a member of the Eagles Lodge and active in the Manette Community Church.
In 1930 Frank married MARGARET S. WING, who was born in Tracyton February 3, 1911. Margaret's mother was a sister of historian Ernest Riddell, and daughter of pioneer John Paul Riddell, who came to Kitsap County in 1891.
Frank died in 1962. Margaret died in 1970. Frank and Margaret had two daughters.
2A. MARLENE ROSE KANTHACK, born in Bremerton September 10, 1932. Marlene grew up in Manette. She attended Manette Grade School, Dewey Junior High School, Bremerton High School and Manette Community Church. Marlene remembers the post office at East 11th Street and Perry Avenue, free wieners at Etten's, Christmas shopping at Aldrich's and the first soft ice cream machine when her mother worked at Martin's. Marlene married R.E. "Bud" LINDSTROM in 1951 and they live on Sylvan Way. Bud works at Puget Sound Power and Light Company. Marlene is employed at Rainier Bank. They have three daughters.
2A1. TERI LINDSTROM, born July 26, 1953. She married Dr. PHILIP LIND. They have two children: TONYA, age 15 (1986) and ANDREW age 11 (1986).
2A2. KRIS LINDSTROM. She married WALT FOX. They have one child, DAVID, born April 19, 1984.
2A3. RANDI LINDSTROM. She lives in Gig Harbor. Randi married MICHAEL GOETZ August 1, 1987.
2B. DONNA KANTHACK, born in Bremerton July 26, 1953. Donna attended Manette Grade School, East High School and Manette Community Church. Donna married MICHAEL SCOTT November 29, 1986.

3. FRED J. KANTHACK was born in 1909. Fred went to high school in Silverdale. He worked for Silverdale Electric Company until Puget Sound Power and Light Company bought it out; he then worked for PSPL for 42 years. He married GERTRUDE PERRIMAN, who was born in Montana in 1912; her mother was Margaret Clare, wife of Walter Clare. Gertrude went to school in Manette, then to Bremerton Union High School. Fred Kanthack died in June 1971. Gert married RAY HILLBERY in 1981 and lives in Shelton. Fred and Gertrude had two children.

3A. LORRAINE KANTHACK, now Mrs. Sarver. Lorraine has two children:

3A1. TONI LEE SUNDSTROM PROBERT, who has one child, and

3A2. STEVE SUNDSTROM.

3B. RICHARD KANTHACK. He has two children, JAN and JOHN.

4. HELEN KANTHACK was born in Bremerton August 19, 1910. Helen married C.E. HUNT. Helen died February 6, 1960.

Margaret "Madge" Clare with daughters Gertrude Perriman (Mrs. Fred) Kanthack and Mae Perriman Tracy, July 1968.

5. ELSIE KANTHACK was born December 4, 1913. Elsie married O.P. HAMER. She died in Bremerton in March 1975.

Fred "Fritz" Kanthack holds granddaughter Toni Sunstrom. Others (from left) are Gertrude Kanthack, Richard Kanthack, Lorraine Kanthack Sunstrom and Lorraine's husband Bill. - Photo from Mae Tracy

6. LOUISE KANTHACK was born August 11, 1918. Louise married A.W. WILLIAMSON and lives in Wenatchee.

RELATIVES
FRANK E. WING, father-in-law of Frank Kanthack, was born September 30, 1855. He married CLARA JANE RIDDELL, born March 31, 1880, in North Dakota. Clara arrived with her family in Tracyton in 1891. She died in 1959. Frank and Clara had four children.

1. JESSE RIDDELL WING, born December 29, 1906, in Tracyton. Jesse died May 15, 1972.

2. FRANK T. WING, born October 9, 1909, in Tracyton. Frank died August 22, 1963.

3. MARGARET S. WING, born February 3, 1911, in Tracyton. Margaret married FRANK KANTHACK in 1930. Margaret died May 17, 1970, in Bremerton.

4. FRED E. WING, born January 16, 1916, in Tracyton. Fred married LEONA RADOVICH.

JOHN PAUL RIDDELL was born July 13, 1836, in Markham Township, Canada. In 1866 John married MARGARET JANE YOUNG, born August 24, 1845, in Nova Scotia. Margaret died in 1910. They came with their family to Tracyton in 1891. John and Margaret had four children.

1. ERNEST E. RIDDELL, born April 22, 1887, in North Dakota. Ernest died September 17, 1962, in Tracyton.

2. EVA RIDDELL, later Mrs. Reeves.

3. MABEL RIDDELL, who married S. H. SHORT.

4. CLARA JANE RIDDELL, born March 31, 1880. Clara married FRANK E. WING. Clara and Frank had four children. Clara died January 5, 1959.

KARST, HENRY
By Jim Karst
1985

ARRIVAL FROM LEHIGH, KANSAS
Henry Karst was born in Echeim in the state of Samara in Russia on the Volga. He arrived in Kansas at age 4. Katherine Pfenning was born in Neu Norka in the state of Samara on the Volga. She arrived in Herington, Kans., at age 16. Henry and Katherine married in 1893 in Lehigh, Kans. Lehigh was settled by Germans and they all spoke the German language. The Karsts had to learn their English in Washington. Henry and Katherine came to Decatur, later to become Manette, in 1902 with their three sons: Adam, Holt and William. A daughter, Esther, was born in Manette. Henry died in 1951. Katherine died in 1946. They are buried in Ivy Green Cemetery, Bremerton.

Henry and Katie Karst moved to Decatur on a recommendation of Katie's brother John Pfenning. Pfenning had come to Decatur when he left the Klondike Gold Rush in the 1890s.

The Karsts were welcomed to Decatur by Katie Karst's three brothers, John, Pete and Adam Pfenning. Henry Karst bought 2 1/4 acres adjoining the Pfennings. This property was on the west side of the county road, now Perry Avenue, and extended from approximately East 15th to East 17th Streets and from Perry to Scott Avenue. All three brothers and one sister built small houses on adjoining properties. Neighbors were Leonard Card, Arthur Bright and Thomas Bright.

There were no streets, just one road and trails leading everywhere through the timber over and under logs. The

Henry and Katherine Karst's home at 1517 Perry Avenue in 1930.

standing trees were from 3 to 4 feet in diameter. These trees were cut down and sawed up for stovewood. Henry built their house on the corner of what is now East 16th Street and Perry Avenue—1517 Perry Avenue. The house still stands but has been enlarged. When Henry built their house he got the lumber at Port Blakely, put it in a large skiff and rowed it to Washington Narrows.

JOBS

Henry was a wheat and sugar beet farmer, diver's helper, millwright and general laborer. He found work with the telephone company and helped lay the first submarine telephone cable to Bainbridge Island and from there to Seattle. Katie took in wash from Manette's Enetai Beach area and the boys delivered it.

Later Henry worked for the paint shop in the navy yard. He used to tell of being sent to work in the double bottoms of the old battleship *Oregon* to chip and scale rust, to wire brush and to paint. The workmen had only candles for light and, as the day wore on, one candle after another would be put out and the employees would go to sleep until, Henry said, he was the only one whose candle was still burning. The other men would cuss him because he made so much noise. Henry advanced to the rating of painter's helper.

A NAME FOR A TOWN

During this period the people of the town were trying to get a post office established. They found that there was already a town in Washington named Decatur. A meeting was held in the home of Adam Pfenning and the name chosen was Manette, the name of a boat in the area.

On September 3, 1905, a girl was born to the Karst family. She was the first white girl born in Manette and was named Esther Manette Karst.

Esther Manette Karst, circa 1905.

GRANDPA PFENNING

Soon after this Katie Karst developed diphtheria and the children were all farmed out to the Pfenning uncles and aunts. Holt and Bill went to stay with Pete and Christina Pfenning. Grandfather Nicolaus Pfenning was living there also. Esther stayed with the John Pfennings for about a year. Adam remained at home to help out.

Holt tells, "I will always remember my grandfather because one evening we were going to have sauerkraut soup for our supper and I did not like it. I decided to go home to eat supper and took off across the acre. I had just gotten to the corner fence post to jump over the picket fence when Grandpa grabbed me by the seat of my pants and warmed my behind. When we ate supper I had to say I liked sauerkraut soup. And I had to eat it to prove it."

Holt also recalls: "Grandpa Pfenning was later killed in the woods up on a ridge above what is known as Clare's Marsh.

He was shot by a hunter who said he thought Grandpa was a bear eating berries. Grandpa was 56 at that time." This was in 1904.

NEW JOBS

By 1909 Henry Karst was a painter in the navy yard, but the turpentine was not good for his health and he began to think of other employment. Bremerton was a wide-open town with 16 saloons and a red-light district. Sailors were much older, rougher men then than now and Henry decided this area was not a good place to raise a young family. In the spring of 1909 the Karsts moved to Nyssa, Oreg., to work with sugar beets. Later the family moved to Shattuck, Okla.

ADAM KARST

Adam Karst attended grade school on Sheridan Road where the Tamarack Apartments now stand. Adam married Bertha Kretz in Shattuck, Okla., May 6, 1917. They moved to Manette with their daughter Virginia in 1919 and lived in one bedroom in the John Pfenning home for 9 months while building their home at 2033 East 16th Street. Most of the lumber was carried by hand from Tracy Lumber Company on the waterfront. Around 1930 the house was remodeled and Virginia remembers living in the garage while the work was being done. The house still stands. Later they moved to 1011 Nipsic Avenue. Adam retired from the navy yard after 38 years as a coppersmith. Adam died in 1970. Bertha still lives in Manette.

HOLT KARST

In February 1917 Holt Karst returned to Manette. He was 19. He worked for his uncle, John Pfenning, who had a dairy. It was Holt's job to deliver milk.

"I soon found out my new job was just another 7-day-a-week job with no time off," Holt said. "Uncle John had 14 milking cows to be milked morning and night. The day would start each morning at 4 or 4:30 with feeding and milking, then running all the milk through the cooler. Next we bottled it in pints and quarts.

"When this was done we had breakfast and then turned the cows out of the barn. Next all the milk was loaded on the wagon and driven to the ferry dock. I carried many cases of bottled milk down the gangway and aboard the launch for Bremerton. Uncle John had a Ford truck in Bremerton and he made the deliveries on that side while I delivered with horse and wagon on the Manette side.

"After the deliveries I had to clean the barn of manure, wash it down with a water hose and take care of the horse and calves and a large bull that was a vicious beast with a ring in his nose. Once while I was cleaning the bull's stall he turned his head towards me and I tapped him on the nose with the fork. He turned back for a minute and then came at me. I saw that the snap had come out of the ring in his nose and I just barely got out of the stall and closed his gate when he crashed against it. If he had caught me he could have crushed the life out of me. The Good Lord was with me that day.

"I had to meet the launch at a certain time and carry all the empty bottles back to the wagon and wash the bottles and cans after first getting up the steam in the boiler to do a good job. Sometimes Uncle John would help me so that I could do other work such as hauling manure and fallen leaves from the alder grove. This mixture he used for fertilizer. I also hauled rock from the field, plowed and harrowed. I found my uncle very hard to please and he demanded more work from me than any man could accomplish. Finally I told my uncle I would work for him until July 1 and then find something else."

Holt Karst went to work at the naval shipyard July 11, 1917. He earned $2.56 for an 8-hour day. He worked as a common laborer for 10 days and then became a helper boatbuilder.

In 1918 Holt sent his family money and they all returned to Manette and built onto the original house on Perry Avenue.

On June 30, 1919, Holt married Olinda Meier in her parents' home in Shattuck, Okla. He brought her to Manette, to live with the Henry Karsts and to start a new family. They had one son, Clyde James "Jim." Holt died in 1977. Olinda lives in Manette.

WILLIAM KARST

William graduated from Union High School in 1922. William never married. He lived at the old family home on Perry Avenue. William retired as a shipfitter in the navy yard after 35 years. He died in 1978.

Thanksgiving at the Karst's in 1926. Back row (from left) Henry, Bertha, Adam and Katie Karst, Kraty and John Pfenning, Holt and Olinda Karst. Front row, William, Kenneth, Virginia and Clyde Jim Karst.

ESTHER MANETTE KARST

Esther Manette Karst—named for the town—was born in Manette in 1904. She married Charles B. Tupper. Esther and Charles had one son, Bruce. Esther lived in California until her death in 1982.

Henry Karst divided his property down what is now East 16th Street, giving a lot to each of his four children. At this time Adam and Bertha Karst with their small daughter Virginia arrived in Manette and built a home on East 16th Street.

Katie Karst died in December of 1946. Henry Karst died in 1951. Both are buried at Ivy Green Cemetery.

RECOLLECTIONS OF OLINDA KARST

"I arrived in Manette on July 9, 1919, as a young bride," Olinda Karst recalls. "We moved in with the Henry Karsts and lived there 5 years. Next we rented a small house on what is now Wheaton Way, and in 1924 we moved into a small house that is now 1134 Ironsides Avenue. In 1929 this house was remodeled into the house it is today."

Olinda does not remember Indians using the beach area or living in Manette when she arrived. Holt told her that when ships came to Bremerton, people had to climb trees to watch them, because there was so much heavy timber no one could see down to the water.

She also recalls seeing George Card walking down the county road to Martins' store for groceries. He would stop and visit with Henry Karst on his way down and again on his way back. It was always a pleasant time for all.

DESCENDANTS

1. ADAM KARST was born December 15, 1884, in Lehigh, Kans. He married BERTHA KRETZ. Adam died in 1970. Bertha died August 5, 1987. Adam and Bertha had a daughter and a son.
1A. VIRGINIA E. KARST, born in September 1918, in Shattuck, Okla. Virginia married EUGENE HANSEN in January, 1949. Virginia and Gene had two children. Eugene died in September 1983. Virginia still lives in Everett, where she and Gene always made their home. Virginia and Eugene's children are:
1A1. JIM E. HANSEN, born in Tulsa in March 1941. Jim attended schools in Everett. He is a truck driver and resides in Mukilteo with his wife MARLENE and two daughters.
1A1a. APRIL J. HANSEN, born in March 1965 in Everett.
1A1b. FRANCINE L. HANSEN, born in April 1969 in Everett.
1A2. KAREN HANSEN, born in November 1954 in Bremerton. She attended schools in Everett and the University of Washington. Karen is an English teacher in Kent, where she lives with her husband, WILLIAM HUKARI. Karen and William have two sons.
1A2a. JONATHAN A. HUKARI, born in December 1978 in Seattle.
1A2b. JEFFREY A. HUKARI, born in December 1981 in Seattle.
1B. KENNETH H. KARST, born August 4, 1920, in Bremerton. Ken married LORNA AMES July 4, 1946. They have five children and reside in Dover, Idaho. Kenneth is retired. The children are:
1B1. JACK E. KARST, born March 30, 1949, in Sandpoint, Idaho. He married MARY G. SYLVESTER December 28, 1970, in Couer d'Alene. Jack is coordinator of Front End Systems for Rosauers Markets. Jack and Mary reside in Newman Lake, Wash. They have three children: CHRISTI, born July 29, 1971; KENNETH, born September 15, 1974, and JACLYN, born April 11, 1982.
1B2. JILL A. KARST, born August 11, 1950 in Sandpoint, Idaho. She married CRAIG BROCKUS September 28, 1968, in Sandpoint. Jill works for General Telephone and they reside in Sandpoint. They have two children: NATHAN, born June 8, 1970, and KAYLEE, born September 25, 1971.
1B3. DENNIS R. KARST, born November 9, 1953. He married GRACE E. RODRIGUEZ July 7, 1973, in Hanford, Calif. Dennis runs computers for Riley Creek Lumber and they reside in Sagle, Idaho. They have two children: ROXANN, born July 14, 1979, and MELODY, born April 5, 1985.
1B4. PENNEY S. KARST, born April 21, 1958, in Sandpoint. She married STEVEN SUMAYA September 16, 1978, in Dover, Idaho. They reside in Hanford, Calif., and have two children: TRACEY, born June 7, 1981, and TIMOTHY, born April 28, 1986.
1B5. SHERRI M. KARST, born October 8, 1960, in Sandpoint. She married JAMES H. HOFFMAN November 17, 1978, in Couer d'Alene. They reside in Kootenai, Idaho, and have two children: PAUL, born May 8, 1978, and AMY, born April 11, 1986.

2. HOLT KARST was born February 19, 1898, in Kansas. He came to Manette with his family in 1902. He returned to Kansas in 1919 for a bride, OLINDA MEIER. They had one son.
2A. CLYDE JAMES "Jim" KARST, born July 9, 1922. Jim married WANDA SCHENCK June 14, 1946. They had three daughters.
2A1. LINDA LORRAINE KARST, born December 6, 1947. Linda married MIKE KROUSE. Later she married WILLIAM WARD and lives in Port

Orchard. Linda and Mike had four children, all born in Bremerton: DAR-
RELL, born in 1966; LISSA, born in 1970; AARON, born in 1973, and
BRANDON, born in 1975.

2A2. SUSAN ELAINE KARST, born May 12, 1949. Susan married PHIL-
LIP PACE in July 1972. They have four children: REBECCA, born May
25, 1974; KATHERINE, born October 1, 1977; BRYAN, born May 10,
1980, and STEVEN, born August 11, 1984.

2A3. CONNIE DIANA KARST, born September 22, 1955. Connie married
CRAIG MUNRO in September 1978 and they live in Tracyton. Connie
and Craig had two children: JENNIFER, born November 29, 1976, and
KEVIN, born February 21, 1980.

3. WILLIAM KARST was born March 3, 1901, in Kansas.

4. ESTHER MANETTE KARST was born September 2, 1904, in Manette.
She married CHARLES B. TUPPER. They had one son.
4A. BRUCE TUPPER, born in California in 1942.

BENJAMIN J. KEAN
(Reprinted from an old newspaper)

Ben Kean was born in
Fossil, Oreg., September
19, 1891. He traveled to
Texas, California, Canada
and Washington with his
family. He went to school
in Port Angeles. In 1908
the Keans moved to
Bremerton, where Ben at-
tended high school and
business college. Ben's
first job was in Puget
Sound Navy Yard.

From 1924 until 1933
Ben operated a fuel and
transfer business in
Manette. Ben became a
Bremerton police officer.

Ben married Mary
Louise Skerik of San
Diego in 1915 and they

Benjamin Kean. - Photo from
Bremerton Searchlight

have two sons, Ben Jr. and Wallace Ray.

Ben Sr. is a member of the Scottish Rite, past master of
Masonic Lodge 117 and past patron of the Eastern Star. His
hobbies are swimming, fishing and boxing.

KEMNER, JOE
By several contributors
1985

ESTELLE MEREDITH:

When I came to Manette in 1922, there was a Joe Kemner
who sharpened saws and knives. He also did yard work for
many people. Once when I asked him to sharpen a knife for
me, he said, "You bought this at the dime store, didn't you?"
I had.

"Don't ever buy anything any time if people are ashamed
to put their name on their product. It's no good."

My knife had no manufacturer's name.

When Joe Kemner needed a place to live, Mr. and Mrs. L.A.
Bender put a stove in their garage and allowed him to live
there for the rest of his life.

JUNE MARTIN SCHWEER:

Joe Kemner was our [the Harry Martin family's] gardener

for many years—at least 18 or 20.

Joe kept rabbits, and much to Grandma (Ella) Bender's dismay they ran loose in his house, which was a garage Benders
had converted into a residence for Joe. I'm sure sanitary conditions left much to be desired.

However, Joe was one of my favorite people.

On days he worked for us, Mother gave him lunch. I must
have been about 2 years old. I would climb into his lap. He
would say, "But I'm all dirty," and mother would put a
newspaper over his muddy coveralls for me to sit on. I do
remember waiting for him to drink his coffee. After each
drink he would pull his long bushy mustache into his mouth
with his lower lip and suck noisily to get the rest of the coffee. I loved it.

A patch of white and pink daisies, those tiny ones, grew in
the middle of our large lawn. Joe would always cut around
them "because June likes to pick them," he would tell Daddy.
Then Daddy would have to get out the hand mower and cut
them down.

Joe carried clippings and starts of flowers and bushes from
garden to garden where he worked and everyone ended up
with anything that was choice and beautiful.

Joe was not over 5 feet 5 inches, very stocky and very dirty.
I can still recall that smell when I think of him. It didn't bother
me at all.

He became ill and bedridden and Ella Bender got him into
an old-folks home in Bremerton. He was heartsick over leaving his rabbits. Mother visited him and didn't recognize him.
He was clean and shaved and miserable. I don't believe he
lived more than a few weeks after being forcibly taken to the
home.

HATTIE ELLIOTT ENGSTROM:

Mr. Kemner used to come to our place and bring Mama
plants, like he did to so many around Manette. He came one
day when Mama was gone. I warmed up some of Mama's
leftovers so he would have a bite to eat. Erik Engstrom was
living with Mr. and Mrs. Hibbard. Next time Mr. Kemner
went to Hibbards he told Erik if he wanted a good wife, he
should get that little Elliott girl, she was a good cook. Hah! I
had only warmed over what Mama had cooked. I don't think
this had anything to do with Erik and me getting married.

Mr. Kemner always called his rabbits "ra bits." He was a
special little ole man but not many people knew very much
about him.

KENNEDY, ROBERT D.
By Robert Kennedy Jr.
1986

Robert D. Kennedy and Bertha Kennedy moved from Seat-
tle to Manette in 1925 with their infant son, Robert "Bob" Jr.
Bertha became an invalid in 1929. Kennedys bought the old
Al Miner home at East 18th Street and Perry Avenue.

Robert Sr. worked at Puget Sound Naval Shipyard as a
driller leadingman. He was active in the Manette Community
Church and was chairman of the board of deacons. He was a
member of the board of the Children's Home Association. He
served as chairman of the board of directors of the Kitsap
County Cooperative Hospital Association in 1967.

Bob Jr. attended kindergarten at Mrs. Hoopes' home,
Manette Grade School and Lincoln Junior High School, and

graduated from Bremerton High School. He also attended services for young people at the church.

Bertha died December 1, 1941, and in 1942 Robert Sr. married Rolena Outland, sister of a Manette neighbor Estelle Meredith. Bob and Rolena took part in activities at the Manette church.

Robert and Rolena Kennedy at their home at 1010 Perry Avenue.

The Robert Kennedy family, circa 1954. Back row (from left), Robert D. Kennedy II, Malcolm D. Kennedy and Beverly Waltz Kennedy. Row 2, Robert D. Kennedy Sr., Rolena Outland Kennedy, Elizabeth "Betsy" Kennedy and Mr. and Mrs. C.J. Waltz. Front row, David Eugene "Gene" Kennedy, Richard Kennedy and Robert D. Kennedy III.

Bob Jr. was in the army during World War II. He married Beverly Waltz of Baker, Oreg., in 1943. Bob graduated from Oregon State University in 1950. Bob and Bev lived in Philadelphia, Pittsburg and California. They now live in Tracyton. Bob worked for Darigold Incorporated for 37 years and recently retired as the company's branch manager. He is also on the board of directors for National Bank of Bremerton. Beverly worked for J.C. Penney and is now a homemaker.

GENEALOGY
ROBERT DARCEY KENNEDY (1894-1968) and BERTHA KENNEDY (1897-1941) had one son.

1. ROBERT DARCEY KENNEDY Jr., born June 21, 1923. Bob married BEVERLY WALTZ and they have four children.
1A. ROBERT D. KENNEDY III, born November 29, 1944. Bob III was in the army 3 years, then graduated from Linfield College. He is a computer analyst for Vector, Inc., and lives in North Bend, Wash. Bob and his wife DIANE have three children, MONICA, MARK and LORI.
1B. DAVID EUGENE "Gene" KENNEDY, born April 9, 1946. Gene was in the intelligence corps for 3 years. He graduated from Linfield College and is now manager at Land Title Company and lives in Bremerton. Gene and his wife MARION have two children, CHRISTINA, born in Bremerton December 27, 1971, and JUSTIN D., born in Bremerton September 20, 1974.
1C. ELIZABETH ANNETTE KENNEDY, born February 28, 1949. She works at Darigold. She married TERRY SCHRAM and they live in Port Orchard. They have two sons, FRANK, born in Bremerton August 30, 1971, and CARY ROBERT, born in Bremerton September 15, 1973.
1D. RICHARD JOSEPH KENNEDY, born February 23, 1951. Richard works for the parks department and lives in Bremerton.

KIMBALL, ERNEST
By Shirley Kimball Jones
1985
Ernest Henry Kimball was born in Fairview May 15, 1904. Fairview was a community between Tracyton and Silverdale. Ernest moved to Manette in 1930 with his wife, Margaret, and their three children, who had been born in Bremerton.

Margaret Kimball was born Margaret Erstad in Brooklyn, N.Y., March 3, 1908. She arrived in Manette in 1919 and married Ernest in 1924 in Shelton.

Ernest worked many years at Puget Sound Naval Shipyard. The family fished commercially in Alaska in the late 1940s. Ernest then returned to PSNS to work as a shipfitter until his

Margaret and Ernest Kimball on 50th wedding anniversary, 1974.
- Photo from Bremerton Sun

retirement in 1961. Margaret worked at the Apex Bakery on 4th Street in Bremerton in the 1930s and later worked at Keyport and in the navy yard as a machinist's helper. The Kimballs lived at 1710 Marlow Avenue in Manette. They now reside in Poulsbo.

Ernest and Margaret's children, Jean Shirley, Ernest Jr. and Robert, attended Manette School and Manette Community Church and went to Sunday School classes at the Hammersburg home.

Shirley married Merle Jones December 25, 1941. Merle's parents, James and Bertha Jones, moved to Manette from Seattle with Merle in 1936. After her husband's death in 1947, Bertha went to Maryland and took care of the children of former Manette residents June and Bill Schweer. Later Bertha returned to Manette and became Mrs. B.F. Harrison's housekeeper for 10 years. She was there until Mrs. Harrison died.

Bertha Jones was killed as a pedestrian in California April 7, 1961.

Merle retired from the Naval Torpedo Station at Keyport in 1972. Shirley worked for 22 years as a meat wrapper in local stores including T.B.&M., now Thriftway, in Perry Avenue Mall for 5 years. Merle and Shirley live in Poulsbo and are enjoying retirement.

GROWING UP IN MANETTE.

My brothers, Ernest and Robert, and I had a lot of fun swimming at the Sandbanks, in front of where Bremerton Gardens now stands. We also enjoyed sledding with all the neighbor children when we had snowstorms.

At the Manette Community Church, Mrs. Wall had the biggest influence on my life. My brothers and I went to her Bible School class. I think we went for the big cookies she gave us but I can remember how sincere she was when she talked about the Lord.

One time the three of us had bad colds and coughs. The school nurse thought we had the croup so she took us home. Mother wasn't home so she took us down to the Children's Home. We always thought that was funny logic, as she was concerned that we would expose our germs to the school children but not concerned about the children at the Home.

I remember our class going to the Bob Kennedy home to sing for Mrs. Kennedy, who was bedridden.

I'm thankful for the friendliness in Manette and a safe place to bring up children.

ERNEST AND MARGARET KIMBALL'S FAMILY

1. JEAN SHIRLEY KIMBALL was born May 30, 1925, in Bremerton. Shirley married MERLE JONES December 25, 1941. Shirley and Merle have a daughter and a son.
1A. SHARON JEAN JONES, born October 7, 1942, in Bremerton. Sharon married LAWRENCE APELAND from Bremerton and they live in Silverdale. Larry is a shipfitter in the navy yard. Sharon and Larry have four children.
1A1. SHARLA JEAN APELAND, born January 15, 1963, in Bremerton.
1A2. MARK LAWRENCE APELAND, born November 11, 1964, in Bremerton. Mark married DARLENE DOW of Elbe in 1984. They live in Silverdale and have one son.
1A2a. CHAD LAWRENCE APELAND, born July 11, 1985, in Bremerton.
1A3. MATTHEW JON APELAND, born August 11, 1968, in Seattle.
1A4. SHAWNA MARIE APELAND, born March 23, 1970, in Bremerton.
1B. DENNIS BYRON JONES, born November 30, 1945, in Bremerton. Dennis married CHERRY D. GREEN from Darrington. Dennis works at Bremerton Glass. Dennis and Cherry have two children.
1B1. JAMES BYRON JONES, born April 24, 1975, in Bremerton.
1B2. JODI ELIZABETH JONES, born June 3, 1982, in Bremerton.

2. ERNEST KIMBALL Jr., born October 7, 1926, in Bremerton. Ernest married PHYLLIS EDENSHAW in 1946. He retired from the pipe shop in the navy yard in 1986. They live in Silverdale. Ernest and Phyllis have six children.
2A. LAVERNE MARIE KIMBALL, born July 20, 1947, in Bremerton. Laverne died November 11, 1965.
2B. ERNEST HENRY KIMBALL III, born August 8, 1948, in Bremerton.
2C. YVONNE KIMBALL, born August 19, 1951, in Bremerton. Yvonne married DAN JOHNSON from Chico in 1984. Later they divorced. Yvonne has a son, EAN, and lives in East Bremerton.
2D. RANDY KIMBALL, born April 30, 1955, in Bremerton.
2E. RENEE KIMBALL, born July 1, 1964, in Bremerton. Renee married TERREL GARDNER of Louisiana. They live in Silverdale. Renee and Terrel have two children, RICHARD and CANDACE.
2F. SCOTT KIMBALL, born December 25, 1967, in Bremerton.

3. ROBERT E. KIMBALL, born September 18, 1927, in Bremerton. Robert married ISABELLE JACK from Brownsville in 1948. Robert works as a brick mason and is semi-retired and living in Ketchikan. Robert and Isabelle have three children.
3A. CHRISTINE KIMBALL, born February 13, 1953, in Bremerton. Christine married EARL NASH of Ephrata. They live in Thorne Bay, Alaska, where Earl is a building contractor. Christine and Earl have two children, SARAH, born August 27, 1979, and MARYANN, born July 8, 1981.
3B. WILLIAM "Bill" KIMBALL, born November 1, 1955, in Bremerton. Bill married ANN WILLOUGHBY from Port Townsend. They live in Ketchikan, where Bill is a furnace repairman. Bill and Ann have two children, TIMOTHY, born July 27, 1982, and JOSHUA, born January 1, 1985.
3C. ROBERT "Bob" KIMBALL, born July 10, 1957, in Bremerton. Bob married DIANNE MARINER from Poulsbo. They live in Chimacum. Bob and Dianne have three children, MASON, born June 24, 1982, CORRINNE, born November 27, 1984, and CHRISTINE VICTORIA, born December 5, 1986.

LEE, EVAN
By Mable Lee Dickson
1985

NORWAY TO MANETTE VIA MINNESOTA

Evan Lee immigrated to Minnesota from Norway in 1904 with his wife, the former Jakobine T. Hurlen, and their three children, Arne, Caroline and Ella. Four children were born to the Lees in Minnesota: Seena, Josephine, Carl and Harold.

Late in 1910, the Bremerton navy yard was recruiting men to work on Dry Dock 1, and Evan left Minnesota for Washington. Accompanying him was Mrs. Lee's sister, Josefine (1869-1950), and her husband, Ole Lillevick (1869-1948).

Mrs. Lee with their seven children followed them west in April of 1911.

They met numerous Scandinavian families in Manette and decided to make their homes here. Mr. Lee bought the Captain Risser home on East 18th Street. A daughter Mable was born to the Lees in Manette October 13, 1915.

The Lee home was destroyed by fire in 1918 but they rebuilt and continued to live in Manette until Mr. Lee, who was associated with Jens Jacobson of the Kitsap Dairy, now Darigold, decided to move to Bremerton in 1920.

When Arne was about 17, in about 1917, he and Manette friends Leo Miller and Morgan Avery drove to Los Angeles in a Model-T Ford to find work. All returned to Manette. In 1930 Arne moved back to Los Angeles to work for a dairy there. He and his family returned to Bremerton and he worked with his father at Kitsap Dairy.

HALL OF FAME

Harold "Hal" Lee was an outstanding basketball player at the University of Washington [see SPORTS]. After World War II he became a basketball referee in the Pacific Coast

Evan and Jakobine Lee's family and home on East 18th Street, circa 1912. Back row (from left) Evan, Jakobine and Caroline. Front row, Seena, Carl, Josephine, Harold, Ella and Arne Lee. - Photo from Mable Lee Dickson

Conference and was inducted into Washington State's basketball Hall of Fame in 1974.

In 1937 Harold married Patricia Bennett. When Pearl Harbor Day came he was playing baseball in the Texas League. He spent 4 years in the army.

ERNIE'S UNION SERVICE

Mable's husband, Ernie Dickson, owned and managed Ernie's Union Service at Harkins Street and Winfield Avenue for 31 years. He retired in 1975. Mable retired in 1975 from the naval retail store system in the navy yard. They live on Trenton Avenue.

Ernie and Mable (Lee) Dickson's 50th wedding anniversary. -Photo from Bremerton Sun

GENEALOGY

EVAN LEE was born in Norway September 21, 1873. He married JAKOBINE T. HURLEN, (1870-1957). They had eight children.

1. ARNE LEE, born June 18, 1900, in Norway. Arne married VERNA BLAISDELL in 1932 in Los Angeles. Verna died in 1947. Arne died in Bremerton in 1973. Arne and Verna had two children.
1A. VIRGINIA LEE, born April 7, 1933, in Torrance, Calif. She married FRED RYEN of Bremerton. They live in Bremerton and have three children.
1A1. CYDNI RYEN, born in 1952 in Bremerton. Cydni married CHARLES LARSON, son of a pioneer Bremerton family. They have two daughters.
1A1a. RYEN LARSON, born in 1979 in Arkansas.
1A1b. LEE LARSON, born in 1981 in Bremerton.
1A2. VICKY RYEN, born in 1955 in Bremerton. Vicky married DEAN HUDSON of Bremerton.
1A3. DENISE "Dee-Dee" RYEN, born in 1958 in Bremerton.
1B. EDWARD ARNE LEE, born October 4, 1935, in Bremerton. Edward married RUTH MORGAN of Philadelphia. Edward died in an auto accident in 1968. Edward and Ruth had one daughter.
1B1. ALISON LEE, born in 1957 in Philadelphia.

2. CAROLINE LEE, born September 1, 1901, in Norway. Caroline married BARTHOLOMEW "Bart" FAHERTY of Boston in 1921. Bart retired as a navy commander. They live in Philadelphia and have three sons.
2A. EDWARD FAHERTY, born in April 1922 in Boston. He married HELEN FEENEY and they live in Pennsylvania. They have six children: MARY LEE, ELIZABETH, SHAWN, BARTHOLOMEW, HELENA and EDWARD Jr.
2B. BERNARD FAHERTY, born in July 1924, in Kitsap County. Bernard married MARGARET HARRIS and they live in New Jersey. They have five children: BARBARA, EARLINE, CAROLINE, PAULA and REGINA.
2C. BARTHOLOMEW FAHERTY Jr., born in August 1925 in Kitsap County. He married MARGARET CONWAY and they live in Pennsylvania. They have six children: MARY, MAUREEN, MARGARET, MARIE, MICHAEL and MONICA.

3. ELLA LEE, born March 28, 1903, in Norway. Ella married WILLIAM "Bill" WEHMEYER in Bremerton in 1922. Ella and Bill had one daughter. Bill died in 1925. Ella married STANLEY "Stan" BLACKWOOD in 1928. Stan was an apprentice in the navy yard. They had one son. Ella died in

1931, leaving two children, one 7 years and one 18 months, who were raised by her sister, Seena.

3A. ARLENE WEHMEYER, born September 29, 1923, in Bremerton. Arlene married HAROLD JOE MARTIN of Manette. Arlene and Joe live in Manette. They have three sons.

3A1. WILLIAM "Bill" MARTIN, born in 1944 in Bremerton. Bill married PAMELA DAVIDSON. They live in Manette. They have two sons.

3A1a. TROY MARTIN, born March 3, 1967, in Bellingham.

3A1b. GUY MARTIN, born January 29, 1969.

3A2. JAMES MARTIN, born in 1948 in Bremerton. He married SUSAN WEBB and they live in California. They have two children, HILARY, born September 18, 1985, and WYATT, born October 12, 1986.

3A3. ALAN MARTIN, born in 1950 in Bremerton. He lives in Lacey.

3B. JOHN BLACKWOOD, born October 29, 1929. John married GAY BENDELE. They live in Seattle. They have two daughters.

3B1. ELLA BLACKWOOD, born in 1959 in Bremerton.

3B2. JULIE BLACKWOOD, born in 1969 in Seattle.

4. SEENA LEE, born May 12, 1905, in Minnesota. Seena married FREDERICK "Fred" DORMAN in 1921. Fred retired as chief quarterman in ordnance from the Naval Torpedo Station at Keyport in 1960. He died in 1969. Seena lives in Manette. Seena and Fred had one son.

4A. MICHAEL FREDERICK DORMAN, born September 11, 1945, in Bremerton. He is a professor at Arizona State University and lives in Tempe.

5. JOSEPHINE LEE, born July 8, 1907, in Minnesota. Josephine married OSCAR SIIRO in 1953. Oscar worked in the ordnance department at the navy yard. He died in 1984. Josephine lives on Warren Avenue.

6. CARL LEE, born December 10, 1908, in Minnesota. Carl married BLANCHE RICH in 1932. He retired as inspector in charge of immigration at Sumas. They live in Tacoma. Carl and Blanche have three children.

6A. LEILA LEE, born January 13, 1934, in Bellingham. Leila married WILLIAM LOEFFLER and they live in Hilo, Hawaii. They have four children: WILLIAM "Buddy," LEE, DANIEL and KATHERINE.

6B. CAROL MARIE LEE, born September 29, 1936, in Bellingham. Carol married THOMAS de WAN and they live in Florida. Carol and Thomas have six children: VAIL, EVAN, LYNN, DEAN, SANDRA and CLAY.

6C. EVAN LEE, born April 4, 1939, in Bellingham. Evan married MARILYN REDLEFF and they live in Tacoma. Evan and Marilyn have two children.

6C1. VIVIENNE LEE, born October 5, 1961, in San Francisco.

6C2. EVAN LEE Jr., born June 9, 1965, in Tacoma.

7. HAROLD LEE, born October 7, 1910, in Minnesota. Harold married PATRICIA BENNETT in 1937. Harold worked at Children's Hospital in Pennsylvania until his retirement in 1969, when he returned to Manette. Harold died in 1977. Harold and Patricia had one son.

7A. HAROLD LEE Jr., born September 18, 1939. Harold married JEANNIE COX and they live in Seattle. Harold and Jeannie have twins, born in Seattle November 22, 1977: DAVID and KATHERINE.

8. MABLE LEE, born October 13, 1915, in Manette. Mable married ERNIE DICKSON in 1935. They have no children.

LEWIS/PARR
By Charles Parr

Sheldon Lyons Lewis, born in Johnstown, Pa., March 17, 1861, came to Sheridan in 1903. With him were his wife, the former Lotta Green, born in Hamburg, Iowa, in 1862, and their daughter, Theo Leota Winnona Lewis, who was born at Man Creek, Colo., in 1891. Lewis worked as a helper machinist in Puget Sound Navy Yard. He died October 9, 1930.

Theo graduated from the eighth grade at Smith School in Bremerton, and from Union High School in Bremerton in 1910. She graduated from Bellingham Normal School in 1915. She taught at the Sheridan and Olympic View School in Bremerton until she retired in 1958.

She often told of rowing across the bay with two other students to attend Union High School; when the weather was not good enough she would ride on a boat that stopped at Lent Lane to pick up or unload.

She was active in Philathea Chapter of Eastern Star, the retired teachers organization and Sheridan Home Economics Club. Theo was a school board member of the Sheridan School.

She married Chadwick M. Parr of Great Falls, Mont., on December 23, 1917.

Chadwick was an auto mechanic in Montana and Manette. He also had a battery shop in Manette. Chadwick retired from PSNS as an electrician. He belonged to Philathea Chapter of Eastern Star and to the Electricians' Union.

After Theo retired she traveled with Chadwick until his death in 1963, and alone or with friends later. Theo died in 1981.

GENEALOGY
CHADWICK and THEO PARR had three sons.

1. NED ARTHUR PARR, born December 27, 1919, in Nampa, Idaho. Ned attended Manette, Sheridan and Lincoln Schools and graduated from Bremerton High School. He worked at Puget Sound Naval Shipyard and at Bangor as a machinist. He married CLARA CARDWELL of Louisville, Ky., in 1944. Ned died May 20, 1981. He and Clara had four children. NED ARTHUR, born June 29, 1946, lives in Spanaway; FRED RICHARD, Ned's twin, born June 29, 1946, lives in King County; JULIE ANN, born November 26, 1952, lives in Wenatchee, and TERRY RAY, born July 18, 1961, lives in Bremerton.

2. JAMES LEWIS PARR, born July 19, 1921, in Sheridan. James attended Manette, Sheridan and Lincoln Schools and graduated from Bremerton High School. He married CHLOE MORRIS. James worked at Puget Sound Naval Shipyard as a machinist. He is now retired.

3. CHARLES SHELDON PARR, born January 24, 1924, at Sheridan. He attended Sheridan and Lincoln Schools and graduated from Bremerton High School. He married CLARICE MOSBARGER of Bremerton in 1947. He worked until retirement as a machinist at Puget Sound Naval Shipyard. Charles and Clarice have three children. SHELDON D., born May 3, 1952, lives in Bremerton; MARSHALL LEE, born October 4, 1953, lives in Bremerton and DARRYL A., born November 19, 1960. Darryl studied for the ministry in Lexington, Ky. He is now pastor of First Christian Church in Bethany, Ill.

LICHTER, NICHOLAS
By Loraine Lichter
1986

The Lichters came from Nelson Landing near Easton, Wash., in about 1913. They wanted to make a home in Manette. Nicholas "Nick" worked in the navy yard. Their home was on 10 acres between what is now East 18th and East 20th Streets west of Perry Avenue. Later they moved to 132 South Wycoff Avenue in Bremerton.

THE LICHTER FAMILY
NICK LICHTER (1866-1944) and his wife MARIE (1863-1939) were born in Germany. They had four children.

1. KATE LICHTER. She married HERB BRUCKMAN and they had two children: HUBERT "Hub" and MARY, who became Mrs. ZWISCHENBERGER. Mary is now deceased.

2. ANTHONY LICHTER. He married LUCILLE PAHRMAN and they had eight children: FRANK, now deceased; ROSE, who became Mrs. SCHULTZ; GEORGIA, who became Mrs. WENZL; ROBERT; MARGARET "Mickey"; DONNA, who became Mrs. WILKE; KATHLEEN, who became Mrs. KRANKEL, and TONY, now deceased.

3. C. NICHOLAS "Nick" LICHTER. He married LORAINE McLEOD and they live in Puyallup. Nick and Loraine had two children: WAYNE, now deceased, and LORNA LEE, who became Mrs. KLARICH.
Of the four Lichter children, Nick is the only one left. He is going strong at 89.

4. MARY LICHTER. She married JAMES STICKELS and they had three children: CHARLES, now deceased; JAMES, and LAVINA, who became Mrs. McNERNEY.

LILLEVICK, OLE
By Mable Lee Dixon
1985

Ole Lillevick (1869-1948) and wife Josefine (1869-1950) came to Manette from Minnesota in 1910, travelling with Evan and Jacobine Lee. Josefine and Jacobine were sisters; their maiden name was Hurlen.

Ole was a carpenter. Four homes he built still stand today south of Bremerton Gardens on Wheaton Way. Lillevicks lived in one of them, 1617 Wheaton Way. The others are 1611, 1613 and 1619 Wheaton Way. Ole worked in the navy yard with Evan Lee.

Josefine and Ole Lillevick.

LINDSEY, FRANK
By Goldie Lindsey Coutts
1986

The Lindseys—Frank D. Lindsey, my father, Rose Silva Lindsey, my mother, Joan, my sister and I—came to Tracyton in 1922 and to Manette in 1932. We lived at 1509 Perry Avenue. My father worked as a supply clerk at the navy yard.

Joan and I attended Manette School and then Lincoln Junior High and Bremerton High School. In 1935 when I was 12 I joined Girl Scout Troop 4 that was being organized in Manette with Neal Meredith as our leader and Hazel Callison as her assistant.

THE LINDSEY FAMILY
FRANK LINDSEY (March 1886-October 1976) and his wife ROSE SILVA LINDSEY (June 1903-April 1956) had two daughters.

1. GOLDIE MAE LINDSEY, born in Tracyton May 19, 1923. Goldie married EDWARD A. COUTTS. He has retired from the U.S. Army, civil service and the California school system. Goldie and Edward have two daughters.
1A. SHARON JOAN COUTTS, born in Bremerton March 21, 1941. Sharon married ANTHONY WAYNE FARLEY, now deceased. Sharon and Anthony had three children.
1A1. HEATHER MARY FARLEY. Heather married ROBERT PIERCE and they have one son, JUSTIN WAYNE.
1A2. NICOLE ADENA FARLEY.
1A3. DAMION WAYNE FARLEY.
Sharon is now married to WILLIAM OTTILIGE and lives in San Diego.
1B. VICTORIA ANN COUTTS, born in Bremerton June 26, 1947. Victoria married CLARK VAN WHY and they live in Grass Valley, Calif. Victoria and Clark have three children; LINDSEY ALLEN, LESLIE ANN and DENISE LYNN.

2. JOAN INEZ LINDSEY, born January 1, 1926, in Bremerton. Joan married CHARLES F. HAINES of Bremerton. They divorced and later Joan married THOMAS O. EVANS. Thomas has retired from the U.S. Navy. Joan and Charles had one daughter. Joan and Thomas have one son.
2A. CHRISTINE JOAN HAINES. Christine married MICHAEL S. DRAGICS. They have two children.
2A1. MICHELLE CHRISTINE DRAGICS, born August 10, 1968.
2A2. JASON TAYLOR DRAGICS, born October 24, 1969.
2B. LINDSEY ROBIN EVANS, born August 15, 1952, in Albuquerque, N.Mex. Lindsey married ELAINE REDDINGTON. They live in Albuquerque and have two children.
2B1. JENNIFER REDDINGTON, born December 16, 1969.
2B2. SEAN REDDINGTON, born May 29, 1973.

MARTIN, JAMES WILLIAM and HARRY
By June Martin Schweer and
Jeane Martin Turnell
1984

JAMES WILLIAM AND FLORA

James William Martin (referred to as "J.W." in newspaper clippings and other Manette records but known to us as "William") and Flora Palmer Martin arrived in Manette in 1893. With them was Flora's son Harry, 13.

William was from Indiana. Flora was from Rockland, Ill., born there in 1853.

Archibald "Asa" S. Martin, William's father, came to Manette from Indiana following the death of his wife in 1894. He lived in Manette for 19 years until his death at age 92 in about 1913.

James William Martin
-Photo from Kitsap
County plat book, 1909

William was county inspector of fruit pests and gave the following report at a monthly meeting of the Horticultural Society of Kitsap County: "Orchards containing 19,505 fruit trees had been inspected. This number...comprised one-fourth of the orchards of the county." At this meeting a report was given on late-keeping apples and samples of the following were shown: Red-Cheek Pippen, grown at East Sound, Orcas Island, and the Northern Spy, Swaar, Ben Davis and Laurien, grown at Lake Washington in Seattle.

William established Pacific Realty Company, one of Manette's early businesses, on the first dock. He then added a grocery and general store. Tracy Lumber Company—subsequently Parker Lumber Company—occupied this site later. Today The Narrows Apartments stand where William Martin built his first store in Manette. Harry went into business with his father. They built a new store across the road

Harry Martin family, 1929. Back row (from left), June, Harry, Jeane. Front row, Grant, Hattie.
-Photo from June Martin Schweer

from the dock and next to the family home. The year was about 1904. When the ferry dock was built at the foot of East 11th Street in 1916, Martin's grocery was moved to a new building at 2105 East 11th Street (occupied today by Manette TV).

Flora graduated from high school at age 15. She taught school until her marriage. She was a member of Elizabeth Ellington Chapter of Daughters of the American Revolution and Philathea Chapter of the Order of Eastern Star. She was a student of American History with a special interest in our Constitution. For many years she was an annual guest speaker at Manette School on Washington's Birthday, when she spoke to school children on what the U.S. flag and Constitution meant to her.

William died in Manette after a lingering illness in 1919.

Martin family members in front of home in the 1900 block of Perry Avenue, about 1900. From left are Harry, Asa, Flora and James William..
- Photo from Jeane Martin Turnell

Flora died in 1947. Her residence at the time was at 2315 East 11th Street.

HARRY AND HATTIE

Harry Martin was born in Rockford, Ill., in 1880. As a 13-year-old in Seattle he was a P.I. paper boy. He remembered the Seattle fire. He married Hattie Sutherland in 1911. Hattie was born in Kansas in 1891. They lived at 104 Winfield Avenue. They had three children. Harry died in 1950. Hattie lived in Manette until 1952. She died in Utah in 1970.

According to an item in the January 25, 1939, *Bremerton Daily News Searchlight* Harry rowed across the bay to Bremerton every day to attend school and was the first to graduate from that school's eighth grade in 1897.

Harry recalled one especially eventful trip rowing across the bay one foggy night when he was about 14. Flora was expecting a child. She started to miscarry and Harry was sent for the doctor in Port Orchard. He rowed unerringly to the Port Orchard dock. Harry brought the doctor to their Manette home but it was too late to save the baby. Harry then rowed back to Port Orchard with the doctor and home again through a solid blanket of fog.

As a young man of 21 Harry spent the winter from October

First home of Harry and Hattie Martin, 1020 Hayward Avenue. On porch are Hattie (left) and Flora. On the steps are James William, Harry's stepfather, and Harry.

-Photo from Jeane Martin Turnell

17, 1901, to about March 1902, in Council, Alaska — a day's trip by dog sled from Nome. This was during the Alaska gold rush. Harry was there to work his employer's claim, protect it from being "jumped" and oversee it during the winter. He returned to Manette and went into business with his stepfather.

Harry Martin was a Manette businessman for nearly 50 years. Harry took great pride in serving his customers. He sold on credit and delivered, as was the custom in those days. Deliveries were made by horse and wagon. Deliveries to Enetai homes were by motorboat.

Each spring Harry planted a vegetable garden in the rich black soil back of the store. Orders for beets, cabbage, carrots, spring onions, turnips, radishes, peas and string beans were filled fresh from the garden. When the sauerkraut crock was getting empty he would spend a Sunday afternoon grating his home-grown, big, fresh cabbages and filling the big stone crocks.

Daddy loved to play pool. In the evening he often went back to the grocery store office to finish the day's bookwork and then would ease up to "Slim" Aldrich's for a relaxing game of pool.

He belonged to the Masonic Lodge, the Elks, Knights of Pythias, Eagles and the Lion's Club.

Hattie was an experimental gardener for the U.S. Department of Agriculture. Big packages of assorted trees and plants fror all over the world arrived via freight delivery. Mother agreed to plant and care for the plants, observe their growth and send reports as to how they did in this area's soil, climate, etc. Our sun porch always had a fascinating assortment of weird looking plants in various stages of growth.

For many years Hattie made huge quantities of mayonnaise to sell in the store. It was ladled out into small cardboard cartons—the white ones that folded closed at the top and had little wire handles. Hattie also baked for sale delicious raisin spice cupcakes—we no longer have the recipe but the aroma lingers on.

Mother never stopped studying and learning. She belonged to the History Club and the Delphian Society that started in Manette in about 1930. Their study included music, poetry, cultures of the world and history. She joined the Sunshine Society that Ella Bender started in Manette; the Lady Lions, Women's Republican Club and the East Bremerton Improvement Club.

Many foods were bought in bulk and packaged in the store. We can remember the pickle barrel and peanut butter, crackers, peanuts being roasted in their shells and brown and white sugar in big barrels and boxes.

In 1938 Daddy bought a newfangled ice-cream machine that mixed and made soft ice cream. We made such amazing (if not memorable) flavors as licorice cherry—colored black—and many peppermint flavors. The ice cream machine made a wonderful product but could never take the place of Martin's soda fountain. There were real wire-backed chairs and little round tables. Patrons sat on high stools at the marble counter and watched as hand-operated soda and syrup dispensers were used to mix real ice cream sodas or root beer floats.

GENEALOGY

JAMES WILLIAM MARTIN came from Indiana in 1893. He married FLORA PALMER, who was born in Picatonica, Ill., August 13, 1853. William died in 1919. Flora died in Manette at age 94 in 1947.

1. HARRY MARTIN, Flora's son, was born in 1880, in Rockford, Ill. Harry, son of Samual Pedlar, was adopted by William Martin. Harry married HATTIE SUTHERLAND, born in Kansas in 1891. They had three children.
1A. JEANE MARTIN, born in 1916 in Manette. Jeane married WILLIAM TURNELL. Jeane lives in Seattle. Jeane and William have two daughters.
1A1. CAROL TURNELL, born in 1937 in Seattle.
1A2. JILL TURNELL, born in 1940 in Seattle.
1B. JUNE MARTIN, born in 1920 in Manette. June married WILLIAM SCHWEER and they live in Utah. June and Bill have three children.
1B1. KURT WOOD SCHWEER, born in 1944 in Bremerton. He now lives in California.
1B2. STEPHEN WILLIAM SCHWEER, born in 1947 in Bethesda, Md.
1B3. CYNTHIA JEANE SCHWEER, born in 1953 in Newport, R.I.
1C. GRANT MARTIN, born in 1922 in Bremerton. Grant married SHARI TAYLOR. Grant and Shari have three daughters: VALI, born in 1953, GABRIELLE, born in 1959, and CHANDRA, born in 1967.

MAWSON, EDITH (MRS. JOHN)
By Berenice Bouchard Root
1984

WESTERN MIGRATION

My maternal grandmother, Edith Louisa Bentley Mawson, was born November 26, 1862, in Argentine, Mich., to Gideon and Mary Case Bentley. Edith was the eldest of triplets, Edith, Mary and Edward.

Their mother died in another childbirth while the triplets were still very young. Their father remarried shortly thereafter and started another family. Apparently the burden of caring for the triplets along with her own expanding family overwhelmed his second wife and the triplets were separated and bonded out to other families. Edith was raised on a farm by a Scottish family named Bird. She was known as Edith Bird.

Edith worked as a practical nurse in Chicago. She met John Henry Mawson in Michigan. John was born September 4, 1862, in Georgetown, N.Y., to Ruben and Ann Carrol Mawson. Edith and John were married in 1888 in Flint, Mich., when they were both 25 years old. For 2 years they lived in Chicago, where John worked as a street car conductor.

In 1900 they moved to a farm in Popejoy, Iowa, where their three children were born: Mildred in 1891, Wendell in 1893,

Work party. At the Wendell J. Mawson home at 1810 Marlow Avenue in 1931 are (from left), George McKeown, Theresa Mawson and a friend, Bruce Walker.
- Photo from Berenice Bouchard Root

and my mother, Novella, August 1, 1898.

Grandfather's health began to decline and farming was hard work with little profit, so in 1904, when Novella was 6, the family of five took a train to the Pacific Northwest, settling in Tenino, south of Olympia, in Thurston County. Here Grandfather Mawson held a variety of jobs, among which were justice of the peace and notary public. He and my uncle Wendell also had a paper route.

Mildred married Jack Stevens. [see STEVENS, JOHN and LOUISE].

In 1914 my grandparents and Wendell, Novella, Mildred and Mildred's husband and children all moved to Condon, Oreg., hoping the desert air would be beneficial to Grandfather's health, but to no avail. He died there after a few months.

Grandmother Edith, along with Wendell and Novella, moved back to Tenino, where she took in boarders, cleaned houses and did private nursing.

It was in Tenino that Novella met her future husband, Archel "Archie" Joseph Bouchard.

KITSAP COUNTY

Grandmother Mawson and several other members of the family came to Kitsap County around the end of 1917 or early 1918.

They lived in the Central Valley and Brownsville area for a short time. Archie Sr. worked at a mill at the end of the lagoon in Brownsville. Some of the pilings from that mill are still visible.

TENT HOUSE

When Grandmother Edith and Uncle Wendell moved to Manette they lived in a tent house at East 18th Street and Marlow Avenue.

The neighborhood had many small houses built by a man named Price to house the families of the men who came to work in the navy yard.

Archie, Novella and Archie Jr. lived across the street from Mawsons at 1939 East 18th Street.

Edith found work as a maid at the old Navy Yard Hotel or, as it was later called, Craven Center.

Next door to the Mawsons on Marlow Avenue lived a young woman and her son, Theresa and George McKeown. Wendell courted Theresa and they were married in 1919 in the little brown house the Bouchards were living in on East 18th Street. They rented a small house near the tent house and in June 1921 purchased the two lots with the house. George McKeown resided in this house at 1816 Marlow Avenue until his death in 1985.

In the navy yard, Uncle Wendell experienced periodic layoffs common in those days. During these layoffs he would find work in Seattle or return to a lifelong hobby of photography, at which he was very adept. Most of the really good family pictures were taken by Wendell. During the Depression he took many fine photographs of the homes in Kitsap County. Wendell retired from Puget Sound Naval Shipyard in 1955 on medical retirement. He died in 1957 at age 63.

Aunt Theresa died in 1974 at 86.

In 1928 Grandmother Edith purchased a lot and small house at 1821 Winfield Avenue, adjacent to Archie and Novella's house.

Edith put her nursing skills to good use and, until she retired at 75, cared for invalids and sick people in their homes. One of her last patients was Dora Hansen of Tracyton.

Edith loved to play cards and was a member of the Jolly 16 Card Club along with Hazel Burton, mother of the Forbes and Burton children, close neighbors of ours.

Edith died in 1957 at age 94.

McKELVY, GEORGE WEBSTER
By Nancy Ann Bledsoe McKelvy
1985

MIGRATION TO MANETTE

George Webster McKelvy was born July 25, 1885, in Glenallen, Mo., just outside St. Louis. He moved to Kitsap County in 1906.

Hazel Lavina Whetstone was born November 29, 1895, in Medford, Oreg., and moved to Kitsap County in 1917.

Somewhere between Port Orchard and Manchester there was a hospital where Hazel Whetstone worked as a nurse's aide in 1917. George McKelvy drove a team of horses by the hospital daily in his job of delivering milk. He met Hazel and on December 22, 1918, they were married.

HOME AND FAMILY

The McKelvys lived in Manette at 2414 East 10th Street near Ironsides Avenue. Three children, Clara, Frances and George H., were born at home and two sets of twins were born in the Bremerton hospital. For the first set of twins the McKelvys' neighbor drove them around through Silverdale. Since it was late at night, the ferry between Manette and Bremerton was not running.

The family attended the Manette Community Church. The children attended Manette School, Smith School, Dewey Junior High School and Bremerton High School.

In 1926 George went to work as a sheetmetal mechanic at Puget Sound Navy Yard. He worked there until he retired in 1946.

GROWING UP IN MANETTE

In the '20s there were very few homes in the area of East 10th Street and Ironsides Avenue — mostly woods. The children would go down to the water to a place called "Wall's raft," and a neighbor, Grandpa Wall, would allow them to use a large rowboat with four oarlocks. They would row out into the Sound and spend the day fishing near the ferry light-buoy. Very little pollution contaminated the water those days. Large crabs could be picked up from the beaches and taken home to eat.

Just down Ironsides Avenue was a home bakery and the aroma of doughnuts drove the children wild. The children enjoyed the large playground that was built in the '30s at East 11th Street and Nipsic Avenue. It had a wading pool, swings, a tennis court and a ball field.

When winter came the children would go sledding down East 11th Street on a large sled owned by the Jacobsens. Axel Jacobsen owned a large automotive garage at East 11th Street and Perry Avenue. Jacobsen also owned a high-speed racing boat and the children liked to watch it race up and down the Sound.

In 1948 George and Hazel moved to Burley, and about 15

years later they moved to Banner Road in South Kitsap, and joined the Harper Evangelical Free Church.

In 1962 George took up hitchhiking within the United States and he continued hitchhiking until shortly before he died in 1976. Hazel died in 1969.

THE FAMILY

1. CLARA ANNABELLE McCKELVY, born in 1919 in Manette. Clara married AL QUICK in 1946. Al worked at Puget Sound Navy Yard until they moved to Portland, Oreg. Clara died in 1983 in Salt Lake City while on a vacation. Clara and Al had one child.
1A. HELEN LEE QUICK, born in Portland. Helen married ROBERT WYMORE. They had a daughter, MELISSA, born in Oregon.

2. FRANCES LOUISE McKELVY, born in 1921 in Manette. Frances married CHARLES HOUR in the 1970s. Charles worked at the Naval Supply Center, from which he retired. They live in Bremerton.

3. MAE VIOLET McKELVY, born July 18, 1923, in Bremerton. Mae married WILLIAM SAUER July 14, 1945, and they live at 5169 Banner Road SE, Port Orchard. William retired from NSCPS, Manchester. Mae and William have four children.
3A. VALERIE SAUER, born November 18, 1956, in Bremerton. Valerie married DAN BORAH. They divorced. Valerie married MICHAEL HART January 12, 1985, in Port Orchard at her parents' home. The Harts have three children: JEFFREY, born May 30, 1977; KRISTI, born October 29, 1978, and JUSTIN MICHAEL, born March 11, 1986.
3B. MIRIAM SAUER, born July 12, 1956, in Ellensburg. Miriam married KENNETH OLESON. They divorced. Miriam lives in Port Orchard. Miriam and Kenneth had three children: AMY, born March 13, 1973; BRIAN, born January 28, 1979, and AMANDA, born June 4, 1984.
3C. DANIEL SAUER, born January 23, 1959, in Bremerton. Daniel married PATTI BITTNER in September 1984. They live in Port Orchard.
3D. REBECCA SAUER, born June 3, 1960, in Bremerton. Rebecca married RICHARD ROBBINS. Rebecca and Richard live in Port Orchard. They have two children: TIMOTHY, born March 24, 1979, in Bremerton, and GREGORY, born January 16, 1984, in Bremerton.

4. JOHN EDWARD McKELVY, Mae's twin, born July 18, 1923, in Bremerton. John married TONI SAN MIGUEL. Toni died. John married JENNIE SWAN, who had a son, STEPHEN. John adopted Stephen. John and Jennie live in Pleasant Hill, Oreg. They have five children.
4A. STEPHEN McKELVY, born in California.
4B. ROBIN McKELVY. Robin married Daniel Compton. Robin and Daniel have two children, PRUDENCE and JENNIFER.
4C. STEVEN McKELVY. Steven and his wife GAYLE have one son, RYAN.
4D. JILL McKELVY. Jill married TIMOTHY CHASE.
4E. CARA McKELVY. Cara married KENT BOLES.

5. GENE AARON McKELVY, born December 11, 1927, in Bremerton. Gene married NANCY ANN BLEDSOE December 5, 1964. Gene retired from Naval Undersea Warfare Engineering Station (NUWES) at Keyport. They live in Bremerton.

6. JAMES WILLIAM McKELVY, Gene's twin. James married EDITH RIMPLE November 27, 1959. James retired from Naval Undersea Warfare Engineering Station. They live in Silverdale.

7. GEORGE HERBERT McKELVY, born March 9, 1930, in Manette. George married SHIRLEY SACKMAN. They divorced. George died March 5, 1982. George and Shirley had two sons.
7A. EDDY ALLEN McKELVY, born June 27, 1956. Eddy married HELEN TOMBLIN June 12, 1976. They have one daughter, MICHELLE MARIE, born April 22, 1983.
7B. JAMES JOSEPH McKELVY, born September 3, 1959. James married JOLENE O'DONOHOE October 15, 1983. They have two sons: PATRICK JOSEPH, born October 3, 1984, and ANDREW JAMES, born July 16, 1986.

McKEOWN, GEORGE
[See also MAWSON, EDITH, family history]
By Berenice Bouchard Root
1985

My step-cousin, George McKeown, became a resident of Manette in 1917. He was born June 29, 1911, in St. Louis and came here when he was 6. He went to Manette School and he

graduated from Union High School in Bremerton in 1929. He also attended Washington State College.

During World War II George worked for 4 years in Puget Sound Naval Shipyard as a sheetmetal worker. At the same time he and Orville Schultz ran Firhaven Trailer Park on George's property at East 19th Street and Marlow Avenue. After that he was a member of the Bremerton Fire Department. He owned and operated the M&M planing mill near the Kitsap County Airport until the mill was destroyed by fire.

George always enjoyed music. He sang and played drums with many different musical groups, such as the Jack Pine Ramblers and the Hometowners Band for dances and other events. He played at the Belfair Barn dance pavilion and for Shelton, Poulsbo and other senior citizens' groups.

George McKeown with his mother Theresa McKeown Mawson and Wendell Mawson about 1921. -Photo from Berenice Bouchard Root

George was a charter member of Boy Scout Troop 505 in 1926.

George loved old cars and was a good mechanic. He overhauled a Model-T Ford and built a body on it to act as a sleeping compartment. It was called a bug. George and Orville Schultz drove it to Yellowstone National Park in 1930 to work as camp roustabouts. In so doing they missed the opening of the new Manette Bridge.

George McKeown.

George died July 5, 1985, in Bremerton.

George married MYRTLE CULBERTSON of Belfair in 1946. They were later divorced. George and Myrtle had one daughter, DIANA.

DIANA married JIM VAN METER and lives near Belfair.

MEICHO, ALBERT
By Thomas Meicho
1986

Albert and Lillian Meicho moved to Manette during the middle '20s with their young daughter, Genevieve. Two more children were born to them here, I, Thomas, in 1929 and Richard in 1937. Albert was employed by Puget Sound Navy Yard as a machinist. There he remained until he retired. I think sometime in 1929 he was laid off for a few months.

My parents became active members of the Manette Community Church almost as soon as they arrived. Over the years, the church became the most important part of their lives. I remember them telling about being chaperones for the young adult group, which included Audrey and Bill Filion. I can remember my mother's work with Vacation Bible School, choir, various women's groups and other meetings. They both taught Sunday School classes. My father taught the high school class for years. I can still see him leading the singing for Sunday evening service when I was a teenager.

If there was a project that required someone to repair or fix something at the church, my father was there along with several other men of the church.

Lillian and Albert Meicho.

My father was the first Scoutmaster of Scout Troop 505 when the troop formed in 1926.

My life in Manette could be divided into two periods, one at what we called the little house on Perry Avenue and the other the big house at 1610 Hayward Avenue. In this loving and nurturing environment I grew up accepting the church and Jesus Christ as Lord and Savior. The activities and programs of the church were natural for me. It was a way of life.

Other images I remember are a kaleidoscope of impressions —potluck suppers with tables laden with food; Bible study classes with Mrs. Wall and Reverend Cooper and the Bible classes he taught in his home; visiting ministers or staff from Linfield College at our Sunday dinner table; the fire that destroyed the church building; the tears that fell from our eyes as we watched our church go up in flames; Reverend Phil Graf; church in the grade school; the radio scripture readings; youth meetings and activities. As these images come to mind

now, my parents are always in the foreground.

My father and mother worked hard to construct the new church. They were just one of the many couples who gave of their lives to make certain that the church would be rebuilt.

Before my parents moved from Manette and Bremerton, their letters always had reference to their life with the church. The church was their life. Even when they moved to Woodburn, Oreg., and joined the Calvary Baptist Church in Salem, their hearts were always with the Manette church. They looked forward to their return trips to share in the life of the congregation.

There are no plaques listing their names or listing the work they completed. They were honest people who believed in their church and were happy to give any way to it. There were probably many others who will be remembered because of Albert and Lillian's leadership. In their own unique, quiet way they served their Lord Jesus Christ and His church in Manette.

THE MEICHO FAMILY
ALBERT O. MEICHO was born January 22, 1895, in Springfield, Ill. He died in Woodburn, Oreg., September 28, 1978. His wife LILLIAN was born October 20, 1900, in Oklahoma City, Okla.; she died April 6, 1974, in Woodburn, Oreg. Albert and Lillian had three children.

1. GENEVIEVE MEICHO, born May 7, 1922. Genevieve attended Sunday School and Vacation Bible School at Manette Church. She attended Manette School. She joined Girl Scout Troop 4 in Manette when she was 12. Genevieve died of pneumonia in Bremerton March 3, 1936.

2. THOMAS MEICHO, born January 27, 1929, in Bremerton. Thomas attended Manette Church Sunday School and Vacation Bible School, Manette School and Lincoln Junior High School. He graduated from Bremerton High School in 1947. Thomas married JEAN WOEST of Yakima in 1950. Thomas graduated from Linfield College in 1951 and from Berkeley Baptist Divinity School in 1954. He was ordained in Manette Community Church in 1954 and served as minister at Lincoln Heights Baptist Church from 1954 to 1957. He has served as admissions counselor, dean of admissions, at Linfield College since 1957. Thomas and Jean have two children.
2A. JAQUELINE JEAN MEICHO BRYANT of McMinnville, Oreg.
2B. GRANT THOMAS MEICHO of Los Angeles, Calif.

3. RICHARD MEICHO, born August 20, 1937, in Bremerton. Richard attended Manette Church and Manette and Bremerton schools. He served in the U.S. Army. He married POK NAM CHOM January 17, 1972. They live in Tacoma. Richard and Pok have one child, MARY INYONG.

MEREDITH, JAMES W.
By Estelle Meredith
1984

MIGRATION TO MANETTE

James Whitfield Meredith came to Walla Walla from Sherman, Tex., with his wife, Marinda Cain Meredith, and their sons Clyde and Fred in 1888, before Washington was a state. They returned to Texas, where another son, Ralph, was born. They then moved on to Oregon to take up a homestead near The Sisters Mountains. James had a store and post office in Oregon on their homestead. They returned to Walla Walla, where a fourth son Malcolm was born, and then came to Seattle. In 1903, J.W. Meredith opened a grocery store on Yesler Way in Seattle.

In 1913 J.W. Meredith traded this store for one at 1102 East 11th Street (at that time Telegraph Avenue) in Manette owned by Harry Martin. This transaction marked the establishment of the Merediths in Manette.

The store that J.W. obtained from Martin was a building with a history. It was originally built by Mr. Lehea for George Fellows in 1904. It is still owned by Estelle Meredith and now rented to "The Gamesters" [see BUSINESS].

FAMILY, FUN AND BUSINESS

Clyde owned a grocery store in Seattle's Green Lake district. He sold that store to form a partnership with his father in Manette.

Clyde married Estelle Outland in 1922.

Estelle was born in Woodland, N.C., in 1894 and came west in 1912 to visit her brother Claude Outland in West Seattle. She worked in his safe-deposit vault in Seattle, then went to Anchorage for 2 years. There she met the Scott Wollovers. After returning from Alaska Estelle came to Manette to visit the Wollevers, who also had returned from Alaska. It was here she met Clyde Meredith.

The night Clyde and Estelle returned to Manette from their honeymoon on Vashon Island, Clyde's Masonic Lodge friends and their families gave the couple a shivaree. Children performed a mock wedding, then celebrated the return of the newlyweds with a chorus of tin pans and other loud noises. Scott Harrington handled the tin pans up the street. There were about 60 people at the Meredith home at 1113 Scott Avenue. J.W. Meredith brought half a barrel of candy from the store and left it on the porch for guests. Nellie Peterson and Marinda Meredith made punch. Joe Tennis, Clyde's cousin, who had a bakery next to the grocery store, made pastries in his brick oven. News of the gathering was broadcast over the radio the—first broadcast from Manette— by Harold Moodie. Friends phoned from Seattle and Tacoma to report that they had heard the program.

Clyde enlarged a small house near his parents'. Their first child was born while they lived in this home at what is now 1106 Pitt Avenue.

Clyde's mother Marinda died February 28, 1925. Clyde, Estelle and their infant daughter Maryjayne moved back to 1113 Scott Avenue to care for J.W.

Clyde and Estelle's son James Lee was born July 4 the following year.

James Whitfield Meredith died in 1927.

Clyde enjoyed camping and fishing in the Olympics with his family. He also went hunting every fall. Some of his hunting partners were Herman Waugh, Renus Bender, Lewis Bender, Jack Carlaw, Warren "Whitey" White and Joe Sibon.

Estelle and Clyde Meredith.

Fred worked in his father's grocery store and was a volunteer fireman in Manette. He married Minnie Odom of Seattle. Fred and Minnie had a son, Fred, known as Fritz. Minnie worked in the grocery store for a few years. Later they moved to Seattle.

Ralph worked in the grocery store, then went to Yakima, where he worked on Charlie Gibson's cattle ranch. He returned to Manette with his wife, Florence. They lived on Shore Drive, next to Cowans and near Von Hoenes. Ralph worked at the state liquor store in Bremerton. After Florence died, Ralph married Pearl, Bruno Lund's widow, of Enetai Beach. They lived in Clyde's "little house" next to Feek's on Pitt Avenue.

Malcolm delivered groceries and worked in his father's grocery. Later he worked with Laverne Painter and Axel Jacobsen in a garage at what is now East 11th Street and Perry Avenue. Tom Bright had the garage earlier. Malcolm married Neal Harrington in 1922 and later worked in the transportation division at Puget Sound Navy Yard. He was a member of Steadfast Lodge and enjoyed fishing. He and Neal shared a summer home on Hood Canal with Neal's parents. Here they entertained many of their friends and family. Malcolm played his accordian to accompany singing around a campfire. They lived on Shore Drive, then built a new home at 1129 Scott Avenue adjacent to Neal's mother and stepfather, Nellie and Nels Peterson. Neal was the first leader of Girl Scout Troop 4 in 1935. She is still a member of Philathea Chapter of Eastern Star. After Malcolm retired, he and Neal spent their winters in Apache Junction, Ariz., and enjoyed collecting, cutting and polishing rocks.

Marinda and James Whitfield Meredith.

Meredith home at 1113 Scott Avenue.

DEVELOPING A BUSINESS AND A TOWN

Manette had dirt streets and board sidewalks. There were three electric street lights: one on the ferry dock, one in front of Meredith's store and one at East 11th Street and Nipsic Avenue.

Freight came from Seattle or Tacoma by boat. The steamer *F.G. Reeve* started its run from Seattle three times each week and made stops at Bainbridge Island, Illahee, Manette, Tracyton and Silverdale. The Merediths and other store owners sent their trucks to the dock to pick up freight.

Passengers went from Manette to Bremerton on a ferry. The last ferry from Bremerton to Manette left at 11:30 p.m. Missing the last boat home meant hiring a taxi to drive the 20 miles around Dyes Inlet through Silverdale or renting a boat from someone and rowing to Manette. Scott Harrington drove the family around the inlet the night J.W. Meredith was dying.

The main floor of the grocery store and the boardwalk in front were at the same height as the horse-drawn wagons that picked up and delivered hay, feed, hardware and groceries. The building was lowered when Manette installed concrete sidewalks. The upper floor was used for the Mason's Steadfast Lodge meetings, Saturday night dancing and Eastern Star's Philathea Chapter. East Bremerton Improvement Club, Scouts, Works Progress Administration officials and Rejene Croxton's ballet classes met here, as did many other groups. During World War II, various volunteers met to sew, knit and collect supplies to support servicemen's families.

After J.W. Meredith died, Clyde managed the grocery business until he retired in 1944. Among the clerks who worked in the store were Bernice Carlaw, Lawrence Root and Grace McNeill. Among those who delivered groceries for the store

were Malcolm Meredith, Willard Muller, Herman Avery, Clifford Waltenberg and Ray Nosker of Manette and Don Erickson of Poulsbo. [See BUSINESS.]

RECREATION

Clyde was an active member of the EBIC and a long-time treasurer of Steadfast Lodge. Estelle belonged to Delphian Society, Garden Club, and Philathea Chapter, and was worthy matron in 1935. She was assistant leader and then leader of Girl Scout Troop 4. Clyde and Estelle belonged to Star and Compass Card Club and the 500 Card Club. During retirement, Clyde and Estelle enjoyed traveling through the Western United States and Canada.

Clyde died in 1962.

Estelle lives in the Meredith home at 1113 Scott Avenue, where she entertains her family and friends. She enjoys woodcarving and stamp collecting and is a charter member of the Bremerton Stamp Club.

FAMILY

Clyde and Estelle had a daughter Maryjayne and a son James.

Maryjayne attended Manette School, graduated from Bremerton High School in 1941. She then graduated from the University of Washington as a nurse. Her husband Dick Hladky studied electrical engineering at the University of Washington and Seattle University. Dick and Maryjayne live in Suquamish. They have two sons, Richard Jr. and Clyde Joseph.

Richard Jr. established a sailmaking business in the upstairs of the Meredith store building. He is now publisher and managing editor for *Waterlines* magazine in Seattle.

Clyde Joseph worked for Trans World Airlines and in an accounting office for the University of Los Angeles. He now lives in Sacramento and is an accountant for the California Department of Transportation.

James, also known as Jim, attended Manette School, Lincoln Junior High School and Bremerton High School. During World War II he left school to work in the navy yard, then served in the army in Japan at the end of World War II. James married Norma Silvernail. They live in Parkwood East. Before retirement James worked as an engraver in the navy yard. James and Norma have two children, Cora Lee and Timothy.

Cora Lee and her husband Gene, who is in the submarine branch of the navy, live in Connecticut with their four children.

Timothy, who is in the air force, recently returned to California from Germany. Tim, his wife Kim and their three daughters live near Sacramento.

GENEALOGY

JAMES WHITFIELD MEREDITH was born May 18, 1857, in Baltimore County, Md. He married MARINDA CAIN, who was born in 1859. Marinda died in 1925; James died November 10, 1927. They had four sons:

1. CLYDE MEREDITH, born November 21, 1885, in Sherman, Tex. Clyde married ESTELLE OUTLAND in 1922 in the First Methodist Church in Seattle. Clyde died in 1962. Clyde and Estelle had a daughter and a son.
1A. MARYJAYNE MEREDITH, born February 15, 1923, in Manette. She married RICHARD HLADKY, from Iowa. They have two sons.
1A1. RICHARD HLADKY Jr., born November 26, 1945, in Bremerton. Rich attended schools in Seattle and graduated from Kirkland High School. He studied physics at the University of Washington. During the Viet Nam War he was assigned to the White House Communication Agency on

President Johnson's Ranch in Texas. He married SANDRA KNOPF. They divorced. Rich lives in Winslow on a sailing trimaran he built. Rich and Sandra have one son.

1A1a. SCOTT HLADKY, born in Fredericksburg, Tex., in July 1968.

1A2. CLYDE HLADKY, born February 22, 1949, in Seattle. Clyde attended schools in Kirkland and Merritt Island, Fla. He went to the University of South Florida in Tampa and graduated in Los Angeles.

1B. JAMES LEE MEREDITH, born July 4, 1926, in Manette. James married NORMA SILVERNAIL of Manette and they have a daughter and a son.

1B1. CORA LEE MEREDITH, born in 1960 in Bremerton. Cora married GENE MILLER. They live in Connecticut with their four children.

1B1a. JAMES DAVID MILLER, born June 22, 1977, in Bremerton.

1B1b. GEOFFERY MICHAEL MILLER, born August 25, 1982, in Bremerton.

1B1c. TIFFANY TABBATHA KAREN MILLER, born September 20, 1984, in Connecticut.

1B1d. ALICIA MARIE MILLER, born September 3, 1986.

1B2. TIMOTHY MEREDITH, born in April 1962. Tim married KIM MICHELLE FRYDAY. Tim and Kim live in California with their three daughters.

1B2a. AMANDA MEREDITH, born March 22, 1983, in Germany.

1B2b. AMY MEREDITH, born August 21, 1984, in Germany.

1B2c. ELIZABETH MEREDITH, born December 9, 1986, in California.

2. FRED MEREDITH (1888-1926), born in Sherman, Tex., married MINNIE ODOM of Seattle. Fred and Minnie had one son.

2A. FRED "Fritz" MEREDITH, born in 1913. Fritz retired from the marine corps and lives in California. Fritz has three children, triplets, born February 8, 1943: ALEX ANTHONY, HENRY WOODIS and CHARLES CLARK.

3. RALPH MEREDITH (1895-1962), born in White Wright, Tex. Ralph and his wife FLORENCE (LOAN) lived in Yakima, then Manette, on Shore Drive. After Florence's death Ralph married PEARL LUND.

4. MALCOLM MEREDITH (1903-1970), born in Walla Walla. Malcolm married NEAL HARRINGTON, whose stepfather was Manette pioneer Nels Peterson. Malcolm died in 1970 in Bremerton. Neal married James Setser and lived in Port Orchard. Jim Setser died in December of 1981. Neal lives at Resthaven in Bremerton.

MINER, ALLEN
[See also STONE, EDWARD]
By Esther Miner Westover
1985

Allen Miner, born in Morton, Wash., in 1892, lived with his mother Anna Miner at 1805 Perry Avenue. Allen married Helen Voigt from Sheridan about 1929. They lived in the house on Perry Avenue until about 1942, when they built a new home on East 18th Street.

Anna Miner died in 1939.

Allen and Helen started greenhouses at the Perry Avenue address. They sold the house about 1942 to the Acme Florist people.

Allen had two brothers, David and Henry. David also lived in Manette. He married Esther Stone.

Allen died in 1984 at age 96.

Allen's brother Henry lived in Port Orchard. After his wife's death in about 1974, Henry married Zelma Jensen and lived in her house on East 16th Street and Trenton Avenue until his death in 1984 at age 96.

MOTTNER, ANTON ALEXANDER
By Valla Mottner Hage
1984

Anton Alexander "Tony" Mottner, our father, was born in Milwaukee, Wis. Prior to moving to Manette he lived in Colville, Wash., where he met and married Martha Marie Verrell. He had a butcher shop in Colville. After a short while they moved to California and lived with his brother Louis.

The Louis Mottner family in later years moved to Washington and settled in the Tracyton area.

From California the Tony Mottners moved to Bellingham, where father owned and operated a service station. The Depression that hit in 1929 forced him to leave this business, and he was one of the fortunate people who was hired as "temporary help" in Puget Sound Naval Shipyard. The "temporary" job in Transportation lasted until about 1949, when a bad heart forced his retirement.

A HOME IN MANETTE

In 1930 Father built a new home at 2606 East 10th Street, where we resided until Father retired. He sold the house and lived in Harper until his death in 1950.

We have many fond memories of the house he built in Manette and of neighbors and friends, who included the Theodore "Tate" Peterson, Frank Clay, Thomas Pidduck, Oscar Etten and Earl Harkins families; also my best girl friend, Genevieve Peters, who lived on Shore Drive.

There were four children in our family, Dick, Marjorie, Valla and Laura.

Mottner family, about 1934. From left, Marie, Tony holding Ernestine, Richard, Marjorie and Valla at their home, 2606 East 10th Street.

-Photo from Valla Mottner Hage

DICK MOTTNER

In 1942 Dick married Virginia Gillard, whose family lived on Shore Drive. Her brother Harold still lives in their family home. Dick and Virginia had two sons. Dick was a heavy-equipment operator. His work for various companies took him from the middle of the Arizona desert to a glacier near Juneau and to Kodiak, Alaska, to repair a dike after the Alaska earthquake of 1964. He now resides in the south during the winter and on Olympic Peninsula in the summer. Dick and Virginia's home is a huge travel trailer and truck.

MARJORIE MOTTNER DILL

In 1947 Marjorie married Richard Max Dill, who worked at PSNS until retirement. Marjorie is an accomplished pianist and organist. She took piano lessons from Mrs. Drum. For many years she played at local functions, at the Masonic Temple or over Meredith's Red & White store where the East Bremerton Improvement Club met. Sometimes sister Valla joined Marjorie for piano and organ duets, such as the ones played at Manette Community Church for family night potluck dinners. Marjorie was employed by the *Bremerton Sun* as secretary to the business manager. She and her husband Richard now live near Allyn. They have two daughters.

VALLA MOTTNER HAGE

Valla recalls popcorn-ball sales at the Manette Playfield carnival. Reverend and Mrs. Walter Laetsch popped the corn and made the popcorn balls, and Margaret Laetsch and Valla sold them.

Valla married Clifford Hage in 1943. They have two daughters.

In 1952 they moved to Anchorage, Alaska, where they stayed for 11 years. Valla is an accomplished pianist and organist. Her time is filled with music and other hobbies of painting, gardening, and handwork. Valla and Cliff were fortunate to be able to buy back the family home in Manette on their return from Alaska in 1963. They lived there until 1978, when they moved into a new home Cliff built on Benson Lake in Mason County.

Clifford was a painting contractor. He then worked for the Bremerton School District until his retirement September 1, 1984. Valla worked as bookkeeper in CPA offices and later as credit manager and bookkeeper for Parker Lumber Company until 1979.

LAURA ERNESTINE MOTTNER TIMBES

Laura Ernestine Mottner was born in Manette in January 1933. She attended Manette Grade School, George Dewey Junior High School and Bremerton High School. In 1950 Mottners moved to Harper. In 1952 Laura went to Alaska with her sister Valla, driving the Alcan Highway with Valla's two small daughters. Laura remained in Alaska, where she married Jack Timbes in Anchorage in 1953. Laura gained a stepdaughter, Jack's Rozanne, who lives in Anchorage. Jack retired in 1980 from Elmendorf Air Force Base, where he was foreman of the propeller shop. Laura cooked at the Elks Club, worked for the First National Bank of Anchorage and then for Anchorage Telephone Utility. She retired in 1980 from Washington Hardware Company, where she worked as office manager and outside salesperson. Her hobbies include fishing, gardening, gourmet cooking, knitting, crocheting and doing charcoal drawings.

FAMILY
The descendants of ANTON and MARTHA MOTTNER are:

1. RICHARD MOTTNER, born in 1921 in Colville Wash. Dick married VIRGINIA GILLARD of Manette in 1942. Dick and Virginia have two sons.
1A. RICHARD MOTTNER Jr., born in 1944 in Manette. Richard married CHERYL MORGAN. They live in LaCenter, Wash. Richard works in Portland. He and Cheryl have five children: RICHARD III; KIM; and triplets, JOHN, LESLIE and LYNN.
1B. ROY MOTTNER, born in 1947 in Manette.

2. MARJORIE MOTTNER, born in 1922 in Colville, Wash. Marjorie married RICHARD M. DILL in 1947. They have two daughters.
2A. LINDA DILL, born in 1948 in Bremerton. Linda married FRANCIS OLSON and they have four children: MARK EDWARD, CAROL JEAN, RICHARD SVERRE and SARAH.

2B. LOUISE DILL, born in 1950 in Bremerton. Louise married ROBERT A. HARRIS. They have two children: PAMELA MARIE and JOSEPH WILKES.

3. VALLA MOTTNER, born in 1925 in Colville, Wash. Valla married CLIFFORD HAGE in 1943. Valla and Clifford have two daughters.
3A. TRENA HAGE, born in 1944 in Everett. Trena married ERROL J. DARLING in 1969. In 1977, Trena married KEVIN BOARDWAY. They live in Port Orchard. Trena and Errol had two daughters. Trena and Kevin have one daughter.
3A1. JAMI LINN DARLING, born July 15, 1970, in Seattle.
3A2. JAHNA PETRINA DARLING, born April 12, 1973, in Vancouver, B.C.
3A3. MEGAN MARIE BOARDWAY, born March 4, 1978.
3B. TONI HAGE, born in 1946 in Bremerton. Toni married LYLE REED MULLER and they lived in Port Orchard. Toni and Reed have one daughter. Toni is now single.
3B1. TAUSHA LAYNE MULLER, born September 23, 1967, in Bremerton.

4. LAURA ERNESTINE "Ernie" MOTTNER, born in 1933 in Manette. Laura married JACK TIMBES in 1953 in Anchorage.

MULLER, CHESTER
By Willard Muller
1985

Chester Rudolph Muller was born in San Antonio, Tex., August 7, 1886. After graduating from Fredericksburg, Tex., High School, he worked on construction jobs in Colorado and Montana. Several years later, while employed as credit manager for a department store in Havre, Mont., he met and married the store president's secretary, Clara C. Hansen, daughter of Scandinavian immigrants to Minnesota. She was born and raised in St. Paul, where she attended business college after completing high school. When Clara's parents moved to Montana to homestead wheat land, she followed them west.

During World War I, Chester and Clara moved to Seattle with their young family of three boys, Ward, Willard and Kenneth. Their only daughter Corinne was born in Seattle on Armistice Day and their youngest son, Wayne, was born there the following year.

The family moved to Port Orchard in 1920, when Chester began working at the Puget Sound Navy Yard. He spent the rest of his working years in the shipfitter shop at PSNY, except for several years when he resigned to set up his own insurance business. He left that venture during the Depression to return to Puget Sound Navy Yard.

The family moved to Manette in 1923. They arrived with their furniture aboard a small chartered vessel at the Manette Dock. By previous arrangement, Oscar Hilstad was waiting with his team and wagon to haul the family and furniture to their new home (the old Bailey place) about 2 miles out Perry Avenue. After living in several other places in downtown Manette, they purchased their own home at 1718 Winfield Avenue in 1931. This remained the family home until after World War II.

Chester Muller was a sturdily built man, stood 6-feet-2, and was often recognized at a distance by friends because of his height and the straight-stem pipe he smoked. His hobbies were working on car engines, reading, hunting and fishing. He always regretted not having gone to college. From the time all five children were small, he encouraged them to plan to attend college. All four boys did, and Corinne became a nurse.

Clara's life was built around her family. Both parents helped their boys with their Scouting merit badge studies, and Clara was a member of the Manette Scout Mothers Club for

Muller home at 1713 Winfield Avenue.
-Photo from Berenice Bouchard Root

a number of years. All four boys were members of Troop 505, Manette, with Ward joining in 1927. Ward and Willard became Eagle Scouts. Kenneth and Wayne became Life Scouts, and Wayne was chosen Pacific Northwest representative to attend the World Scout Jamboree in Edinburgh, Scotland, in the summer of 1939.

All five children attended Manette Grade School, with the oldest three beginning there in 1923. All five were graduated from both Lincoln Junior High and Bremerton High School. Until 1930 they crossed daily to Bremerton aboard the *Pioneer.*

Following high school, Ward, the oldest son, worked as a carpenter's apprentice in Bremerton until World War II, when he joined the Army Air Corps as an aviation cadet. He was in a plane which caught fire during cadet training, and all six aboard had to parachute out. Ward received an injury and was given a medical discharge. After the war he studied engineering at the University of Washington for several years, then became a surveyor. Later, he organized his own surveying company in Port Orchard, which he operated for more than 30 years.

Willard worked 2 years (1934-36) at the Manette post office, following Floyd Buchanan in the job. The postmistress was Etta R. Harkins. As assistant postmaster, janitor and flag-raiser Willard saved enough to go to college. After graduating from Stanford University and the Maxwell Graduate School of Public Affairs at Syracuse University, he served as a junior naval officer, on a destroyer in the Pacific during World War II, advancing from ensign to lieutenant.

In 1945 he was stationed in Puget Sound Navy Yard. He spent nearly all his working career in the U.S. Department of State, where he achieved a top career rank. He was assigned in western Europe, Asia, Africa and Washington, D.C. He retired in 1973 with 33 years of service. After retiring he became a free-lance writer and dabbles in real estate.

Kenneth became a stockholder in the Parker Lumber Company in Manette following high school, and worked there until he entered the army during the war. He served in Australia and New Guinea and became a master sergeant. After the war he attended the University of Washington and spent 5 years as a log cost accountant for Weyerhaeuser. For the remainder of his career he has been a CPA.

Corinne studied nursing at St. Joseph's Hospital in Tacoma. She was working as a nurse at the Bremerton hospital when she met and married Robert T. Ohrt, who later became a career air force officer and jet pilot. Following his retirement from the service, he became a successful real estate broker and syndicator in Anchorage, Alaska.

Wayne, the youngest son, became an apprentice draftsman in the Puget Sound Navy Yard. After World War II he studied electrical engineering at the University of Washington, and spent his working career as an electrical engineer with the Navy Department in Bremerton and Washington, D.C. During the war he served as an enlisted man in the army in the Philippines and Japan.

Chester Muller died in 1940. Clara died in 1960.

DESCENDANTS
CHESTER and CLARA had five children.

1. WARD CHARLES MULLER, born December 11, 1914, in Havre, Mont. Ward married LYNN WEIRICH in 1943. They live in Port Orchard and have one son.
1A. LYLE REED MULLER, born in January 1944 in Bremerton.

2. WILLARD CHESTER MULLER, born May 7, 1916, in Havre. Willard married CAROLYN BUE in 1945. They now live in Port Angeles. Willard and Carolyn have three children:
2A. MAROLYN JEAN MULLER, born in August 1949 in Munich, Germany. Marolyn is now Mrs. RUSSELL.
2B. BARBARA ANNE MULLER, born May 4, 1951, in Washington, D.C.
2C. NANCY ELEANOR MULLER, born October 30, 1952, in Truk, Caroline Islands.

3. KENNETH LYLE MULLER, born June 18, 1917, in Havre. Kenneth married MILDRED STONE [see STONE, ERNEST] in 1944. They live in Marysville. Ken and Mildred have two children.
3A. CRAIG WILLARD MULLER, born September 9, 1954, in Seattle.
3B. TANYA SUSANNE MULLER, born October 19, 1955, in Everett. Tanya is now Mrs. POKSWINSKI.

4. CORINNE FAITH MULLER, born November 11, 1918, in Seattle. Corinne married ROBERT OHRT in 1943. They live in Anchorage and have two children.
4A. KATHLEEN SHARON OHRT, born April 8, 1948, in Moultrie, Ga. Kathleen is now Mrs. KENNEDY.
4B. ROBERT OHRT, born July 15, 1951, in Spokane.

5. WAYNE DWIGHT MULLER, born October 16, 1919, in Seattle. Wayne married VIRGINIA KETCHAM in 1943. Virginia is a niece of Eugene and Grace Jack of Manette. Wayne and Virginia have two children.
5A. LEANNA PATRICIA MULLER, born in March 1947 in Seattle. Leanna is now Mrs. WHISNANT.
5B. KEVIN DWIGHT MULLER, born in July 1952 in Bremerton.

NELSON, MARK A.
By Roger Paquette and Judy Mulhauser
1986

Mark A. and Grace Nelson moved their family from Plainview, Minn., to Manette in 1920. They lived at 1936 Perry Avenue. Three of their sons saw action during World War II in the European Theater. Two lost their lives there.

Sergeant John Y. Nelson, U.S. Air Force, a gunner on a B-17, met his death in a mid-air collision over England while returning from his 20th mission over Germany. He was permanently buried in Cambridge, England. He had a son, Ronald Owen Nelson.

Private First Class Clyde E. Nelson was killed on maneuvers in Italy on June 12, 1945, a bare 4 months after his brother John met his death. Clyde was attached to the ground crew of the 36th Air Depot Group. Services were conducted by the Reverend Sidney Cooper of the Manette Com-

Mark and Grace Nelson's home at 1936 Perry Avenue. 1987 photo.

munity Church and a tribute
was given by Earl Harkins,
long-time friend of the family. Participating at the inter-
ment in the veterans' plot at
Ivy Green Cemetery was the
John and Clyde Nelson Post
7498 of the VFW. Honorary
pallbearers were Darwin
Johnston, Ray Nosker,
August Halverson, George
G. Baker Jr. and Ward and
Kenneth Muller.

Clyde Nelson.

Another son, Neil F. Nel-
son, returned from the war
and moved to Monterey,
Calif. He was a corporal in
the 515th Field Artillery. Two other sons, Marion E. and Mark
Nelson, settled in Virginia. There
were two daughters, Genevieve
(Mrs. Frank Hawes) and Julia
"Judy." The Nelson family was active in Scouting, the Moose Lodge
and other organizations.

Mr. Nelson died a few years
after John and Clyde, and Mrs.
Nelson died in 1952.

Judy married Charles Eslick and
their daughter Janet was born in
Bremerton. When Charles died
Judy moved to Missoula to be near
Janet.

Judy Nelson Muhlhauser.

A national magazine, *Women's Household,* had a feature about how a doll-making hobby of Judy's had expanded to a full-time project of creating toys of all descriptions for ill and under-privileged children. The toys were shipped to hospitals and homes throughout the West, Canada, England and even Vietnam. While living in Missoula, Judy met and married Ted Muhlhauser.

Judy has been featured in Missoula as senior-of-the-month. After Ted died Julia volunteered full time to the Missoula

Senior Citizen Center and her church. Although Julia depends on a cane since she had a stroke she says "quit is just a word in the dictionary."

Julia's Aunt Merle married George Baker of Manette. Their children were Phyllis, who has passed away, George Jr. and Ruth.

FAMILY
MARK and GRACE NELSON'S descendants include:

1. MARION NELSON, born in Wisconsin in 1909, now deceased.

2. JULIA "Judy" NELSON, born in Wisconsin in 1911. Julia married CHARLES ESLICK. Charles died in 1959. Julia moved to Montana. Julia married TED MUHLHAUSER. Ted died in 1974. Julia and Charles had one daughter.
2A. JANET ESLICK, born in Bremerton in 1936. Janet married PAUL DOOLITTLE. Janet and Paul divorced. Later Janet married JACK MARTIN and lives in Montana. Janet and Paul had two children.
2A1. MIKE DOOLITTLE, born in Montana in 1952. Mike lives in Missoula, is chef at "The Rocking Horse" and is a drummer.
2A2. JOAN DOOLITTLE, known as Joanie. Joan married JOHN BEEKMAN and they live in Hawaii with their three children.

3. MARK NELSON, born in Minnesota in 1912. Mark's wife and family live in Bellevue.

4. GENEVIEVE NELSON, born in Minnesota in 1913. She married FRANK HAWES and they have one daughter, JUDITH. Judith married WAYNE WALKER. Both families live in California.

5. CLYDE NELSON, born in Minnesota in 1914. He did not marry. Clyde died in Italy in 1945.

6. JOHN Y. NELSON, born in Minnesota. John died in England during World War II in 1945. John had one son, RONALD OWEN NELSON, born in Bremerton.

7. ARLINE NELSON, born in Minnesota in 1917. Arline died in 1921.

8. NEIL F. NELSON, born in Minnesota. He attended school in Manette. Neil married ELAINE GRAFF. Elaine was killed in an auto accident while Neil was overseas. Later Neil married FRANCES O'DONELL. They have three children and live in California. One of their children, NEALANN, married VINCENT BRADLEY. Nealann and Vincent have four children and live in California.

OLSEN, EMIL
By Bonny Olsen Pettit
1985

The Emil Olsens arrived at MacTeigh's Garden Tracts in 1924. The address of their property today is 1622 Jacobsen Boulevard. They moved from Bremerton. Emil was the eldest son of the Rudolph Olsens of Bremerton and Whidbey Island. Emil was born in Minnesota in 1884 and came west when he was 3. He began working in the navy yard in 1898 as a boy of 14 and was in the first apprentice school. He was a supervisor in the outside machine shop and had worked in the navy yard 42 years at the time of his death in 1940.

Emil's wife Ethel was the daughter of the Andrew Gus Andersons and granddaughter of the Riley Hoskinsons, all early Bainbridge Island homesteaders. She was born in 1885 on Bainbridge Island, where her grandparents and mother settled in 1878. Emil and Ethel were married in Bremerton in 1910.

Emil and Ethel had two daughters, Bonny and Billie.

The Olsens were members of the East Bremerton Improvement Club.

Mrs. Olsen died in 1938 and the family moved to

Bainbridge Island, where Mr. Olsen died 2 years later.

Bonny and Billie live in Seattle and have fond memories of growing up in Manette. They attended Manette Grade School and Manette Community Church and were Girl Scouts.

Bonny was born in Bremerton in 1922. She graduated from Bremerton High School in 1939. She worked on the *Manette Gazette* and later worked on the *Daily News Searchlight* and the *Kitsap County News.*

Billie completed her education on Bainbridge Island and later worked for Aetna Insurance in Seattle. She married Jerry Randall of Bainbridge Island. Jerry is retired from National Oceanic and Atmospheric Administration (NOAA) and spent many seasons in Alaska with the Coast and Geodetic Survey. Jerry and Billie live in West Seattle.

GENEALOGY
EMIL OLSEN, born in Minnesota in 1884, married ETHEL ANDERSON, born on Bainbridge Island in 1885. They had two daughters.

1. BONNY OLSEN, born in Bremerton in 1922. Bonny married GAIL A. FOWLER. Bonny was divorced. Bonny married WARD PETTIT. Bonny and Gail had two children.
1A. ALLISON FOWLER, born in Seattle in 1950. Allison married ROBERT E. BERGSTROM Jr. Allison and Robert live in Seattle and have two children born in Seattle: KENDRA, born in 1975, and ERIK, born in 1978.
1B. THOMAS FOWLER, born in Seattle in 1952. Thomas married THERESA SCHULLER and they live in Seattle.

2. BILLIE OLSEN, born in Bremerton in 1928. Billie married JERRY RAN-DALL. They have four children.
2A. DEBRA RANDALL, born in Seattle in 1953. Debra married RON GARROW and they live in Kent.
2B. KAREN RANDALL, born in Seattle in 1954. Karen married ROGER HARRINGTON. Karen and Roger live in California.
2C. CHERYL RANDALL, born in Seattle in 1960. Cheryl married SCOTT STEWART. Cheryl and Scott live in Renton and have two sons born in Seattle: ANDREW, born in 1984, and KIRK, born in 1986.
2D. JERRY RANDALL, born in Seattle in 1967. Jerry lives with his parents while attending Highline Community College.

OLSEN, TOLLEF
By Gladys Olsen Solid
1984

FROM NORWAY TO MANETTE

My father, Tollef Olsen, was born in Stavanger, Norway, February 22, 1861. He and two brothers came to America in 1880. They went to Chicago and later moved to Marshalltown, Iowa. Tollef received his first naturalization papers in 1886 and final papers in 1908.

He married Lottie Severtsen. Lottie was born in Sandnes, Norway, in May, 1865. She came to America when she was 16. She came with her brother, who was 21.

Tollef and Lottie had nine children.

Tollef was a boilermaker and was the first man hired by Dave Lennox, founder of Lennox Furnace Company in Marshalltown. They made wood-and-coal-burning furnaces. The company still manufactures heating and cooling systems.

In September of 1907 Father received a provisional appointment at 65 cents an hour to work for about 2 years on the Isthmus of Panama as a boilermaker. He received free transportation on the steamer *Advance* from New York City.

In May of 1909 we moved to Salem, Oreg., where Father was employed as a boilermaker. In February of 1917 we came to Manette and he worked as a flange turner in the boiler shop of the navy yard.

Tollef and Lottie Olsen in 1917.
- Photo from Gladys Olsen Solid

Father received a certificate in 1918 from the government for "commendable work" on an improvement in the process of bending the plates for torpedo tubes. Production was increased from five plates to eight plates per day — 60 percent.

FRIENDS AND HAZARDS

I recall sledding down the hill on a bobsled in front of Hermanson's house in Manette. I was with Esther Karst, Len and Earl Bright and my sister Marguerite.

Mr. Wood had a store in the building shared by the old post office on the corner of East 11th Street and Perry Avenue. A side door of the store entered the post office. Etta Eggleston, who later was Mrs. Earl Harkins, was the postmistress and store manager. I worked in the store for her.

One day in 1920 when my father was coming home from Bremerton there was an accident at the Manette ferry dock. To get on and off the boat, passengers went down a ramp to a float. This time when the boat unloaded passengers the float flipped. The tide was running out. The weight of passengers pushing one side of the float down and the tide pushing the other side up was enough to turn it over. Dad was cautious. He decided, "Well, I'm not going to get off on that float until they're all off," and he held onto a post on the boat while the rest of them went into the water. One person drowned.

In 1923 Father and Mother returned to Salem. Father passed away in May of 1933. Mother passed away in October 1947.

Mother was a homemaker and a perfect mother. She had started the first Sunday School for Elim Lutheran Church in Marshalltown, Iowa. The first classes were held in our home in the 1880s. When we moved to Manette she enjoyed association with a group of Scandinavian women. They were Mrs. Jens (Minnie) Jacobsen, Mrs. Chris (Valborg) Jensen, Mrs. Ole Lillivick, Mrs. August (Marta) Wall and Mrs. Sanford Peterson. They sewed for the Children's Home in Poulsbo and enjoyed coffee hours.

Lottie Olsen and daughters, circa 1930. Back row (from left), Beatrice Fischer, Marguerite Bright, Gladys Solid, Lucile (Wilcox) Van Dyke. Front row, Lottie Olsen, Anna Anderson.

TOLLEF AND LOTTIE OLSEN'S DESCENDANTS

Of the nine Olsen children, four came to Manette: Anna, Lucile, Gladys and Margaret. Lucile, Gladys and Margaret attended Manette School.

1. ANNA OLSEN, born in 1885. She married ERNEST ANDERSON. They came from Salem, Oreg., to live in Manette for a time. Anne started the first cradle roll class at Manette Community Church. Ernest, a sheet metal worker, made a small church of metal, painted it and put a slot in the steeple for children to put their birthday pennies in. A bell rang when the pennies were dropped in. Ernest and Anne had four children.
1A. ESTHER ANDERSON, born March 29, 1905.
1B. CARL ANDERSON, born November 4, 1906.
1C. CONRAD ANDERSON, born in 1908.
1D. MARJORIE ANDERSON, born November 17, 1912.

2. CONRAD OLSEN, born in 1890.

3. LILLIAN OLSEN, born in 1892.

4. BEATA OLSEN, born in 1894.

5. BEATRICE OLSEN, born in 1895.

6. ORVAL OLSEN, born in 1897.

7. LUCILE OLSEN, born July 16, 1900. She came with her parents to Manette in 1917. Lucile married LUCIAN WILCOX, a navy yard boat-shop employee. They moved to Oregon in 1920. Lucian died in 1945. Lucile married VERN VAN DYKE in 1946. Lucile and Lucian's children were:
7A. HARRY WILCOX, born July 29, 1921. Harry was killed while serving on the destroyer *Brain* off Okinawa in 1945.
7B. MARY WILCOX, born August 15, 1922. Mary married RICHARD REMENTERIA. Mary and Richard had two sons and two daughters. RICHARD Jr., MARY, ANN and MICHAEL.

7C. MONICA WILCOX, born October 12, 1923. She married RICHARD LARSON. They have seven children: KYLE, born in 1946; SUZAN, 1948; LUCIA, 1950; MONICA, 1954; CELIA, 1958; ERIC, 1960; and JUSTIN, 1962. Monica divorced and later married DON McLEAN in Eugene, Oreg., in 1983.

8. GLADYS OLSEN, born August 21, 1902. I came to Manette in 1917. I married LLOYD C. SOLID. Lloyd was a machinist in the navy yard. In 1923 we bought property on Ironsides Avenue, north of the Manette School. On the property was an old crumbling water tower that had belonged to the Manette Water Works. Our contract for the property stated that when the tank was no longer used it would revert to whoever owned the property. We tore it down and used the timbers under our house when additions were made. The house is now 1327 Ironsides Avenue.
Lloyd enjoyed his home, gardening and fishing. He was a member of the Manette Community Church and worked diligently in the East Bremerton Improvement Club. Lloyd retired in 1952 with a heart disability. He passed away in January of 1969. I, Gladys, am a member of the Manette Community Church and a 66-year member of the Order of Eastern Star. I prepared hot lunches for Manette School children during 1923. I reside in Bremerton Gardens.
Gladys and Lloyd had one son.
8A. STANLEY SOLID, born July 3, 1922, in Portland, Oreg. He attended Manette School, Lincoln Junior High School and Bremerton High School. He was an army pilot and retired on a disability. Stan married NANCY JOHNSTON.
The *Manette Newsletter* of May 11, 1944, gives the following information: "SOLID COMING HOME. Stanley Solid, U.S. Army, his wife and their son will arrive here soon to visit his parents, Mr. and Mrs. Lloyd Solid, 1327 Ironsides Avenue. Stanley recently spent three months in the Army hospital at Gardener Field, Taft, Calif."
Stan and Nancy divorced. Stan married GLORIA PARK. Stanley died December 25, 1985. Stan and Nancy had two sons and a daughter. Stan and Gloria had one son.

8A1. STANLEY RICHARD SOLID, born December 16, 1943. Stanley lives in Santa Clara, Calif.
8A2. RAYMOND LLOYD SOLID, born September 25, 1945. Raymond lives in San Jose, Calif.
8A3. LARK SOLID, born September 27, 1950. Lark lives in Cupertino, Calif.
8A4. KARL SOLID, born in Long Beach, Calif., May 11, 1964. Karl lives in Olympia.

9. MARGUERITE OLSEN, born in 1904 in Marshaltown, Iowa. She came to Manette in 1917. She married LENNOX BRIGHT of Manette September 1, 1923. Marguerite enjoyed music and played piano and organ. Lennox died in February 1968. Marguerite died December 25, 1987. Marguerite and Lennox had a son and a daughter.
9A. LENNOX BRIGHT Jr. was born September 28, 1925. He married RUTH BURROUGHS. He and Ruth have two sons and two daughters: GREGORY BRIGHT, born May 16, 1954; KATHLEEN BRIGHT, born August 3, 1956; STEVEN BRIGHT, born November 4, 1958, and CAROLYN BRIGHT, born May 4, 1960.
9B. GLORIA MAY BRIGHT was born December 20, 1929. She married ELVIN LEONARD of Port Orchard. Gloria is now widowed and lives in Port Orchard. Gloria and Elvin had two sons and two daughters.
9B1. THOMAS LEONARD, born May 27, 1956.
9B2. PAUL LEONARD, born June 7, 1958.
9B3. KAREN LEONARD, born April 27, 1961. Karen is now Mrs. SANBORN.
9B4. BETTY LEONARD, born October 15, 1962.

OLSON, EDVARD
By Louise Ashenberg
With information from *Manette Newsletter*, May 11, 1944.

Edvard Olson bought 240 feet of waterfront in Manette and built his home at what is now 315 Shore Drive in about 1902. Ed worked for 24 years as a machinist in Puget Sound Navy

The Edvard Olson family. With Edvard (right) are (from left): son-in-law Ray Harris, wife Mathilda, daughter Esther (Harris) and daughter Hilda.
- Photo from Louise Parsons Ashenberg

Yard before retiring in 1934. Louise Ashenberg saved his badge #3839 from a bonfire.

In Sweden where he grew up, Edvard became interested in plants. A schoolmaster asked him to deliver horticultural specimens from the post office and express station to the student gardens. This was Ed's first exposure to the field of botany.

Ed's hobby was raising and developing roses. He constructed shallow rose beds enclosed in concrete frames that were 20-by-4-foot rectangles. Each rose bush was marked with a tag telling the year the plant was bred and its number. He numbered his roses rather than naming them. He main-

The Edvard and Mathilda Olson home at 315 Shore Drive.

tained a record book with information about each rose bush.

Ed was proud to display the roses he had nurtured from seed in his hothouse. He used a syringe to apply a measured amount of water to each young plant. Besides the expected red, pink and yellow roses some of his roses were a startling blue or green.

THE OLSON FAMILY

Edvard and his wife Mathilda had two daughters and one son. One daughter, HILDA, married PEDER SVENDSEN and moved back to Scandinavia, where she died. Hilda considered herself the last surviving member of the Olson family. She is now deceased. The other two children were ESTHER and JOHN.

PALMER, RICHARD
By Helen Palmer McCallum
and Thomas McCallum
1983

Richard Hugh Palmer was born in Angelica, N.Y., in 1893. He came to the Northwest in 1910 with some of his brothers. They traveled by train to Seattle, by steamer to Clallam Bay and by horse and wagon to Forks, where an older brother was farming.

Richard Palmer worked as a store clerk and a mail carrier. He carried the mail from Clallam Bay down the coast as far as the Hoh River.

In 1914 he married Delphine Merchant of Forks, and after a year they moved to Seattle, where he worked as a streetcar conductor.

With World War I they moved to Manette and both went to work in the shipyard. They lived in a duplex in Manette just off Trenton Avenue, later renting a house on the waterfront, now Shore Drive.

Dad had a beautiful banjo inlaid with mother-of-pearl. On summer evenings Dad would sit on the deck and play his banjo. I remember particularly "Drifting and Dreaming."

Many canoes and rowboats would stop near our house so the people aboard could listen to the music.

Mom wanted to live out far enough so she could have a cow, raise chickens and pigs and have a big garden.

In 1927 we bought a house on Cascade Trail near Trenton Avenue. I think I must have been 6 years old. People seeking directions to the Palmers' were told to proceed up Perry or Trenton Avenue to Cascade Trail and watch for the "red-heads." There were four of us, plus Dad: Martha, Helen, Phyllis, and Wayne.

The first years we lived on Cascade Trail our house had but two bedrooms. The folks put up a tent in the back yard and Martha slept there until an addition could be put on our house.

Mom bought a cow. It was a super cow, named Christmas, who gave us very rich milk. Mom sold the milk our family couldn't use to Meredith's store and to neighbors. When pasteurization was introduced for milk sold commercially the milk from our farm had such a low bacterial count that pasteurization was not required.

Martha was interested in learning to drive. Dad had a Model-A Ford at the time. Martha carefully watched Dad driving and one day while he was under the house doing something, she got in the car and drove off. Dad didn't mind.

Punishment for kids' pranks or mischief was dealt with promptly. No waiting until Dad came home. More than likely Mom would hand the faulty kid a kitchen knife to cut a "good" switch from the willow patch. This was brought back to Mom and she would use it on the culprit.

Mom was the flower gardener. Her specialty was the bearded iris. She knew them all by name and color and spent many hours poring over flower and bulb catalogs in the winter months picking and choosing new favorites to order when the time came. Dad grew the vegetables and dahlias and roses.

Sunday afternoon and summer day boredom was relieved with walks down through Pop Jensen's property to the canyon.

Strawberry time always reminds me of the Jensen strawberry fields. The local kids always worked then, although Martha was the only one of us old enough to help. I can still see Mr. Jensen standing at our back door with a dishpan full of so-called "culls" that he said were not good enough to sell. My mother made delicious jam from them.

Once while we were walking home from school we had a visitor follow us up Trenton Avenue—a baby deer had been separated from its mother and had been chased by dogs. When we ran, it ran. If we stopped, it stopped. We led it home and Mom managed to get a rope on it and feed it. Next she called the Woodland Park Zoo in Seattle. They sent someone over the next day to pick up the fawn.

The house on Cascade Trail was our family home until the deaths of our parents. Delphine died in 1963. Richard died in 1964.

GENEALOGY
RICHARD and DELPHINE PALMER had four children.

1. MARTHA ANNETTE PALMER, born in Forks in 1915. Martha married ALBERT WILLIAM RAPP. Martha worked as a clerk-typist and homemaker. Albert retired from the U.S. Navy. They are both deceased. Martha and Albert had six children: DELPHINE, now deceased, RICHARD, HUGH, WALLACE, KATHLEEN and WILLIAM.

2. HELEN JOYCE PALMER, born in Manette in 1920. Helen married THOMAS ALEXANDER McCALLUM whom the U.S. Army had sent to Manette in 1941. His unit placed anti-aircraft guns at Cascade Trail and Nip-

sic Avenue, not far from the Palmer home. Helen and Thomas now live in Port Orchard. They have four children.
2A. THOMAS LEE McCALLUM, born in 1944. Thomas married CHERYL SAMSON and they live in Port Orchard.
2B. JUANITA JOYCE McCALLUM, born in 1946. Juanita lives in Tacoma with her husband, ROBERT BRAND.
2C. DAWN ELIZABETH McCALLUM, born in 1950. Dawn married JAMES BORDER and they live in Manchester.
2D. ROBBIN EDGAR McCALLUM, born in 1954. Robbin lives in Port Orchard.

3. PHYLLIS JUNE PALMER, born in Manette in 1922. Phyllis married CORBETT FOYSTON. Phyllis was administrative assistant in the Seattle liaison office of Alaska Indian Affairs Bureau. Phyllis and Corbett live in Manchester.

4. WAYNE LEE PALMER, born in Manette in 1924. Wayne married HELEN JOSEPHINE. Wayne works at PSNS and lives in Manette. Wayne and Josephine have three children: PATRICIA, TERRY and KAREN.

PAQUETTE, JOSEPH A.
By Roger Paquette
1985

THE FAMILY'S BEGINNING

Joseph Alfred "Fred" Paquette was born in Lawrence, Massachusetts, in 1889. Fred was a machinist. He learned the machinist's trade in shoe factories in Lawrence and he worked for railroads in Montreal and Edmonton and lumber mills in Vancouver, B.C.

He first came to Bremerton as a crewman on the U.S.S. *Pennsylvania* about 1909. The area made an impression on him, and 16 years later he took a job in the shipyard and returned to settle with his family. He married Maria St. Pierre in 1914 in Montreal. Maria was born in Ontario in 1894. I was born in Montreal in 1915. My brother, Richard Hermas, was born in Edmonton in 1921.

We arrived in Manette on a warm summer day in 1925. We boarded the *Pioneer* in Bremerton and when it pulled out, Maria let out a shriek. She thought we were just sitting there waiting for the ferry to come in.

Fred and Maria Paquette, circa 1930.

The ride on that ferry was the first of thousands for us. The ferry went past Tracy's lumber yard and Ben Kean's coal and wood yard. The Paquettes saw the rest of the commercial area on the walk to our new home at what is now 1302 Perry Avenue.

First, at the upper end of the ferry slip, was the waiting room in which was located Hall's Confectionery. Adjacent to this was W.H. Hawkes' real estate office. Then up the dock was Aldrich's card room and smoke shop. Up on the brow of what is now East 11th Street we passed Stone's meat market, gas station and parking garage; Ben Kean's gas station; Martin's grocery; Meredith's grocery; a candy store; the post office; and finally, on what is now East 11th Street and Perry Avenue, Painter and Meredith's garage.

ANOTHER HOME

In 1926 we moved into a house Fred bought from the Allens at what is now 1624 Hayward Avenue. He put in several

Fred and Maria Paquette home at 1624 Hayward Avenue.

Roger, Maria and Richard Paquette, 1930s.

years of hard work remodeling. The foundation was rotting so he dug a basement (by hand) and put in a new foundation.

Hardpan is the indigenous opponent of the digger in Manette. The ally of the digger then was dynamite. So Fred proceeded to blast under the house. Every time he would get ready to shoot, Maria would run to the neighbor's house, hysterically waiting to see how high the house would go.

Over time, Fred tore down the woodshed, workshop and garage. Roger was given the honor of removing nails from the shiplap and structural lumber, sorting and stacking the lumber, then straightening the nails so all could be used in future projects.

Fred built and installed a septic tank system which allowed him to get rid of the cesspool and install an indoor toilet. Then, instead of tearing down the privy, he burned it down along with the chicken house. Again this sent Maria flying off to the neighbors, but Richard and Roger thought it a great show (especially Roger, who wouldn't have to pull out and straighten those contrary nails).

Next Fred bought a Kerrihard hot water furnace, built radiators, bought a 500-gallon oil barrel and installed a hot-water heating system, discarding the wood heater. (We seem to have come full cycle with people now re-installing wood heaters.) Roger liked that, too. It meant less wood to split.

Ralph Elliott was a handsome western, Marlboro-type man who owned a fine looking pair of mules. He used them hitched to a two-handled scraper to move dirt on regrading jobs. So when Fred was ready to landscape, Elliott came with his mules. Richard and Roger had an entrancing two days. Elliott was an artist with the mules and scraper. The language used to communicate with the mules was evidently an important facet of the art because the air became quite blue. The next time Roger was to hear similar language was when Wheaton Way was being constructed across the canyon that divides Bremerton Gardens. The contracting logger used a donkey engine and a highline to clear out the timber before the fill was made. It seems there are many things that can go wrong in such an operation (or he may have been an inept logger or was using inferior equipment). In any event, more blue air.

SCHOOL DAYS

Both Roger and Richard graduated from the sixth grade at Manette School, seventh and eighth grades at Lincoln Junior High, then Bremerton High School, Roger in 1933 and Richard in 1938. Both went to Sunday School at Manette Community Church and have fond memories of Amy Hoopes

—Richard's kindergarten teacher, Roger's Sunday School teacher. Other Sunday School teachers were Mr. and Mrs. Ammerman, Mrs. Nichols and Al Meicho, who was also our Scoutmaster.

Reverend Robert and Mrs. Mary Thompson had a son, Bob, who went to Linfield College in McMinnville, Oreg. He drowned while on a fraternity rush party at the ocean. Their grief, however, did not destroy their faith in the Baptist college, and Mrs. Thompson was active in recruiting students for Linfield for the duration of Reverend Thompson's pastorate in Manette. Among those she sent there were Jessie Crowell, Ruth and Dorothy Wall, Merrick McHenry, Russel Quay, Dorothy Cole and Roger Paquette. Roger attended for 2 1/2 years and then left to serve an apprenticeship in the shipyard.

ANOTHER GENERATION

In 1940 Roger married Anne McDougald from Portland, whom he had met at Linfield College. At the end of World War II he went back to Linfield to complete his degree in physics. In 1947 he was hired by Olympic College to teach in the apprentice program in the shipyard. He retired from there in 1980. Anne, who had previously taught high school in Oregon, taught music in the Bremerton schools for 20 years and also retired in 1980.

Richard worked for the Bremer Estate and on the Manette Gazette with Earl Harkins and Kenneth and Wayne Muller. He served an electrician apprenticeship in the shipyard during the war. He and Wayne Muller dated sisters, Virginia and Katherine Ketcham, who visited their Manette relatives, the E.C. Jacks, in the summers. Wayne married Virginia. Richard married Katherine.

At the end of the war Richard was drafted and served 2 years in the army. He stayed in the army reserve, retiring as a full colonel. He attended the University of Washington and worked as a food salesman and distributor in Seattle.

Katherine Paquette died in 1973. Richard later married Barbara Maxwell, a long-time staff member of the Department of Anthropology at the University of Washington. They now own and run two delis in the Queen Anne district of Seattle, both called Beba's.

Fred and Maria separated in 1940. Fred re-married and moved to Portland, where he worked as a machinery inspector for the navy during World War II, then later for the Bonneville Power Administration. After retirement he worked for Kaiser in Vancouver. He died there in 1968.

Maria worked in the cafeteria in the shipyard during the war and later as housekeeper in some of the wealthier homes in Seattle. She married Jean Charette; then, on his death, went back to Montreal to live with her sister. She died there in 1971.

GENEALOGY
JOSEPH ALFRED "FRED" PAQUETTE was born in 1889. In 1914 he married MARIA ST. PIERRE. They had two sons.

1. ROGER JOHN MARK PAQUETTE, born in Montreal, Quebec, in 1915. He married ANNE McDOUGALD from Portland in 1940. They have two daughters:
1A. TERRY ANNE PAQUETTE, born in Manette in September 1945. She presently lives in Reno, Nev., where she works at the community college. She has two sons:
1A1. MICHAEL MCPHILLIPS, born in 1967 in McMinnville, Oreg.
1A2. JOSHUA STRANGE, born in 1979 in Tahoe City, Calif.
1B. JEANNE ELIZABETH PAQUETTE, born in Bremerton in September 1949. She married JOHN H. ATKINS. They now live in Beaverton, Oreg. They have one son:
1B1. JOHN PAQUETTE ATKINS, born in Arlington, Va.

2. RICHARD HERMAS PAQUETTE, born in 1921 in Edmonton, Alberta. He married KATHERINE KETCHAM. Richard and Katherine lived in Seattle. She died in 1973. Richard married BARBARA MAXWELL. Richard and Katherine had three children.
2A. VIRGINIA THEONA PAQUETTE, born in Virginia in 1947. She married WILLIAM O. SMITH. They live in Seattle. Virginia and William have two children.
2B. JOHN MARK PAQUETTE, born in Seattle in 1951. He married JAN DENSON. They presently live in Portland, Oreg. John and Jan have a daughter and a son born in Illinois: ALIA KATHERINE, born in 1982 and ASHER DAMAS, born in 1983.
2C. CAROLYN GEORGIA PAQUETTE, born in Seattle in 1952. Carolyn lives in Seattle.

PARKER, HARLAN
By Mrs. Harlan Parker Jr.
1986

Harlan Edwin Parker was born in Ashville, N.C. He came to Seattle and worked as a logger until he was badly injured. He met and married Emma Deane Hubbell. They moved to Manette to truck garden. They lived on Sheridan Hill, now 203 East 31st Street, below Atkinsons and near the Carters. Later they moved to Shelton, where Harlan worked for a sand and gravel company.

DESCENDANTS
HARLAN (May 10, 1899-August 19, 1954) and EMMA PARKER had three children.

1. LOUISE PARKER was born in Wilburton, Wash., in April 1915. Louise married WALTER ANDERSON. Louise divorced and later married a Mr. FREDRICKSON. Louise had no children. She died in 1955 in California.

2. EILEEN PARKER was born in Wilburton, Wash., in 1917. She married TONY DeBARDI in 1939. Eileen and Tony had six children: DONA, LARRY, MARY LOU, JOSEPH, JANICE and MICHAEL.

3. HARLAN PARKER Jr. was born in Manette February 7, 1923. Harlan went to school at Sheridan and high school at Silveredale. Harlan became a

heavy equipment operator. He married GERTRUDE LARKIN in 1941. They divorced. Harlan married IRENE THOMAS. They live in Silverdale. Harlan has three children, two by Gertrude and one by Irene. The three are:
3A. GERALDINE PARKER, born in Bremerton in 1941. She attended school in Shelton and Poulsbo and graduated from Central Kitsap High School. Geraldine married SAM YOUNGER. They divorced and later Geraldine married NISN POUSIMA. They divorced. Geraldine kept the Younger name. She and Sam had three children: STEVEN, BRIAN and GREGORY.
3B. GARY PARKER, born in Bremerton in 1943. Gary went to school in Shelton and Poulsbo and graduated from Central Kitsap High School. Gary owns Parker Auto Supply stores in Poulsbo, Silverdale, Bremerton and Port Orchard. He married VICKI OEFFNER, and they live in Silverdale. They have three children STEPHANIE, KATHLEEN and GREGORY.
3C. DONALD PARKER, born in Bremerton in 1959. Donald attended school in Trego, Mont., Renton and Kent. He is self-employed, working in Bremerton as an auto mechanic. He lives in Silverdale.

PECKENPAUGH, SILAS
By Dorothy Peckenpaugh McAlinden
1986

The Peckenpaugh family came to the United States from Eiterbach, Germany, in 1750, arriving in Maryland. My grandfather, Silas Peckenpaugh (born March 1851, died June 1918), worked as a horse trader, road builder and farmer. He met and married Sidney Caroline Gordon (born October 1853, died October 1937) in Finley, Mo., in 1872. They were married 46 years and raised eight children. They settled in Cedar County, Mo. About 1883 they sold their farm and traveled by covered wagon to Salmon River, Idaho. There they bought some property and remained for about 3 years, until Sidney and the younger children were ready for further travel.

In 1887 they sold the property in Idaho and continued on their journey to Seattle. Once there they sold all but one team of horses and purchased a homestead at what is now the northwest corner of Brownsville Highway and McWilliams Road. Then Silas built two rafts and loaded on their household goods, wagons and the horses. He hired a small workboat to tug the rafts to an area of the Sheridan-Tracyton beach, and unloaded. Silas then built a skid road to the homestead. This

Silas Peckenpaugh

skid road remained for many years.

Silas and Sidney's seven children were with them, Anne (1873-1964), John (1875-1893), Louise (1879-1967), James (1881-1950), Ethel (1884-1984), Ira (1886-1969) and Harold (1888-1968). Vera (1900-1970) was born later.

When Silas was seriously injured in a logging accident he sold the homestead. They bought 5 acres on what is now Tracyton Boulevard in Sheridan, about a block north of where the Sheridan Dock then stood. There they built a four-bedroom, two-story house, which still stands at 2824 Tracyton Boulevard.

Silas was a county road supervisor for many years and built many of the original roads in the Sheridan-Tracyton area. He also worked as a logger and was an expert tree faller. In ad-

Peckenpaugh home at 2824 Tracyton Boulevard.

dition, during those years, the family raised horses, cows and poultry and maintained a large fruit and vegetable garden.

Silas and Sidney both rest at the Tracyton Cemetery alongside their oldest son John and granddaughter Caroline.

JAMES AND HARRIET PECKENPAUGH

James Albert Peckenpaugh (born October 1881, died April 1950) was born in Cedar County, Mo., the second son and fourth child of Silas and Sidney Peckenpaugh. He married Harriet Bagshaw (born July 1888, died December 1937). Harriet was the ninth of 12 children of Edward Francis Bagshaw (died 1920) and Elizabeth Harriet Williams (died 1913).

The Bagshaws came from Wales. They traveled to London and then by steamship to New York. There they took the railroad train to Seattle. They arrived in Seattle about 1890, when Harriet was 2 years old. Edward homesteaded 180 acres in Seattle, across from the Broadway High School and close by the old Carnation plant. There he set up a successful fuel business.

Jim and Harriet built a house in Sheridan after their marriage in 1910. The house still stands at 3227 Pine Road just above the apartment complex The Willows. There they raised chickens and sold fryers and eggs. They sold this property to the Larsen family shortly after Silas died in 1918.

Jim's mother, Sidney, decided to move to Seattle to live

Sidney Peckenpaugh and youngest daughter Vera, in 1903.

near her daughters. So Jim and Harriet bought her house on what is now Tracyton Boulevard. They had four children: Caroline (September 1913-December 1913), Dorothy Harriet (born June 1915), James Albert Jr., (December 1917-March 1986), and Martha Louise (born February 1922).

In his early years Jim worked with his father in farming, logging and road building. He also worked for a short time in Alaska. Upon his return he entered PSNY as an apprentice shipfitter and worked up to leadingman. He retired in 1941 after 35 years of service.

Jim and Harriet were very active in community affairs. They were members of the Grange and the Tracyton Methodist Church. They helped with community building projects such as building the Grange Hall and a school playshed and raising the church to add a basement.

They took an active part in getting the Pacific Telephone Company and the Puget Sound Power and Light Company to extend their services to the Sheridan community. When the Bremerton-Manette bridge was proposed they attended the meetings and invested money to get the project developed.

After electricity was available, Jim wired the house. They dug a new well and installed a pump. They added a bathroom and installed fixtures. And they added a washroom and bought a new Maytag washer.

Jim was a charter member of the Masonic Steadfast Lodge. Harriet was a member of the Get-together Club and the Ladies Aid and was active in 4-H club work. At various times she was the leader of the garden, sewing, rabbit and canning clubs. She helped young children in showing their produce at the local fairs each fall.

Harriet had a lovely soprano voice and sang solo at the church. She also sang lead in the community operettas. She was artistic and painted water color pictures, some of which we still have. She made the costumes for the children for the annual Easter, Christmas and May Day Festival programs. She was on the decorating committees for many community functions.

Both Jim and Harriet were talented gardeners. They both had a strong work ethic and ran an organized and scheduled household. After buying the Tracyton Beach home they added fruit trees, berry bushes and flowering trees and shrubs. Each year they planted large vegetable gardens. They always had a lot of flowers. Every summer Harriet canned several hundred jars of fruit, vegetables, salmon and jams. Each fall the basement bins were filled with potatoes, apples, pumpkins, squash and onions. They also raised chickens, ducks, turkeys and geese. We had "Blossom," a milk cow, "Red," a horse and "Silver," an Alaskan spitz dog. There were always two or three cats in the barn and woodshed.

Jim and Harriet were generous with their produce and loved to give it away at any opportunity. We were little affected by the Depression. Our parents left us a rich heritage.

They rest together at Tracyton Cemetery.

DESCENDANTS OF JAMES AND HARRIET PECKENPAUGH
Dorothy, James Jr. and Martha Peckenpaugh, the children of James and Harriet Peckenpaugh, were born and raised in Sheridan. They attended the Tracyton Grade School and the Union High School in Silverdale, both of which have been torn down and replaced. All the children were good students and made the honor rolls.

They attended the Tracyton Methodist Church and participated in activities there. They remember especially The Reverend Mary McKee and her innovative ideas. They were members of the various 4-H clubs and planted separate gardens and raised New Zealand Red rabbits in some of their projects. They showed the results of their work at the local fairs and won ribbons.

1. DOROTHY PECKENPAUGH took dancing lessons and was called upon to dance at many of the community programs. These dances included the Highland Fling and the Irish Jig. After graduating from Silverdale High School in 1932 she attended Bremerton Business College. She worked as secretary for Move-by-Heck/Puget Sound Express. On May 29, 1936, she married J. EMMETT McALINDEN, (born October 1912) and moved to Tacoma. Before retiring, Dorothy worked as a librarian for 22 years. The McAlindens have two children.

1A. MICHAEL E. McALINDEN, born August 1941 in Tacoma. Mike graduated from Los Altos High School in 1960, from American River College, then University of Nevada in Reno. He served as a corporal in the U.S. Marine Corps Reserve in 1960-1966. He has worked in the mental health field for over 16 years and is presently a program coordinator with the Sierra Developmental Center at Reno, Nev.

1B. PATRICIA E. McALINDEN, born in January 1945 in Burbank, Calif. She graduated from La Sierra High School, from American River College, then from the University of California at San Francisco. She married JAMES WESTLAKE in 1975. She worked in the insurance field for several years and is with Porche Cars-North America-Reno as a compensation/benefits coordinator. Pat and Jim raise Appaloosa horses in Golden Valley, Nev. They have one daughter TARA KATHLEEN, born December 1981.

2. JAMES PECKENPAUGH Jr. attended Washington State University after graduating from high school in 1935. Against his father's wishes, he entered PSNS as an apprentice shipfitter. He became a superintendent and had a very successful career, retiring in 1973. James married MARGARET PETERSON of Port Orchard, June 7, 1941. They have two sons.

2A. JAMES A. PECKENPAUGH II, born in April 1942 in Bremerton. After graduation from South Kitsap High School in 1960 he attended Olympic Junior College in Bremerton. He then joined the air force and earned his B.A. degree at the University of Wisconsin. While stationed at Andrews Air Force Base he earned a master's degree at George Washington University. He and his wife, SUSAN PARTNOW, reside in Seattle, where he has his own tax consulting business. They have two children: JESSICA PARTNOW, born February 1981 and TYLER JAMES, born October 1985.

2B. JOHN E."Jack" PECKENPAUGH, born in July 1943 in Bremerton. He graduated from South Kitsap High School in 1962 and attended Olympic Junior College for 2 years. He graduated from the University of Puget Sound in business administration. He is regional claims manager for Universal Underwriters Group. Jack married JOAN SILVER in Bremerton in 1964. They live in Edmonds and have two sons: JOHN EDWARD, born in September 1967, and JEFFREY BEN, born in December 1969.

3. MARTHA PECKENPAUGH was the most gregarious member of the family and always had a host of friends. Martha was 15 when our mother Harriet died. Martha remembers spending many days with Mrs. Jessie Morton and Mrs. Grace Carter, who were like surrogate mothers to her. Upon graduating from high school in 1940 she attended Metropolitan Business College in Seattle. She went to work at Pacific Telephone Company as an operator. When the war started she went to work as a clerk at PSNS. In October of 1942 she married navy Chief RICHARD A. SMITH (born December 1920). The family traveled and lived in several states during Richard's career in the navy. After Richard's retirement from the navy in 1959, Martha and her family settled in White Bear Lake, Minn. Martha is now divorced. She retired in 1984 and lives in Virginia near her son Curtis. The Smiths had three children.

3A. RICHARD SMITH, born in June 1943 in Bremerton. After graduating from White Bear Lake High School in Minnesota in 1962, he spent 4 years in the navy. He is now an electrician in Burnsville, Minn. Dick married MARY CATHERINE CARLSON in October 1968 and they reside in Rosemount, Minn. They have two daughters: MICHELLE LEE, born in December 1969 and NICOLE LYNN, born in August 1971.

3B. LINDA SMITH, born in July 1945 in Fort Lauderdale, Fla. She graduated from White Bear Lake High School in Minnesota in 1963. She married JERRY O. PRESFIELD in February 1964. They have retired and reside in Homosassa Springs, Fla.

3C. CURTIS JAMES SMITH, born in January 1953, in Groton, Conn. He graduated from Mounds View High School in Minnesota in 1971 and then enlisted in the navy as a submarine sailor. He earned the rank of chief in 1980 and plans to make the navy his career. He married CYNTHIA MARION BRAZEE. They live in Hampton, Va. They have a son and a daughter: MATTHEW STEVEN, born in April 1978 and COURTNEY LEIGH, born in August 1980.

VERA PECKENPAUGH

Vera was Silas and Sidney's youngest child. She was born at home (Brownsville Highway and McWilliams Road) in 1900. She married Joel Erickson about 1919. They are both deceased. Vera and Joel had three children, Barbara, Roger and Joan.

PERRIMAN, MARGARET
By Mae Perriman Tracy
1985

Mother, Margaret Perriman, came to Washington with me and my sister Gertrude in 1924. Mother's parents, Mary Ann and John Gabelhie, lived in Tracyton and Mother's sister- Norma (Mrs. Charlie) Clare, lived in Manette near Fellows' greenhouse on East 11th Street. I went to Tracyton School for several years. Mother and I helped Grandpa and Grandma on the place. Grandma was a midwife for several families. She also sold butter, eggs and cream to people in Tracyton and walked long distances to do it. When Grandma was away Mother kept house. They had a cow and a big garden with all sorts of vegetables, a big patch of lovely big red Marshall strawberries plus loganberries. We helped in picking those and helping mom's dad get things ready for market. They lived a mile and a half from town. He took those things on a flat-bed wheelbarrow to Tracyton and on the boat to Bremerton and sometimes to Seattle.

Later Mom, Gertrude and I went to Seattle where Mom worked in an office of a fuel yard and then, during World War I, in a laundry. I attended Central School in Seattle for a couple of years. My sister was not old enough to enter school, but I was taking her with me every day. The school sent word to Mom that I shouldn't bring her; Mom sent a note saying that if she didn't go, I'd have to stay home and care for her. They OK'd it and she was put in a "small" first grade. It was a long walk to that school—and later a long one to Tracyton school when we came back after the war.

In about 1915 we returned to Bremerton and lived in a small house at 6th Street and Callow. I graduated from Washington

Mary Ann Gabelhie and her daughter Margaret Perriman Clare. - Photo from Mae Perriman Tracy.

Grammar School and attended Union High School. I had to quit high school and do housework and child-care to help provide for Mom, my sister and me.

Gertrude married Fred "Fritz" Kanthack and they lived on Nipsic Avenue.

Mother married Walt Clare and we moved to Manette in about 1920. Walt was a brother of Charlie Clare, to whom Mother's sister Norma was married.

I went to work at the Woolworth Store and at the Rialto Theater, where I met my future husband, Bert Tracy, shortly after we moved to Manette.

Bert and I had two sons, Rodney and Leon Tracy.

[see TRACY, RALPH]

PERSONETTE, ARTHUR
By George Personette
1984

Arthur J. Personette arrived in Manette in 1913. He returned to Illinois and married Georgia Dean Felts. Arthur came back to Manette with Georgia and their 3-year-old son George in 1918. Arthur worked in Puget Sound Navy Yard in Bremerton from 1918 until 1950. He retired in 1950 as master painter.

MEMORIES OF MANETTE

One of my earliest memories of my years in Manette was the blowing of the navy yard whistle daily and the sirens on all the ships in the navy yard when World War I was declared over in 1919—a very impressive happening for a 3-year-old. At that time my folks and I lived in a little three-room house made over from an old chicken house owned by Mr. Dan Salt. Salt was a wealthy Seattle boxing promoter who had his summer home, "Salt Air Rest," on the old beach road that was replaced by Jacobsen Boulevard. Orville Schultz was a neighbor at that time and still lives in the home his folks built (1700 Jacobsen Boulevard) on the old Salt Air home property.

During those early years I remember playing on the beach and in the waves made by the stern-wheeler ferries *Bailey Gatzert* and *Tourist* as they made Seattle-Bremerton runs. I also recall the launch *Chickaree* which ran from Brownsville and Fletcher's Bay to the navy yard. We kids knew that when the *Chickaree* went by it wouldn't be long before our dads would be home. They didn't walk quite as fast as the *Chickaree* ran.

When I was 5 my folks built a home at East 13th Street and Trenton Avenue. From here it was just one block to good old Manette Elementary. What an exciting day it was when Orville took me to school my first day. He was a veteran as he had started school the year before. It took me a few years to catch up with him, but I finally did in the sixth grade as my folks weren't too smart and let the teacher skip me over the fifth grade—I still have a hard time with fractions and decimals, which I was supposed to have learned in the fifth grade. I spent 6 great years in Manette school and have many memories of Miss Turner, Miss Johnson, Mr. Cash and Mr. Miller—all super teachers.

The eighth grade year was spent in Bremerton at Lincoln Junior High School, where we mixed with students from Central and Smith Elementary Schools. To them we were the "hicks from the sticks." I chuckle at how many of those same people grew up and moved over to the "sticks."

These were great years for growing up in Manette, since hunting, fishing and clam digging were in vogue the year around. Bicycles were also in vogue and we roamed far and wide. We never seemed to lack things to do. One favorite spring activity was kite flying and the most popular place to launch our kites was from the water tower on Fellows' Ranch. There was an apple orchard near the tower and we kids always helped with the "early picking." One day either Walt or Charley Fellows caught me helping myself to the apples and decided to teach me a lesson. The town fire truck, an old solid-tire, chain-driven rig, was stored in their barn. They smeared my hands and face with heavy black grease from the truck and sent me on my way. I could not get the grease off without getting it on my clothes and so had to go home and tell my mother what happened.

Summertime brought baseball games and the Manette town team was sponsored by D.S. "Slim" Aldrich, who gave to us kids, who chased and returned foul balls, either an ice cream cone or a nickel. We got in a lot of hard running to get to the ball first. Those nickels went a long way at Meredith's store or at Mrs. Sam Hall's candy counter on the Manette Dock, where she was the freight agent.

When Orville Schultz and I were kids our moms used to take us to the area where the Illahee State Park now stands. It was only a 20-minute walk down the beach from where we lived. Later, when we were in high school, Roger Paquette, Ray Cole, Orville and I used to camp out overnight there.

High school years brought sports into my life and I enjoyed earning my "B" in basketball and baseball. After high school, softball became the thing to do and our team, playing under the name East Bremerton Improvement Club and Tony's Tavern, enjoyed considerable success. We won state softball championships twice—mainly on the good pitching of Ervin and Alfred Jensen.

I spent the years 1935 through 1939 at the University of Washington, where I earned four letters in swimming, football and track.

In the spring of 1940 I finished my 5th year at the U. of W. and registered at the teacher placement office. Jobs were scarce—about three out of five teachers were placed that year. The superintendent from Tieton came to the U. of W. looking for a commercial teacher and when he found one that was qualified not only to handle the commercial subjects but could handle coaching positions also, I had a job. He could then drop out of coaching himself as previously all other faculty were women or had no talents for coaching sports.

I took a job teaching commercial subjects—typing, shorthand and bookkeeping—plus coaching baseball and track at Tieton High School.

After teaching and coaching 3 years I spent the next 3 years as a gunnery officer in the USNR, roaming around the South Pacific. While I was away in the navy three small schools in the area west of Yakima—Cowiche, Tieton and Naches Heights Schools—consolidated and formed the Highland School District.

I returned to my teaching position at Highland High School in February, 1946. In 1947 I was appointed Highland High School principal and served the next 29 years in that position, retiring in 1977. I am currently operating a 20-acre apple orchard in Tieton.

GENEALOGY

ARTHUR J. PERSONETTE was born in Bernard, Kans. In 1912 he married GEORGIA DEAN FELTS, who was born in Litchfield, Ill. They had two children.

1. GEORGE A. PERSONETTE, born August 17, 1915, in Litchfield, Ill. He married VIOLET REID in 1941. They live in Tieton and have one daughter.
1A. LINDA M. PERSONETTE, born January 30, 1943, in Yakima. Linda married LARRY MARVIN in 1969. They live in Yakima and have one child.
1A1. REID PATRICK MARVIN, born January 1, 1979, in Yakima.

2. MARY A. PERSONETTE, born February 14, 1919, in Litchfield, Ill. Mary married VIRGIL MARVIN in 1937 while he was stationed at the naval hospital in Bremerton. Virgil and Larry are not related. Virgil retired from the navy and worked at Stanford University for 24 years. He retired a second time 9 years ago. Mary and Virgil live in Mountain View, Calif., and have one daughter.
2A. BETTE LEE MARVIN, born in 1939 in Bremerton. Bette married ALAN TIPPETT. They have three children and two grandchildren.

PETERSON, ANDREW M.
By Ted Peterson
1985

Andrew M. Peterson was born April 18, 1865, in Yislof, Sweden. His wife, Hannah Erickson Peterson, was born January 22, 1865, also in Yislof. They came to Manette by way of Breckenridge, Minn., and Tacoma, arriving here in 1901. With them were their three chidren, Carrie Bertha, Theodore "Theo" and Walter James.

Andrew died October 10, 1929. Hannah died May 12, 1930.

The three children became well-known Manette residents.

Carrie Bertha married Hugo Berglind [see BERGLIND, HUGO].

Theodore [see PETERSON, THEODORE] married Alyce Card, member of another pioneer Manette family.

Walter James Peterson, the third of the three, was born May 6, 1892, in Minnesota. He went to school in Manette. He married Ruth Kelsey who lives in Seattle. Walter died August 14, 1968. A son Ralph lives in Bremerton.

Ralph married Marjorie Smith, daughter of Al Smith.

Another son of Walter and Ruth is Dale Peterson who lives in Seattle. Dale has three sons and two daughters.

PETERSON, AUGUSTUS
By Eleanor Harrington
1986

Augustus Peterson came to Manette from Minnesota in 1888. With him were his wife Karen and their four children: Clara, Nels, Willie and Annie.

The family homesteaded on a piece of property in Illahee, a land grant awarded to Augustus W. Peterson, Nels' father, for service in the Civil War. This piece of property near the famous "Big Rock" is now part of Illahee State Park.

THE FAMILY
AUGUSTUS W. PETERSON and KAREN MARTHA PETERSON (1847-1927) had four children.

1. CLARA PETERSON (1866-1948). Clara married ALEXANDER WATT. Clara and Alexander had two children: CORA and GUSSIE.

2. NELS PETERSON (1868-1948). [See PETERSON, NELS history]

3. WILLIE H. PETERSON (1879-1901)

4. ANNIE WILHEMIA PETERSON (1882-1901).

PETERSON, NELS
By Eleanor Harrington
1986

[For photo see HARRINGTON, HERBERT]

Nels E. Peterson was 17 when he, his parents, August and Martha, two sisters, Clara and Annie, and a brother, Willie, came to the area from Minnesota in March 1888. With Clara was her husband Alexander "Alex" Watt. They had been lured by reports of mild weather in Washington. Nels told of working in his shirt-sleeves all of the first winter he was here, a wonderful respite from freezing temperatures, heavy snows and tornadoes with winds strong enough to drive a straw into a fence post.

Nels first worked at logging camps at Clare's Marsh, Chico, Brownsville and the Indian Reservation near Agate Pass. Logging was done with teams of oxen and horses, and loggers used springboards to cut down the virgin timber. Logs were then rolled to the water, rafted and towed to the mills when tides were right. The mill at Port Blakely on Bainbridge Island was the only mill with extended tracks which could accommodate the huge trees, some of them 300 feet long. From these trees the mill cut sailing masts and spars up to 120 feet in length.

Clara and Alex Watt's first daughter Cora was born in a logging camp. Gussie was born after they were more permanently located.

The *Bern* was the first passenger ferry to run from Bremerton to Manette, but if Nels had work to do on the Bremerton side he would drive the horse team and wagon into the water near the Bender place and come out near the present location of Evergreen Park. To get supplies he would row across the bay and back.

The *Yosemite*, a side-wheeler ferry, would come from Seattle and then stop at any of the little communities where the ferry could land. It was equipped with an apron ramp for the loading and unloading of horses and cattle. At unloading time the apron was dropped, letting livestock into the water; they would swim ashore and were rounded up by someone on the beach. Later the *Yosemite* burned and sank in the narrows off Bainbridge Island and the debris drifted ashore on the northern side of the lighthouse near Flapjack Point. Nels, his father and possibly others towed the pilot house, which was still intact, back to the homestead and used it for a privy. More spacious than most, it remained a subject for conversation for years.

Nels was still working here at the time of the Seattle fire and he took his team and wagon to Seattle to help move people and their goods. As soon as the fire was under control he continued to guard property to prevent looting.

INDIANS

He told wonderful stories of those early days and, working often among the Indians, he learned much of their dialect. Once while working at the Chico logging camp he arose at 5 a.m. to get wood so the camphouse cook could start breakfast. When he opened the door and looked toward the bay there was an Indian standing in a canoe yelling for help. The tide was out and the Indian had a fish on the line that was too big to handle. He gave the line to Nels and told him to run up the beach as fast as he could. Together they landed a salmon which weighed between 80 and 90 pounds. The Indian promptly sold it to the camphouse cook for a dollar.

Another tale concerned the son of Chief Chico. It was a winter day with a strong wind blowing when he came by in his canoe. He stood up suddenly and the canoe overturned. He made it to shore but in doing so lost his revolver. The following June at extreme low tide, Nels went to the spot and waded barefoot until he found the pistol. It had survived the winter. It was a .44 Smith and Wesson navy model, and today it is owned by Robert Carlson.

Nels married Florence Johnson of Tracyton and they built a house in Bremerton at 4th Street and Pacific Avenue. Sometime later they moved to Northville, Mich., but returned in 1909 and settled in Manette. He built three more houses; the last was at 1119 Perry Avenue.

He and his brother William worked in the navy yard, Nels operating the big hammerhead crane until he retired. The crane is still referred to as "Big Pete." Nels was also one of the participants when the first flag was raised over the navy yard September 16, 1891.

Not much is known about the termination of his marriage but in 1916 he married Nellie Harrington, a widow, and became "Daddy Pete" to Neal and Scott Harrington.

Nels was active in community affairs and lodge work, was a life member and noble grand of Bremerton Encampment 145, I.O.O.F. He was an active member of the Good Roads Club and the EBIC. He was one of the initiators and builders of Steadfast Masonic Lodge 216, and one of its masters. He also was a patron of Philathea Chapter 174, Order of Eastern Star.

During the flu epidemic in World War I, Nels would go each day to several houses where there was illness. He chopped wood, carried it in, brought groceries and did whatever else was needed. Until his death in 1948 his life could be described by the Bible's definition of true religion— "to help the widowed and the fatherless and to keep oneself unspotted from the world."

PETERSON, THEODORE
By Ted Peterson and Arthur Card (1923-1986)
1985

Theodore "Theo" Peterson, also known as "Tate," was born March 28, 1890, in Breckenridge, Minn. He came to Manette from Tacoma when he was 11 with his parents, Andrew M. and Hannah Peterson, his sister, Carrie Bertha, and his brother, Walter James.

Alyce Card, the girl Theo was to marry, was born July 21, 1892. She came to Manette from Seattle in 1898 with her parents, George and Jane Card, a sister, Ethel (later Mrs. Hausdorf) and brothers, Leonard and Harry.

Theo worked as grocer Harry Martin's delivery boy and drove the wagon everywhere around Manette. He started an apprenticeship as a machinist in the navy yard in 1906. His father, A.M. Peterson, Mr. Olson and Theo used to row back and forth to work and tied their boat up in the navy yard. Theo worked as an apprentice from 1906 until 1910. He went to Washington State College in Pullman from 1911 to 1914 and was a member of Gamma Delta Fraternity, which was organized January 17, 1912, and later affiliated with Beta Theta Pi, national Greek letter organization. Theo was freshman

Petersons and relatives. Back row (from left), Ethel and Elvin Hausdorf, Theodore Peterson Sr. and George Card. Front row, Lillian and Leonard Card, Jane Card, Alyce Peterson, Theodore "Ted" Peterson and Ted's fiancee Charlotte Yowell.
- Photo from Ted Peterson

class president. He was also a member of the drama guild in college.

Alyce attended Sheridan School, then high school in Bremerton. She and Ethel often spent summers with the family of George Card's brother in Cardston, Alberta, Canada.

Theo and Alyce were married August 1, 1917. They moved into a house Theo had built at 2604 East 9th Street.

Theo returned to the navy yard and in 1936 was appointed master mechanic of the inside machine shop.

He was a member of Master and Foreman's Association and was head of it for a while. He became a member of the Bremerton Board of Civil Service Examiners in 1943. He retired from the shipyard in August 1951 after 42 1/2 years.

RECREATION AND COMMUNITY SERVICE

Theo became a member of: the Washington State rifle team that won the national meet in 1914; the Steadfast Masonic Lodge, where he attained 32nd degree; was president of the East Bremerton Improvement Club in 1932; member of Kitsap Golf and Country Club (playing golf was his main recreation); head of the Bremerton School Board 1932-1937; 30-year member of the library board and its chairman from 1935 until 1959. He was a member of the Red Cross and was its chairman around 1953-54; member of Elks Lodge 1181.

Theodore and Alyce Peterson home built in 1917 at 2604 East 9th Street. - Photo from Ted Peterson

He helped start First Federal Savings and Loan, which is now Great Northwest, was on the board of directors and was elected chairman of the board in 1941, holding the position until his death.

Alyce was active in Philathea Chapter of Eastern Star, the History Club, Manette Ladies Aid and the Bremerton Garden Club.

Theo and Alyce built a summer cottage on beach property near Seabeck. They entertained friends and social organizations there.

Theo died September 20, 1959. Alyce is 95 and lives at Forest Ridge Convalescent Center in Bremerton.

THE FAMILY
Theo and Alyce Peterson had two children.

1. MURIEL LOUISE PETERSON, born March 4, 1919, in Bremerton. Muriel attended Manette School, Lincoln Junior High and Bremerton High School, graduating in 1936. She attended Washington State University, majoring in home economics. She was a member of Pi Beta Phi sorority. September 23, 1939, Muriel married Dr. EDWARD TUGAW of Omak at her home. The ceremony was read by Reverend Walter Wall. Muriel and Ed met at WSU, where he graduated as a veterinarian. Ed was a veterinarian in Salt Lake City until his death in 1980. Muriel lives in Salt Lake City. They had three sons and a daughter.
1A. EDWARD ANTHONY TUGAW Jr., born December 23, 1942. Edward married MARY LYNN TIMPSON. They have two daughters.
1A1. STEPHANIE LYNN TUGAW, born August 3, 1970, in Salt Lake City.
1A2. TIFFANY ANN TUGAW, Stephanie's twin.
1B. JAY RONALD TUGAW, born July 17, 1946. He married KAREN CHAMBERS. They live in Salt Lake City. They have two daughters and a son.
1B1. BRITTNEY KAY TUGAW, born May 7, 1977, in Salt Lake City.
1B2. HEATHER MARIE TUGAW, born May 5, 1980, in Salt Lake City.
1B3. EDWARD JASON TUGAW, born January 7, 1983, in Salt Lake City.
1C. WILLIAM GERALD TUGAW, born October 18, 1950. William married DIANE TENNANT. William and Diane have one son.
1C1. DANIEL JERALD TUGAW, born December 10, 1985, in San Carlos, Calif.
1D. TANYA ANN TUGAW, born May 19, 1959. She lives in Salt Lake City.

2. THEODORE "TED" PETERSON, born May 16, 1922, in Bremerton. Ted attended Manette and Lincoln Schools and graduated from Bremerton High School in 1940. Following graduation he entered the apprentice machinist program at PSNS. He worked as a machinist until 1950, then as an equipment specialist in the supply department. In 1966 Ted was transferred to navy headquarters in Washington, D.C., as a program analyst until his retirement in 1970 after 33 years. Ted married CHARLOTTE YOWELL of Halfway, Oreg., in 1946. Charlotte was a clerk-typist in the machine shop at PSNS from 1941 to 1945. Following Ted's retirement they built a home at 15280 NW Maple Lane near Maple Beach, Seabeck, on property that had been Alyce and Theo's summer home. Ted and Charlotte have two children.
2A. LA DONNA GAIL PETERSON, born January 28, 1947, in Bremerton. La Donna married JAMES HUGHES and they live in Tacoma. They have two sons.
2A1. TROY HUGHES, born December 11, 1973, in Boise.
2A2. TODD HUGHES, born January 20, 1977, in Tacoma.
2B. GREGORY DUANE PETERSON, born October 14, 1953, in Bremerton. Greg lives in Bremerton and works in the Trident Refit Facility in the machine shop at Bangor.

PFENNING, JOHN
By Jim Karst
1985

John Pfenning was born in Russia, February 27, 1869. His grandfather had immigrated to Russia from Germany. John's father, Nicolaus Pfenning, born in 1841, was a fur trader and immigrated to Kansas with his wife, Margaret Starkel Pfenning. They came with their four sons, John, Peter, Adam and Henry, and two daughters, Katherine (later to become Mrs. Henry Karst) and Elizabeth (known as Lizzie). Margaret,

Marguerita "Kraty" (Karst) Pfenning and John Pfenning.   - Photo from A. Karst

mother of the six, died during the immigration. The remainder of the family first settled in Harrington, Kans.

From Kansas, son John worked his way west to Portland and in 1898 went to Alaska during the gold rush. He came back in 1900 and purchased 5 acres of land in Manette (Decatur). He found work in the shipyard as a blacksmith. He was also a dairy farmer and truck gardener. (One customer was Meredith's grocery.) John married Marguerita Schlappe, known as "Kraty," who was born in Switzerland and lived in Portland, Oreg. They had no children.

Two of John's brothers, Pete and Adam, arrived and bought acreage next to John Pfenning at East 17th Street and Perry Avenue. They helped each other build two-room houses. The brothers all worked in the shipyard.

In the spring of 1902 they welcomed their sister, Katie Pfenning Karst, her husband Henry Karst and their three boys, Adam, Holt and Bill. They shared their homes until Henry could buy land and build a home. The property involved was on the west side of the county road, now Perry Avenue, between East 15th and East 18th Streets.

Henry Pfenning died in 1904. Grandfather Nicolaus Pfenning, whose second wife had died, was living with his son John in 1904 when he was mistakenly shot for a bear while picking blackberries in the area commonly known as Clare's Marsh. Pete Pfenning moved to Gatsby, Alberta. Elizabeth (Lizzie) finally settled in Russell, Kans. Adam lived out his years in Seattle and John Pfenning stayed in Manette until his death April 28, 1952.

[See KARST family history.]

Pfenning - Karst family members at home of Peter and Christina Pfenning, East 17th Street and Perry Avenue, circa 1903. From left are Adam Karst, Christina Pfenning, Katherine "Katie" Karst and Holt Karst.   -Photo from Jim Karst

John Pfenning home, East 18th Street and Perry Avenue. Holt Karst wrote "This picture was taken about 1903. The picture is of Grandfather Nicolaus Pfenning and Kraty Pfenning, wife of John Pfenning. The child on Grandpa's lap is William Karst."

- Photo from Jim Karst

PRICE, CLIVE EMSLEY
By Lloyd L. Price
1985

ALASKA YUKON EXPOSITION
BROUGHT US TO WASHINGTON

Clive Emsley Price was born January 25, 1879, in Ontario, Canada. He served in the Spanish-American War. He married Carrie Lockhart in Michigan in 1903. In 1909 he brought his family west to see the Alaska Yukon Exposition at the University of Washington. He decided to remain in Washington and moved to Colby with his wife Carrie and their first three children, Sidney, Lloyd and Dorothy. I remember our neighbors, the Shaw family, in Colby. I watched Mr. Shaw and his boys milking their cows and squirting milk into my face. We moved to Manette in about 1912. Later the Shaws moved to Manette. We rented a house from Al Bubb while our home was being built. Dad had to chop his way into the woods that were thick in Manette at this time.

We ferried to get to Colby, and to get to Bremerton we rode the S.S. *Tourist*, an old sternwheeler. To get between towns we rode the Mosquito Fleet's small boats. The white battleships in Bremerton's navy yard were known as Teddy Roosevelt's "Great White Fleet."

The *Bern*, the *Swan* and one other smaller boat ferried passengers between Bremerton and Manette. Later the ferry dock was expanded for the automobile ferry *Pioneer*. Once the safety chain on the ferry was released too soon and a car with a couple in it plunged into the water. Harry Hansen's crew took a pike pole and dove down, broke a window in the auto and saved the couple.

Clive Price home at 2002 Winfield Avenue, 1912.

and Mercer Island—real estate—buying tax properties, remodeling, re-selling and building. Clive also worked at Seattle City Light as a painter. Later he retired to Mercer Island and worked with Scott Realty. In his last years he and his second wife, Nettie, sold their Mercer Island home and moved to Monrovia, Calif. Clive died in California in the Veteran's Hospital October 25, 1960. Nettie sold the Monrovia home and came to Redmond, Wash., to live near her son from a previous marriage, Sherman Howard. She died in 1966.

Clive was active in Manette Steadfast F and AM Lodge and the Constellation Lodge in Seattle, where he was in charge of the library. He wrote several articles and poems for the Masonic magazine.

Price family. The boys from left, Father Clive, Sidney, Lloyd. The girls, Esther, Mother Carrie, Dorothy.
-Photo from Lloyd Price

CLIVE'S BUSINESS INTERESTS

In 1916-17 we bought the Ryther Estate in Manette and divided it into more than 200 lots. The north side of our property bordered the Hillman Addition near the Parker home. The original Ryther Estate later became Eastpark. Clive Price's business interests in Manette included building houses and buying and selling real estate. He helped construct the first Masonic meeting place in the area over Meredith's store. In later years he continued in similar activity in Seattle

GENEALOGY

CLIVE EMSLEY PRICE (1879-1960), born in Bangor, Ontario, Canada, married CARRIE LOUISE LOCKHART of Michigan (1882-1942) in 1903. After Carrie died in 1942 Clive married NETTIE NAAB HOWARD. Clive and Carrie had four children.

1. SIDNEY ROLAND PRICE was born in Michigan in 1904. He died in 1978. He became a painter for Seattle City Light. Sidney married EDNA IRENE THOMAS (born in Minnesota, 1908) in 1928. Sidney died March 8, 1978. Edna lives on the water near Kingston. Sidney and Edna had three daughters.
1A. DORIS JEAN PRICE, born in Seattle in 1930. She married LEROY MEEK in 1949. They lived in Seattle and Ellensburg and in Gary, Ind. They now live in North Carolina, where Leroy works for Reynolds Tobacco Company. They have two children.
1A1. LINDA DIANE MEEK, born in Seattle in 1951. Linda married RON INGRAM. Linda died of leukemia in 1981. Linda and Ron had a son, IVAN.
1A2. THOMAS MEEK. Thomas' wife MARY had a daughter, RACHEL. Tom and Mary had three children. LISA, ROBERT and KENNY.
1B. ELIZABETH LOUISE PRICE, born in Seattle in 1933. She married WILLIAM B. AREND in Seattle. They had five sons: WILLIAM Jr., born in Great Falls, Mont.; MARK, born in Seattle; GREGORY, born in Seattle; STEVEN, born in Seattle, and MICHAEL, born in Seattle.
1C. SHARON MAE PRICE, born in Seattle in November 1942. She married ROBERT NICHOLS in 1959. They have three children: TAMBORAH, CHRISTINA and MADRIGAL.

2. LLOYD LOCKHART PRICE, born in Michigan January 22, 1906. In 1925 Lloyd married BEATHIA PROVEN (born in Scotland July 5, 1896). In 1945 Lloyd married MAYME SWORD LINDSAY (born in Kiuruvesi, Finland, June 30, 1915).
Lloyd and Mayme held U.S. Civil Service positions in Washington, Alaska and California. He was in supply. Her positions included one as secretary to the commanding officer of the U.S. Ammunition Depot at Bangor, in 1955. Lloyd retired from the Naval Weapons Center in China Lake, Calif., in 1963, with a disability from a massive heart attack. Mayme retired in 1973 from the U.S. Naval Torpedo Station in Keyport. They now live in Manette.

Lloyd is a member of Steadfast Lodge 216 in Manette and Mayme is a member of Philathea chapter, Order of Eastern Star, in Manette.

Lloyd had one child by Beathia, adopted a child of Mayme's and had one more by Mayme. The three children are:

2A. DAVID LOCKHART PRICE, born in Tacoma July 27, 1926. He married DAISY L. COLBERT in 1943. David is a doctor of optometry in El Centro, Calif. David and Daisy have two children:

2A1. SHERRIE LYNN PRICE, born March 18, 1953. Sherrie has one child, MEGAN NOEL GILMOUR, born in 1981.

2A2. GARY STEPHEN PRICE, born February 18, 1956.

2B. JOHN LLOYD PRICE (Mayme's son), born May 25, 1938. He was adopted by Lloyd. John graduated from Olympic College and electronics apprentice school at PSNS. John married JANICE LaVONNE ANDERSON in 1959. He works in laser-beam technology at Naval Weapons Center, China Lake, Calif. John and Janice's children are:

2B1. JANELLE LYNN PRICE, born November 27, 1960. She married JEFFREY JORDAN December 21, 1977. They have one daughter, JESSICA LEIGH, born June 15, 1980.

2B2. JOHN LLOYD PRICE Jr., born March 23, 1961.

2B3. JANENE LOUISE PRICE, born December 20, 1966.

2C. RONALD CLIVE PRICE, born November 19, 1945. He married VICKI LYNN COPE July 18, 1970. Ronald graduated from Olympic College, then from Eastern Washington University, with a degree in psychiatry. He, his wife and son are in Germany working in a drug and alcohol program for the army. Ronald and Vicki's son CHRISTOPHER BRIAN was born May 20, 1972.

3. DOROTHY LUCILLE PRICE, born in Au Gres, Mich., June 30, 1907. She married KARL AXEL LINDALL, born in Marblemount, Wash., December 5, 1910. They have two children.

3A. ERVIN DURANT LINDALL, born July 23, 1944. He lives in Mt. Vernon, Wash., where he works for Mt. Vernon Fire Department.

3B. DAMON EUGENE LINDALL, born November 5, 1946. He lives in Wyoming.

4. ESTHER KATHRYN PRICE, born in Manette April 25, 1910, in a house we were renting from Al Bubb while our house was being built. Esther married JACK VERNON NEFFEW, born November 11, 1910. They have two children.

4A. JACK RICHARD NEFFEW, born in Vallejo, Calif., August 24, 1937. Jack and his wife PATRICIA live in California. They have two daughters, SUSAN and CARRIE.

4B. VERNON DAVID NEFFEW, born at Keyport May 27, 1945. Vernon lives in San Diego, where he works for an electronics firm. He and his wife TERRY have two sons.

RATH, PETER
By Robert Ballew
1985

Peter and Lydia Rath home at 2405 East 9th Street and Hayward Avenue. Same house, remodeled, is now at 2405 East 9th Street. -Photo from Bob Ballew

Peter Rath (born in New York 1870; died 1937), whom I knew as Grandfather, and his wife Lydia Elizabeth (born in Pennsylvania February 6, 1886; died January 5, 1963), my grandmother, lived in a house that Peter built at the southeast corner of East 9th Street and Hayward Avenue. When they married, Lydia had three daughters from previous marriages: Alma and Esther Holt, and Vera Fern Washburn, my mother. Peter and Lydia had one daughter: Edna Mae Rath.

Pete was a member of the Manette Volunteer Fire Department, while Lydia—a midwife—was active in helping several children come into this world.

Pete lived in the East 9th Street and Hayward Avenue house until about 1930. In 1937 Fred Fitzwater and his wife Lillian purchased the house, turned it to face East 9th Street instead of Hayward Avenue, and remodeled it. The present address is 2405 East 9th Street.

(Mrs. Fitzwater is the sister of the late Art Morken, who was Bremerton police chief and later Kitsap County sheriff.)

REA, WELBY
By Marjorie Rea Ray
1984

Welby L. Rea was born in Madison, Ind., April 3, 1890. He came to Seattle in 1912 with a friend who was coming west for his health. Welby worked as a motorman on a streetcar in Seattle before coming to Bremerton. In 1914 he came to a job in the Bremerton shipyard, where he worked for 36 years as a clerk.

A fellow worker, Roy Ellis, arranged for a double date. It was on that date that Welby met Mabel Bragdon. They were married in 1919. Mabel was born in Pipestone, Minn., June 15, 1887. She was raised in the Seattle area and came to Bremerton in 1916 to teach at Smith School. Several of the girls that taught with her became good neighbors when the Reas moved to Manette.

In 1918 Welby joined the navy as a radioman for an 18-month tour of duty. He married Mabel while he was in boot camp at the University of Washington. When he was discharged in 1919 they built a small home at 1901 East 13th Street in Manette. It was on an acre of ground that extended from Winfield Avenue to the water. Welby and Mabel had three children.

Welby commuted to the navy yard on the ferry *Pioneer* that ran between Manette and Bremerton. On weekends and after hours there was the *Urania*, a small passenger steamer. One Sunday evening in December of 1919, Welby, Mabel and Gladys, Mabel's sister, went to catch the *Urania*. The boat crew misjudged the tide and hit a loading float with such force that it threw everyone from the float into the water. Mabel ended up under the dock, clinging to a piling. She was picked up by someone in a rowboat. Since she landed near home she found help there. Other people were taken into homes along the beach. Welby and Gladys spent an anxious time trying to find Mabel. What a relief to meet someone who knew she had been taken home and was safe.

CLUES TO THE PAST

All along the beach there was evidence that Indians had used this area as a campground. Welby found several primitive tools in the deep layer of shells when he sifted the dirt to put in a lawn. This happened when the Reas built a larger brick house down by the water. The property nearby where the Children's Home stood had been an Indian burial site and several skeletons were uncovered. A complete Indian skeleton was found between the Renus Bender and Rea properties.

With the beach at the doorstep, this was an ideal place to raise a family. Swimming, boating, fishing and beach-combing kept the children busy. Mothers along the beach would take turns keeping an eye out when the children were swimming.

Welby drove a 1923 Franklin and the family looked forward to Sunday drives that took them all over the Kitsap Peninsula.

The Reas belonged to a card club, the Masons and Eastern Star. They were active in Boy and Girl Scout organizations, garden club and the Manette Community Church. There were Scout picnics and swimming at Hood Canal, church picnics at Island Lake and the Bremerton city park, corn feeds with neighbors at harvest time, and dances at the Masonic Temple.

The family built a cabin at Mount Rainier. There was always a gang around the table in the outdoor kitchen. The Scouts, church groups and the card club often enjoyed outings there.

There were evening picnics down at the Sandbanks and rowboat trips around to the beach at Illahee or across the bay to the city park with its slides and swings.

We remember the bobsled rides in winters when the snow was deep enough in Manette. We looked forward to the fires and hot chocolate at the end of the hill.

Welby retired from the shipyard in 1949 and the Reas sold their home at 1901 East 13th Street. They lived for a while at 1123 Vandalia Avenue before moving to the Seattle area, where their girls Marjorie and Frances had settled. Welby died in 1964; Mabel died in 1970.

DESCENDANTS

WELBY and MABEL REA had three children: FRANCES, MARJORIE and LAWRENCE. They went to grade school in Manette and then were bused to Bremerton to junior high and high school.

1. FRANCES REA was born in Bremerton in 1921. She married HAROLD HORN of Bremerton. They built their first home near Lawrence's grocery store, near Perry Avenue and Sheridan Road. Harold was a pilot. He was killed in 1959 in a plane crash on Mount Rainier while he was dropping medical supplies to a research group in the Rainier crater. After Harold's death, Frances married GENE WEBER. Frances and Harold had three children. Frances and Gene have one son.
1A. JANET HORN, born in Bremerton in 1941. Janet married DARYLL OLSON. They have two children, DARYLL and DEANA.
1B. JAMES HORN, born in Bremerton in 1943. James married CHERYL CLARK. They live in Lacey, Wash. They have three children, JAMIE, born in 1970; TIMMY, born in 1972; and CHRISTI, born in 1983.
1C. RAY HORN, born in Bremerton in 1946. He married JUDY KLEPPE. Ray is a career member of the United States Air Force. He and Judy have two children, TERRY, born in 1969, and TRACY, born in 1971.
1D. KEVIN WEBER, born in 1969. He married DAWN BROWN and they live in Joline, Ill. They have one child, ADAM WEBER, born in 1985.

2. MARJORIE REA was born in 1923 in Bremerton. Marjorie studied art at Washington State College in Pullman. She is a wood-carver in Puyallup. Marjorie married JAMES RAY. They live in Puyallup and have four children.
2A. STEPHEN RAY, born in 1948 in Seattle. Stephen married KATHY SHEPARD. Stephen and Kathy have four children: MATTHEW, born in 1974, NATHAN, born in 1977, PETER, born in 1979 and ELIZABETH, born in 1985.
2B. JAMES RAY, born in 1950 in Seattle. James married GINA KNUT-ZEN. They have three children: AMIE, born in 1975, BEN, born in 1978 and DANIEL, born in 1982.

2C. SANDRA RAY, born in 1954 in Renton. Sandra married ROBERT BRITTEN. They have two children: KATI, born in 1978 and JEREMY, born in 1979.
2D. JON RAY, born in 1958 in Renton. Jon married RENE BENSON.

3. LAWRENCE REA was born in Bremerton in 1924. Lawrence became a missionary with the Conservative Baptist Church and has been in Brazil since 1956. He married MARIE PETERSON. They have four children.
3A. REBECCA REA, born in 1958 in Brazil. She married MIGUEL HADJI. They have two children: SARA, born in 1980, and MICHAEL, born in 1982.
3B. SAMUEL REA, born in 1959 in Minnesota.
3C. EUNICE REA, born in 1960 in Brazil.
3D. ELIZABETH REA, born in 1961 in Seattle.

REANIER, BURTON
By Beatrice "Bee" Greenameyer
and Harold Reanier
1986

Burton Reanier, his wife Violet, and their children Sylvia, Beatrice and Harold, came from North Crandon, Wis., in 1916 at the urging of Burton's father, Henry. The father was one of the first Civil War veterans to be placed in the new Veterans' Home at Retsil; he had been a drummer boy in the Union Army at age 13. He is buried at Retsil Cemetery.

Burton and his family first came to Edmonds, then to Manette to work in the navy yard in 1918. Burton worked as a carpenter. They lived on what is now East 13th Street, then moved out to what is now North Perry Avenue. After their arrival here, Clifford, Charles, Glenn, Betty Mae, then Shirley were born. We attended Manette Community Church. The children started to school in Manette and then went to Sheridan School, from which we all graduated. In those days you had to pass a state exam and there were regular graduation exercises, similar to high school now, from eighth grade.

I (Harold) remember the flu epidemic of 1919-20. My mother used to go to Seattle one Saturday a month to shop, and always took me with her. We had to wear masks over our mouths. I remember the lines of horse-drawn wagons stacked high with flag-draped coffins of the sailors and marines who had died from the flu being shipped home. In those days the ferries had either side wheels or stern wheels—the *Bailey Gatzert* and the *Tourist*. The *F. G. Reeve*, a propeller-driven boat owned by the Reeve family in Silverdale, hauled all the freight up and down the sound.

Burton and Violet both are buried at Forest Lawn Cemetery.

THE REANIER FAMILY

BURTON A. REANIER was born in Wisconsin June 24, 1880. He married VIOLET REANIER, who was born in 1880. They had 11 children, three of whom died in infancy. Burton died in 1965; Violet died in 1971. Their eight surviving children were:

1. SYLVIA REANIER, born December 21, 1910, in Wisconsin. Sylvia married RAY LYNCH. Ray died. Later Sylvia married MAC KALISZEWSKI. Sylvia died in Illinois in 1974 and is buried in Bakersfield. Sylvia and Ray had three children, DOTTIE, PATTY and RAY.

2. BEATRICE REANIER, born June 9, 1912, in Wisconsin. Beatrice married ROBERT GREENAMEYER January 4, 1928. They live in Medford, Oreg. They had two children.
2A. ROBERTA GREENAMEYER, (now deceased).
2B. ROBERT GREENAMEYER. Robert lives in San Jose, Calif.

3. HAROLD REANIER, born September 22, 1914, in Wisconsin. Harold married ELINORE PARK, now deceased. Harold lives in Manchester. Harold and Elinore had three children: THOMAS, born October 12, 1936; BURTON F., born November 2, 1937, and GAIL, born July 25, 1939.

4. CLIFFORD REANIER, born May 12, 1917, in Manette. He married MAE

VASGIAN. They had three children, WILLIAM, ROBERT and RENA. Later Clifford married EVELYN and they had a daughter, SELINDA. Clifford died and is buried at Retsil.

5. CHARLES REANIER, born May 30, 1918, in Manette. Charles married EDITH JONES. They were later divorced. Charles lives on Shore Drive in Manette. Charles and Edith had three children, DENNIS, NANETTE and TRACY.

6. GLENN REANIER, born August 19, 1924, in Manette. Glenn and his wife MARY LOU had three daughters.
Later Glenn remarried. He and his wife JUANITA live in Bremerton. They had a son. [Glenn died February 9, 1988.]

7. BETTY MAE REANIER, born November 26, 1928, in Manette. Betty Mae married CLARENCE STAYMEN. They have two daughters, THERESA and JACEYLYN.
Betty later married DICK CRANE, and they live in Duarte, Calif.

8. SHIRLEY REANIER, born September 24, 1930, in Manette. Shirley married DON COLEMAN and they live in Lake Havasu, Ariz. They have three children, RICHARD, BARBARA and DENISE.

RENN, JOHN WILLIAM
By Oliver Melvin Renn
1984

MIGRATION:
GERMANY TO MANETTE VIA TEXAS

My grandfather, John William Renn, also known as Bill, was born in Germany in 1858. He and his wife, Melvina Gallas Renn, came to Seattle about 1885. They moved to Washington from Texas because of hard times in Texas. John Renn was a carpenter.

In 1886 the family moved to Sidney, now Port Orchard, with their two sons, Herman (my father) and Edward; and John's brother Fred. A third child, Clara, was born in 1888. She was said to be the first white girl born in Sidney.

The Manette chapter of the Renn family history started in 1900 with the purchase of 10 acres of land from the Schwabacker brothers. The price was $200. The property is located between Trenton and Perry Avenues and is divided by East 18th Street. My grandmother, Melvina Renn Matteson, acquired the property in a divorce settlement in 1902 and gave each of her children one acre with the stipulation

Renn family members and some jumbo firewood, circa 1920s. Twenty fir trees like the one just felled here stood in the vicinity of East 18th Street and Nipsic Avenue, near the Renn home. Individuals in photo are (from left) Melvina Renn Matteson, Mabel Renn, Duane Matteson, Joseph Trucky and Olive Millington Bauer Trucky, mother of Mabel.
-Photo from Melvin Renn

they could not mortgage, sell or give away the land or it would immediately revert to their heirs, Melvina's grandchildren.

When Herman was a teenager one of his close friends was Frank Clay, another Manette pioneer. Frank was best man at my parents' wedding. The two families used to go on fishing trips together. Frank's daughter, Kathryn Clay Dickerson, lives near Gorst.

FRED RENN

Fred Renn logged and trapped for animal furs around Puget Sound, finishing out his life—as John did—living on the shores of Hood Canal.

HERMAN RENN

Herman Renn, my father, was born in Texas. He was 7 years old when he arrived in Seattle. He recalled standing on the old Grand Street Bridge watching the Seattle fire in '89.

Herman Renn home. The old family house built in 1914 now stands on the Southeast corner of East 18th Street and Trenton Avenue (1735 Trenton Avenue). When the house was built, East 18th Street did not exist.

He started to work in Puget Sound Navy Yard in 1901 as a boilermaker and riveter. In 1905 he built a home on 5th Street between Pacific and Park Avenues in Bremerton. He married Mabel Millington Bauer. Their son Oliver Melvin was born in 1913.

Herman was Bremerton's first night marshal (1911-1916) and later police chief (1922-24). He belonged to the city's first volunteer fire department.

Herman built the first house on the Manette property in 1914 on the Southeast corner of East 18th Street and Trenton Avenue, now 1735 Trenton.

The Renns moved to Seattle, where Herman was in charge of the swing-shift riveting gang at Skinner and Eddy Shipyard during World War I. We returned to Manette in 1920, moved to Bremerton in 1921, and back to Manette in 1924. Herman returned to work in the navy yard in 1924 and resumed living in the family home at 1735 Trenton Avenue in Manette.

In about 1928 while Herman was driving rivets overhead with a 40-pound air gun, a helper pushed a white hot rivet up to his ear, causing him to drop the air gun on his face, breaking his nose and doing other facial damage. During his recovery he was transferred to the pipe shop, where he remained until his retirement in 1943 after 28 years service.

Herman and Mabel bought property on Hood Canal, where they built and enjoyed a summer home "Camp Olivus."

Herman was a member of the Washington State Pioneers; Thomas M. Reed Masonic Lodge 225, Seattle; and Eagles Aerie 192, Bremerton. He lived with Melvin and Edythe in Seattle from 1956 until he died in 1959 at age 76.

MABEL MILLINGTON RENN

Mabel Millington, my mother, was born in Victoria, B.C. She was Bremerton's first telephone operator and sent the initial message to Seattle over Peninsular Telephone and Telegraph Company wires from Bremerton. Mother was a charter member of Philathea Chapter, Order of Eastern Star, in Manette. She died in Bremerton in 1946.

THE McMANNS

Edward's wife, Sidney, had a sister, Hattie McMann, who lived in Manette near what is now Pitt Avenue and Harkins Street. Hattie had one daughter, Marion, who married Hi Garrett. They had no children.

THE BASICS

From 1920 until 1930 living on Trenton Avenue was very basic. Our water supply came from a 30-foot well that liked to go dry in August or September. We carried water into the house and carried it out again. We spent our weekends at Camp Olivus.

The house was originally wired for electricity but we used coal-oil lamps until about 1928, when my father and Adrian Daley had to buy four light poles from Puget Sound Power and Light Company to get the wires strung up to the property line.

Each year in November the family car was put up on blocks and stayed in the garage until spring. Our only road was Trenton Avenue, which became a bog to Kidder's corner (East 13th Street and Trenton Avenue) and the clay too slick to climb up the Trenton hill from Jacobsen's canyon (East 16th Street and Trenton Avenue).

One year County Commissioner John Carlson loaned us a broken-down county gravel truck. Some neighbors, John Youngs, Adrian Daley, Lawrence Meagher, and I think Svend, Ervin and Viggo Jensen, helped load gravel and spread it on Trenton Avenue to make it an all-winter road. The truck lost its transmission after about five trips and sat alongside the road for a number of years.

Our fuel for heating and cooking came from the back acres plus some $12-a-ton coal from Hilstad's fuel yard down by the ferry dock. On the peak of the hill where Nipsic Avenue and East 18th Street meet there was a stand of old-growth fir trees that measured 3 to 6 feet at the stump. There were about 20 trees in the stand and all these were cut up for firewood. Today they would build four or five houses. My grandmother's second husband, Duane Matteson, hauled most of the wood to heat an apartment house on 5th Street in Bremerton. He transported the wood in his old Overland touring car (reported to be the first one sold in Kitsap County). The car was 'way ahead of its time, having an automatic transmission controlled by electric switches on the steering column.

EARLY NEWSBOYS

For a period of time five of us controlled the newspaper distribution in Manette. Bill Schweer and Floyd Buchanan took care of the *Bremerton Searchlight*. Eugene "Pogey" Parkins delivered the *Union Record* for a time. Harold Christensen had the *Post-Intelligencer* and I had the *Times*. We combined efforts to handle the routes and each would deliver half the morning and half the evening papers. On Saturday nights we would get our combined Sunday papers off the ferry *Pioneer* about 9 o'clock, load half of them in my old Model-T Ford and deliver the hill customers, sometimes picking up Don Rodger to go along for the ride, then back to the dock for another load to cover the beach down to the Croxtons.

During my school years in Manette and Bremerton I started working in 1928 at Shorties Garage on 7th Street in Bremerton. In 1931 I entered the navy yard as a supply department messenger. The summer of 1934 I was the engineer on McMicken's yacht, *Lotus*. With Harold Christensen's father as captain and Bill Schweer as cabin boy we spent 3 months in Alaska. I started a toolmaker apprenticeship in the navy yard in 1934 and moved to the shop superintendent's office in 1943 with a mechanical engineer rating. There was a reduction in force in the navy yard in 1949 and I started over with Military Sea Transport Service in Seattle in 1950. I transferred to Keyport Torpedo Station, then to Boeing Aerospace plant in Seattle; then to Portland, Oreg., in 1965 to become chief of production for the Defense Contract Administration office. I retired in July, 1970, with 38 years of government service.

Oliver Melvin and Edythe Renn, circa 1951.

JOHN McDONNELL'S FAMILY

A branch of the family of my wife, Edythe Toothaker Renn, pioneered in Manette. Her sister Zilda was Mrs. John McDonnell. John was a navy yard printer and was also instrumental in freeing the Manette Bridge from tolls. John's brother Dan was a yard boatbuilder and lived in Manette. He never married. John and Zilda's children are Cleo, wife of Boyde Gilbert, living in Kennewick; Agnes, wife of Dr. John C. McMillan, now living in Bellevue; and Norma, who married Dr. Hawley Jackson. Norma died in May, 1983. Cleo had no children, Agnes had three boys, and Norma had a girl, Dayna, and two boys, Robert and Richard.

THE JOHN RENN FAMILY

JOHN WILLIAM RENN was born in Germany in 1858. He married MEL-VINA GALLAS. John died in 1934. They had three children.

1. EDWARD ADOLF RENN. Edward was a carpenter and built many homes in north Seattle, Edmonds and Manette. He worked on Seattle's famous Big Dipper rollercoaster in Playland at Bitter Lake. Edward married SIDNEY THOMPSON about 1905. They had one son.
1A. HARVEY RENN. Harvey married DOROTHY (maiden name unknown) about 1938. Harvey served a coppersmith apprenticeship in the navy yard, became a safety engineer and later the fire chief at a naval installation on Bainbridge Island. Dorothy died in about 1962. Harvey and Dorothy had two children.
1A1. DARLENE RENN. Darlene married BIRGER HERTZ. They live in Arkansas. Darlene and Birger have four children, KIMBERLY, KARRY, KIRSTEN and KANDIE.
1A2. DARRELL RENN. Darrell married and had one son, MARK.

2. HERMAN RENN. Herman was born in Tyler, Tex., in 1881. He married MABEL MILLINGTON BAUER, who was born in Victoria, B.C., in 1882. They had one son.
2A. OLIVER MELVIN RENN was born February 7, 1913. He married EDYTHE TOOTHAKER of Hover, Wash., on July 3, 1935, in the Manette Community Church. Edythe was assistant leader of a troop of Girl Mariners in 1938-39. Melvin and Edythe lived at 2619 East 18th Street until 1950; they now live in Seattle. Melvin and Edythe have two sons.
2A1. JOHN OLIVER RENN, born May 4, 1942, in Bremerton. John is engineering department manager for CX Corporation in Seattle. In 1966 John married JANICE BRUKETTA. They have two daughters.
2A1a. DIANA CHRISTINE RENN, born February 16, 1971.
2A1b. DARCIE ELIZABETH RENN, born October 9, 1977.
2A2. WILLIAM ARTHUR RENN, born September 21, 1945, in Bremerton. Bill owns and operates Color Art Printing, Inc., in Seattle.

3. CLARA RENN. Clara was born in 1888, in Sidney, now Port Orchard. She married PATRICK McGUERN. Clara and Patrick divorced. Clara later married GEORGE REED and they wintered in Seattle and spent summers on Hood Canal. Both are now deceased. Clara and Patrick had one daughter.
3A. VIOLET McGUERN. Violet married JOSEF DIAMOND, Seattle attorney and parking lot owner. They have a son and a daughter, JOEL RENN DIAMOND and DIANE DIAMOND FROEMAN.

RODGER, JAMES
By Roger Paquette
1985

James Rodger (1878-1957) was born in Glasgow, Scotland. His family came to America when his father received a bid to be the boss blacksmith of San Francisco's Union Ironworks. James served his shipfitter apprenticeship (1893-1897) with the same firm. He worked on the U.S.S. *Olympia* (Admiral Dewey's flagship) and a sister ship built for the Japanese, and also helped build the U.S.S. *Ohio*. He was a personal escort for President William McKinley's party when the president appeared for the commissioning ceremony for the *Ohio* in 1901. (McKinley was assassinated 2 weeks later in Buffalo.)

In 1902, he came to Bremerton to work in the shipyard, and soon made a name for himself as a result of structural work on the U.S.S. *Oregon*. The Moran Shipbuilding Company of Seattle sought him out when faced with the task of building the U.S.S. *Nebraska*. Rodger, who, on his own terms, was granted 6 months' leave, supervised the laying of the keel of that ship. This was the first of several times Rodger shuttled between commercial and government jobs. During World War I he was superintendent for Seattle's J.F. Duthie Company. He retired from the shipyard in 1938 with 30 years of government service including 16 years as a supervisor and 5 as a planner and estimator.

Lena R. Brownlee (1886-1964) was born in Ohio and while a schoolteacher in Youngstown, came to Seattle in 1909 to spend her vacation at the Alaska Yukon Pacific Exposition.

She met James Rodger there and married him. After his death she married John C. Hall, a long-time family friend. She was a charter member and past matron of the Philathea Chapter 174 of the Order of Eastern Star, and a member of the Manette Community Church. Rodger was a past patron of the Philathea Chapter and served as past master of Steadfast Masonic Lodge of Manette. He was also a charter member of Boilermakers and Shipfitters Navy Yard Lodge 290.

Rodger had purchased property in Manette in the early 1900s. He was quoted as saying that "In the early days we used to row to and from work—and to union meetings, for that matter." The family home was at 2224 Perry Avenue.

The Rodgers had two children: Muriel (1910-1978) and Donald (1912-1980).

Muriel attended Manette School and graduated from Bremerton High School in 1929. She married Donald Young, son of another pioneer Manette family. They lived at 1616 Jacobsen Boulevard.

Muriel was employed by the Horton Nursing Home for 13 years and served 30 years with the Kitsap County Tuberculosis League. She was an active member of the state and local P-TAs, a member of the Philathea Chapter of the Eastern Star, the Altrusa Club and the Washington State HAUS.

Muriel and Don had two children: a son, Clyde "Tyke," deceased, and a daughter, Diane, of Bremerton.

Donald Rodger graduated from Manette Grade School and Bremerton High School. He retired from PSNS in 1972. He also worked at a shipyard in Balboa, Calif., and at Martha and Mary Nursing Home in Poulsbo. At the time of his death he was living in Kingston. He married Josephine Griffin (1909-1964) in 1940 in Bremerton. They had two daughters, Donna and Karen.

ROGERS, JOHN FRANCIS
By Jack Rogers

FROM UTAH TO MANETTE

John Francis Rogers, known as Frank, his wife Minnie, 6-year-old son Harold and 2-year old son Jack came from Juab County, Utah, to Pleasant Beach on Bainbridge Island and then, in 1917, to Manette. Frank worked in the navy yard. They rented a house and an acre of garden space from the Johnson family near the Waltenburgs out what is now Perry Avenue. Later they moved to Bremerton, where a daughter, Margaret Fern, was born.

Son Jack Rogers graduated from Bremerton High School in 1933 and attended the University of Washington. He left school in 1935 when hired as the first reporter employed by *The Bremerton Sun* when it was established July 15, 1935. He worked as reporter and city editor of the *Sun* from 1935 until 1942, when he became editor of *The Bremerton Daily News-Searchlight*. Jack was editor and publisher of the weekly *Port Orchard Independent* from 1947 until 1966 and proprietor of the Bremerton Printing Company from 1959 until 1969.

Jack married Dorothy Cole of Manette February 5, 1937.

PUBLICATIONS AND A GIFT SHOP

Jack and Dorothy paid Earl Harkins $100 for his *Manette News-Letter* and this paper eventually became the *Kitsap County News*, published on the Manette Peninsula until it was ultimately combined with the *Silverdale Breeze*, which Jack

Rogers and Dave Averill purchased from George Harrison.

In 1945, Jack and Dorothy and Wendell and Betty Arnold purchased the Treasure Chest, a gift shop in Bremerton, and operated it until 1956.

PUBLIC SERVICE

Jack began his public service career in 1940, when he was elected Kitsap County coroner. In 1941 he was appointed chairman of the Kitsap County Rationing Board by Governor Arthur B. Langlie and served in that position through World War II.

Jack Rogers was elected to the State Senate from 23rd District (Kitsap County) in 1944 and served 12 years, until 1957, in the senate. He was elected to the House of Representatives of the State Legislature and served there from 1963 until 1966. In 1966 he was elected as county commissioner in Kitsap County and served until 1969, when he was employed as executive director of Washington State Association of Counties.

In October of 1969 he moved from Bremerton to Olympia to act as legislative lobbyist for the county governments of the state of Washington. From 1971 to 1981 he served as member of the Public Employees Retirement System board of trustees and also as member of the Law Enforcement Officers and Fire Fighters Retirement System board of trustees. In 1980 he retired as executive director of the counties' association and in April of 1981 was appointed by Governor John Spellman to the State Investment Board, serving as chairman in 1983-84. In Feburary of 1985 he was reappointed by Governor Booth Gardner. This board has jurisdiction over investment of the state's pension and other trust funds.

CIVIC POSITIONS

Jack's civic experience includes membership in the Chambers of Commerce of Bremerton and Port Orchard, the Kiwanis and Lions Clubs of Bremerton, the Rotary Club of Olympia, the Audubon Society and the State Capital Historical Museum, of which he is a past president.

DOROTHY'S ACTIVITIES

After Jack and Dorothy moved from Chico to Olympia in 1969, Dorothy operated Fernbrook Herbs, a wholesale herb-growing nursery, and joined Karman McReynolds in writing a cookbook of favorite recipes featuring home-grown herbs. Karman and her husband Donald operated Cederbrook Herb Farm at Sequim. They formerly operated The Melody Lane restaurant in Bremerton when they lived in Tracyton.

Dorothy has been very active in volunteer work, both in Bremerton and Olympia. She has been chairman of the Herb Garden Committee at the Washington State Capitol Museum and she also has given many volunteer hours to the St. Peter's Hospital Auxiliary and the Puget Sound Blood Bank, and to serve as docent, guiding tours through the Governor's Mansion in Olympia.

ROMANCE

When Jack was courting Dorothy Cole of Manette in the early 1930s, the bridge to Manette charged tolls and we always will remember the cheery face and friendly words of George Baker as he collected 5 cents from pedestrians. Things were so money-tight in those Depression days that Jack often

would arrange to meet Dorothy at the toll booth at the Bremerton end of the bridge after she had paid for her crossing. Jack and Dorothy married February 5, 1937. They live in Chico.

GENEALOGY

1. HAROLD ROGERS, born August 28, 1911, in Mammoth, Utah. Harold married EVELYN CRAFT August 28, 1936. They had three children.
1A. SHARON ROGERS, who lives in Holly.
1B. PAMELA ROGERS, now Pamela MILLER, who lives in Seattle.
1C. PATRICK BRIAN ROGERS, now a physician in Bozeman, Mont.

2. JACK HENRY ROGERS, born October 8, 1915, in Juab County, Utah. Jack married DOROTHY COLE of Manette February 5, 1937. [See COLE history.]

3. MARGARET FERN ROGERS, known as Fern, born February 3, 1921, in Bremerton. Fern married JAMES WEBB and they live in East Bremerton. Fern and Jim have one daughter, CANDACE.

ROSS, GEORGE HERBERT
By John Ross
and Mildred Ross Hughes
1985

ENGLAND TO MANETTE

George Herbert Ross was born in Newcastle on Tyne in England April 7, 1872. He married Evelyn Booth from Sunderland, England, in 1904. George found work at Puget Sound Navy Yard. A daughter, Mildred, was born in Seattle October 16, 1910. Ross moved to Manette from Seattle with his wife, their 5-year-old son John (called Jack) and 6-month-old Mildred in April of 1911. The Ross family lived at 1154 Winfield Avenue in Manette. John recalls red trim on the window and door frames and madrona trees in the yard of their first home near East 11th Street and Hayward Avenue. George worked as a machinist at Puget Sound Naval Shipyard.

George Ross was active in the Masonic Lodge and was patron of Philathea Chapter of the Eastern Star in 1935. Daughter Mildred belonged to the Rainbow Girls.

Mail was brought to the post office on a wheelbarrow by Mr. Ed Aird, who met the ferry every day. Mrs. Eggleston was postmistress. She later became Mrs. Harkins.

JACK ROSS RECALLS

We moved to a larger place on Winfield Avenue on the corner of a road that connected Winfield to Perry Avenue. The Olsens with their three girls— Lucile, Gladys and Marguerite—and the Aldriches lived on the same side of our street. In about 1918 my parents bought a lot closer to town. Mr. Dewar and his boys helped clear the land and Mr. Armstrong and Chris Hilstad dug the basement using a horse and a hand-held scraper. A contractor constructed the house. Egglestons lived next to us until their house burned. I recall shooting pheasants from our back porch.

In 1911 I started to school in the two-room Manette School. My first grade teacher was Mrs. Drake. She was very nice although she reprimanded me sternly for rubbing charcoal on Earl McNeill's face in class. Later in the four-room school I remember Miss Vida Bean, who later became Mrs. Cornell. A Miss Pumpelli taught there one year. Mrs. Kallander in the seventh and eighth grades was motherly and had a profound influence on my life.

The last half of the eighth grade we all had to go to Smith School in Bremerton to graduate, since Manette School got too crowded. Ray Elliot was my teacher and we had a pleasant relationship. I enjoyed Halloween parties in the Manette School basement, playing ball on the field below the school and the games everyone played around the school building. Strange to say, I even enjoyed school work and learning.

There was a village blacksmith shop under the spreading prune tree that would be 1113 Perry Avenue today. I cranked the blower on the forge as Mr. Brown heated the iron or horseshoes to work on. I loved to hear the sound of the hammer on the anvil and to see the sparks fly as things were shaped or forged together. Mr. Brown and I always had good conversations. He taught me many things about the work and life.

The number 1 edition of the *East Bremerton Foghorn* was published by the Pursells November 18, 1920. It states,"Clyde Meredith is building a new house on his lots across from Martin's Store." The paper was published weekly. I helped set the type and print it.

I remember the Meredith family well and have a faint recollection of the older J.W. Meredith. I remember the Meredith and Martin grocery stores and a general merchandise store. They delivered orders by horse and wagon. One of the horses bit me on the hand, turning me against horses.

A volunteer fire department operated on the one-way dirt roads. Wooden sidewalks ran up the hill on what is now Perry Avenue. There was an old dock and all supplies came by water. Boats such as the *F.G. Reeve* ran the water route from Seattle with stops at Bainbridge Island, Manette, Sheridan, Chico, Silverdale, Bremerton, Charleston, Port Orchard and Waterman.

The launch *Bern* carried 20 people. The *Bern* landed at a float attached to the dock with a gangplank. I fished many times from this float.

The *Reeve* and others landed at the outer end of the dock with supplies, which were then hauled from a side door up a ramp on two-wheel hand carts pulled by a winch.

I remember seeing loggers cut timber and haul it by horse down to the bay at Sheridan on a skidroad.

I explored McDougal's Creek and canyon many times and I learned to swim at the mouth of the creek, not far from the present Bremerton Gardens.

Tom Fellows had a greenhouse that Mr. Shimasaki managed. I played house at Fellows' with Florence Fellows and Margaret Hixon.

I remember hikes to Big Rock above Illahee. On the way we hunted trilliums and also found licorice root to chew.

In the winter we would slide on our sleds from the top of the hill on Perry Avenue all the way down to the dock. Many of us loved to ice skate on Renner's pond and Clare's Marsh.

Manette was a very vital part of my life, especially the caring people who were friends and neighbors. My fondest, most treasured memories are about the old community church where the foundation was laid for my religious beliefs which have stayed with me all my life. Reverend Guy Nokes slept in the attic above the classrooms at the back of the church. I enjoyed being able to ring the church bell now and then. James Eggleston and I did the janitor work at one time.

At a Christian Endeavor meeting I saw for the first time Wynona Whitcomb, who years later was to become my dear wife, the greatest blessing in my life.

Many times I worked for Ben Kean wheeling coal, sand or gravel from barges to the storage area on the dock, as all material came by water in those days.

Later I worked at Martin's grocery store, driving a truck, picking up supplies and delivering groceries. It was an enjoyable experience but a far cry from present-day merchandising, such as at the supermarket at Silverdale.

Most of us boys loved swimming in the summer and in the early years skinny-dipped at the Sandbanks. I remember Mrs. Dewar wondering how William could get sunburned through his bathing suit. Later we swam in front of Hunton's, Boe's and Jacobsen's.

The Hunton boys and I dug a fortune out of the ground in front of Hunton's, now the 1300 block of Jacobsen Boulevard. We noticed the corner of a chest showing out of the ground above the beach. We dug it out and it was filled with wampum beads the Hudson Bay Company had used in trading with Indians. None of us knew what its being here meant. I don't know what happened to it.

I remember school picnics at Chico and at Enetai, in the vicinity of where the Carlsons lived later. I also remember Masonic picnics at Bainbridge Island.

I remember an unchaperoned beach party at Sandy Point, near the present Illahee State Park. We used rowboats for transportation. Parents, especially the girls' parents, were horrified when they found out. It was a good clean party and no one had anything to be ashamed of.

Since I quit school and went to work at 16, my childhood was short-lived. I was forced to start growing up and assume the responsibilities of life.

I belonged to the volunteer fire department. I still have a badge I was awarded as a memento. Our hose cart was handdrawn and we were slow getting to fires, especially on an uphill grade.

We had many friends, some especially dear, such as the William Abbotts, Theodore Petersons, Hugo Berglinds and Saunders Ford Dewars. My close friends were James Eggleston, Richard and Lendall Hunton, Bill, Charlie, and Warren Dewar and Earl McNeill.

I first started to work in the navy yard in 1922 as a messenger boy in the commander's office at $1 per day. My next job was at Mount Rainier on road construction. I then went to the Port Gamble sawmill, then to concrete pier construction at the navy yard. While working at Martin's grocery on August 9, 1923, I was accepted and started an apprenticeship in the electrical shop at the naval shipyard. During that time I went to night school and finished my high school education, graduating in September, 1927. I worked up to chief quarterman electrician, a job I held until I retired in 1961.

I met Wynona Whitcomb in 1926. In 1932 we became engaged. In October 1932, Wynona quit her job as head cashier and bookkeeper at Bremerton J.C. Penney store and came to Honolulu where I was working, and we were married. Emily McHenry Mecklenburg, her friend of many years, was her matron of honor. We lived in Honolulu 6 months until I was able to transfer back to Bremerton. We found waterfront property on Erland's Point and established our permanent home there. Eighteen years after our family grew up we moved to Panorama City, Wash., in 1974.

Our son Wyman is a National Forest supervisor at Packwood Ranger District and is district fire commissioner. Our daughter Joan is psychophysical therapist at Federal Way Medical Clinic and her husband is a physician there.

MILDRED ROSS REMEMBERS

Manette was a great place to me, and one outstanding thing in my memory were the visits to the Carlson home on Manette beach. I went with a lady called Mrs. Andrew Peterson.

I married a Manette boy, Darrell Z. Jones, who lived on Scott Avenue. He went to Manette School and his father worked at Puget Sound Navy Yard. Darrell and I lived at 1154 Winfield Avenue and Darrell worked at the navy yard. We moved to Bremerton in 1932. In 1938 we moved to Portsmouth, Va.,where Darrell worked in the Norfolk Naval Shipyard. Ten years later we moved to Virginia Beach, where we lived for 19 years. Darrell passed away in 1976. I married W. Gordon Hughes and now live in Blounts Creek, N. C.

Although I have lived in many places since those days long ago—I will never forget Manette.

My son, Norman Ross Jones, graduated from North Carolina State University and today is a corporate executive for the Scott Paper Company. He lives in West Chester, Pa., with his wife Melissa and three children, Heather, Ross and Aaron.

FAMILY SUMMARY

GEORGE ROSS (England 1872-Bremerton 1969) married EVELYN BOOTH (England 1871-Bremerton 1921) in 1904. George and Evelyn had two children.

1. JOHN B. "Jack" ROSS, born in Seattle November 16, 1905. Jack married WYNONA M. WHITCOMB in 1932. Jack and Wynona live in Panorama City, Wash. They have a son and a daughter.
1A. WYMAN GEORGE ROSS, born August 10, 1933, in Bremerton. Wyman married GAYLE L. DAVIS in 1968. They have two children.
1A1. JONATHAN A. ROSS, born November 15, 1969, in Chehalis.
1A2. MICHAEL J. ROSS, born October 5, 1971, in Chehalis.
1B. JOAN L. ROSS, born August 15, 1935, in Bremerton. She married Dr. MAXWELL WALDRON in 1956. They had three children.
1B1. LIANE B. WALDRON, born March 3, 1961, in Burien.
1B2. GRANT R. WALDRON, born August 26, 1964, in Burien.
1B3. BLAKE D. WALDRON, born July 3, 1966, in Burien.

2. MARTHA MILDRED ROSS, born in Seattle October 16, 1910. Martha married DARREL Z. JONES of Manette in 1929. Darrell died in 1976. Later Martha married GORDON W. HUGHES. Martha and Darrel had a son.
2A. NORMAN ROSS JONES, born in Virginia October 28, 1945. He married MELISSA ANNE MURRAY February 15, 1969. They have one daughter and twin sons.
2A1. HEATHER JONES, born December 13, 1970, in Goldsboro, N.C.
2A2. ROSS JONES, born July 20, 1976, in Dover, Del.
2A3. AARON JONES, born July 20, 1976, in Dover.

RULEY, PAUL E.

The 1909 Kitsap County Plat Book introduces "Paul Ruley, Farmer.... Born in Stuttgart, Germany, fifty years ago" at the age 2 1/2 he "came with his parents to America and settled in Oneida County, N.Y., where he remained with them, going to school until his eleventh year. Since that time he has shifted for himself. Twenty-five years ago he took up his present place, where he has resided ever since and raised his family. Mr. Ruley is an industrious citizen of integrity, and having been deprived of the advantages of an early education, is a zealous advocate for the educational advantages not only of his own children but the young of the community. He has a good backer in his wife, Jane E. Ruley, who was educated for a teacher and served her day and generation for several years in that capacity. Mr. Ruley has served for a number of years on the School Board of his district, which position he now fills." Dianne Robinson's *Kitsap County Black History* states, "Mrs. Jane A. Ruley was born Lilly Jane Archer in Berkley, Virginia, in 1856. The daughter of a slave and considered a very gifted child, she was educated in the General Armstrong School in Hampton, Virginia (now Hampton Institute), where she was the valedictorian of her class. As was reported in the *Bremerton News* on November 23, 1915, one of her most notable classmates was Booker T. Washington with whom she shared the same date of birth....

"After graduating from General Armstrong School in 1875, she moved to the Northwest where she settled down in Kitsap County to work in her profession as a teacher. Here she proved herself as a woman of excellent scholarship and was prominent in the educational affairs of her community and dedicated community worker....

"Mr. and Mrs. Ruley had two children, a son, Archie and a daughter Gertrude....

"It is said that in the early days, Mrs. Ruley held school in a barn on the Ruley Ranch which was called the "Sleepy Hollow Ranch." Later on they helped establish the first Sheridan School #22 and became instrumental in the support and upkeep of this Bremerton early school....

"March 27, 1897, records of the Sheridan #22 School show that Mrs. Ruley was selected as first teacher of the school. Other records indicate she was the first black school teacher in Kitsap County and first black school teacher in the State of Washington.

"Mrs. Ruley also taught the first Sunday School for the Manette Church, introduced music to its members and served as an organist....

"Archie was known in the Sheridan and Manette area as one of the greatest pitchers during his time who kept the name of the ball team going. As reported in the *Bremerton News* of July 2, 1915, he was given a surprise party by his team members for his 21st birthday. He also played ball at the Washington College where he attended school.

"Gertrude was known in the community as a very talented young lady....she played the piano. She finished Union High School in 1914 and was the class salutatorian.

"At the age of 17, Gertrude entered Washington State College in Pullman.... Her major was in the field of muisic and she graduated in 1918 with a degree of Bachelor of Arts in Music."

Paul Ruley died September 18, 1913 and Jane died in 1927.

SCHLAGEL, CHARLES
By Mary H. Schlagel Wagner
1987

Charles Frederick Schlagel was born in Prussia, Germany, in 1867. His father left home when Charles was a small child. His mother was a midwife who practiced medicine and raised three children.

Charles wanted to be in the navy when he grew up, but was too short and the government wanted to put him in the army. He ran away from Germany and shipped on a Norwegian sailing ship. After years of sailing to various countries and after many adventures including being shipwrecked, he came to Seattle. While in Seattle working on ship repairs, he fell from a mast to the deck and was badly injured. When the hospital released him the ship had already sailed. In 1897 or 1898 he came to the Bremerton to work as a carpenter in the navy yard.

Charles Schlagel home at 3125 Rickey Road. Mary and her husband Warren Wagner live in this home.

He lived at the Antone Hitzell place in Bremerton and ate meals at the George Hefner boarding house in Bremerton. He met Francisco Romaine Reiml at the boarding house, where she worked. Mr. and Mrs. Hefner had sent to Germany for her to work for them. Francisco's grandmother was Mrs. Hefner's sister. Francisco was born in Bavaria, Germany, and arrived in Bremerton in 1898. She was petite and had brown eyes, dark brown hair and olive skin.

Charles was short with dark, curly hair and blue eyes. They were married December 17, 1899, in Bremerton. She was 19 and he was 32. Their marriage was recorded December 20, 1899, in Sidney (now Port Orchard).

Charles Schlagel drawing water by rope and pulley from his well on Sheridan hill, about 1910.

Charles and Francisco first lived in a small house behind where the Kitsap Dairy used to be on Park Avenue. Charles built them a nice home on 5th Street. Their son, George, was born there in 1900. Their first daughter, Frances, was born in 1902. Then came Beatrice, Margaret, Emelia and Mary. The first five children were born in Bremerton and Mary was born on Sheridan Hill.

The children were all baptized in the Catholic church, located (I believe) at 5th and Washington. We went there by rowboat, landing where Kenyon Lumber Yard was and walking from there. Later years we went on boats that ran from Erland's Point, Chico, Silverdale, Fairview, Tracyton and Sheridan to Bremerton.

In the early 1900s Charles purchased 9.79 acres on Sheridan Hill from Joseph E. and Clara A. Pitt. This property was part of the Joseph E. Pitt homestead and the deed was filed in Port Orchard on June 27, 1908. They evidently started buying the property before 1908 as they spent some time there in the summertime in a tent house before they built their home.

In 1908 Charles started to build the barn on the property. The family was all in the tent house for the summer. When Francisco realized she was going to have another baby, Charles just added two more big rooms on the front of the barn and it turned out to be a house. It was built of 1x12's up and down with battens on the seams and tar paper over them. The kitchen living area was 16x20 and the other two rooms were 12x16. Mary Helen was born in the front room on February 5, 1909. Mary and her husband of 56 years still live there.

In 1909 Charles sold the 5th Street house to the Lewis Funeral Home. Lewis built the funeral chapel on the site in 1909 or 1910 after moving our house to a different location.

Francisco was not too well, and the stress of six small children, the new home and pressures from certain neighbors took their toll and she passed away December 25, 1909, at age 29.

German friends, Mr. and Mrs. Frank Melzer, took care of Mary until she was a year or so old and Charles could manage us all. Charles stayed home with the children for about 2 years until Emelia and Mary were older and could be left with good neighbors when Charles worked and the other children were in school. I cannot imagine how he could manage six small children alone, but he did. He would always say, "I would do it again without any hesitation." He washed, cooked, baked, sewed and mended.

From then on our lives were intermingled with all the good neighbors on the hillside: the Hefners, Hitzels, Pitts and others who had moved to the neighborhood from Bremerton. Mrs. Hefner was Francisco's great aunt and Mrs. Hitzel was somehow related to her.

Frances and George Schlagel and possibly Beatrice went to the one-room Sheridan School. They had to walk about 2 miles. Charles Schlagel built the two-room schoolhouse that followed the one-room school. We were in the Tracyton School District but Sheridan School was closer, so Charles went to Port Orchard and had the school district boundaries changed. By the time the youngest girl, Mary, was ready for school, Frances had graduated from grade school. So Frances was the little mother at home. Emelia didn't start to school until Mary was old enough to go to school. The older children would take Emelia and Mary to some of the neighbors on their way to school. Among our favorite neighbors were Grandpa

Charles Schlagel family, about 1916. Back row (from left), Frances, Charles, Beatrice and George.
Front row, Margaret, Emelia and Mary.   - Photo from Mary Schlagel Wagner

and Grandma Hodges, not really our grandparents, but very dear, and kind. Grandma Hodges was small, rather plump, red-headed and fiery-tempered when crossed. The Hodgeses raised their grandson, Charlie Holland, and their granddaughter, Hazel Hodges.

Charles built homes and buildings around the neighborhood, in Bremerton and around the bay. He would take the wheelbarrow and his carpenter tools down to the bay and row to Bremerton, or around Rocky Point, or to Oyster Bay or Phinney Bay. He built two boats, and would take all the children on outings on summer days, usually on Sunday afternoon.

People worked 6 days a week back in those times. Charles built the Lewis house which is still on Lewis Lane. He worked on the Wallace Building in Bremerton. The original home he built for Jim and Harriet Peckenpaugh is still standing behind The Willows retirement home. He worked in a cabinet shop in Bremerton for a man named Hornbogan.

We always raised a big garden and had cows, chickens and pigs for winter meat. We had to work in the garden in the summertime until noon. Papa would outline just what he wanted done before we could go to the beach to swim. We always waited until after 12 o'clock to go the beach so Mrs. Hubbell wouldn't think we hadn't had our lunch. The neighbor women would worry about us because we didn't have a mother.

What fun we had at the beach with all the Hubbell children and others! We used to stay until the boat went by to get the working men from the navy yard. We waited to swim in the waves the boat made; then we would hurry home to get supper for Papa and do the chores. One of our greatest pleasures was to run down the road, hide and wait for Papa to come up the road from work; we would jump out of the hiding place

and say "Boo!" He would always pretend to be real frightened, and he probably saw us all the time.

Harry Martin used to solicit for our grocery order once a week and then deliver the groceries later. He first used a horse and buggy and in later years a car. In the wintertime he would sometimes have to leave the groceries at the bottom of the road and we would have to go and get them with a sled. There was a real steep hill by our place then. Even cars had a time getting up there in the winter. The road ended at our barn.

It seems as if the weather was colder in the winter than it is now. In 1916 there was the big snow—4 feet at least. It was quite a bit of snow to shovel to clear a path to the barn and the "chic sales." The older boys had bobsleds and had great times starting at Smith's Hill and trying to go all the way to the bay. One time one bobsled went off the bridge down by Lewis' place. I think brother George was on that one. They took some extra precautions after that incident. The Clare boys had their bobsled too. They lived out at Clare's Marsh, across the road from what is now Value Giant. There was ice skating in the wintertime on the marsh.

In later years, Charles Schlagel continued to be a help and a comfort to his children and grandchildren. He loved to go with Warren and Mary and family on fishing trips; he loved to fish.

Mary and Warren, Frances and Russell continued to trade at Martin's grocery store in Manette, and at Etten's meat market. Charles always traded there. He had a Model-T Ford. He would come over on the *Pioneer* and do his buying. Before Mary was married she would come home on Sunday. Papa would meet her on the other side and he would cook T-bone steaks and eggs for breakfast.

Charles continued to work until he was about 75 years old.

He always provided for his family: not luxury, but meat and potatoes and love; he raised a big garden, made dill pickles and smoked hams and bacon. Papa always made the dressing for the turkey even in later years. He was not too well in later years; he had arthritis and that foot of his that was injured on the sailing vessel gave him much pain. He had to have it amputated when he was about 80 years old. With help from Frances, Mary and Margaret he managed to stay in his little cabin. He passed away on October 12, 1956, at age 89.

GEORGE SCHLAGEL

George Schlagel was a quiet but ambitious boy. He was protective to his sisters and a joy to his father. After graduating from Sheridan School he went to work in the navy yard as an apprentice machinist at age 14. He and Papa traveled back and forth on the boat to Bremerton. In October 1918, he finished his apprenticeship. This was during World War I. One week later he contracted the flu and died. Many people were dying and doctors were difficult to get out here.

FRANCES SCHLAGEL

When Frances was about 14 she went to work as a mother's helper in Bremerton. As she got older she worked at Jackson's Book Store, then in the 5-and-10-cent store for Edith Hull. Her best friend, "Glo" Hubbell, worked there also. Frances met Russell William Rickey when she was working in Bre...erton. He had been a soldier in World War I. They were married in 1920. Before their first son, Harold, was born they moved out to Grandpa Hodges' place. When Harold was 9 months old, he got ill with convulsions. He died on the *Pioneer* on the way to the hospital.

Soon after Harold's death Frances and Russell moved back to Bremerton. They had another son, Robert, in 1924. They bought a home up on Yantic Avenue. Their third son, William "Billy" died of spinal meningitis in 1933. They moved back to Sheridan Heights and built their permanent home there. Their fourth son, Charles, was born there in 1936.

Russell Rickey was active in the neighborhood and was responsible for the road being named Rickey Road. Russell died while they were on a trailer trip to Arizona in 1964.

Frances worked for the Sheridan Village Laundromat, and then helped her sister Mary at the Manette Station post office when Mary got the office in 1964. This was a contract station. When Mary retired, Frances helped Winona Seymour at the post office.

BEATRICE SCHLAGEL

Beatrice met her future husband, William James Parrott, in 1921. He had come to work in the navy yard and was staying with our good friends, the Van Stralens. When his job ran out in the navy yard he went back to Michigan. Beatrice and Bill had an understanding when he left and she went to Michigan, where they were married.

When their first boy, Charles "Buddy," was 9 months old they packed their Model-T Ford with all their worldly possessions and came back to the beautiful Northwest. It took them a month to get here. They lived in Manette for awhile and then moved to Seattle, where Vera was born. They moved back to Manette and lived in Grandpa Hodges' house. Bill couldn't find work here and they went back to Michigan, where two more boys, Lawrence and Maurice, were born. Beatrice died

in Romeo, Mich., in 1930.

MARGARET SCHLAGEL

Margaret went to work for F.J. Perry sewing machine shop in Bremerton in 1919, when she was 14. When she was 19, she opened her own hemstitching shop on Second Street. She married William D. Fountaine in 1924. Bill was in the navy so Margaret spent some time traveling. When Bill was stationed in Bremerton she worked at Pizers department store. They built their home on Sheridan Hill and still reside there after 63 years of marriage.

After the war Bill and Margaret developed a resort at Tahuya. It is now Sandy's Resort. They then bought a general store at Riffe, Wash. It is now under Riffe Lake.

EMELIA SCHLAGEL

Emelia stayed at home with Mary until Mary could go to school. The older children would drop us off at the good neighbors' houses on their way to school and pick us up on their way home. Emelia went to the two-room Sheridan School up on the north side of Sheridan Road—the school where the big boys from Manette used to turn over the outside "chic sales" every Halloween. The big boys and some of the fathers had to turn them back up, but until they were righted "thank goodness for the woods."

As the older girls left home and Emelia was out of grade school, Emelia and Mary were soon alone with Papa. Emelia tended the house.

MARY SCHLAGEL

Mary graduated from Union High School in Bremerton in 1927. She went to Wilson's Business College in Seattle. She worked at Christenson's Bakery in Bremerton, at Edith Hull's 5-and-10-cent store, and at D.D. Ellis' drug store in Charleston.

Mary met Warren E. Wagner while she was working at the drug store. Warren was born in Port Orchard and worked in the navy yard. Warren and Mary eloped and were married in Prosser July 13, 1931. Mary worked 5 years in the school lunch program. Mary and Warren celebrated their 55th wedding anniversary in 1986. They moved out to Sheridan Heights in February of 1933 to the old Charles Schlagel home.

Warren retired in 1959. Mary took over the contract post office on Second Street in Bremerton. She continued to operate it until 1961, when the Wycoff Station was completed. Mary then did babysitting, enumerated for the city directory, and worked at the Sheridan Village Laundromat. In 1964 she was the successful bidder on the contract to operate the Manette Station post office on Scott Avenue.

Mary and Warren had three children, Jerry, Sylvia and Dale. Jerry went to Sheridan Grade School and Bremerton High School. He became an Eagle Scout and was active in 4-H. He worked in the navy yard as an apprentice, then went into the army for 3 years during the Korean War. He took an apprentice printer's course at the Everett Herald.

Sylvia was active in 4-H. She attended Olympic View School and Bremerton High School. She graduated from beauty school and worked for Isabelle Birkenfeld in Bremerton. Sylvia went to college for 2 years in Seattle and is a medical records technician.

Dale was in scouting. He went to View Ridge Elementary

School and East High School. He attended Olympic College and University of Washington. Dale works at Boeing in graphic art.

In 1967 Warren and Mary Schlagel moved the Manette post office to its present location at 2106 East 11th Street. They have since retired. Gardening, trailering, fishing, neighborhood involvement and grandchildren now keep them busy.

GENEALOGY

CHARLES FREDERICK SCHLAGEL (8-3-1867 to 10-12-1956) and FRANCISCO ROMAINE REIML SCHLAGEL (1880 to 12-25-1909) had six children.

1. GEORGE FREDERICK SCHLAGEL, born in October of 1900 in Bremerton. George died in 1918.

2. FRANCES KATHERINE SCHLAGEL, born January 20, 1902, in Bremerton. Frances married RUSSELL WILLIAM RICKEY in 1920. Russell died in 1964. Frances died April 3, 1978. Frances and Russell had four sons.
2A. HAROLD DESMOND RICKEY, born in Bremerton in 1921. Harold died at age 9 months.
2B. ROBERT RICKEY, born in Bremerton in February 1924. Robert and his wife SALLY had two children, LAURA and WILLIAM.
2C. WILLIAM R. RICKEY, born in Bremerton in 1926. William died in 1933.
2D. CHARLES RICKEY, born at Sheridan Heights in 1936. Charles and his wife FLORA have three children: BRUCE, CHERIS and CHARLEEN.

3. BEATRICE EDITH SCHLAGEL, born in May 1903 in Bremerton. Beatrice married WILLIAM JAMES PARROTT. Beatrice died in 1930. She and William had four children.
3A. CHARLES "Buddy" PARROTT, born in Michigan. Charles and his wife JOYCE had four children; two died in infancy.
3B. VERA PARROTT, born in Seattle. Vera married JIM FROST and they have four sons and a daughter.
3C. LAWRENCE PARROTT, born in Michigan. Lawrence and his wife have two children.
3D. MAURICE PARROTT, born in Michigan. Maurice and his wife FRANCES have four sons.

4. MARGARET MARY SCHLAGEL, born April 1, 1905, in Bremerton. Margaret married WILLIAM D. FOUNTAINE in August 1924. They still live on part of the Schlagel property.

5. EMELIA ELIZABETH SCHLAGEL, born November 22, 1907, in Bremerton. When she was 16 she married LLOYD SIMS and lived in Bremerton. She divorced Lloyd, remarried him, then divorced again. Emelia married JOHN FLOORE, divorced him and later married CLYDE ECHOLS. Clyde died in 1983. Emelia lives in Texas.

6. MARY HELEN SCHLAGEL, born February 5, 1909, at home in Sheridan. Mary married WARREN E. WAGNER July 13, 1931. They have three children.
6A. JERRY E. WAGNER, born September 19, 1933, in Bremerton. Jerry married JANET HARSHBARGAR in the Manette Community Church January 18, 1957. They have three children.
6A1. JEANNINE WAGNER, born June 2, 1960, in Everett. Jeannine married BILL THURN.
6A2. DARRELL WAGNER, born March 12, 1962, in Everett.
6A3. ALLISON WAGNER, born July 17, 1965, in Seattle. Allison married SCOTT STERLAND.
6B. SYLVIA G. WAGNER, born April 3, 1937, in Bremerton. Sylvia married JOSEPH HOFMANN September 27, 1958. They have two children.
6B1. ANITA HOFMANN, born June 20, 1959. Anita married MONOLITA MUNAR
6B2. ROBERT HOFMANN, born December 21, 1962.
6C. DALE W. WAGNER, born June 6, 1946, in Bremerton. Dale married CAROL KING in 1978. They have one daughter, JENNIFER, born October 2, 1978.

SCHOONOVER, EDWARD
By Ada Schoonover Matteson
1984

Edward Schoonover was born in West Virginia on March 21, 1874, and died in Bremerton April 19, 1956. In 1897 he went to Alaska, where he spent 20 years prospecting. As one of the survivors of the Chilkoot Trail he rafted down the Yukon River, made a few strikes and wrote poetry and stories.

Gertrude Green was born in Juliette, Idaho, November 6, 1884, and died June 29, 1971. She was educated in Idaho, attended Central Washington College in Ellensburg and did some teaching. She married Charles Brallier and lived in Yakima. Charles Brallier drowned 3 months before the birth of their son, Leroy. Leroy was 3 years old when Gertrude married Edward Schoonover in Grandview, Wash., on January 30, 1912.

A son Raymond was born July 26, 1914, in Grandview and a daughter Ada was born January 16, 1916, in Prosser. The family moved to Seattle and, in December of 1916, to Bremerton. A daughter Margaret "Margie" was born December 14, 1918, in Bremerton. In the spring of 1919 the family moved to Manette, where a third daughter Bernice was born September 6, 1921. Dr. John Schutt came to the house in his Ford to deliver her.

Our one-bedroom house was small for such a large family. In the mid-1920s our father added three rooms. We had no electricity or running water but we had a good well under our porch. Our mother had a box on a pulley. She kept meat, milk, butter and other perishables in the box, which she would lower into the well just above the water line. We always had good cold milk to drink. John Pfenning delivered the milk. He had a pasture between Perry and Winfield Avenues south of East 18th Street where he kept his cows.

Our home was on the south side of East 16th Street, west of Trenton Avenue. We had an acre of land inside the city

Schoonover home at 2703 East 16th Street in 1919.

limits. Across the road was the county line.

Our outhouse, which we called Mrs. Jones, caught fire one night. This was great. There was my dad in his underwear getting water from the well on our back porch, yelling his head off, "Fire in Mrs. Jones!" Of course we had to help, so we all scrambled out of bed. We had to pump water from the well, run down the steps and about 200 feet to throw water on the fire. And do you know, we saved about half of that old toilet.

Every June my father, being an outdoor man, took the kitchen door off the hinges and put it away until September. We had no screen door like today. The windows were left wide open at night, so we could hear the coyotes and cougars cry. We missed a lot of sleep at night fretting about that.

Schoonover family in 1943. Back row (from left): Raymond; Bernice (Mrs. Jones); Leroy Brallier (Mrs. Schoonover's son by previous marriage). Front row, Marjorie (Mrs. Rhodes), Edward, Gertrude and Ada (now Mrs. Matteson).

Our father enjoyed gardening. We had an abundance of vegetables and all kinds of fruit trees and berries.

Leroy and Raymond were hunters. When they got a deer during hunting season, Mother, a hard-working woman, promptly canned the venison. She would carefully cut the meat off the neck, add it to our apples and make jars of mincemeat (no equal). She canned the rest of the meat in jars. She canned hundreds of jars of food during the summer to see us through the winter. We didn't have electricity or city water until about the time the Manette Bridge was built in 1930. She scrubbed our clothes on a scrub board and hung them out to dry.

I remember when we finally did get electricity. The men came and spent the day wiring our house. The cords hung down from the ceilings, with a bulb hanging on each, and a long chain which we could pull to turn the light on or off. Well, this man stuck his finger up into the socket, pulled the string and said, "Yep, there's juice." So after they left, I climbed on a chair, pulled the string, stuck my finger in the socket, nearly fell off, but I said to my two sisters, "Yep, there's juice." My first big jolt.

We had a fold-up rubber bathtub. Every Saturday evening our father would place galvanized tubs on the stove, fill them with water from the well and stoke the stove to heat the water

for our baths. After our baths, our clothes were all ready for us, starched and polished, for next day's Sunday School.

The school, which was a big square brown-on-top and white-on-the-bottom building, housed a basement, two rooms on the first floor and two rooms with an office on the top floor. Each classroom had a cloak room, where we hung our coats and put our galoshes. It reeked with various odors. When we were bad, we had to spend time meditating our sins in the cloak room. The principal's office was a dreaded place. When we were really bad we were sent there to receive a spanking or lecture.

The ferryboat that crossed from Manette to Bremerton had cabins on either side, one side for the ladies and the other for the men (the men smoked on their side). Two benches were in each cabin—one along the outside and the other along the inside. The center part of the boat was for cars. Eight cars was about the capacity.

One day we docked on the Manette side on our way home from Lincoln Junior High School. A rowboat pulled up at the end of the ferry with Bill Schweer in it urging the kids to get in and he would take them ashore. Harold Christiansen decided that was a great idea, so he attempted to climb aboard. In doing so, he upset the rowboat and all aboard had a good ducking.

In the wintertime after the bridge was built we'd take our sleds, ride down Perry Avenue and make the turn down the main street of Manette. Then we would walk up the incline of the bridge as far as the span, being careful not to be seen by the toll takers on the Bremerton side. Down we would slide, ending up by the Harkins house at the end of the street.

Church and school were the meeting places of the Manette community. We had plays, musicals and get-togethers for many occasions. Everyone turned out and it was always fun. Some of our best memories were Christmas Eve at the church. We could hardly wait. We had pieces to say, songs to sing. Elizabeth von Hoene played the piano and Mrs. Hawthorne led the music. Mr. Hoopes was the superintendent. What we all looked forward to and listened for were the sleigh bells from Santa Claus, alias Tom Bright. He would come down the aisle shouting "Merry Christmas" and shaking the sleigh bells. We would all get excited. There was always an orange and a little pasteboard box of hard candy—the best candy of all—and something nice from our Sunday School teacher.

Our father retired from the navy yard in 1936 after 20 years as a tile setter. The folks sold the home and moved to Silverdale, where they lived for 7 years. They then moved back to Manette, living at 4005 North Perry Avenue for the duration of their lives.

THE FAMILY

EDWARD and GERTRUDE SCHOONOVER's descendants include:

1. LEROY BRALLIER, son of CHARLES BRALLIER, Gertrude's first husband.

2. RAYMOND SCHOONOVER, born July 26, 1914, in Grandview. Raymond married ELLEN BRALLIER, a cousin of Leroy Brallier. Raymond and Ellen lived in Bremerton. Raymond worked at Sears. Ellen died in 1965. Later Raymond married FRANCIS ERICKSON. Raymond died in 1983. Raymond and Ellen had two daughters.
2A. CAROLYN SCHOONOVER, born September 28, 1936, in Bremerton. Carolyn married CALVIN ROBINSON in 1953. They had two sons and two daughters. In 1965 Carolyn married ALVIN MERCER and her two younger children changed their name to Mercer.
2A1. KAREN ROBINSON, born September 1, 1953. Karen married chiropractor TOM NESS in 1972. They live in Bremerton. They have a son and a daughter: BRENT, born February 26, 1975, and JESSICA, born July 24, 1980.
2A2. KURT ROBINSON, born August 16, 1954. Kurt married JAN NELSON October 16, 1983. They live in Port Orchard and have sons: JOSH and NICHOLAS.
2A3. KIM RAY MERCER, born March 14, 1956. He married RACHEL SMALLEY October 20, 1984. They have a son TREVER and a daughter ASHLEY. They live in Bremerton.
2A4. KELLY MERCER, born May 31, 1958. She lives at Lake Symington.
2B. JUNE SCHOONOVER, born June 20, 1946, in Bremerton. June married CARL FRANCOM and they lived in Bremerton. June died in 1984. June and Carl had a son, RAYMOND, born in Bremerton.

3. ADA SCHOONOVER, born January 16, 1916, in Prosser. Ada married BURL MATTESON. They have lived at 2923 Wheaton Way since 1940. They have four daughters.
3A. JOAN MATTESON, born in Bremerton. Joan married DENNIS RAINIER. Joan and Dennis live in Seattle and have a son and a daughter: TIMOTHY, born September 7, 1966, and JODEEN, born May 30, 1968.
3B. SUSAN MATTESON, born April 6, 1941, in Bremerton. Susan married PHILLIP WEBER. They live in Bremerton and have three sons and a daughter:
3B1. WENDY WEBER, born January 15, 1959. Wendy married SALVITOR LAZZARA and they live in Virginia. They have four children: SALVATOR, born November 23, 1978; NICKOLE, born July 19, 1981; RYAN, born July 15, 1983, and AMBER, born May 6, 1985.
3B2. PHILIP A. "Tony" WEBER, born December 28, 1961. Tony married Dana Van Buskirk and they have two sons: JOSHUA, born January 8, 1980, and SAM, born April 4, 1983.
3B3. JOSEPH WEBER, born April 24, 1968.
3B4. DAVID WEBER, born February 24, 1971.

3C. GAY MATTESON, born April 8, 1943, in Bremerton. Gay married JACK SCHMIDT and they live in Lynnwood, Wash. They have one daughter: CONSTANCE, born June 19, 1964.
3D. DONNA MATTESON, born January 29, 1950, in Bremerton. Donna married SCOTT DAVIS. They live in Port Orchard and have a son and a daughter: TODD, born December 11, 1968, and TRACI, born April 2, 1973.

4. MARJORIE SCHOONOVER, born December 14, 1918, in Bremerton. Marjorie married COY RHODES. They made their home on Harbel Drive. Coy died in 1980; Marjorie died in 1983. They had one son.
4A. DAN COY RHODES, born January 30, 1943, in Bremerton. Dan married JOANN BRUNSTEAD and they have three children:
4A1. JEFF RHODES, born June 4, 1964. Jeff married DENA SARTOR. They have a son: DUSTIN, born August 29, 1986. They live in Port Orchard.
4A2. JULIE RHODES, born August 14, 1969.
4A3. DAN RHODES, born April 10, 1975.

5. BERNICE SCHOONOVER, born September 6, 1921, in Manette. Bernice married DEAN JONES. They live on Dora Avenue. Dean Jones was sheriff of Kitsap County for 20 years, a position now held by a son, Patrick. Dean and Bernice Jones have four children.
5A. DEAN "Bud" JONES, born September 21, 1941, in Bremerton. He married YVONNE FULBRIGHT. They have a son and a daughter: SUZANNE, born May 26, 1977, and DEAN RYAN, born February 1, 1980.
5B. LINDA JONES, born May 14, 1944, in Bremerton. Linda married KENNETH HUGHES in 1966. They have one son and one daughter: MELINDA, born May 31, 1968, and MARK, born October 12, 1972.
5C. PATRICK JONES, born December 12, 1949, in Bremerton. Patrick married PAULETTE BENKE. They have a son, DEREK, born in 1986.
5D. DENICE JONES, born May 10, 1956, in Bremerton. Denice married THOMAS HUFFMAN. They have one son and one daughter: THOMAS, born June 10, 1977, and JENNIFER, born June 28, 1983.

We, as a family, are proud and happy to be included in the history of Manette. We have seen progress far beyond our dreams. We have survived wars, depressions and hard times, and enjoyed love and happiness and have made many good friends.

SCHULTZ, WILLIAM
By Orville Schultz
1984

FROM IOWA TO MANETTE

William H. Schultz, third in line in a family of 10, was born in Whitmore, Iowa, January 18, 1892, to Henry and Bertha Miller Schultz.

The Henry Schultz family moved to Davenport, Iowa, in 1901 and later to Hartline in Eastern Washington to dry-farm the wheat lands. They moved to Wadena, then to Cass Lake, Minn., where Bertha Schultz passed away. In August of 1907 Henry split up the family among relatives and friends and disappeared.

William Schultz at the age of 15 was on his own and worked on farms and logging crews. In 1911 at age 19 he came west to Spokane to begin working in logging camps and sawmills in Idaho, British Columbia and Washington.

He met and married Eva Beatrice Nichol in Kamloops, B.C., in 1912. Orville F. Schultz, their only child, was born February 22, 1914, in Colville, Wash. In 1917 they moved to Coeur D'Alene, Idaho, where William worked as a millwright in the Weyerhaeuser sawmill for $2.80 a day for a 12-hour shift.

The U.S. Navy was recruiting general helpers in 1918 for the Bremerton navy yard at $2.80 a day for an 8-hour day, but working a 10-hour shift with 2 hours at overtime pay. It looked very inviting, so William Schultz came to Bremerton.

He found no housing available for his family in Bremerton

Schultz home at 1700 Jacobsen Boulevard in 1920.

so they lived in one room in a Seattle hotel. Eventually they moved into a summer cottage on Enetai Beach owned by a land developer, Tom Kashel. He rented this cottage for the winter but renters had to move out in the summer. The Schultz family moved into a tent erected on a floor and framework on a vacant lot in what is now the 1800 block of Jacobsen Boulevard, on Enetai Beach. Neighbors helped build the floor and framework.

While in this tent the three Schultzes contracted but survived the flu, which took so many lives during World War I.

Navy yard workers who lived along Enetai Beach rowed to a raft anchored offshore. From there they were picked up by the passenger boat *Chickaree* and taken to Bremerton. If they

Schultz family about 1930. From left are Eva, Orville and William.   - Photo from Orville Schultz

had to work overtime on weekends a navy tug came out to pick them up.

In 1920 Schultz moved his family into an old barn on the beach of what is now 1700 Jacobsen Boulevard, and eventually purchased the land from Mrs. Daniel (Louise) Salt, a neighbor, whose husband had been a fight promoter in Seattle. The barn was added to, remodeled and converted into the present beach home.

OCCUPATIONS, RECREATION AND RETIREMENT

William Schultz retired from PSNS as a quarterman shipfitter in 1947. In his later years he lived in the second family home, built in 1940 on "upper" 1700 Jacobsen Boulevard. He drove his own car until he was 92. He lived to be 96.

Orville attended the old Manette four-room school, grades 1 through 7, and graduated from the eighth grade at Lincoln Junior High School in Bremerton. He then attended Bremerton High School, graduating in 1932. He commuted to school, first on the ferry *Pioneer*, and finally walking over the newly completed bridge built in 1930. He graduated from Washington State College in the Department of Agriculture in 1936 and shortly thereafter went into partnership with George McKeown in managing the Fircrest Trailer Park at the end of Marlowe Avenue in Manette. This trailer park was in operation all during World War II.

Orville married Virginia May Shephard of Bremerton in 1941. She had attended the Charleston grade schools and graduated from Bremerton High School in 1937. They live in the original family home on the beach.

Orville joined Boy Scout Troop 505 of Manette in the charter year of 1926. He came back into scouting as Scoutmaster of the troop in 1959, when his son Steven entered Scouting. Orville now has over 30 years of Scouting experience and has participated in National and World Scout Jamborees at council and national levels. He received the Silver Beaver Award in 1969 for his years as a volunteer in the Boy Scout program. He remembers the experiences of exploring and establishing, with Honor Scouts and Explorer Scouts, the historical Press Trail of 1889-90 in 1973 and the O'Neil trail of 1890 in 1983, within the boundaries of the Olympic National Park. The J.C. Penney Golden Rule Award was given to him in 1983 for his years of outstanding volunteer service in the community.

Orville retired from PSNS in 1971 as a fire control mechanic (gun control). Orville and Virginia are ardent historians and since they retired in 1971 they have trailered in 48 states and visited the remaining two by boat and plane. They have also toured Europe and visited their son Steven when he lived in Japan and their daughter Susan when she lived in the Bahamas.

They have been involved in establishing and maintaining street-end parks in Manette. They volunteer at the Kitsap Day Care Center, where Virginia has been on the board for 20 years.

GENEALOGY

WILLIAM H. SCHULTZ was born January 18, 1892. He married EVA BEATRICE NICHOL. Beatrice passed away in 1971. William died in February 1988. William and Beatrice had one son.

1. ORVILLE FRANK SCHULTZ, born February 22, 1914, in Colville,

Wash. He married VIRGINIA SHEPHARD of Bremerton in 1941. Virginia was born April 27, 1919, in St. Lawrence, S.Dak. Orville and Virginia live in the original family home on the beach. They have three children.

1A. SUSAN MAY SCHULTZ, born October 4, 1943, in Bremerton. She graduated from Whitworth College. Susan married CHARLES BROWN, who was raised in Bremerton. They currently live in Manette with their two daughters at 1333 East Hope Street near Clare's Marsh.

1A1. MARY HELEN BROWN, born August 24, 1966, in Bremerton.

1A2. ANNE KATHERINE "Katy" BROWN, born March 10, 1970, in Bremerton.

1B. JAN MARIE SCHULTZ, born March 29, 1945, in Bremerton. She graduated from Central Washington State College. Jan married ALAN McMANAMNA of Astoria, Oreg. They lived throughout the Pacific Northwest, following his carrer in wood products industry. Alan died December 31, 1985. Jan moved to Bremerton with their three sons.

1B1. EDWARD AARON McMANAMNA, born May 8, 1968, in Bremerton.

1B2. MICHAEL JASON McMANAMNA, born May 1, 1972, in Seattle.

1B3. THOMAS BARRETT McMANAMNA, born April 15, 1975, in Olympia.

1C. STEVEN WILLIAM SCHULTZ, born March 21, 1947, in Bremerton. He graduated from the University of Washington. Steven married BARBARA BAKKER of Bremerton. Steven is a naval architect and the third generation of Schultzes at PSNS. They live at 1806 Chester Avenue, Bremerton. Steve and Barbara have three children.

1C1. KIRSTEN ALANA "Krissy" SCHULTZ, born January 4, 1971, in Bremerton.

1C2. KATRINA AILEEN "Trina" SCHULTZ, born January 30, 1974, in Bremerton.

1C3. KEVIN MICHAEL SCHULTZ, born May 15, 1975, in Bremerton.

SCHWEER, EUGENE
By Bill and June Martin Schweer
1984

Eugene W. "Gene" Schweer came to Bremerton in January 1920 from Monroe City, Mo., to run a store for J.E. Wood. Mr. Wood was a brother of Gene's wife, Daisy.

J.E. Wood at that time had a dry goods store, the J.E. Wood Co.—later to become Bremer's Department Store—in Bremerton. He also had a store in Monroe, Wash., and one in Manette. Gene Schweer managed the Manette store. The location was at East 11th Street and Perry Avenue, where the old post office was located. Casa Del Sol Apartments are now on this land.

Daisy Schweer and their son William "Bill," age 6, followed Gene to Bremerton in March 1920.

The Schweers purchased a house on pilings over the beach at the foot of Hobson Street, now East 14th, for a summer home. It was built by Mr. McAlmond, who was building it to use as a houseboat. He was planning to tow it to Alaska with a boat he was building in a small drainage gulch near the beach, later the site of the Renus Bender home.

Chris Hilstad bought and finished the boat and named it the *Evelyn Sharp* after one of his daughters. It was a craft of about 40 to 50 feet in

The Gene Schweer home in 1920 at the foot of what is now East 14th Street.

The Schweers, circa 1937. From left, Bill, Daisy and Gene.   - Photo from Bill Schweer

Bill Schweer. He started carrying papers at age 8.
-Photo from News Searchlight

June and Bill Schweer, 1940.
- Photo from June Martin Schweer

length. This boat was used later as a passenger launch to carry Navy Yard workmen from Bainbridge Island to Bremerton. It burned and sank when a spark from a lunch pail striking a piece of metal ignited gas fumes and caused an explosion.

The Schweers ran the store in Manette for about a year until J. E. Wood sold his stores. By this time they liked the beach house so well they decided to live in the it year 'round.

Daisy was very active in the Manette School P-TA, social and fraternal organizations for many years. She was the only woman—the director—in the Womanless Wedding sponsored by the P-TA in the 1920s as a money raiser for school equipment.

Gene Schweer went to work for the North Pacific Public Service Company. This company was later bought out by Puget Sound Power and Light Company. Gene became the Western District extension representative and worked for Puget Power for more than 25 years, retiring at the age of 65. He died while on a trip to Key West, Fla., in 1960. Daisy lived in their Manette home at 1801 East 14th Street until her death in 1965.

DESCENDANTS

1. WILLIAM SCHWEER, Gene and Daisy's son, was born in Kirkland, Mo., in 1914. He went through elementary school in Manette and through junior high school and high school in Bremerton. As an 8-year old, he and Floyd Buchanan (also 8) became Manette's first paper boys. They delivered the *Bremerton News-Searchlight*. Bill started in 1922 with 25 customers and kept the route for 10 years, ending with 125 customers. He earned 25 cents a month for each customer.

Bill went to sea in 1933, serving on U. S. and foreign ships. He married JUNE MARTIN, daughter of Harry and Hattie Martin, another pioneer Manette family, in December 1940. Bill then was working as acting chief engineer on one of the Bremerton-Seattle ferries. World War II was imminent. Bill enlisted in the U. S. Navy and served there for 28 years, retiring with the rank of captain in 1968. Bill and June now live in Leeds, Utah. They have three children.

1A. KURT WOOD SCHWEER, born in 1944 in Bremerton.

1B. STEPHEN WILLIAM SCHWEER, born in 1947 in Bethesda, Md.

1C. CYNTHIA JEANE SCHWEER, born in 1953 in Newport, R. I.

SHANLEY, JOHN T.
By Jack Shanley
1985

In the spring of 1905, my father, John T. Shanley, arrived in Seattle from Newton, Kans.

He had served his apprenticeship at the Santa Fe Railroad in Wichita and was going to Alaska to work on the Alaska Railroad. While in Seattle he met a Mr. Fogg, who suggested he apply for work at the navy yard in Bremerton. He was hired immediately as an outside machinist.

The following year he and Isabel Monahan, also from Newton, were married in Bellingham.

I was born when the family lived on Perry Avenue. My brother Edward was born in a house my father built at East 11th Street and Ironsides Avenue. The peach tree Father planted is still there. Kiernan followed. He is now deceased. James was next. He, too, is deceased. After James was born we moved to Bremerton, where Raymond, the last of five boys, was born.

In 1910 my father became a member of the Manette Water Company that had been founded in 1906.

As a kid I sloshed through the mud of Manette "streets," fall through spring, to deliver newspapers, the Bremerton *News Searchlight*. I had a miner's lamp on my cap. More often than not it did no good. I started carrying a lantern even

The Shanley home built in 1909 at 914 Perry Avenue (since remodeled).   - Photo from Jack Shanley

though it was cumbersome. At that time there were no street lights.

Other memories I have of early Manette are the camping trips we took with friends and neighbors. We went to Sherwood Creek near Allyn and the Staircase area above Lake Cushman. At the "old burn" near Port Gamble we picked blackberries and huckleberries, which my mother put up for winter use.

John and Isabel Shanley with sons John "Jack" and Edward in 1910. - Photo from Jack Shanley

We seldom traveled any place in our car without some kind of trouble. During the winter the engine was taken apart piece by piece, cleaned, blued and put together again. We were then ready for the next year's trips.

I was employed by PSNS during World War II as an electrician. After the war I worked as a photographic salesman, wholesale and retail for 25 years. I retired from Washington State Department of Natural Resources, where I worked as a copy technician and photographer. I now live in Tacoma with my wife Helen. We have a son who lives in Waco, Tex., with his family. Our daughter lives in Lacey, Wash., with her family.

Edward lived in Bremerton. He retired from PSNS as an estimater and planner. Edward had four daughters, all of whom live in Bremerton. His son resides in California.

James was a shipfitter at Mare Island in Vallejo, Calif.

The son and daughter of Kiernan are both in California and so are the two sons of James.

Raymond has lived in Alaska for many years. He and his family have remained there. He now lives in Anchorage.

In December of 1928 my father died of a heart attack. He was 48 years of age.

My mother was 79 when she died in September 1959.

THE SHANLEY FAMILY
JOHN T. SHANLEY married ISABEL MONAHAN in 1906. They had five sons.

1. JACK SHANLEY, born in June 1908 in Manette. Jack married HELEN CARLSON. Jack and Helen live in Tacoma. They have a son and a daughter.
1A. RICHARD SHANLEY. He married HELEN ANN FARNEY. They are both at Baylor University in Waco, Tex. He is an associate professor of clarinet and chairman of the woodwind department. She is a lecturer and teacher of flute. They have two daughters.
1A1. ALISON SHANLEY, born June 17, 1973, in Waco, Tex.
1A2. MELISSA SHANLEY, born September 16, 1975, in Waco, Tex.
1B. PAMELA SHANLEY. She married CHARLES CARELLI, who is a planner in the water division of the state ecology department. She is an educational assistant in the North Thurston County School District. They have two daughters.
1B1. MARLICE CARELLI, born March 26, 1969, in Tacoma.
1B2. MICHELLE CARELLI, born November 19, 1971, in Tacoma.

2. EDWARD SHANLEY, born in December 1909 in Bremerton. Edward married ISABEL TURNER. She died in December 1983. Edward died February 1988. Edward and Isabel had four daughters and a son.
2A. JOAN SHANLEY. She is now married to BOB ROBINSON, who is retired from PSNS. Joan teaches English to non-English-speaking students at Olympic College. Joan has three children.
2A1. LESLIE LARSON. She is married to PAUL POZNANTER. They have two sons and live in Croton-on-Hudson in New York.
2A1a. DAN POZNANTER, born July 4, 1977.
2A1b. DAVID POZNANTER, born May 21, 1979.
2A2. LAURIE LARSON. She is single. She lives and teaches school in Sunnymead, Calif.
2A3. KENNETH ROBERT LARSON. He is single and lives in Seattle. He recently received a master's degree in business administration and is employed at Boeing as a financial systems analyst.
2B. PATRICIA SHANLEY. She is now married to JACK KNOWLES, who works at PSNS. She is employed by the Bremerton School District. She has two daughters and a son.
2B1. DEBBIE HERRELL. She is married to GARY DAVIS. They live in Chico. Both Debbie and Gary are employed at PSNS. They have a son and a daughter.
2B1a. CARLI ANN DAVIS, born March, 17, 1978.
2B1b. COYLE DAVIS, born June 12, 1981.
2B2. TONI HERRELL CLAPPÉ. She works at PSNS. She has one son.
2B2a. CHRISTOPHER CLAPPÉ, born April 7, 1983.
2B3. RICK HERRELL. He married DENISE HARNELL. Rick works for the Bremerton *Sun*. Denise works at Bangor. They have one son.
2B3a. RYAN EDWARD HERRELL, born December 26, 1983.
2C. CARMEN SHANLEY. She married EDWARD LINSTROM. They have four daughters and a son. Edward works at PSNS. Carmen is a homemaker.
2C1. CAROLE LINSTROM. She is married to MARK THOMPSON. Mark

is on the Bremerton police force. Carole and Mark have a son.
2C1a. KYLE THOMPSON, born October 15, 1985.
2C2. KRIS LINSTROM. Kris is married to RANDY GIESE, who is employed by Honeywell. Kris is employed by PSNS. They have one daughter.
2C2a. SHELBY GIESE, born April 22, 1986.
2C3. KARLA LINSTROM. She is single, lives in Federal Way and works at Boeing in Seattle.
2C4. ROSS LINSTROM. He is single, and sells insurance. He lives in Bremerton.
2C5. KIM LINSTROM. She lives in Bremerton and works at Safeway.
2D. NANCY SHANLEY. She is now married to FRED DENSON, who is retired. Nancy works at the Golden Star restaurant in East Bremerton. She has two sons and two daughters.
2D1. RODNEY STANSBERY. He lives at Kitsap Lake and is a building contractor.
2D2. MARTY STANSBERY. He works at PSNS and has a son.
2D2a. JOE STANSBERY, born September 16, 1975.
2D3. JODI STANSBERY. She is married to SCOTT DOSS, who works for K-2 Corporation on Vashon Island. Jodi is employed at Bremer's in Port Orchard. They have two sons.
2D3a. BRENT DOSS, born July 9, 1982.
2D3b. JARED DOSS, born March 22, 1984.
2D4. RANDI STANSBERY. She is single. Randi is employed by the Golden Star restaurant.
2E. PHILLIP SHANLEY. He is a car salesman. He has a son.
2E1. THOMAS SHANLEY is stationed in Germany with the U.S. Army. Thomas has one son.
2E1a. STEVEN PHILLIP SHANLEY, born August 28, 1986.

3. KIERNAN SHANLEY, born in April 1913 in Bremerton. He was married to FRANCES TYREE. Kiernan died in March 1976. They had a daughter and a son. Both live in California.
3A. KAREN SHANLEY. She is an Avon representative and her husband, BILL HART, is a truck driver for Bay City Building Concrete. They have two daughters.
3A1. LISA HART is a waitress in San Francisco.
3A2. DERILYN HART is in the National Guard training program.
3B. NORMAN PAUL SHANLEY. He married PATRICIA ANN JACINTO. He is an attorney in Sacramento, Calif. She is a teacher. They have two sons.
3B1. BRETT SHANLEY, born in 1982.
3B2. TRAVIS SHANLEY, born in 1985.

4. JAMES SHANLEY, born in January 1915 in Bremerton. He married NOLA CUNNINGHAM. James died in 1962. They had two children who live in California.
4A. MICHAEL SHANLEY. He married MARY STONER; both work in the California welfare department in Vallejo. They have a son.
4A1. COREY SHANLEY, born November 27, 1984.
4B. ROBERT SHANLEY. He married KRISTINE HOLM; both work for California State Industrial Insurance in Redding. They have a son and a daughter.
4B1. TYLER SHANLEY, born October 17, 1982.
4B2. CAITLIN SHANLEY, born October 13, 1984.

5. RAYMOND SHANLEY, born in January 1917 in Bremerton. Raymond and his wife, BETTY JENKINS, live in Alaska. Raymond is retired from the naval base at Kodiak. They have three children.
5A. STARR SHANLEY, born February 8, 1957. Starr married LARRY VAN MERSBERGEN. Starr is employed by Alaska Pacific University as an administrative assistant. Larry is a full-time student, junior year, and works for National Bank of Alaska.
5B. LLOYD RAYMOND SHANLEY, born May 4, 1959. Lloyd is single. He is employed by a marine diesel company, N.C. Machinery, as a representative in parts and service.
5C. MARY LOU SHANLEY, born January 22, 1962. Mary Lou married ROBERT QUARTERMAN. They have one son.
5C1. EVAN PEACE QUARTERMAN.

SIDAM, ALFRED
By Harold Christensen and
Dorothy Sullivan Sidam (1903-1985)
1985

Alfred Sidam came to Manette in 1907. He returned to Michigan to sell his farm and in 1908 brought his wife Emma and son Charles to live here permanently.

Alfred and Emma Sidam had seven children, five of whom came west. Of the five, William, Charles and Maggie lived in the Bremerton and Manette area. Edyth and Mary lived in the outlying areas of Seattle at various times.

Alfred and Emma managed the Sound Hotel in Bremerton near the navy yard gate. Later they moved to Enetai and were caretakers for the summer homes of Seattle residents. Maggie also worked there.

They bought a place at what is now 1153 Scott Avenue that extended to Pitt Avenue and included a large orchard and a big garden. That home was sold after Emma died in 1930 and Alfred moved to East 16th Street to live with his daughter, Maggie Christensen. He lived with the Christensens until his death at 97 in 1944.

Maggie's book of records states that Queen Victoria was Emma Sidam's second cousin.

DOROTHY SULLIVAN SIDAM

I landed here May 28, 1923. I was 19.

I had been teaching school in Idaho for 2 years. Bremerton authorities looked askance at my age and my having taught, but I managed to convince them that I really had. They hired me for the fall season for the munificent wage of $100 a month. I was rich. I taught at Smith and Manette Schools.

The thing that interested me most on my arrival here was the fact that two young men of the community knew that two new girls were coming to town and they each picked one as their prey, you might say. The two girls got here and had minds of their own. As it turned out there was a little bit of shuffling. We each wound up with a different man than had picked us. I eventually married one of the two, Charles Sidam of Manette, in 1925.

The day I arrived I would have turned around and gone back on the next boat if I'd had any money. I hated the place. It was one of those springs when it rained and rained and rained. It was foggy. Mother would say, "There's Mount Rainier over there—the Olympics are over there." I'd say, "Where?"

You couldn't see any of them.

Besides that—it was one of those springs when the whole countryside was covered with caterpillars. I loathed them. They were terrible. My small sister, Harriet, who was 16 years younger than I, adored them. She would pick them up and let them crawl up and down her arms. They were dropping down the back of your neck all the time.

The trees crowded in on me. I felt stifled. It was a long time before some of that Puget Sound sunshine made its way through.

Now I love it.

I joined the Manette Community Church and taught Sunday School there.

In 1958 we moved to Tracyton.

My sister Harriet, now Mrs. James Morton of Bremerton, was born in Idaho. She lived in Manette and now lives in Tracyton.

CHARLES AND DOROTHY SIDAM'S FAMILY

CHARLES L. SIDAM (born April 16, 1896, in Billings, Mich., died March 3, 1964, in Bremerton) married DOROTHY SULLIVAN (born December 11, 1903, in Illinois; died October 28, 1985, in Bremerton) in Manette in 1925.

Mrs. Sidam was active in P-TA and a member of Manette Community Church, where she taught Sunday School. She also enjoyed camping, fishing, gardening and hiking.

Dorothy and Charles had one daughter and one son.

1. MARY SUSAN SIDAM, born in Bremerton in 1940. Mary "Susie" attended school in Bremerton. She was married and is now divorced. Susie is now a school teacher in Central Kitsap School District.

2. PAUL SIDAM, born November 18, 1925, in Bremerton. Paul married ROSE MARY ZIMMERMAN. Paul died in September 1970. Paul and Rose Mary had four children, LAURA JANE, KATHLEEN FAY, ROBERT DAVID and RICHARD PAUL.

SMITH, SHELDON
By Ruth Byrne Lockwood
1985

Sheldon Hiram Smith was born in 1844 in Versailles, N.Y. He came to Dyes Inlet in 1880, accompanied by his brother Warren. Sheldon took a homestead in Sheridan, where he farmed. Warren took one on the future site of Bremerton. Sheldon's original cabin stood on Sheridan Road, probably at Schley Boulevard. Now, Church of the Nazarene stands on the site.

Sheldon Smith home at what is now 924 Sheridan Road, site of Church of the Nazarene. Standing is Ella Smith and seated on steps is her daughter Olive. Sitting on the porch railing is a friend, Theo Lewis.

- Photo from Ruth Lockwood

Sheldon and Warren were from Fort Ticonderoga, N.Y., and were descendants of Col. Ethan Allen, Revolutionary War hero. In the Smith families, the oldest son of the oldest son was always named David Allen Smith.

In 1886 Sheldon brought his cousin, Ella Matteson, to Sheridan as his bride. Ella was born in 1857 in Pennsylvania.

Ella was frightened of the cries of animals in the forest. She was also frightened—with good reason—of the Indians who gathered clams and peered in at the windows of the log cabin. Only 2 years earlier the Indians had gone on the warpath.

Ella had to carry all water uphill from a creek a quarter of a mile away. Life was hard. She lost her first baby, by not getting to a midwife in time.

Her second child, Olive Mabel, was born in 1888, and her son, David Allen, was born in 1892. Sheldon's eldest brother, living in California, had had no son, so gave up his right to the name.

Ella belonged to Philathea Chapter of Eastern Star, to Amaranth, and to Daughters of the Nile.

Sheldon was an avid reader and a believer in education. In 1897, when Olive was 9, School District 22 was formed, and Sheldon, one of the directors, offered to sell a piece of his land for a school for $1. The offer was accepted and Sheridan

Sheldon and Ella Smith's children Olive (left) and David, circa 1896. - Photo from Ruth Lockwood

School was built. Edith Case was the teacher. Manette children also attended there until 1903. Olive and David completed eight grades there.

Sheldon belonged to Knights Templar and other Masonic lodges.

Sheldon died in 1925. Ella died in 1938.

OLIVE

Olive told of walking to school on a trail through the forest, being treed by a bear on one occasion and followed by a cougar on another. She attended the area's first Sunday School, held at Sheridan School in 1898, and later at the Baptist Church in Manette.

Olive attended high school in Bremerton, held at Smith School on land given by Warren Smith. She then attended Stanford University. In 1913 Olive married A. Clifford Byrne of Bremerton, a lieutenant in the navy. They lived in the Philippine Islands 2 years, in Washington, D.C., 2 years, New York City one year, then Bremerton, Manette, and finally Seattle.

RUTH

I was born to them in 1915 in the Philippines. I first came to Sheridan in 1920, at the age of 5. We came across on the ferry *Pioneer* and grandfather Sheldon drove us to the farm in his wagon. We stayed a year, and after that spent every summer and most weekends at the farm. I remember walking the gravel road to the ferry landing in Manette, or to the inlet in Sheridan. I remember beach picnics when a washtubful of gravel yielded a water-bucketful of clams. We cooked them over the glowing coals of a bonfire, on a piece of rusty metal that we found.

I remember expeditions to gather dogwood, trilliums or the avalanche lilies that grew by the thousands near Tracyton and Silverdale. Rhododendrons grew thickly in the uninhabited woods near Hood Canal, and the stream below Lilliwaup Falls was alive with spawning salmon. In the summer wild blackberries grew plentifully all through the woods, and in the fall we picked huckleberries. Every farmwife guarded her secret—her favorite berry patch.

I remember the fascinating sights and smells in Martin's store in Manette. I recall quiet winter evenings reading Dante and Gibbon around our pot-bellied stove, or playing cribbage at the dining-room table.

In 1938, I married an architect, Francis Lockwood. He worked for Bremerton Lumber and for architects Branch and Branch. We built a small house on Vandalia Avenue. From it we could visit the farm frequently. When World War II came, my parents sold the farm and moved to New York. We sold the Vandalia house and moved to California.

DAVID

David was a "doughboy" in World War I. Later he owned a store in Seattle for a time, then returned to Sheridan and worked in Puget Sound Navy Yard as a pipefitter. David married at age 50 during World War II, and his wife Mary also worked in the pipe shop. When the war ended, they moved to Olympia, where Mary had relatives.

DESCENDANTS

SHELDON and ELLA SMITH had two children.

1. OLIVE MABEL SMITH, born in Tracyton in 1888. Olive married ALBERT CLIFFORD BYRNE in 1913. They had one child.
1A. RUTH ELIZABETH BYRNE, born October 6, 1915. Ruth married FRANCIS LOCKWOOD. They have one child.
1A1. BARBARA ARDEN LOCKWOOD, born in 1947 in Los Angeles. She is a lawyer with her own practice in Woodinville, Wash. She married CRAIG JOHNSTON. They have two children.
1A1a. IAN BRUCE JOHNSTON.
1A1b. DAVID ALLEN JOHNSTON.

2. DAVID ALLEN SMITH, born in 1892 in Tracyton. He and his wife MARY had no children.

SOLID, LLOYD
By Gladys Olsen Solid
1986

Lloyd Solid home at 1327 Ironsides Avenue.

Gladys and Lloyd Solid, 1922.

- Photo from Gladys Solid

Lloyd Solid was born in Colfax, Wis., July 29, 1898. He was raised by his grandparents, who resided at Coupeville, Wash.

His grandfather, Christian Solid, was born in Tromso, Norway. His grandmother, Kristina, was born there too.

Christian Solid was one of the early Alaska settlers. He built the first hotel in Dawson City in 1897, and later went farther north as far as Nome.

Lloyd came to Bremerton to work in the navy yard in 1919. He and a boyhood friend, Edgar Strong, lived in a boarding house on Burwell Street near Pacific Avenue.

Lloyd's sister Frances was married to Hershal Van Sant and they lived in Manette. It was at their home that Lloyd first met Gladys Olsen, whom he married September 1, 1921, at her parents' home.

He remodeled the three-room house he first bought at 1327 Ironsides Avenue. There was a water tank on the back corner of the property. It had at one time been used to supply water to part of Manette. It was made of large timbers. Lloyd paid $40 for this tank. He tore down the tank and base and used the lumber in the house.

Stanley Solid, 1941.

In 1931 Lloyd received an engraved silver medal from the East Bremerton Improvement Club for his outstanding service to the club.

Lloyd died in January of 1969. Gladys lives in Bremerton.

Lloyd and Gladys had one son, Stanley. Stanley was born in Portland, Oreg., on July 3, 1922. Stanley attended Manette school, Lincoln Junior High, and graduated from Bremerton High School in 1941. Stanley died in Tacoma December 27, 1985.

[See also OLSEN, TOLLEF].

STAREVICH, STEVE
By Helen Starevich Cuellar
1986

Stefan Starcevic, who was a Croatian, was born in Lic', Austria (now Yugoslavia), August 20, 1885. He came to the United States in 1899, and his name was Americanized to Steve Starevich. After some years in Minnesota he came to Ronald, Wash., a small coal mining town near Roslyn and Cle Elum. Steve worked as a blaster in the coal mines.

Mary Starcevic, a fourth cousin to Steve, was also born in Lic', in 1900. She came with her mother to join her father in Ronald about 1912. When she started to school she changed her name to Starkovich. She met and married Steve when she was 15.

Steve and Mary had five children: Mildred, Robert, Helen, Anna and Katherine "Chinkey."

Steve and Mary were separated and in 1924 Steve, five small children and four suitcases arrived in Manette via the *Seattle* and *Pioneer* ferries.

Until our Dad could establish a home for us we lived in the

Mary Starevich with her children Mildred, Helen, Robert, Anna and Katherine "Chinkey" (front), about 1925.

- Photo from Anna Starevich Hepworth

The Starevich home at 2600 East 11th Street. Photo taken in 1986.

Manette Childrens' Home. Mrs. O'Donnell was the matron. There were many memories—some good, some not so good—as in all childhood memories. The good ones were: having Christmas aboard the navy ships; Mrs. King, the cook at the Children's Home; swimming in the Sound in the summertime. The bad ones were: mass vaccinations, measles, chicken pox, whooping cough, and castor oil given for all misdemeanors.

We, as a family, were relatively unknown to the Manette neighbors until we moved to 2600 East 11th Street and Nipsic Avenue 6-1/2 years later in 1930.

Manette was a wonderful place to call home and we are proud to have our roots here. We remember most of the old Manette families fondly and I'm sure they remember the Starevich clan.

Steve Starevich retired as a chipper and caulker from Puget Sound Navy Yard in 1947. He died August 13,

Steve Starevich.

1956. Mary, who lived in Seattle, died in Brownsville August 4, 1952.

DESCENDANTS
STEVE and MARY STAREVICH's five children were:

1. MILDRED STAREVICH, born in Ronald, Wash., September 18, 1916. Mildred married WILLIAM GIBBONS in 1941. They both retired from PSNS. Bill died in 1968. Mildred in now married to AUGUST HUYGHE and they live at Miami Beach near Seabeck. Mildred has two stepdaughters, three stepgrandchildren, and three stepgreatgrandchildren.

2. ROBERT "Bob" STAREVICH, born in Ronald, Wash., December 20, 1917. Bob, was a crew chief in the Army Air Corps. He was awarded the

Distinguished Flying Cross, Airman's Medal, Silver Star and several battle stars and campaign ribbons. He was shot down over Saipan in August 1945. His wife LUETTA (now Slagle) lives in Salt Lake City as does their daughter, ROBYN, whom Bob never saw.
2A. ROBYN married RON GONZALES. They live in Salt Lake City and have three daughters, KRISTY, LYNN and JENNIFER, and one son, DAVID.

3. HELEN STAREVICH, born June 17, 1919, in Ronald. She married MANUEL W. CUELLAR. Ronald retired from the navy and PSNS. They live at Illahee and have no children.

4. ANNA STAREVICH, born September 9, 1920, in Ronald. She married RAYMOND HEPWORTH, who retired from PSNS. They live at Illahee. Annie and Raymond have three sons.
4A. JACK HEPWORTH lives in Anchorage, Alaska. He has a son and a daughter.
4A1. MARK HEPWORTH. Mark has one daughter.
4A2. ARLAN HEPWORTH. He died at 3 years.
4A3. ARLENE HEPWORTH.
4B. RAYMOND HEPWORTH. Raymond and his wife JAN live in Illahee. He has two daughters, two stepdaughters, and a stepson. The two daughters are:
4B1. KAREN HEPWORTH.
4B2. KARLA HEPWORTH.
4C. WILLIAM HEPWORTH. He lives in Anchorage. He has two sons:
4C1. KENNETH HEPWORTH.
4C2. KEVIN HEPWORTH. He has one daughter.

5. KATHERINE "Chinkey" STAREVICH, born June 27, 1922, in Ronald. She married RONALD J. DAVIS, who retired from PSNS. They live at Olympic Manor in Manette. They have two children:
5A. MICHAEL DAVIS.
5B. KATHERINE DAVIS. She and her husband live in Bremerton; they have two daughters.
5B1. CHERYL SOROS.
5B2. NICOLE SOROS.

STEVENS, JOHN and LOUISE
By Berenice Bouchard Root

My twin cousins, John M. and Louise Stevens, were living in Kelso with their parents, Mr. and Mrs. Jack Stevens, when their mother, Mildred Mawson Stevens, died in 1927. John and Louise were in their teens and came to live with us [the Bouchards] in Manette at different times after their mother's death.

John married Arlene Wilsen, also a twin [for photos see BOUCHARD-MAWSON history], who was a member of a well-known Manette family. Their first home was in our grandmother Mawson's little house at what is now 1821 Winfield Avenue. They had two daughters, Roberta and Aileen. Roberta was also born in grandmother's house. In 1940, when Aileen was only 4 months old, her mother Arlene died from injuries sustained in an automobile accident. Roberta and Aileen were adopted by Arlene's sister Grace Wilsen McNeill [see WILSEN family history].

John was drafted into the army during World War II and served in Italy.

After John was discharged from the army in 1945, he returned to Manette and the Bouchard household and found work as a gardener in the Puget Sound Naval Shipyard.

John married Lulu Bowen of Tracyton and they have one son, Michael, who resides at Buckley, Wash.

John retired from PSNS as head gardener. He and Lulu reside in Tracyton.

John and Arlene have two daughters: Roberta, who married Grover Bowers and Aileen, who married Richard Mueller. They have families and reside in Kitsap County. Aileen recently moved back into the old family home at 2215 Winfield Avenue built by her Grandfather Wilsen.

John's twin, Louise, married Leo Meadows and lived in the

Manette area for awhile. Their first child, Babs, was born in my grandmother's little cabin-like house at 1821 Winfield Avenue. Leo worked in lumber mills in southern Washington and eventually they settled in Oregon, where a son, Charles, was born.

After Leo's death in the late 1940s, Louise married Dave McCauley and they have a son, Dave III, and reside in Astoria.

STEWART, ROY
By Audrey Stewart Filion
1984

My father, Roy Thompson Stewart, came to work as a puncher and shearer with the shipfitters in Puget Sound Navy Yard early in 1918 during World War I. He brought his wife, Mathilda Mae, known as Mae, and daughter, Audrey, to Bremerton from Vancouver, B.C., in 1919.

Roy Stewart was born in South Dakota in 1882 and came with his parents from the Black Hills to Seattle by train in 1890. Roy's father was a carpenter for Great Northern Railroad Company, constructing railroad stations. The family lived in Seattle one year, then moved to Everett, where Roy was raised. Roy married Mathilda Mae Daum from Winnipeg, Manitoba, in Vancouver, B.C., in 1907 and I was born in Tacoma in 1908.

When we came to Bremerton, I remember we stayed about a week in a hotel on 2nd Street across from the Rialto Theater while looking for a place to live.

My parents bought a small three-room house on the beach at the foot of East 9th Street in Manette. They could not buy the property, just the house; and they paid a small yearly ground rent to the owner, Walter Jacobs, who had a coffee business in Bremerton. There was no house address; everyone got mail at the Manette post office.

The Roy Stewart 1919 home, 811 Shore Drive.

I started school in the seventh grade at Manette School. There were two grades to a room and our teacher for the seventh and eighth grades was Mrs. Alice Kallander, who was also the principal. Once a week the girls took domestic science and the boys took manual training at Smith School in Bremerton. That was a fun day, taking the ferry *Pioneer* to town and stopping on our way to Smith School to spend our nickel on a doughnut or a cup of hot chocolate.

My parents never owned a car and often used their rowboat to go to Bremerton during those early years. There was a dock at the end of 2nd Street to tie up to. In 1920 my mother had pneumonia and Father rowed over to the 2nd Street dock in Bremerton to get Dr. John Schutt, and took him back the same way.

Grocery stores had delivery service so shopping was easy. Harry Martin's grocery sent a clerk door-to-door Friday mornings to take orders for delivery. Groceries were charged on a weekly bill.

In 1930 my parents purchased from J.H. and Margaret Martin Lots 10 and 11, Block 3, Grandview Addition to Decatur, together with the tidelands abutting, for $800. In 1934 they built their home on this piece of property,

Mathilda and Roy Stewart, 1952. - Photo from Audrey Stewart Filion

which is now 1115 Shore Drive, and lived there until their deaths, Mother in 1956, and Father in 1968. My father had retired in 1946.

In 1928 I married William A. Filion, who was in his fourth year of machinist apprenticeship at PSNS. He was raised in Butte, Mont., and came to Bremerton in 1925 as an apprentice. At the time of our marriage I was working at the Puget Sound Power and Light Company. I worked there for 2 years.

In 1930 we purchased a house at 1121 Perry Avenue on Lots 6,7 and 8, Fellows Addition to Decatur, from Mr. and Mrs. Lester Tubbs. Mr. Tubbs was an engineer with the firm that built the Manette Bridge.

This was our home for 38 years, where we reared our family of three sons: Ralph, Arthur and Donald.

Ralph was born June 18, 1929, in Bremerton. He graduated from Linfield College in McMinnville, with a degree in business administration. He married Grace Bowen of Yakima and they have four sons, two daughters and six grandchildren.

William and Audrey Stewart Filion family in 1946. From left, Arthur, Audrey, Ralph and Bill, with Donald standing in front.

They live in Kansas City, Mo., where Ralph owns his own business: Offshore Sourcing Specialists.

Arthur was born April 30, 1934. He graduated from the University of Washington with a degree in mechanical engineering. He married Grace Martin of Bremerton (daughter of the late Olympic College instructor George Martin "Mr. Mountaineer," of Bremerton). They have three sons. They live near Philadelphia, where Arthur is an engineer at the U.S. Naval Base.

Donald was born March 29, 1938. He graduated from Washington State College with a degree in chemistry. He married Nancy Rice of Centralia and they have one son and three daughters. They live in Webster, N.Y., where Donald is a radio-chemist with Rochester Gas and Electric Company.

In 1962 my husband Bill retired from PSNS as a supervisor in the instrument shop.

In 1968 we moved into my family home on the beach, where we live today, 1115 Shore Drive. We spend winters in Arizona and summers in Manette.

Ernest and Harriet Stone home, built in 1919 at approximately 2010 East 11th Street..
- Photo from Esther Miner Westover

The Roy Stewart home from 1934 until 1968, at 1115 Shore Drive. Since 1968 this has been the home of William and Audrey Stewart Filion.

STONE, ERNEST
By Mildred Stone Muller
and Esther Miner Westover
1985

Ernest Edward Stone was born in Ogden, Utah, January 17, 1889. Ernest married Harriett Harms of Grand Junction, Colo., in 1914. Ernest and Harriett, with their son, Eugene, moved to Manette in 1917. Ernest was a farmer who came to work in the navy yard. They first lived in a rental house in Bremerton but later moved to Manette and lived in a tent house. Ernest and Harriett had five more children.

Ernest worked in the shipyard for about 2 years. He then built two small houses and a meat market on Manette's main street, now East 11th Street.

Later Ernest Stone's parents, Edward and Esther, arrived with another son, Jess, and daughter, Esther Pauline.

Edward was a very talented, self-taught musician. He had played violin for dances for many years. He tuned pianos, taught violin and studied the art of violin making. He found

a huge maple burl near Enetai Beach. He cut the burl into thin slabs and over the next 25 years made and sold several violins from that maple burl. The curly grain in the maple burl made beautiful violins.

Ernest's brother Jess and their father Ed built a garage and gas station near the Manette end of the bridge, now Wheaton Way and Harkins Street. Jess and Ed Stone operated the garage and gas station. From the garage they also had taxi service for customers' convenience.

The Manette Garage and the Manette Meat Market, located

The Stone and Miner families taken at the Miner home at East 18th Street and Perry Avenue in 1923. Back row: Esther Stone, Allen and David Miner, and Esther Stone Miner (David's wife). In front: Melissa Dayton (mother of Esther Stone); Anna Miner (mother of Allen and David); grandson Ernest Juneau (behind Anna); Eugene Stone (son of Ernest Stone); Esther Miner (daughter of David Miner); Hattie Stone with Margaret, and Ernest Stone, holding Mildred.

- Photo from Esther Miner Westover.

side by side on the north side of what is now East 11th Street between Winfield and Pitt Avenues, were operated by the Stones from approximately 1919 until 1927. Ernest learned the meat cutting trade from his father Ed.

Edward and sons Ernest, Jess and Joseph moved the meat market building across from the north to the south side of East 11th Street. In 1927 they sold the market to Oscar Etten.

The Ernest Stones' son Eugene and their first daughter Mildred attended Manette School. The children were also enrolled in the cradle rolls of the Manette Community Church.

Ernest Stone was a member of the Masonic Lodge in Manette.

The Stone family moved to Seattle for a time, then moved to Lakebay, a peninsula near Gig Harbor, where Ernest farmed until retirement. Then Ernest and Harriett moved back to Marguerite Avenue in Bremerton.

Ernest died in 1970.

Harriett lives near a daughter in Hadlock. She enjoys a healthy, active life.

EARLY IMPRESSIONS

I remember:

- The wooden sidewalks with the wide cracks in them and all the blackberry vines that lined the wooden sidewalks.

- The grocery stores on the main street, now East 11th Street, and a gift shop during the Christmas season, had the mos. beautiful German-made Christmas ornaments.

- The fire siren that blew whenever necessary and the church bells ringing on Sunday.

- The gypsies that would come into town frequently—how colorfully they seemed to be dressed! And the many children with them, hanging out the car windows. They would come into the meat market and one would try to distract Mr. Stone while several others would attempt to pick up some items. I can remember my father calling for another member of the family to come and help him one time as so many of them had come into the market.

LINEAGE
Descendants of ERNEST and HARRIETT STONE include:

1. EUGENE ERNEST STONE, born April 5, 1915, at Grand Junction, Colo. Eugene married ADA SORENSON October 20, 1938. They live in Lakebay, Wash. Eugene and Ada have two daughters.
1A. MARILYN STONE, born in 1940 in Tacoma. Marilyn married SONNY ANDERSON, and they have three children, ERIC, KRIS and KREG.
1B. LINDA STONE, born in 1942. Linda married ROY BARTH and they live in Tacoma. They have one son, KARL RAYMOND.

2. HOWARD IVAN STONE, born February 8, 1917, in Bremerton. Howard died from a heart condition in 1920.

3. MILDRED MAXINE STONE, born April 22, 1919, in Bremerton. Mildred married KENNETH L. MULLER October 20, 1944. They have a son and a daughter.
3A. CRAIG WILLARD MULLER, born September 9, 1954, in Seattle. He married HEIDI THOMPSON in 1983. They live in Poulsbo and have no children.
3B. TANYA SUSANNE MULLER, born October 19, 1955, in Everett. She married MARK POKSWINSKI in 1975 and they live in Everett. They have three children, JOEL, SUSAN and TODD.

4. MARGARET DOROTHY STONE, born May 13, 1920, in Bremerton. Margaret married EARL McSPADDEN in December 1980. Margaret has three children by a former marriage.
4A. GENA ELIZABETH ELDRIDGE. She is married to Cmdr. Robert Schultz. They live in Fairfax, Va., and have two children, TODD and VICTORIA.
4B. RODNEY HARMS ELDRIDGE. He lives in Charleston, S.C.

4C. JOHN PAUL ELDRIDGE. He also lives in Charleston.

5. GEORGE DOUGLAS STONE, born October 26, 1924, in Bremerton. George married NINA LATHAM May 24, 1945. They have two sons.
5A. KIM STONE, who resides in Littleton, Colo.
5B. JEFF STONE. He and his wife CINDY reside in Littleton, Colo., and have a son and two daughters: JONATHAN, EMILY and VICTORIA.

6. MARIAN VALDEEN STONE, born January 7, 1929, in Lakebay, Wash. Marian married EARL GREEN November 24, 1948. They have a son and two daughters.
6A. BONNIE GREEN. She is married to DON MINNEMAN. They live in Tacoma and have two children, PAUL and HEATHER.
6B. JANET GREEN. Janet is married to BILL THOMPSON. They live in Tacoma and have two children, TRACEY and AARON.
6C. MICHAEL GREEN. He and his wife KATHY live in Port Ludlow and have three children, STEPHANIE, APRIL and DAVID.

STONE, EDWARD
By Mildred Stone Muller
1985

EDWARD and ESTHER STONE came to Manette a few years after their son Ernest arrived in 1917. [See STONE, ERNEST] Ed died in Lakebay, Wash., in June 1945; Esther died in Manette in 1954.

DESCENDANTS
Edward and Esther Stone had four children:

1. ERNEST STONE, born in 1889.

2. JESS STONE, born in Utah in 1890. Jess married AGNES McLEOD, a sister to Grace Carlaw Jess was a member of the Masonic Lodge, and Agnes was a member of the Philathea Chapter of Eastern Star. Jess' sister Pauline (Esther) was also a member of the Philathea Chapter.
Jess Stone died about 1955 while living near Gig Harbor.

3. ESTHER PAULINE STONE, known as Pauline, born in Mercur, Utah, in February 1899. Pauline was a member of Philathea Chapter. Pauline married DAVID MINER (born February 1897, in Morton, Wash.) at the courthouse in Port Orchard on February 28, 1920, and they lived at East 18th Street and Perry Avenue in a large house which became Acme Florists during the 1950s and 60s.
David Miner and his brother Allen bought the house together and made it into a duplex; Allen and his mother Anna lived in half and David and Pauline in the other half.
In 1924 David and Pauline moved to Kent, Wash., for 1 1/2 years, then came back to Manette and bought a house on Shore Drive, where they lived for 2 years. They then sold and moved back to the duplex on Perry Avenue for a year. In June of 1929 they moved to the Key Peninsula near Gig Harbor to be near the Stone family. They returned to Bremerton in 1934.
Pauline died in 1961. David later remarried and lived in Port Orchard. He died in July 1980. Pauline and David had one daughter.
3A. ESTHER LOUISE MINER, born in Manette February 4, 1921. She attended the first and second grades in Manette School. In 1941, she married DAVID WESTOVER, an equipment specialist in design at PSNS. He retired in 1973 and died in 1980.
Esther worked for 13 years as an educational secretary for the Bremerton School District—mainly at Coontz Junior High School. She retired in 1972. She has a home in Eldorado Hills and a mobile home in a park near Palm Springs, Calif., where she has spent winter months since 1981. Esther and David had one daughter.
3A1. DIANE WESTOVER. She had two daughters.
3A1a. LISA WILCOX, born in Bremerton in 1972.
3A1b. MELANIE WILCOX, born in Bremerton in 1974.

4. JOSEPH STONE, born in Utah in 1891. Joseph lived with the family in Manette for a short time. He worked periodically with the brothers and later lived near the family at Lakebay, Wash. He died about 1958. He had no children.

SUTHERLAND, WILLIAM
By Lelah G. Sutherland
1987

William George Sutherland was born in Salamon, Kans., in 1860. He married Ladora Grant Beck, born in Niles, Kans., in 1868. They moved to Manette in 1908, to Ballard, then returned to Manette in 1913 with their five children.

William was a shipright and worked in the navy yard. He died in 1921 in an accident in the navy yard.

His son, William Beck "Bill" Sutherland, went to school in Manette and graduated from Union High School. He became a machinist and worked in the navy yard 34 years, 10 months and 4 days. He married Lelah McDonald of Sequim, who came to Manette in 1925. They lived at 1149 Scott Avenue.

Bill enjoyed studying and collecting rocks and belonged to a rock club. Bill died in Bremerton in 1975 from a heart problem.

Lelah belonged to the Eastern Star, was first guardian for Job's Daughters and is now a member of Belfair Senior Citizens.

DESCENDANTS:
WILLIAM GEORGE and LADORA SUTHERLAND had eight children.

1. HATTIE AMELIA SUTHERLAND, born in Kansas in 1891. Hattie married HARRY MARTIN of Manette. [See MARTIN history.]

2. ADA ESTHER SUTHERLAND, born in Kansas in 1893. Ada married CHARLES OSTER.

3. DAVID ARLINGTON SUTHERLAND, born in Kansas in 1894. David died in 1909 in Seattle.

4. LILLIAS AMARYLLIS SUTHERLAND, born in Mexico in 1896. Lillias married ROY WALLS. Later she married ED MILLHOUSE. Lillias had one son, ELWOOD, who died in California.

5. WILLIAM BECK SUTHERLAND, born in Ballard in 1900. Bill married LELAH McDONALD of Sequim. Bill and Lelah had four children.
5A. LETA MAY SUTHERLAND, born in 1927 in Manette. She attended Manette School and graduated from Bremerton High School. Leta May married JOHN L. TAYLOR.
5B. DONALD WILLIAM SUTHERLAND, born in 1933 in Manette. He attended Manette School and Bremerton High School. Donald died in 1971.
5C. LELAH ESTHER SUTHERLAND, born in Manette in 1937. Lelah married WILLIAM E. SCHLOSSER of Bremerton. They live in Sunnyslope. Lelah Esther and William have four children.
5D. JOHN ARLINGTON SUTHERLAND, Lelah's twin, born in 1937. John lives in Seattle.

6. ARTHUR BURTON SUTHERLAND, born in Ballard in 1905. Arthur married JENNIE BACILE.

7. LADORA ELIZABETH SUTHERLAND, born in Manette in 1910. Ladora married THOMAS ERDMAN.

8. MARY MARGARET SUTHERLAND, born in Chico in 1914. Mary married Mr. EMPETT. Mary died in Shelton.

SWAN, HUGH
By Vivian Swan Graves
1986

ACROSS WASHINGTON

Hugh W. Swan came to Manette in 1916 from Spokane, where he had lived for several years. He was 35 years old. World War I was on and workers were needed in the navy yard. He went to work in the shipfitter shop, where he worked until his retirement in 1943.

There was no housing available for the influx of navy yard workers. People were living two and three families to a house, if one were lucky enough to find a house. People were putting up tent houses and small cabin type houses, not more than shacks. Tim Cole arrived at the same time and was one of the lucky ones to find a house to rent. It was on the beach on the east side of Manette. Hugh Swan and another man boarded and roomed with the Coles while Hugh was building a tent

house about a block south of the Coles' house. Hugh built on the beach side of the road where East 11th Street would have ended had it continued on over the hill to Shore Drive. A much-traveled trail took off where East 11th Street ended, went through the woods, curved around the hill and ended at the beach road.

The tent house was built in 1917 across from the present home of Marie Gould at 1102 Shore Drive. It was about 12 by 20 feet, divided into two rooms and had a wooden floor and wooden sides up about three feet, covered with tar paper. It had a tent top and a fly over the tent.

At this time, summer of 1917, Hugh sent for his wife, Opal, and two children. Opal

Grandma Allen with Vivian and Forrest Swan in 1917, soon after their arrival in Manette.

stored most of the furniture from a large house, bringing only necessities to Manette. This was very primitive living but many more families were living under similar conditions. We carried our water from the Tim Cole residence. We had a three-burner kerosene stove for cooking. It had a portable oven that covered two burners. We had kerosene lamps and

Hugh and Forrest Swan, 1917.

an outside toilet.

Hugh, our dad, immediately began to build a two-room house, papered on the inside with a felt-type building paper. When the house was finished we used the tent house for sleeping quarters. It joined the house with a tent-covered walkway.

Hugh went to Spokane and sold most of the furniture which could not be used in a two-room house, including Opal's prized possession, her pump organ.

We now had a cookstove and a wood heater. I think we had electricity soon after the house was completed. Hugh then dug a well that had a pitcher pump on it. We never did have running water in the house but did not have to carry water any more.

Ed Frith built a house almost identical to ours right next to us and we shared our well with Friths and with two or three other families in nearby tent houses.

SCHOOL DAYS

I started at Manette School in second grade and attended the second, third and fourth grades there. My brother Forrest attended the first grade there. I think the school had only four rooms at this time, two grades to a room. At least there were two grades in my rooms.

FUEL

Hugh built a very small rowboat, just big enough for two, and went on wood-and-log-hunting trips weekly. At this time there was a lot of floating and beached driftwood and logs that had been separated from booms. These logs were stamped with the owner's brand or initials and were not supposed to be gathered up, but wood was expensive and whoever got to them first was considered very lucky. The marked ends were immediately sawed off and burned. It was our daily job to gather beached wood and to watch for floating wood.

FOOD AND CLOTHES FOR THE FAMILY

Hugh went deer hunting every season and I can remember havi..g venison so often that I have never liked it since. Mother canned it as we had no ice box. I'm not sure if ice was available in Manette at this time. Dad also fished a lot and we had too much fish for my liking.

We raised chickens and rabbits. One year a banty hen hatched six Plymouth Rock eggs. The chicks were bigger than she was in a very short time and they would try to get under her wing. She was just standing on top of them. The rabbits got out of their pen and we had rabbits running all over the nearby hillside.

Mother was a former seamstress and milliner so she made almost all of her own and my clothes and part of Forrest's. Mother bought a piano and I took lessons once a week from Nellie K. Wagner in Bremerton.

CHURCH AND SOCIAL LIFE

We attended the First Baptist Church in Bremerton, where we were members. Much of every Sunday was spent in church activities. Wednesday night was prayer night. Opal was a Sunday School teacher and a lifetime deaconess. Both Hugh and Opal sang in the choir, and much of their social life was in some way church-connected.

Hugh was one of the original members of the Bremerton Sportsman's Association and was presented a lifetime membership. He was also a member of the Boilermaker's Union and the Retired Men's Club. He belonged to Masonic Lodge 117 and both he and Opal were members of Reliance Chapter 70, Order of Eastern Star.

In 1920, the Swan family moved to 1106 Elizabeth Avenue in Bremerton, where Hugh and Opal lived until their deaths.

Opal started to use her real first name, Lillie, when she reached 65, for Social Security reasons.

On July 4, 1978, Lillie Opal was the guest of honor at the Port Orchard Fathoms O' Fun Centennial. She was the oldest resident of Kitsap County born on the 4th of July. It was a huge celebration, held on her 99th birthday.

She had two more large birthday parties and open-house celebrations on her 100th and 102nd birthdays. They were held at the Tamarack Apartments, where she lived from the time they were built until she was almost 104 years old. She passed away in October 1983 at Resthaven Nursing Home in Bremerton at the age of 104.

GENEALOGY

HUGH W. SWAN was born in Knoxville, Tenn., on June 5, 1881. He married LILLIE OPAL ALLEN, who was born July 4, 1879. Hugh died in 1957; Opal died in 1983. They had three children:

1. VIOLET JUANITA SWAN was born January 29, 1909, and died March 2, 1909.

2. VIVIAN SWAN was born April 18, 1910. She married ROBERT GRAVES. They have no children. They have lived at 124 Northwest 130th in Seattle since 1958, and are retired.

3. FORREST SWAN was born November 23, 1913. He married CHARLOTTE ANNE MITCHELL. Charlotte was born in Vancouver, B.C., in 1920. Forrest owned the Bremerton Sport Shop; he was in business for 45 years. Forrest died in October 1986. Charlotte still lives in their home at 2133 East 17th Street. Forrest and Charlotte had two daughters.
3A. LESLIE ANNE SWAN, born August 7, 1945, in Bremerton. Leslie married DAVID MARKHAM. Leslie is now married to JACK JENSEN. They live in Yakima. Leslie and David had one daughter: TRACY MARKHAM, born August 7, 1972, in Bremerton.
3B. ALAYNE SWAN, born May 26, 1950, in Bremerton. Alayne married THOMAS THORSEN of Brownsville. Alayne is now married to GREGORY VANDIVER and lives in Bremerton. Alayne and Thomas had four children, all born in Bremerton: KELLY JEAN, born March 8, 1976; GUNNAR, born February 3, 1978; LARS born September 11, 1980, and SHANNON born October 12, 1983.

TAFT, FLOYD
By John E. Holmes (Ellsworth Danel)
and Jean Anderson Taft Bland
1987

Floyd Taft was born in 1916 and died in 1947. He is buried at Sunset Lane Cemetery in Port Orchard.

Floyd's father left the family when Floyd was very small and was never heard from. Floyd's mother died when he was 4 or 5 and Floyd grew up in Manette Childrens' Home. He was the last resident of the Home [see ORGANIZATIONS].

He graduated with honors from Bremerton High School in 1936.

Floyd married Jean Anderson from Port Orchard in 1941.

Floyd was employed by Standard Stations in Port Orchard. He worked in the sheet metal shop, Shop 11, of the navy yard during World War II. He was employed by the Bremerton Fire Department until early in the spring of 1947. Then, while employed building houses in the Moses Lake area, and in the process of moving there, he was killed in a traffic accident. His wife and two children; Barbara, 5 and Douglas, 8 months, continued to live in Port Orchard for about a year. Jean sold the house and moved to Spokane, where she later married Chester Bland.

DESCENDANTS

Floyd and Jean had three children.

1. ROBERT FLOYD TAFT, born October 1, 1941, lived only 4 months.

2. BARBARA LYNETTE TAFT, born October 21, 1942. Barbara married ROBERT PERRY and has two sons: RICHARD PERRY, who has two sons, CASEY and DANIEL, and MICHAEL PERRY.

3. DOUGLAS BILL TAFT, born February 4, 1947.

TENGE, GEORGE E.
By Jewell Tenge Sollie
1985

George E. Tenge was born January 3, 1890, in Milwaukee, Wis., where he began working for the Chicago, Milwaukee & St. Paul Railway when he was 14. He graduated from the company's master boilermaker apprentice program, continuing to work in Milwaukee until he moved to the railway's station in Deer Lodge, Mont.

Bernice Slaughtner was born in Pioneer, Mont., August 21, 1897. She and George were married January 1, 1919, in the home of her parents in Pioneer, and in the same month moved to Seattle, then to Bremerton. Dad worked as a boilermaker in what was then known as Puget Sound Navy Yard.

Bremerton was not to mother's liking—she was homesick—and later in the year they returned to Deer Lodge, where Dad resumed his work with the Milwaukee Railroad. In 1921, with their first child, they moved to the small railroad town of Avery, Idaho. While living there 6 years, Mother returned briefly to Deer Lodge in 1922 and 1924 to give birth to their second and third children.

Then in 1927 the memories of the Puget Sound country with its good year-round climate, beautiful water and mountains lured them back, first to Seattle and then to Manette in 1928. With them were the three children born in Montana: Jewell, Kenneth and Wilbur. A fourth child, Carolyn, was born in Bremerton.

SHORE AND RECREATION

The house on Shore Drive on the waterfront afforded a front yard of water in which we neighbor children literally lived in the summertime. The water somehow was not as cold then and we swam, rafted and rowed boats together. When the tide changed we gathered seaweed and long ropes of kelp and made designs on the beach. We also played on logs that the menfolk had towed in from the bay and left high on the beach to dry for firewood. There was always the sound of dragsaws as neighbors helped each other saw the logs. We all had wood stoves for cooking and heating.

There were lots of pheasants where the Manette playfield is now, and deer wandered into town as far south as East 11th Street. There were lots of woods where we climbed trees, built trails and camps and played hide-and-seek.

Dad had our house moved across the street in 1932. Wintertime found us busy at Manette School and Manette Community Church and active in Girl Scouts, Boy Scouts, Rainbow Girls and Job's Daughters. We all attended Lincoln Junior High School and Bremerton High School in Bremerton.

Dad and Mother belonged to Masonic organizations. Many family-oriented programs and parties were enjoyed in the beautiful new Manette Masonic Temple, built in 1927. Years later, in 1956-57, Mother was worthy matron of Philathea Chapter 174, Order of the Eastern Star. Another oldtimer, Earl "Dutch" McNeill, was Worthy Patron.

Most families had gardens and raised chickens and rabbits. Some families, like the Chris Jensens, also produced fields of wonderful strawberries, and if we wanted any for the dinner table we children went and picked them. The blazing sun beat down on us but the strawberry shortcake for dinner made it all worthwhile.

ROADS, BRIDGE AND AIRPLANES

We had only narrow, dusty dirt roads and not many cars, and we remember everyone turning out to rake the roads when the oil-spraying truck was coming.

It was fascinating to watch the bridge being built in 1930. The variety store and barber shop were located on the ferry dock and we had reason to be there often. When the bridge was completed a group of young boys heard rumors that it was going to fall because of swift tides and not enough rock around the cement piers. Those boys were at the popular nearby Ben Kean's Service Station waiting for it to fall down. When it didn't, they often found great pleasure and were challenged to climb around on the structure under the bridge, over the water. Luckily, no one fell off and drowned.

One of the most dramatic happenings was when one of Mr. Gorst's amphibians crashed into the bay near Manette. The two pilots were the only ones aboard and both were killed. Gorst ran his air service to Seattle from 1929 to 1931. More than 19,000 passengers were carried in the first 6 months.

BARRAGE BALLOONS AND BARRACKS

When World War II came the army moved in. Manette was well covered with barrage balloons and barracks. One of each was literally in our backyard. The soldiers were from the east coast and were most happy to be around the local people who befriended them. One soldier who married when he went home on leave to New Jersey brought his bride back with him. She lived at our house and filled a void, because our boys were called up in the army and were gone. Kenneth was in Mississippi in training to be an infantryman and Wilbur was in Texas in training to be a medic. Needless to say, the friendship made between New Jersey and Manette has lasted.

THE FAMILY
GEORGE E. TENGE (1890-1982) married BERNICE SLAUGHTNER (1897-1984). They had four children:

1. JEWELL L. TENGE, born October 29, 1919, in Deer Lodge, Mont. Jewell married BERNARR SOLLIE of Bremerton in 1950. Bernarr died in May 1984. They had two daughters.
1A. YVONNE L. SOLLIE, born June 18, 1951, in Bremerton. Yvonne married JAMES OLDROYD III of Bremerton in 1976. They live in Bremerton. They have two children.
1A1. JASON S. OLDROYD, born February 4, 1970, in Bremerton.
1A2. JARED A. OLDROYD, born April 2, 1981, in Tacoma.
1B. SONJA M. SOLLIE, born February 18, 1953, in Bremerton. Sonja is unmarried.

2. KENNETH G. TENGE, born May 17, 1922, in Deer Lodge. Ken is unmarried.

3. WILBUR L. TENGE, born April 2, 1924, in Deer Lodge. Wilbur married VIRGINIA STENCIL of Bremerton in 1948. They live in Seattle and have two children.
3A. STEVEN G. TENGE, born April 3, 1954, in Bellingham.
3B. BRADLEY J. TENGE, born June 22, 1961, in Seattle. Bradley married TERESA SCOTT of Seattle.

4. CAROLYN J. TENGE, born August 15, 1928, in Bremerton. Carolyn married EDWARD "Gene" O'NEAL of Bremerton in 1950. They live in Bremerton and have no children.

TRACY, RALPH
By Mae Perriman Tracy
1985

Ralph Tracy with his wife Rose, their son Bertram, and Ralph's brother Foster Tracy came to Manette from Maine in 1917. Foster boarded with Ralph and his family.

Ralph started the Tracy Lumber Yard in Manette in 1919 or 1920. It was located where The Narrows Apartments are now. All materials came in by barge at high tide.

Ralph died January 31, 1961. Rose died January 27, 1966. Bert Tracy attended Manette School and later Bremerton Union High. Bert worked in the navy yard for a short time and then was needed to help his dad in the lumber yard, where he assisted with the bookkeeping and delivering lumber in a flat-bed truck.

When I met Bert in 1923 or 24, he was driving a Ford. We started going to dances together. He let me drive his Ford to my work at the Rialto Theater. Mother was upset when she saw me driving.

Bert and I were married in 1926. We had one son, Rodney.

I remember working at the lumber yard when Ralph Tracy was sick. I answered the phone and I weighed and sold nails, paint and other supplies. I wrote down the order or took the phone number so Bert could call the customer when he returned from a delivery. Hay and feed were also sold at the lumber yard. After a lot of sickness, Ralph sold the lumber yard and he and Rose moved to Gorst.

FOSTER AND BERTRAM TRACY

Foster Tracy, Bert's uncle, worked in the navy yard for several years. Just before retirement he married Marie, who also worked in the navy yard. After Foster's death Marie lived at Lacey, Wash.

When Ralph sold the lumber yard, Bert went to work selling electrical and oil equipment in Bremerton from 1939 until 1941. He sold and repaired oil burners, pumps and light plants. After Pearl Harbor Bert worked in navy yard shop 67 as an electrician. Later he worked on radar and was sent to Alaska twice to install radar equipment when Elmendorf Air Base was being built. Bert retired with an ear injury in 1965.

Bert played the piano with local dance bands throughout the county during the 1930s. Bert was a life member of the Musicians' Union. He bought a Hammond organ, which he enjoyed playing at home.

ANOTHER GENERATION

BERTRAM TRACY, son of Ralph and Rose Tracy, was born November 30, 1902, in Calais, Maine. He married ELLEN MAE PERRIMAN August 16, 1926. Mae had come to Manette with her mother Margaret Clare, step-father Walter Clare and sister Gertrude [see PERRIMAN and KANTHACK histories]. Bert died in 1985. Mae lives in Manette. Bert and Mae had two sons.

1. RODNEY TRACY, born in Bremerton July 10, 1932. Bert and Mae had prayed for a boy, since Ralph and Foster were the last of the Tracys. Rod went to school in Bremerton. When Rod got out of high school he got a job at Bangor. He started an apprenticeship as a machinist but was drafted and sent to Korea in 1950. When he returned from Korea he finished his apprenticeship. He now works in the navy yard as a supervisor in planning and is often sent as a consultant to other navy facilities. Rod married WANDA SOUTHERLAND and they live in Navy Yard City. Rod and Wanda have three children.

1A. DALE TRACY, born in Bremerton in 1956. Dale has a marine license and has traveled extensively to Alaska, China and the Indian Ocean. He now works for Marine Logistics Corporation in Seattle.

1B. DEAN TRACY, born in Bremerton in 1958. Dean attends the University of Washington and works part-time for an architect.

1C. CARRIE TRACY, born in Bremerton in 1960. Carrie married MICHAEL HAYES and they live near Erland's Point. Carrie has worked for Kitsap Physicians Service since she graduated from high

Four generations of Tracys, 1956. From left, Ralph (holding Dale), Bert and Rodney.

school and is now a supervisor. Carrie and Michael have a son, BRYAN MICHAEL HAYES, born January 9, 1985.

2. LEON TRACY was born February 23, 1940, in Bremerton. Leon went to school in Bremerton. He is a widower and lives in Phillipsburg, Mont. Leon and his wife BETTY JEAN had a son and a daughter.
2A. RICK LEON TRACY, born in Bremerton in 1959. He grew up in Montana. Rick completed air force basic training in Lackland, Tex. and then went to Keesler AFB, Miss. to take a course in operating communications systems. Rick now lives in Seattle.
2B. ATHIE LYN TRACY, born in Bremerton in 1960. She grew up in Montana. She is married and has three children. She lives in Everett.

VOLL, OTTO
By Jack Voll
1987

Otto Voll and his wife Lillian (Streeter) Voll came from Seattle to Manette in 1919. Their home was at 2310 East 9th Street. Otto worked as a sign painter in Manette and Bremerton.

He belonged to the Kiwanis Club and East Bremerton Improvement Club. Otto also enjoyed gardening and boat building. He played handball on the Bremerton team during state championship competition. Lillian was well known for her flower garden. She specialized in raising roses and many varieties of rockery plants. Her other hobbies included music and art. She was one of 17 members at the first meeting of the Manette Garden Club in 1935. She also belonged to the Community Concert Society and the Sunshine Society.

Otto, Jack and Lillian Voll, 1922.

Otto and Lillian had a son Jack. Jack and his father built four sailboats. When Jack was 8, they built a 6-foot boat in their dining room. When Jack was 12, they built an 8-foot boat; when he was 14, a 12-foot boat, and when 17, a 21-foot boat. Jack has also built a 14-foot Port Madison pram, a 15-foot runabout and two 6-foot dinghies.

Jack attended Manette School and Lincoln Junior High and graduated from Bremerton High School in 1939. He worked in the navy yard boat shop and machine shop. In 1942 he enlisted in the U.S. Army Air Force and was discharged in 1946. Jack attended Olympic College in '46 and '47, University of Washington in '47 and '48 and Cal Aero Tech. He worked at Boeing as tooling inspector and production planner, then at U.W. as maintenance supervisor of machine and sheet metal shops. Jack retired in 1981.

Jack married Beth Huntsman in 1956 and they live on Bainbridge Island. Beth has a son and daughter, Lee and Lynn, from a previous marriage. They also live on Bainbridge.

Jack has belonged to the Port Madison Yacht Club for 25 years and served as commodore in 1965. In 1977, 78 and 79 he was president of Pacific Handicap Racing Fleet.

Lillian, Jack and Otto Voll with 21-foot sailboat—the fourth boat built by Jack and Otto. Photo was taken in 1939.

VON HOENE, WILLIAM
By Elizabeth von Hoene Waters

My father and mother, William and Ethel von Hoene, with my sister Margaret and me, moved to Manette in 1917. Father started to work in the Puget Sound Navy Yard in 1910 and commuted from our home in Seattle until 1917.

The Von Hoenes' first Manette house was on the beach near the end of Trenton Avenue. It was a rustic sort of place —housing was scarce because of the war—no electricity and little else except the beach to recommend it. My best memory of the place involves one of the few spankings I ever received because I threw a biscuit at Margaret and knocked over the coal oil lamp on our supper table.

A few years later we moved to a tent house Dad built on the lots next door. There were many tent houses in those days of the war. Later he bought a house next door at the end of Trenton Avenue from a Mr. Cropp.

We lived there for many years—until about 1934 or 35

The von Hoene home at 1133 Hayward Avenue. Photo taken 1987.

when we moved to 1133 Hayward Avenue. In those early years the Walter Walls and the McHenrys were across the street. The Fellows family lived in the big house nearby with the old time music box in the hallway that fascinated us all.

The Japanese gardener was next to Fellows' home. None of old Manette would have been as pretty as it was without his geraniums each spring.

Our first house on the beach was later home to the Russell Elliotts, then to the Tom Pidduck family. Other neighbors in those beach days were the Frank Holbergs, the Tenges, the Barretts, the Gilmans and the Wrights. Farther down the beach were the Stewart and Parkins families and others.

Many families moved in during those World War I years but left during the Depression. As I remember, Manette was not too hard hit by the Depression for most who lost their jobs

Von Hoene family, 1942. Back row (from left), Elizabeth, Frances and Margaret. Front row, William and Ethel.

moved on and we were left with only those who still had jobs.

Grocery shopping was done at Meredith's or Martin's stores and groceries were carried home since few people had cars. I remember Martin's store vividly. During the great flu epidemic I was sent to Martin's to buy groceries. Both Mother and Dad were ill. I wore a gauze mask, went up to the loading platform in the rear of the store, shouted for Mr. Martin and gave him my order. He brought it out to me and I carried it home.

Meredith's store stands out in my memory for its boxes of cookies arranged on a slant with a glass lid. You reached in and selected the amount you wanted—no plastic packages in those days.

There was Wood's Department Store on the corner [East 11th Street and Perry Avenue] next to the old post office. I remember it well, for it was there that Audrey Stewart informed me that one said "vaz" not "vase." She was saved from being called snooty by me as Frank Holberg stopped to tell us he had another son.

I remember that Stewarts had the first radio on the beach.

Mrs. Stewart called us all in one day [in 1927] to tell us Lindberg had landed in Paris. Mrs. Stewart was even more famous for the delicious chocolates she made and so generously shared with her neighbors.

Mother and Dad belonged to the Knights of Pythias for many years but when Dad became very involved with the newly organized East Bremerton Improvement Club, that interest waned. As I remember, Dad and Earl Harkins, through the improvement club, were among the leaders in getting the first Manette Bridge built and a state park at Illahee.

Frances von Hoene, who was adopted by the Von Hoenes in 1933 when both Margaret and Elizabeth were grown, cut the ribbon on the bridge when it was freed of tolls in 1939.

Says Frances, "I was lucky enough to have been adopted by a very caring and loving couple who were willing at a later time in their lives to take in a sickly 3-year-old who, through love, was brought back to good health. I remember the many trees and the large picnic table we had in the yard at the beach house, where we often ate outside during the summer. I also had a swing between two fir trees which I enjoyed.

"I became a teacher and taught at Olympic View, Lincoln, East Bremerton, Manette, Navy Yard City, Olympic View, and Bremerton High Schools. During 30 years of teaching I taught mostly fifth grade, with third-, fourth- and sixth-grade classes along the way. I am now retired and live in the old family home at 1133 Hayward Avenue with my two cats, Adam and Eve.

"I feel proud, lucky and honored to have had such a wonderful understanding family take me into their lives and I feel I was a very lucky person to have had such a happy and wonderful life."

Margaret and I both attended Manette School and Bremerton High School. Margaret was in the first grade and I was in the second when we moved to Manette. I can still sing our old school song if anyone is interested. Each room had two grades and I remember the teachers: Miss Woods, Miss Ryan, Miss Crofoot, Miss Mendham and Mrs. Howard. The principal was Alice Kallander, whom many of us met once again in high school—sometimes to our sorrow since she was strict.

We all attended Manette Community Church. For years I was convinced it was really Isaac and Amy Hoopes church for without them I'm not sure there would have been a church. I can still see Isaac hunching up his shoulders and telling all the children at Christmas Eve Sunday School programs that Santa Claus would soon be there. It was some time before many of us realized why Tom Bright was never there to sit with Mrs. Bright; he was busy being Santa for many years. I still miss those Christmas boxes of sticky candy and realized one day I must be growing up when I was asked to help fill boxes. Little Dicky Feek in his black velvet suit was often one of the star performers welcoming all to the service.

For years I played the piano for Sunday School and church; Margaret helped run the Vacation Bible School and Mother helped keep the Ladies Aid and WCTU on an even keel. After my dad's last retirement I think they both helped with the church custodial duties. Both were very proud of the church and anxious to keep it in good shape. My favorite Sunday School teachers were Mrs. Card for her very gentle ways and soft voice and Amy Hoopes, who taught us all to be tolerant of others.

Entertainment in those days for small children and older ones was usually of our own contrivance. We had the woods and the beach; plenty of room for games like Run Sheep Run, Kick the Can, and Anti-I-Over; trees to climb; clams to dig; swimming, play acting, and hiking out to Big Rock and Sandy Beach as dating time came along.

I'm not sure what other parents did but ours were always involved in church affairs, P-TA, improvement club parties (remember those box suppers?), and neighborhood card games, campfires, camping and fishing.

We, as well as everyone else in town, went to Bremerton on the old *Pioneer* ferry. That was where I learned to be on time for the rest of my life. Missing a ferry meant a long cold wait on the dock or in a very smelly, creaky old waiting room. I'm sure Bob Carter, the boatman, could have retired on all the nickels we kids owed him on the days we forgot our money. When we began our Rainbow days we carried our dress shoes in a paper sack to the ferry, changed from our wet and dusty old shoes and tucked the old ones in among the life preservers in the ladies' cabin. I don't think anyone ever lost her shoes.

I don't think Manette in those days was ever a Peyton Place and what scandal there was, was so hushed up by grownups that we never knew much about it. Years later I understood but by then I'd forgotten any names and it was just as well.

My dad was paymaster in the navy yard from 1910 until he retired. He couldn't stand retirement so accepted a job in a parking lot. He stayed with that until they retired him. Then the state hired him to help with the construction of Illahee State Park. He and Mother both worked there, felling trees, making trails and transplanting shrubs until once again he was retired.

Whenever you cross the old bridge or go to Illahee Park I hope you'll say a quiet thank you to Ethel and Bill von Hoene and Earl and Etta Harkins, who was postmistress, for all their efforts. I know there were many others who helped too. I think the old post office was the real hub of early Manette. It was our link with the outside world, where all the kids met to take the ferry to Bremerton, where dates were made, gossip exchanged and friendships either begun or broken.

Just up the street a bit was the old blacksmith shop—not under a spreading chestnut tree but under a great plum tree. The smith had "hard and sinewy hands" and a beautiful beard. His shop was a fascinating place and one that made us all believe Longfellow.

The children growing up in Manette these days don't know what they missed.

I left Manette in 1939 to attend Mills College in California. I was married in California in 1940 and have been home only for visits since then. After 48 years away I'm not sure now whether I'm back in Manette or not. One of the few names I still recognize on a building is the Masonic Temple. I miss the old post office, the row of maple trees on the same street, Benders' lilac borders, Fellows' big house and the greenhouses. Someone even cut down the maple tree that dad planted on Armistice Day in the garden at the old beach house. I'll never forget his telling us that this was the war to end all wars. At the time of World War I the War Department informed him he'd have to drop the "von" from his name - too German. During World War II he was informed he could once again use it. Somewhere during those years even though we were once again fighting the Germans, the "von" had lost its sting.

Let me digress for one more memory—how many of you remember when all the school children were taken to see the Kaiser's flagship, a spoil of the war brought to the navy yard for overhaul and decommissioning? We saw the Kaiser's throne, a lot of gold and glitter. Best of all, the cooks in the galley gave our class fried egg sandwiches.

THE VON HOENE FAMILY

William and Ethel von Hoene had three daughters.

1. ELIZABETH VON HOENE, born in Seattle May 31, 1910. Elizabeth married ARRON C. WATERS, born in Waterville, Wash., May 6, 1905. Two children were born to them. Arron was a university geology professor. He has taught in various universities and taken field trips to Europe. Elizabeth accompanied him when he was training astronauts for their first trip to the moon.

2. MARGARET VON HOENE, born in Seattle June 18, 1911. Margaret married BRUCE PAINTER, born in North Carolina July 12, 1912. They lived in the Philippines, where Bruce was in business. They now live in Eatonville and he makes frequent trips to the islands.

3. FRANCES VON HOENE, born in Seattle January 19, 1930. Frances was adopted by Bill and Ethel. She attended Manette School, Lincoln Junior High and Bremerton High Schools. Frances is a retired teacher and lives in the family home at 1133 Hayward Avenue.

WALKER, ROBERT
By Bruce Walker
1983

My father, Robert Walker, came to Manette in about 1916 to seek employment in the shipyard. He bought a lot or two with a lean-to shack on it in an area which, after Pearl Harbor, became known as Eastpark housing project. Dad's lots were about due west (across McDougal's Creek) from Gideon Hermanson's and McNeill's on north Perry Avenue. At one time Gideon's parents were our next door neighbors.

Although Dad was born in Amity, Oreg., he spent much of his younger life in the Yakima, Ellensburg and Cle Elum area of Central Washington. His father, Henry Walker, was a buyer for Frye and Company meat packers of Seattle. Grandfather had what was known as the "Northwest Triangle" for his territory; that is, Seattle, Spokane and Portland. Dad, in his early years, worked for his father handling sheep and cattle and transporting them to Seattle.

Dad married Gertrude Louise Miller in Victoria, British Columbia, in 1909. They lived in the Ellensburg area. Since Dad was away from home a lot, Mom sometimes worked in Ellensburg or Yakima. After I was born in 1912 she spent some time with me at her parents', the George Millers, on their homestead near Naneum Canyon north of Ellensburg. When she returned to work I continued to live with my grandparents.

When I was about 4 years old Dad got a job with Brooks-Scanlon Lumber Company in Bend, Oreg., and sent for Mom and me. After a year or two there, Dad found a better job with the Puget Sound Navy Yard in Bremerton. Mom and I returned to Ellensburg, but Dad soon sent for us again, and I began to take root in Manette.

Due to irregular boundary lines of school districts, I was obliged to go to the Sheridan School, a two-room country school about a mile or so up the power line to the north of us. Yet my boyhood chum, George McKeown, lived only about a half-mile south and a little east of us and went to Manette School. However, all of us kids had to go to high school in Bremerton.

In my circle of friends were George McKeown, Bill Schweer, Mel Renn, Floyd Buchanan, Orville Schultz, Jack Geiser, George Personette, and a boy from Bremerton, Fritz Graebke. Harold Christensen was another Manette boy who joined us.

Our group was the ACS, or the Alley Cat Society. Our logo was a Halloween cat with arched back and a bottle brush tail.

Although my family lived outside the town of Manette, our everyday life was somehow entwined with Manette activities.

I substituted as paper carrier for George McKeown, who delivered the *Seattle Star*, and Bill Schweer, who handled the *Bremerton News Searchlight*. George's *Star* route took him down toward Enetai as well as around town. Bill's *Searchlight* route covered somewhat the same downtown area but ended up way out North Perry Avenue then west up over Sheridan Hill to Bubb's Corner (now Wheaton Way) and back to Manette. When George and Bill both took off at the same time I had to cover a lot of territory in one afternoon—on a bicycle. Many customers took both papers, some only took one. I think that is why I have such a poor memory today. I tried too hard to remember who took what.

Most of our shopping was done in Manette—Oscar Etten's meat market where hamburger was 15 cents a pound; Harry Martin's Price-Rite grocery; Clyde Meredith's Red and White Store; Jake Jacobsen's garage for car maintenance; Dick Feek's Union Station for gas.

I recall the fawn that wandered into town (or perhaps was chased into town by hunting dogs). It became quite tame and wandered the streets at will. Often it would try to board the ferry *Pioneer* for a free ferry ride to Bremerton. However, Bob Carter, the only crew member, managed to prevent stowaways from boarding the ferry.

The deer followed the kids around like a dog would. Finally it started sprouting two spikes. It was feared that some kid would inadvertantly lose an eye as the deer frolicked with the youngsters. It was finally taken out of circulation by being placed in a wire pen built between Clyde's Red and White Store and the fire house. Finally it was shipped to the Woodland Park Zoo in Seattle.

Some of my memories of Manette involved the kids living at the Children's Home up in back of Bill Schweer's home on the beach. Names of some of the kids were Stephona (Tony) Soyat, Floyd Taft and the Starevich family. I liked them all.

Since the government developed Eastpark, which enveloped the couple of lots that my folks had owned, I can't find the spot where my Dad's house stood. Evolution takes its toll. I feel like a man who has lost his roots.

In 1935 I married Myrle Bates of West Seattle. We were watchmen of the Manette Point (Point Herron) fog horn for a little over a year, about 1936-37. The magic eye was in operation then, so we did not have much to do.

I started to work in the Puget Sound Navy Yard in 1940. I left there in 1953. Since that time I have worked in Portland; in the San Francisco Bay area at Naval Materials Redistribution Center; and at Stockton, Port Hueneme, and Point Mugu, Calif. I retired in 1967 and we moved to central Oregon.

My mother passed away in July 1934. Dad married Adelaide Fredlund in 1936. Father died December 6, 1942.

OUR FAMILY
ROBERT and GERTRUDE WALKER had one son.

1. BRUCE WALKER, born in 1912 in Ellensburg. Bruce married MYRLE BLANCHE BATES. Bruce and Myrle have three children.
1A. GERTRUDE BLANCHE WALKER, born February 17, 1936, in Bremerton. Gertrude married JAMES PRATER. Gertrude and James have four children.
1A1. LYNNETTE JOYCE PRATER. Lynnette married MIKE LEGGETT. Lynnette and Mike had a son STEVEN. Lynnette and Mike divorced. Later Lynnette married CHARLES HENDRICKSON. Lynnette, Charles and Steven live in Flagstaff, Ariz., where Charles and Lynnette are employed at Coconino National Forest.
1A2. SANDRA LOU PRATER. Sandra married MIKE PIAZZA. Mike and Sandra are employed at Fremont National Forest, Paisley, Oreg. Sandra and Mike have two children, CARRIE and SCOTT.
1A3. JAMES THOMAS PRATER. James married CANDY FIFIELD. Later James married JANET WILSON. James and Candy had three children, JAMES, JENNIFER and AMANDA.
1A4. STEVEN BRUCE PRATER, born in Oxnard, Calif. Steven married LEE HOFFMAN. Steven is in the U.S. Marine Corps in Okinawa.
1B. GERALDINE RAE WALKER, born May 2, 1938, in Bremerton. Geraldine married RUSSELL GIBSON JR. They had three children born in Los Angeles: LAURA, born in 1957; RUSSELL Jr., born in 1958, and DEBRA, born in 1958. Russell Sr. was killed in an auto accident. Geraldine and children moved to Missoula, where Geraldine married RAIDER OLSEN. Raider died after they had one son, RAIDER A. OLSEN. Geraldine then married TOM HECK. They divorced. She is now married to DON GETTY of Lakeview, Oreg. They live in Burns, Oreg. Young Raider A. also lives in Burns.
1C. DOUGLAS BRUCE WALKER, born May 16, 1944, in Portland. Douglas was raised in California. He married SHIRLEY PADEN of Santa Barbara. Doug adopted Shirley's daughter CAROL, who was born in 1960. Doug and Shirley had three more children, MALINDA RAE, born in 1966; KATHY JOY, born in 1968, and BRUCE DOUGLAS, born in 1971. Carol has a son JEREMY. Doug is a computer engineer in National Service Division of IBM and works out of the Portland office.

WALL, ERIK AUGUST
By Gertrude Wall Carr
1984

MIGRATION FROM SWEDEN
TO KITSAP COUNTY

Erik August Wall, known as August, was born Erik August Vall in Hudiksvall, Sweden, April 29, 1862. When August arrived in 1900, Bremerton was an open pioneering town. Washington had been a state for only 11 years (admitted to the Union November 18, 1889). Bremerton itself was only a few hastily erected, rough wooden buildings surrounded by fields roughly cleared of brush so that tents and cabins could be set up.

The main interest was the newly established Puget Sound Navy Yard. This was just a few buildings and docks, but there

August and Marta Wall's home at 222 Shore Drive in 1903. - Photo from Gertrude Wall Carr

Copper shop built in 1906 by August Wall on Shore Drive, Wall home in background.
-1987 Photo from Orville Schultz

were ships anchored off the cove and these few buildings and docks were swarming with workmen.

August's son Walter arrived July 1, 1901, and went to work in the navy yard the day he arrived. Walter, then 16 years old, was a big lad, strong for his age, and intelligent. He was already taller than his father, and had learned enough coppersmithing to be more qualified for the job than many of the men who applied.

August's job was to establish a copper shop at the navy yard. He was the first coppersmith employed, and rose to be the first quarterman coppersmith, the highest rank a coppersmith could hold at that time.

FINDING A HOME

August got a tent and built the then-customary tent-stand in a field north of the navy yard in what is now the Burwell Street area. To this tent he brought his wife Marta, born Jorlin Marta Edlund May 16, 1864, in Sweden. He had married her in Sweden in 1885. Three additional children, Walda, 13, Erik August Jr., 11, and Eda Christine, 5, came with Marta.

August Wall was impressed with the natural beauty of the country. For the first time in his life he felt the need to buy land and build a permanent home. It was beautiful around Bremerton, for the water lay between hills that were covered with evergreen timber down to the water's edge. It was very similar to the mountain fjords he had left in Sweden when he came to the United States in 1892. There was one important difference—the climate was much milder.

The water was a constantly changing source of beauty. Whether it was placidly calm, a sheet of reflecting glass dimpled by shadows or a seething, lead-colored tumult of waves, it was beautiful. There were snow-capped mountains in the distance and magnificent sunsets behind them.

WE MOVE TO DECATUR

August wanted to buy land across the water from the town of Bremerton, away from the noise of the shipyard and the turmoil of activity. Marta objected. There was no possible way to reach the opposite shore except by rowboat, and she—with a family to look after—had no time for rowing a boat across the channel every time she wanted to go shopping.

Erik August and Marta Wall family, circa 1910. Back row (from left), Walda Wall Solibakke, Oscar Solibakke, Walter Wall, Eda Christine Wall. Front row, Erik August, Gertrude and Marta Wall.

Her arguments were useless. August bought 10 acres in Decatur township, later called Manette, in the Shore Drive and Perry Avenue area. He also bought 25 acres in the Enetai Beach area. He had the second house built in Manette. W.E. Harris built the first and Edward and Mathilda Olson, who lived at what is now 315 Shore Drive, are thought to have built the third. Other buildings in the area included an Indian fort and an Indian school.

August wasn't the only one who thought the east shore of the sound looked more inviting than the booming, sprawling navy yard city of Bremerton. The land was quickly bought up and the small community of Manette came into being.

The house August built at what is now 222 Shore Drive was a large two-story house with an attached woodshed. The house had a parlor, living room, kitchen and pantry on the ground floor and three bedrooms upstairs. It was equipped with a carbide gas plant for indoor gas lighting. There was a well with a hand pump—like the motive power on the old-fashioned railroad hand cars—that pumped water to a reservoir on the roof so there was running water in the kitchen. Out in the woodshed was a water closet with the old-fashioned pull-chain—a new fashion at that time—and there was an open breezeway between the woodshed and the kitchen door which was screened with lattice worked into a diamond pattern. The kitchen porch had a wooden floor with a trapdoor to the cement cellar.

A white picket fence around the yard and house encompassed three city lots. The street, now Pitt Avenue, passed directly by the back door, so one could open the lattice porch door and step out onto the roadway. A concrete walkway ran nearly 50 feet across the front yard to the front gate on Upper Shore Drive. Beside this gate was a 10-foot-high stump of an enormous tree. There was a footpath from the front gate down a steep incline to the shore. Here August had earlier built a one-room shop 20 x 30 feet and two stories high. Here he set up a forge and a workbench and kept a complete set of coppersmithing tools and equipment.

Although Marta had brought furniture with her from previous dwellings, this new home swallowed it up. So she bought furniture in Seattle—deep maroon-colored wooden rocking chairs inlaid with mother-of-pearl scrolls and flowers and elaborately turned legs and slatted backs; a delicate writing desk with carvings on the front and a narrow mirror in the back, and a round occasional table.

Lace curtains were at the windows, and a lovely green carpet with garlands of roses and ribbons was on the floor. Straw matting carpeted the bedrooms, which were reached by a narrow stairway in the center of the house between the kitchen and the living room.

No sooner was the house finished and furnished than social gatherings began. Many Scandinavians known to the Walls were now living in Bremerton, and in addition, August's new social status as boss of the copper shop brought him many friends.

Every Sunday boatloads of Scandinavians came from Seattle to join the round of partyings from house to house. Among these were two eligible bachelors, Mr. Frederick and Mr. Nelson. One was short and the other was tall. These young men were doubly welcome because of their habit of bringing a gift to the hostess at whichever home they visited. They had a general merchandise store in Seattle, Frederick & Nelson's, and it was there that Marta had purchased her house furnishings. On one occasion, the hostess' gift to Marta was a beautiful damask linen tablecloth as heavy and glossy as glass.

The parties were usually picnics and outdoor romps where there would be lots of games involving running and boys catching girls. One favorite game was "Last Couple Out." It consisted of several couples—a man and a woman, naturally—standing in a double row all facing the same direction with one single person at the head of the row. This single one would call "Last Couple Out" and the last couple in the row would break into a run, one on each side of the row, and try to meet and join hands at the front of the line before the "leader" could catch the partner of the opposite sex. This was very popular because it permitted lots of sly hugging and coy resistance between the young men and women.

There was one spot in particular that was a favorite for picnics. This was the beach of the 25 acres August had purchased at Enetai. Boatloads of young people—with baskets and boxes of food—would row ashore there. August had built a long table of rough boards. This would be covered with tablecloths and then loaded down with food.

RELIGION ENTERS THE PICTURE

At this time Manette was a frontier town with no regular church. However, it wasn't long before a Baptist missionary was sent to form a church group. A young couple, Mr. and Mrs. Sam Galotte, were active in this work, and it wasn't long before they had a young people's group started. Enthusiasm grew fast and in 1906 Bethany Baptist Church, now Manette Community Church, was built at East 13th and Hayward Avenue.

August had imbibed the opinions of Ingersoll and the Socialists of that time and had no use for God or the church.

Young Walter, on the other hand, was converted and took to the church heart and soul. He was the one most deeply affected, although Walda and the nearly teen-age Eda went to the meetings, too. The church was the focal point of the young people's activities and its influence was so deep that even Marta was affected. She was accepted into the church by baptism in the fall of 1906.

Marta's piety was inarticulate and she did not attend church often, but her conversion was genuine and deeply felt. She could read and write English to a limited extent—enough to read a newspaper—but not enough to enable her to read the fast-paced hymns or participate in congregational responses. So, rather than be embarrassed by having to stand with her mouth closed while others around her were reading aloud or singing, she stayed home and read her Bible.

WALTER

During these years in Manette, Walter made the decision to dedicate his life to God. He started to save what little money he got—for although he was working in the navy yard he turned over his wages to his parents and received in return only a little pocket money. He decided to become a missionary and with the encouragement of the Galottes, attended Nyack College in Nyack, N.Y.

Walter worked as a coppersmith in the navy yard until his retirement. In addition he alternately pastored churches at the Washington Veterans Home in Retsil and Scandia Bible Church in Poulsbo.

WALDA

Walda attended school at Tracyton. When she was graduated from grade school she went to Bellingham to attend the Bellingham Normal School and was graduated with a teacher's accreditation. She first taught in Edgewood, behind what is now Port Orchard. Her next assignment was in Poulsbo. Here she met a young man, Oscar Solibakke. Oscar was one of a large family whose father was the acting Lutheran minister in Poulsbo. Oscar was a tall, handsome, wavy-haired young man and took a decided liking to Walda.

Walda taught 2 years in Poulsbo. She and Oscar married mid-term of the second year. She finished out the teaching year but stopped teaching after that.

AUGUST JR.

August Jr. was growing up to be a lively rascal with an impish sense of humor. He had a round face and two round blue eyes, topped by straight blond hair that stood up on his head as though he'd just grabbed an electric wire. One day in 1904 he was scuffling in a public swimming pool in Seattle, fell against some exposed plumbing and injured his spine. He developed spinal meningitis and was sent home to Manette. He lay sick for three weeks and then died. He was 14 years old.

EDA CHRISTINE

Eda Christine had heavy chestnut hair with auburn lights in it, and it was her fervent hope that it would darken to the dark auburn of her maternal grandmother. She loved music. She had a strong, vibrant contralto voice—even when quite a young girl. She also had a talent for the piano. After 11 years of being the baby of the family, suddenly Christine found herself supplanted by another little girl whom she was allowed to name, Gertrude Martha.

GERTRUDE

On April 18, 1907, Walter was sent rowing across the sound to get Dr. Acton. Walter had to go because his father was upstairs in bed with a sore foot. He had accidentally shot a toe off.

I was a comparatively puny baby—as Marta's babies went—weighing in at only 10 pounds. But then, Marta was well along in years by that time, 43 years old.

In 1908, as soon the baby was old enough to travel, Marta took a trip back home to Sweden to visit her father. Her mother had been dead for many years, but her father, a sister and brother were still alive. Marta had been homesick for a long time; now there was money enough so they could afford the trip. We stayed 18 months.

ROWING TO WORK

Since August and his family first built their home in Manette the town had grown into almost unrecognizable proportions. Originally the only access was by rowboat. Every morning and evening he and Walter rowed across the channel to work in the navy yard. Walter described it: "We'd grab a bite of breakfast, then the lunch pails, run for the beach, drag the boat to the water and get in. Out would come the oars, then row for all we were worth. Finally we'd land and drag the boat up and tie it to a tree, hide the oars, run for the navy yard, drop our muster checks and start the day's work. The work was usually aboard the U.S.S. *Oregon*, *Wisconsin*, or the *Monterey*."

Years later, after the ferries were put into service, the men would walk the few blocks from their home to the Manette ferry dock, board the ferry *Pioneer* or *Urania* and walk 2 blocks on the Bremerton side to the navy yard.

Preparation for his breakfast later became a ritual for August. Before he went to bed at night, he would shake out the ashes from the grates in the stove and prepare the stove so that when Marta came down in the morning about 6 a.m., she could light the fire, put the coffee pot on the hottest part of the stove and start mixing batter for August's waffles or pancakes. August usually ate 10 or 12 waffles or pancakes spread lavishly with butter and jam or jelly. He would then pick up his lunch box and amble down to catch the 7:45 ferry.

When August first came to Manette he was active in community affairs and belonged to the East Bremerton Improvement and Investment Club. He participated in practically everything that came along, except for one thing. There was a salesman who came around with a promotional scheme for writing up the early "History of Manette." This book was to cost $75, which in the early 1900s was practically a month's pay. August didn't go along with this promotion. When the book was published—and a beautiful job of bookbinding it was—the only pioneers featured with a whole page were those who had paid money in advance. The more they paid, the bigger the feature. Others got scant mention.

In 1910 August moved the family to Tacoma, where he started his own coppersmith business. The business did not prosper after Walter married and left for the ministry in 1912. During World War I August went to Seattle and worked in the Duthie Shipbuilding Company. He returned to PSNY in 1926.

When August came back to live in Manette the second time, he found an entirely new set of public figures. The Improvement and Investment Club had fallen into disuse. Few of the old timers remained. Edvard Olson still lived in his big house below Wall's, with a big stone bulkhead holding back the waters of Puget Sound from reaching his rose garden. Olson was a machinist in the navy yard, but in his spare time he grew roses. He belonged to several horticultural societies, developed several new roses and had articles and pictures in rose growers' magazines. He wore his choicest blooms to work. He was tall and thin with twinkling eyes and a pointed Vandyke beard of a rich brown color. It was an incongruous sight to see this tall, gangly machinist with a lovely, delicate rose pinned to his cap.

In 1930 August Wall retired from the navy yard. He was given a big celebration. He rode out of the copper shop for the last time in an official car with naval officers beside him. His retirement gift from the copper shop was a genuine cowhide suitcase. He made good use of it.

Although he had been hit by the bank failures of the Depression in 1928/29 he still had enough money to carry out a cherished dream. August had finally contacted his half-brother, Karl Kilander, who was a port dockmaster in East London, South Africa, and the two returned to their home in Hudiksvall, Sweden.

August died in 1946 and Marta in 1947. They are buried in Forest Lawn Cemetery.

GENEALOGY

ERIK AUGUST WALL (1862-1946) changed his name from Vall to Wall when he migrated to the United States with his wife MARTA (1864-1947) and their four children. Four more children were born in the United States.

1. WALTER VICTOR WALL, born in Sweden December 23, 1885. He married HULDA SWANSON in June 1912. He met Hulda at Nyack Missionary College. Walter died in 1968. Hulda died in 1972. Walter and Hulda had five children:
1A. RUTH EVANGELINE WALL, born May 24, 1913, in Florence, Oreg., where Walter pastored a church for one year. Ruth married BRUCE HENSLEY. They divorced and he is now deceased. Ruth lives in the Kona Apartments on Sheridan Road. Ruth and Bruce had two sons, twelve grandchildren and four great granddaughters. The two sons are:
1A1. JACK HENSLEY, who lives in the home of his grandparents, 1134 Hayward Avenue.
1A2. WALTER HENSLEY, who lives in Seattle.
1B. DOROTHY EVELYN WALL, born June 11, 1915. She married ROY HELSER and they live in Oregon. Dorothy and Roy have two sons and a daughter: DENNIS, SUSAN AND ROY.
1C. WALTER ROBERT WALL, known as Robert, born June 30, 1917. He married BETTY ERNISSY of Yakima. Robert and Betty have two daughters and a son: ALIDA, KATHY, and ROBERT, who is a professor at Seattle Pacific College.
1D. CHARLES RAYMOND WALL, born November 26, 1920. He and his wife MARY live in Wheaton, Ill. Charles and Mary have four daughters.
1E. MARION WALL, born December 1, 1922. She married ROY SMITHEY. Roy died in 1963. Their children are: JEAN (Jean died in 1985.), who has two sons: PATRICK, who has a son and a daughter; and MICHAEL, who has two daughters.

2. WALDA VICTORIA WALL, born in Sweden December 1, 1887. Walda married OSCAR SOLIBAKKE. Walda and Oscar had three children.
2A. HERBERT OSCAR SOLIBAKKE. Herbert and his wife LOUISE had a daughter and two sons. Louise died in a fire in the Bahamas. Later Herbert married NELLIE BRUGGEMAN.
2B. EDA MARGARET SOLIBAKKE. Margaret married RICHARD SHAGRIN and lives in Seattle. Margaret and Richard have a son, RICHARD JR., and a daughter, JOLIE, who is now Mrs. BREWER and has an adopted daughter.
2C. GERTRUDE MARTHA "PATTY" SOLIBAKKE. Patty is now Mrs. FRANK PORTER, a widow. She lives in Hawaii. Patty and Frank had four children.

3. ERIK AUGUST WALL Jr., born in Sweden December 26, 1889. Erik died in 1903.

4. VALENTIN GUSTAF WALL, born in Sweden January 3, 1892. Valentin drowned at about age 6.

5. EDA CHRISTINE (originally IDA KRISTINA) WALL, born in Wisconsin November 3, 1895. She married JESSE PARSONS. Eda and Jesse divorced and Eda married, then divorced, BRUCE PLANTT. Eda, until recently, lived on one of the lots, 917 Perry Avenue, of the original family property. She is now in a rest home. Eda and Jesse had one daughter.
5A. LOUISE PARSONS. She married JAY ASHENBERG and lives on the family property at 917 Perry Avenue. Louise and Jay have two daughters and four grandchildren. The two daughters are:
5A1. STEPHANIE ASHENBERG. Stephanie married CHRIS DOERR and lives in Avon, Conn. Stephanie and Chris have two daughters: ALLISON and KRISTINA.
5A2. GENEVIEVE "GENNA," now Mrs. JOHNSON. She is divorced and lives in Bremerton with her two sons, TIMOTHY and CHRISTIAN.

6. CARL GUSTAV WALL, born in the spring of 1897. Carl died at the age of 18 months.

7. An infant son, born in the summer of 1898, died 2 hours after birth.

8. GERTRUDE WALL, born in Manette April 18, 1907. Gertrude was married to HANCE "Henry" JACOBSON. They had one son, Eric. They divorced. Gertrude married FRANK CARR, and Eric took the name Carr. Gertrude and Frank live in Seattle.
8A. ERIC CARR attended Manette School, Lincoln Junior High, Bremerton High School and the University of Washington. Eric married GLORIA TRASK, also of Manette. Eric and Gloria divorced. Eric married PRISCILLA. They divorced. Eric lives in Manette on his sailboat *Genna*. He and Gloria had four children.
8A1. GREGORY CARR. Gregory and his wife MARGARET live in Portland. They have two daughters: GLORIA and MARTHA ANN.
8A2. CHRISTINE MARIE CARR. Christine married JAMES SCHULTZ and they live in Keyport.

8A3. MARY ANNE CARR. Mary Anne married and divorced TOM REEVES and DAVID DUES. She had two boys and two girls. One girl, EILEEN, is deceased. THOMAS, DAVID and JACQUE ANN live on Shore Drive.
8A4. JOHN CARR. John died in a diving accident at age 23.

WALSH AND BORGEN
By Joyce Walsh Walter
1986

THE BORGENS ARRIVE

Martha K. Borgen, who was to become my mother, was born in Helena, Mont., in 1898. Her parents were John and Julia Borgen, who were born in Norway. They operated a county "poor farm" for elderly men in Anaconda or Helena, Mont. Martha attended business college in Anaconda and worked for the telephone company.

In 1918 John and Julia Borgen moved to Manette with their daughter, Lillian (who became Mrs. Schultz), and son Joe. They lived a mile out of town on what is now Wheaton Way. Martha came out the following year.

John Borgen worked in the navy yard. Julia and John died and were buried in Acacia in Seattle in approximately 1933 and 1931 respectively.

"SHORTY" WALSH COMES

Charles Vernon "Shorty" Walsh, my father, was born in Oakland, Calif., in 1898. He came to Manette in 1919. Shorty was in the navy, then worked in the Puget Sound Navy Yard and became a leadingman rigger.

Shorty Walsh and Martha Borgen were married in 1920. They established their home on Marlow Avenue across from the Children's Home.

[Shorty's mother was Emelita Walsh, aunt of Joaquina Feek. See FEEK family history.]

FAMILY AND JOB

Shorty and Martha's son, John Vernon Walsh, known as Jack, was born in Bremerton in 1921, and I, Charlotte Joyce Walsh, in 1923. When we were children, Dad was laid off several times, along with a good many other men. At that time he cut firewood and sold it, caught and sold salmon and did garden work for Hattie Martin.

CHILDHOOD IN MANETTE

My brother and I enjoyed life—growing up in Manette, we hiked a lot. We attended Manette School, Lincoln Junior High and Bremerton High School. We spent our time on the beach in the summertime. The "big boys" swam nude at the Sandbanks, an out-of-bounds area for girls and "little kids." Our neighborhood gang included the Hilstad boys, the Holden girls and Wayne Burlew. Steve Hilstad and I were the youngest and were left out of the big kids' fun. However, we entertained ourselves by gathering hazelnuts, one for you and one for me; picking all the trilliums we could find; catching bees—which I mixed with mud pies; and catching snakes. We threw the snakes into the Hilstad's chicken pen. Mrs. Hilstad was cleaning a chicken one day and pulled a dead snake out of the chicken. She screamed.

Steve and I ran. We kept our mouths shut.

Later Shirley Bright and I were pals. We received bicycles with balloon tires for Christmas in 1935 and regularly rode out to Tracyton or out toward Island Lake.

Jack was a Boy Scout and I was a Girl Scout. My Girl Scout Troop still has yearly get-togethers, with three of our leaders, Neal Meredith, Hazel Callison and Estelle Meredith joining us.

While Jack was in the Marines he was stationed in Japan from September 1945 until June 1946. He worked for the army in Japan from 1949 until 1964, and in Hawaii from 1964 until 1968. He also worked in the navy yard.

THE FAMILY
CHARLES AND MARTHA WALSH's descendants are:

1. JOHN "Jack" WALSH, born July 8, 1921, in Bremerton. Jack married SAEKO FUJISAKI in Japan in 1950. Jack is retired and lives in Bremerton. Saeko died October 14, 1987. Jack and Saeko had two children.
1A. MARY WALSH, born November 11, 1950, in Japan. Mary married ALAN BAIN. They have one son.
1A1. ALEX BAIN, born June 1, 1978, in Seattle. Alex is a student in Everett.
1B. MICHAEL WALSH, born March 1, 1957, in Japan. Michael is single.

2. CHARLOTTE JOYCE WALSH, born March 18, 1923, in Bremerton. Joyce married Lt. (jg.) DELTON EARL WALTER, USNR, in 1943. Del was contract manager for Bethlehem Steel. He died at their summer home near Tahuya in 1981. Joyce lives on Magnolia Bluff in Seattle. Joyce and Delton had three sons.
2A. KENT WALTER, born March 10, 1945, in Brooklyn, N.Y. Kent married JULIE ANNE CAGLE. They have two children.
2A1. JAMES KENT WALTER, born October 7, 1964, in San Mateo, Calif. James is a student at Montana State University.
2A2. JENNIFER ANNE WALTER, born May 13, 1969, in Seattle. Jennifer is a student in Seattle.
2B. LYNN WALTER, born December 12, 1946, in Seattle. Lynn married LAUREL NIST. They divorced. Lynn and Laurel had a daughter.
2B1. HEATHER CHRISTINE WALTER, born May 23, 1970, in Seattle. Heather is a student in Port Orchard.
Lynn married NANCI EWART March 17, 1985, in Seattle.
2C. LANCE WALTER, born February 4, 1949, in Seattle. Lance is single and lives in California.

WALTENBURG, JACOB
By Margaret Avery Bruemmer
1985

Jacob Edson "Jake" Waltenburg was born July 9, 1864, in Oakdale, Wis. He died in June 1952. Jacob married Lucy Mary Grondin, who was born June 3, 1873, in Oscola, Wis. She died June 29, 1945. Jacob and Lucy had eight children: Kathryn Mae, Maybelle, Mary, Elmer, Agnes, Violet, Clifford and Helen.

In 1911 Jake came west from North Dakota with the oldest

Elmer Waltenburg in Meredith's delivery truck.
                              -Photo from Violet Avery

daughter, Kathryn Mae, on the train. The Waltenburgs had received letters from their former hired man, John Emel, about Silverdale. John had come west 2 years before and had written letters back about the good opportunities here. Kathryn Mae met her future husband George Fischer on the train ride out here.

Jacob and Kathryn Mae—she was always called Mae—got to Silverdale in 1911. Lucy Mary with six more children came about 4 months later. The little house they lived in still stands between the old Boy Scout hall and the water in Silverdale. They stayed there a little while, then moved to Pleasant Avenue in Bremerton.

On Violet's birthday, May 10, 1912, a terrible accident happened with blasting caps—Violet lost her thumb and two fingers.

HOME IN MANETTE

In June 1912 the Waltenburgs moved to Manette next to "Fisherman" Johnson on Shore Drive. Within the next few months they moved up to Cascade Trail and Perry Avenue; the house is still there. Their next move was to a green house on Perry Avenue where the Emmanuel Lutheran Church now stands. At this time Jacob, with the help of Mr. Farmer and Charlie Martin, was building a house in "Pumpkin Center," nearby. Helen, their last child, was born in the new Pumpkin Center house on January 26, 1914.

Around this time, a big forest fire came roaring up from the Sandbanks, near where the Community Theater now stands. Jacob built back-fires to halt the rush of fire.

EARLY DAYS IN MANETTE

Jake Waltenburg worked as a gardener at the Officer's Club in the navy yard for about $2 a day.

Mary, Elmer, Agnes, Violet and Clifford went to Sheridan School. There were boardwalks up Perry Avenue to the road to Pumpkin Center. Dallas "Dolly" Cowen had worked on building the boardwalk.

There were several places to dance. One was in Hillman City where the Bremerton Community Theater is today; another in Tracyton, and later one in Lincoln Heights at the end of the boardwalk on Perry Avenue.

PUMPKIN CENTER RESIDENTS

Some of the other families living in Pumpkin Center were Lamont, Jim Robinson, Charlie Robinson, Chase, Morris, Walker and Christenson.

Jake took parties of hunters cougar and bear hunting. They hunted all around Kitsap County. They hunted where Illahee State Park is now. Some of the people they took were officers from the navy yard, even Admiral Greg Wire.

Elmer Waltenburg worked at Meredith's store in early 1920. He also had a coal yard with Ben Kean. It was where the laundromat at East 11th Street and Shore Drive is today. Oscar Hilstad also owned a coal yard.

Mail was delivered by a trotter horse and buggy. Bill Avery was the driver. The route went all the way to Brownsville, returning through Tracyton.

If doctors were needed at night after the 12-passenger boat *Berne* stopped running, the doctor was rowed across from Bremerton and he stayed all night at the home of the patient. Early doctors were Dr. John Schutt, Dr. Munns (father of recently retired Dr. Edward Munns) and Dr. Taggert. Dr. Ray Schutt came to Bremerton after World War I. Elmer Waltenburg was his first patient; Elmer had mumps.

DESCENDANTS

Following are sketches of the eight children of JACOB and LUCY WALTENBURG

1. KATHRYN MAE WALTENBURG was born February 25, 1894, in Wisconsin. She died October 12, 1955. Kathryn married GEORGE FISCHER, born July 24, 1888, in Holland. George died August 18, 1959. [For their descendants see FISCHER, JOHN GEORGE, family history.]

2. MAYBELLE DELIA WALTENBURG was born June 28, 1896, in Wisconsin. She died June 16, 1967. Maybelle married WILLIAM EARL HEPWORTH, born September 26, 1889, in Bountiful, Utah. William died December 3, 1959. Their children are ALICE, born in 1917 in Manette; RAYMOND, born in 1919 in Manette; LUCY, born in 1921 in Manette, and WILLIAM, born in 1937 in Manette. William died April 22, 1943.

3. MARY ISABELLE WALTENBURG was born September 20, 1898, in Wisconsin. She died February 22, 1985. Mary married JUDSEN DAVIS, who died in 1929. She then married BONNY HOWERTON, who was born in 1905 and died in 1969. Mary had no children.

4. ELMER JACOB WALTENBURG was born March 2, 1900, in Minnesota. He died July 2, 1970. Elmer married PEARL JONAS, who was born October 31, 1904, in Colville, Wash. She died July 2, 1977. Elmer and Pearl had three children: WILLIS, born in Bremerton November 9, 1921; DONALD, born in Bremerton in 1923, and EDWIN, born in Bremerton in 1929.
Elmer and Pearl were divorced; Elmer later married AUDRY HAMELTON. She died in 1947. Later Elmer married AGNES JOHNSON.

5. AGNES MARTHA WALTENBURG was born May 24, 1902, in North Dakota. Agnes married DOUGLAS EUBANKS. They were divorced. Agnes second husband was GEORGE PHILLIPS, whom she married in 1920. They were divorced. Agnes married CHARLES RAABE, born January 19, 1892, in Germany. He died June 22, 1970.
Agnes' second husband, George E. Phillips (1889-1952), came from California when he was about 2 years old. He had a younger brother Ray. They went to school at Sheridan and were taught by Mrs. Ruley. George lived here 63 years, when he died. He had no children. His family homesteaded 80 acres on North Perry Avenue near where Dr. David Relling now lives. George's parents are buried on the hill at the end of Barnett Street. They were strawberry farmers.
Agnes and Charles had three children: JOHN, born in Bremerton in 1937; FRANCIS, born in Seattle in 1939, and RAYMOND, born in Seattle in 1943. Agnes died November 19, 1970.

6. VIOLET MARGARET WALTENBURG was born May 10, 1904, in North Dakota. On May 10, 1929 she married DALLAS HARLEY AVERY, who was born January 27, 1904, in Sidney, now Port Orchard. Dallas' family lived in many locations in Kitsap County. They moved to Manette from Brownsville in 1928. Dallas started to work in the navy yard in 1919, when he was 15. After a reduction in force, Dallas joined the United States Marine Corps. After his enlistment he returned to Puget Sound Navy Yard, where he retired 32 years later. Dallas' parents were Bud and Leath Avery. His brothers and sisters were Ollie, Marian, Helen, Dick and Jim. Dallas worked at different jobs when the navy yard would have a reduction in force. He helped pour cement for Manette's sidewalks, worked on water lines and did any kind of work to earn a living in those days.
Dallas and Violet have lived at 4800 Fir Drive NE all their married life. Their children are MARGARET, born in Bremerton in 1930; PATRICIA, born in Bremerton in 1932; MARY ELLEN, born in Bremerton in 1936, and DALLAS Jr., born in Bremerton in 1940.

7. CLIFFORD ALEXANDER WALTENBURG was born July 16, 1910, in North Dakota. He married HELEN AVERY. They had no children. They were divorced. Clifford later married PAT WAGNER. They had a son, DARRELL, born in 1939.
Clifford and Pat were divorced; he married MYRTLE WILDER BLYSTONE. They had a son, DOUGLAS, born in Seattle in 1945.

8. HELEN FLORENCE WALTENBURG, born January 26, 1914, in Manette. Helen married JAMES HALL. They were divorced. Later Helen married FRED HART. They too were divorced. Helen has no children. She died June 14, 1987.

Jacob and Lucy, the first "Manette" generation, now have descendants down to the sixth generation. Most live in the Pacific Northwest.

WAUGH, HERMAN
By Esther Waugh Fischer
1987

Herman Waugh and his wife Eva came to Manette in 1924 from Weiser, Idaho. They lived at 1614 Winfield Avenue. Herman worked in the navy yard at the power plant. He enjoyed hunting deer with Clyde Meredith. Eva Waugh and Gertrude Schoonover, another Manette pioneer, were sisters. Herman Waugh and Edward Schoonover, Gertrude;s husband, were cousins. Herman and Eva Waugh had three daughters and a son: Esther, Harold, Evelyn and Louise.

Esther taught piano to Manette and Bremerton children for 35 years.

THE FAMILY

HERMAN and EVA WAUGH'S descendants are:

1. ESTHER WAUGH, born in Grandview, Wash. Esther married SIG SIGURDSON. Later she married BOB FISCHER. Bob died May 7, 1985. Esther lives in Bremerton. Esther's foster daughter, BARBARA (now Mrs. LOUTOCKY), born September 16, 1926, lives in Coos Bay, Oreg.

2. HAROLD WAUGH, born in Seattle. Harold married JULIE DEUTRACH of Fargo, N.Dak. He worked in the shipyard and played basketball. Harold also played the banjo. He was a guide in Alaska until his death in 1973. Harold had two sons.
2A. GARY WAUGH was born in Everett in 1943.
2B. DAN WAUGH was born in Alaska in 1948.

3. EVELYN RUTH WAUGH, born in New Meadows, Idaho. Evelyn married CHARLES KRAMER and they lived in Longview. Evelyn died in June 1958. Evelyn and Charles had one son.
3A. MICHEAL KRAMER. Micheal and his wife SYLVIA have a daughter KRISTI. Micheal and Sylvia live in Eugene, Oreg.

4. LOUISE WAUGH, born in Weiser, Idaho. Louise married LEE REESE of San Diego. Louise died February 14, 1984. Louise had four children.
4A. SHIRLEY REESE, born in 1939. Shirley married FRANK LEAHY. Shirley and Frank had five children: SHELLY, born in 1958; MICHEAL, born in 1960; ROBIE, born in 1963, and twins KATHY and KRISTY, born in 1968.
4B. TERRY REESE, born in 1943. Terry has a son SCOTT, born January 7, 1980, and a daughter DEONE, born June 23, 1981.
4C. MARILYN REESE, born August 27, 1948. Marilyn has a son MICHEAL, born in 1966.
4D. DAVID REESE, born March 23, 1954. David has a son RYAN, born August 4, 1984.

Herman and Eva Waugh family, 1934. From left, Esther, Louise, Herman, Eva, Harold and Evelyn.
-Photo from Ada Schoonover Matteson

Esther Waugh's music class, 1927. Back row (from left), Ada Schoonover, Louise Waugh, Selma Wilsen, Dorothy Wall, Jeane Martin, Freda Walker, Esther Waugh, Zola Walker, Betty Bender, Ruth Wall, Bob Davidson, Margaret Hoopes, Opal Cowan, Delcie May Walker, David Morris, Barbara Christensen, Margie Schoonover, Muriel Peterson, Alice Sherman, Maryjayne Meredith, Helen Holden, Blossom Bright, Genevieve Painter, Doris Welborn, Eleanor Pidduck.

WHEATON, DAVID
By Roger Paquette
1986

The man for whom Wheaton Way was named came to Manette in 1928. He and an associate were partners in the Union Bridge Company of Portland. He was the superintendent in charge of construction for that company and he served in that capacity in the construction of the Manette Bridge. Before that, he had had a long history of building bridges (three across the Columbia), roads, railroads, sewers, streets and tunnels. Some of these projects brought citations from professional associations because of their degree of difficulty.

During the Depression years of the 1930s he was superintendent of WPA projects in Bremerton. He did contract work at the Bremerton NAD Annex and the shipyard. At the start of World War II he built the first housing units at Eastpark.

In 1949 he was elected public works commissioner and served Bremerton in that capacity for 10 years. Major projects of his administration were the Casad Dam on Union River, water reservoirs and the Warren Avenue Bridge. It was this last project which appropriately led to the naming of the road in Manette between its two bridges as Wheaton Way.

David Wheaton was born in Manitoba, Canada, in 1887. The death of his mother forced the termination of his formal education in the sixth grade. He was on his own in his early teens. At 16 he came to Eastern Washington and then to Bellingham, where, in 1918, he received his naturalization papers. His engineering know-how came through correspondence study and experience, coupled with hard work and resourcefulness.

His obituary in the *Bremerton Sun* of February 19, 1960, summarized his many outside activities. "He had been active on the Kitsap County Fair Board, State Good Roads Association and Kitsap County Historical Society.

"He was a member of the Manette Community Church and former deacon there; member and past vice president of Bremerton Gideons; was on the Youth for Christ Board and was active in the founding of the Bremerton Servicemen's Center. He was a Kiwanian."

Wheaton was married in 1913 to Lettie Mullen of Nova Scotia, who had come to Bellingham. They had a daughter, Elsie Louise. When the family moved to Manette they bought the Mikkelson home at 1147 Perry Avenue. Lettie Wheaton died in 1937. In 1952 David Wheaton married Mrs. Chester R. (Clara) Muller. They lived in the Muller family home at 1718 Winfield Avenue. Dave and Lettie's daughter Elsie married Dale Aldrich. They had three children: David Kirk "Robin" Aldrich, Gerald Norman Aldrich and Jacklynn Dale Aldrich.

WILLIAMS, ALBERT
By Alexa Brown and Fred Williams
1983

Our grandparents, Albert Bonaparte Williams and Lizzie Francis (nee Smith) Williams, came here from Minnesota in 1890 with their five children. They came west because business wasn't too good in Minnesota where they lived.

Albert Williams was a storekeeper by occupation. He operated A.B. Williams store in Manette. The house the family lived in was close to the store. Since all transportation was by water, early homes and businesses were near the water.

When Albert married Lizzie he insisted on having biscuits every morning for breakfast. Being a loving, dutiful wife, she

Albert and Lizzie Williams family in the early 1920s. Back row (from left), Theresa Williams, Harriet Williams Holden, Nathan Williams. Front row, Ella, Lizzie, Albert and Theodore Williams.

complied. Where she got the recipe for her biscuits, nobody knows. She never wrote it down or gave it to anybody. It was her own secret and she guarded it well. When she died, it died with her.

She became noted around the area for her biscuits and many people made their way to the Williams table just to get a few of her biscuits. Biscuits were always served for breakfast and Sunday dinner. Many years later, when she moved in with her daughter Theresa at a house Grandpa built in Seattle, we used to go there for dinner occasionally. When she made biscuits the kitchen was off-limits. However, getting to the bathroom required going through the kitchen. Mom (Linna Williams) forgot about Grandma in the kitchen and went through the swinging door, and there was Grandma making biscuits—with Bisquick! Theresa knew about it because she bought the groceries, but she never told anyone. We never knew just when Grandma changed to Bisquick.

The Williamses were early members of the Port Orchard Historical Society.

Grandpa was a large man, but without an ounce of fat, just big. One day when he was about 79 one of the rabbits he kept got out. He saw it under the hutch and went after it. That is where Grandpa died. Grandma died peacefully in her sleep at 88.

NATHAN WILLIAMS

Nathan Williams, Albert and Lizzie's eldest child, was a carpenter, millwright and shipwright. For a time, he was a farmer at Yakima, Sunnyside, Grandview and Mabton.

He and his brother Theodore operated a small boat, the *City of Manette*, out of Manette.

While working on the *City of Manette* Nathan became acquainted with and enamored of the cook, a Norwegian lady named Annie Kleven, and they were married. Nathan and Annie had four children.

Co-author Fred reminisces about his uncle Nathan, "Some things I remember about him...he smoked White Owl cigars, liked to play pinochle and cribbage, and I loved him dearly. A big Saturday night for me was to go to his house in West Seattle, play cribbage and drink a pot of coffee. He always wore his beat-up felt hat on the back of his head, partly exposing his balding head. He died of a heart attack in the summer of 1948 while cutting the wet grass."

HARRIET WILLIAMS

Albert and Lizzie's second child was Harriet, known as Hattie. Hattie married Arthur Holden, a master draftsman at the Bremerton navy yard. She worked for several years for "Prints of Wales", a photography studio in Bremerton. She made many portraits of Bremerton and Manette old-timers. Arthur served at one time as a councilman in Manette. [See HOLDEN, ARTHUR, history.]

THERESA WILLIAMS

The third child, Theresa, graduated from the University of Minnesota with a degree in education. She served as kindergarten teacher at West Woodland School in Seattle until she retired at age 75. She never married.

ELLA WILLIAMS

Ella, the fourth child, married Walter H. Gray, a cabinet maker turned camera repairman. For several years they owned the Walter H. Gray Kodak repair at 107 Seneca in Seattle. They had no children. Ella lives in Seattle. At age 94, she is still active in High Episcopal Church, in bowling and in a bridge club.

THEODORE WILLIAMS

The last child, Theodore, known to everybody except his brother and sisters as Ted, worked for a time with his brother on the *City of Manette*, then left and worked for the Alaska Steamship Company as an able-bodied seaman on the SS *Northwestern*. Shortly after 1918, he left their employ and began his trade as a job printer, which he worked at the rest of his life.

Ted had a big wolfhound named Ted who liked to hunt rats near the docks. Theodore told of hearing wildcats near the house at night. The dog Ted, despite his size, respected the wildcats. He left them alone.

EXCERPTS FROM *The Bremerton News*

April 12, 1902: Mr. Williams of Bremerton is clearing his (Decatur) lot with the intention of building.

May 17, 1902: A.B. Williams has let contract for store building to be ready by the 1st of July.

December 26, 1906: A.B. Williams has opened up a hardware store in the old store building near the wharf.

April 27, 1907: Nathan Williams has purchased the Davis property near Fellows Hall.

May 18, 1907: Mr. and Mrs. A.B. Williams announce the coming marriage of their daughter Hattie to Arthur Holden next June.

THE FAMILY

ALBERT BONAPARTE WILLIAMS was born June 26, 1851, in Eaton Rapids, Mich. He died in 1930. His wife, LIZZIE FRANCIS SMITH WILLIAMS, was born August 22, 1851, in Wilton, N.H. They had five children:

1. NATHAN WILLIAMS, born May 3, 1882, in Minnesota. He married ANNIE KLEVEN, who was born in Skien, Norway, May 26, 1884. Nathan died in Seattle in September 1948. Annie died in Seattle in November 1964. Nathan and Annie had four children.
1A. CLIFFORD BONAPARTE WILLIAMS, born in Manette October 31, 1906. He married OLGA PATTERSON in Seattle in 1930. They had one daughter.
1A1. GLORIA WILLIAMS. Gloria has four sons and one daughter.
1B. ALEXA WILLIAMS, born in Manette in 1908. Alexa married RUSSELL BROWN (1905-1976). They had two daughters and a son.
1B1. BARBARA BROWN. Barbara married FRANCIS CLYDE. They had three children, RONNIE, LINDA and LARRY.
1B2. LIAM BROWN. Liam and his wife KAREN had six children, JOELLEN, WILLIE, DEANNA, TIMMY, ALEXA and NATHAN.
1B3. LOIS BROWN. Lois married WILLIAM WHITE. They had four children, STEVEN, MICHAEL, PATTY and ROBERT.
1C. AGNES WILLIAMS, born in Manette March 15, 1913. She married HERCEL WADE in Prosser, Wash., on October 6, 1932. Hercel was born in Markham, Wash., May 29, 1910. They had three children.
1C1. CARL HERCEL WADE was born in Grandview October 11, 1934. Carl married JANET VANDERLIP, who was born October 15, 1937. They were married in Seattle August 3, 1957. Carl and Janet had three children: BRUCE, born June 17, 1959, in Seattle; DIANE, born January 25, 1965, in Seattle, and MARK, born May 8, 1968, in Seattle.
1C2. DALE ELMAN WADE was born in Renton April 10, 1940. He married SANDRA WRESSEL in Renton in December 1961. Sandra was born April 30, 1937. Dale and Sandra had two children: KENNY, born in Renton May 11, 1963, and ARLENE, born in Renton January 29, 1965.
1C3. GLENN ROBERT WADE was born in Renton June 22, 1945. He married CLAUDIA WOODS in Centralia September 16, 1967. Claudia was born April 7, 1945. Glenn and Claudia had two children: CHRISTINE, born in Germany May 2, 1971, and BRIAN, born in Tacoma June 22, 1974.
1D. DONALD HIRAM WILLIAMS, born in Sunnyside in 1919. Donald and his wife GAYLE had two children, BRIAN and DONNA. Donna married in 1967 and has two children.

2. HARRIET WILLIAMS, born June 26, 1884, in Bremerton. She married ARTHUR HOLDEN [See HOLDEN, ARTHUR, history.]

3. THERESA WILLIAMS, born November 20, 1886, in Minnesota. She died in December 1977 in Seattle.

4. ELLA WILLIAMS, born February 11, 1889, in Minnesota. Ella married WALTER H. GRAY. They had no children. Ella lives at 900 Queen Anne Avenue in Seattle.

5. THEODORE SYLVESTER WILLIAMS, born July 25, 1890, in Morris, Minn. He married AMELIA LINNA UHLMANN, known as Linna, in Seattle May 4, 1918. Ted died in San Francisco September 13, 1954. Ted and Amelia had two children.
5A. DOROTHY MARIE WILLIAMS, born in Seattle February 7, 1919. She married ARTHUR GAGNE in Seattle in 1938. They had no children. Dorothy and Arthur divorced. Later Dorothy married WILLIAM A. GRYDER. Dorothy and William had one son, BILLY.
5B. FREDERICK ARTHUR WILLIAMS, born in Seattle July 30, 1920. He married SARAH ELIZABETH STARK at Tinker Air Force Base, Okla., August 4, 1951. Sarah was born at Eldon, Mo., February 4, 1923.

Nathan and Annie Williams family, circa 1908. Back row (from left), Annie Kleven, Albert and Nathan Williams. Front row, Mrs. Smith (Lizzie William's mother), Lizzie Williams with grandchildren Clifford and Alexa Williams.
-Photo from Alexa Williams Brown

WILSEN, CHARLES
By Elsie Wilsen Sayler
1985

NORWAY TO MANETTE

Charles L. Wilsen was born in Stavanger, Norway, in 1870. He arrived in Manette in 1902. He married Agnes H. Garland, who was born in Portland, Oreg., in 1877. Charles was a painter at Puget Sound Navy Yard. The Wilsens lived on 5 acres of wooded land they bought from John Mikkelson along what is now Winfield Avenue. They worked hard, cleared land, started fruit trees and built a house and barn. They had one or two cows, chickens and a pig.

The Mikkelson house was sold to John Morris and later became Gideon Hermanson's property. The Wilsen house still stands at what is now 2215 Winfield Avenue and is owned and being remodeled by a granddaughter and her husband, Ailene (McNeill) and Richard Mueller.

GETTING AROUND IN MANETTE

There were boardwalks, made of two large planks with a small board in the middle, up Perry Avenue. It was treacherous walking. I was always getting my shoes caught between the boards and falling. Perry Avenue was a very steep hill before it was graded and blacktopped.

We had a lane from our property to Perry Avenue and a small path to Winfield Avenue, which was just a narrow road. The road wound down East 18th Street to Marlow Avenue and by a narrow bridge across a canyon to what is now Wheaton Way, finally coming out on the beach road to Tracyton. I was a fourth grader when I made my first trip by car. It was a Model-T and we went to Tracyton. Quite an event.

My dad had to walk to the Manette Dock and take a small launch to work. In still earlier days he went across the narrow, in a rowboat. The Manette Dock was located at the site that became Parker Lumber, now The Narrows Apartments.

SCHOOL AND NEIGHBORS

When I was in grade school there were approximately 200 families living in Manette so we knew 'most everyone. I remember Len Bright, and an Indian family, the Halls. The Olsens had a big house on the beach. There were also the Tom Fellowses, the Millers, Mikkelsons, Karsts, Pfennings, Morrises, Averys, Brewsters, Cards, Farmers, and, of course, the Wilsens with all the girls.

I graduated from the eighth grade in 1926, which was the last year the eighth grade was taught in Manette. After that when students finished the sixth grade they went to Lincoln Junior High School in Bremerton. I attended Union High School, later called Bremerton High School. The building, later Coontz Junior High, was located between Fourth and Fifth on High Avenue.

Mother died in 1929 of cancer and Dad died in 1933 of a heart attack. They are buried in Ivy Green Cemetery.

NEW GENERATIONS

Five of the Wilsens' nine children lived to be adults and I am the only one living of those five.

1. LEONARD GERARD WILSEN was born in 1903. He died in 1904.

2. ESTHER H. WILSEN was born in 1905. She died in 1926 at age 21 of tuberculosis.

3. VERNIE WILSEN was born in 1906. Vernie died in 1918 at age 14 of influenza.

4. GRACE L. WILSEN was born in 1907. She married EARL "Dutch" McNEILL. Dutch lived on Cascade Trail and later at 2221 Winfield Avenue. When he and Grace were married in 1930 they moved to Corvallis, Oreg., where Dutch was employed by Shell Oil Company. He was laid off in 1933 during Depression days. He and Grace moved back to our home place at 2215 Winfield Avenue. Earl worked at different jobs—for Tracy,

Gillette and Parker Lumber Companies—for more than 40 years. Grace and Dutch had no children of their own but raised her sister Arlene's two girls when Arlene was killed in an automobile accident in 1940. Grace died in 1964. Dutch died in 1978.

5. A son died at birth.

6. ELSIE M. WILSEN was born in 1910. Elsie married OSCAR D. "Jack" JACKSON, an electrician in the navy yard, in 1936. Elsie and Jack had three children.
6A. RODERICK JACKSON, Jack's son, was 2 when Elsie and Jack married. Roderick has three children, RODERICK Jr. of Salt Lake City, JANIE of Everett and DIANE of Mississippi.
6B. CHARLES JACKSON was born in 1938. Charles and his wife have two sons, MARK of Coos Bay, Oreg., and HUGH of West Virginia.
Oscar Jackson died in 1940. In 1952 Elsie married EDWIN SAYLER, a sheetmetal worker at PSNS. Edwin Sayler died in 1978. Elsie lives at 2217 Winfield Avenue on property owned by her parents and next door to the original family home now owned by her niece. Elsie and Edwin had one daughter.
6C. CAROLE SAYLER, born in 1953. Carole married JAMES SCHWANDT and they live in Port Orchard. They have a daughter, JIMI CARLA, born in 1982.

7. SELMA L. WILSEN was born in 1913 and married ALBERT PETERSON. Albert was a leading man in PSNS supply department. They lived on Jacobsen Boulevard and later moved to Illahee Shores. Albert died in 1972. Selma died in 1976. Albert and Selma had three children.
7A. JOAN PETERSON, born in 1936. She died of a ruptured appendix in 1941.
7B. RUTH ELLEN PETERSON, born April 8, 1939. She married WILLIAM FELIX REESE. William is employed by PSNS at the old Manette School navy facility. For several years Ruth operated the Keyport Mercantile, which she and Bill owned. They live in Keyport in the home her grandparents, Alfred and Ellen Peterson, owned. Ruth and William have three children.
7B1. DOUGLAS MARK REESE, born September 10, 1958, in Bremerton. He graduated as an apprentice pipefitter at PSNS. He works at PSNS and lives in Keyport. Douglas is engaged to KARMON HANSON.
7B2. SCOTT ALAN REESE, born September 17, 1962. He married LORIE LEE STONE. Scott is a student at Olympic College and a student aide at Bangor. Scott and Lorie have one son.
7B2a. DARRIK SCOTT REESE, born November 19, 1982.
7B3. ELLEN JOANNE REESE, born November 27, 1970, in Bremerton. She is a student at Bremerton Christian School.
7C. ANN LOUISE PETERSON, born in 1945 in Bremerton. Ann married JULIUS TEMPLETON. Julius was born in Bremerton. They own Templeton's Market Deli on Charleston Beach Road, Templeton's groceries in Tracyton and Silverdale and on Trenton Avenue, and Perry Avenue Automotive. Ann and Julius have three daughters.
7C1. ROBIN ANN TEMPLETON, born in 1964 in Bremerton. Robin graduated from Central Washington University and currently teaches at Bremerton Christian School. Robin married JIM WALTER.
7C2. HEIDI JULIANE TEMPLETON, born in 1967 in Bremerton. Heidi is a student at Western Washington College.
7C3. TARA LYNN TEMPLETON, born in 1970 in Bremerton. Tara is a student at Bremerton Christian School.

8. ARLENE A. WILSEN, a twin sister of Selma, was born in 1913. Arlene married JOHN STEVENS. John worked as gardener at PSNS. He lives in Tracyton. Arlene died in 1940. They had two girls, Roberta and Aileen, who were adopted and raised by Arlene's sister Grace McNeill.
8A. ROBERTA STEVENS/McNEILL was 5 when Arlene died in 1940. Roberta married GROVER BOWERS and lives in Bremerton. They have 6 children, JEAN, SANDRA, GREGORY, CHRISTOPHER, DEBRA and EARL.
8B. AILENE STEVENS/McNEILL was born in 1940. She married DONALD ANDREWS. Their two sons are:
8B1. STANLEY EUGENE ANDREWS, born April 6, 1961. He married PATRICIA LAW from Moses Lake. They live in Kennewick where Stanley works for Payless stores. Stanley and Patricia have one son.
8B1a. CHRISTOPHER SCOTT ANDREWS, born September 1987.
8B2. JEFFERY EARL ANDREWS, born July 13, 1963. He graduated with a degree in chemical engineering from Washington State University. He graduated from navy officers candidate school and is entering a nuclear power program.
Ailene and Donald divorced and Ailene married RICHARD MUELLER. Richard works in planning and estimating at PSNS. Ailene is a checker and florist at Safeway.

9. A daughter born in 1916 died at birth.

WOMAC, FRANK
By Wesley Langrell and Bruce Womac
1986

Frank Womac was born in Ketchum, Idaho, August 19, 1897, to Emma Hunt and Jethro Womack Sr. The family name originally had been spelled Womack, Frank and his brother, Jethro Jr., dropped the "k" from the name when they left Idaho.

Frank moved to Manette with Jethro Jr. and their mother Emma in the early 1900s. Jethro Sr. had died and Mrs. Womac had married Edwin P. McWilliams.

Frank Womac married Helen G. McLin July 25, 1917, in Seattle. Helen was born in St. Louis December 6, 1898, to Robert D. McLinn Jr. (The name was originally spelled McLinn) and Hennriette Ross. Frank worked in the supply department at PSNY 40 years, meanwhile moving to Paulson Road in Central Valley. Frank served 16 years on school boards at Tracyton, Brownsville and Silverdale.

FRANK AND HELEN'S FAMILY
FRANK and HELEN WOMAC had four children.

1. FRANK WOMAC Jr., born March 7, 1919, in Seattle. Frank attended grade school in Tracyton and high school in Silverdale. He played football and held the county pole vault record for years. Frank married VIRGINIA BRAUN in St. Louis in 1942. Frank served in the army in World War II in the European theater. He and Virginia had one daughter.

2. BRUCE D. WOMAC, born August 29, 1923, in Tracyton. Bruce attended grade school in Tracyton and Brownsville and high school in Silverdale. He served an apprenticship as a machinist in PSNY and worked there throughout World War II. Bruce married RUTH L. DeMENT in Silverdale April 2, 1943. Her parents were James and Mai B. DeMent of Clear Creek. Bruce and Ruth had four children.
2A. ALLAN K. WOMAC, born June 1, 1946, in Bremerton. Allan graduated from the University of Washington and served in Germany and Viet Nam as a first lieutenant. Allan married MARY ANN ENGLE September 13, 1968, in Seattle. They have two children, STEFFANI and ALLAN Jr. and live in Redmond.
2B. JANIS MARIE WOMAC, born December 19, 1948, in Bremerton. She graduated from the U. of W. Janis married ROBERT MARSICEK in Port Angeles September 19, 1970. They have two daughters, JENNIFER and MOLLY. Janis is divorced and works as a legal assistant in Bellevue.
2C. DENNIS B. WOMAC, born November 4, 1950, in Bremerton. He graduated from U. of W. and served in the U.S. Marine Corps during the Viet Nam conflict. Dennis married ANNETTE ALLEN in Port Angeles August 18, 1973. They have three boys. Dennis is a music teacher at Tumwater High School. Annette is an attorney in the attorney general's office in Olympia.
2D. BEVERLY ANN WOMAC, born April 9, 1958, in Port Angeles. She married TOD EISELE August 27, 1983. Beverly works for the state highway maintenance division and Tod is a logger.

3. JEAN BELLE WOMAC, born April 14, 1929, in Tracyton. She graduated from Central Kitsap High School where, she was active in musical productions. She sang as soloist with Bremerton Symphony and the Corale Society. Jean married ARTHUR THORSEN September 18, 1948, in Silverdale. They had six children. Jean died June 10, 1976, in Bremerton. Arthur died in 1985.

4. JAMES ORVILLE WOMAC, born September 24, 1935, in Central Valley. He graduated from Central Kitsap High School. James married ROSANNE BERRYHILL October 25, 1954, in Port Orchard. They live 1/4 mile from the McWilliams homestead on Brownsville Highway. Jim works at Bangor and Rosanne is a nurse at Harrison Memorial Hospital. They have six children.

WOMAC, JETHRO Jr.
By June Womac Wilmot
and Ann Guy Womac
1986

Jethro Womac Jr., born in Idaho in 1894, came to Manette from Carey, Idaho, in the early 1900s with his mother Emma and his brother Frank. Jethro Jr. worked at Puget Sound Navy Yard. His wife, Edith, was born Edith Nyberg in Grand Marais, Mich., May 14, 1899. Her father was Andrew Nyberg and her mother's maiden name was Hilda Johanneson.

Edith and Jethro married in 1916. They spent the next few years on High Avenue in Bremerton; then they purchased an older farm home on 5 acres on the County Road, now Perry Avenue. They took great pride in remodeling and modernizing the home. They turned the yard into a park with natural fish ponds, trees and flowers.

Jethro was a member of the Fraternal Order of Eagles. Both Jethro and Edith belonged to Philathea Chapter of Eastern Star.

Womacs' property was taken from them under eminent domain, and Dewey Junior High School was built on the grounds [and since torn down]. The original home was moved one block south on Perry Avenue. The Womacs then purchased a home at 1350 Jacobsen Boulevard. Jethro died there in 1945. Edith married Hugh O'Bell and continued to live on Jacobsen Boulevard until her death in 1969.

JETHRO JR. AND EDITH'S FAMILY
JETHRO Jr. and EDITH WOMAC had three children.

1. THEODORE "Ted" WOMAC was born June 26, 1917, in Bremerton. Ted was a Boy Scout in Troop 505 and played on the Bremerton High School football team. He graduated in 1936. Ted married ANN GUY of Bremerton. The family enjoyed camping and fishing. Ted worked at the navy yard

Edith and Jethro Womac.
-Photo from June Womac Wilmot

as a pipefitter. He died in 1972. Ann lives in Bremerton. Ted and Ann had three daughters.

1A. KAREN WOMAC, born August 29, 1940, in Bremerton. Karen and her sisters were Girl Scouts and Rainbow Girls. Karen married BUD CAMERON. They had three sons. Karen and Bud divorced and Karen married RUSS JOHANSON, who had two sons, John and Eric. Karen and Bud's children are:

1A1. DOUGLAS CAMERON, born February 18, 1957, in Bremerton. Douglas lives in Longview and is a logger.

1A2. CHARLES CAMERON, born November 20, 1959, in Bremerton. Charles is married and has two children. He works at Keyport.

1A3. TODD CAMERON, born August 27, 1962, in Bremerton. Todd is married and has one daughter. He is a fisherman in Alaska.

1B. NANCY WOMAC, born November 20, 1943, in Bremerton. Nancy married SAM JOSEPHSON and they had two daughters. Sam and Nancy were divorced and Nancy married DONALD COODY. They live in Olympia. The two daughters are:

1B1. KELLY JOSEPHSON COODY, born August 24, 1960. Kelly married RICHARD SPENCER and they live in Bremerton. They have one daughter, ASHLEY SPENCER.

1B2. JULIE JOSEPHSON COODY, born November 9, 1962. Julie married BRIAN FINGERSON. Brian works in Kent as a draftsman and they live in Tacoma.

1C. BETTY WOMAC, born July 12, 1945, in Bremerton. Betty married JACK SUHDOLNIK, who had two boys by a previous marriage. Betty is a teacher and Jack is a dentist in Everett.

Ted and Ann Womac with Karen and Nancy, circa 1945.
-Photo from
June Womac Wilmot

2. LYLE WOMAC, born February 7, 1919, in Bremerton. Lyle belonged to Boy Scout Troop 505 and played on the Bremerton High School football team. He graduated in 1938. Lyle served in the U.S. Navy through World War II. Lyle married ALYCE DRAPER, born in 1920 in Pocatello, Idaho. Lyle and Alyce have no children. Lyle is retired and they live in Puyallup.

3. JUNE WOMAC, born June 22, 1923, in Bremerton. She was a member of Girl Scout Troop 4 and belonged to the Rainbow Girls. June graduated from Bremerton High School in 1942. She married CLIFFORD CALLISON in 1942 and they had two sons, LARRY and ROD. June and Cliff divorced in 1952. June married DON WILMOT in 1954. June and Don live in Bullhead City, Ariz. Don adopted June's two sons.

3A. LARRY JETHRO WILMOT, born December 16, 1942. Larry married SHERIE BOSTRUP of Woodland Hills, Calif. Larry and Sherie live in Simi Valley, Calif., where Larry is superintendent for a construction company in Los Angeles. Larry and Sherie have four daughters: KIM, born January 11, 1963; JAN, born December 2, 1964; LISA, born December 10, 1966; and JULIE, born September 12, 1969.

3B. RODNEY "Rod" WILMOT, born July 30, 1947. Rod married SUSAN WILLIAMS of Woodland Hills, Calif. Rod and Sue live in Thousand Oaks, Calif. Rod is a fire chief in the city of Los Angeles. Rod and Sue have three daughters: JENNIFER, born August 4, 1970; LAURIE, born October 3, 1973; and KELLY, born August 27, 1976.

LANGRELL, MAYBELLE
By Wesley Langrell (1986)

Maybelle Irene Fatour (later Langrell) was born in 1892 in Carey, Idaho. She was the daughter of Fred Fatour and Emma Hunt Fatour. She spent time in Manette in the early 1900s. Her father had died and her mother (Emma) had married Jethro Womac Sr. Jethro died and Emma then married Edwin P. McWilliams. (McWilliams is the man for whom McWilliams Road off Brownsville Highway is named. The original McWilliams home still stands near McWilliams Road.)

Maybelle married William Frederick Langrell, born in

1895 in Langrell, Oreg. They lived in Oregon until William died in 1937. In 1938 Maybelle returned to Manette with her sons Jack and Wesley. She opened a beauty shop in 1939 at 1145 Scott Avenue and operated it 8 years.

Jack Langrell married Sigrid Scheving and lives in Seattle. Jack raises orchids commercially in his greenhouse. He retired from his job as a machinist with Continental Can Company.

Wesley Langrell married Vernice Ivalee Bryson who was born in 1919 in Mansford, Wash. She died in Bremerton in 1983. Wesley is postmaster in the post office sub-station in Manette.

WORKMAN, ERNEST
By Roy Vernon Workman
1986

I was born in Yakima. My father Ernest Robert Workman took my mother Laura Theresa Curl Workman, my sister Daphne and me to Victoria, where another sister Vera was born. We lived in Vancouver, New Westminister, Victoria and Seattle; then, in 1916, when I was 5, settled in Stewart, British Columbia.

In Stewart we rented a building to live in from a George Benjamin "Ben" Lawrence. Ben and my father formed a partnership and built a water-powered sawmill and two electric power plants.

On July 8, 1920, my mother gave birth to another little sister, just for me. She was christened Josephine Emma.

In 1924 my parents separated. Father left and Ben managed the International Electric Company for himself, my mother and the stockholders. Daphne was in nurses' training in Vancouver, B.C., and I was working at the power plants. Mother moved to Manette with Vera and Jo, occupying a house next door to mother's cousin Alice Anley Conway at East 11th Street and Trenton Avenue.

Christmas of 1925 I took the steamship from Stewart to Seattle and the ferry to Bremerton to spend a week with my mother, Vera and Jo. Mother insisted I not go back.

It was difficult to convince anyone that at 16 I had completed a correspondence course in electrical engineering. I used to make crystal and tube sets and although we heard no complaints I bet they interfered with radio programs. I worked briefly at the Puget Sound Power and Light Company office in Bremerton as a clerk for $2.50 a day.

Finally I was hired as a messenger boy in the commandant's office in the navy yard at $600 a year.

Ben Lawrence moved to Manette and married my mother June 14, 1927. He offered to adopt me but I decided to keep the Workman name. Ben was like a father to me in Stewart even before my father left.

I had been a Boy Scout in Canada. In Manette I joined Troop 505. One of the boys in the Scout troop was Floyd Buchanan. Floyd was a good swimmer and offered to teach me so I could become a first class Scout. We went to the YMCA pool. I would not let on that I was afraid so I followed Floyd's instructions and put my face in the water. He even told me to open my eyes. Finally, when I was 21, I was swimming at Twanoh State Park and realized that I was actually enjoying having my eyes open under water—after 5 years of learning to like the water.

Mother and Dad Lawrence lived in the old Casey place at

the corner of East 11th Street and Trenton Avenue. They decided to buy a house with 2.5 acres of land on Cascade Trail, halfway between Perry and Trenton Avenues.

On May 14, 1928, my mother gave birth to George Benjamin Lawrence Jr.

I was a car buff. I bought a Model-T Ford for $25 from Mr. Palmer, who lived across Cascade Trail from us. When it wore out I managed to acquire a Chevrolet 490. In 1928 Dad Lawrence bought a new Chevrolet sedan.

Our family joined the Manette Community Church. The Sunday School superintendent was Isaac Hoopes, and his wife Amy was Sunday School teacher for high school-age kids. I learned much more about the Bible from Mrs. Hoopes than I had learned in Stewart. I will always be grateful to her.

Isaac Hoopes worked in the production office in the navy yard. When a worker contracted tuberculosis I was accepted to fill his position temporarily. I finally had enough time in civil service and passed the examination with a grade far above other applicants and was appointed mimeograph operator earning $1020 a year.

On November 15, 1930, I had saved enough money to buy a new Model A Ford Roadster for $569. I used to go to dances twice a week at the Masonic Temple in Manette and the Moose Hall in Bremerton. I became acquainted with Walt Fellows and we used to stag it to dances in Silverdale, Poulsbo and other out-of-town places.

My sister Vera brought home friends she had met at the Baptist Youth Camp on Vashon Island. They were Eloise Carty and her sister Alice from Tacoma. When I saw Alice I thought to myself "That is for me." When it was time for them to go home I asked to take them in my Ford roadster. They accepted. From then until Alice and I were married on September 2, 1933, I spent every weekend with the Cartys in Tacoma.

Alice had been married before. I not only had a beautiful wife but inherited a beautiful baby daughter, Roberta Jean, who was born on June 24, 1931. We rented a house for $25 a month in Bremerton.

In 1935 I received my GS-3 rating and $1620 a year—just in time, because Ronald Allen Workman was born December 10, 1935.

We bought a 60-foot lot from Mother and Dad Lawrence on East 14th Street in Manette just west of Perry Avenue. Dad Lawrence helped us build a new house there and we moved into it in April 1939, and transferred back to the Manette Community Church. Our home was next to the Scout hall that was owned by the Manette church, sponsor of Troop 505. I transferred from the planning office back into the production office at the navy yard this same year.

Paul Almon was a friend who used to play baseball and attend church and Sunday School with me. Paul was killed in action during World War II.

The church had a pick-up basketball team in the Bremerton City League. When I was 16 I used to play with the team. When our son Ron was in junior high school he played basketball and I became the team's coach. Our church building burned and when the new church was built it included a basketball gym with a 24-foot ceiling that was also used as a

general-purpose room. A retired machinist, Al Meicho, rigged the baskets with an acme-thread screw mounting so they could be set at any height from 8 to 10 feet. We would start the little kids out with volleyballs and the baskets at 8 feet.

THE FAMILY

ERNEST WORKMAN married LAURA THERESA CURL WORKMAN. They had five children. Ernest and Laura divorced. Laura married GEORGE BENJAMIN LAWRENCE, July 14, 1927. They had one son.

1. DAPHNE WORKMAN, born August 12, 1907.

2. ROY ELD WORKMAN, born September 16, 1909. Roy died December 17, 1909.

3. ROY VERNON WORKMAN, born September 14, 1910, in Yakima. Roy married ALICE CARTY and adopted her daughter, Roberta. Roy and Alice moved to Beaverton, Oreg., in 1983. They have two sons.
3A. ROBERTA JEAN YAWN WORKMAN, born June 24, 1931, in Tacoma. Roberta attended Manette School, Bremerton High School and Olympic College. She married GERALD "Jerry" DEAN YATES of Bremerton. They lived in the home built by Grandpa Ben Lawrence at Sheridan Road and Perry Avenue. Jerry retired from the navy and is a homicide detective on the Seattle police force. Roberta and Jerry live in Renton. They have two sons.
3A1. WILLIAM CARTY YATES, born September 13, 1952, in Tacoma. William lives in San Jose, Calif., and is purchasing agent for Stanford Medical Center.
3A2. DARRELL ALAN YATES, born February 9, 1956, in Tacoma. Darrell is manager at a steel mill in Seattle. He lives in Renton.
3B. RONALD ALLEN WORKMAN, born December 10, 1935, in Bremerton. Ron attended Manette School, Bremerton High School, Linfield College and Oregon State University. Ronald married JOAN K. KANGAS of Bremerton. Joan's mother, Nita Kangas, lives on Nipsic Avenue in Manette. Ron and Joan live in San Jose, Calif., where Ron is manager and computer expert at a manufacturing plant. Ron and Joan have four children.
3B1. MIKE BLAINE WORKMAN, born April 8, 1959, in Beaverton, Oreg. He is an Eagle Scout. Mike graduates in 1986 from Cal Poly as a metallurgist.
3B2. BONNIE SUE WORKMAN, born December 4, 1961, in Conoga Park, Calif. She works for a computer software company and lives in Santa Barbara.
3B3. STEVEN CORY WORKMAN, born November 18, 1967, in LaCanada, Calif. He lives with his parents and is an Eagle Scout. Steven joined the marine reserves in June of 1986.
3B4. PAMELA LYNNE WORKMAN, born April 14, 1969, in San Jose. She lives with her parents and is studying to be a medical doctor.
3C. WILLIAM EDWARD WORKMAN, born May 20, 1941, in Bremerton. Bill attended Manette School, East [Bremerton] High School and Linfield College. Bill married BARBARA LEE MORTON. They live in Renton, where Bill works as a computer consultant for Boeing. Bill and Barbara have two children.
3C1. SANDRA LEE WORKMAN, born June 15, 1976, in Santa Clara, Calif.
3C2. STEVEN WORKMAN, born January 14, 1981, in Santa Clara.

4. VERA WILLENA WORKMAN, born November 6, 1914, in Victoria. Vera was adopted by GEORGE BENJAMIN LAWRENCE. She attended school in Bremerton. Vera married EUGENE "Pogy" PARKINS of Manette. Vera and Pogy have three children.
4A. WILLENA GENE PARKINS, born June 28, 1934, in Bremerton.
4B. EUGENE RUSSELL PARKINS, born September 19, 1935, in Bremerton.
4C. GEORGE LAWRENCE PARKINS, born April 11, 1937, in Bremerton.

5. JOSEPHINE EMMA WORKMAN, born July 8, 1920, in Stewart, B.C. Josephine was adopted by BENJAMIN LAWRENCE. Josephine married DONALD LAUCKHART. Jo and Don have three children.
5A. ROGER WILLIAM LAUCKHART, born February 11, 1946.
5B. JOHN RICHARD LAUCKHART, born May 15, 1948.
5C. JENNIE LORRAINE LAUCKHART, born April 8, 1950.

6. GEORGE BENJAMIN LAWRENCE Jr., born May 14, 1928, in Bremerton. He attended Sheridan School. Ben and his wife LOUISE live in Boulder, Colo. They have five children, KIM, KAREN, KURT, KATHY and KEES.

WORLAND, GEORGE
By Larry Worland and
Teckla Worland Sunderland
1983

FROM MINNESOTA TO MANETTE

George Thomas Worland was born to Thomas Clement and Alice Marie Worland on October 10, 1885, at Wayzata, Minn. On July 3, 1886, Thomas, George's father, fell from a wagon and was killed. About 1890, Alice Worland, George's mother, moved George and his five brothers and sisters by horse and wagon to Havre, Mont.

Teckla Euphemia Orne was born to Theodore Oscar and Sarah E. (nee Woods) Orne on November 15, 1889, at Pullman, Ill.

About 1903 Theodore, Sarah and Teckla moved to Butte, Mont., where Theodore and Sarah managed the Columbia Gardens fair grounds.

Teckla and George T. Worland, 2220 Perry Avenue, July 4, 1926. -Photo from George W. Worland

George Worland and Teckla Orne were married at Havre February 8, 1911. They lived in Havre from 1911 to 1917. George worked as a fireman and for the Great Northern Railroad.

In 1917 George and Teckla arrived in Kitsap County with children Martha, Mary and George. They settled in Silverdale on 5 acres in a house they bought from Mr. and Mrs. Wolcott. Four more children were added to the family: Genevieve, Lucine and Lawrence—the third set of twins born in Silverdale—and Teckla.

Our family came to Manette in the spring of 1926. We lived on Perry Avenue for about one year, then moved to 1118 Scott Avenue, where another son, John, was added to the family. The folks rented this home from Mr. and Mrs. George Card for $14 a month. We lived at this address until the spring of 1935, when we moved onto 12 acres in Central Valley.

George T. and Teckla Worland's children, 1926. Back row (from left), Mary, George, Martha. Middle row, Genevieve, Lucine, Lawrence. Front row, Teckla.
-Photo from George W. Worland

THE FAMILY
The descendants of GEORGE and TECKLA WORLAND are:

1. THOMAS THEODORE WORLAND, born January 25, 1912, in Havre, Mont. He died April 15, 1912.

2. MARTHA ALICE ELIZABETH WORLAND, born March 17, 1913, in Devils Lake, N. Dak. She died February 8, 1930.

3. MARY LAVINA WORLAND, born January 5, 1915, in Havre, Mont. Mary married HENRY LeCLAIR, then DON WALLER. Mary passed away January 22, 1973, in Dayton, Ohio. Her children are:
3A. FRANKLIN ANTHONY LeCLAIR, born October 7, 1933, in Manette.
3B. MARGARET MARIE LeCLAIR, born August 29, 1937, in Port Townsend. Margaret married BERTRAM PAXTON. They live in Bellingham. Margaret and Bertram have one son.
3B1. STEVEN WAYNE PAXTON, born November 22, 1954, in New Westminster, B.C. Steven married DEBRA TODAHL and lives in Bellingham. They have three children.
3B1a. KATHI ANN PAXTON, born June 17, 1971, in Bellingham.
3B1b. RICHARD LEE PAXTON, born June 27, 1975, in Bellingham.
3B1c. BRIAN WAYNE PAXTON, born November 29, 1977, in Bellingham.
3C. PATRICIA NATALIE LeCLAIR, born April 15, 1939, in Portland, Oreg. Patty married Mr. WILLIAMS, divorced, and then married CLARION HAROLD LUDTKE. They live in Bellingham. Patricia has four children and two stepchildren.
3C1. RICHARD JOHN WILLIAMS, born July 14, 1959. He married LEE ANN PETERSON and they live in Bellingham. They have a son.
3C1a. ERIC SCOTT WILLIAMS, born April 24, 1986, in Bellingham.
3C2. RHONDA JEAN WILLIAMS, born June 4, 1960, in Bellingham. She married GREGORY L. WILLET, who died in a motorcycle accident May 25, 1985. They have two children.
3C2a. ROBERT GREGORY WILLET, born July 1, 1979, in Bellingham.
3C2b. BROOKE LIVI WILLET, born October 2, 1980, in Bellingham.
3C3. JOANIE MARIE WILLIAMS, born December 12, 1961, in Bellingham.
3C4. DAVID WAYNE LUDTKE, born February 2, 1968, in Bellingham.
3C5. DEBORAH KAY LUDTKE, born April 9, 1955, in Bellingham. Deborah married THOMAS REED. They have two children and live in Bellingham.
3C5a. SCOTT THOMAS REED, born July 15, 1966, in Vallejo, Calif.
3C5b. CHRISTINE MARIE REED, born December 6, 1970, in Bellingham.
3C6. PAMELA JO LUDTKE, born September 16, 1956, in Bellingham. She married Mr. TINCKER and is now divorced. She has two children.
3C6a. RYAN WINFIELD TINCKER, born September 16, 1977, in Bellingham.
3C6b. CHRISTOPHER LAWRENCE TINCKER, born September 7, 1981 in Seattle.
3D. FRANCES JEAN LeCLAIR, born May 6, 1940, in Bellingham. She married Mr. Dolan. They divorced and Frances lives in Bellingham. She has four children.
3D1. KELLY LYNN DOLAN, born July 22, 1960, in Bellingham. Kelly married JAMES CANNARD and they live in Bellingham. Kelly and James have three children.
3D1a. BRIAN SCOTT CANNARD, born June 1, 1981, in Medford, Oreg. He died June 2.
3D1b. JAMES MATTHEW CANNARD, born May 17, 1982, in Gold Beach, Oreg.
3D1c. NATHAN WALLACE CANNARD, born May 8, 1983, in Bellingham.
3D2. KARL LAWRENCE DOLAN, born October 2, 1961, in Bellingham.
3D3. KENNETH RAY DOLAN, born March 23, 1963, in Bellingham.
3D4. BRUCE HENRY DOLAN, born April 1, 1966, in Bellingham.

4. GEORGE WORLAND, born September 26, 1916, in Havre, Mont. He married Viola Bredeson in 1944. He is now married to Alice Venard. George and Alice live in Silverdale. His children are:
4A. COLLEEN WORLAND, born August 31, 1945, in Bremerton. Colleen married THOMAS KNAPP, is now divorced, and lives in Silverdale. Colleen's children are:
4A1. DONALD KNAPP, born October 21, 1965, in Bremerton.
4A2. TIMOTHY KNAPP, born July 25, 1967, in Bremerton.
4B. ALICE WORLAND, born August 11, 1953, in Bremerton. Alice married DAVID SHOFFNER and lives in Honolulu. Her children are:
4B1. DAVID S. SHOFFNER, born July 25, 1974, in Bremerton.
4B2. JASON L. SHOFFNER, born February 4, 1978, in Groton, Conn.

George's stepchildren are: WALTER VENARD, born January 23, 1941, in South Colby, Wash.; DONALD VENARD, born January 26, 1943, in Fragaria, Wash.; and HAROLD VENARD, born March 8, 1946, in Bremerton.

5. MAUDE GENEVIEVE "Gene" WORLAND, born in Silverdale September 6, 1918. Gene married RALPH JOHNSON, then KENNETH PADDEN (deceased). She lives in Centralia. Her children are:
5A. JO ANN JOHNSON, born April 1, 1937. She married DON BANGS and lives in Yakima. They have five children.
5A1. SUSAN BEVERLEY BANGS, born July 26, 1957, in Fairbanks. Susan married GENE DAYS.
5A2. MICHAEL DONALD BANGS, born December 27, 1958, in Ellensburg.
5A3. MARK LEROY BANGS, born January 11, 1961, in Othello, Wash. Mark died in Alaska, November 4, 1964.
5A4. RICHARD KENNETH BANGS, born August 21, 1965, in Yakima.
5A5. CARRIE ANN BANGS, born May 3, 1969, in Yakima.
5B. JOSEPH W.R. JOHNSON, born May 16, 1938. He married BETTY KAUFMAN and lives in Bellingham. Their children are:
5B1. BRUCE WILLIAM JOHNSON, born March 8, 1970, in Bellingham.
5B2. JENNIFER REBECCA JOHNSON, born October 14, 1971, in Bellingham.
5B3. WILLIAM ROBERT JOHNSON, born December 14, 1975, in Bellingham.
5C. LORI PADDEN, born November 5, 1951. Laurie married Sergeant M. HINES and lives in Lacey. Their children are:
5C1. WILLIAM MATTHEW HINES, born September 24, 1979, in Nuremberg, Germany.
5C2. KENNETH ROGER HINES, born September 19, 1982, in Stuttgart, Germany.
5C3. TARA JEAN HINES, born October 23, 1983, in Stuttgart.
5D. PATRICIA PADDEN, born May 7, 1957. She lives in Chehalis.
5E. KATHERYN PADDEN, born October 15, 1955. She lives in Garfield, Wash.
5F. DEBORA PADDEN, born July 11, 1953. She lives in Seattle.
5G. PAMELA PADDEN, born May 17, 1959. Pamela married Mr. WOOD. She is divorced and lives in Centralia. She has one child.
5G1. DUSTIN LEE WOOD, born April 26, 1982, in Centralia.

6. FLORENCE LUCINE WORLAND, born in Silverdale April 19, 1920. Lucine married CHARLES SLATON and lives in Port Hueneme, Calif. They have three children.
6A. BERNICE FAYE SLATON, born June 2, 1939, in Bremerton. She married GREG NANCE and is now divorced. Bernice lives in Port Hueneme, Calif. Her children are:
6A1. SUZZANNE ELIZABETH NANCE, born May 26, 1962, in Oakland.
6A2. PAMELA DIANE NANCE, born June 16, 1963, in Oxnard.
6A3. LINDA ADELE NANCE, born September 26, 1965, in Huntsville, Ala.
6B. CHARLES PHILIP SLATON, born April 20, 1943, in Bremerton. Charles married HELEN HAYNES and is now divorced. He lives in Carpenteria, Calif. He has three children.
6B1. CHARLES COREY SLATON, born May 24, 1973, in Ojai, Calif. Charles died January 3, 1976.
6B2. KATHLEEN SLATON, born April 7, 1975, in Ojai.
6B3. ELIZABETH ANN SLATON (adopted), born September 18, 1979, in Korea.
6C. WILLIAM SLATON, born August 16, 1952, in Port Hueneme. Wil-

liam married KRISTAN WHEELER and lives in Oxnard. They have two children.
6C1. AMY ELIZABETH SLATON, born April 16, 1977, in Ventura.
6C2. MICHAEL PATRICK SLATON, born July 12, 1982, in Ventura.

7. LAWRENCE "Larry" WORLAND, born in Silverdale April 19, 1920. He married GERALDINE REESER. They live in Port Orchard. Their children are:
7A. LAWRENCE "Larry" WORLAND, born August 22, 1942. Larry is married and lives in Bremerton. He has three children: JODY MARIE, born July 22, 1967; WENDI ANN, born September 8, 1969; and MARGI ELIZABETH, born April 11, 1972.
7B. EDWARD WORLAND, born June 30, 1943. Edward married MARILYN ALLRED and lives in Port Orchard. He has two children: KRISTIN DAWN, born February 12, 1969, and BRYAN DEAN, born October 10, 1972.
7C. JENNIFER WORLAND, born October 15, 1946. Jennifer married FRED VOSKUHL. They live in Bremerton and have two children: JEFFREY ALAN, born March 29, 1966; and KILY WORLAND, born January 7, 1971.

8. TECKLA BERNICE WORLAND, born in Silverdale January 14, 1923. Teckla married JOSEPH NAZAROWSKI, then JAMES DEARDORFF Jr. She is now married to LYLE SUNDERLAND and lives in Tracyton. Teckla worked in the navy yard in the production engineering division and retired in 1984. Her children are:
8A. TINA NAZAROWSKI, born July 7, 1944, in Chicago. She married LEN COYLE, then DARRELL LANHAM and later CLIFF GEROU. She is divorced and lives in Bremerton. She has four children.
8A1. DALE COYLE, born September 26, 1967, in Bremerton.
8A2. SHELLEY COYLE, born June 3, 1970, in Bremerton.
8A3. DARRIN J. LANHAM, born January 22, 1976, in Bremerton.
8A4. JOSEPH GEROU, born November 28, 1978, in Bremerton.
8B. KAREN ANN DEARDORFF, born October 31, 1946, in Bremerton. She married DENNIS WALLACE and lives in Valdez, Alaska. They have one child.
8B1. AARON BRENT WALLACE, born September 4, 1975, in Othello, Wash.
8C. JAMES DEARDORFF III, born October 27, 1947, in Seattle. James married DIANE WING and lives in Tracyton. They have two children.
8C1. ANGELA DIANE DEARDORFF, born August 7, 1980, in Bremerton.
8C2. MICHAEL JAMES DEARDORFF, born November 5, 1983, in Bremerton.
8D. THOMAS SUNDERLAND, born April 10, 1960, in Bremerton. Thomas lives in Seattle.
8E. SUSAN SUNDERLAND, born May 8, 1962, in Bremerton. Susan lives in Bremerton.

9. JOHN WORLAND, born in Manette April 26, 1930. John married HELEN BRUNS and lives in Bremerton. John worked in Shop 17, PSNS, 34 years and retired May 3, 1985. John and Helen have three children.
9A. CHERYL WORLAND, born June 28, 1956, in Bremerton. Cheryl lives in Tacoma. Cheryl married DON WAYBRIGHT in 1985.
9B. STEVEN WORLAND, born September 24, 1959, in Bremerton. Steven lives in Bremerton.
9C. NEIL WORLAND, born April 21, 1964, in Bremerton. Neil lives in Bremerton. He married JANET FOLTZ of Bremerton in 1986.

CHAPTER 13

A TREASURY OF MEMORIES
... Sentiments of old ...
From many Manette citizens, past and present ...

WENDELL ABERNATHY: On Christmas Eve in 1919, when I was 4-1/2, we went to the Manette Community Church celebration for the kiddies. We were new in attendance. All the kids got gifts of candy and fruit—I remember a tangerine. There was none for me and we were told [by someone not authorized to say it] that only the kids who belonged to the church got them. My feelings were really hurt. Somehow Ma found one for me. My tears didn't last long. When Ma became a member of that church she made sure such a thing wouldn't happen again.

EVELYN ALDRICH WALKER: My recollections are of the escapades I got into between ages 10 and about 14, in the early 1920s...I recall a New Year's Eve party at Margaret and Elizabeth von Hoene's house. We left the party—12 of us—with Don Young in his big old touring car. He drove over the Illahee dips. Oh, that used to be fun. There were 13 of us in that car of his.... It was 4 a.m. when I walked into the house. I had my tail between my legs. Dad inquired as to where I had been. I squeaked something at him and was told that I had to be in the house every night during January by 6 p.m.

At the Sandbanks below Bremerton Gardens we spent hours in the summer. We used to slide down the bank, swim, lie out in the sun to warm up and go slide some more.

A family named Emerson lived on the upper road. Russell Emerson was born the same day as I—July 1, 1910. The kids used to call us twins. When Russell was ejected from the classroom by the teacher for misbehaving he would go down in the basement and bang on the hot air register leading to our classroom. What a racket!

The Whites lived up at the head of our street. Mr. White used to sit on their front porch in the evening and play his banjo. It was beautiful. They had a little boy named Billy who had only one leg. The other was off at the knee and he had a little wooden leg. I can still see him running down our street— he had golden curls like an angel and was just as good...He died soon after.

(From the December 7, 1938, *Manette Gazette*, quoting the *Fog Horn* of January 27, 1921:) "Miss Evelyn Aldrich entertained seven of her girlfriends on Wednesday afternoon in honor of Mildred Ross, daughter of George Ross.... Those present were Mildred Ross, Alice Fellows, Nellie Clark, Marguerite Pursell, Margaret and Elizabeth von Hoene, Vivian Swan, and the hostess."

LENORA ALINDER YEAGER: While living with the Trasks I helped with summer Bible School of Manette Community Church. The first person to arrive at Bible School got to carry the flag into the church. One night one of the Trask kids broke the Trasks' clock. Elmer Trask fixed it and, not thinking about it, set the time an hour ahead of the actual time. He arrived at work in the navy yard an hour early and I arrived at the church an hour early. Not a soul was around. Reverend Walter Laetsch came over. We found out the clock was an hour fast—so I carried one of the flags into the church.

On a camping trip, when Girl Scout Troop 4 went to Neal Meredith's camp on Hood Canal, I remember sitting in the woods with a pillow case and a flashlight waiting for the snipe to arrive so I could catch them in the pillow case.

MARGARET AVERY BRUEMMER: My memories of Manette are of good times. Since we lived out of town we didn't know too many of the city kids...I was 13 before I saw anyone play tennis.

...My mom, Grandma, and Aunt Maybelle Hepworth used to can together. There would be rows and rows of fruit, vegetables and canned meat.

When World War II came we all grew up fast. Bill Hunter was 15 and worked in the navy yard, as some of his friends did...We went to swing-shift dances at Island Lake, roller skated at the roller rink where the railroad office at PSNS is now, and fished off all the docks around Bremerton, Manette, Illahee and Port Orchard.

BIRDIE MAY AVERY HILSTAD (1899-1979): [from previously written memories] I recall sitting on the front steps of our house [near present Latter-Day Saints Church] when I was 2 or 3 years old [about 1902]. Bennie Brewster, a red-haired neighbor boy of 5 or 6, gave me a pretty metal cup. I can remember just how it looked. It might have been for my birthday.

Later we moved to a new house Pop built.... My folks had chickens.... A big red rooster flew at me when I was throwing some grain out to feed them. It gave me such a scare I avoided going out to play when he was anywhere in sight.

It was such fun to make mud pies. Veva Hearn and I made them and put huckleberries on top. We put them on a board out in the sun to bake—we ate some, too. We thought they were good with huckleberries.

One day when I was 4, Mom and I were visiting a neighbor, Cordelia Martin. She had little red and white daisies. I could not resist the temptation to pick a handful. When Mom looked at me she asked if I had been picking Cord's flowers. I said, "No." She said, "Do you know where bad girls go who tell stories?" I said, "To Sunday School." Cord never let me forget that.

When I was 4 Uncle Jim Armstrong helped John Morris clear his land. Several stumps had to be blasted out with dynamite. Uncle Jim wrapped the extra dynamite caps in paper and put them in his lunch pail to keep them safe and dry. That evening Aunt Matt opened the lunch pail and dropped the paper and dynamite caps into the wood range. Soon caps were exploding. Stove lids, sparks and burning wood were flying. Lucky the old Monarch range didn't fly apart.

My first day at school was in Manette in 1905. Cousin Morgan Avery and I started school together. Our teacher was Miss Hester from Port Orchard. I liked her and thought she was very pretty. Classmates were Lola Thompson, Lena Miles, Lucille Short, Morgan Avery, Earl Martin and Raymond Carlson.

Our second-grade teacher was a pretty blond, Miss Chloe Sutton. She, too, was from Port Orchard. She taught us a wand-drill with wands wrapped in white crepe paper and decorated with pink paper flowers. We sang this song as we went through the exercise:

> Bring wand to the shoulder right
> Twice left to the arms full height
> Like with left, be softly deft
> And down to the floor again.
> Right hand, change left
> Wand to the front
> And clasp with both
> Forward twice then
> Downward and up the same.

Once Lennox Bright was reading from the textbook and didn't recognize the word "bright." Someone in class started to laugh. Miss Sutton said, "We all know a boy by that name." He finally got it....

Mama took Loran and me by rowboat to the 4th of July celebration at Evergreen Park. There were crowds of people and the first merry-go-round I had seen. There was cotton candy, a pie-eating contest, races, climbing the greased pole and catching the greased pig. There were sawing, chopping and log-rolling exhibitions, for logging was one of the main industries.... It was here that Uncle Jim Armstrong first began exhibiting his fruit and garden produce and Aunt Matt displayed her preserves and jellies.

The winter of 1906, when I was 6 or 7, there was a terrible windstorm. Many trees were blown down in the woods around us. The steamship *Valencia* was driven on the rocks off Vancouver Island. The captain and crew were lost. Only two or three people survived. Our neighbors, Mr. and Mrs. Gamage, lost their son Charles, who was a member of the crew.

When I was about 8 we moved to the Sheridan district, about 2 miles farther out, into a house Pop had built on 5 1/2 acres. I saw my new playmates, Ethel and Isabelle Smith.... They were dressed in blue overalls and boys' shirts. They wore their hair in a long "Dutch cut." Mr. and Mrs. Albert G. Smith had been born in England. We were fond of little Mrs. Smith. She called us all "Lambie" and often gave us gingerbread. We always made a May basket for her. Mr.

Smith was away most of the time. He was a cook aboard sailing ships that traveled all over the world. He wrote long letters and brought Ethel and Isabelle pretty things from places he had been.

An old bachelor, George Bachman, lived a mile down the road in a little one-room shack. One day he told Pop about his magic lantern—this was an early day form of showing films on a screen. He invited us to see his pictures. One evening we visited him and saw dozens of pictures of women which he had taken from magazines and newspapers. Many were popular stage stars mostly in scanty attire.

One night when I was 10 Mom awakened me and we stood at the window looking out at Halley's Comet for a long time—a mysterious visitor from space, not to be seen again for 80 years.

Stores and markets were far away so we welcomed the Watkins man with his tins of spices, bottles of flavoring, and linaments. The Raleigh man sold soaps, linaments and home remedies. The Caswell's Coffee man sold coffee and tea. Each of them drove a horse and buggy to carry their wares. Then there was the little peddler who came our way once or twice a year. He walked all the way carrying two big heavy leather cases. Whenever he came Mom needed something so we would gather 'round and enjoy looking at the interesting things he carried—laces, ribbons, needles, thread, scissors, pins, buttons, cotton and wool dress fabrics, strings of beads and some fur pieces. Sometimes he would ask Mom if she would fix him a bite to eat. We always had eggs, bread, butter and milk so that was no problem. He would give her lace or ribbon in exchange.

Mr. and Mrs. Paul Ruley lived 2 or 3 miles away, over near Thelma Henderson's folks. The Ruleys' two children, Gertrude and Archer, went to Sheridan School. Mr. Ruley was German, Mrs. Ruley was black. She was 12 years old when slavery was abolished. She had gone to school with Booker T. Washington.... Both Gertrude and Archer were musicians. Gertrude was a pianist and Archer played the violin. They were several years older than I.... In about 1920 Mrs. Ruley's former owner, Mrs. Baker, came to visit her.

DORIS BAILEY HARKNESS: I have wonderful recollections of my cousins playing games in the evenings with the Pentz kids from next door [North Perry Avenue], and the Lynch kids, across the street. We played Tap the Icebox; Annie, Annie, I Over; Hide-and-Go-Seek, and Kick the Can.... Grandma ordered her groceries from Meredith's store by telephone and they were actually delivered to her door. What a luxury!.... It was in Grandma Bailey's kitchen that I first discovered my life-long love of cooking. My cousins, Jean, Phyllis and I would make fresh blackberry pies and were allowed sips of Grandma's homemade blackberry and loganberry wine...but watching her singe the pin feathers off a freshly killed chicken—I'll never forget that odor.

BOB "Buster" BALLEW: A cougar used to roam Manette [early 1930s]. Once it followed my brother Charlie "Bud" Ballew and Kenny Hendrickson through the woods. They ran to Kenny's house. Once inside they heard the family dog barking like crazy and it sounded like he was running around the Hendrickson house. It seems the cougar was circling the house and killed the dog.

ROSEMARIE BOE HUDSON: My mother, Agnes Ericksen, arrived from Norway in 1899 to make her home with her aunt Bertha Johnson in Sheridan. I believe Bertha was the first white woman in that area—all the others were Indian.

Dad, James Boe, arrived in 1900 from Norway and he married Agnes that year. Dad was a well-known building contractor in Bremerton. My folks were close friends of Minnie Jacobsen and her family. We used to ferry over to her place to pick strawberries.

Dad built his first home on 4th Street where the Sears store was later located. Then he built on 4 acres where Olympic College now stands. That property is now known as the Boe Addition to Bremerton.

Mother rowed a small boat from Sheridan to Bremerton to buy groceries in 1899. One day the current was so strong that her boat tipped over and she hung on the bottom of the boat until help arrived over an hour later. She also told us of the time she rowed to Bremerton to get meat for dinner. A cougar followed her, wanting the meat, and she had to throw pieces of it behind her as she ran to the boat to get home.

MAE BRENDEN: We came here in 1926 from Everett, although I am a native of Kitsap County because I was born in Poulsbo. I've only missed 4 years in the Manette area.... When we first moved here we lived out where the Family Pancake House is now and later we moved to where Bremerton Gardens is. I remember when we first moved here people came with their sleds in the wintertime and sleighed because it was all a hill.

Another memory is the East Bremerton Improvement Club's big festival. They had ball games and races. We had a hamburger stand. I remember cooking hamburgers for—I don't know how many dozens a day. It was really a fun time.

FERRIS BUCHANAN: I used to like to fish on the old dock with my brother. Other days we'd go up with Erv Jensen and fish down in their canyon.

EVERTS BURLEW: On the day the Armistice was signed ending World War I, I was sent to ring the church bell in the Manette Community Church.... One year I had the job of tending the pump that brought water across the Sound from Bremerton. I oiled it and turned it on each morning and turned it off each evening. Jack Martin paid me 50 cents per day for this work.... In addition to swimming at the Sandbanks I can remember how grown up it felt to jump off the ferry dock....

Later, riding the ferry out a short way and swimming back to the dock.... Some of the boys I did things with were Paul Almon, Oval Martin and LeRoy Brallier. I also had many good times and hunting trips with Scott Harrington and George Grantham.... I remember my mother, Cora Palmer Burlew, working at the Children's Home. She told about the struggle she and the others had when taking the children to the navy ships for dinners and parties the sailors would provide for Christmas and other holidays.

HAROLD CHRISTENSEN: At the west end of the Sandbanks stood the remains of an old dock. At the land end of this pier was a large plank which bore the legend, "HILLMAN CITY." It seems that a real-estate entrepreneur by the name of C.D. Hillman started several of these develop-

ments, including this one near Manette. The whole venture seemed to have ended in legal litigation when it was found that several of the plots had been sold to more than one party.

The mode of operation included the chartering of the steamer *Yosemite* out of Seattle. The steamer was loaded with prospective customers, barrels of beer, free lunch and music, supplied by a calliope. It was said that the calliope could be heard before the steamer hove in sight with flags flying, people laughing and singing and having a great time. By the time the boat got from Seattle to the development near Manette, the prospective customers were probably pretty mellow, full of free lunch and good cheer and ready for the sales pitch.

On one such trip in 1909 the crew is reported to have been mellower than the prospective customers and ran the *Yosemite* on the rocks in the passage between Waterman lighthouse and Fort Ward. For many years there was a pilot house sitting on a flat near the beach approaching Fort Ward on the Manchester side, said to be from the wreckage of the ill-fated trip to Hillman City.

Growing up in Manette was an experience to be long remembered. We in Manette had certain parameters by which we measured our friends and neighbors. To a small boy in Manette it seemed that God, mail box, plumbing and garbage can were the important things.

Now it seemed necessary to have a God. Our family went to Sunday School, morning services, evening services and on Wednesday it was prayer meeting with ladies aid, missionary society and the WCTU.

If you had a mail box it seemed to raise you one step up the social ladder from the galoot who would stop in the post office occasionally to inquire if there was any mail. We had a mail box in the post office so I guess you could say we were safe on that point.

We had indoor plumbing, but in deference to Grandpa, who believed that indoor plumbing was unsanitary, unnecessary, immoral, indecent, uncivilized and unpatriotic, we maintained a two-hole outhouse nestled in a grove of hazlenut brush out near the woodshed.

Few may remember the Manette Telegraph Company owned and operated by Melvin Renn and Harold Christensen. The two owner-operators had secured two telegraph sets and constructed a transmission line of bits and pieces of all kinds of wire run through the necks of broken bottles acting as insulators. The return circuit was an earthen ground fastened to a water pipe at the Christensen end and a ground rod at the Renn end. Battery operation was out of the question due to cost, so a small light globe cut the house electricity to a usable level. The line ran through several wooded acres belonging to Tom Bright. The raw alternating current gave the telegraph sounder a buzzing sound that made it ideal for Morse code. Early problems were caused by operators' lack of expertise with the Morse code. They were often forced to call each other on the telephone to verify the contents of messages. PR problems were a reality for the company. Mrs. Christensen claimed that when watering the garden she had attempted to turn off the outside faucet and received a strong electrical shock. The Renns claimed the system generated so much static they couldn't hear Amos and Andy on their new battery-operated radio receiver.

People were trying to figure out how to get a piano up the narrow back stairs of Meredith's store, with a corner involved. They set the piano up on end and all the menfolks carried it up by brute strength and force. I wish I knew how many hernias could be traced to this operation.

I remember dances held upstairs; the Danish Polka remains in my mind. Mr. Meredith came running up the stairs yelling, "Stop, stop! Don't do that dance any more. I am afraid if you do the upstairs will end up in the downstairs."

One evening about dusk Alvin Hansen was piloting *Pioneer* and ran over a large Christmas tree. It got jammed in the front wheel. Men on deck got a rope on one end of the tree and Alvin reversed the engine while the men pulled on the rope and got the tree dislodged.

Mr. Jacobson was Manette's lighthouse tender. His job was to place a lighted lantern on the platform off the Manette beach. This light was later replaced with an electric beacon.

Manette was a close-knit family in those days before the bridge. Not a lot of families had cars, and one walked to the post office for mail and the store for groceries. As kids we walked to school, even to Lincoln Junior High and high school in Bremerton. Remember walking across the bridge and getting your legs soaked with the wind-lashed rain?.... We all remember the days the battleships came in the narrows to the navy yard and fired salutes. We would all run to the window to see the big battleship go by.

Some folks who worked in Bremerton wrapped their garbage in old newspaper and tossed it off the ferry on the way to Bremerton. The more fastidious would enclose a rock with the garbage so it would sink.... One chap, who brown-bagged his lunch, had both his lunch and garbage one morning. He tossed his lunch off the ferry and carried his garbage to work.

WALTER P. CLAUSEN: My family settled at Illahee. I used to visit the Akers family who lived on the shore between Manette Point and Illahee State Park. Mr. Akers worked at the naval shipyard in Bremerton for years. Their son Howard was an especially good friend and I visited him from time to time after the family moved to Manette from Illahee.

I remember the Manette Meat Market and deliveries of meat to Illahee. Illahee residents would leave orders in mailboxes and after the delivery man read the note he left the customer's meat in the mailbox.

The ferry *Pioneer* I recall vividly as I was allowed to steer the boat part way by the owner, Mr. Hansen, since he was a friend of Howard Akers, who was my friend.

Axel Jacobsen had a speed-boat. He towed us kids on a home-made surf-board.

During the Depression years of the 1930s I worked in Illahee woods with Mr. Hugh Kane of Gilberton, who was in the cordwood business. Since I lived with my folks in Seattle at that time, I traveled back and forth on the steamers of that day.

I remember people fishing off the Manette ferry dock for salmon. The current would spin the fishermens' spoons, thus attracting the fish. Many good catches were made.

DOROTHY CROWELL GERMAINE FIALLO: When we walked across the bridge to high school on foggy days we kept our hands on the railing so we wouldn't fall off the sidewalk. It would be so foggy we couldn't see the walk clearly. I believe it was Bonnie Booth that fell off one day, and turned her ankle badly. It was really spooky, with the fog horns moaning in the distance! And, oh so cold on the frosty,

foggy mornings. Most of us didn't have the dime to ride the bus, or a nickel for the jitney up 4th Street to school. Some days it was a long, long walk. Coming home always went too fast, particularly if you were walking with someone special!

During World War II one night there was an emergency; an unidentified flying object was seen. All men were called back to camp and the barrage balloons were put up in a hurry. The alert lasted several hours. Meanwhile, my son, Lee, age 8, and "Skeeter" Hall came sneaking into the house giggling. They finally told me they had been flying a kite with a flashlight tied to it, just to see what would happen.

We were visiting the New York World Fair with my son, Lee Sherman, who was doing his 2-week stint for the National Guard. A marine was standing guard by a rocket display. Lee asked about the nose cone. The marine's spiel went something like this, "This is called the Sherman Sleeve. Scientists all over the world tried to design a cone for a rocket to go into space that could stand the shock of breaking free of our gravity. There had been several failures, when someone remembered a guy at Puget Sound Naval Station who was exceptional with his calipers. They contacted Mr. Sherman and he was successful in figuring out the technical angles of pressure per inch and all that.... So they have named this cone the Sherman Sleeve...."

That Mr. Sherman was Lee's father George "Mitch" Sherman, my first husband, who designed the sleeve while employed in PSNS.

The Manette School was on a hill. To the west I could see over Bremerton to the sharp, white-capped Olympic Mountains, so different from the rolling mountains of Montana where I was born. I could look down at the water, sometimes as smooth as glass and other times dancing with little whitecaps. When I looked out the south windows of the school, I could see Port Orchard and Waterman and felt superior to those who had to live over there.

The school consisted of four rooms, with two grades in each room. There was a full basement with half windows above ground. The bathrooms and furnace room were in the basement. On cold days the janitor, Mr. Armstrong, would let students who brought their lunches eat by the furnace. I only got to eat in there once, but how I cherished the memory of having my lunch in that nice warm room.

Whichever one of us got to school first would be allowed to ring the bell. The rope from the bell tower hung near the inside of the front door. When you rang the bell you had to hold the big rope tightly, because the rope would pull you up off the floor.

We were allowed to skate in the school basement on rainy days. Other days we played outdoors...I remember the baseball games, marbles, tag, Cock-On-the-Rock, Whip the Cat. We were never bored. There were bars to swing on, skin the cat and do other acrobatics.

Once a week our redheaded Scottish gym instructor Mr. MacIntyre came from Bremerton. He would line up all the students in front of the school for calisthenics and stand on the front porch above us and shout out his orders like a drill sergeant. None of us ever thought of not doing what he said when he said to do it.

My third-grade teacher [1921-22] was Mrs. Nagel. She taught third and fourth grades. When one class was reciting, the other class studied. Discipline was excellent due to the rubber hose that Mrs. Copley, the principal, kept in the library. It was rarely used but was a good persuader.

Since I was restless, Mrs. Nagel would send me on errands. I jumped at the chance to race upstairs to the library for supplies and then down the bannister I would slide. Often the principal would catch me, even though I looked around to see if she was watching. I'd be grounded for sliding down the bannister—no recess.

We all loved our fifth-grade teacher, Dorothy Sullivan, soon to be Mrs. Charlie Sidam. She was replaced by my first man teacher, Mr. Teagarden. We had to do our work, no matter what, as we had to pass the state tests before we could advance a grade. In the sixth grade we had tiny Myrna Woods for our teacher. I believe I was the only one in class who was smaller than she. Mr. Miller was our seventh-grade teacher. He was so handsome I think he had a problem with all us girls falling for him.

Our class of 1927 was the last Manette eighth-grade class to have graduation exercises at the Manette School. What a day of mixed emotions! Happiness that we'd made it and were standing on the stage of the Manette Community Church to receive diplomas from Mr. Tillman Peterson, county superintendent of schools. Sadness that we were leaving Manette School and this particular group of classmates—forever. Next year we would have to catch the *Pioneer* and go to Bremerton, that terrible town, to high school. My graduation dress was ash rose and white silk crepe material that Dad, whom I hadn't seen since I was 2 years old, sent to me. I also had my first pair of silk stockings and a little bouquet of flowers.

How much the people in the Manette Community Church fashioned my life! Mr. Hoopes, Sunday School superintendent; Mrs. Hoopes, his adorable little happy wife who taught Sunday School; sweet little Mrs. Dewar and Mrs. Sprague, who always had a hug and a kind word for a little girl.

Our families used to go camping at Long Lake, Spencer Lake or Island Lake. We'd find a wide spot at the side of the road, pull off and set up our tents. Cooking was done over an open fire. It would take several hours to get to the lakes. We carried a little shovel and a few gunny sacks for traction under the tires when we got stuck in the mud. Fishing for catfish in Long Lake provided fish for dinner. When Helene, Mom's friend, cooked catfish she put the lid over the fish in our big old iron skillet. She piled big stones on top of the lid to keep the fish from knocking it off and flipping out of the pans.

Beyond the Children's Home was McDougal's Creek and then the Sandbanks. How many picnic dinners we had at the creek. Ben, my stepfather, would build a fire on the beach.... We would get some water out of the creek and mix it with lemon juice and sugar for lemonade. We brought ham sandwiches and potato salad and raw spuds that we would throw in the coals of the fire to bake. How good those "mickeys" tasted smothered with butter, salt and pepper.

There was the girls' Sandbank and the boys' Sandbank about half a block away. A big tree had fallen down from the bank that separated the beaches. It was understood the boys would circle up over the top of the bank to approach the beach and we girls wouldn't go near the boys' Sandbank beach. Everyone knew we all went skinny dipping. You might wear a suit into the water, but it came off as soon as you were in. One day my family was visiting friends that lived in the last house on Pacific Avenue. They told of watching through their binoculars and seeing kids skinny-dipping at the Sandbanks. Mother said to me, "You hadn't better be one of them."

Water played an important part in our lives. The Parkinses had a raft in front of their home at Nipsic Avenue and Lower Shore Drive which we used all the time. On George Washington's birthday we would have a big bonfire, roast weenies and go swimming. It was understood that when the tide was running, either in or out, you stayed out of the water. My sister, Jessie, was about 12 and a very strong swimmer. She decided to swim out to the raft one more time as the tide was just beginning to run. She was swept away by the current. It was fortunate Mr. Parkins and Mr. Lossee were home. By the time they got the rowboat in the water and caught up with Jessie she was almost down to the Manette Dock....

Some of us kids had our own private madrona trees. They were our houses. The madrona limbs were just right for one to be a living room, another the kitchen, another the bedroom. We'd go calling on each other and talk on our tin-can phones with lines strung from tree to tree. When no one else could come out to play, I would spend hours sitting in "my frontroom" reading a fairy story.

On the corner of East 11th Street and Perry Avenue was Daddy Green's big old hardware store. My greatest delight was to count nuts and bolts for him. He took the place of the Grandad I didn't have. If I was careful he would let me fill his little bins with all the shiny hardware. One day Mother said I couldn't go down there any more. A few days later the doors were locked. It was years before I knew he had died, but I was one broken-hearted little girl when he wasn't there any more.... Mr. Painter bought the building and made a garage out of it. Later he sold the place to Axel Jacobsen, who had a garage and later sold cars.

On the southwest corner of East 11th Street and Perry Avenue was a dry-goods store. Later the post office with Mrs. Harkins as postmaster took part of the building and Mr. Harrison became the new barber in town in another part of the building. In the 1930s Mr. Mitchell opened a third grocery store there.

Mr. Aldrich had a little store and card room down on the dock...Mr. Harrington was the barber. His daughter Mae was in the grade behind me. She used to delight in going down on the beach by the dock and wading in the seaweed at low tide. One day an octopus wrapped a tentacle around her ankle. She screamed like a banshee and several men from the barber shop and card room ran down and had a real struggle pulling her out. That ended the wading in the seaweed.

There were two grocery stores on the main street, now East 11th Street; Martin's and Meredith & Son. Clyde Meredith used to grow asparagus in a swampy piece of land where Vernon Powers' jewelry store is now. Joaquina Feek worked for Harry Martin and made the best fudge sundaes ever made.

Meredith's store was a favorite—they had a big cookie barrel in the middle of the floor. It was high enough so we kids couldn't see in it but we'd reach our arm over and swipe a cookie. When we got outside we would compare notes about what kind we had gotten. I think the ones with the pink marshmallow center and coconut on top were my favorites. We never thought of it as stealing. Someone had said, "Oh, he doesn't care," and we believed it.... One day my sis and I were in the store with Mom. She didn't see us take our cookies, but when we got outside and started to compare our cookies, mother came unglued. First we got a lecture about what constituted stealing; then she marched us back into the store and made us return the cookies. Mr. Meredith protested that it was OK, all the kids swiped cookies and he knew it. He said he'd have to throw away part of the barrel of cookies as they would become stale unless the kids took some. We still had to give the cookies back and Mother insisted that he put 20 cents on her bill which we would work out at home.... After that Mr. Meredith always gave me a cookie when I came in for groceries. When he married Estelle, the town celebrated with the noisiest shivaree.

Next to Meredith's was a small store that sold material and sewing notions. They had a grand penny-candy case. How long it would take us, with our faces pressed against the glass, to decide just which piece of candy we would buy with our penny—a jaw breaker, a little box of candy hearts, a licorice stick or a tootsie roll.... This store was Bushy's confectionery. In 1924 they came out with a great big O'Henry for 10 cents.

There was a blacksmith shop, not under the spreading chestnut, but under a big plum tree. They were the best plums ever, but I was terrified of the blacksmith. I never knew his name but he was a big man. His muscles bulged. He tolerated me standing around watching him work, but he never talked to me. When he scowled in a certain way, I knew it was time to leave.

Around 1928 Mr. Etten opened his meat market. Later Harold Reanier worked there. About the time World War II started, Mr. Etten enlarged the building and added a grocery line.

Oscar Hilstad had a coal and wood business down on the waterfront near the dock. Down the street was Ralph Tracy's lumber yard. The owner's son's name was Bert and he married Gert Kanthack's sister, Mae.

Next to Fellows' home on East 11th Street was a greenhouse. For years it was leased to a Japanese man named Mr. Shimasaki. He raised vegetables and sold them to the officers in the navy yard.

The Lewis Benders lived next to the dock. They had a magnificent row of lilacs in front of their place. Mrs. Ella Bender always had one of the girls from the Children's Home living at her home and working for her board and room. Lillian Peterman was one of the girls.... One time Mrs. Bender had all of us Girl Scouts in her home so Lillian could demonstrate to us how to make a bed properly. We toured the spotlessly clean house. During the tour Mrs. Bender showed us her bathroom—a thing of beauty to most of us that had our bathroom at the end of a path.... We also had a big round tub set in front of the wood stove every Saturday night for our baths. Mrs. Bender told us that when we were to be married, we could come down the day before and have a bath in her tub. How I looked forward to that special occasion. What a disappointment when my mother installed plumbing in our home when I was 15.

Up near the old post office was the fire bell tower. If there was a fire, one would run to the center of town and ring that bell. The men of the volunteer fire department ran to Fellows' big barn and brought out the fire engine. At one time they had a fire wagon and kept horses there to pull it. By the time we moved there, they had a fire truck.

The first fire I recall was Morgan's house on East 10th Street and Hayward Avenue. It burned down and the Manette "city fathers" worked long hours to help build a new one for him. I can still see Ben, my stepfather, come home late at night, dog-tired from working on that house. He seemed to take it as a personal responsibility. Ben had an artificial leg,

from his knee down, and it was very painful from so much time up on ladders and crawling around on the roof. But he stayed with it until the last board was placed.

The town sidewalks consisted of pairs of two-by-twelves. Every Halloween they were torn up and used to make barricades across the streets. I think it was about 1933 that Mr. Adkins graded the roads and put in concrete sidewalks. The old wooden sidewalks went out Perry Avenue as far as Brewsters, today Latter-Day Saints Church. To make it easier to step from their sidewalk into a horse-drawn carriage, Brewsters had a big concrete carriage block with steps. It had to be removed to put in new sidewalks. The next year dwarf Japanese cherry trees were planted along the sidewalks throughout much of Manette.

Ben, my stepdad, always put our Studebaker up on blocks and removed the tires the day after Labor Day. He had the tires put back on and pumped up ready for our first time out on Memorial Day. Even then you would get stuck in the mud and everyone in the car would have to pile out and push, except me. I was the smallest so I got to steer the car and push on the brakes when Ben hollered "Whoa!"

One winter night I missed the last ferry from Bremerton to Manette. My dates, George Dayton and Ed Day, asked a taxi driver to take me around through Silverdale but the roads were closed. George was scared enough of my mother that he and his buddy Ed "borrowed" someone's rowboat and rowed me across the bay. Fortunately the water was still and rowing easy. It was a gorgeous night with a million stars shining in the deep-blue crystal sky. Shining bubbles bounced around the boat and away from the oars. The boys took me home, then turned the boat over and slept under it. They woke the next morning to face a policeman looking for the culprits that had stolen the boat. After they returned the boat and explained what had happened, all was forgiven.

Manette and its people were my mother and father. It and they shaped my life. I was taught kindness, compassion, truthfulness, consideration for others, joy and happiness. It was part of me, my heritage. Anyone who lived there was doubly blessed. It taught me love.

RUTH DANEL BLASBERG: I was born in Seattle and came over here in my mother's arms in 1919. I remember in 1922 those three boards going up the south side of East 11th Street. I thought Pop had them put in for my tricycle to ride on.... I remember we'd fly our kites from Fellows' tower. I guess one of my fondest memories is when I used to help Earl Harkins at the improvement club. Margaret Hoopes and I did the handwriting on all the letters that he stormed Washington, D.C., with so he could get Illahee Park established.... I remember meeting Senator Magnuson and how charming he was. I almost melted to think that I got to meet him back in '36.

I remember when my father drove the first car across the Manette Bridge. It was for the dedication ceremonies [1930]. Jack Martin was the honorary mayor and we had him and an Indian woman from Tracyton, Jane Garrison, who was 106 years old, in that car. We were in the news and that was great!

Manette holds cherished memories for all of us. We also recall the brown paper pay envelopes from the navy yard...East 11th Street closed off for sledding...riding the ferry *Pioneer* with the Driscolls to attend Star of the Sea Catholic School...Constable Charlie Young's night-

First car across Manette Bridge, 1930. Ralph Danel drove car over during dedication ceremonies. Honorary Mayor J.H. "Jack" Martin sits beside Ralph. In back seat are (from left) Mrs. William Abbott, whose husband helped promote the bridge; Jane Garrison, 106-year-old granddaughter of Chief Seattle and resident of Tracyton; and Marguerite Olsen Bright of a well-known Manette family.   -Prints of Wales photo

stick...Art and Melba Morken's shivaree...Genevieve "Ginger" Painter getting to sing with a band...skating on Clare's Marsh...the board bridge going to Gilberton...our Sunday rides...the exchange holiday dinners with the H. Hunter and E. Earing families...Wendy Martin's pet monkey...Earl Harkins' dedication in founding the East Bremerton Improvement Club and establishing Illahee State Park...the EBIC softball team with those Forbes and Jensen brothers. Most of all—classmates and friends who served our country and didn't return to add their page or two in our history book. Manette holds cherished memories for all of us.

JANE ELLEN DIXON QUINN: My Uncle Harry Hansen started the ferry service when he was a teen-age boy with a motor launch. I think it was the *Rainier*. It didn't carry cars. Connor was a deck-hand.

Harry Hansen married my mother's sister, Ellen Gertrude Swisher. Ellen was born in Ruske County, Kans., March 11, 1880. She came to Kitsap County in 1906. My mother came west at that time and stayed with Aunt Ellen for a long time. Mother was on her way back to Kansas when she met my father in Portland...She never returned to Kansas except for an occasional visit.

Remember going down at night and getting on the dark *Urania* and sitting by the motor waiting for the lights to come on?

An elderly cousin of Aunt Ellen, Laura Terry, lived with Aunt Ellen and Uncle Harry on the waterfront at Tracyton. Laura and her husband had worked all their lives as teachers on Indian reservations. In the early 1930s the state of Washington presented Aunt Laura with a huge bell from one of the reservations because of her long and outstanding service at that reservation. The bell, which would have taken at least two big men to lift, sat in our front yard at 7th Street and Naval Avenue for at least 2 two years because nobody knew what to do with it. Then one dark night somebody stole it and we never found out what happened to that bell....

Harry died in 1970 when he was 83. Aunt Ellen died November 19, 1946 at the age of 66. She suffered a stroke.

HATTIE ELLIOTT ENGSTROM: We came here in 1913 and I didn't get to see the town because we lived outside a ways. I remember the boardwalk. I worked for Mrs. Hattie Martin before I was married. I bought my first piano from Mrs. Feek. Mrs. Martin made our wedding cake.

Lincoln Heights Hall was on the property where the Medicine Shoppe is today, 2541 Perry Avenue. One winter, I think it was 1916, a deep snow caused the collapse of the hall. Papa could hear the roof cracking and called people, but no one could do anything about it. I can still recall the sight of the ruined building when I walked to school the next day.

RUSS ELLIOTT: We lived in a beach house with the bathroom out over the beach.... The pipes froze so my mother chopped a hole in the bathroom floor and poured boiling water down to thaw the pipes. Dad was real upset when he came home—about the hole in the floor.

One of my fondest memories is of the play *Womanless Wedding*, enacted in the hall above Meredith's store. Bill Schweer's mother was the director, as I remember. The gales of laughter still ring in my ears from that event.

The thing that still impresses me is the closeness that we had as a community. Everybody knew everybody else in the neighborhood. The old Manette School; the old wooden church; the glass of the old greenhouse sparkling in the sun; the sound of the navy yard whistle; taps being played at Retsil (the old soldier's home)—those all come back and I hear them in my memory and there is a part of me that is forever locked there—that never left Manette. The hours I spent on the beach with my toy boats; other hours fishing from the skiff. Many are the times I came home from school, jumped into the skiff and fished out in front of the house. I would catch enough for supper and have them on the stove cooking before Dad got home from the navy yard.

Who of us that lived on the beach—the Schultzes, Driscolls, Palmers, Von Hoenes, Stewarts, Pidducks—can forget the fleet of boats that fanned out from the dock in Bremerton to take home the workers that lived as far away as Poulsbo. The *Chickaree*, among them, passed by our front door every working day.

Who could forget the forays of clamming that we enjoyed so much on those minus tides—the grotesque shadows that the lanterns we carried cast as we walked the beach with lantern, shovel and pail. The sweet nectar that came from the steaming kettle that Mom had on the old wood-burning stove in the kitchen. (I warmed my bottom many times on cold mornings standing on the oven door while dressing. They don't make stoves with doors like that anymore.)

Manette—it was the dearest homespot a child could ever have. A book could be written by every individual that ever lived there, and even all these stories combined could never adequately tell the history of the fondest years of our lives.

HELGA ENKEBOLL BEHR: When I was going to Manette School [1921-27], students gathered in the large basement. They lined up according to their grade. Then, with the beat on a metal triangle, they marched upstairs, in turn, to their classrooms...There was a small school library located on the upper level under the bell tower...The fire escape from the upper level was a metal slide. Fire drills were exciting with this method of descending...Our teachers included Miss Turner, Miss Johnson, Miss Kingsbury and Miss Lappenbusch. Mr. Cash was principal...Students noticed when Miss Johnson had been to the hairdresser. Her hair had neatly arranged marcel waves. Miss Irene Kingsbury had the nickname "OK/IK"; this was the way she signed student passes. Miss Lappenbusch's sisters, Marie and Lulu, were teachers in Bremerton.... In the fourth grade Duncan Buchanan had polio. When he returned to school they cheered for him.

Duncan was the first boy to flatter me. We were swinging like monkeys on the playground bar. My long hair brushed him. He said, "You have fine, soft hair." I said, "Oh." He said, "You really do."

A new student, Roger Paquette, came from Canada. He wore knee pants. The boys teased him, but the girls giggled and thought he was special, because of his good looks.

At one time in the classroom Roger turned to a girl (either Jeane Martin or Dorothy Cole) sitting at a desk near him. Seeing an orange with SUNKIST on it he said, "I am the SUN and you are the KIST."

One Christmas Manette students participated with Bremerton elementary students in a Christmas program at the Rialto Theater. Willard Muller was Santa Claus and I was Mrs. Claus....

A play about Hiawatha was performed by older students at the church. William, my brother, was in the play as a squirrel. Mama made his costume of burlap sacks. He had a few peanuts tucked away to munch on....

The walk home from school followed a path through a wooded area. There I picked johnny-jump-up flowers and small delicious wild strawberries. Next there was the road (Perry Avenue) and the blacksmith shop, a place to watch the smith shoe horses and to get plums from a nearby tree.

Further down the road were horse chestnut trees and many large nuts on the ground. The nuts were inedible, but it was fun to remove the spiney green husks to see the glossy brown

shell inside. Then onward was a row of huge maple trees which provided winged seeds to be thrown up in the air to whirl to the ground.

After a rain this street had mud puddles that were a challenge to walk through. A few times my rubbers would get stuck and I would come home minus a rubber, left behind in a puddle.

Sometimes my friends walked home with me to get bunches of grapes from our grape vine. Mama was generous about this, but sometimes she objected, because she wanted the grapes for wine she made.

Hikes with friends were along the shore trail to the Akers' at Enetai and beyond, or in the other direction, on the trail to the Sandbanks. We picked trilliums in the wooded area above the banks. Another hike was up the hill to the Jensens' place. Our family got milk from the Jensens.

Mama had many Valentine birthday parties for me—I was born on February 14, Valentine's Day. Weather for February 14 was unpredictable. Once there was a snowstorm the night before, leaving more than a foot of snow. That time my birthday lasted a week, as different friends came each day, thinking the snow had melted enough so that the party would be then...another time the weather was so mild violets were blooming, and I picked a bouquet for each friend.

When there was a large quantity of snow, sledding was permitted on the sloping main street in the evenings. My brother and I would come home cold and exhilarated from this fun.

I am sure the class that started in 1921 will agree with me that these early years in Manette were some of the happiest in our lives.

ADDIE ETTEN: When I first met Oscar Etten I fell in love with his overcoat.... I worked in the navy yard until 1921, when Oscar and I were married. Then Roy and June came along...and later Keith. We had a home on Shore Drive that we bought [1920] for $2300. It had a fireplace...and a full concrete basement.... When we sold it for $2600 we thought we'd done well.... My husband had the meat market he bought from Mr. Stone. Later we added groceries.... Oscar gave all his good customers at the meat market a pound of bacon for Christmas each year. Bacon was 19 cents a pound.

Our daughter June used to sing on the radio—Uncle Frank's broadcast on Saturday from Seattle.

JUNE ETTEN JARSTAD: In 1935 the old Manette School acquired a new principal, Florence Holman. She encouraged the children to use their talents. We used to have Major Bowes Amateur Hours at assemblies (Major Bowes was then a popular radio show featuring non-professional talent.) This gave the children an opportunity to perform his or her specialty. We had a harmonica band instructed by Miss Holman. Those were very happy years...we had some real snowfalls, and my brother Roy and I coaxed our folks to buy us each a sled. We slid down Fellows' pasture just below the old school.

Before 1930 there was no Manette Bridge. Whenever we needed a doctor, Dr. Ray Schutt would come across on the ferry and make his house call. Those were the "good ole days" when doctors made house calls. Whenever we had childhood diseases—measles, mumps, chicken pox or smallpox—we would be quarantined. The health department would send someone around to tack up a big yellow sign with black letters that said "Quarantined." Father Oscar could not stay at home while the house was quarantined because he handled meat. So he would bring the family groceries and ice and fill the coal bucket, which we left on the porch. He stayed with friends. Roy had smallpox, but no one else in the family caught it.... One winter when there was a particularly good snowfall Addie and Oscar and friends went sledding down Jacobsen Boulevard...several friends built a bonfire in front of Constable Charlie Young's house and roasted hot dogs (kind of nervy!).... On Halloween Sally Painter's husband and a friend of his went out to have some fun—they got confused and knocked over their own outhouse, and some one fell in.

ALICE FELLOWS LAWSON: The Fellowses had the first Cadillac in town. It must have been about 1910. There was a certain hill that was kind of sandy. When one guy that had a team of horses saw us coming he'd get out his team so he could pull us up that sandy hill.

Mrs. Abbott had a parrot and that was really wonderful. I'd never seen one.... Joaquina Feek came to our house and ate cherries...she was as much of a cherry eater as I.... All the kids gathered at our place because we had about a block of territory there and we'd play in the summer evenings until the curfew blew at 9 o'clock. Everybody really ran like crazy for home when that curfew blew.

I went swimming at the end of Trenton Avenue every day in the summertime with the Von Hoene girls. We had a big water tower in our yard. I remember when the first airplane came over there. All us kids climbed that water tower and watched that airplane all day.

Grandpa Hixon brought the mail off the ferry with his wheelbarrow. He went down to the ferry, picked up the mail, took it to the post office and came home with his empty wheelbarrow. When he got a car that was really a disappointment because us kids would have to get off the street so he could go by in his car.

In 1917 George, my oldest brother, caught mumps from his girl friend, Regina Peppard. Very soon, Walter came down with it, but on one side only. Just as they recovered Clifford and Mom developed mumps, then Florence and the cat, then Charlie and I. We just got over the mumps when school started and I caught whooping cough...we had a big orange sign on the front of the house, announcing quarantine. We changed signs from mumps to whooping cough. In about 1918 John Shanley and I broke out with measles at school. Our teachers and the principal looked us over out in the hall and sent us home. I was so embarrassed. When my sister Florence came home for lunch, Mom handed her some clothes out the window and she went to stay with her friend, Helen Siefert.

WALT FELLOWS: I was born here in 1901. I remember when I was about 9 years old, the Manette Church had an excavation along one side of it, filled with water and ice. Us kids went up to play on the ice. The church had acetylene gas for light. We had the same thing at home so I knew how it worked. It froze up and blew out the bottom of the tank—white wash all over the place. Reverend MacIntosh, as I remember, came out and accused us kids of blowing that thing up. Of course we knew what happened because we had it happen at home.

I remember "String Town," they used to call it, because everybody went up the county road, now Perry Avenue, on

that sidewalk made of two 12-inch boards with an inch or so in between them. It made a beautiful sled run in the winter. We'd go up above Tom Bright's and you didn't amount to much unless you'd go clear down and out to the end of the dock, which I believe would be East 10th Street now. I've been within a few feet of the end.

Mr. Pfenning, George Card and Tom Bright all had cows and they took milk to Bremerton about 10 o'clock every morning in a rowboat. If you wanted to go to Bremerton shopping you got a ride with them in the rowboat and came back when they did.

Shorty Shimasaki leased greenhouses and lived on our property with his wife. He had a girl about 18 years old that worked for him for awhile. She lived with the Shimasakis and may have been related. He bought her a piano to keep her happy. His doors were too small to get the piano through, so he cut a hole in the side of his house to get the piano in.

Shorty's produce crops included leaf lettuce, cucumbers and tomatoes. He sold some locally but most of it went to Seattle. I remember he took loaded wagons down to the dock at the end of East 10th Street and put crates of produce aboard the *Norwood* to be ferried to Seattle. The *Norwood* or the *Reeve* would stop in Manette about 7 a.m.

There were two cherry trees and one plum tree on his place. He had nine large greenhouses and one small one.

Two boys from the O'Hara family that lived up on the County Road, now Perry Avenue, used to visit Shorty. We knew them as Sam and Kozol.

MARIE GALLEHER (1895-1986): I recall the two Skagit sternwheelers, *Skagit Belle* and *Skagit Queen*, woodburners with tall, skinny smokestacks, coming in alternately on Tuesdays and Fridays, leaving their scalloped wakes.

In Enetai we had a neighbor, Canady, who was the father of Mrs. Croxton. Canady had been all over the world as ship's cook on sailing ships. He was a widower when I knew him. He lived north of us on 5 acres where he had a very fine apple orchard. Canady died at a veterans hospital at the age of 78 of pneumonia in about 1920.

ROWENA HARKINS HINSHAW: Our German shepherd/police dog, King, became part of the family and community. In 1929 or 1930, King followed the Bremerton mayor to a meeting at our house one evening and stayed for 19 years. King slept with me, pulled my sled when there was snow, and guarded the post office, our home and the neighborhood. He carried sacks home from the grocery store and followed at Dad's heels, or wheels if Dad were traveling in our Oakland automobile—even as far as Illahee State Park. After being given a bone at Etten's butcher shop many times, he learned to help himself when the butchers were busy.

We enlisted King in the U.S. Marine Corps. Later two of his offspring served in the K-9 corps in Alaska during World War II. King served as "dogface" for about a month until we could no longer stand his absence. We drove to Camp Wesley Harris to see our military son. When we called, he came, jumped on Mother's lap, and put his paws around her neck and his head on her shoulder. We all cried and took King home AWOL.... When he died several years later, news of his demise was on the front page of the *Bremerton Sun*.

Reverend Walter Laetsch came to our home to visit when I was reading a banned magazine, *True Story*. I yanked off my glasses, left them on the couch and hid the magazine under the couch. The reverend sat on my glasses...but they didn't break! I never brought another *True Story* into our house!

John McKelvy chased me down the hill past the Manette Community Church with a garter snake he was trying to put down my neck. I have been afraid of snakes ever since.

Dorthea Spencer was my third-grade teacher. She had 30 students that year. She passed 15 into the fourth grade and kept 15 back. I was in the latter group, thus enjoying one extra year at Manette School.

I was awakened by Dad on December 7, 1941, with news of the Pearl Harbor attack. What a change in our lives—nets were installed across the bay to protect the navy yard from enemy submarines, army posts were set up all over Manette and barrage balloons were flying to protect the area from air attack. Many of us left high school early to fill jobs left vacant by young men who had enlisted in military services. Hundreds of people came into town from all over the United States to take jobs in the navy yard. My folks delivered mail on holidays and opened the post office on holidays, if necessary, to deliver V-Mail. Mother was postmistress.

I sang at June Etten and Glenn Jarstad's wedding. Later June sang at my wedding when I married George Hinshaw. I sang at another wedding when Maryjayne Meredith married Dick Hladky.

Although Manette was incorporated into Bremerton, to me it never changed—You can take the girl out of Manette, but never Manette out of the girl.

I remember my little friends Hatsu and Edai Yamashida, Shorty Shimasaki's nieces. They lived with Shorty and his wife. I had lunch with them at Shorty's home next to his greenhouse on Fellows property.

JEAN HARRISON GLUDE: My first night in Manette in 1925 I slept on the top of a trunk at Aunt Dell's (Mrs. Dell Brewster Harrison's).... There were concrete steps at the side of the road in front of her home on Perry Avenue. These were used in the horse-and-carriage days—a way to get up into the carriage. My sister EmmaBelle, June Womac and I played by the hour on those steps.... Manette had wooden sidewalks and low bridges over the small gullies. As I'd walk down Perry Avenue from Cascade Trail to go to kindergarten at Mrs. Amy Hoopes's on East 16th Street I'd cross over these low bridges that had nettles and blackberries fighting to get higher than we were. We'd take big sticks and whack at those nettles to keep them down. The smell of disturbed nettles today brings back those memories.... Very few streets had names in those days.

When Dad was clearing land for our home on Hayward Avenue, Brights, Paquettes and Meichos came over and we'd wrap potatoes in newspaper, dunk them in a bucket of water and throw them into the hot coals to bake. Never were there any better tasting baked potatoes, no matter how black the outside got.

When my brothers Howard and Earl would go on Boy Scout hikes in the Olympic Mountains, EmmaBelle and I had to deliver the *Shopping News* for them. Manette seemed pretty big to us and the papers very heavy at that tender age.

Dad always raised a big vegetable garden and when Mother would be canning string beans we kids would sit around a big washtub of string beans and cut beans all day. We'd cover our thumbs with adhesive tape to keep from getting all cut up and

when the day's work was done, Mother would give us each 5 cents. We'd get to spend it on anything we wanted. I usually went down to Meredith's or Martin's grocery store and bought animal cookies—one small box for 5 cents.... I've lived and traveled the world over but Manette will always be home to me.

ELVA HIBBARD: A minister, Reverend C.S. Morrison, and his wife moved into the Lincoln Heights district, now north Perry Avenue. Since there was no church, he conducted services in the big house where he and his wife lived.

MADORA HICKS: I moved here in 1920. Mother Bender (Mrs. Lewis, Ella), took me under her wing.... I met Quina Feek...she had black hair and was the most beautiful woman in Manette.... A group of us played 500 (card game like bridge) for over 40 years.... One of the best things that happened, happened after my husband Fred was hurt very badly in the navy yard. We were trading with Clyde Meredith. Clyde knew Fred would be in the hospital for a long time. He came down to see me and said, "Now, I know you're young, and if you need groceries, or money or whatever you need, don't hesitate to come to me." That always impressed me.

When Clyde and Estelle were married in 1922 we had a shivaree on them. Estelle had never heard of a shivaree. It was a pretty lively, loud party that night.

ELGIE HOFFMAN: While in an early elementary grade I had a favorite teacher, Miss Florence May McClain. When Bill Glud took her for his wife, it took me several months to forgive Bill. In later years, I realized my beloved teacher couldn't have married a nicer man.... Miss McClain commuted to school by horse and buggy. She used Mr. Glud's barn, across the road from school, to house her horse until time to go home. This daily contact with Bill grew into courtship.

EVELYN HOLDEN NEWKIRK: Albert B. Williams landed in Phinney Bay in 1900. He had five children. One was my mother, Harriet.... My father, Art Holden, bought material for his house from Fellows' sawmill.... Grandmother took her kids from Phinney Bay to Tracyton school by boat—there were no roads. Later they lived on Highland Avenue and my mom went to the 4th Street school.

They moved to Manette in about 1904.... Meredith's store belonged to my grandfather, Albert Williams, and George Card. Before that Albert had A.B. Williams Hardware Store at the base of East 10th Street. Later it became Williams and Son.... One of my uncles ran the *City of Manette* ferry.

Out in Sheridan was the big hall, Lincoln Heights Hall, where they had square dancing. Wayne Burlew's father was the caller. I remember when I was a little kid we would go home from that hall about 3 or 4 in the morning. My father carried my sister Alice and a lantern. Everybody had so much fun dancing, time didn't mean a thing. There were bunks where they threw the kids—there were no baby sitters. It took hours to get the coffee hot. When they had the snow in 1916 the structure couldn't withstand the snow and collapsed.

JOHN ELLSWORTH (Danel) HOLMES: My mother and I came to Manette in 1922. The first thing I saw was those three boards going up the south side of East 11th Street. I thought Pop had them put in for my tricycle to ride on.... I remember we'd fly our kites from Fellows' tower.

GENEVA HOWERTON PICKERING: I remember my first day at school. It was September 1913 when I started to the first grade of school in the two-room Manette School.

I walked alone over a mile to get there. Everything was new to me.

Mama had packed me a lunch. When the noon hour came and we were supposed to eat, I was very upset. The problem was that Mama had taught me—and stressed—to share. "Share and don't be piggy," she always said.

Well, there were lots of children inside the school room and out in the yard. I looked in my lunch box. There was a sandwich, an apple and two cookies. There was not enough to share with so many children. I closed the box and put it back on the shelf. I didn't want those children to think that I was piggy.

When school was out, I started to walk home. My new shoes made a blister on my heel, I was hungry and it was raining. By the time I got home, I was crying real hard.

Mama explained that the lunch she had packed was for me and I didn't have to share.

JESSE HOWERTON: We had one of the old reliable water pumps called rams. Ours was a medium size: 1-1/2-inch intake, 3/4-inch discharge. Water rushed down the 1-1/2-inch pipe and produced hydraulic pressure to propel the water up the little pipe to a big tank on the canyon rim....

The ram to operate had to be approximately 25 feet lower than the supply of water. The water went into the big tank at the rate of approximately 1000 gallons in 24 hours. The tank was always full and running over with delicious cold water...Expense: one leather foot valve and two gaskets, replaced once a year.

In 1985 I was on Kitsap County jury duty for 15 minutes. The judge asked all of us on the jury if we had ever committed a crime or broken the law, and I said, "I have on several occasions." The judge said, "How badly were you punished?"

I said, "Fortunately, I wasn't caught."

The judge said, "For a remark like that you can go home, Mr. Howerton."

LENDALL HUNTON: I recall one day we came home from school and my mother was dripping wet as she came up from the beach where she had just swum out into the bay and rescued a 2-year-old child whose mother was screaming and hysterical on the beach.

I also recall the night we all got out of bed and went down on the beach and pounded on the beached hull of a large tugboat to wake the skipper, who had fallen asleep at the wheel. The propeller was still turning and dug a huge crater in the beach. The scow in tow was also beached nearby.

My brother Dick and I were witnesses to the tragedy of the float capsizing at the Manette Dock in 1919. We had just escorted Ethel Ward, who later married Bob Louden, to the dock as the *Urania* pulled up to the float. Ethel made a leap to the boat as the float went under, and helped others on board. We made certain she was OK and then helped others up the gangway. [For an account of the tragedy see TRANSPORTATION; FERRIES]

I remember finding Indian beads on our place...the community wiener roasts on the beach...hunting, fishing and clam digging...skinny dipping at Sandy Point...our Triple B clubhouse in Jacobsen's draw...helping to build the Manette Community Church...all the picnics on all the beaches from Manette to Agate Pass.

Most of all I remember Axel Waldemar Jacobsen. He was the strongest, had the first outboard motor, motorcycle, dragsaw and radio receiver, and could repair most anything.

I remember well a violent storm that hit our beach area in 1927. The barometer had been dropping all morning and intermittent rain squalls were passing through. I had a date to play tennis and some golf at Enetai and started out walking there when the wind picked up to gale force as I got past the Jacobsen property. I saw the bay turn greenish in color—the tops of the waves were being whipped off in white foam—and then it hit the beach area. First I saw Boe's garage under a big madrona tree lifted off of its foundation and dumped on Jacobsen's beach; then our small skiff and someone's rowboat came flying through the air and landed somewhere between Jensen's and Lund's property.

By this time I was soaking wet as the wind had blown all the water out of the mudpuddles and I ran and hid behind a telephone post in front of Akers' property and watched the wind rip through the large fir trees in Bruno and Pearl Lund's front yard. Large limbs were broken off and several of these big trees were twisted and split up the trunk. Needless to say, after the storm subsided I didn't play golf or tennis, but when I returned home I could see where our front porch roof—about 10 x 25 feet—had been torn off and was resting on Jacobsen's front porch and in small poplar trees in their front yard. Also a large whale bone about 8 feet long, which was over the archway of our front door, was planted upright in Jacobsen's tomato patch. Now when I speak of this storm I ask people if they have ever seen flying rowboats.

HELEN PALMER McCALLUM : We lived down on the beach, now Shore Drive, in 1927. Phyllis [my sister] and I were playing outdoors by our basement when the wind hit. Phyllis had an open umbrella. The wind caught the umbrella and she started to rise. Martha saw her, grabbed her feet and dragged her into the basement where we hid from the storm. We had a big madrona tree in the yard that split. We got in the house and watched the cyclone head out the water toward Bainbridge Island, carring one of the neighbors garages with it, along with lots of debris."

[Roger Paquette provides the following additional information about the "Manette tornado."]

"MINIATURE CYCLONE SWEEPS MANETTE BEACH"

This was a banner headline on the front page of the *Daily News Searchlight* January 3, 1927. About 4 p.m. on Sunday, the 2nd, gale force winds converged in Port Orchard Bay off Bremerton. They then formed a twister that raced in a northeasterly direction across the Manette beach and on to the Bainbridge Island shore at Crystal Springs. The 3-mile trip took about 3 minutes, but the 300-foot swath did considerable damage to some beach homes. Quoting from the *Searchlight*:

"The two-story frame home of C.O. Parmley, [about the 1300 block Jacobsen Boulevard] on the beach a half mile from the Manette point, unoccupied for the winter, was demolished. Doors and other substantial parts were found strewn over a range of several hundred feet. Not a part of the structure remained in an original position.

"A beach home owned by L.E. Hunton, [1300 block, Jacobsen Boulevard], and rented and occupied by E.B. Deyo was unroofed and badly shattered. Mr. Deyo and family were in Tacoma for the day. Returning last night they found their home shelterless.

"A residence owned by Mr. Frederickson [Charles Frederickson, 1618 Jacobsen Boulevard] also on Manette beach, was shorn of a big veranda, part of the roof thrown away and smaller utilities strewn about. L.E. Hunton lost a garage that was blown down and mingled with wreckage that covered a considerable territory."

On arriving at Bainbridge, the twister tore out the power line mast for the island and disrupted electric and phone service there.

BERNICE JACK THOMPSON and GRACE JACK BARLOW: We remember running out to see the sternwheeler go by...tobogganing in the winter down the hills...ice skating at Clare's Marsh...playing in the church orchestra and singing in the choir...taking the ferry to Bremerton before the bridge was built and playing on the underpinnings of the bridge after it was built...rowing out toward the ferries from Seattle and toward the battleships when they fired 21-gun salutes as they came into the navy yard...going on picnics at the Sandbanks, below what is now Bremerton Gardens...going up to Aldrichs' on the ferry dock for ice cream after dinner...buying horehound at the little store by the ferry dock...walking to the post office to pick up the mail...piano lessons from Esther Waugh and piano recitals...community club meetings over Merediths' grocery store....

We remember the Children's Home. We thought it was great to have so many kids to play with, but Mother said they had enough work to do without looking after us, too.... We always met the kids at the street and walked to school together.

We remember walking up to the Manette Playfield, sitting in the bleachers and watching the Jensen brothers hit home runs in the long summer evenings.

As we got older, our favorite destination for swimming was Twanoh State Park on Hood Canal. We also remember growing prize tomatoes. Every year the community club sponsored a garden contest for the kids and we enjoyed that.

RAY JACOBSEN: Ollie Avery's truck provided a job for many young fellows in Manette [1940s], among them Wayne Palmer, Gene and Ted Howerton, Ollie's younger brother Jim, and me.

Working for Ollie was inspirational. In spite of his crippling physical infirmities from polio, he always went with the driver on a job no matter how cold, wet, long or difficult, helping in any way he could and never voicing a complaint. Even today, when I start feeling sorry for myself and want to complain hoping for some sympathy, Ollie nearly always comes to mind along with the realization that my imagined problems are just that—imagined.

WALTER LAWSON: The first time I came here was in 1928 aboard the battleship *California*. We were in here about 6 months getting guns for the ship. We used to go to dances in the old American Legion Hall in West Bremerton. I married Alice Fellows in 1930.

MABEL LEE DICKSON: Entertainment consisted of picnics and swimming at the Sandbanks; baseball; ice skating at Clare's Marsh; school and Sunday School plays and recitals. For the adults—the Ladies Aid and get-togethers at one anothers' homes.... Fourth of July was a big event, with prizes for catching the pig and climbing the greased pole. Christmas was a time for the Manette Community Church pageant. After the pageant, small net bags were given to each child with a gift, an orange, nuts and ribbon candy.

Memories also include the dirt roads, board sidewalks, Mr. Bender's and Parker's sawmills, plums received and eaten at the blacksmith shop, the Childrens' Home, strawberries growing on the hillside of Jacobsen's home, Mr. Jacobsen's printing press and the poetry that came so readily to him, the principals at Manette School, including Mrs. Kallander, Mrs. Cornell and Mrs. Mills, who was the first principal—and always the baseball team.

DICK LINKLETTER: I have a connection with early Manette history. When I was young I stayed with my grandmother Emily Marlow in Seattle. Aunt Clare Peterson, a pseudo aunt who lived next door to Grandmother, took care of me when my grandmother was busy. Aunt Clare married Don Pitt. Don Pitt was an early sheriff here and Pitt Avenue was named for him.

Gideon Hermanson was active in getting the Manette Bridge built. He also worked with EBIC to make the bridge free. The bridge shows what community spirit can do. It is a monument to the spirit we have in this community.

JUNE MARTIN SCHWEER and JEANE MARTIN TURNELL: Perhaps some may remember a dog that frequented the soda fountain area at Martin's store and chewed off the ABC—already been chewed—gum deposited by customers on the under side of the stools. This dog was readily recognizable as he never learned to spit. When he was tired of chewing, the gum was transferred to his tongue and stuck onto his front legs. His legs had a very odd look.

ESTELLE MEREDITH: My first visit to Manette was as a guest at a party given to welcome the Wollevers home from Alaska in 1921. They had been my neighbors in 1916-17 when I worked in Anchorage. I was invited from Seattle, where I worked in my brother's (Claude Outland's) safe-deposit vault.

When Wollevers moved to Alaska they sold their house. When they returned they bought the same house back for twice as much as they had sold it for. Ferris Buchanan lives in the house at 220 Shore Drive today.

The party I attended was given by the Star and Compass 500 Club of the Eastern Star and Masonic Lodge to welcome Wollevers back into Manette. At the party, guests played a variation of the card game 500. I had never played cards since my family was Quaker. Clyde Meredith explained the game to me. Later we were married.

Clyde's partner was a girl nicknamed Happy. Other guests were Lewis and Ella Bender and their son Arthur with his wife Kate; Nels and Nellie Peterson; Len and Hulda Hunton; Arthur and Georgia Personette; Albert and Alma Gilman; Louis and Edna Bailey; Jack and Margaret Martin; Jack and Grace Carlaw; Ben and Mary Kean, and Bill and Jean Abbott.

Businesses I remember in the 1920s were Meredith and Son's grocery and feed store, with Joe and Ruby Tennis' bakery next door; Harry Martin's grocery store down East 11th Street; the post office with Mrs. Etta Eggleston, postmaster; Harrison's barber shop; Ben Kean's oil station down where the laundromat is now; Stone's meat market. Jack Martin built a general store on the corner of what is now East 11th Street and Perry Avenue. Mr. Harrison later had his barber shop in the same building.

The volunteer fire department bell was across the street from Meredith's store. When a fire was reported to the store, phone 425, Clyde would run across the street and ring the bell, calling volunteer firemen, who ran to the fire equipment that was kept in a garage next to Tennis' bakery.

Meredith's store building on the corner of East 11th Street and Scott Avenue was built for a general store. People had lived in it, too.... Later George Mitchell opened a grocery store next to the post office at East 11th Street and Perry Avenue.

At the dock for the Manette-Bremerton ferry was an open waiting room. Mr. and Mrs. Aldrich had an ice cream parlor at the shore end of the dock, Mr. Hawkes had a real estate office near the dock. Later he built an office on Winfield Avenue.

The Lewis Benders built a house down by the bridge during World War I and rented it out to officers off the navy ships.

Mrs. Perry and her son Olmstead were Clyde's parents' neighbors to the south. To the north were two Myers sisters. Between Merediths' house and Pitt Avenue Joaquina Feek's family were neighbors. Other early pioneers were the Cards and the Fellowses.

Everyone in Manette was friendly and helped neighbors in case of need. Families could leave for a week or two and never lock a door. Very few people had locks on their doors.

"Shorty" Shimasaki was a Japanese gardener who rented the greenhouses from Fellows. At that time non-citizens could not own property. Shorty raised fresh tomatoes and other fruits and vegetables that he sold to grocers in Manette and Bremerton. Shorty had no car at first so he delivered produce in a wheelbarrow or the grocer had his delivery truck pick up the order....

When his "mail-order" bride arrived from Japan, she was dressed in a beautiful dress with lace and ribbons. Shorty met her with his wheelbarrow and took her from the ferry dock up East 11th Street to their home.

That afternoon I took something up from our grocery store to where they lived behind the greenhouse. The bride sat in the living room dressed in her finery and Shorty was preparing dinner.

The next day I was up there again. The new bride was dressed in old clothes. She had a shovel and was working in the garden....

Clyde Meredith, my husband, put a railing around our grocery store entrance platform so children wouldn't fall off. He built a flower box around the top of the rail and Shorty kept flowering plants growing tn the box.

MARYJAYNE MEREDITH HLADKY: My father's uncle Frank, J.W. Meredith's brother, visited us for a few months each winter. He dealt cards in gambling houses in Alaska. He taught me to play pinochle before I started to school.

When Hoover was elected President in 1928 we were invited to Hugo and Carrie Berglind's home to hear the election returns on their radio.

Swimming at Nels and Nellie Peterson's camp on Hood Canal was an exciting treat. My father drove the Red & White delivery truck on the rough, narrow road from Manette to the canal and never exceeded 25 miles an hour. When we met another car, there were places where we had to pull off the road, not wide enough for two cars. Campfires in the evening when my Uncle Malcolm played his accordian and we sang were favorite times. Malcolm and Neal's shepherd dog, Kenney, joined the circle.

I took piano lessons from Esther Waugh when I was 4. Rejene Croxton taught ballet lessons in the hall over my father's grocery store and I was an avid student. Kate Bender gave singing lessons to several of us at her home after she spent the day teaching fourth and fifth grade classes at school. When I started seventh grade, I selected the flute and took lessons. When I went to the University of Washington I had to decide between music and nursing as a career.

When I was in the fourth grade, a classmate—George Cowan—contracted polio. He lived next door to my uncle Ralph and aunt Florence on Shore Drive near Von Hoene's. George died and I decided then that I would become a nurse and help prevent such tragedies. This feeling was reinforced when Norma Silvernail, who later became my sister-in-law, was crippled with polio. When I became nursing director in a health department in Florida, I was adamant about the school immunization program.

DICK MOTTNER: This is a story I recall about Orville Schultz: The navy used to have some funny looking little airplanes that would fly from Sand Point to Bellingham. One came in on my beach one time. It was about school time for Orville and he came walking by. The pilot got out of the cockpit all decked out in this big fuzzy suit. He asked Orville how he could get to Bremerton and to the navy yard. Orville said, "You walk right up that trail and straight to the end of the road. There's a ferry there—but it won't take airplanes."

WILLARD MULLER: Some of the Muller children's earliest memories of Manette:

The only grocery stores in Manette: Meredith's (groceries, hardware & feed), and Martin's. Your family was either a Meredith's or Martin's customer. Loyalty to one or the other was virtually complete.... The steamer *F.G. Reeve*, painted white, coming into the Manette Dock every afternoon at around 3 to offload freight and an occasional passenger before going on to Silverdale.

going on to Silverdale.

Other memories: Old man Moody, who lived at the top of the hill, on Hayward Avenue, about three or four houses past Mr. Shimasaki's greenhouses. Moody, tall, ancient looking, with a long white beard, was perhaps Manette's only Civil War veteran, and said he had been on Sherman's March to the Sea... Charlie Young, our fearless town constable...the Ruley family, who lived on the corner just west of Meredith's store. The Ruleys included the elderly mother, a grown son who attended Washington State College, where he played on the football team, and a grown daughter, and her little girl, Mercedes.

Still other memories: Scouts of Troop 505 going on over-night camping trips to Barker's Creek, between Tracyton and Silverdale, and being taught by the older boys about "snipe hunting." High-spirited boys gathering on Halloween night and pushing over outhouses. Once we were surprised, about the time we put our shoulders to Louie Bailey's privy, to hear his voice from inside threatening unbelievable consequences if we didn't cease and desist immediately. We did— and ran. Another time we braced against Ed Olson's outhouse stand-ing on his bulkhead. It went over, hit rocks below and split into kindling wood. We decided that was going beyond good fun, and after that reined in our privy pushing.... Mr. Jacobson's boatbuilding shop down on the beach, near the Hawthorne home, Ernie Stone and Booth homes. The Manette Community Church, attended by all except Catholics, who went to Bremerton. Every Christmas Eve there was the Christmas program. Always at one end of the platform stood a tall, beautifully decorated tree—lighted with big candles...this until the late 1920s. Isaac Hoopes, Sunday School superintendent, presided, children recited, Walter Wall played the violin, and Santa arrived, feet stomping, shouting merry greetings. He passed red or green netting stockings filled with ribbon candy and oranges to every child.

And still more memories: Kids doing their first ice skating in winter at Clare's Marsh (now part of the Brownsville high-way), and skiing on barrel staves down the Manette School hill. The Danel family, who lived kitty-corner from the Masonic Temple (after it was built in 1927), bringing their Atwater Kent radio, one of the very first in town, out to the front porch on summer evenings.... Townfolks gathered, stood in the yard, marveled at this new invention and listened to Amos and Andy...summer swimming and picnics at Island Lake Park. A whole generation of Manette boys learning to swim (in the buff) at the Sandbanks, a quarter-mile beyond McCougall's Creek.... People dancing to the western music of the Wicklund brothers' "Cascade Rangers" band at the Masonic Temple in the middle 1930s.

BONNY OLSEN PETTIT: I remember riding the *Pioneer* ferry...the bridge opening...the cherry trees everyone planted...kindergarten at Mrs. Hoopes' house. I enjoyed Girl Scouts and church activities.

The Enetai Beach road was in front of our house; then Jacobsen Boulevard went in [1933].... We used to sled on that one.

Roberta "Bobbie" Rue and her sister, Melva, lived farther down on the beach, at Illahee. Her father was county commis-sioner.... She had great Halloween parties. Shirley Bright had great birthday parties.... Other friends were the Akers kids, Orville Schultz, Bob Carlson, Virginia Galleher.... We had

Martin McGovern, 1920, in shoe repair shop in his home at 1376 Jacobsen Boulevard.-Photo from Anne Jacobsen

our shoes soled at Mr. [Martin] McGovern's and our hair cut by Cecil Owens. We bought our first candy from "Grampa Walker" at his little store next to Pearl and Bruno Lund's.

ROGER PAQUETTE: One of my most poignant memories of the early days is waking up on a foggy morning to the many different whistles used by the ferries to warn each other as they brought navy yard workers to the Bremerton docking spaces. The closer they approached their assigned piers, the more frequently they blew, until they sometimes overlapped. Each ferry had a distinct whistle: the lordly steam whistle on the *City of Bremerton,* the squeal of the smaller boats like the *Chickaree,* the *Evelyn Sharp,* the Port Orchard and Annapolis boats, and the *Pioneer* from Manette. Best of all was the *Pioneer!* It had an insolent squeal, a *peee-o-weet!.* Then all would be quiet for awhile, for they all docked at ap-proximately the same time.

When we bought our house at East 17th Street and Hayward Avenue in 1926, we became subscribers to the Bright water system ($1 per month) until the City of Bremerton, in the early 1930s, erected a new water tower across the street. The tank leaked when filled, and Lee Harrison, who had built a house just south of it, had a fine irrigation system for his garden.

One ride on the *Pioneer* I shall always remember took place on the 5 p.m. run from Bremerton. Nearly all yard workers rode this ferry home and no cars were allowed on this run as it was packed with foot passengers. A dozen or so men always stood in front of the restraining chain at the bow to be the first to jump off before the boat had properly docked. On this par-ticular run, as Harry Hansen, the pilot, threw the controls to reverse the propellers to slow the boat down, I heard the con-trol cable snap. There was no slowing down. The *Pioneer* went into the slip at a high speed. The men forward of the chain had no time to get back but they alertly jumped up onto the apron as the boat hit the slip then bounced back into the stream. The men who had jumped off turned around and waved at us as Harry put the boat back into forward thrust and slowly docked. Nobody was hurt.

The Sandbanks, located below Bremerton Gardens and

across from City Park, was a popular nude bathing area for young boys. How we stood the cold water I don't know. Its popularity came to an end in the early 30s when numerous complaints sent a Bremerton police officer to arrest us one summer afternoon. [See account in Chapter 10].

The Manette Dock was a fascinating place for a pre-teen boy. Loading and unloading cars on the *Pioneer* at low tide was not just routine. The ramp was quite steep and could lead to excitement when a truck tipped back and had to be pushed up...or when my mother put our 1922 Dodge in low gear to go down the ramp and then stepped on the clutch.... The *F.G. Reeve* would unload freight...scows would come with coal, sand, gravel or lumber for Ben Kean's fuel yard or Tracy's lumber yard. There was all kinds of fishing off the dock; salmon, perch, rock cod, pogies, bullheads, dog fish. Herring and smelt were taken with a snagging line.

One year we had an honest-to-gosh oil spill. The story went that somebody goofed on an oil line valve in the navy yard. Anyhow, it ruined the summer because Manette beaches, as well as others in the area, had a nice black gooey coating, which had the same effect as oil spills today. It took several years for the beaches to get back to normal.

George Personette said to me a few years ago, "You know, Roger, I've always felt very lucky that I grew up in Manette at the time we did. You could hunt, fish (fresh or salt water), steal Gravensteins from Fellows' orchard, go swimming at "bare pickle beach," and you didn't have to go far to do it—all within a 15-minute walk. Or you could go camping overnight with an hour's hike." They were wonderful years. So much for nostalgia!

DOROTHY PECKENPAUGH McALINDEN: The Fourth of July was always a big holiday when we were growing up in Sheridan. We looked forward to it with anticipation because some of our cousins would come from Seattle and there was usually a picnic in the neighborhood. And then there were fireworks.

Our father would buy a big bag of firecrackers, rockets and other noisemakers and hide the bag someplace until the big day. In the evening we would walk down to the Sheridan Dock, where our father would set up a trough to shoot our rockets in the direction of the bay. He would give each of us our share of fireworks and we would have a great time shooting them off toward the bay.

In 1921 I was 6 and ready for the first grade. Sheridan School was almost 2 miles distant. There were no school busses and I walked to school.

Since I was the oldest of three children, this first day of school was an especially big family event.

The first day of school arrived and our family was up early to help me get ready. We children dressed downstairs by the pot-bellied heater. First I put on my new underwear, which had long legs and arms like long johns. It also had garters attached so when I pulled on my long black stockings I fastened them to the garters. Next I put on my new black bloomers, a white petticoat and my new red plaid dress. All of these garments had been made by my mother. Mother helped me pull on my black high-top shoes and laced them and tied them with a double knot. To all this I added a sweater, a raincoat, a bonnet and gloves.

I picked up my lunch bucket and book bag and started for school. The road to the school was uphill. I'm positive no other child wore as many clothes as I did.

I was thrilled with school and loved the teacher, Miss Clemmons. She had a sweet face and fluffy white hair piled high. She put letters on the blackboard and had us sound them out: a, e, i, o and u. What fun!

At recess I would rush out to watch the other children play. I was shy so did not take part in their games.... The bathroom was a gray wooden building called a "four-holer." With all the clothes I wore, it was a big job to go to the bathroom. It was hard to get the buttons undone and even harder to get them fastened. Sometimes this operation took up a whole recess.

At lunchtime we would go out behind the school and sit on logs and tree stumps to eat. It was great fun to exchange sandwiches and cake and cookies. Then we would wander through the brush and eat huckleberries.

Since it was downhill, walking home was easy. At the bottom of one long hill there was a bridge that crossed a stream. The Ammerman family lived nearby. David Ammerman used to hide beneath the bridge and moan and cry to frighten me. I peered over the railing and soon figured out who was making the noise.

MARTHA PECKENPAUGH BECKER: Our mother baked the best nut bread I've ever tasted. One of my fondest memories is coming in from school, when Mother would slice off a good-sized piece and smother it with fresh butter for our after-school snack.... Midgie, Mother's canary, was a beautiful singer, as was our mother. When Mother was preparing supper she would stand at the sink peeling potatoes and she and Midgie would sing together. To me it was the most beautiful music I have ever heard.

Christmas was a special occasion. One Christmas I received (from Santa) a beautiful silver cradle for my newest baby doll. The cradle was actually a doll carriage which had belonged to my sister. Father had taken the wheels off, put rockers on and painted it a shiny silver color. Mother had lined and quilted the inside.... Our parents were very talented with making do with what they had. Many of our gifts were handmade by Daddy with his hammer and saw and Mama with her sewing machine or needle and thread.

It was great to get sick in our house.... Mother would make delicious fresh egg custard and a pot of tea.... At age 11 I came down with the mumps. I went downstairs and told her I hurt near my ears. She put me to bed and tied my mumps with a dish towel. She gave me a bite from a dill pickle. When I cried that it hurt she said,"You've got the mumps all right." I knew I'd be getting some egg custard and tea and felt better right away.

ESTHER PRICE: I was born in our home across the road from Fellows' home on Perry Avenue. Alice [Fellows] and I played together. After Dad built our home on Ryther Estate property, our playground was part of what later became the Maple Leaf Tavern grounds.

LLOYD L. PRICE: I recall ice-skating on Clare's Marsh; Bright's bottling works and their soda-pop delivery by horse and buggy; the Ryther family—across from the Price's in 1911-12; the Lee family—Hal Lee was to become famous in basketball; the Fellows family—with a 50-foot water tower, a carbide lighting plant and a greenhouse operated by a

Japanese, Mr. Shimasaki...Grandpa Jake Waltenburg—a government hunter who hunted cougars in and around Manette.... The Hilstad Dray Company had great draft horses that hauled coal and fuel; the Parker family had horses that hauled building materials and groceries; the Meredith family had cayuse horses that delivered groceries.... My brother Sid and I picked cherries at Grandma Peterson's place in Illahee and sold them at the navy yard gate.

Our address was simply Manette. Our mail came to the post office in Martin's Dry Goods Store.

Archie Ruley and Heinie Johnson were pitchers on the Manette baseball team in the early days...the Bledsoe family sold cosmetics from door to door.... School teachers I remember were Miss Iverson, Miss Pompelli and Miss Kallander.

We fished in McMicken's Creek in Enetai. We used to go by 1914 Ford on a bumpy, narrow road to Island Lake, which was surrounded entirely by forest. We enjoyed many picnics there.

Clifford Fellows, a Manette neighbor, was my real buddy. We roomed together in Seattle.

My father went up into the thick woods near where Harrison Memorial Hospital is today, bought two lots, whacked out a little clearing, plowed an area for a garden, built a house, dug a well, built an outhouse and moved the family into this one-room house...there were four of us children.... My brother Sidney, sister Dorothy and I all went to the old one-room Manette School. After a couple of years they built a four-room schoolhouse and we transferred to it.

During that time my father built a new 6-room house next to the one-room house. He went into the woods and packed out timbers for the sills.... We used the one-room house for the kitchen after that.... Father contracted to take lumber from the old hotels and other buildings standing where the navy yard was going to expand near the YMCA.

A man named Parker lived between the high-tension tower and Sheridan Road.... The hills in that area have been leveled now, but they were steep in those days. Parker had to whip his horses to make them go up those hills. He was quite a man, bootlegging on the side, I guess.... During World War I, Dad built many houses...house tents, and anything people could live in; he would build to rent or sell. He had taken over the Ryther Estate that had a big square 10-room house on the beach.... We had chickens and ducks, a well and an outhouse.

MELVIN RENN: In the 1920s early logging had left the land clear except for a few tall single trees. Our view from East 18th Street and Trenton Avenue covered the area from north of the Waterman dock to Port Orchard.

There were only three houses besides ours in this landscape. They were located southeast of us on the edge of the hill overlooking the beach.

The first house was on the edge of Jacobsen's canyon and known as the Javi place. The house sat empty from about 1924 until the influx of World War II people. In all that time no one broke the windows, stole the furniture or otherwise bothered the place except to hunt pheasants and pick the cherries—part of the good old days. The inside walls were painted with murals from floor to ceiling and they were works of art. The walls had been entirely covered with wallpaper and the paintings didn't show up until years later when dampness allowed the wallpaper to come loose.

The story behind the house was that three brothers from Belgium built it before World War I. At the start of that war they returned to Belgium to join their army; one brother was killed the first week and another was killed the last day of the war; the third brother returned to Manette and raised rabbits for awhile. He left again about 1924.

The next house north was occupied by another Belgian family named Van Almond. They were older people and had a very old grandmother who was dying. My mother, who did practical nursing at times, walked over to the house every day for a month or more to take care of the old lady until the end. My mother's pay was an old family picture worth about $10.

The next family in the house was the Vandenbrocks, also from Belgium. They had escaped from Antwerp during the invasion. The father was a diamond cutter and told about sewing diamonds in the lining of the children's clothing to keep the Germans from confiscating them.

The two children in the family were Felix and Marie. The old man became homesick and returned the whole family to Antwerp about 2 years before World War II. Felix survived the whole war in the king's army. Marie married into the English royal family. The father was killed in a bombing. The mother made a brief visit to her sister's in Manette and Bremerton after the war and then returned to England.

The third house was occupied by part of the Van Almond family and later by the Adrian Daley family. The Daleys had a son, Eugene, and two daughters, Margaret and Ruth. Ruth, the youngest child, was badly burned by a grass fire one hot summer day. She survived after weeks of skin grafts and medical care. The fire spread through the grass and the orchard, nearly taking the house. It then spread into Jensen's canyon, where we fought it for about a week.

ADA SCHOONOVER MATTESON: I remember when we finally got electricity. Men came and spent the day wiring our house. Cords hung from the ceilings, with a bulb hanging in each, and a long chain which we could pull to turn the light on or off.... This man stuck his finger up into the socket, pulled the string and said "Yep, there's juice." So after they left, I climbed on a chair, pulled the string, stuck my finger in the socket, nearly fell off, but I said to my two sisters, "Yep, there's juice." My first big jolt.

My uncle, Herman Waugh, sold insurance. He had a customer who didn't have much money but had an old white horse. So dear Uncle Herman (God rest his soul) took the old white horse in trade. Since they lived on a city lot and we had 2 acres, he brought the horse to our place to pasture. This was great. It was summer and no school, so us kids and all the kids from Manette had a great time. We rode that old plug from morning till night. We had a real great summer.

The poor old horse got tired, I guess, because Uncle Herman gave him away to a man in Silverdale. Well, the poor old horse died and the man didn't know quite how to dispose of him, so he left him in the pasture hoping the poor thing would just disappear. The neighbors "caught wind" of the situation and started to voice their opinion. Since the man had some dynamite which was left over from blowing up stumps earlier, he figured this was a good way to dispose of the carcass. He planted the dynamite under the horse and blew it over a large part of Silverdale.

Sure did miss that old horse, and the fun summer.

Manette School, which was a big square brown-on-top and white-on-the-bottom building, housed a basement, two rooms on the first floor and two rooms with an office on the top floor. Each classroom had a cloak room where we hung our coats and put our galoshes. It often reeked with various odors. When we were bad, we had to spend time meditating our sins in the cloak room.... The principal's office was a dreaded place. When we were really bad we were sent there to receive a spanking.

The ferry boat that crossed from Manette to Bremerton had cabins on either side, one side for the ladies and the other for the men (the men smoked on their side). Two benches were in each cabin—one along the outside and the other along the inside. The center part of the boat was for cars. I think eight cars was the capacity.

One day in the late 1920s we docked on the Manette side on our way home from Lincoln Junior High School. A rowboat pulled up at the end of the ferry with Bill Schweer in it urging the kids to get in and he would take them ashore. Harold Christensen decided that was a great idea, so he attempted to climb aboard. In doing so, he upset the rowboat and all aboard had a good ducking.

In the winter time after the bridge was built we'd take our sleds, ride down Perry Avenue and make the turn down the main street of Manette. Then we'd walk up the incline of the bridge as far as the span, being careful not to be seen by the tolltakers on the other side. Down we would slide, ending up by the Harkins house at the end of the street.

Church and school were the basis of the Manette community. We had plays, musicals and get-togethers for many occasions. Everyone turned out and it was always fun. Some of our best memories were Christmas Eve at the church. We could hardly wait. We had pieces to say and songs to sing. Elizabeth von Hoene played the piano and Mrs. Hawthorne led the music. Mr. Hoopes was the superintendent. What we all looked forward to and listened for were the sleigh bells from Santa Claus, alias Tom Bright. He would come down the aisle shouting "Merry Christmas!" and shaking the sleigh bells. We would all get excited. There was always an orange and a little pasteboard box of hard candy—the best candy of all—and something nice from our Sunday School teacher.

ORVILLE SCHULTZ: I recall—learning to row a boat and rowing from Enetai to Waterman Dock for ice cream...bringing in logs to be cut up for firewood...living in a tent...walking along the beach and trails to Manette School...running to catch the ferry *Pioneer* to get to Lincoln School in 1928...standing in line for the "movie show" in Bremerton...playing soccer at Manette School...watching Dad with an old crystal set which was our radio. There was no electricity or modern radio in those days...being sick with the flu. Many people died during the epidemic of World War I...Clare's Marsh for ice skating...Mr. Fellows' greenhouses...the fire siren on the pole...Charlie Young, the Manette constable, and Halloween trick-or-treats...Enetai Point at low tide with its old ballast rocks...the delivery man bringing groceries from Meredith's store and Archie Bouchard from Etten's with his meat truck...early cars on the beach—Bruno Lund's, Dad's, Emil Olsen's, Charley Frederickson's—and the old one-way road down on Enetai Beach. The tides coming in and washing out the roads...watching the sternwheeler *Bailey Gatzert* go by...Grandpa Walker's little store...digging clams and geoducks at Enetai Point.

BILL SCHWEER: Wendell Abernathy or his older brother drove a Model-T Ford taxi that sometimes met the *Pioneer* and drove people home. One day he parked down on the dock and went to Slim Aldrich's pool hall for coffee. Some of the "Vandals" (an athletic club with Axel Jacobsen, Scott Harrington, Paul Almon and others) saw the taxi and carried it down and set it crossways on the ferry slip and then disappeared to watch from a distance. When the ferry arrived, the passengers all had to help carry the taxi back up the slip while Abernathy tried to explain how it happened.

Manette's summertime sport was skinny dipping at the Sandbanks, just beyond McDougals' canyon, below what is now Bremerton Gardens. Swimming consisted of warming oneself to a fine toast in the hot sand, running into the cold 58-degree water, swimming furiously and running out thoroughly chilled to bury into the warm sand again. Civilization began its usual erosion of the simple pleasures when the swift incoming tide forced boats and the Silverdale ferry, *F.G. Reeve*, close to the beach each evening. Also, across the bay at Evergreen City Park, people were training binoculars on the Sandbanks. Complaints of the nude swimming in Manette flooded in.

Poor Charlie Young, our constable, tried to enforce the new rules. Excuses such as "I can't afford a swim suit" fell on deaf ears as Charlie explained how a suit could be fashioned from a gunny sack by cutting holes in the corners. Charlie and the Bremerton police hatched a cunning plan...[Several persons wrote accounts of the police raid on the Sandbanks. For one of them, see "The Last Swim" in Chapter 10.]

The swimming continued, of course, but those lucky enough to be arrested gained great prestige and envy within their circles of influence.

It was fun growing up in a small town. I remember walking along Manette's wooded trails eating sour grass...picking trilliums in the spring...hiking to Big Rock to dig for licorice root...walking through McDougal's Canyon on a hot afternoon and drinking from the stream of water coming out of a small hole in an exposed pipe...swiping cherries at night at the Benders' and strawberries at Jensens' farm...joining a group of kids after dinner, choosing up sides and playing Run Sheep Run, Red Light, Duck on the Rock or baseball in the long summer evenings.

When it snowed, coasting all the way from Nelson's to the end of the dock. On Halloween, making Constable Charlie Young's outhouse the number one target...figuring the evening was not complete until the water was turned off to Enetai, the fire alarm rung and a couple of fire hydrants turned on.

At Manette School, playing Crack the Whip in the morning, especially when a new kid could be maneuvered to the "whip" end and, strangely enough, be flipped off into the septic tank outflow area at the bottom of the hill.... Waiting with the "gang" upstairs in the school for Jim Armstrong to pull the school bell rope on the floor below and then pulling him up off the floor as the rope came up; collecting the best and biggest ripe horse chestnuts from the tree across from Wheaton's place...playing hookey to go ice skating on Clare's Marsh.

Smelling the lilacs at Ella Bender's in the spring; playing Follow-the-Leader on bicycles and trying to master, with equally disastrous results, teeter board and ladder acts seen at the circus; fishing for perch under the Manette ferry slip and watching the *Reeve* offload freight onto the dock.

And the night we were waiting in Bremerton to go home on the *Urania*. The luminous white jellyfish caught our attention so we caught them and smeared the luminous slime around our eyes so we would look like the Phantom of the Opera in the movie we had just seen.

Do kids still spin tops in the spring? Roll hoops? Or take their best girls to the Saturday matinee weekly serial, "Casey of the Coast Guard"?

VIVIAN SWAN GRAVES: I remember the frigid dip in the bay each November by Opal Swan, Annie Frith and Mrs. Tim Cole...My brother Forrest, at about age 5, falling into the water off our float. The water was over Opal's head and she could not swim. She put her leg through a space between the boards and could just barely reach his sleeve. She pulled him up.

My almost daily trips down the beach to Jacobsen's for milk...The trail through the woods and over the hill that all the beach residents used daily...the large trees that Hugh felled on top of the hill, cut into stove lengths and rolled to the beach. Someone had to stand guard on the trail to see that no one was there. One time a tree knocked down a yellow-jacket nest and Hugh had quite an experience getting around them. He cut the tree from each end but I do not remember how he solved getting the wood near the nest.

The little boat that took us back and forth to Bremerton. People went down a gangplank to a float to get on the boat. One day the float tipped, dumping all the people into the water. One woman drowned. All the rest were pulled from the water. I remember Dad telling about helping roll the woman over a barrel trying to get the water out of her. Dad was at the top of the gangplank so was not thrown into the water, but he went to help pull the others to safety.

The time Dad and Forrest were towing a long log with the rowboat out by the lighthouse and were caught in a rip tide. The log started to swirl around them, and Dad was barely able to get it untied and turned loose. They were both mighty scared.

Shopping at Martin's store when it was down by the waterfront...picking up the mail at the little post office next door to the Fryett Department Store on Perry Avenue...Mrs. Eggleston was the postmistress.... A little hummingbird built its nest for 2 years in a row on a branch of a tree in our yard, so low that even I could look into it. The bird was not afraid of us.

November 11, 1918, the day the Armistice was signed. Hundreds of people, mostly navy yard workers, gathered in the street at the corner of First and Pacific and did they celebrate! They danced, sang, yelled, blew horns and burned an effigy of the Kaiser. They celebrated for hours. Dad took us over to Bremerton and we watched from a distance.

JEWELL TENGE SOLLIE: We moved here in 1928. I remember the fun bob-sledding on East 11th Street from the top of the hill clear down onto the dock. It was a long walk back but the whole community was out there and we were all getting lots of exercise and having a lot of fun—no cars. Constable Charlie Young blocked off the best street for sledding, so the few cars in town had to use another route.

I'm one of the few of my age group that stayed here. Many of my friends moved away but I've never been sorry that I stayed.

CARL LEE TENNISON (Remembrances of Manette from my diary):

1942, March 6 -A new Safeway and Aldrich Drug Store opened in Manette..

1943, January 19 -Eighteen inches of snow!...

1943, February 18 -Fuel oil and grocery ration books received. I got 12 gallons of gas for $2.58...

1948, June 17 -Ground was broken for a new school in Manette...

1951, June 11 -45-year-old Manette Church burned down...

1958, November 26 -Warren Avenue Bridge opened...

1972, October 24 -Warren Avenue Bridge toll-free. First car across was a 1916 Buick which I drove..

1979, February 13 -Hood Canal Bridge sank in 105-mph wind.

MARGARET VON HOENE PAINTER: I remember at Christmas—at Meredith's store Clyde Meredith gave each of us children a piece of sugar cane—this big.... Later, when we were living in the Philippines, every time I saw the sugar cane I thought of Clyde Meredith and Manette. He also gave us candies every time we paid our bill.

Frances von Hoene was official ribbon-cutter when the Manette Bridge was freed. She still has a piece of the ribbon.

I remember Mrs. Croxton had a very long, graceful neck. She wore a black velvet ribbon around it with sometimes a pearl and sometimes a diamond pin. I thought—if only I could have a neck like that.

BRUCE WALKER: I remember Bill Schweer digging for arrowheads. One day he found a skull up·on the Children's Home grounds. He cleaned it up and Dr. Bender (dentist) cemented the teeth back into it. Bill had it up in his den. He had a small microphone behind it that was wired to the radio downstairs. Whenever the radio downstairs played, the skull up there was singing to him.

My wife Myrle and I were living in the upstairs flat of a beach house along Shore Drive. The house was owned by a well-known boat-builder, Jacobson, who had a contract with the government to operate the beacon light and foghorn on the dolphin off Point Herron. Underwater cables ran from the dolphin to the upstairs porch of the Jacobson house.

The beacon light was activated automatically by a light-sensitive "magic eye" but the foghorn had to be switched on manually from the porch. That was Myrle's and my responsibility—24 hours a day. That was how we paid the rent.

The trick was to develop a feel for fog. One learned to smell it.

Around 1:30 a.m. Myrle and I were just about scared out of our pajamas by distress signals—short blasts from the *Chippewa*. The blasts seemed to come from just outside the window.

"My God!" we thought, as we leaped out of bed and dashed for the porch, "the fog must have sneaked in on us and we didn't turn the horn on!"

To our great relief the stars were visible and there was no fog. However, we could see the running lights of the *Chippewa* offshore, much too close for comfort but not quite aground.

The crew managed to wrestle the huge anchor to the bow's edge and over into the water with sufficient line attached to reach the bottom, thus arresting the drifting of the helpless ferry.... Myrle and I did not get booted out for what could have been a dereliction of duty.

ELSIE WILSEN SAYLER: Our church was the Manette Community Church. Dad was one of the founders.... We went by small launch with all our lunch baskets and ice cream in 5-gallon containers to picnics at Chico and Waterman.... The old Manette Dock was located at the site that became Parker's lumber yard. Martin's grocery store was across Shore Drive, where the plumbing shop is now. Martin's store later was moved to 2105 East 11th Street where Manette TV is today.

We had boardwalks with two large planks up Perry Avenue. I was always getting my shoes caught between the boards and falling. Perry Avenue was a very steep hill before it was graded down and blacktopped.

When I was very small a solicitor from Martin's grocery came on Tuesdays and took orders for groceries. Groceries were delivered on Fridays by a wagon pulled by two horses.

We had a lane from our property to Perry Avenue and a small path across to Winfield Avenue, which was a narrow road. The road wound around down East 18th to Marlow and by a narrow bridge across a canyon to what is now Wheaton Way, then finally came out on a beach road to Tracyton.... I was a fourth grader when I made my first trip by car. It was a Model-T and we went to Tracyton. Quite an event.... We used to have lots of snow when I was in grade and high school.... Axel Jacobsen made a big bobsled out of planks. It would hold 15 adults—what fun we had sliding.

When I was in grade school (1920s) there were approximately 200 families living in Manette, so we knew 'most everyone.

I graduated from the eighth grade in 1926. I attended Union High School, later called Bremerton High School, located between 4th and 5th Streets on High Avenue.

In 1930 the Manette Bridge was opened. How sad we were when a Bremerton girl won the contest to be queen at the ceremony. A bunch of us staged our own ceremony the night before the official opening of the bridge. Mary Soyat, runner-up in the contest, was a Manette girl and she was queen for us that night. We had songs and fun.

People I remember are Len Bright, Ed Warren, Ken Tappe, Callow Mason, Ellen Munson and the Indians—I think their name was Saxon.

After our family arrived in Seattle from Ohio in 1909 we took a hack to the Galbreth Pier, where we boarded the old *Norwood*.

I recall Bill Harris' real estate office, Martin's grocery and the Manette Improvement and Investment Company office.

The Tom Fellowses were among the Manette residents, and the Millers, Mikkelsons, Karsts, Brights, Pfennings, Morrises, Averys, Brewsters, Cards, and Farmers—and the Wilsens with all the girls.... Most people had their own wells for water but the down-towners had a water system of wooden pipes.... The Bright boys made and sold pop by the bottle in the early days.

ROY WORKMAN: Sometime in 1942 or 1943 a barrage balloon at the southwest corner of the old Manette School grounds raised suddenly, broke its cable, and continued raising, heading north, with a long cable trailing.... It was a unique incident for anyone at anytime to see.

LARRY WORLAND: Manette was a community. We were separated from Bremerton. The only thing that joined us was a water main across the narrows and the ferry *Pioneer*, operated by Harry Hansen and Bob Carter. It cost a nickle to cross on that ferry. A lot of times we kids didn't have a nickle and Bob would put us on anyway.

While I was in Manette as a child I had many a "father." Manette was a community. If someone saw you getting out-of-hand he took you under his wing and straightened you out like a father.

...Those board sidewalks—we had a bicycle and we'd come down East 11th Street. The planks ran parallel with the street. There was a crack between the planks wide enough to catch the front wheel of your bike and throw you clear out.

The Manette Volunteer Fire Department had a Model-T Ford fire truck, garaged in an old shed that Clyde Meredith owned east of his store. The town fathers worked hard getting that truck started for the run. It took a lot of cranking, frustration, and eventually a push down the hill.... The fire bell hung from a tower down the hill from the post office on East 11th Street between Perry and Scott Avenues.

...A construction crew dug up a large granite rock at East 11th Street and Perry Avenue. This rock was moved to the east end of the Manette Bridge to mark the location of the old Indian fort. My father, George T. Worland, built a sled.... The rock was loaded on it and pulled behind the gas shovel used on the street project. This rock still marks the location of Manette's Indian fort.

DON YOUNG: Alice (Fellows) Lawson was one of my old girlfriends. She was born September 6, 1910, and I was born September 6, 1909. My dad was heading for Montana to work in the mines when there was no work here...he'd taken our old horse up to Ralph Elliott and traded him for a big fur coat.... Lincoln Heights dance hall up on Perry Avenue was where we went with our folks. We'd dance around for awhile and then they'd lay us out in the back room on benches to go to sleep.

I had two sisters on the float that Sunday night when the float for the ferries *Pioneer* and *Urania* tipped over and dumped about 40 people into the bay. One person lost her life. The accident happened when the *Urania* pulled in to tie up. The tide was running out strong and when all those people got on one side of the float it flipped the thing right up and dumped everybody into the bay. Some younger kids swam to shore. My sisters hung on to a piling and someone pulled them in through the windows of the boat. David Swan said his folks were going over to church and his dad had forgotten his wallet and went back home to get it [and so missed the experience]. That was in 1919. [See the account in TRANSPORTATION]

...The county road workers came down to Smith Hill gravel pit hauling gravel.... They'd have a donkey on one end and the trucker back under...he couldn't see when the scraper came up, so I used to sit on top of the bank and whistle when the scraper came up. I was just a little kid.... They logged with a donkey engine that pulled logs out of the woods.

Charley Parker had two mules down at Hillman City. That whole greasewood hill was staked out in lots. This promoter Hillman would bring excursions over every weekend on the little steamer *Yosemite*, then sell the people a lot. He piled the

Yosemite up on the rocks at Fort Ward and that pilot house was on top of those rocks for years.

I recall when the ferry *City of Bremerton* ran aground. The old quartermaster, a big red-faced guy, came around Waterman Point and never straightened her up. He ran right into the beach full blast. It was about midnight. We didn't get off that beach until high tide came in early in the morning.

A navy tug came out and pulled a tight pull on the *City of Bremerton*. He pretty near burned his tug up. Then another tug came out...J. Smith was the chief in charge. He hooked a one-inch cable on the cleat and made a run. He pulled the cleat and all the boards in the deck apart. Then he said, "I can't do nothing for you," and left.

...Jay Burlew and Art Holden were great horseshoe players. When I was a little kid we used to come down to Aldrich's store on the upper end of the dock to pick up a newspaper. Jay and Art were always down there playing horseshoes.

PHOTO MEMORIES

WORLD WAR II

Gasoline ration stamps.

In the service, circa 1942. From left are Elwood Walls (Grant Martin's cousin), Grant Martin and Jack Bender.
-Photo from Bill Schweer

Barrage balloon, sandbagged down at Manette School. Balloons, cable-tethered, were sent aloft as hazards to enemy airplanes.   -Photo from Elmine Ricks

Barrage balloon crew and quarters (tents) near Manette School.   -Photo from Gladys Solid

ROADS AND TRAILS

Manette waterfront, 1920s. This trail led north from the Manette Dock toward the Sandbanks.

Tom McManamna and Kevin Schultz, grandsons of Orville and Virginia Schultz, on Big Rock in 1986. Old-timers recall the rock as being at the end of a trail through the woods. Today it is seen from the paved Illahee Road.   -Photo from Orville Schultz

Clare's Marsh, February 11, 1951. Water flooded Brownsville Highway near Wheaton Way and Riddell Road—again.

CARS AND SUCH

Walter Fellows' 1918 Velie. Bill Filion changing tire.
          -Photo from Walt Fellows

Sam Hall in his E.M.F. The car was one of the first in Manette.   -Photo from Ken Hall

William Enkeboll in his Overland roadster, 1922.
-Photo from William Enkeboll

Logging Sheridan School land, circa 1920. Standing on truck bed, dwarfed by fir butt, is David Smith.
-Photo from Ruth Smith-Byrne Lockwood

Charles Ballew's 1929 Studebaker. Peter Rath's home at right rear.   -Photo from Robert Ballew

George Abernathy's Model-T Ford, 1918. In back seat is Allie Abernathy with Wendell. Front seat, Elton. Standing (from left), Earl Huff Abernathy, George Abernathy and Archibald Thistle Huff.
-Photo from Wendell Abernathy

Bill Schultz's 1921 Model-T Ford.
-Photo from Orville Schultz

Road job. Grader works on East 16th Street.   -Photo from Holden album

Hot rods and hot rodders, 1937. Ford 1 (left): Betty Thompson, Henry Fischer, Donald Waltenburg, Willis Waltenburg. Ford 2: David Lawing, Larry Worland. Ford 3: Joe Fischer, Jerry Fischer, Eugene Howerton, Fred Hunter.

CAMARADERIE

Constable Charlie Young feeding Manette's pet deer "Honey Boy" circa 1930. Worlands' home in background. Deer was believed driven into town by dogs; was later sent to Woodland Park Zoo in Seattle.

Hannah Hibbard and friend. Hannah was wife of Puget Sound Navy Yard master sheet metal worker Ralph Hibbard. The Hibbards had acreage at Sylvan Way and Trenton Avenue. Hannah lived to be 103 (1859-1962).
-Photo from Evelyn Holden Newkirk

Bill Schultz (center), son Orville (left) and Bruno Lund playing three-handed pinochle in front of Schultz home on Enetai Beach, 1922.   -Photo from Orville Schultz.

Bill Schweer, Floyd Buchanan and George McKeown camping out, 1920s.   -Photo from Bill Schweer

*Fellows' burro "Prinny," 1906. Rider is Harold Steven, whose father later became a clerk at Martin's grocery.
-Photo from Walt Fellow*

*Playmates, circa 1929. From left are Jean Hendrickson, Joe Martin, Faith Martin and Joyce Walsh.
-Photo from Lou and Hazel (Hendrickson) Nagle*

*Buddies, circa 1932. From left are Jack Geiser, Bruce Walker, Fritz Graebke, Bill Schweer, Harold Christensen, Melvin Renn and George McKeown.
-Photo from Bill Schweer*

Fun on Sunday, 1926. Back row (from left), Mildred Ross, Florence Fellows, Alice Fellows, Mrs. Mary Fellows, Elizabeth von Hoene, Evelyn Aldrich, Mrs. Ethel Aldrich. Front row, Anna Parkins, Evelyn Holden, Muriel Rodger, Margaret von Hoene.

Jake Williams driving his mules, early 1930s. Along for the ride are (from left), Donald and Edwin Walten-burg, Frances and Ray Hall and Robert Ballew.   -Photo from Robert Ballew

SUMMER FUN

Boating, circa 1916. Axel Jacobsen is at motor and his parents Jens and Minnie and brother Olav amidships. Either this motor or another Axel owned was a Motorgo but Axel's father dubbed it "Motorstop."

-Photo from Gertrude Wall Carr

Wet feet, circa 1929. Wading in Port Washington Nar-rows are Laura Ellis and Bernice, Grace and Ruth Jack. Manette Dock in background.

-Photo from Bernice Jack Thompson

Manette bathing beauties, early 1920s. From left are Edna Hoopes, Emily McHenry, Ruth Nosker, Hazel Nosker and Grace Hook. Walt Fellows' Velie at right.   -Photo from Walt Fellows

Members of the Hubbell family of Sheridan afloat, circa 1910. From left, Mary, Hallie, Eliza, Dot and Alice.
                                    -Photo from Irene Parker

Picknicking at the Sandbanks, early 1920s. The picknickers are (from left) Merwin McKnight, Mrs. McKnight and son, and Helga, Anna and William Enkeboll.
                        -Photo from Helga Enkeboll Behr

Fun at the Sandbanks, 1918. From left are Anna Anderson's two children; Anna; Gladys Olsen Solid; Marguerite Olsen Bright; Lucille Olsen Van Dyke, and Lucian Wilcox.   -Photo from Gladys Olsen Solid

The Sandbanks. Photo taken in 1941 after Eastpark was built.   -Photo from Edna Hoopes Brookman

HOLIDAY FUN

Children's Day Parade, East 11th Street, 1935

Ruth Danel (left) and Esther Buchanan in May Day costumes, 1926. -Photo from Ruth Danel Blasberg

Valentines, 1918-1925 style. Margaret von Hoene received these. Margaret is now Mrs. Bruce Painter and lives in Eatonville.

Elgie Hoffman speaking at an Independence Day celebration in 1911. Platform was built just north of present Manette Bridge approach. Hoffman now lives at 827 6th Street in Bremerton.
-Photo from Elgie Hoffman

May Day sailors' hornpipe dance group, 1920s. Back row (from left), _____, Arlene Wilsen, Anna Jo Harkins, Martha Palmer, Jeane Martin, Ada Schoonover, Bernice Pedersen, Helga Enkeboll. Front row, Margaret Hoopes, Mayzie Ballew, Mildred Starevich, Edna Mae Rath, Louise Waugh, Helen Akers. -Photo from Helga Enkeboll Behr

Show biz. These Manette School fourth-graders performed in a colonial days school play in February 1914. From left are Neal Harrington, Florence Clark, Emma Whitehead, Regina Peppard, Mayme Collins, Lois Casey, Ella Jennings, Morgan Avery, Will Dewar, John McDougall, Earl Bright, Charles Dewar, Bert Card and Malcolm Meredith.
-Photo from Neal Harrington Meredith

Halloween Party at Enkeboll home (324 Shore Drive), circa 1925. Back row (from left), Ervin Jensen, dressed as a girl; William Enkeboll, ghost; Bill Schweer; Laska Clark; Edith Jensen, dressed as a boy; _____. Middle row, Helga Enkeboll, _____, Kenneth Hall, Marjorie Woods, Katherine Bratt. Front row, Dorothy Crowell., Edna Mae Rath, _____, _____, _____, _____ McKnight
- Photo from Helga Enkeboll Behr

Christmas Cheer. Manette's Tom Bright was a department store Santa Claus for many years. This photo was taken in 1956 at Frederick and Nelson's in Seattle. With Santa are his wife Carrie as "Aunt Hollie" and grandchildren (from left), Timothy, Sheryl and Dan Baker.

OLD HOUSES

A few of the residences of early Manette still stand but many have been lost to time. Some of those shown here date back to the turn of the century.

John Morris, "Melrose Farm."
-Photo from Kitsap County plat book, 1909

Omar and Rometta Senn, 2704 East 13th Street.
-Photo from Orville Schultz

OLD MANETTE HOUSES, continued

Neil McDougall, west end of East 16th Street.
-Photo from Kitsap County plat book, 1909

Peter Highstead, 305 Shore Drive.
-Photo from Gertrude Wall Carr

John H. "Jack" and Margaret Martin, 2612 East 13th Street.

John and Grace McNeill, 2315 Cascade Trail.

Ole and Josefine Lillevick, 1617 Wheaton Way.

Robert and Mary McKeown, 4410 Perry Avenue.
-Photo from Hattie Engstrom

M. R. and Mary Brewster, "Fernwood Ranch," where Latter-Day Saints Church stands today at 2225 Perry Avenue. -Photo from Kitsap County plat book, 1909

Soren Mikkelson, County Road, now 1146 Perry Avenue. -Photo from Kitsap County plat book, 1909

OLD MANETTE HOUSES, continued

Oscar and Walda Solibakke's rented home at 1105 Perry Avenue. Standing, (back to front), are Gertrude Wall (now Carr) and Herbert, Eda Margaret and Gertrude "Patty" Solibakke. This later became the Danel home.
-Photo from Gertrude Wall Carr

Scott Wollever, 220 Shore Drive.

W. G. Miles, "Summit Ranch," Manette Heights.
-Photo from Kitsap County plat book, 1909

Mystery photo. This picture appeared in the Manette History Club files from an unknown source. It is identified as "Lovers' Lane, Wheaton Way, about 1930," but the exact location is not given.

MEMORIES OF A YOUNGER GENERATION
By Wesley W. Langrell

Friend, where is Manette under the sun?
It's down on the point of East Bremerton,
Down where the old bridge crosses the bay.
Manette has been there many a day.

Manette is a fine community
Though many things we no longer see.
My home town offers recollection
To one of a younger generation.

Remember all of the grocery stores?
At one time the markets came in fours.
Gas stations, drug stores and shoe repair -
Look around, there are none of them there.

There was a fine white church which later burned
Where the souls of men for God had yearned.
The lumber yard was down on the shore.
The post office leaned against the store.

Manette's old brown school stood very tall
But who remembers a school at all
Few things are eternal (most are brief).
Hail great Olympics! Hail Maple Leaf!

Sheridan had a fine brown school too
Sitting atop the hill with a view.
Bay Theatre was our only movie,
Hamburger Heaven an eatery.

In Summer there was skinny-dipping
Below the narrows bluff a-dripping.
The thrill of Winter was ice-skating
On cold Clare's Marsh, perhaps while dating.

Did you sail the one-ended *Iroquois*
And ride the silver *Kalakala?*
Did you drive on Galloping Gertie
And ride the Point Fosdick ferry?

The tie with Bremerton is very clear -
Puget Sound Naval Shipyard is here
Giving the city its life, its gain.
Symbolized by the hammerhead crane.

World War II brought the greatest change -
Housing and people, sudden and strange.
Recall the blacked-out city at night,
Air raid sirens and balloons in flight.

As souvenirs of the price war took
You may still have a rationing book
And a small flag which hung in the window bold
With a star of blue, perhaps of gold.

When asked "Remember the old hotel,
Children's home, ferry dock, fire bell?"
I only answer in negation,
"I'm from a younger generation."

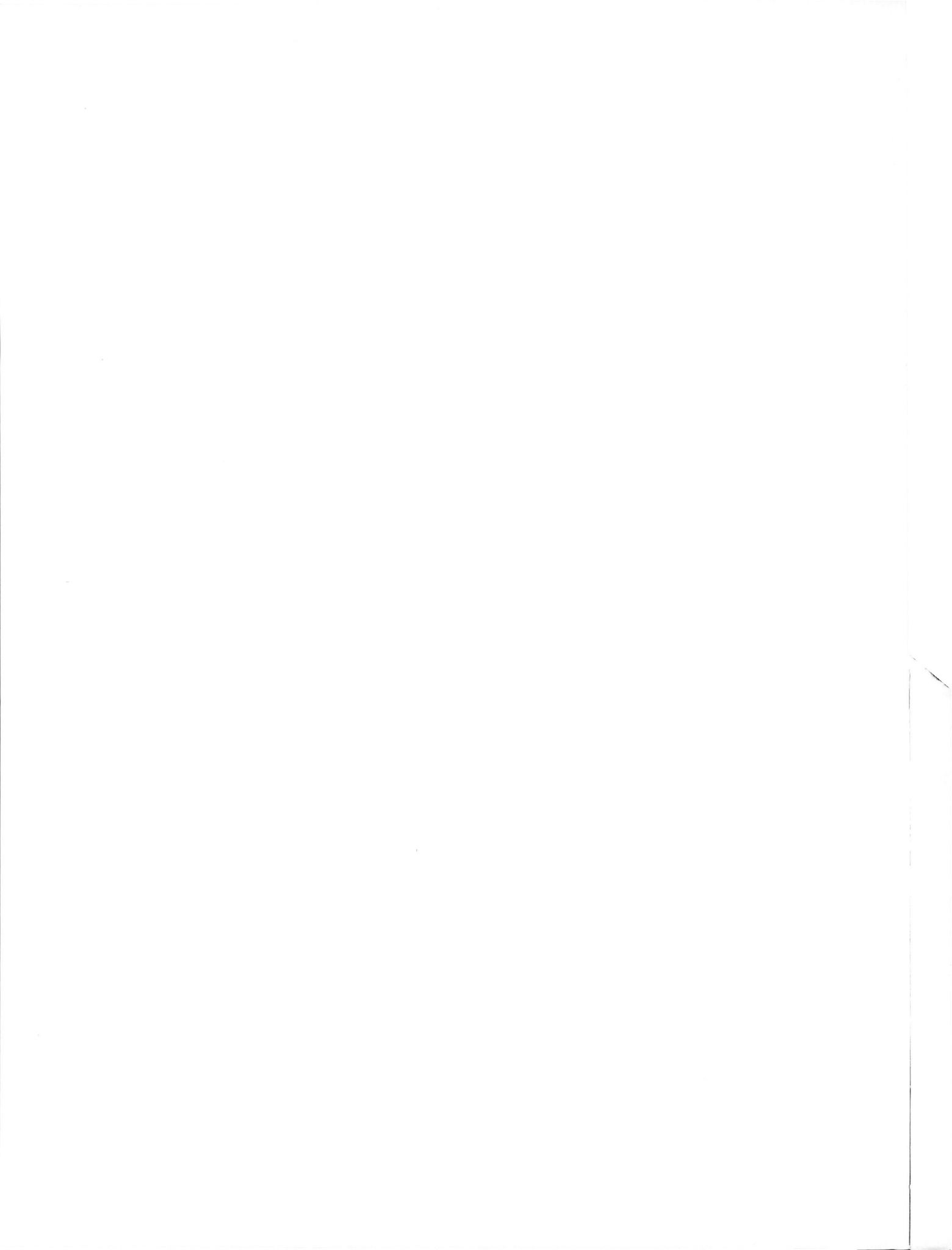

www.ingramcontent.com/pod-product-compliance
Lightning Source LLC
Chambersburg PA
CBHW062016090426
42811CB00005B/878